DATE DUE

FE 1 '94			
FE 22 '94			
APR MR 23 '94			

Her Name Is Barbra

HER NAME IS

Barbra

An Intimate Portrait of the Real Barbra Streisand

by Randall Riese

A BIRCH LANE PRESS BOOK
Published by Carol Publishing Group

A Birch Lane Press Book
Published by Carol Publishing Group
Birch Lane Press is a registered trademark of Carol Communications, Inc.
Editorial Offices: 600 Madison Avenue, New York, N.Y. 10022
Sales and Distribution Offices: 120 Enterprise Avenue, Secaucus, N.J. 07094
In Canada: Canadian Manda Group, P.O. Box 920, Station U, Toronto, Ontario M8Z 5P9
Queries regarding rights and permissions should be addressed to Carol Publishing Group, 600 Madison Avenue, New York, N.Y. 10022

Carol Publishing Group books are available at special discounts for bulk purchases, for sales promotion, fund-raising, or educational purposes. Special editions can be created to specifications. For details, contact: Special Sales Department, Carol Publishing Group, 120 Enterprise Avenue, Secaucus, N.J. 07094

Manufactured in the United States of America
10 9 8 7 6 5 4 3 2 1

Library of Congress Cataloging-in-Publication Data
Riese, Randall.
    Her name is Barbra : an intimate portrait of the real Barbra
Streisand / by Randall Riese.
        p.   cm.
    "A Birch Lane Press Book."
    ISBN 1-55972-203-7
    1. Streisand, Barbra.   2. Singers—United States—Biography.
I. Title.
ML420.S915R5   1993
782.42164'092—dc20   88 765   93-2521
[B]   CIP
                                                             MN

To Mark Goins and Neal Hitchens

"If I do not rouse my soul to higher things, who will rouse it?"

—MAIMONIDES

Contents

One

Conducting Symphonies

*S*he stood in front of the bathroom mirror in Brooklyn at the age of sixteen. She was not a pretty girl, as her own mother reminded her often enough. Hers was not an ugly face, but an improbable one. Bangs fell down her forehead and into eyes, big and blue and spaced too far apart. Her nose was crooked and obtrusive and summoned unwanted stares. Her mouth was wide and misshapen and usually downturned. It was a face in which nothing seemed to fit. But she was a girl of other qualities. Her mind was sharp, and more important, her imagination was vast and powerful. Locked outside of the bathroom door were pain and alienation. Inside, she could go wherever she wanted, become whoever she wanted. Fantasy was her friend.

On this particular day, as she stood before her mirror, and as the imaginary sounds of Stravinsky swelled in her ears, she raised her outstretched arms with the grandeur of the maestro and proceeded to conduct a full orchestra to an audience of none. The other girls at school talked about getting married, having kids, and saving enough money for a fur coat and a house in the suburbs. Her dreams, however, were far greater. She was going to become a symphony conductor for the New York Philharmonic. With the sweep of her arms, she commanded a chorus of violins, and as she did, she caught a glimpse of herself in the mirror of her bathroom in Brooklyn. And she was beautiful.

When not directing symphonies, Barbra Joan Streisand has always been directing everyone and everything around her. When, at the age of nineteen, she auditioned for a part in the Broadway musical *I Can Get It for You Wholesale,* she asked if she could sing sitting in a chair. She was less

1

nervous sitting than standing, and it seemed an appropriate and potentially humorous prop for her role of the secretary.

Later, after she was cast in the part, director Arthur Laurents instructed her, despite her frequent and tersely worded protestations that
it had been more effective with the chair, as to how *he* wanted the number staged. The night before the show opened in tryouts in Philadelphia,
Laurents, exasperated by her repeated requests and seeming impertinence, snapped, "Do it in your goddamned chair!" His words gave her
permission, but his tone distinctly and sadistically implied, "It's *your* funeral."

That night, Streisand's performance of "Miss Marmelstein," delivered
from the chair, stopped the show, as it later would on Broadway. "I
couldn't understand why they were mad at me for being right," Barbra
later reflected. It was a question she would ask herself again and again
over the succeeding years.

Streisand legend abounds with stories of her recording, over and over,
a single lyric or phrase until she deems it perfect, much to the frustration
of the exhausted studio engineers who are kept up until all hours of the
morning. On one occasion, while listening to an album of hers before
giving it her approval to be released, Barbra heard awkward dead space
between phrases. She summoned the technician and found out that he
had, without her permission, excised her audible gasps for breath between phrases. Incensed, Barbra castigated the technician and commanded that not one utterance of her breathing was to be censored. The
technician was duly rebuked, and the breathing was restored.

While finishing up another album, and after much consideration, Barbra selected a certain photograph to appear on the cover. After it was
sent to the lab for retouching, the photo was resubmitted to her for her
approval. Upon examining the photo, however, Barbra was overcome by
a disquieting feeling. Something was different about the photograph.
Something was wrong. Something was missing. The bump on her nose
had been cosmetically and unceremoniously removed.

Barbra called the retoucher at the lab, who had thought she would be
pleased, and informed him in no uncertain tone that if she had wanted
the bump on her nose removed, she would have gone to a doctor. The
bump, like the breathing, was restored.

Are these indications of bitchery, as some would suggest, or merely
examples of a woman who knows what she wants—and doesn't want—
done to *her* bump, and *her* breathing?

Then, of course, there is her fanaticism for decorating, or rather *re*decorating, the various rooms of her various homes. She's been known to take a series of Polaroid snapshots of any given room to see if a certain, say, settee is in aesthetic concert with the rest of the room; to see if each and every piece is in its proper place. She studies the resulting photographs, rearranges the room accordingly, takes another series of Polaroids, followed by more rearranging, and the process continues until every detail has met with her complete satisfaction. When after a while she becomes bored by the static perfection of a room, she opts to redecorate it in another look, style, or period. The rooms of her homes are exquisitely stylish, color-coordinated perhaps to a fault, and created with the intent of conveying a certain atmospheric mood. They aren't "homey" in the "lived-in" sense, but instead resemble the perfect and production-designed sets from some of her movies.

During the filming of *Funny Girl,* her first movie, Barbra, age twenty-five, used to watch the dailies at the end of each day's shooting, and, in her mind, she would edit the picture. She would decide which sentences from which takes should be used and which takes of which close-ups should be kept or dismissed. She would give the other actors, most of whom were far more experienced in pictures than she, unsolicited advice on how to play a particular scene. And she was certainly not too shy to make suggestions to her sixty-five-year-old and much Oscared director, William Wyler, the talented powerhouse who had tamed the beast in, among others, Bette Davis. When the picture wrapped production, Wyler, sincere but with his wicked sense of humor wonderfully intact, presented Barbra with a director's megaphone and some advice of his own: "You should be a director," he told her. The words stuck.

But then, Barbra Streisand has been directing ashtrays and sofas—and symphonies—for years.

Pat Conroy is the author of *The Water Is Wide* (adapted for the screen as *Conrack,* starring Jon Voight, in 1974), *The Great Santini* (produced in 1980 with Robert Duvall), and *The Lords of Discipline* (a 1983 picture with David Keith). It took Conroy six years to write *The Prince of Tides.* Published by Houghton Mifflin in 1986, the book stayed on the best-seller lists for a year. The paperback sold to Bantam for $1.5 million and had a remarkable 4.1 million copies in print after some thirty-four printings.

The Prince of Tides is set primarily in the fictional town of Colleton, South Carolina, and unfolds in rich, rambling, and often verbose narrative. It is the story of Tom Wingo, a shrimper's son who goes to Manhattan to help his twin sister, Savannah, a renowned but deeply disturbed feminist poet, after her latest in a series of suicide attempts. He is engaged by Dr. Susan Lowenstein, Savannah's psychiatrist, to assist in her treatment by unearthing the violent and embedded secrets of their fractured family's past. He becomes, in a sense, his sister's memory.

Conroy's story is unabashedly autobiographical. His real-life sister, Carol, also a writer, underwent her own series of emotional problems and suicide attempts. On one such occasion, Conroy went to live with her while she was institutionalized. When she learned that her brother was writing about their family in *Tides,* Carol informed him, "You can't write about me. You can't steal my life." But write about her he did, and she hasn't spoken to him since.

His father, Col. Donald Conroy, who also inspired *Santini,* was, in Conroy's words, "a consummately violent man. His beating of me, my mother, my brothers and sisters is a central fact of both my life and my art." Tellingly, Conroy adds, "In my fiction no child is ever safe."

Lila Wingo, the repressed and social-climbing matriarch of *The Prince of Tides,* was largely based on Conroy's own mother, who passed away in 1984. The book, in fact, is something of an homage to Peg Conroy, and much of what it has to say is about forgiving one's own mother, about confronting one's own past, no matter how painful and disturbing, so that one can live in the present and have hope for the future.

It is easy, then, to understand Barbra Streisand's initial attraction to, and eventual obsession with, the project. Then in her mid-forties, she was herself the mother of a young adult, and perhaps the preeminent performer of her generation. Yet she had not resolved the emotional scars left by her own seriously flawed childhood. In *The Prince of Tides,* she saw the opportunity to tell, in a sense, and on various levels, her own story, confront and deal with her own pain, and hopefully grow and heal from the process.

It was while she was finishing *Nuts,* which she was starring in and producing, that the music editor on the picture suggested *Tides* to Barbra as a story she should direct. The suggestion was dismissed until months later, when, according to an industry source, her paramour at the time, actor Don Johnson, read passages of the book to her in bed. Sufficiently intrigued, Barbra went out and bought a copy of the book, which she proceeded to read with abandon. Upon completing it, she knew that it was a picture she wanted to make. "When I read the book," she would later insist, "I saw the movie. I felt what would be the important themes: how everyone's relationship has changed through compassion and love."

Predictably, she envisioned Johnson as her Tom Wingo. With "Miami Vice" in television ratings decline, Johnson was reattempting a film career. The two of them engaged in animated discussions about the book and exchanged and interpreted Conroy's dialogue. The book provoked conversations about and references to their own childhoods and the impact those childhoods were still having on their adult lives. They talked about how the material should and shouldn't be filmed, and it would be fair to say that the developmental origins of what became the movie version of *The Prince of Tides* emerged not in the sterility of a studio boardroom, but, rather, right there in bed, between friends and lovers and under cotton sheets.

However, Streisand and Johnson were not the only ones interested in *The Prince of Tides.* CBS Theatrical Films purchased the rights in 1986 from Conroy, who, in this age of high-tech agenting warfare, did all of his own negotiating. When CBS eventually disbanded its feature film division, Conroy reacquired the rights to the property. He then wrote his own screenplay, which was purchased and accepted for production by MGM/UA.

At the time, KCR Productions, comprising producer Andrew Karsch, Conroy, and James Roe, Conroy's business manager, was going to produce the picture, with Jay Presson Allen (who wrote the film version of *Cabaret*) adapting the screenplay. According to an inside source, Conroy was paid $250,000 for *his* screenplay, on top of the $600,000 he received for the film rights. It was Karsch's agreement with MGM/UA that the picture would be produced *without* stars and with a moderate budget of $10 million.

But the project stalled in limbo at the financially distressed studio throughout 1986 and into 1987. Various directors, including Robert Mandel and Luis Mandoki *(White Palace)* were attached to *Tides.* Then Robert Redford, a Conroy fan since reading *The Great Santini,* entered the picture.

John Voland, who has covered the movie industry for years, first for the *Los Angeles Times* and then for the *Hollywood Reporter,* was privy to Tinseltown buzz about Redford and *Tides.* "I know that he had expressed to his agent and around town that the picture was something that he really wanted to make and something that he felt he could do very well."

Redford eventually took the project over from KCR and signed an agreement with MGM/UA to star in and produce the picture under his Wildwood Enterprises banner.

When Barbra learned that Redford, the former Hubbell Gardiner to her Katie Morosky, had acquired the project, she called him to discuss the possibility of a collaboration. By then, the intensity of her relationship with Johnson was waning and she was more than willing to alter her vision to feature Redford as her Wingo. The two had been wanting to work together again since *The Way We Were* some fifteen years before. More important, Robert Redford was, in many ways, the ideal actor to portray Tom Wingo, the fair-haired all-American boy grown older, wiser, more cynical, a man whose casual good looks belied the childhood pain that lurked deep within. "All my life," Redford once said, "I've been dogged by guilt because I feel there is this difference between the way I look and the way I feel inside."

According to one source, they talked about Redford directing Barbra as Lowenstein. It was, after all, *his* property, and he had certainly proven his mettle with *Ordinary People,* for which he won a 1980 Oscar. Primarily, though, they talked about Barbra directing Redford as Wingo. However, after several lengthy conversations, it was apparent to Redford, a forceful personality himself, that the proposed "collaboration" was doomed. Film, for some, is the ultimate collaborative art form. For Streisand the director, it is primarily an auteuristic one. If she was to direct the picture, it was to be *her* picture, *her* message, *her* vision, from a line in the screenplay and how it was to be read to an armchair in the set design and where it was to be placed.

"Once Streisand was set to direct," offers John Voland, "it's my understanding that Redford's interest in playing the Tom Wingo character ended at that point. It was my understanding that Redford finally just— it's not that he disliked her or had trouble with the way she was working—but it was just obvious to him that it was being taken in a direction that he didn't want to go."

Barbra later intimated that the essence of her "artistic differences" with Redford was rooted in his unwillingness to strip himself emotionally naked and become totally vulnerable, which was, understandably, the central prerequisite Barbra required from the actor who would be Wingo. "Artistic differences?" one source warily questioned. *"Ego differences, more likely."*

What happened next is a mystery to almost everyone concerned, even to Pat Conroy. Bonni Lee, who worked closely with Redford for three years at Wildwood Enterprises between 1988 and 1991, is also uncertain about what happened. "It was really odd because it was just so much between Bob and Barbra. I don't think anybody really knows except

Redford and Streisand what the agreement was between them."

Perhaps it was because he was exhausted after producing and directing the then recently released picture *The Milagro Beanfield War*. Perhaps it was because he was engrossed with other activities, which included a visit with Fidel Castro in Cuba, a ten-day trip through the Soviet Union, campaigning for presidential candidate Michael Dukakis, and other ventures related to his Utah-based Sundance Institute. Possibly it was because Redford was having difficulty adapting the Conroy story for the screen, or perhaps he was simply bowing to what he recognized to be Streisand's greater passion for the material. Whatever his motivation, Robert Redford relinquished his rights to *The Prince of Tides*, clearing the way for Streisand.

It's interesting to consider what might've happened had he not. The complex and textured role of the tortured Tom Wingo would have provided Redford with the role of his career and might well have resurrected his diminishing stature in Hollywood. (Later, Redford would have a box office, if not critical, success with the 1993 picture *Indecent Proposal*.) Instead, he opted to star in the megabudget *Havana*, a well-intentioned political drama that failed dismally upon its release in 1991.

Meanwhile, the embattled MGM/UA, which had produced *Yentl* several years before, was barely surviving and subject to various takeover attempts. One such effort was made by the high-powered threesome of Bert Sugarman, Peter Guber, and Jon Peters—the latter, of course, being Barbra's former longtime lover. It was not a coincidence that the only MGM/UA project slated for production that the trio wanted to retain was *The Prince of Tides*. The attempted purchase, however, faltered in negotiations, and the studio was left to stand, for a time, on its own unsturdy legs.

For much of 1989, Barbra was in and out of negotiations with MGM/UA to direct the picture. According to a studio insider, the principal holdup was money. The studio had allotted her $14.5 million to make *Yentl* and had initially projected spending only $10 million on *Tides*. Barbra insisted on a budget of $25 million, an average amount for any major production of the period, but a bit too heady by MGM/UA standards, particularly for an adult drama. The picture, as Barbra envisioned it, was an old-fashioned romance set against a psychological backdrop, not exactly the kind of inane comedy or bloodfest action picture that was drawing big money at the box office. Furthermore, Streisand's last two pictures had both been something of a commercial disappointment.

"Remember," says Anne Thompson, a professional expert on the business aspects of Hollywood moviemaking, "she was coming off of *Nuts,* which was a disaster. It was a really bad commercial venture." John Voland adds, "People kept thinking that *Yentl,* although it was quite successful in a number of ways, was not the biggest performer in the world, financially. And there was concern that a picture that Barbra was insisting on directing and starring in herself might not have the financial attractiveness to make such a big budget worthwhile."

There were others in Hollywood who believed that she was no longer the star that she once was; that she had betrayed the loyalty of her fans, who wanted to see her in musical comedy; that she was, as a box-office commodity, tarnished goods, if not all washed up.

Nevertheless, Barbra proceeded to adapt *Tides* into a workable script. She started by trying to reach Conroy, leaving repeated messages for him to phone her. She was perplexed when he didn't return the calls. Naturally, she assumed that her reputation for bitchery had preceded her, or that Conroy simply had some unknown something against her, as people who didn't know her sometimes did. Still, Barbra is nothing if not determined, and her calls to Conroy persisted, and they continued to go unreturned.

It seems that Conroy had a friend in Atlanta named Bernie who was fond of perpetrating phone pranks of the offbeat kind. Typically, Bernie would call Conroy in a disguised voice and leave a message from former president Jimmy Carter inviting him to attend some important gala event for dignitaries. Bernie frequently executed variations of the long-distance charade, and Conroy surmised that the calls from "Streisand" had also been staged by Bernie.

Then one day Barbra learned that Conroy was staying in Los Angeles and she telephoned his hotel room. Conroy picked up the phone. "This is Barbra Streisand," said the familiar and somewhat strident voice at the other end of the line. "Why aren't you returning my calls?"

Still suspecting Bernie, Conroy asked the caller-who-would-be-Barbra to prove her identity by singing "People." Startled, and more frustrated than offended, Barbra sang into the telephone mouthpiece the first few bars of the song to which she had become irrevocably linked.

Sufficiently satisfied, and more than a little sheepish, Conroy apologized profusely and accepted Barbra's request that he fly to New York to collaborate with her on the script. Later she would find revenge when she coerced Conroy into crooning "Will You Still Love Me Tomorrow," to clarify a reference in the book to the Shirelles.

Upon their introduction at Barbra's apartment, Conroy, who exudes

Southern politeness and the impeccable good breeding instilled in him by his mother, told Barbra that he had written *Tides* while listening to her records. Pleased by the thought, which further encouraged her that she was somehow destined to direct the film, Barbra presented him with her copy of the book and requested that he sign it.

"Barbra, I have nothing against you," Conroy then began as Barbra braced herself for the worst. "I write to your music—what a voice you have—but my father said you eat writers alive, and I'd prefer not to have that experience, if you don't mind."

Barbra considered what she had just heard, then, looking Conroy directly in the eye, she asked, "How long has your father known me?"

If such things can be traced to a single moment, a freeze-frame in time, it was then and there that their collaboration and genuine affinity for one another began.

For the next three weeks, Conroy and Barbra, not terribly unlike Wingo and Lowenstein, worked together behind closed doors to attain a shared goal. Barbra wanted to understand every reference in the book, every detail, every nuance, even if it was not to be a part of the screenplay. At one point, her probing prompted her to ask about the "shag," a regional dance referred to in the book. Sensing the opportunity, Conroy stood up on cue and proceeded to teach Streisand to shag.

Having mastered the dance, or a reasonable facsimile of it, Barbra continued to labor over every line in the book and assaulted Conroy with a barrage of questions: "What were you thinking when you wrote *this?*" "What did the character mean when he said *that?*" Of Barbra, Conroy would later quip, "One assumes she does not even make a salad without considering the ingredients mightily." He was further astonished to learn that she had essentially memorized the entire book. She would sometimes pepper their discussions with questions prefaced with, for example, "On page 262, you say . . ." Conroy would have to flip through the pages of his own book to find out what she was talking about. He was also probably surprised to find that Barbra, although she would not take screen credit for it and would probably deny it if asked, was secretly writing a good deal of the script herself.

It was a harmonious collaboration, partially because Conroy discarded all semblance of ego and usually acceded to Barbra's decisions. To be fair to Streisand, it is also partially because, contrary to her reputation, she generally gets along well with people whom she respects, a select group of which Conroy was thankfully a member.

"We talked a great deal. There would be differences, and whenever we had one of those differences or an argument, Barbra usually won," Conroy related. "It would go like this: I'd say, 'I like the way *this* line sounds.' She'd say she liked the way *that* line sounds. And we'd go through it like that. It was never with raised voices. Just discussions. But she won most of those."

Revealingly, Conroy adds, regarding his experience on the film, and the fate of the writer in Hollywood in general, "I now know my place in Hollywood—I'm a writer—the scum of the earth. [But] I've never complained about Hollywood, because whatever pain you may feel, they throw zillions of dollars at you to assuage that pain."

It was fortunate for Conroy that he had no delusions of grandeur, no exaggerated idea of his importance to Hollywood, and hence to the film version of *Tides*. According to a studio source, his draft of the screenplay of *his* book was eventually all but scrapped by Streisand, although he would receive a shared screen credit nonetheless. Interestingly, Conroy would not even be introduced to Becky Johnston, the writer responsible for most of the final script.

Following her extensive sessions with Conroy, Barbra submitted the script to several therapists, including Dr. Harvey Corman, husband of her longtime best friend, Cis Corman. Barbra was certainly no stranger to psychoanalysis herself, having been in therapy for over twenty years, ever since attaining stardom on Broadway. Still, for the next several months, she consulted with her assemblage of experts and doctors and incorporated some of their ideas into her script and discarded others that didn't accord with her own theories. She also met with untold dozens of other writers (Joan Tewkesbury and Robert Getchell among them) and solicited their ideas.

Becky Johnston made a distinctly favorable impression on Barbra, despite having had only one script theretofore produced, *Under the Cherry Moon,* which was a 1986 failure for recording artist Prince. The two women shared many of the same ideas about the script and the direction it should take, and according to entertainment reporter Mitchell Fink, Johnston virtually moved into Barbra's home during the course of the writing. Then with the *Los Angeles Herald-Examiner,* Fink reported at the time that Johnston, along with Barbra's other "aides," was "available around-the-clock for *Prince of Tides* brainstorming. Barbra is said sometimes to wake her helpers in the middle of the night to say, 'I've thought of something I want you to remind me of tomorrow morning.' "

With its financial woes increasingly insurmountable, MGM/UA placed *Tides* in "turnaround" by the end of 1989. What this means, essentially, is that the studio opted to halt development on the project and make it available to other studios that might be interested.

"It's my understanding," offers John Voland, "that budget projections got to the point that they said, 'Well, you know, in all good faith, we can't afford to make this.' This was happening just at the beginning of the whole [Giancarlo] Perretti buyout scam [of the studio], and they didn't feel that they had enough money on hand to do any sort of justice to it. The budget scared a lot of people, so they just let it go."

Curiously, the response at other studios to *Tides* was tepid. One would assume that a Streisand-driven vehicle adapted from a major best-selling novel would elicit a good deal of excitement from, and perhaps even a bidding war waged by, the Hollywood powerbrokers. Such, however, was not the case.

"It is rather amazing that [other studios] didn't agree to do it," says industry expert Anne Thompson. "It surprises me. But I would say to you that Hollywood doesn't make that many adult dramas anymore. They are considered hard sells at the box office. And a lot of people had a perception before *The Prince of Tides* that Barbra Streisand was most marketable in a musical. It was an expensive picture, and a drama with no comedy elements. I can see, and I'm not saying that they were right or wrong, but I can just see the studios not jumping up and down about doing this picture. There could also be other reasons. Perhaps there was a sense that—and I'm not saying that this was the reason—but it is possible that they perceived that working with Streisand would be a challenge, that she's a handful."

Naturally alarmed about the considerable amount of time, money, and not to mention *passion,* she had already expended on it, Barbra took the project to Warner Brothers, for which she had made *Nuts,* and where she had an ongoing production deal through her New York–based company, Barwood Productions.

John Voland recalls, "There was momentary chat about it being made at Warner Brothers. That, however, disappeared pretty fast." When Warners also passed, as did, reportedly, every other major studio in town, Barbra turned, reluctantly, and not without humility, to Jon Peters.

Former hairdresser and beauty salon owner Jon Peters had, with undeniable and inestimable assistance from his girlfriend Barbra, propelled himself to the ranks of movie producers in the 1970s, much to the salacious and drooling delight of Hollywood wags who dubbed the couple a joke: the superstar and her shampoo boy. With his partner Peter Guber,

Peters became something of a mogul in the eighties with, among other pictures, the blockbuster *Batman,* the biggest-grossing film in Warner Brothers history. Theirs was an interesting partnership that provoked considerable speculation in Hollywood.

"There was a lot of curiosity about *what* Jon Peters brought to that relationship with Peter Guber," surmises Nina J. Easton, who spent a couple of months getting to know Peters for a feature-length story she was doing on him for the *Los Angeles Times.* "I think what it was was that Jon Peters can play the bad guy, the hatchet man. Peter Guber is very, very uncomfortable with confrontation. He was also very focused on, or liked to think of himself as being focused on, 'high quality' projects, the Oscar kind of movies. I think it was kind of useful to have [as a partner] somebody like Jon Peters, who does the *Batman* kind of movies. And they were very close."

On November 16, 1989, the Japanese electronics giant Sony purchased Columbia Pictures Entertainment and installed Guber and Peters as cochairmen of the conglomeration that included Columbia Pictures, Tri-Star Pictures, and Columbia Pictures Television. The deal included Sony's purchasing of Guber-Peters Entertainment Company for a reported $200 million, and an annual salary for the pair of $2.75 million each, in addition to various guaranteed bonuses worth reported multiple millions. "It was," says Easton, "a very, very rich deal. One could argue that it cost $700 million to get them. I think that Sony ended up looking a bit embarrassed."

Not surprisingly, one of Peters's first decisions in his new position of power was to "green-light" *The Prince of Tides.* In private, Barbra would quip to friends, in the guise of a joke, "Ex-boyfriends come in handy."

"It was one of his very, very first moves," says Nina J. Easton of Peters's acquisition of *Tides.* "I think for Jon Peters, this was a big-name project to bring to Columbia, and a project belonging to a good friend of his. Keep in mind that there was nobody else in charge at the studio at that time. It was just Jon Peters and Peter Guber. There were not any Mike Medavoys or Frank Prices there yet. For several months after they first took over, Peters and Guber were running the studio very 'hands-on.' So it was no surprise that Peters comes in and reaches out to people he knows well, like Barbra Streisand. He is also the kind of person who goes for big-name projects. He likes 'star quality' kinds of projects. Peters was the one who set it up at the studio and the one who championed it."

As for his personal relationship with Barbra, Easton relates, "Yes, I did talk to him about that. They were *not* lovers [at that point]. They talked about each other as good friends. And she speaks in glowing terms about him."

There couldn't have been a more appropriate vehicle to reunite Jon Peters with Barbra Streisand. Years before, Peters, alternately charming and brash and full of bravado, confided to Barbra that he had been abused as a child. Like her, he had been forced to live in the home of a stepfather who despised him. They shared the battle scars left by the traumas of their respective childhoods, stirring their mutual understanding and deepening their bond. With *Tides,* their relationship would come full circle.

On January 25, 1990, Columbia Pictures announced that it was finalizing negotiations with MGM/UA to acquire *Tides* with Streisand as producer, director, and star. Holding up the deal, however, was money, according to John Voland, who adds, "And it was funny because the Columbia brass, after all of the decisions had been made to shepherd the project over there, started balking at the budget, which was something they should've known ahead of time if they'd have listened to anyone from MGM. But, of course, in Hollywood, no one listens to anyone else."

According to one studio source, Columbia wanted Barbra to accept $1 million less than the reported $7 million fee that had been previously agreed upon—$2 million to produce and direct, and $5 million to act. Barbra balked. At first, she refused to lower her fee at all. She was, after all, no Julia Roberts–come-lately. She was arguably the biggest female movie star in the world, and had been for decades. Later, she handed Columbia a humbling ultimatum: she was willing to concede to a $500,000 cut, but no more. If this compromise was deemed unacceptable by the studio, Barbra threatened to halt all further negotiations.

While obviously wildly outrageous by any rational standards, a $5 million acting fee is not only reasonable by Hollywood standards, it is a relatively small amount compared to the exorbitant sums paid to some male actors. Despite its liberal pretensions, Hollywood is decidedly though discreetly sexist when it comes to paying women equal pay for equal work.

"Until Julia Roberts came along, Barbra was the best paid of the women stars," industry expert Anne Thompson says. "I don't think that Meryl Streep, Goldie Hawn, Cher, or Bette Midler have topped the $5 million mark. I think that Meryl has gotten up to $4 million."

Comparatively, Redford got $7 million to act in *Havana.* Jack Nicholson's standard fee is $11 million. Arnold Schwarzenegger and Sylvester Stallone also command $11 million. Tom Cruise was paid $12 million to star in *Far and Away* and another $12 million for *The Firm*. In addition to their flat fee, some performers demand, and get, lucrative "back-end" deals which give them a percentage of a film's profits and sometimes of a film's gross.

By the fall of 1991, while the president of the United States was still dulled by denial, Hollywood acknowledged the economic recession as its impact sent reverberations throughout the industry. Fees, however, still bordered on the ludicrous. Six-million-dollar actors lowered their price to $4 million; $2 million actors agreed to accept $750,000. Even Disney chairman Michael Eisner had to content himself in 1991 with *half* the bonus money he received the previous year: a mere $5.44 million, compared to the $10.48 million he had pocketed in 1990.

Meanwhile, while waiting for Columbia's final decision on her $500,000 compromise, Barbra began having last-minute jitters about her commitment to *Tides*. It wasn't, after all, the only project she had in development. Even before becoming immersed in *Tides*, Barbra had been wrapped up in discussions with producer Linda Yellen about collaborating on a motion picture biography of Margaret Bourke-White, the ambitious photographer for *Life* magazine in the 1930s and 1940s who had an affair with writer Erskine Caldwell. Plans for the proposed production were deterred but not altogether shelved by Lawrence Schiller's 1989 telefilm on the same subject starring Farrah Fawcett.

She was also planning a big-budget, full-scale remake of Claude Lelouch's 1975 French romance, *And Now, My Love*. The picture had starred Marthe Keller as a wealthy woman, with André Dussollier as her good-for-*almost*-nothing lover. The proposed remake was to be produced by Faye Schwab for Warner Brothers.

Another project which Barbra optioned and has had in various stages of development for years is the Larry Kramer play about AIDS, *The Normal Heart*. Not surprisingly, she has had some difficulty casting and finding financing for the project. If Hollywood is discreetly sexist, it is blatantly homophobic. Barbra has also undoubtedly found Kramer, a highly outspoken AIDS activist, to be far less amenable in adapting the material than was Pat Conroy, despite the fact that he is an unabashed Streisand fan.

Riddled with fear and insecurity about whether to proceed with *Tides* as her next project, Barbra, seeking some paranormal or spiritual guidance, asked for a "sign." Months before, she had, on a whim, redecorated her New York penthouse apartment, making it more commensurate with her lofty standards of comfort. *Tides* was to be shot, in part, in New York. Barbra took this fact as something of a sign, however vague. She would, after all, be able to live in her renovated apartment while making the picture. But she wanted something more. She wanted something definitive. She didn't want a sign, she wanted a billboard from above.

Before committing to do *Yentl,* which was intended by Barbra as a tribute to her father, she went to New York and, for the first time in her adult life, visited his grave. Uncertain about whether to do the picture, Barbra extended her arms out toward the universe and asked for some kind of sign. Later, when examining a photograph that had been taken of her at the cemetery, she noticed the tombstone that stood next to her father's. The name on the tombstone read "Anshel." In the movie, Anshel was the name of Yentl's dead brother. (It's also the name Yentl took as a "boy.") Barbra took this as her sign to make the movie.

So while Columbia deliberated over her ultimatum regarding *The Prince of Tides,* Barbra again turned to what she calls her "higher power" and asked for a sign. That night, overcome with uncertainty, she turned out all the lights in her bedroom and crawled into bed. Suddenly, in the middle of the night, she was awakened by the sound of a simple click. She sat up in bed, erect, alert. Hanging over her bed was a painting of a beautiful woman in pink. Over the painting was a light. The clicking sound had been the light switching on. Her painting had been illuminated.

As she sat up in her bed, Barbra was stricken by a thought that persisted: *Light up your art.* The thought resonated in her head. The words were similar and the idea identical to the advice Tom Wingo gives to the troubled Savannah in the book of *Tides:* "Use your art," brother tells sister.

Barbra had her sign, but was still in doubt. She studied the painting and observed that it had been done in 1900. The present year was 1990. "Even the numbers were the same," she later enthused, while professing at the same time that she was not a "woo-woo" type of person. Still, she doubted, giving benefit to the negative.

She turned off the light over the painting and went back to bed. A few hours later, she was again awakened by the sound of a click. Barbra later reflected, "It was like, 'What, you didn't believe me?'" It is contingent on such tenuous things that movies are made—and not made—in Hollywood.

Finally, she was resolute about the *rightness* of her making the picture. To Streisand, this is essential. She doesn't select projects casually, nor does she simply "make" a movie, hence her propensity for doing only one picture every four years. She nurtures it, breathes it, becomes it. It is a major investment of heart, soul, and self, the privacy and preservation of which she characteristically guards with narrowed eyes and icy reserve. This is *not* a woman who gives of herself—whether it be to a motion picture or to another living person—easily.

The following morning, the telephone rang. It was an executive from Columbia Pictures. The studio had acceded to her compromise. The contracts were ready to be signed. Twenty-five million dollars was at her disposal, waiting to be spent. This dichotomous Hollywood icon who conquers motion picture studios and yet is afraid to get on a train by herself, this veritable *industry* who earns a phenomenal living by being a public figure and yet is afraid to use a public lavatory (or to do anything else in public, for that matter), got off the phone that morning and heaved a sigh of relief. For such a complicated, contradiction-filled character, her subsequent reaction was the most basic and simple of human emotions. For one brief moment, Barbra Streisand rejoiced. For after over two years of an exhausting roller-coaster-like ride of ebb and flow, her fated tide had finally come in.

And so the little girl from Brooklyn stood before the mirror in her bathroom. She picked up her maestro's baton, lifted her head, and raised her outstretched arms. She was ready to light up her art, wondrous art.

Two

Tea Sets and Party Dresses

There were few toys, little laughter, and for Barbara Joan Streisand, a childhood that was anything *but* wondrous. In the 1990s, the abhorrent atrocity that is child abuse has begun to emerge out of the proverbial family closet, but back in the early 1950s, in the days of Ozzie and Harriet, it was denied, disguised, and dismissed. Deemed to be "discipline," it was hidden, determinedly, under a cloak of family secrecy. It's no wonder then that, more than three decades later, Barbra would be obsessed with uncovering and exorcising the tragic, embedded secrets of the Wingo family in *The Prince of Tides.* She had, after all, some family secrets of her own.

She was born in Brooklyn, the "broken land," and would be raised by a mother with a broken spirit. But the prospects for her young life had not always been so bleak. She made her entrance into the world on April 24, 1942. It was a spectacular and much anticipated debut. Outside, a world war waged its horrors and untold thousands of Jews were methodically slaughtered, but inside the home of Emanuel and Diana Streisand, aged thirty-four and thirty-three, respectively, there was music and laughter and genuine *hope* for a future that held much promise. For the Streisands, much of that promise was embodied in their newborn child.

She was a bald—family legend has it that not a hair grew on her head until she was two—but beautiful baby. Blue eyes sparkling, and even then, questioning. Friends would later suggest to Diana that Barbara (note the traditional spelling) was a picture-perfect "Gerber baby" and should be put into television commercials, which were then just beginning to burgeon into the public consciousness. Diana, however, rejected the notion. She had very strong ideas about what was right, and even stronger views on what wasn't, and the idea of exploiting her baby for profit was, well, *vulgar.*

Diana Rosen was one of four children of a tailor, who also served as a cantor, from whom she inherited, among other things, a beautiful singing voice. Born in 1908, she was a simple young woman of modest ambition. "She's mainly interested in basic things," Barbra would later say of her mother, with varying degrees of admiration and disdain, "like eating and breathing. She's a very secure person, sort of like, uh, normal."

Growing up the quintessential "nice Jewish girl," Diana's few aspirations included marriage to a good (Jewish, naturally) man, a kosher, middle-class home, and, of course, children. She found the man of her dreams in Emanuel Streisand. They were introduced at the home of her girlfriend, and it was, according to Diana, "love at first sight, oh boy."

Manny Streisand, the son of an immigrant fishmonger who owned a store in Brooklyn, was a student working on his master's degree in education. Dark, handsome, fiercely serious, and extremely intelligent, he seemed to have a future of infinite possibilities. Twenty years old at the time he met Diana Rosen, Manny worked as a lifeguard to support his studies. For the next year, their romance burned with poetry and passion, but was abruptly extinguished after a heated, though utterly forgettable, argument. It is likely that Diana, with her pragmatic mind, pressed for the logical next step in their relationship, and Manny, financially insecure, was reluctant to commit. Whatever the reason, the young lovers parted.

Diana waited for his apologetic return. "If he likes me enough, he'll call me," she told her friends, family, and self. She waited by the telephone for a year. When the call finally came, she was out of the house, engaged at a Saturday afternoon matinee. Upon receiving the message, she feigned girlish indifference. Actually, she decided to play hard-to-get and not return the call, at least not immediately.

Soon afterward, with the call still unreturned, Diana had a brush with fate at the local trolley car station when she bumped into a familiar and anxious young man. "It was Manny," Diana later related. "I was dumbfounded. If that wasn't an act of God, nothing else was." She had her sign from above, and the two reignited and resumed their romance the following year.

Married in 1930, with the country in the throes of the great economic depression, the conscientious young couple postponed the expansion of their family. Their first child, Sheldon, was not born until five years later. Diana desperately wanted another child, a daughter, but the couple decided to wait further until they were more financially stable. The importance of money, the pleasure that comes from searching for and securing a good bargain, and the distinction between those who had and those who didn't were principles Diana would later instill in her daughter. To each of her children, she would also impart the words of worry and wisdom, "Hold on to what you've got—it might not be there tomorrow." It was a lesson Diana learned all too well for herself.

With Barbara's birth in 1942, twelve years after their marriage, Diana finally, joyously, had the fulfillment of her idealized family. There may have been a war going on, but for the Streisands, their baby was healthy, their hearts were full, and all seemed right with the world. And then, inexplicably, all went terribly, tragically wrong.

Manny's teaching career had begun to thrive. He was a respected and well-liked English teacher at the George Westinghouse Vocational High School in Brooklyn. He was happy in his marriage, elated with his family, and in vigorous good health. "He played squash and tennis when Jewish boys didn't do things like that," his daughter would later enthuse in awe. "He was an *adventurer.*"

As the spring term of 1943 came to a close, Manny began to look for summer employment to earn extra money to cover the costs incurred with the birth of his daughter. It was Nathan Spiro, a fellow teacher at George Westinghouse, and one of Manny's best friends, who came to the rescue. One of the things that the two men had in common was that they both had a son named Sheldon. It is possible, in fact, that Nathan Spiro named his son, born two years after Manny's son, as an homage to his good friend. Sheldon Spiro, today fifty-five years old, recalls the events of that fateful summer:

"My father was an industrial arts teacher. We had five children in our family, and my father felt it was more economical to rent a summer camp and run it as a business, rather than to send us all away to summer camp, which would've cost a fortune. So, in his infinite wisdom, he rented a camp by the name of Camp Cascade. It was up in Highmount, New York, which was about forty miles north of Kingston. Highmount is where the Bel Air Ski Resort now is. It's a beautiful place. Anyway, there was a camp that he rented for the season. You bring your own campers up. And he hired Manny Streisand to be his head counselor."

Diana, for one, was reluctant to make the trip. Cautious and high-strung by nature, she felt a gnawing at her gut. She would later reflect, "I don't know, something within me was nervous." Besides, she didn't long to be outdoors as her husband did. She was not an adventurer. She loathed the prospect of the long train ride and she thought with distaste about eating meals prepared by the camp cook. Her own meals, she argued, were undoubtedly more kosher, better tasting, and more nutritious for their children. Besides, Diana adored the security and solace of their apartment at 457 Schenectady Avenue in Brooklyn. Nevertheless, when the school term ended in June, Manny Streisand, imbued with the promise of summer fun, packed up his family, and together they boarded the train headed for the country, the Catskill Mountains, and Camp Cascade.

Sheldon Spiro continues the story. "So Manny came up, of course, with his family. Barbara was just an infant. The camp probably had about 150 campers, boys and girls. The whole thing was a two-month situation. They came up at the end of June, and they leave the end of August. Manny, apparently, was a very healthy person. The job of head camp counselor is a pretty rigorous thing, walking up and down these hills, supervising loads of kids and counselors and so forth."

During the course of the summer, Nathan Spiro found himself in trouble when several of his counselors quit without notice. Unable to find hasty replacements, Nathan and his friend Manny doubled their already hectic work schedules. Then, one particularly hot, humid day, Manny complained of a headache. Not much was made of it because he was prone to migraines. He was left alone to lie down and rest. When he failed to awaken from his slumber, Diana nervously paced the floor of their room, clutching baby Barbara in her arms. "Everything's going to be okay, everything's going to be okay," she whispered urgently to her baby and herself. As Diana would later allow, "It was a frightening situation, being so far away from home."

Finally, Diana summoned the help of Nathan Spiro. According to Sheldon, "My older sister, Helene, baby-sat Barbara while my mother went to the hospital with her mother. It was a small hospital, a poor infirmary named Fleischmanns Hospital located in a small rural town called Fleischmanns, New York."

Within twenty-four hours of being admitted to the hospital, Emanuel Streisand, bounding with energy only days before, was pronounced dead. It was August 4, 1943. The cause of death was shrouded in secrecy. For years afterward, Diana told everyone, including her children, that he had died from a cerebral hemorrhage caused by overwork. Not only was this explanation untrue, it would also have an unfortunate consequence. Both Barbara and Shelley would grow up with the fear that they, too, would die a sudden and premature death brought on by overwork.

Actually, Manny Streisand died from an improperly treated epileptic seizure following a mysterious, though not fatal, head injury. Apparently, at Fleischmanns Hospital, a doctor administered morphine into Manny's neck to halt an epileptic seizure. Manny then went into respiratory failure, probably precipitated by an adverse reaction to the morphine.

The motivation for Diana's deception is curious. Perhaps, in a misguided effort to ensure her husband's respectability, she decided to avoid any reference to epilepsy, therefore also avoiding the absurd stigma that was then attached to it. Or, perhaps, lost in her own haze of hysteria and despair, she herself was confused about the cause of her husband's death.

Diana, then thirty-five, understandably went into shock. She couldn't speak, she couldn't comprehend, she couldn't cry. She sat, stiff-backed, eyes forward, in stunned silence. Far away from her beloved home in Brooklyn, far from almost everything she knew and loved and was comforted by, her world had collapsed and crumbled with the prick of a needle injection; the bright, white picket-fence future she had envisioned for herself and her family suddenly ceased to exist. Many years later, reflecting back upon her life, Diana would still shake her head in sad disbelief. He was "such a healthy, strapping man, an athlete," she would lament, adding that he "had everything to look forward to." At the time of his death, Emanuel Streisand was thirty-five years old. He left behind a wife, two small children, and a plethora of what-might-have-beens.

And so the inconsolable widow sat with her two fatherless children as the train took them back to their home in Brooklyn. Financially incapable of maintaining their apartment, Diana had little choice but to cram her young family into the home of her parents. It was a small, drab, three-room apartment located in a poor area of town on Pulaski Street in the Bedford-Stuyvesant projects. Diana's parents slept in one room, Diana and Barbara shared a bed in another, and eight-year-old Shelley slept on a folding cot in the third room, which also featured a table and a credenza. Conspicuously absent was a living room, or even a couch. As Barbra would later relate, "We never had a couch. Couches to me were, like, what rich people had."

If love existed in that overcrowded three-room apartment, and one presumes that in some form it did, it wasn't often or openly expressed. The Rosen family was curiously stoic, dispassionate, more likely to dispense punishment than affection, or even approval. Everybody had a job to do, a role to play, and in that tiny apartment on Pulaski Street, the boundaries were clearly drawn. One of the first words little Barbara ever learned was "no"—it would be a word she would hear ringing in her ears—and one she would object to for the course of her life.

According to Sheldon Streisand, the Rosens were "decent, hardworking people, but there was no love in that house. I remember there was a huge table in the dining room and Barbara and I would scuttle under it to avoid beatings."

Diana, meanwhile, continued to wallow in her great tragedy and withdrew from her children. Little Barbara would sometimes crawl across the apartment floor to the window overlooking the street and peer out, as though waiting for her father to come home. Seeing her this way broke Diana's heart, but she offered her daughter little solace. "Emotionally," Barbra would later reflect, "my mother left me at the same time [as my father]. She was in her own trauma."

Diana's plaintive cry grew louder every time she walked out the door and onto the Brooklyn streets. Every place, everything, everyone, reminded her of her dear departed Manny. She was so consumed by what was, and what could've been, that she was blinded, sadly, to what still could be. Eventually, finances dictated that Diana get a job. The war had ended, and in the spirit of triumph and optimism, businesses were beginning to spring up everywhere. Easily enough, she found a job in downtown Brooklyn as a bookkeeper.

In the years that followed, Shelley and Barbara were raised, essentially, by their asthmatic grandmother, and by an amiable woman with a penchant for knitting by the name of Toby Berakow. Every morning when Diana left for work, Barbara, shaking with fear, certain of an impending traffic accident, wondered if her mother would return home that night. Parents, she had learned, sometimes didn't.

When Diana *did* return home at night, she was almost always too tired and too impatient to tolerate Barbara's litany of questions about the outside world. "Go away and play," was a phrase frequently employed to dismiss Barbara. "I didn't have any toys to play with," she would later relate. "All I had was a hot-water bottle with a little sweater on it. That was my doll." Interestingly, many years later, when she had become a mother herself, Barbra was asked if she intended to spoil Jason, her recently born son. "He can play with a walnut," she quipped in response, "or [he can] explore the carpet."

She improvised with other toys as well. At the age of two, Barbara climbed atop a chair beside her grandmother's dresser, and, using the edge of her favorite blanket, smeared lipstick all over her face. Reprimanded and rejected and "shhhh'd" away (often done with one menacing finger placed over the lips), Barbara retreated into her own world where little girls had tea sets and party dresses and daddies upon whose laps they sat.

She would spend hours in front of the mirror, attempting to put on her mother's makeup, and when that wasn't available, she substituted her brother's crayolas. Sheldon, meanwhile, entertained himself with an interest in Indian lore. He would spend hours collecting and playing with feathers. Among his impressive creations was a chieftain's headdress, which Barbara loved to parade in and model before the mirror. Once, she raided Shelley's dresser drawers and pretended she was the father of the country, George Washington. Barbara had a thing about fathers of all kinds. She always would.

On another occasion, after watching him shave, she tried using her grandfather's razor. She cut her lip and was rushed to the hospital. The blood was disquieting, but little Barbara reveled in the attention.

In September 1946, at the age of four, Barbara was sent to kindergarten at the nearby Yeshiva of Brooklyn. Diana saw her daughter off on the first day armed with a brown paper bag lunch and an inventory of *don'ts*. "Don't talk to strangers," "don't cross the street," "don't go near the water," Diana instructed. "Don't do this," and "don't do that." As Barbra would later say, "I was raised to be frightened of everything."

Terrified by the horrors that surely awaited her, Barbara sat obediently at her desk under the big pink ribbon which adorned her hair. In time, however, she came to enjoy school, if for no other reason than that it provided an outlet for her questions, and a reprieve from the grim and claustrophobic cubicle that was her home.

After school, Barbara sought refuge from her grandmother's disapproving glances in the apartment of Toby Berakow, who lived in the same tenement building, and whom Barbra referred to as "the Knitting Lady." Berakow and her husband had a son named Irving who attended school with Barbra. More important, they were among the first in the neighborhood to have a television set. It was a miniature with a seven-and-a-half-inch screen, and as Barbra recalled years later, "I remember his mother cooking stuffed cabbage and knitting every afternoon while we watched Laurel and Hardy through a magnifying window." It was on that tiny television set that Barbara was introduced to a world she would grow to covet, the world outside of Brooklyn.

Typical, perhaps, of the stereotypical "Jewish mother," one of the primary ways Diana demonstrated love for her children was by making them eat—and eat. Once, she chased Shelley around the apartment, plate in hand, while he pedaled ahead of her on his small bicycle.

Usually, though, it was her daughter's lack of appetite that drove Diana to distraction. Barbara was skinny and gangling and had protruding bones. It wasn't so much that she refused to eat, she was just particular about *what* she ate, and wasn't prone to gaining weight. Even then, her energy was unrivaled. Still, Barbara secretly delighted in her mother's show of concern. She learned how to manipulate her mother. If she wanted attention, she simply had to withhold the fork from her mouth.

Afraid that her daughter was anemic, Diana sent Barbara, at age five, off to what has been described as a summer "health camp." For Barbara, it was a distressing, even painful experience. Her introduction to the camp was particularly disconcerting. "I remember their taking off my clothes and dumping me into this bath like I was a piece of dirt," Barbra later related. "They scrubbed me and washed me and put this lice disinfectant in my hair, then they put me into their uniform."

Homesick, she made crying an everyday ritual, which provoked merciless ridicule from the other kids in the camp. Wiping the tears from her eyes, Barbara, with defiant ardor, insisted that she hadn't been crying at all—that she simply had a loose tear duct that couldn't be controlled. Mocked by her peers, Barbara was befriended by an older girl named Marie. Interestingly, as a child and over the years, Barbra would always be more comfortable with people older than herself.

One day at camp, Barbara boldly jumped into a pool of water. Hysterical, and certain that she was going to drown, Barbara was rescued by Marie. From that day on, and for the course of her life, Barbara would be afraid of the water. Beginning with that summer, she would also suffer from periodic psychosomatic asthma attacks when she went to the country.

Back home in Brooklyn, dubbed "the City of Churches" because it had a church on every corner, Barbara, then in the first grade, engaged in a debate with her friends, Rosalyn Arenstein and Joanne Micelli. Rosalyn was an atheist, Joanne was Catholic, and Barbara, of course, was a Jew. When Rosalyn insisted that there was no God, Barbara argued adamantly that she was misinformed. "I believed in God very strongly," she later related. "We were on her fire escape, and I said I am going to pray to God that that man on the curb steps into the gutter [on the side of the street] . . . and sure enough, the man walked across the street." When Joanne, who attended Saint Joseph's, proclaimed, "The Jews killed Christ," Barbara, a member of the Yeshiva of Brooklyn, took it personally and shot back, "No they didn't!"

Still, she couldn't resist a little rebellion at the yeshiva, which she attended until the third grade. From early on, she defied her assigned role of the stereotypical "nice Jewish girl." She hated being marginalized, although she didn't have the vocabulary for it. She wanted emancipation. Sometimes when the rabbi would leave the room, Barbara would cause an uproar in class with the pronouncement of a single profanity. The word? "Christmas!"

She used to fantasize about being Catholic. She adored the nuns, the priests, and their clothes, and would raise a few eyebrows in the neighborhood by walking around saying, "Hello, Father," to this person and that. She loved the beauty and the pageantry of the Church, particularly when compared to the drabness of the yeshiva.

In the summer of 1949, despite an arduous protest, Barbara, at the age of seven, was again sent away to camp. Perhaps one reason Diana sent her children away was that she had begun dating. After six years of mourning, Diana wanted a home of her own and a father for her children, and at the age of forty, she sensed that her time was limited.

During her mother's dates, Barbara used to hide under her grandmother's table and eavesdrop. "I remember listening to the adults misinterpret each other," Barbra would later recall. "I remember thinking, 'Oh no, he's talking about one thing, she's talking about another, and they don't know it.'" She adds, tellingly, "I hated those men. Once I saw a man kissing my mother. I thought he was killing her. Except she was laughing."

It is possible, of course, that Barbara would not have liked any man eventually settled upon by her mother. She certainly did not like Louis Kind, whom she was first introduced to when Diana brought him with her on a visit to the summer camp. Fourteen years older than Diana, Kind, aged fifty-five, worked at various times peddling real estate and used cars, in addition to a stint as a tailor, and hardly resembled the gallant knight on the white horse that Barbara envisioned as her stepfather.

On both sides, there was suspicion, jealousy, and dislike at first sight. Barbara, crying, related the cruelty of her cocampers. Kind attempted to reassure Barbara that the camp was not such a bad place, and that she just needed to try harder to make friends. Barbara's crying grew louder. She stomped her feet and told her mother in no uncertain terms, "You are *not* leaving here without me!" Caught in the middle of the fray, as would happen repeatedly in the years to come, Diana nervously packed Barbara's bags and the three of them drove back to Brooklyn in silence. It was Barbara's feeling that Louis Kind had hated her ever since.

Whenever he showed up at the door of the Pulaski Street apartment, Kind braced himself for an outburst of hysterics from Barbara. "Don't go with *him,* Mommy, stay with *me,"* she would plead as she clung to Diana's skirt. Partly, Barbara was convinced that Diana would get hurt in a car accident or some other calamity if she walked out the door. Mostly, though, she was afraid that her mother, who represented the only stability that she knew, was being taken away from her by this strange and unpleasant man. Barbara sensed that the life she knew was about to change for the worse. And she would be right.

Diana married Louis Kind later that year, and the family moved out of the Bedford-Stuyvesant projects and into Flatbush, to a middle-class building known, somewhat pretentiously, as the Vanderveer Estates. Located at 3102 Newkirk Avenue, near the corner of Nostrand, the apartment was hardly a palace, but certainly an improvement over their previous one. On the first night in their new home, Barbara cried and insisted that she be allowed to sleep, as she was accustomed to, in the bed with her mother.

When she woke up the following morning, Barbara complained to Diana that she had a click in her ears. The click, Barbara feared, was some kind of a psychic warning. Diana, perturbed that she hadn't been able to sleep with her new husband, dismissed her daughter with, "Well, sleep on a hot-water bottle!" From that day on, Barbara kept the mysterious clicks in her ears to herself. Two years later, the clicks would be replaced by a high-pitched wail that would remain with her for the rest of her life. She walked around the neighborhood with a scarf around her head to block out the sound, which only made it worse. She kept the noise a secret and retreated into her own world, certain that she had been singled out, certain that she was marked for tragedy—or for greatness.

Surprisingly, Barbara Streisand's first venture into show business was not as a singer, or even as an actress, but, rather, as a ballet dancer. Against her better judgment, Diana enrolled Barbara in Miss Marsh's ballet school. "I always wanted to be a classical ballerina," Barbra related, "but my mother thought I was too skinny and my bones would break. The first few times I pointed my toes, I got a pain in my arch." Nonetheless, Diana conceded to Barbara's continued lessons, and even purchased for her a tall black hat and a stick for a proposed tap dance routine.

The lessons, however, along with Barbara's aspirations of pirouetting grandeur, came to an abrupt end after six months when Miss Marsh moved out of the neighborhood. "Was I happy," Diana confessed, "when this instructor moved away."

Barbara had to content herself, much to her mother's further chagrin, with roller-skating in the Brooklyn gutters. She later recounted, "I used to go to the Roller Dome, you know, inside, where you rented skates, and my dream was always to have a pair of my own, but I never got them. I wanted the good kind, with shoes, not the kind you clamp on that tear the sole right off your shoe." Such were the signs of status on the streets of Brooklyn.

The neighborhood may have been an improvement over their previous one, but Barbara's living conditions changed little. She still had no bedroom of her own. "I lived with my mother in Brooklyn until I left high school," Barbra later said, "and in all that time I never had a room of my own. I slept on a couch. Ever sleep on a couch night after night? All you think about is, 'How can I get a room of my own?' You get to the point where you *have* to make good!"

Her mother and stepfather shared one room, her brother, in the middle of his adolescence, got the other, and Barbara was relegated to sleeping on the front room davenport. The one perceptible difference was that, along with all of his other baggage, Mr. Kind came blessedly equipped with a television set, which was installed in the front room. Delighted with this addition to the family, and with such programs as "Arthur Godfrey's Talent Scouts," "Your Show of Shows," "Texaco Star Theater," and "Philco Television Playhouse," Barbara became a devoted member of the first television generation.

As much as she enjoyed these and other shows, she was equally entertained by the commercials. She began spending an inordinate amount of time in front of the bathroom mirror, the only one in the apartment, hawking, among other things, toothpaste, shaving cream, and cigarettes. She became so adept at "doing commercials" that she decided to perform them for her mother and stepfather. Louis Kind, however, was unamused, and Diana was preoccupied by another addition to the family, a baby girl named Roslyn. Besides, Diana viewed the television set, as she did most everything, with suspicion. "Don't get too close to it," Diana warned, concerned about her daughter's already slightly crossed eyes, "you'll go blind."

Undaunted, in front of that hallowed bathroom mirror, Barbara convinced herself that she was going to be a movie star, an accomplished dramatic actress, and a television commercial spokesperson. "I'll show them," she said to herself as she practiced her repertoire of facial expressions, "I'll show them." She would be the greatest, the biggest, the best.

"I remember a long time ago, when I was a kid, I hadda be somebody," said Barbra in later years. "I hadda be great. I couldn't be medium. My mouth was too big."

It wasn't just her mother and stepfather whom she wanted to "show," it was everybody who had ever uttered a "no" in her direction, or ever given her a disparaging glance, including the other kids in the neighborhood. Once, she was pushed into the pond of the Botanical Gardens in Prospect Park. The other girls laughed. Barbara, drenched, ran away crying. She was easy to pick on. Children seldom need a reason for their cruelty, attacking anyone who looks or seems different. Barbara bristled at any sign of rejection by others, which, of course, only made them pick on her more.

She later related, "When I was nine years old, sometimes the girls would gang up on me in my neighborhood, make a circle around me, make fun of me, and I'd start to cry and then run away. I'm still trying to find out why."

Barbara's few allies at the time included two of her classmates at her new school, P.S. 89, who lived in the same building, Maxine Eddelson and Ed Frankel. "We were very close," says Frankel, today a financial adviser. "I lived in apartment 3A and Barbara lived up on 4G, I think it was. Our families knew each other from the old neighborhood, Bedford-Stuyvesant. Her grandparents owned the fish market where we used to purchase fish."

"We lived at Vanderveer Estates," Frankel relates, "an apartment complex that was a part of the Vanderveer Projects. It was the biggest apartment complex in the city and covered quite a few square blocks. Public School 89 was right across the street. We had a large courtyard, which all of the apartments surrounded, and there was a parklike setting with benches, where people could sit, or take care of their children, and wheel their baby carriages. There was a sandbox and swings, where the kids would play. Barbara and I used to play at the swings and carry on with other friends.

"Nostrand Avenue was the main street with all the stores," he goes on. "On the corner was Vanderveer Drugs, a pharmacy/luncheonette. There was an Ebinger's Bakery, a famous old Brooklyn German bakery, right next to the drugstore. Next to it was a Smilen's fruit and vegetable stand. Next to that was a butcher shop and a dry cleaners. Across the street was the pizza place where we would stop in the afternoon for pizza and sodas, and next to that was a shoe store. They were all predominantly mom-and-pop type of stores, except for the A&P, which was a major market.

"There was a gal named Maxine Eddelson," says Frankel, when asked to name some of their other friends. "When we were real small, eight or nine years old, we used to gather around and carry on like all kids did. And one day we were in Barbara's apartment—I don't know if she remembers this—but we were playing doctor. I was the doctor, and Barbara was the nurse, and"—he laughs—"Maxine was the 'victim.' We called her the victim because we stripped her down, powdered her up, and did all those good things that all kids do. When it came Barbara's turn to be the victim, she chickened out.

"She had a flair for creating characters," Frankel continues. "We used to put on little shows. She had a very vivid imagination about setting up themes and different stories. One time, when it was just Barbara and myself, she told me that her mother was a descendant of some Hawaiian tribe, and she had all these secret formulas and stuff. So, Barbara concocted a fruit drink for me. She was also taking Hawaiian dance. She was doing the hula."

Meanwhile, Barbara's relationship with Louis Kind worsened. He had little tolerance for what he considered to be her self-absorbed antics and her manipulative ploys for her mother's attention. Once, when Barbara refused to eat, Diana ordered her to go to bed. When she was in bed, Diana proceeded to force-feed Barbara as though she were an infant. "I've never seen a happier look on a child's face," Kind later recalled with disdain. "Not only did she lap up the food, but also the attention she was getting."

On another occasion, over some domestic disobedience, Diana slapped Barbara across the ear. Vengeful, for the next several hours Barbara walked around the apartment with a blank look on her face, insisting that she was deaf. Diana, filled with remorse, panicked, and Barbara, pleased with her charade, was now certain that she could act.

Kind, however, was infuriated by the theatrics. For the most part, though, he literally ignored Barbara. She would ask him a question, and he would pretend that she wasn't there. She would try again, and again she would be silently turned away.

The marriage between Mr. and Mrs. Kind was shrouded in fear, hostility, and violence. Today, there are various support systems for a child growing up in an abusive home, but for Barbara Joan Streisand, it was a way of life, and one that she was ordered, just as Tom Wingo was, to keep secret. Sometimes, when Kind would be abusive to Diana, Barbara watched through a fury of tears. "He was mean to my mother," she would say nearly forty years later in understatement, still, perhaps, unable to articulate the atrocity. "I saw him be mean to her. This was not a nice man."

Barbara watched as her mother was being beaten down by Kind, and a future feminist was born. No man would ever put *her* down without a fight. No man would ever imprison her in a life of subordination. No man would ever make her feel *insignificant.*

Sometimes, it was Barbara herself who got hit. "I know that she never got along with her stepfather," Ed Frankel grimly relates. "He used to [emotionally] abuse her. I know he verbally abused her. I know he hit her at least once or twice. She did not have a good childhood at that point. I used to hear shouting and carrying on from upstairs. Her mother's best friend was my mother. They used to have tea in the afternoon together, and her mother used to confide to my mother what was going on."

Frank Volpe was a good friend of Toby Berakow's in the last years of her life (she passed away circa 1990); "Toby was always telling me," Volpe says, "that Louis Kind was very mean to Barbara. He would taunt her and tell her that she wasn't pretty, and that she would never amount to anything. And he was verbally abusive, to the point that Barbara would run away crying all the time."

Like many abused children, Barbara thought that it was she, somehow, who was at fault. "I just thought that *I* was awful. I must be so awful," she later related. Barbara braved the beatings, but like many child abuse victims, it was the emotional abuse that was most traumatic and had the greatest impact. Once, Kind, with astonishing cruelty, told Barbara that she couldn't have an ice cream cone because she was too ugly. "He was really mean to Barbara," concurred Sheldon Streisand. "He taunted her continually, telling her how plain she was compared to Roslyn." In fact, when addressing the two girls, Kind would refer to them sadistically as "the beauty and the beast," and he made no bones about which one of them was the beauty and which one wasn't.

"Barbara was a typical Cinderella story," says Ed Frankel. "Her mother was a nice person, but her mother showed the affection toward Roslyn and her husband, not toward Barbara. I guess that he was a domineering husband, and that was what he required. Barbara was basically forced to wash the floors, and do all of the chores, everything. Her mother and stepfather were always going, 'Barbara do this, Barbara do that!' And she wasn't even thanked or rewarded for it. And the reward that she wanted, like any child, was affection.

"Barbara was really closed about that aspect of her life," says Ed Frankel, "but we *knew*. It was very easy to know that there was friction between her and her stepfather. Back then, there *was* child abuse, but there was nothing known about child abuse, or the different forms of child abuse. We were very closed people. We would not discuss the things that really troubled us."

It's little wonder that when Barbara stood before her mirror, she despised what she saw. It's a difficult moment in the life of a young girl when she confronts the mirror and comprehends that her face is not quite what it should be. Her beloved television had been airing a series of 1930s movies, and Barbara wanted desperately to look like Shirley Temple. Instead, her hair hung down, limp and straight. Her eyes were crossed. Her nose jumped out of her face. Her mouth was too big.

She was too ugly to live. Literally. One day, she came across a pamphlet on cancer which listed nine symptoms of the disease, and she became certain that she had every one of them. In her self-loathing, she had convinced herself that she had only six months to live. Within days, she began to develop psychosomatic illnesses. "I'll show them," she thought to herself, with the back of one hand held woefully against her forehead. "I'll die a tragic death," she vowed, thinking of the ill-fated heroines she had seen on television, "and then they'll be sorry." And so, as she sat atop the roof of her apartment building, nine-year-old Barbara Streisand took a deep, dramatic drag on her cigarette as she plotted her early demise.

Three

Metamorphosis

*W*ay, way, *way* off-Broadway, 1952, Barbara Joan Streisand, aged ten, sat atop the stoop in front of her parents' apartment building on New-kirk Avenue as she unveiled her singing voice upon a dreary, work-weary world. It was a less than auspicious debut, what with young Barbara at-tempting to sound like Joni James, her favorite singer on the hit parade (along with Johnny Mathis and Peggy Lee), while her friends, Ed Fran-kel among them, harmonized with their off-key "oohs" and their high-pitched "ahhs." Parents stuck their heads out of their windows and politely applauded when the kids finished their repertoire.

Actually, she had been singing for years, to an audience of brick and mortar. "I remember singing in the hallways of my Brooklyn apart-ment," Barbra related years later, "and there was a great echo sound in this hallway and I thought, 'Oh, that's pleasant. That doesn't sound bad.'" "We used to sit out on the front stoop on summer nights," recalls Ed Frankel. "In the winter, we'd sit on the staircase in the apartment building. It would be Barbara, me, Maxine, and a couple of other people who lived in the building. Sometimes, Melvin Brown would come around. We'd sing the popular songs of the day. Show tunes too. Some-times, Barbara and I would do duets."

Although the response to her warbling was less than enthusiastic, it was, at least, an overture of approval and gave her the attention she craved. She was to make her official debut at a local PTA meeting. The day of the event, however, she came down with a bad cold and was or-dered to stay in bed. That night, defying her mother's command, Bar-bara slipped into her new dress and, in between sneezes, gave her first public performance as scheduled. And so, Barbara continued to sing, as one day yawned at another, and in time, she came to be known in the neighborhood as "that funny-looking kid with the good voice."

"Barbara and I were also in the chorus in P.S. 89," relates Ed Frankel. "Our teacher was Mrs. Beach. I was a really rotten kid in school, and I used to carry on and do all types of crazy things. I was always in trouble. Barbara was the 'A' student. She always performed well in anything she did. Everybody knew she had a voice. *She* knew that she had a good voice. I told her that she could be a singing star. I was the very first fan she ever had."

Diana regarded her older daughter's singing voice as palatable but weak, and in the years that followed, she even suggested that it was Roslyn and not Barbara who had the superior gift. And so it was with reluctance that Diana escorted a determined Barbara to auditions at the Steve Allen studio, and the MGM recording studio. On the occasion of the latter, Barbara, aged ten, wore a blue dress with a white collar and cuffs from the Abraham and Straus department store, and she sang Joni James's "Have You Heard?" behind a glass booth. "I felt sure they'd want me," Barbra would later say, "but they just said 'Thank you' and that was it." Actually, according to Diana, both auditions went favorably, but "when they said, 'No pay,' I said, 'No child.' "

The rejections rolled off Barbara's skinny back. She was used to them. Back at home, the walls of the apartment were her prison, and she spent much of her young life with her hands clasped behind her head, staring at the ceiling, plotting, scheming, dreaming up a plan for the day she would make her departure. Until then, though, she escaped in the solace of a darkened movie theater and a ritual of Saturday afternoon matinees. She had her favorites, of course. She sat, eyes fixed to the screen, and fell in love with, among others, Gregory Peck and Marlon Brando. "Now, *they're* what I call men," Barbara thought dreamily to herself as she put their pictures up on the wall over her couch of a bed. She vowed that one day (when she became a star of equal stature, of course), she would *have* such men for herself.

Of the women, Barbara was awed by the beauties of the day: the cool, classic, Aryan elegance of Grace Kelly, the sultry sexiness of Rita Hayworth, the wide-eyed innocence of Natalie Wood, and the smoldering perfection of Elizabeth Taylor.

Audrey Hepburn was another favorite, and the one to whom Barbara could most relate. At the age of twenty-one, Audrey had triumphed on Broadway in *Gigi*. Three years later, she attained international movie stardom with *Roman Holiday* (1953), in which she portrayed an unorthodox princess. In *Sabrina* (1954), she was the poor chauffeur's daughter who commands the love of her father's employer's wealthy sons—both of them. She is swept off her feet and out of poverty and into princessdom. In *Funny Face* (1957), she was the object of Fred Astaire's desire. He loved her nontraditional beauty and her "funny face," and not only did he fall in love with her, he turned her into a high-fashion model. Of such things, the teenage Barbara Streisand's dreams were made.

Like Audrey's, Barbara's looks were unconventional. Like Audrey, Barbara was criticized for being too thin. On the night she would win an Oscar for *Roman Holiday,* Audrey was sped via limousine from the Broadway theater where she was starring in *Ondine* to the NBC Century Theatre, where the Oscars were being held. Upon her arrival, Audrey was rushed to a dressing room where she hastily took off her stage makeup. A photographer from *Life* magazine who was accompanying her pounded on the dressing room door and bellowed, "Hey, skinny, come on out!" The words, Barbara fantasized as she devoured the press reports of that evening, could have been meant for *her.* She read further about how, after the awards ceremony, Audrey joined her fiancé, Mel Ferrer, and Deborah Kerr for a celebration drink at the Persian Room, and how Audrey, three nights later, won the Best Actress Tony award for *Ondine.*

She read breathlessly about these and other stories in the movie magazines which she collected. When she returned home from her glorious Saturday sojourns, Barbara sulked miserably around the apartment. She was an extremely moody child by nature, but never more so than after going to the movies.

"My mother hated it when I went to the movies," Barbra related. "I was always grouchy for a couple of days afterward. After looking at all those beautiful clothes, apartments, and furniture, coming back to the place where we lived used to depress me."

Compounding her depression was her own lack of glamour. Back then, she *yearned* for glamour. "I used to spend a lot of time and money in the penny arcades," she would confess, "taking pictures of myself in those little booths. I'd experiment with different colored mascara on my eyes, [and] try out all kinds of different hairstyles and sexy poses."

She wanted to be a Tennessee Williams heroine, but, instead, she was a Paddy Chayefsky reject. And she was reminded of this every time she looked at those four-in-a-strip arcade photos, or in the mirror after returning home from the movies. Still, she would spend hours in front of that mirror, determinedly applying various brazen shades of lipstick and eyeshadow that had been purchased with her school-lunch money. When money for makeup wasn't available, she would dip into her mother's cosmetics, mixing this with that, and come up with violet lips or some other concoction. Or, she would take her brother's colored pencils and use them for eye makeup. "Somehow," Barbara reflected, "it made me think I was attractive."

"I was a very strange kid," she allows. "Every day when I came home from school, I'd put on these old ballet shoes and go to the bathroom to sneak a smoke. I'd put on false eyelashes and do cigarette commercials in front of the mirror."

Diana, meanwhile, continued to try to get Barbara to eat, with little success. Barbara sustained herself, instead, with her dreams of glamour and escape, intertwined with "I'll show you!" drive. She smoked cigarettes in the bathroom and on the roof not for the rebelliousness but for the Bette Davis drama of it. "Fasten your seat belts—" puff, puff, "it's going to be a bumpy night!"

Throughout her childhood, Barbara was always fictionalizing her life story, because she didn't like the one that had been written for her. She would create and re-create herself, because she didn't like what fate and heredity had given her. She hated her Jewish nose, and she willed herself to be Italian. Italians, after all, also had prominent (though to her somehow more aesthetically pleasing) noses. Later, while living in Manhattan, she would occasionally employ an Italian alias, Angelina Scarangella, which she claimed to pick out of the phone book on a whim.

The selection of an Italian identity, however, was anything but a whim. Back in Brooklyn, she read books on the culture, studied the language, and remade herself Italian. She also remade herself Catholic. She remade herself Oriental. She tried on, for size, different looks, different names, and different personas. It's no wonder that her parents were troubled by her moodiness; little did they know that she was always changing her identity.

"I always knew I would be famous," Barbra professed. "I knew it; I wanted it. I always wanted to be out of what I was in. Out of Brooklyn. I had to get out. I was never contented. I was always trying to be something I wasn't. I wanted to prove to the world that they shouldn't make fun of me."

She really wanted to prove to the world that she could not be ignored. She vowed with a vengeance that she would flaunt her eventual success in the faces of her stepfather and mother for, respectively, abusing and underestimating her. At first, Diana dismissed Barbara's talk of movie star glory as passing adolescent dribble. When she realized, however, that her daughter was serious, Diana put her down. "Movie stars are *pretty*," she told her daughter, and suggested that she think instead of a more suitable, more practical, more attainable ambition.

Curiously, Diana rarely complimented Barbara on anything, despite the fact that she invariably brought home school report cards that would enthrall most mothers. Barbara would lament, "My mother never said to me, 'You're smart, you're pretty . . . you can do what you want.' She never told me anything like that." She adds, "I was always trying to prove to her that I was worthwhile, that I wasn't just a skinny little *ma-rink*." Interestingly, over the years, Barbra would masochistically take over where her mother left off, and be even harder on herself than her mother ever was.

While growing up, Barbara despaired at her mother's uncharitable indifference. Furthermore, she resented her for allowing Louis Kind into their lives, and once in, for permitting him to stay. Diana even tried to rationalize, if not excuse, his behavior by telling Barbara, "He's allergic to kids." In 1953, Kind made his exit from the family, to Barbara's great relief, but it was not at Diana's command. And it was not for good. "He went off and then came back on several occasions," recalls Ed Frankel. Finally, one day he went out for the proverbial pack of cigarettes and never returned. Instead of feeling abandoned, however, Barbara was elated. The rest of her days in Brooklyn might be boring, but at least they would be bearable. Barely.

Distanced from her mother, Barbara longed to know more about her biological father. The absence of a father left her with an insurmountable emotional void. Sometimes, she looked at her mother and saw a stranger. Surely, she hoped, she was more *connected* to her father. But she knew little about him except that he had been an "educator," a word Barbra would come to revere. She didn't even have a photograph of the two of them together. All that was left of him were his books, which were tied up with string in the cellar.

Diana, certainly, was of no help. For reasons of her own, she kept her reminiscences of Emanuel Streisand to herself. She did not tell Barbara that his dream, like hers, was to one day go to California, or that his secret ambition was to become a writer. Nor did she tell Barbara that she had inherited her interest in drama from her father.

With Louis Kind at least temporarily excised from the family portrait (he would leave for good in 1956), Diana returned to work in 1953, and

Barbara, eleven, secured a job of her own, baby-sitting for a neighbor, Muriel Choy. Mrs. Choy and her family owned a local restaurant named Choy's Chinese, and in time, Barbara, who was particularly adept at math, was put on the payroll as a cashier. Sometimes, when business was slow, she also worked as the hostess; sometimes, she took phone orders for take-out; other times, she waited on tables and tried out her few words of Chinese on the bemused, egg-roll-eating customers.

"Jimmy and Muriel Choy lived in our building," relates Ed Frankel. "They had two very cute daughters. The restaurant was on Nostrand Avenue, within a block of where we lived. Barbara just walked to work. Jimmy's mother and father were also involved in the restaurant for a long period of time. The Choys," Frankel recalls affectionately, "were very warm, open people."

Barbara was all but adopted by the Choys. She remade herself Chinese, and delighted in being a member of a minority. Being Jewish in Brooklyn was commonplace, and she loathed the commonplace. It was them against the world at Choy's Chinese, and Barbara frequently loitered there after hours, engrossed in conversation with Muriel Choy. It was Muriel who talked to Barbara about the things Diana dared not mention: boys, romance, sex. She also talked to Barbara about makeup and manicures, and in time, Barbara flashed inch-long nails to complement her long, slender fingers. She would later quip to reporters that she had grown her nails to ward off typing lessons. Actually, they served another purpose. Painted fire engine red, they gave Barbara, in her teenage mind, an illusion of the glamour she so desperately wanted.

And then, of course, there was the food. To Diana, Chinese food was wickedly sinful, and smacked of betrayal. It also represented something of a rival, because her daughter seemed to prefer dishes with names like "sweet and sour" this, and "moo shoo" that, to her own, less exotic cooking. To Barbara, Chinese food was liberating. Each delectable bite represented a revolt against her upbringing. She came to love it all with a passion, from the crispy fried wonton, to the fresh baked bread stuffed with shrimp, to the obligatory, meal-ending fortune cookie. During her tenure at Choy's Chinese, Barbara would go through untold hundreds of fortune cookies, searching for a printed validation of the future she *knew* would be hers.

Late at night, Barbara indulged in another passion, the late-late-late movies on television. The problem was privacy. She now shared the front room with her younger sister, eight years her junior, who could not sleep with the blaring cinematic commotion. "She'd pay her dues by putting me to sleep tickling my back with her long nails," Roslyn would later confide, "[and] she'd bribe me with coffee ice cream." Unlike Barbara, Diana had no problem whatsoever in getting little Roslyn to eat.

In fact, little Roslyn was *not* so little. In the third grade, she played a fat Peter Pan in the school play. Says Roslyn, with self-deprecating humor, "They couldn't fly me across the stage." In her teenage years, Roslyn ballooned up to 189 pounds and a 20½ dress size. Still, that wouldn't be enough for Diana. "Mother and her chicken soup, already," Roslyn exclaimed, exasperated. "If I didn't eat it she'd say, 'You're so thin I could break you.' " But dutiful Roslyn, unlike Barbara, always ate for her mother.

By the time she entered high school in September 1955 at the age of thirteen, not only had Barbara braved years of rejection, she was a pro at it. She was not going to be rejected by society. She would reject *it.* It was a teenager's way of taking control, of self-preservation. And so she withdrew, went about her business, and lived for her future. She maintained her grades, which provided her with only a nominal challenge, and for the most part, she kept to herself. She was quiet, until drawn out; a loner, until approached.

But, and this is important in understanding her self-perception, then and in later years, she was hardly the ridiculed, "absolute misfit" of a punching bag that she and her previous biographers have repeatedly made her out to be. Nor was she perceived in high school to be this hideous, practically deformed, freak of nature. It is possible that, upon her success, *Barbra* revised her life story and fed such anecdotes to the press because they made good copy. Since she hadn't been deemed the most beautiful girl in school, or the most popular, or even the most likely to succeed, she may have decided to recast herself as the most outrageous, if not the most pathetic.

It is more likely, however, that Barbara actually *believed* that she was *thought of* as the high school doormat. Like many victims of child abuse, she was always hardest on herself. Similarly, she perceived herself to be the perennial victim, with "Why me? Why me? Why me?" topping her list of questions.

In fact, instead of having the outlandish, "kooky" hairdos, makeup, and clothing that she has been characterized as wearing, Barbara groomed herself meticulously in front of the mirror every morning before school. She was still striving for glamour, and one of her favorite accessories was a strand of fake pearls, hardly the accessory of choice for beatnik rebellion. She would abandon the all-consuming pursuit of being pretty in favor of flamboyance only *after* she graduated from high school. In school, she *was* one of the few girls to wear makeup, a fact which made her envied, rather than pitied, by her peers. By then, she had become proficient at makeup application, and had affected some semblance of attractiveness. About the most "radical" things Barbara did in high school was to refuse to cut her beloved nails; and she sported a streak of bleached blond hair. Instead of being scorned, however, it was a fashion statement that would be emulated by the other Jewish girls at the time.

And, contrary to the pathos inherent in the often told drama of the lone wolf, Barbara had her share of good friends. First of all, there were Maxine Eddelson and Ed Frankel from the Vanderveer Estates, both of whom attended high school with Barbara. And there were others. Over thirty-five years later, and for the first time, one of Barbara's high school friends agreed to be interviewed for this book. Diane Silverstein, today Diane Lemm, an accountant, was one of Barbara's best friends in high school.

"I met Barbara on the first day of school when we were both freshmen," Diane relates. "They used to sit you in alphabetical order, and I was Silverstein and she was Streisand, and apparently there was nobody in between us, because she was always seated right behind me."

Erasmus Hall High School, located on Flatbush Avenue, was the oldest secondary school in the state, founded in 1787 as an all-boys institution. In 1955, it was a highly prestigious school, with a reputation for turning out honor students and a succession of Westinghouse science winners. It also turned out a large number of renowned figures, including Barbara Stanwyck.

Diane Lemm continues, "Upon graduating from the eighth grade, and this was also true of Barbara's public school, those students who graduated with all A's, and were tested, were deemed to be what was known as 'honor students.' I was one of those students, and so was Barbara. Then, in those days, school officials would lump students together depending upon what foreign language they chose. They gave you three choices—French, Spanish, or Latin. I picked Spanish, naturally, as the majority of us were doing. The Puerto Ricans had come to New York, that was the big influx at the time, and people started moving into the neighborhood who were speaking Spanish. So, those students who graduated from the 'feeder' eighth-grade public schools, who were deemed to be honor students, and who took Spanish, were put into one class. Barbara and I met the first day of school in class 1102. It was always 'Miss Streisand,' this,

'Miss Silverstein,' that. It was funny, when we got to Spanish it was 'Señorita Silverstein,' 'Señorita Streisand.'

"I was excellent in Spanish, and so was Barbara. I think our first Spanish teacher was Mrs. Thomas, a Jewish lady who spoke with a lisp. We had some corkers over the years, like Miss Frizzita, who would get really mad at us. Her real name was Mrs. Fried, another Jewish lady, but she was known as Miss Frizzita. They used to have these Spanish movies that they would run at the Astor Theatre next door to the school. So, very often on Saturday mornings, we had to go to school and see these movies with subtitles. I remember being very jealous of Barbara in Spanish because, at the end of the term, she got an award for having the highest Spanish average in the whole high school.

"Barbara was quiet," Lemm continues, "but everyone liked her. I was with a clique, and she was shy until she was with us. She'd come up with these funny comments—we used to mumble a lot under our breath—and in class, we'd always be leaning over, whispering back and forth. She was smart. She was fun. She was very honest. She appeared to be lonely and aloof, and so we took her into our circle, especially this one gal, Linda Ashendorf. Linda was a *beautiful* girl."

Bonding Señoritas Streisand and Silverstein were, among other things, the skinny legs and long, flashy fingernails they had in common. "We were always comparing nails," Lemm says. "Even now, when I see her in movies, I check out her nails." They were also the only two girls in class to wear makeup. "Her eyes were absolutely gorgeous, and we all used to tell her that. I think she was the first one in school who wore real mascara. She used to do wonders with eyeshadow. One day, Linda Ashendorf said to Barbara, 'God, Barbara, you're always so *colorful!*' Barbara wore this blue eyeshadow, and she was the forerunner of blush.

"She was *very* neat. She wore the long skirts and the white socks. We all wore sweater sets, you know, short-sleeved shirts with a sweater over it, and a neckerchief. We weren't allowed to wear sneakers in school. We had to wear leather shoes—loafers or saddle shoes, or white bucks that were dirty. We were very normal, we were all good kids, every last one of us. Except we all tried to act older, and we all smoked. We had to walk away from the building to smoke. The only thing against school rules back then was cutting class and going down to the local pool room. Mel Shanman, the boy's dean, used to go and yank them out. We girls didn't cut class."

When confronted with previously published stories that Barbara, in high school, was some sort of unattractive fashion freak, Diane balks. "I don't think those people [who are saying that] really knew Barbara. I knew her for four years. I always thought she was attractive. All of us thought she was good-looking. There was *never* any pity. I know that there was some envy from other classmates, you know, 'Oh, that Barbara. Look at that hair, look at that eye makeup, look at her nails, look at how neat.' Also, she didn't have a weight problem like some of the rest of us. Barbara did *not* look bizarre, I beg your pardon. She was a very pretty young lady. I won't buy that. Not in high school. *No way.*"

When asked why Barbara herself fed such stories to the press, Diane responds, "I don't know. Maybe that was the way she wanted it to be known." When asked if Barbara was teased about her nose in school, Diane laughs. "No! We *all* had Jewish noses. We all talked about getting nose jobs, all of us. None of us did it that I know of, maybe in later years. I didn't do it, that's for sure."

Others confirm Diane Lemm's depiction of Barbara as a fairly attractive girl who did not appear to be outlandish. Most of the Erasmus alumni contacted for this book had no recollection of her whatsoever. Surely, no matter how populated the school, if Barbara was indeed the pathetic freak that she and others have characterized her as being, she would have been remembered, if nothing else.

Marilyn Saposh was Barbara's first biology teacher. "Let me just tell you that she was in a biology class of many, many bright youngsters. It was a school that had exceedingly bright students, and Barbara was among those. She followed a curriculum that we would've called 'college prep.' She was very bright. I think I gave her a mark of 92 or 93. I don't think she came from a well-to-do family. She was rather quiet. She *wasn't* a class clown. She didn't make a big impact on the class. She was a good student, and she did well in the course, but not so much so that I would be able to single her out as being extraordinary."

Frederic Ansis, the student body president and the big man on campus at the time, also confirms Barbara's relative anonymity. "I never *heard* of this woman until she released her first album. Once, years later, I was in a coffee shop in the Century Plaza Hotel [in Los Angeles] and Barbra was sitting at the next table. I just really didn't have the nerve to go over and do the whole high school routine. In retrospect, I think all of us would've loved to have known her back then. Take us back thirty-five years, and we all probably would be hanging around her. She was there, this unpolished gem, right in our midst."

"Barbara and I got into a lot of trouble in gym class," Diane Lemm continues. "Mrs. Dorney and Mrs. Johnson were the gym teachers. They both looked like lesbians, but they weren't. Married women, you know? They just liked to play ball. Anyway, they were always *on* us because of our nails. They would check us, and we used to try and hide our hands, [but] you try and hold a basketball and catch it with long nails. So, we both got marked down, demerits, or whatever the heck they were called, because we wouldn't cut our nails."

Barbara loathed gym class, and, in particular, a required swimming test. "If you didn't pass the test," Lemm recalls with mock fear, "you had to take swimming and wear their bathing suits, these god-awful one-piece tank jobs." The pool was located in the dank basement, a cavernous room which reeked of chlorine. Observing the testing process was a matron dressed in white. "It was," Lemm says, "like something you'd see in a mental institution."

Prior to the start of class, Barbara, Diane, and Maxine concocted a plot: if one of them hesitated before jumping into the pool, then another girl would push her in. "None of us were swimmers," Lemm relates, "but we could stay afloat." They would each stay afloat long enough to pass the dreaded test, but only by clinging onto the edge of the pool.

Later, Barbara and Diane circumvented the system by taking an elective physical education course dubbed "dance gym."

"Barbara wasn't athletic," offers Diane. "None of us were athletic, those of us in dance gym. In dance gym, we didn't have to put on those ugly gym suits. We could wear leotards! And we could wear ballet slippers instead of sneakers! And they didn't care if we had long nails! So we learned modern dance, and Barbara was my dance gym partner. We had to do a dance of 'Slaughter on Tenth Avenue,' and our girlfriend Judy Jacobson—she was a ballet student—was the choreographer."

They hung out at Garfield's cafeteria and lunched on coffee and grapefruit, or a scoop of egg salad on a piece of lettuce. They talked about all the usual things: clothes, school, boys, other girls, makeup, and allowances. "That was a problem," Lemm recalls, "trying to make your allowance last." There were several sororities on campus at Erasmus, but Barbara, Diane, and their group were not among them. They called the sorority girls "cashmeres," because they wore cashmere sweaters to school. "None of us owned a cashmere sweater," Lemm relates, "we couldn't afford it." Sherry Bronson was a cashmere. So too were Michelle Weiss and Barbara Solomon.

Barbara was acutely aware of the differences between herself and the "cashmeres," and she envied them desperately. Living glamorously was difficult on her meager paychecks from Choy's Chinese. And so, sometimes when she was broke, she took to shoplifting. She wasn't, however, your ordinary teenage thief. With cunning, Barbara used to walk around a store until she found a discarded receipt. She would then retrieve the items listed on the receipt, take them to the register, and return them for cash. Then she'd go to another store and purchase whatever it was that she wanted. Sometimes, she'd just pocket some makeup. Sometimes, it was books. Sometimes, as Barbara related, it was other things as well. "I used to steal candy too. Cinnamon hots, jujubes, and even salt shakers. I love salt shakers, especially those fancy ones."

Previously published reports have repeatedly asserted that Barbara never sang in high school, and, further, that no one *knew* she could sing. That, too, like the depiction of her as the freakish, woebegone waif, is a fallacy.

"During our first year at Erasmus," recalls Diane Lemm, "we had to take Freshman Chorus. It was mandatory. And that was when I first knew that Barbara could sing. Our teacher was Mr. Johnson, a tall, balding old man. All of us would go into this big room with tiered chairs. He would go around the room and have each of us do a "do, re, mi, fa, so, la, ti, do." Barbara and I were both second sopranos. You had your sopranos, your altos, and the boys were bass, tenor, and baritone. All of us sopranos were grouped together. Barbara's friend, Maxine, she was with us too. Anyway, when it was Barbara's turn, *well,* she just came out sounding *so* gorgeous, so professional sounding. And that's when I first learned that Barbara could sing.

And *what* did the chorus, comprised of mostly Jewish students, learn to sing? Christmas carols, of course. Erasmus was famous at the time for its annual Christmas concerts. "If it wasn't for us Jewish kids who sang in these choruses," Diane Lemm proffers, "Erasmus would not have been able to have its Christmas concerts. Back then, Hanukkah wasn't even discussed in school, it was only Christmas."

From the Freshman Chorus, Barbra was chosen to be a member of the Choral Club, where she fell in (puppy) love, as did all of the other girls in the school, with the group's director, Cosimo Depietto. "He was known as Mr. D.," Diane Lemm recalls, "and he was a very handsome Italian man. He had *hair,* lots of hair."

"I remember we went to a party," Lemm continues, "and somebody said, 'Come on, Barbara, sing for us.' She was shy. You had to cajole her to do it. You practically had to push her to do it. She *knew* she was good. We always told her how good she was."

Back in the summer of of 1955, Barbara and her mother, with Roslyn in tow, returned to the Catskills for a vacation. It was there, a dozen summers before, that Emanuel Streisand had suddenly passed away. While there, they met a piano player who told them about a place called the Nola Recording Studios where, for a few dollars, they could record a couple of songs. Months later, on December 29, 1955, with the pianist as her accompanist, Barbara Streisand, at the age of thirteen, had her very first recording session. Diana, singing "One Kiss" and another operetta piece, went first, and Barbara watched intently as the piano player hogged the session with his endless refrains. When it came time for *her* to record, Barbara instructed the startled, and presumably humbled, pianist, "We'll just do a *little* interlude and then *I'll* come back in." The first songs she ever recorded, were "You'll Never Know" and "Zing! Went the Strings of My Heart."

Upon returning home to Brooklyn, Barbara went to the apartment of her friend Ed Frankel. Ed says today, with a measure of pride, "The first record that Barbara ever recorded as a demo was played on my phonograph. Why? Because her mother didn't have a 45 rpm record player." Still, Frankel was not terribly impressed by the record. "The voice quality on that demo," he recalls, "was not as good as her natural voice. I remember remarking about that. I said, 'It sounds like Barbara, but Barbara has a better voice.' "

Although she sang in the high school chorus, Barbara did *not* try out for any of the school's dramatic productions. It is possible that she didn't want to set herself up for another rejection. It's more likely, however, that she did not wish to associate herself with anything she regarded as decidedly amateur in calibre. At thirteen, she auditioned as an actress for a professional radio program. "I did a speech from *Saint Joan,*" she later related, 'He who tells the truth shall surely be caught.' I always felt that about myself."

After much prodding, in April 1956, Diana took Barbara into Manhattan for her fourteenth birthday to see a Broadway play, her first, *The Diary of Anne Frank.* Their tickets were for the cheap seats way up in the balcony. Barbara sat, enthralled, as the curtain was raised from the stage. By the time she left the Cort Theatre, however, she was both depressed and disillusioned. The show depicted real life. Barbara had had her fill of "real life" back in Brooklyn. Broadway, she decided, had none of the glamour of Hollywood. "it was a sad play," she would later say, "and the setting was so dreary. It was drab compared to the movies. I've always tried to avoid what was drab or ordinary."

The show would have an impact on her nonetheless. Barbara related to Anne Frank. She too was Jewish. She too had suffered. "It seems to me that neither I—nor, for that matter, anyone else, will be interested in the unbosomings of a 13-year-old schoolgirl," Anne Frank wrote in her diary, and Barbara understood.

She related, too, when Mr. Van Daan chastised Anne by saying, "A man likes a girl who'll listen to him. A domestic girl who likes to cook and sew. Why do you show off all the time? Why not be nice and quiet like your sister Margo?" The words could have been Diana's. Anne responds victoriously, "I'll open my veins first! I'm going to be *remarkable!*" The words could've been Barbara's.

The Diary of Anne Frank would leave Barbara with one important lesson. "I remember thinking that I could go up on [that] stage and play any role without any trouble at all," Barbra said of the experience. While Hollywood remained her eventual goal, it was miles, and perhaps years, away. Broadway was in her backyard. Furthermore, after having been there, and after seeing the actors who had been cast, she surmised herself to be, at the very least, their equal. Susan Strasberg won a Best Actress Tony nomination for her performance as Anne Frank, but Barbara felt certain that *she* would've been equally Tony-worthy in the part. Moreover, she learned that you didn't have to be Elizabeth Taylor beautiful to be on Broadway. Perhaps for the first time, she clearly saw her road out of Brooklyn. She was Broadway-bound.

In the summer of 1957, with $150 Diana gave her, Barbara attended the Malden Bridge Playhouse in the Adirondacks in upstate New York. "She couldn't stand me saying no to her," Diana acknowledged. Later, Barbara learned that the money had actually come from a legacy her grandfather had left her.

"At the last minute," Barbra related, "it was a question of using the money for summer stock or to fix my teeth. I had gone to the dentist, and he discovered that I still had my baby teeth on each side, bicuspids, I think they're called, and the other ones had never come down. He pulled one on each side, then wanted to pull two more and give me braces, but I wouldn't let him. For the next year, I went around with these holes on both sides of my mouth. Imagine an actress without her teeth! I used Aspergum. It was the closest color I could get to real teeth. I would press a piece in each side of my mouth, like false teeth."

To gain admittance into Malden Bridge, Barbara lied about her age, claiming to be seventeen. Her experience there was completely unlike the horrendous summers she had spent away from home in the "health camps" of her childhood; this time, Barbara loved being away from home. At Malden Bridge, she found the encouragement she had never found at home. She was cast as Millie Owens, the sixteen-year-old tomboy from Kansas in *Picnic,* and as Elsa, the sexy secretary on the prowl in *Desk Set.* "Can't you just see me at fifteen," Barbra wondered, bemused, "coming on the stage, sitting down on a desk, swinging my leg and playing sexy?" And she was successful at it too. The first review she ever got read, "The girl who plays the office vamp is very sexy, and her name is Barbara Streisand. *Down boys!*" It was the last two words in particular that delighted Barbra.

Perhaps to irritate her mother, or just to grouse, Barbara wrote home saying that the cook at the playhouse had made an abrupt departure. Diana related, aghast, "Can you imagine how I felt hearing such news, when what she needed most was good food and rest to go on with her studies in the fall? Well, she finally got home and I thought she was cured of her acting ideas, but no way."

Back at school, *boys* became an increasingly important topic of conversation among Barbara's group of friends. "I remember," Diane Lemm continues, "there were these dances that were held at the various Jewish Centers in Brooklyn, and Barbara went with us. It was the two Lindas, [Ashendorf and Silverman], Judy, Roberta Weiss, and myself. I forget if we shared a taxi, or what, but Barbara went over to one of the Lindas' houses, and we all went to the dance together. This particular Jewish Center was on Ocean Avenue. All of the senior boys were there at the dance, and some of the alumni boys as well. As a matter of fact, Doug Moe [later a professional basketball player] asked me to dance that night. And Barbara would dance when she was asked.

"We went to a party once in which we triple-dated," continues Lemm. "Two of the boys were twins. Barbara had one twin and I had the other. It was a blind date set up by Linda Ashendorf. The twins were short and had no personality. They were from Queens, and they didn't like it very much that they had to come to Brooklyn to pick us up. Then we had to take the subway to the party. It wasn't much of a date. None of us drank. There was no booze in those days. But, the party was held at an apartment in Forest Hills in Queens, and what made these apartments so special to us was that they were in these new buildings, and they had two bedrooms instead of one. Forest Hills was a ritzy area in those days. Maybe it still is."

Other than that occasion, Diane doesn't recall Barbara going out on dates. The only boy in school on whom Barbara had a crush (or at least the only boy she later professed to caring about) was future chess champion Bobby Fischer. She was attracted to his eccentricities and peculiarities and would cast amorous glances in his direction as he flipped through the pages of the *Mad* magazines he was always reading.

Actually, when it came to boys, Barbara was the proverbial late bloomer. Other than what Muriel Choy told her, and what she gleaned from the hushed conversations of her girlfriends, she knew nothing about sex. Diana's tutelage on the subject can be summed up with a single word, "don't," and one often-repeated aphorism, "Don't show your brains. Men don't like girls who are too smart."

"In my family," Barbra would confide, "sex was taboo. You don't screw anybody until you get married, you don't hold hands, you don't kiss, because you'll get a disease. It was all so awful that I had to develop a fantasy life."

Diane Lemm shrugs her shoulders when asked why she thought Barbara was apparently less popular with the boys than the rest of their group. "I don't know. I do know that we all had boobs, and Barbara, well, Barbara didn't have such boobs. She was very skinny and flat-chested. I know that you photograph heavier, but I always wonder, when I see Barbra in the movies, *where* did she get those boobs from?"

According to Ed Frankel, as Barbara progressed through high school, her attire became somewhat more avant-garde. "She used to wear high boots, black stockings, and long print dresses," Frankel recalls. "But," he adds, "she wasn't kooky. There was no purple eyebrows or green teeth. That's just nonsense."

At fifteen, while still attending Erasmus, Barbara boldly started taking frequent evening and weekend excursions into Manhattan. "Half a block from where we lived," says Frankel, "on the corner of Nostrand Avenue and Newkirk, was the I.R.T. subway, which took you into Manhattan. I remember her going into the Village all the time. She used to go with friends, especially that little girl, Susan [her new friend, Susan Dworkowitz].

Soon, Barbara landed a volunteer job, as a backstage apprentice sweeping floors at the Cherry Lane Theatre in Greenwich Village. Bursting with energy, and ecstatic to be working in a real "theatuh," Barbara was eventually promoted to assistant stage manager, and then cast as an understudy for the part of Avril in a production of *Purple Dust.* It was then that Barbara met, and was befriended by, Anita Miller, one of the actresses in the cast. Anita's husband, Allan Miller, worked as an acting teacher in the city, and in time, Barbara became a student in his class. She still lived in Brooklyn, but in a sense, she had found her home.

Today Miller teaches acting in Los Angeles. He recalls, "She came to me through my ex-wife, who was working as an actress in an Off-Broadway theater called the Cherry Lane. And my wife kept talking to me about this girl. She kept saying, 'There's *something* about her. I don't know, there's just something about her.' I said, 'Well, what do you want me to do about it?' She said, 'You should talk to her. You should teach her.' And I said, 'I'm not encouraging a fifteen-year-old girl to go into the theater.'

"But then, one night, lo and behold, guess who was invited to dinner? The *creature.* And then, at the end of dinner, they had another surprise for me: they had prepared an audition. It was the single *worst* audition I think I've ever seen in my entire life. I don't remember the scene they did. But in what she did, there was no cohesion between what her body did, and the way her feelings were going, and what would come out of her mouth. She was like an infant where the hands would go one kind of way while the thoughts and feelings would be flying in another kind of way.

"I was so struck by the rawness," Miller relates. "She didn't even try to imitate other actors. There was something striving in her to be really genuinely available to herself, but she didn't know how to put it together. She was so *desiring.* She was so full of this young, raw eagerness that I finally said, 'Okay, listen. I'll give you a scholarship to my class.' She had no money, that came up very quickly. She was working as a cashier at a Chinese restaurant. And so I offered her a scholarship to one of my classes. And she said, 'I'll take them *all.'* "

A whole new world opened up for Barbara. She was wide-eyed and ebullient, and intuitively receptive to signs of intelligent life. It wasn't just the acting classes, it was the people she met, and the possibilities of the city itself. Suddenly, anything seemed possible. She entertained thoughts of becoming a doctor, a biologist, a landscape architect, a scholar like her father, a symphony conductor, and a violinist.

"Once, I thought about becoming a great violinist," she would acknowledge in later years. "[But] it was either my nails or Horowitz. Horowitz went out the window." Unquestionably, Barbara wanted desperately to become a great dramatic actress to rival Sarah Bernhardt and Eleanora Duse. Still, she cursed the unwritten law that said you could have only one profession.

She read Victorien Sardou and Alexandre Dumas. Tolstoy's *Anna Karenina* would change her life. In Anna, Barbara found a heroine who suffered because she had become a social outcast. But she did so glamorously. She carried on a passionate, adulterous affair with the handsome Count Vronsky, a relationship she wanted to flaunt in the face of a snickering society. When she had to suppress the relationship, and herself, it drove her insane, and to a tragic death on a railroad track. Recklessly throwing her mother's echoing words of caution to the wind, Barbara vowed that, unlike Anna, she would no longer care what society—or her mother—dictated as proper and acceptable. Not unlike Anne Frank, she would be "remarkable."

But first she had to graduate from high school.

It was a difficult rite of passage for Barbara, to go from the promise of her new life in Manhattan, back to the vapid, textbook lessons of Erasmus Hall. Though only a subway ride away, the two were worlds apart. For Barbara, there was no turning back. She didn't want to read about history, she wanted to make it. She wanted out so badly that her bones nearly jumped out of her skin.

And so she did extra credit. And she went to summer school. And in January 1959, she picked up her diploma and never looked back. For Erasmus had committed the cardinal sin. It had ignored her. At the school's year-end ceremonies, Harriet Mersel would be named the "Class Actress," and Trudy Wallace was named the "Class Singer." It had been Trudy, too, who had been picked over Barbara to sing most of the solos in the school's choral club. Barbra later related with a trace of irony, "They had this other girl, an opera singer. *She* was going to be a big star, they said."

Back on Newkirk, Diana Kind was not about to let go of her daughter without a fight. She can't be blamed, really. Diana wanted for Barbara what most Jewish mothers wished for their daughters in the Brooklyn of the late 1950s: steady employment (with health benefits and pension), marriage, and children. As author Letty Cottin Pogrebin, a contemporary of Barbra's, succinctly wrote, "In my day, womanhood *was* motherhood."

Besides, Diana could not see beyond what she considered to be the obvious. It wasn't the girls at Erasmus who corroborated Barbara's view of herself as unattractive, it was her own mother. Later, of course, there would be many others who concurred. "She was not a good-looking girl," Diana attests, "[and] in show business at that time, there were very pretty girls around. And I thought, really, she is taking a big chance."

Undaunted, Barbara continued her subway sojourns to and from

Manhattan, and even took to following her acting teacher as he got on the bus. She would sit in the seat next to him and utilize their time together with a barrage of questions and an informal, not to mention, *free,* lesson. "She was always asking me questions," Allan Miller relates. "Always, always, always. I was coaching her and teaching her on the bus, for God's sakes!"

One day, according to Miller, Barbara turned to him and pronounced, " 'You know, listen, I'll sit for yuh.' We had two little kids, and she became our baby-sitter. And in no time at all, she was living with us.

"Her mother called me on the phone and accused me of taking this young girl under my wing and ruining her child's life. I took her away from her one paying job, working as a cashier at the Chinese restaurant. I was seducing her daughter away from her."

It is possible that one of reasons Barbara has demeaned her singing voice over the years ("I'm an actress, not a singer"; "I just open my mouth and sing. What's the big deal?") is that she got her voice from her mother. A matter of inheritance, a stroke of genetics, it had nothing to do with Barbara's own acquired abilities. In Barbara's heart, Diana always vied with the ghost of Emanuel Streisand. It was an unfair competition, of course. Diana, after all, could never match up to a man who had been idealized in death. It had been in her father's shadow that Barbara lived out the mostly unhappy days of her childhood.

"When a kid grows up missing one parent," she would say, "there's a big gap that has to be filled. It's like someone being blind, they hear better. With me, I felt more. I sensed more." And she adds, tellingly, "I wanted more."

She sat on the subway which was transporting her from the childhood she would try to block out. After years of dreaming before the bathroom mirror of her mother's apartment, and fantasizing in the penny arcades of Flatbush Avenue, Barbara Joan Streisand, sixteen, was on her way.

But even she could not imagine the enormity of what awaited her.

Four

The Fountainhead

*T*hey sat in their seats, sucking on their cigarettes. Smoke filled the room. Amorous glances were cast back and forth, and back again. Lips were moistened with the roll of a seductive tongue. Such was the setting as the lights dimmed and the singer took the stage. It wasn't a "stage," really, just a square of floor space beside a piano that faced out to the tables. It was amateur night at The Lion, a mostly gay bar and restaurant, located at 62 West Ninth Street in Greenwich Village, the haven for New York misfits. Each week, four performers bared their vocal wares and competed for a parcel of approval and a one-week engagement with pay. It wasn't much, maybe, but it was *more*.

The singer looked out into the audience. The audience looked back and saw a nose on an unlikely face. The singer ignored the cruel rejection. She summoned her nerve, closed her eyes, and opened her mouth to sing. The song was "A Sleepin' Bee" by Harold Arlen and Truman Capote, introduced by Diahann Carroll in the unsuccessful Broadway musical, *House of Flowers*. It was hardly a typical show-stopping song. Devoid of opportunities for what would, decades later, be characterized as "Star Search" bombast and histrionics, it was a simple, plaintive number about newfound love. Still, as she sang sweetly about the bee that lay in the palm of her hand, the singer held the audience rapt in attention with the startling highness of her upper range, and the piercing, perhaps unparalleled, clarity of her voice.

There was something else, not so much in her voice, but in her *being*. The audience had no way of knowing that she had lost her unemployment insurance, was nearly destitute, and had only agreed to sing as a last resort. But they sensed her desperation. She was an outcast like them, and they recognized it. She longed for love and acceptance, but would not beg for it, and they understood. She defied the definition of beauty as big-bosomed cheerleader. They defied the definition of everything a man was supposed to be in the America of the late fifties and early sixties.

When she finished the number, there was a pause, followed by a burst of applause. With one song, the singer with the improbable face had become beautiful. And The Lion roared. "Barbara Streisand," they said to one another as they excited the club, "remember that name." "Barbara Streisand," they said to one another as they ascended the two steps back into the Ninth Street night, "remember that name. Remember that name."

Her first taste of triumph in the lion's den came at the age of eighteen in June 1960, over a year after her move to Manhattan. She had spent the interval consumed, primarily, with redefining her image, and a succession of her beloved acting classes. Allan Miller, a member of the Actors Studio and a protégé of Lee Strasberg, recalls, "She was so awkward and unknowing, that I wouldn't let her talk for many months in my class. She had to do all of her scenes in *sounds*. She had to make noises to express what was going on. She was very, very awkward, emotionally and physically, in her expression of herself."

When asked what he hoped to accomplish by limiting Barbara to scenes without speech, Miller responds, "The most immediate way to express what a person is thinking and feeling is without all the coverage of words. If somebody is going out on a first date, they have to get through all the claptrap of 'How long have you been living here?' and 'blah, blah, blah,' before they get to what is really going on inside of them. But with just noises and sounds, you could find out in five minutes if you wanted to be with this person. Barbara accepted the challenge. She respected what I was doing and how I was doing it. She understood what it would eventually get to. She was *very* bright.

"The very first scene she did in my acting class in which she was allowed to speak was from *The Rose Tattoo* by Tennessee Williams. The role called for a very young girl, about fifteen or sixteen, from a very strict, Catholic mother, who is a very *earthy* mother. The mother reserves the right to fling herself around sexually, but the girl has to be very well brought up. The girl meets a young sailor and brings him home. The mother confronts the sailor and makes him promise that he will not touch her daughter, who is a virgin. The boy is a decent boy and he promises. Then they have a scene alone together, the boy and the girl. She's really hot and bothered and wants him to make love to her, but he refuses because of his promise. Finally, she says, at the end of this scene, that she's going to wait for him at this hotel.

"One day, Barbara said to me that she was really dying to do a scene. So I said, 'Okay. The scene I want you to do is from *The Rose Tattoo.*' She said, 'What's that?' And I told her, and she said she would read it. The next day she said to me, 'I can't do *that* scene.' I said, 'Why can't you do that scene?' And she said, 'Well, you *know.*' What she was really saying was that she was a virgin. She didn't know anything yet about sexuality. So, I said to her, 'Barbara, find some way of behaving, like you think the way this girl behaves in this scene, but it must have *nothing to do with sex.*' That was the way I would work with her. I would give her a *physical* thing to do.

"A week or two later, she comes in with this scene. Within one minute, the boy in the scene with her was beet red with embarrassment. It was the sexiest scene I think I have ever seen in my life, and it had *nothing* to do with sex, except that"—he laughs—"of course it did. As soon as it was over, the whole class applauded. I said, 'Wait, wait, wait. Barbara, tell everybody what you had worked on.' And she mumbled something. And I said, 'Louder, come on, say it.' And she said, 'I tried to touch every part of his body with every part of my body, without ever touching the same part twice.'

"The poor guy in the scene with her couldn't deal with it. He could hardly put his hand on her without her turning it into a red-hot iron. It was wonderfully expressive of what the situation called for, and it was done with a kind of choice that most actors and most acting teachers did not use. What I learned to do with Barbara, sometimes I had to make up. It helped me enormously, both as a teacher and as an actor, to explore things for, and around, and with her, because, as I say, she was just so raw and innocent. It was quite an amazing time."

The scene would have a profound impact on Barbara too. Over the years, she would affectionately relate the experience to friends, and in 1977, she told an interviewer, "It was the kind of moment I'm always striving to feel again. . . . I think it's what they call inspiration, which I've experienced very few times."

During this period, Barbara appeared in an off-off-*off*-Broadway "production," if it can be called that, entitled *Seawood.* Written and produced by Armand de Beauchamp, the play was staged in an attic above an apartment in the West Seventies. Joan Molinsky, another aspiring young actress, played a knife-wielding lesbian who lusts after Barbara. "I liked the high school girl with the big nose who was funny and made jokes," she would later relate of Barbara. "We had immediate rapport, maybe because she seemed a tough little hustler." She also admired that Barbara, despite being the youngest member of the company, was extremely serious about the craft of acting. Years later, Molinsky would attain enormous success as a performer under the name of Joan Rivers.

In the summer of 1959, Allan and Anita Miller decided to spend their "vacation" performing in summer stock at the Clinton Playhouse in Connecticut. Barbara accompanied them on the trip as the baby-sitter of their children. "She was a great baby-sitter," enthuses Miller. "She liked kids. She was very childlike herself. She knew the kinds of things they enjoyed. And when she took them out to play, she played with them like a kid would. They both liked her a lot." While in Connecticut, Barbara was cast as Ellie May in a Clinton Playhouse production of *Tobacco Road.* Coincidentally, another young actor was also working at the playhouse that summer. His name was Warren Beatty.

A few months after returning to Manhattan, Barbara moved out of the Millers' apartment on West Seventy-fifth Street. "We had become sort of surrogate parents," Miller explains, "and we were encouraging her to mingle more on her own. She was extremely, extremely shy. To get her to go out with other people was hard. She was sort of clinging to me. I felt she was a little too dependent."

Barbara moved into an apartment on Thirty-fourth Street with her friend from Erasmus, Susan Dworkowitz. She also got a job doing general office work (finally, something of which her mother approved) and answering phones at the Michael Press printing company. By day, she toiled, miserable with the paper-pushing mundaneness of it all. By night, she raced to Miller's classes at his theater workshop on West Forty-eighth Street. Often, she arrived late, disheveled and out of breath, and with a hamburger or a yogurt, or some other quick, makeshift dinner. When Diana Kind would hear of her daughter's decidedly sloppy nutritional habits, she would rant over the telephone.

Barbara was frugal with her money, and got her meals free, whenever possible, at the apartment of one kindly friend or another. She opened up a bank account at Seamen's Savings, an account she has to this day, and cashed her weekly paychecks. She would then return to her apartment and divide the money into a set of well-organized envelopes. In the one marked "phone," she'd deposit five dollars; "laundry" would get ten dollars; "food" would get twenty dollars; "rent" would get twenty-five dollars; and "miscellaneous" merited five dollars. Among her "miscellaneous" splurges was an occasional taxi. To Barbara, taxi rides were a luxury of the rich and famous.

Meanwhile, Allan Miller cast her in Christopher Fry's *A Phoenix Too Frequent,* a one-act play which was to be a part of a showcase program he was directing. Barbara would play a young servant girl to a wealthy, recently widowed woman. Two other actors were cast in the production, including Cis Corman as the widow. "I had four kids. I had roots," Cis would later say. "I had a refrigerator full of food." Like the Millers, Cis and her husband, Harvey, would become surrogate parents to Barbara. Unlike her friendship with the Millers, however, her relationship with the Cormans would endure over the years.

The play was a comedy set in ancient Greece, where custom dictated that the widow had to commit suicide in honor of her dead husband. As part of the custom, she was allowed to take a favored servant with her, and the widow in the play chooses, as her reluctant companion, the character played by Barbara. Distraught, the servant girl delivers a speech in the kitchen in which she bemoans the imminent loss of her young life, her beloved kitchen, and the boyfriends she would leave behind.

In rehearsals, Miller wanted Barbara to cry during a pivotal scene. The moment came, however, and not a teardrop appeared. They tried it again and again, to no avail. It wasn't that Barbara refused to cry, she just couldn't. "She had blockaded herself over the years from any form of self-pity, including crying," Miller later said. "Tears seemed unknown to her."

The day before dress rehearsal, having exhausted his usual motivational techniques, Miller took Barbara out to lunch. He looked across the table and saw a girl who was totally consumed with the craft of acting and the idea of having a future in the theater. Suddenly, a question occurred to him. Surely, he thought, the prospect of a life without acting would hit an emotional chord. So he asked Barbara what she would do if she *couldn't* act. He was floored when she responded, brightly, and without hesitation, "Open a bakery shop." She proceeded to tell the astonished Miller that she had always wanted to be able to have her own bakery where she could make any breads that she desired, where she would design her own cakes and pastries for every occasion. "I love the smell of bakeries. I love the look of bakeries. "I could spend my whole life in a bakery!" she announced, pleased with the thought.

Another idea occurred to Miller. He asked Barbara to describe what kind of a cake she would make for her own twenty-first birthday. She proceeded to describe, and then *pantomime,* how she would make a spectacular, two-foot-high, multilayered cake gorged with creams and fudge, and crowned with a delectable whipped cream image of herself at the top. When she finished, Miller, playing along, drooled at the imaginary cake and asked for a slice. Barbara refused. It was a cherished cake, made for *her* twenty-first birthday, she protested. Undaunted, Miller proceeded to sing a few bars of "Happy Birthday." While he was singing, Barbara, touched, started to tear up. "All right," she submitted, "you can have a slice."

Barbara pantomimed the slicing of a generous piece of cake and gingerly, lovingly presented it to her teacher. "I hope you will like it," she beamed, proudly. But as he accepted the imaginary slice of cake, Miller suddenly dropped it to the floor. "Oh no!" Barbara wailed with true feeling. "Why did you drop my cake?" she asked in horror. *"Why?!"* she cried, as the tears came gushing out.

At the following evening's rehearsal, Miller informed Barbara that he had changed a piece of staging. As she began her monologue about being too young to die, he wanted her to turn stage right. Uncertain of his motive, she agreed, nevertheless. When it came time for her to deliver her speech, she turned stage right and was jolted by what she saw. There, devouring an elaborate piece of pastry, in lieu of a two-foot cake, was Miller's unsuspecting stage manager. Suddenly, the tears again poured out as Barbara evoked, without interrupting the flow of the play, the servant girl's tragic lament.

Punished for some insubordination or another, Barbara was fired from her job at the Michael Press printing company. Instead of being disconsolate, however, she rejoiced in the seemingly sinful joys of unemployment insurance. With the skills and the confidence gained from her nightly classes, she was ready to join the legions of other dedicated young New York actors and actresses. She was ready to hit the streets, knock on doors, and make the proverbial rounds.

Or was she?

Two days after embarking on her new effort, Barbara threw up her hands in disgust and vowed never again to put herself in such a position. She couldn't even get into some of the offices, and at those that she did get into, the agents had little to say, but their message was clear: "Change your name. Change your nose. Change your profession." She was savvy enough to know that she didn't come off well in snap judgments. Her appeal was one that took time, was beyond the obvious, beneath the surface.

"I wasn't the ingenue type those casting creeps were looking for," she would say, not without bitterness. "I could have changed the way I looked, had my nose fixed or something, but I just wouldn't. That wouldn't have been honest, right?"

"Name?" they would invariably ask. Sometimes, Barbara would employ her alias, Angelina Scarangella, for protection. That way, when they rejected her, it wouldn't be *her* that they turned down. "What have you done?" they would ask. "Nothing," she would answer, adding quickly, "You wanna hear me read? Look, you'd better sign me up. I'm terrific!"

"Sorry," they would say. "Next!"

Influenced by the beatnik trend prevalent at the time, Barbara at seventeen was anything *but* the fresh-faced ingenue. Her hair was straight and stringy and dyed dark. She dressed primarily in funereal black, to complement the intensity of her disposition. It was the winter of 1959–60, and she made her rounds wearing black tights, under a black trenchcoat. "People looked at me as though I was nuts," she recalled. Sometimes, she would have lunch with her brother, Sheldon, who had gotten a job at a Manhattan advertising agency. While walking to their given destination, he used to insist that she walk three steps behind him because he was embarrassed to be seen with her. Usually, her stockings were torn, revealing unstylish glimpses of the back of her legs. "I can't see it, so it doesn't bother me," Barbara would say to her brother. "Why should it bother you?" Sheldon offered to lend her money. She refused. He offered to buy her a new pair of stockings. She refused that too. And so he offered to take her out to lunch. This she accepted. Somehow, her pride never restricted her from accepting a free meal.

"Wanted: female beatnik type," read one of the notices in the industry trade papers. "Perfect," Barbara thought to herself, "They've gotta cast me as *that.*" She learned otherwise, however, upon arriving at the audition.

"We have to see your work," the woman behind the desk informed her.

"Whaddya mean, you hafta see my work," Barbara objected, "it's only a walk-on!"

"We have to see your work," the woman behind the desk repeated, this time with slight agitation.

"Why?" Barbara insisted. "I mean, you don't hafta be Eleanore Duse to do a walk-on! I'll never get work if people like you keep telling me that you hafta see my work. When do I get that first shot?"

The protest, of course, was in vain. "It was so depressing," she would later relate. "I cried in practically every office. I made terrible enemies." "You'll be sorry," she promised. "You'll come after me, I'm not going to come after you. I'm not going to bang on your door and say 'Hire me.' That's *your* problem." Her parting words were heartfelt but hardly original. "Screw you!" she pronounced as another door closed in her face.

The dynamics of such auditions would bother her for years. "I *knew* I was good," she would say, "but no one would let me read till I had experience, so how could I get experience?" For Barbara, it was a degrading process, and a manipulative power play of agents over actors. She wanted desperately to become an actress, but she was unwilling to grovel and lay herself at the feet of those people who, in her view, couldn't evaluate talent. "I can't force myself down somebody's throat," she said. "I'm not going to beg for nobody."

Instead of letting the rejection defeat her, however, Barbara seemed ignited with "I'll show you" drive. In addition to her mother, her stepfather, and all the kids back in Brooklyn, she now also had to prove herself to all the agents in Manhattan who had dismissed her with a shrug, a yawn, a banishing "Next!"

She turned to her acting classes for sustenance. She would later claim that the idea to see other drama coaches had been hers. She would even explain how she used her alias, Angelina Scarangella, in one of the classes so that her teachers wouldn't suspect her disloyalty to Allan Miller, with whom she had been studying for a year and a half.

Miller, however, contends that he had suggested to Barbara the other teachers with whom she should study. Miller recalls, "I made the arrangements for her to go to *four* different other acting teachers, Eli Rill, Curt Conway, Lee Strasberg, and I can't remember the other one. Each of these instructors said to me afterwards, '*Why* are you bothering with this girl? This girl has no talent. And she's a pain in the ass.' "

Eli Rill has distinct memories of Barbara sitting in his class, but he has no recollection of having had an unfavorable impression of her. He acknowledges, "What did surprise me, in all honesty, is the levels to which she rose. I did *not* know at the time that she sang. Oddly enough, one of the exercises I would do quite often at the time was a singing exercise. This was started by my teacher, Lee Strasberg, at the Actors Studio. It used singing not as a vocal lesson but to deal with and connect with certain areas of tension and freedom, as some kind of a release. It was an exercise which helped an actor to be able to come into certain areas of self-consciousness and expressiveness. If I had thirty students in a class, I probably gave this exercise to twenty-nine of them. But I never gave it to Barbara Streisand. Why? Because she didn't need it.

"She was rather skinny, as I remember. *Very* slender. She always looked as if she was in a hurry. It didn't seem as if she primped in front of the mirror and had to make a vital life decision as to which sweatshirt, or whatever, she was going to wear. She was always in a hurry to get there, and always in a hurry to leave.

"She was always working. If somebody else was doing a scene, she was watching. Her body language was always leaning forward. 'What's going on? What can I absorb?' There's a young man in my class right now who reminds me of her. His eyes are always narrowed.

"She had, from what I recall, no humor. Don't misunderstand me, she had humor, but she was *not* there as a social event. I don't recall her buddying up to people. Even with the best intentions, some of the students I've had over the many years, they're dedicated and involved, but they also have an occasional laugh over a cup of coffee. Not her."

Barbara was rejected in her bid to become a member of the Actors Studio, which was then the hallowed home of all serious New York actors. The reason is shrouded in some controversy. It has been suggested that she was rejected because she cited Mae West or Rita Hayworth as her favorite actress on her membership application. More likely, during her audition scene, she broke down uncontrollably in tears, perhaps mistakenly believing that the excess would impress her judges.

According to actress Renée Taylor, a member of the Studio and later a friend of Barbara's, acceptance for membership "didn't have anything to do with talent. Some people got in who weren't too good. A lot of people didn't get in that were good. It was just very political."

In her acting classes, Barbara was generally younger and less experienced than her classmates. Still, this didn't preclude her from speaking up for herself. She challenged authority, even then. "Very often, I would be leery of taking younger people in," Eli Rill relates, "because they are sometimes intimidated or inhibited by older people. But I never worried about Barbara. She was not intimidated by anybody, including me. She was not shy as a student. She was one of the few people who would argue a point."

"She had a natural bent to humor," Rill recalls, "it wasn't just the *way* she spoke. If she perhaps didn't speak with that kind of Brooklyn Yiddish inflection, she may or may not have been as funny, I really don't know. It's hard to separate. But I associate her humor with having a certain manner and style, with accent being only one of the small items.

"I said to her, 'There's nothing wrong with that, Barbara; we are laughing because we enjoy what you're doing.' She would do something, let's say she'd make a gesture with her hand, and we'd laugh. And I said, 'You have a very particular way of behaving that appeals to us.' I think I even compared her to a friend of mine, Zero Mostel, who could hardly say anything without people laughing, and he's an extremely sensitive, intelligent man. He has a certain impulse, an expression of life, that creates humor around what he is saying. And I remember saying to her, 'There will come a time, time will pass, and there will be certain serious tones that come alive in you. But for the time being, accept graciously the fact that you have a certain natural capacity to be humorous.' "

Rill adds, "I remember, very vividly, her standing there in class and being very direct. I don't remember her exact words, but the substance was, 'Look, if you're so good as a teacher, make it so that people don't laugh.' And I remember being very struck by this person's concern with not being laughed at."

Eli Rill did not know about the derisive laughter she had been subjected to through much of her childhood. Nor did he know that it was in Barbara's nature to deny and negate anything that came too easily to her. Just as singing came easily to, and emanated naturally from, Barbara, so too did making people laugh. But she wanted little to do with either. She was going to be a *serious,* perhaps Shakespearean, tragedienne.

One of her favorite assignments as a young acting student had been to play Medea. She wanted to make people cry, not laugh, as though pain were somehow the more valid emotion. She would not be ignored, or so went her childhood vow, and she would not be laughed at, either. The companion maxims, however, would soon conflict, as her first big successes would come in musical comedy.

Something happened to Barbara around the time she made "the rounds" in Manhattan. Perhaps she got a good look at the other actresses in her age range and realized that, physically speaking, she couldn't compete. Eli Rill expresses the conventional wisdom of those who knew her at the time. "I felt very concerned about this young lady. I didn't know how far she could go. Notwithstanding her talent, I felt there would be limited use of her in the business. At that time, the people who were being cast fit more the mold of what one would call conventionally attractive. For instance, I may have said the same thing of Al

Pacino if he had been in my class thirty years ago. Or Dustin Hoffman. I may have said, 'Well, he's talented, but he doesn't look like Tyrone Power.' "

It's easy to understand the concern of Rill and others. No one expected much out of Barbara at that stage. The women making a splash on Broadway at the time were such young, talented, extremely *attractive* actresses as Anne Bancroft (*Two for the Seesaw, The Miracle Worker*), Julie Andrews (*My Fair Lady*), Barbara Cook (*The Music Man*), Carol Lawrence (*West Side Story*), France Nuyen (*The World of Suzie Wong*), and Jane Fonda (*There Was a Girl*). Eighteen-year-old Barbara Streisand, did not fit the mold. Who could've known then that it was a mold she would eventually shatter.

And so she made a calculated decision: if she wasn't going to be beautiful, she was going to be, in a word, *conspicuous*. She would be bold and brash and Anne Frank "remarkable." Inside, she was still the shy, quiet girl from Erasmus Hall High School, but outside, everything about her became loud. She even talked loud. She dyed her hair red, painted her face with white powder and her mouth with purple lipstick, and wore clothes that were sure to command attention even on a New York City street corner.

Meanwhile, money became more scarce. Her friend Susan Dworkowitz moved back to her home, family, and security in Brooklyn. To Barbara, it was an act of betrayal. She found a tiny four-flight walk-up at 339 West Forty-eighth Street, next door to Allan Miller's workshop. However, she needed a roommate to be able to afford the rent, and posted a notice on the bulletin board at Actors Equity. Marilyn Fried, an aspiring young actress who had run away from her parents' home in the South Bronx, answered the ad.

To earn extra cash to supplement her weekly unemployment checks, Barbara took a job ushering at the Lunt-Fontanne Theatre on Broadway. She kept the job a secret, even from her friends. And when she walked up and down the aisles, flashlight in hand, she kept her head lowered, so as not to be noticed. Once famous, she didn't want theatergoers to be able to recall her as the lowly usherette who had once showed them to their seat.

Playing at the Lunt-Fontanne at the time was the smash hit *The Sound of Music*. When she got word that the producers of the show were looking for a replacement for the part of Lisl, Barbara managed to finagle an audition with Eddie Blum of the Rodgers and Hammerstein casting office. Blum was instantly smitten by her singing voice, so much so that he had her sing for three hours, knowing full well that there wasn't a place for her in *The Sound of Music* as Lisl, or in the chorus. There was something incongruous about Barbara Streisand as a singing nun or a von Trapp family wannabe. Streisand was not, nor would she ever be, the Rodgers and Hammerstein type.

Late one night, at the West Forty-eighth Street apartment that she shared with Barbara, Marilyn Fried was preparing for bed when she was stricken by a glorious sound emanating from a radio in the other room. Curious, she went over to investigate and was amazed to discover that the remarkable sound came from her roommate, who was practicing for her audition with the Hammerstein office. Encouraged by the ecstatic response, Barbara sheepishly pulled out her old Nola Recording Studios demo of "You'll Never Know" and put it on the phonograph. *"What* are you doing struggling to be an actress?" Marilyn exclaimed after listening to the record. "You're a *singer!"*

"I'm an actress, *not* a singer," Barbara corrected her openmouthed roommate. It would be a statement that she would repeat many, many times in the years to come.

Through Marilyn, Barbara was introduced to Terry Leong, an aspiring male fashion designer who would become a good friend. "I was designing clothes on Seventh Avenue, after having studied at F.I.T. [Fashion Institute of Technology]," Leong recalls. "I was introduced to Barbara, and she needed clothes for auditions, so I started designing for her. She had a very strong fashion sense. I guess she read magazines and things. She wanted to start dressing *up,* and I sort of helped her." It was Terry Leong who introduced Barbara to the treasures that could be found in the thrift shops of the city.

"I turned her on to antique clothes," Leong says, "She really wasn't into it before then. We would find these antique clothes in the thrift shops, and I would accessorize them and make them into dresses that she could wear. They were very *theatrical* kinds of things. Beaded tops from 1900, dresses from the 1920s. There was one coat we found that she subsequently had copied for the movie version of *Funny Girl.* She had it done in leopard and, I think, fox.

"It was great fun doing clothes for her. We would go to Ninth Avenue, there were a lot of thrift shops in that area. And I had outlets on Seventh Avenue when I was designing there. So, between that and the fabrics and things that we found, we would pull things together. It was great fun because she had such style." Barbara also had two friends who were window dressers at Lord & Taylor's who would supply her with scraps of leftovers.

There was virtually nothing she wouldn't try. According to other friends, at times she resembled a walking Christmas tree.

"She could practically wear anything and look terrific," Leong recalls. "She was very striking. She had long limbs, very elegant, and very tapered. She was very thin in those days. She had a very good figure to carry clothes.

The designer adds, "I thought anything 1900 or 1920s worked for her. And then she discovered slips, which was an introduction to the 1930s, but we never got around to doing that. The clothes she wore were all different colors—pales, purples, blacks, blues. I thought those worked best for her. She also liked pastels. I would also accesorize things with antique shoes and jewelry. I shelled out some money, and she paid a little for these things. She was struggling at the time."

"I bought that stuff because it was cheap," Barbra later said. "Besides, I figured anybody that's rich enough to donate to a thrift shop gotta dress clean, know what I mean? They're rich enough to take a bath, huh?

"[In thrift shops] you could buy designer clothes for a song—good thing I sing," she would later quip to a reporter. "Maybe they were last season's, or twenty seasons ago, but they were beautiful originals. They became even more original because, in altering them to fit me, I might change a neckline or add beading."

She invariably forgot to mention that it was not she, but Terry Leong, who did the alterations and the redesigning, in his Chrystie Street apartment. Somehow, she would always have a problem giving the friends who helped her when she needed it their just due.

During this period, she devoted her considerable energies to a rather tacky, embarrassing production of Karel and Josef Capek's esoteric *The Insect Comedy,* a.k.a. *The World We Live In,* which was promoted as "a parable of the human condition." It ran for three nights in May 1960 at the Jan Hus Theatre, with Barbara in multiple roles, playing the messenger, the second butterfly, and the second moth.

In another project, Eli Rill cast her in a full-length play he was directing at the Actors Studio. It was called *Cancer: An American Comedy,* and there were two parts in it for which Rill wanted to cast Barbara. "It was one of those cast situations [like *The Insect Comedy*] in which people could double doing small roles," Rill explains. The problem was political. An Actors Studio member of some twenty years' standing had already been cast in the production. "So," Rill relates, "when this other actress, who will remain nameless, was having problems with the professional juggling of doing my play and a television show, I sort of made it easy for her to leave." Barbara replaced her in the play, and according to Rill, "She never let me down."

In describing the experience of directing her, Rill says, "Even at that age, Barbara did not observe what I would call the political correctness, the political niceties of how you relate to people who hire you or teach you. Let's say, me putting her in the play, one would imagine that she would've said, 'Thank you very much,' and 'Call me again,' or so forth, but she just did her job and I did my job, and she didn't feel it was necessary to call me up and make points with me. I think what she was saying to me, more or less, was, 'If you hired me to do this job, and if I did a good job, if you need me, you'll hire me again. I don't have to go through all the hoopla. I don't have to be flirtatious, as some people are, or brownnosing. She treated me like a peer, and I didn't mind that at all. [But] she does leave out spaces as far as what you're supposed to do when you're dealing with somebody who's been around for a while."

Meanwhile, Barbara, eighteen, was befriended by a twenty-two-year-old actor named Barry Dennen, who then spelled his first name Barré. He had played a cricket and a snail in the ill-fated *The Insect Comedy*. The two shared a camp kind of sensibility, based largely in the 1930s movie comedies of Mae West, W. C. Fields, and Groucho Marx. They became compatriots in the offbeat and unexpected, and spoke in a language that was their own.

Soon, they were spending a lot of time together in Dennen's apartment at 69 West Ninth Street in Greenwich Village. He was attracted to her naïveté, her audacity, and the genius of her eccentricity. She was awed by the vast range of his intelligence as he taught her about art, literature, music, and theater. He was so unlike the boys she had met and known back in Brooklyn. In Dennen, Barbara had finally found a worthy, and willing, receptacle for her endless questions.

He was also what she only envisioned herself to be, a Shakespearean actor. It was Barbara's dream to play Juliet, and for a while, with his apartment as their stage, Barry Dennen played her Romeo. They danced atop the worn furniture, and snuggled as they watched old Fred Astaire and Ginger Rogers movies on television.

It was a fine, if brief, romance.

One prophetic day, Barbara asked Barry if she could use his tape recorder. An agent had requested a tape of her singing. "When I heard the first playback," Dennen later said, "I went insane." He told Barbara not only that she could sing, but that she *had* to sing. It was her calling. "But I'm an actress," she feebly protested, "not a singer."

Undaunted, Dennen attempted another approach. Why couldn't she take a song, break it down into three acts, and *act* it out while she sang it? After all, while the city's agents could prevent her from acting on a Broadway stage, they had no power to prevent her from acting on a *nightclub* stage. She would later relate, "I thought, If they won't let me become an actress, what's to stop me from making it by yelling?" "Yelling," of course, was Barbara's disdainful characterization of her own singing.

Dennen told Barbara about the weekly amateur contests at The Lion, which was located, conveniently, right across the street from his apartment. He promised that if she agreed to enter the contest, and won, he would help her with rehearsals and with the selection of her repertoire. He also agreed to direct her act.

Certainly, Barbara rationalized, she could use the fifty dollars in prize money. She was no longer working at the switchboard, or as an usherette, and her thirty-two-dollars-a-week unemployment checks had stopped coming. Her financial situation had deteriorated from difficult to desperate. She could do without rent and food money. But she could not, would not, do without money for her acting classes. And so she agreed, albeit with much reluctance, to set her reservations aside, at least for a night, and "yell" for her supper. Before she did, however, she went to the apartments of some of her various friends, insisted that they turn toward the wall, and unveiled, to unsuspecting ears, the full force of her remarkable singing voice. Invariably, when her friends turned around to face her, she saw awe on their faces, and tears in their eyes.

It was June 1960. And Barbara Streisand, eighteen, was ready to enter the lion's den.

Five

Illusions

$\mathscr{B}$urke McHugh remembers the moment he first laid eyes on her. "I managed The Lion—the dining room, the bar, the show, the whole works," he relates. "Every Monday night, I decided to put on talent contests. I used to audition the contestants, along with my male pianist, every Monday morning. We'd select four of them to come back for the contest that night. They came in and out, in and out. Most of them were *not* very good, you know. So we'd say, 'We'll let you know if we want you back.' That was the only morning that they could audition, and they had to be available to perform that night.

"God, was it a hot day. We were having the auditions out in the bar, in the front room, and we decided to go outside and cool off. And this girl came along wearing a pair of dungarees, with her hair down to her shoulders, uncombed, and really messy. She looked like a hooker—no, not a hooker, 'cause she wasn't sexy. She looked like a kid off the streets who hadn't been home to change her clothes. I said to the piano player, 'Oh boy, here comes a winner.' And then I said to her, 'Oh, hello. Did you come to audition?' And she said, 'Audition for what?' She acted like she was just walking by. So I explained the whole thing to her, and she said, 'Well, I've never sung in public before, but I'll give it a try.'

"So we brought her out into the front room. I heard about two lines come out and I said to the piano player, 'Oh my God, this girl is *unbelievable!*' So I said to her, 'Hold it a minute. Let's go in the back room with the grand piano.' So we moved into the back room, where there was a microphone. We didn't have a mike in the front room. I turned the mike on and I asked her her name. She said her name was Barbara Strinberg. So I said, 'Okay, Miss Strinberg, do a number for us.' When she sang, the piano player looked at me and I looked at him. We just couldn't *believe* what we were hearing. When she finished, I said to her, 'Oh my God, Barbara, that was really magnificent!'

"And then I said, 'Okay, now how do you spell Strinberg, I want to get it correct.' And she kind of paused and said, 'I've gotta change the name. I can't stand it.' I said, 'Barbara, what do you want to change it to? I think Strinberg is fine.' And she said, 'It sounds too Jewish. It sounds too Jewish.' So I said, 'Okay, let's sit down for a minute and think about names.' The radio was on and there was a song, 'Footsteps in the Sand' or something like that, and she said, 'Sand, I like that,' that's a good last syllable.' I laughed and said, 'Yes, that's very nice.' And she said, 'Oh good, the last syllable is sand. Barbara Streisand.'

"She was lying, of course. I guess she was lying with 'Strinberg,' and then when she saw that we were interested in her, she decided to use her real name." It was one of Barbara's occasionally employed techniques. She used an alias to buffer rejection. It would not be until she was accepted that she would entrust someone and provide her real name. It wasn't so much deceit, just self-preservation.

Contrary to previously published reports, Burke McHugh insists that Barbara's competition that night did *not* include an opera singer, or a comedian. He seems to recall that her primary competition came from a black girl, Dawn Hampton, who was Lionel Hampton's niece.

McHugh recalls, "She was a jazz belter and she sang like there was no tomorrow. She sang in an awful lot of places later on. That night, against Barbara was tough competition."

Barbara sang two songs, "When Sunny Gets Blue" and "A Sleepin' Bee," the latter of which was cowritten by Truman Capote. Ironically, although he was an early advocate of Streisand's, Capote did not like her version of his song. "She certainly doesn't do it very well," he told writer Lawrence Grobel. "It's good, but it's not as good as Diahann Carroll's, who sang it originally." He added, "Streisand turned it into a three-act opera and it's not."

Those who were there that night at The Lion disagreed. "I just wept the first time I heard her sing," Terry Leong relates. "It was just so unbelievable. I don't know, so pure." Barbara was the unanimous winner of the contest. Her prize? Fifty dollars in cash and a one-week engagement, the latter of which would be extended by popular demand.

"There was definitely a buzz about Barbara," McHugh recalls. "It started that first night at The Lion. A lot of agents came down to see her.

Noel Coward saw her at The Lion. He was right here, and her mike was right there, and she just belted in his face. Did she know who he was? Oh God! Is the Pope Catholic? He went bananas. He thought she was brilliant."

McHugh is perturbed by the characterization of The Lion as a "gay bar." Arguably, and to varying degrees, *every* bar was gay in the Greenwich Village of the early 1960s. The fact is that, while the front bar of The Lion *was* predominantly gay, the showroom in which Barbara performed was mixed, and drew such celebrities as Ethel Merman, Lynn Fontanne, and Tallulah Bankhead. "I remember Veronica Lake used to come in and hang out at the bar," McHugh relates. "She was one of Barbara's earliest fans."

Among those to make the trek to The Lion during Barbara's extended engagement were Anita and Allan Miller. The latter relates, "She called up one night, this was about two years after we started together, and she said, 'Hey, listen. I won a talent contest. You gonna come down and see me? It's at a place called The Lion.' I said, 'Where is that? I've never heard of that theater.' And she said, 'No, no. It's like, umm, a little, you know, restaurant kind of thing.' And I said, 'Doing what? What's the play?' And she said, 'No, no, it's not a play. I'm *singing.*' "

Despite the closeness of their relationship with her, not only had the Millers never heard Barbara sing, they didn't even know that she *could* sing. And so it was with trepidation that they took their seats at their front row table. "We were clinging to each other," he relates, "hoping she wouldn't be too terrible. I mean, it was like our daughter was performing for the first time."

As the spotlight hit the stage, illuminating Barbara in her ill-fitting thrift shop regalia, the Millers braced themselves. Allan Miller says, "She looked like the worst cartoon mixture.

"And then she started to sing. We were floored. Totally floored. Later, we talked about it at home, and Gregory, who was the older boy, I guess he was six or seven, he said, 'Yeah, when we used to go to the park, she would go off there singing.' She had been practicing her singing at the playground."

Opportunities presented themselves. *Men* presented themselves. Suddenly, Barbara was desirable, attractive. She had been relatively late in discovering men, and, at the age of eighteen, was determined to make up for it. Part of her new attitude had to do with defiance in general. Part could be attributed to rebellion against her mother and everyone else who had ever thought she was unattractive, and therefore undesirable to men. Her first love, Barry Dennen, was quickly joined by a second. During her run at The Lion, Barbara began seeing Veronica Lake's teenage son.

A friend at the time relates. "Veronica used to live across the street from The Lion. Sometimes, Barbara would be late for performances, and she'd be found with the son in Veronica's apartment across the street."

Since her graduation from Erasmus Hall High School, and her arrival in Manhattan, Barbara had been defining and redefining her image. "She was desperately fishing around for a better image for herself," Allan Miller relates. During her engagement at The Lion, she decided to make one other alteration, not so much to her image, but to her *identity*. As a slap in the face to all of the wide-hipped and narrow-visioned agents who had told her to change her name to Barbara Sands, or some other homogenized, de-ethnicized configuration, she decided to comply. But she didn't want to change it *too* much, because she wanted all of those very agents, and all of the kids back in Flatbush, to remember that she was the same big-nosed girl at whom they had once scoffed.

"There was much talk about everybody wanting her to change her last name so it would be easier to pronounce," recalls her friend Terry Leong. "And then one day, she told me she changed her name. I said, 'To what?' And she said—he breaks into laughter—'Bar-bra.' It was so funny. Instead of three syllables, it was two. She explained it as being easier to remember."

"Every day, listening to that *a* in the middle of Barbara, who needs it?" she once told a reporter. "Two *a*s are plenty. For nineteen years [actually, eighteen and two months], I had three *a*'s, and enough is enough. Now," she said, "I'm Barbra." To other reporters she would quip, "Just be sure to spell my name—*wrong.*"

There was, of course, another reason she changed her name. There had, after all, been other Barbaras before her—Stanwyck, Payton, Bates, to name a few. But there had never been another *Barbra*. And there never would.

Six

Crossroads

$\mathcal{I}$t was early summer, 1960. While the rest of the country vacillated between Nixon and Kennedy, and two very different Americas, Barbra Streisand's eyes, crossed though they may have been, were clearly focused on the prize that was now within her grasp. Her virgin taste of fame was sweet, however slight, and intoxicating with its promise. Her next step seemed logical. While The Lion had opened the proverbial door, it could now do little more than take a bow and get out of the way. It was decidedly Greenwich Village, where Broadway slummed and mingled with the bohemian. Many of the city's power elite stayed away, contemptuous of the club's gay association and bargain prices. She needed a venue that could give her credibility and put her on the cabaret map. She needed the Bon Soir.

Along with a few others, the Bon Soir was one of the premier clubs in the city. It opened in September 1949 in a basement at 40 West Eighth Street in Greenwich Village. It was right around the corner, but a world of prestige apart, from The Lion. Typically, the shows were emceed by the club's front man, Jimmie Daniels, who had been the toast of Paris for several years, and featured a comic and a singer. Over the years, the club presented such name acts as Kaye Ballard, Phyllis Diller, Alice Ghostley, Jimmie Komack, Felicia Sanders, Sylvia Sims, Larry Storch, and, perhaps the most revered of all cabaret singers, Mabel Mercer.

Burke McHugh recalls, "One night Barbra dropped over to the Bon Soir in between shows at our place. She was quite impressed with it because they had [the combo] The Three Flames. The two owners were great friends of mine. One of them was Ernie Sgroi, Sr., the father of my partner at The Lion. So, I took her over there myself and asked them to please give her a listen, and she did a couple of songs."

"We had Sunday night tryouts," explains Tiger Haynes, the leader of The Three Flames. "I remember the night when Mike Nichols and Elaine May went on. The room was practically empty. These kids had to go on and work to tablecloths, practically. They were scared shitless, but they were funny. My piano player, my bass player, and I sat at a table so that they would have somebody to work to and bounce off of. Then the waiters came and sat, too, and the kids ended up doing a hell of a show. But they didn't get hired."

Haynes also remembers the Sunday night that Barbra Streisand first walked onto the stage. "I had been at the Bon Soir for so many years," he relates. "Whenever you do something for a long time, you develop something. If you've been driving a cab for a long time and you're picking up customers, you have an idea of what they're like before they get in your cab. And I knew that Barbra Streisand was going to be a star. She had that *attitude* of 'I belong here.' She was wearing a black velveteen kind of thing that looked like she got it at a thrift shop. First," says Haynes, not one to mince words, "you looked at the nose. Then you looked at the dress. Then you heard the voice—and that was it."

Ernie Sgroi, Sr., and his partner were also quite taken with Barbra, and they sat at the table with her and Burke McHugh to discuss an arrangement. Barbra, who didn't yet have an agent, did her own negotiating.

McHugh recalls the conversation. "They said, 'Yes! Absolutely! We want you as soon as we can get you.' And Barbra's big line was 'Do I get my meals free?' She wanted a sirloin steak and a baked potato. That was the first thing she said. She didn't even say 'Thank you.' I'm not trying to make her sound hard, this is just the way she was. And she said, 'And once more, I'll get some eight-by-ten glossies and I want them out front. I want one of them at the top, and one at the bottom.' And they said, 'Well, the other people that perform here are also very talented and they only get one photo.' And she said, 'Take it or leave it. I want those eight-by-tens, and I want a very good meal every night. That's the deal.'

Barbra could have made prompt use of the $125 weekly paychecks, actually, $108 after taxes, *and* the free meals. Unfortunately, her engagement at the club could not begin for three months. "The Bon Soir," explains Tiger Haynes, "usually closed for the month of July and did not open until September. But Streisand, whom I had never heard of before, was so liked, so professional, that on that last Sunday in June, they hired her on the spot to open on the Friday after Labor Day."

It was the summer of little money and much anticipation. Barbra, eighteen, and her coterie of friends, mostly male, and mostly gay, were living in poverty, or somewhere in the vicinity. Still, she was heady with excitement, and surrounded by a community of support, encouragement, and inspiration. When one of the guys got invited to a party, he sometimes took Barbra along as a "date." Together, they raided the free food at the banquet table. They snuck into movie theaters. Sometimes, they went to a revival at the New Yorker Theatre, propped their legs up on the seats before them, and reveled in old thirties and forties pictures.

They made do with what they had, and schemed to get what they didn't have. Barbra, for example, devised a way to get hold of complimentary sheet music for her upcoming engagement. She called around to the town's music publishers and pretended to be singer Vaughn Monroe's secretary. "Mr. Monroe is looking for some music," she would say with an affected nasal inflection, "could you send some over?" She worked odd jobs, including a short-term assignment as a switchboard operator at her brother's advertising agency. She entertained herself, and friends who would call, by employing a variety of accents. Tiger Haynes insists that she also worked for a time checking coats at The Lion. She continued with her acting classes and landed a small part as a French maid in a production of *The Boy Friend*. Unfortunately, it was not staged on Broadway, but in Fishkill, New York, where it played at the Cecilwood Theater from August 16 through August 30.

Back in Manhattan, she labored over her repertoire with Barry Dennen, whom she continued to see. She also worked on refining her image. Through Dennen, she was introduced to Bob Schulenberg, a young artist who had just arrived in the city from Los Angeles. They would become fast, close friends.

"It was the first night that I got to New York," Schulenberg recalls. "Barry and I were going out for a hamburger at the Pam Pam on Sixth Avenue. She was just leaving The Lion, picking up her clothes. She had these shopping bags full of stuff, and I was fascinated by these *things* coming out of these bags, you know, costumes, feather boas, all kinds of marvelous stuff. She also had a monkey hat in her bag, and she was wearing these 1927 red satin and gold kid shoes that were in perfect shape. She looked like she just stepped out of a division of Western Costume. And she came running down the sidewalk after us, carrying these bags, and yelling, 'Barry!'

"She was fascinated that I had awakened and had lunch on Beverly

Glen in West Los Angeles and was suddenly having dinner in Manhattan," Schulenberg says. "She wanted to know what that experience was like."

A lack of finances forced Barbra to move out of her West Forty-eighth Street apartment. She resorted to commuting back and forth from Brooklyn. Diana Kind was relieved to have her wayward daughter back, even if only to eat and sleep. Still, she worried constantly about Barbra, and stayed up nights waiting for her safe return on the I.R.T. Sometimes, Barbra stayed in Manhattan and slept over at the apartment of one friend or another. She had a fold-up cot she lugged around with her. "Any place I hang my hat is home," she would sing at the Bon Soir. The words were Arlen's; the sentiment, however, was Streisand.

Sometimes, it was Barry Dennen with whom she stayed. Sometimes, it was Veronica Lake's son. "As a matter of fact," Bob Schulenberg says, "the first time I met her, Barry said to her, 'Barbra, Bob is going to be staying with me, so you can't crash over.' And she said, 'That's okay. I'm staying over at Veronica Lake's.' And I thought, Excuse me? And it turned out that she was a friend of Veronica Lake's son."

Schulenberg says, "I know that what brought us together was that she had a tremendous interest in the 1920s—the personalities, the lifestyles, the clothing. She had a considerable quantity of the clothing, in perfect shape. And she *knew* about them. And I *knew* about them. It wasn't just anything old that she was attracted to—and this has certainly followed her in her life—it was an attraction to something finely made. She wasn't interested in, say, a Bill Blass suit that wasn't lined in silk. Or in an all-wool suit that was *kind of* all wool—really, it was polyester with a wool percentage, and yet you still paid $1,500 for it. Barbra could absolutely tell the difference."

Beyond sharing Dennen as a friend, Schulenberg had something Barbra could use. Upon meeting people, Streisand shrewdly sized them up. If they had something she wanted to possess, or knew something she wanted to learn, or had connections which could facilitate her journey, she befriended them. If they didn't, she was not interested. "I think that that can make her appear to be ruthless," Schulenberg says. She was the quintessential sponge.

In addition to being an artist, Bob Schulenberg had been a costume designer for Western Costume in Hollywood. He also had expertise in makeup application. "My brother was probably my first model," Schulenberg says. "I'd put stage makeup on him. I'd use my mother's lipstick and put feathers from her hat boxes on him. He'd come down to dinner parties and stand there in the hallway dressed like an Inca [not unlike Barbara at age five].

Schulenberg recalls, "In college, I was playing around with the sorority girls, putting makeup on them. I had an old MG sports car and I'd ride down Sunset Boulevard with these girls who were wearing false eyelashes and looking very movie star glamorous, and people were always looking and saying, 'Who is that?'"

It was a brand of glamour that Barbra had wanted for herself.

When asked if Barbra thought of herself as attractive back then, Schulenberg is adamant. "No, I'm certain that she realized, like so many young women, that she didn't look the way she was supposed to look. The terrible thing is that anything someone could've said that was bad about her, you could really be sure that she had said much worse about herself."

Over the years, Barbra has made much of the fact that when she was first starting out, various agents, producers, and industry types encouraged her to get corrective cosmetic surgery on her nose. At least one would-be mentor even offered to pay for Barbra's proposed rhinoplasty. But the very suggestion, she has implied, was demeaning. For Barbra, it was the stuff of which lifelong grudges were made.

However, according to Bob Schulenberg, it was Barbra herself who most wanted to have her nose fixed. *"She* wanted a nose job. I said to her that I thought her voice might change if she had it done. I got so sick of hearing her talk about how she really wanted a nose job to have a prettier nose."

Allan Miller concurs. "We didn't fight her about taking the *a* out of her name, but when Barbra said that she wanted to fix her nose, my wife and I were livid. My wife told her that if she had a nose job, she could never stay with us again. And I told her that if she did it, she could never be in my acting class again. I wasn't worried about her appearance. Just like Dustin Hoffman and George Scott, and every misbegotten face I can think of, the talent finds a place for you to be."

Barbra eventually abandoned the idea of surgery, because, according to her mother, "She was afraid to [go through with it]. They said it would change her voice."

From June 29, 1960, to July 16, 1960, Barry Dennen was appearing in Shakespeare's *King Henry V* in Central Park. Schulenberg used the opportunity to try out a new look he had in mind for Barbra. It was part Martha Graham, part Audrey Hepburn in *Breakfast at Tiffany's* (which was being shot in New York at the time). "I had been wanting to *change* Barbra," Schulenberg says. "So I said, 'Why don't we go to the play and surprise Barry? Why don't I do a makeup job on you that's totally different? He might not even recognize you." Elated by the prospect of "an all-new me," Barbra agreed.

Schulenberg started by painstakingly *hand-trimming* each individual strand of hair on a pair of false eyelashes. Then came the greasepaint. *"Heavy* greasepaint," Schulenberg says, "because she had that bumpy teenage skin. She was glad when I covered it up." When doing her eyes, Schulenberg discovered that the way to make them appear bigger, and less crossed, was to extend the bottom line out with eyeliner. Later, almost invariably, Barbra sported in some fashion the so-called Cleopatra line. *"That,"* Schulenberg says, "was something that I taught Barbra."

He then "regularized" her nose with shadow, making it appear less bulbous. Throughout the makeover, Barbra hounded Schulenberg with questions. "Why are we doing this?" "What is this?" "How do you do this?"

Finally came the matter of her dress. Barbra, of course, was used to *over*dressing. Prior to that night, if someone had asked, "What is she wearing?" the answer would have been, *"Everything."* But, Schulenberg dressed her in a simple black leotard, a black cardigan sweater, and a pair of narrow, black, Audrey Hepburnesque pants. The only jewelry adorning Barbra's stark new look was some Venetian glass bracelets and a pair of Venetian glass earrings. Her hair was piled atop her head.

"Well, it took so long to do Barbra's makeup," Schulenberg relates, "that we missed Barry's performance. He was really pissed. He waited the whole time. He was *really* annoyed and he *gave it* to us. He wasn't in the mood to see how beautiful Barbra looked. But it didn't matter, because the point of the evening was made. Everybody was looking at Barbra like, *'Who* is she?' She was very aware of it."

Dennen's anger, of course, was justified. It wasn't just that his friends had missed the play. It was that *his* moment of triumph had been turned into another Barbra Streisand melodrama. There was an imbalance in friendships with Barbra. They were all tilted in her direction. When asked if Barbra had been interested in and supportive of *his* fledgling career, Bob Schulenberg replies, "Well, she would *think* that she was. She was as interested in mine as she's been in anyone's."

It was the summer of little money and much music. While planning her repertoire for the Bon Soir, Barry Dennen introduced Barbra to numerous records from his extensive collection. Sometimes, Bob Schulenberg joined them. "We listened to all the thirties stuff," Schulenberg says. "Mabel Mercer, Helen Morgan. Those charismatic women who brought 'the whole thing' with them, who turned songs into drama."

They also played recordings of Fanny Brice, Edith Piaf, and others. Schulenberg says, "I told Barbra about the time that I had seen Edith Piaf perform at the old Biltmore Theatre in Los Angeles and how a friend had taken me backstage to meet her. I told her about Piaf's look. It was the 1950s, and everybody was wearing sequins and feathers. I used to jokingly say to Barbra, 'I can't stand the singers who have a big grin on their face while they're singing "I'll Never Smile Again." ' Or, about how poor they are, while they're wearing sequins and furs. Barbra was fascinated by Piaf. I told Barbra that Piaf used minimal gestures when she sang, that she didn't do anything but stand there."

Critics of Barbra's club performances would later compare her to Piaf and Morgan. Others would compare her to Judy Garland, Lena Horne, Julie London, and Morgana King. Barbra, however, would contend that she was an absolute original. "I hadn't really heard anybody," she would claim. "I'd never been to a nightclub until I worked in one." The latter part of the statement was true, but the former, of course, was not. She had listened to and studied hundreds of records and dozens of singers in Barry Dennen's apartment.

"It seems to me," Schulenberg continues, "that Barbra just brought theatrical concepts from her acting classes to the stage. She thought, 'Why should you stop drama when you're singing? They're not two different disciplines.' "

"From what Barry told me," says Terry Leong, "it was he who shaped a lot of Barbra's sensibilities as far as acting and singing go."

Bob Schulenberg agrees "Barry *was* the one, as I understood it, who liberated the idea that you could have your own little play by the selection and *sequence* of songs. It was his idea, as I remember it, that her show be *Aspects of a Young Woman,* an autobiography of what a young woman would be going through. 'A Sleepin' Bee' was about first-time love; 'Lover Come Back to Me' was about losing the love; and 'Who's Afraid of the Big Bad Wolf?' was a little whimsy in between."

Barbra, of course, would never credit Barry Dennen. "I'm an actress," she would tell a reporter, "and the songs are all little plays that I present. In one evening, I'm half a dozen different people, a whole repertory theater, kind of. Singing, or whatever it is that I do, is harder than acting. I'm up there alone. I've got nobody to back me up or bounce my stuff off of, like other actors. It's tough, but I love it, I guess. But you never know. Maybe I'll wind up in the construction business."

For reasons of her own, Barbra would also want to give the impression that her singing career was something that just happened. Perhaps she figured that people might be more impressed if they thought her singing was totally unpracticed and had no history. "I never sang around the house or anything like that," she would contend, obviously forgetting about singing in the hallways and on the front stoop and in the school choirs of her Brooklyn childhood.

Diana Kind, meanwhile, was the mother who wouldn't go away. Sometimes, when Barbra hadn't returned home for a while, Diana would track her down and show up at her doorstep, unannounced, with mason jars filled with chicken soup. Says Bob Schulenberg of Mrs. Kind, "I was always with Barbra when I saw her. I think she's a *distant* woman. I think Barbra's distance comes from her mother. There was an awful lot of 'get out of my face' kind of stuff that Barbra would give to her mother. I can remember her mother getting on her case about something, and Barbra saying, 'Leave me alone!' in no uncertain terms, and in *quite* salty language."

Meanwhile, Barbra continued with her acting classes. "She talked about the exercises that she was learning," Schulenberg relates, "and once she described to me a sensory exercise in which she was a chocolate chip cookie in the oven. She described how she goes into the oven raw, with her chocolate chips. The oven gets hotter and she says, 'Parts of me are drying, cooking, melting, feeling hotter.' Then she goes, 'Oh my God, Oh my God, my chocolate's melting!' And she just loved going through what it would feel like to be a chocolate chip cookie.

On Friday, September 9, 1960, Barbra Streisand opened as the second- or third-billed act at the Bon Soir. She wore a black velvet skirt and a black beaded top from the 1890s. She stood fairly still on the stage, and sang. There was very little patter and very little stage movement. Her hands, long and slender, did all of the dancing. She was Piaf incarnated. And she would be such an unqualified success that her engagement would be extended and reextended into the month of December. The Bon Soir didn't make Streisand a star, it made her a *happening.* The city was abuzz, if not afire, with word of this weird-looking new girl singer from Brooklyn. Eventually, the city's agents and producers and record company executives made their way into the Bon Soir, but it was the gay community that provided her with her staunchest support. To them, she was not just a cabaret singer, she was a *cause.*

Robert Richards, a young illustrator, made frequent forays into the Bon Soir and witnessed the beginning of the Streisand phenomenon. "The Bon Soir was, in its way, legendary," Richards relates. "You played at the Upstairs at the Downstairs, the Living Room, the Blue Angel, the Bon Soir. Those were the great pubs. The Bon Soir was a little cellar on Eighth Street. You walked down this perilous flight of stairs into this black little hole. It was painted black, black, black, and had these crooked white sconces. The decor had seen better days. There was nothing posh about it. It was terribly smoky. It was basically a straight club, but over to one side, nearest the entrance, there was a bar that would be *packed* with men only. It was a very serious kind of gay scene. The minute the lights would go down, the club would be pitched into total blackness. There was just this one little light at the register for the bartender to see. And the men would engage in this sort of juvenile kind of sex play, hands and flies and unzippered pants, and all that sort of thing. So you could sort of 'shop' at the Bon Soir bar, and you could see a show at the same time.

"Generally speaking," Richards recalls, "there would be a comic, always sort of an avant-garde thing, and usually, the star of the show would be one of the legendary New York cabaret singers. They were older women, generally speaking, who sang the kinds of songs that I guess people still sing, those sad or witty or very sophisticated Cole Porter and Harold Arlen sort of songs. So you would have all these people at the bar with this divided loyalty—what was going on on the stage, and what was going on at the bar."

And into this scene came Barbra Streisand, who looked and acted nothing at all like what cabaret aficionados had come to expect from their divas. But emerging from beneath her tiny frame, with its shapeless contours, and her irregular face, with its pounds of eye makeup, was not only a remarkable voice but also a surprising inner strength that was at once heroic.

"Back then," Richards continues, "she was really, really *raw.* And she would just *do* things that you had never heard anybody ever do. The intensity of her singing was just incredible. She was a hurricane of a certain kind of unbridled passion. The wailings of a young girl. It always worked because it was so excessive. She would just hold notes until she would turn blue. And she would just gasp at the end of words, you know, like, *'uuuhhh!'* She was very bad, musically, but that really didn't matter. It was revolutionary in its way.

"There was always a sort of edge, the sense that she was giving you more than you deserved, as opposed to Liza Minnelli, who was just begging you to love her. Streisand never did that, not even in the beginning."

She was only eighteen years old, but almost immediately, she attracted the same kind of lines that were typically formed for Mabel Mercer, Sylvia Sims, and Felicia Sanders, *the* cabaret elite. She became a phenomenon in the gay community in particular. For some, congregating at the Bon Soir bar became a religion. They caught every show and spread word of the great new savior of New York nightlife.

Part of her appeal, certainly, was her insistence on individuality in an age of vanilla-flavored conformity. Barbra said and sang what she wanted, how she wanted. She made no apologies for not being polite. And she certainly made none for not being pretty. Clearly, she was a new breed of woman, who was going to use different, atypically feminine weapons to attain her goals.

Seven

Before Stonewall

*I*t can be argued that Barbra Streisand owes her career to gay men. Certainly, it was the gay male population that discovered her. And it was the gay male population that, over the years, would comprise her most ardent following.

The reasons for this appeal are complex. Before a gay audience, Streisand was a misfit among misfits. At eighteen, she had suffered. And when she sang about the pain of being unloved, she really *felt* the lyrics. Gay men related to that pain, that brand of rejection. Both Barbra and her gay audience had been rejected by a society that expected them to be something that they were not and could never be.

She related, too, to their humor, their "camp" sensibility. "I don't know what it is that gay people thought was funny about Bette Davis when other people thought she was a tragedienne," Robert Richards reflects. "I don't know why gay people *knew* Joan Crawford was weird, long before we knew about the wire hangers. And I don't know why Barbra Streisand had the same mentality that gay men of that era, for some reason, had. She just *did*. She sang songs like "Ding Dong the Witch Is Dead," and there was something just unbelievably homosexual about the whole thing."

To understand her relationship to the gay community, one has to put Streisand's arrival in context. It was pre-Stonewall (the Stonewall riots of the late 1960s marked the advent of the gay rights movement), at a time when gay men were repressed and invalidated. The public perception was that they were somehow psychologically defective and consigned to living lives that were empty and spent sitting atop a bar stool, or slumped in a darkened alley.

It was in this context that there came this eighteen-year-old ragamuffin *kid* who not only refused to suppress her differences, she was flaunting them in the face of a straitlaced, suit-and-tie society—and she was being accepted. She was giving the finger to the centuries-old unwritten code of acceptable conduct—and she was getting away with it. She was breaking all of the rules—and she was *winning.* To some gay men, she provided a vicarious thrill. To many others, she was downright liberating.

And so they made her their own. Years later, gay men would find another idol in Madonna. Reflective of the times, Madonna would not play victim as Judy Garland did, nor would she simply say, "Take me as I am," as Streisand defiantly did over twenty years before. Taking an activist stance, Madonna would not only express herself, in her songs, videos, movies, and any other available media, she would also proceed to blatantly market herself (and her sexual fantasies) down the collective throats of a sometimes adoring, sometimes appalled public—and she would get away with it. Madonna, it could be said, is the ACT UP entertainer of the current generation. But it can also be said that there probably would never have been a Madonna if there hadn't first been a Streisand.

As she became more of a public personality, Barbra suppressed her innate shyness, reserving that side of herself only for the closest of friends. Publicly, she was brash, swaggering. "I think I'm a great actress," she would say with the kind of bravado that would make some shudder at her apparent and inelegant egotism. "A great actress makes people feel the emotion behind the lines; a great singer does the same. There's no trick in getting up in front of an audience and closing your eyes and singing. That's easy. But to get up there and keep your eyes open and look at your audience and make them feel what you want them to, that's hard. Standing up there without doing anything at all, that's the hardest." She would add, with characteristic candor and cocky conceit, "I can do that too!"

What she *would* demand from her audience was complete quiet and absolute attention. She was known to start her act by unleashing a scream into the microphone, just to get everyone's attention. She would then calmly retrieve the chewing gum from her mouth, stick it into the mike, and start to sing. What this also did, of course, was set the audience up. It was the element of surprise. Generally, her audience laughed when she took the stage, and was then stunned into silence as she began to sing. Barbra sensed their shift in mood, and she reveled in that power. She could make them laugh. She could make them cry. She could make them be quiet.

"I sometimes feel guilty, because I've put them through the wringer," she would say. "But I can't help it." She would add, "On my good nights, I *do* control them. And on my bad nights, they control me. I think an audience has to be led."

One night, the audience refused to be silenced. Inwardly, Barbra panicked. Outwardly, however, she just stood there immobile, and refused to sing. Peter Daniels started playing the piano introduction to "A Sleepin' Bee," but the audience continued to buzz and Barbra still refused to sing. She just stood there on the stage and stared the audience down. Finally, a few people in the audience "shhh'd" the others down, and finally, she launched into the opening bars of the song. To Barbra, a silenced room was a sign of respect.

"People shut up," she would say of her singing. "What can I tell you?" It was a daring approach for a seasoned professional. For an eighteen-year-old newcomer, it was audacious.

Barbra's repertoire at the time, which had been worked out with Barry Dennen, included Fats Waller's "Keepin' Out of Mischief Now," on which she oozed with sex. By the time she finished the song, every straight man in the audience, and a few who were not so, *wanted* her and was surprised that he did; Rodgers and Hart's "Nobody's Heart," on which she ended her notes with a biting *"zuh!"*—"That's the least of my cares-zuh!" and "Nobody's arms-zuh belonged to me!"; "Lover, Come Back to Me," which she belted in parts, and virtually *shrieked* in others; "Cry Me a River," the standard made famous by Julie London, on which Barbra seethed with aggression and bitterness, "Come on, come on, cry me a river!" she taunted; and, of course, "Who's Afraid of the Big Bad Wolf?" a high-strung reworking of the children's song. Barbra mockingly told her audience, when introducing the latter, that people complained that she didn't sing standards.

Among those entranced by Streisand was Truman Capote, despite his dislike for her version of "A Sleepin' Bee." "She's very extraordinary," he would say of her. "She is one of the real phenomenons of today. My favorites are Bea Lillie and Billie Holiday, and she's the only one I've heard to equal them." Other early fans were Johnny Mercer, George Abbott, and Harold Arlen.

She was thrilled to meet Arlen, her favorite composer. One day, Arlen invited Barbra to his apartment, where he proceeded to perform hours of his music for her. Later, she would perform and record several of his songs, including "Down with Love," "Right as the Rain," and "I Had Myself a True Love." She would also guest on one of his albums, for which she reportedly insisted on receiving half of all of his royalties.

Anne Jackson and Eli Wallach were also ardent, early supporters. They were both successful in their acting careers, and would give parties in their apartment which were attended by an assortment of distinguished guests. They would then have Barbra go in front of the room and sing. And, like the Choys and the Millers and the Cormans before them, the Wallachs took Barbra under their wing. She had lost a father in infancy and was not particularly close to her mother, but she had an expanding list of couples who were more than willing to be her surrogate parents.

During her early appearances at the Bon Soir, Barbra was not the headlining act, although, in time, she drew most of the crowds. Renée Taylor performed as one of the headliners.

"We were working the same club," Taylor—who was involved with, and would later marry, actor-writer Joe Bologna—recalls. "I was a little older. Barbra didn't have any money. I really didn't have any money, either. I wore a pair of stockings, and when I came offstage, I used to take them off and lend them to her to wear. We also shared a dressing room. It was a tiny room with two chairs. Only two people could fit into the room. Barbra had all these old antique clothes hanging up.

"We were always talking about fellas," Taylor remembers. "I fixed her up with Joe's cousin, Bobby Aldermari.' I said to her, 'Maybe you'll like Bobby.' But I don't think she liked him." Taylor adds, "We always talked about career and boys. I think Barbra is still doing that, career and boys. Only, her nails have gotten shorter."

Another of the Bon Soir's headliners at the time was Phyllis Diller. Diller instantly sympathized with Barbra. She had started her own career in her mid-thirties, a destitute housewife and a mother of five. She knew what it was like to be the unattractive underdog. And she played her lack of good looks for all they were worth, shooting to fame with her own brand of self-deprecating humor. "You probably think this is *hair*," she quipped to her audience. "You're sweet . . . these are *nerve ends!*" she screeched, followed, of course, by her now trademark cackle, "Ha-ha-ha-ha-ha!"

By all accounts, Diller was very gracious, going so far as to buy Barbra clothing, a cocktail dress which Barbra accepted but did not like. She also introduced her to people who could further her career.

What Barbra needed was an agent. Although the Bon Soir kept extending her engagement, it was bound to end sometime, and she wanted to be prepared when it did. She was living at the time at the Hotel Earle in the Village, and she didn't want to have to return to Brooklyn. Among those that she approached to be her agent was Burke McHugh. He flatly declined. For one thing, he was busy with his work at The Lion, and with a modeling agency which he owned. He had other reasons too. "She was cocky," he says. "No, she was determined," he corrects. "Single-minded? Definitely. I'd rule out shy. Abrupt. Abrupt was a good word for her. She didn't listen too closely to things because she already had her mind made up."

Another man who figured prominently in the early career of Barbra Streisand was Ted Rozar. His contributions are not well known in Streisand lore, because, according to Ted, "Barbra forgets about it because I can't help her anymore. I can't do her any good anymore."

It was November 1960 when Rozar ventured into the Bon Soir to catch the act of comic Paul Dooley. Sitting with him was Orson Bean, whose career he then managed. Bean was a regular guest host of "The Jack Paar Show" (a.k.a. "The Tonight Show") and would be one of two finalists (Johnny Carson was the other) to replace Paar in 1962.

Rozar doesn't recall much about Dooley's performance. He was too mesmerized by the second-billed, unheralded girl singer. When she completed her first number, Rozar, mouth still dropped open, turned to Bean and pronounced, "*That* is one of the three most talented singers alive." The other two being, in his opinion, Judy Garland and Eydie Gorme.

Following her act, Rozar marched backstage, walked up to Barbra, and kissed her. The first words out of his mouth were "I love you." And then he asked her if she had a manager.

The following Wednesday, November 23, 1960, Barbra walked into Rozar's office at 53 East Fifty-fourth Street and signed an agreement making Ted Rozar her first manager. The contract was for three years and gave Rozar 20 percent of her earnings, with another 5 percent going to anyone outside of the city who assisted Rozar with out-of-town negotiations. Potentially, it stood to earn Rozar an enormous amount of money. Upon signing the contract, Barbra was disturbed by a factor which had nothing whatsoever to do with finances. She took her pen and scratched out the extra *a* which had been inadvertently included in the spelling of her name. As she got up to leave, she shook hands with her newly signed manager and pronounced, "My name is *Barbra*."

There is no doubt that Ted Rozar recognized and believed in his client's talent. In 1964, when Barbra was the toast of Broadway with *Funny Girl*, Charles McHarry wrote in his "On the Town" column in the New York *Daily News*, "As recently as three years ago there were perhaps but two people who were absolutely certain Barbra Streisand would make it to the top. One was Miss Streisand and the other one was Ted Rozar. . . . Rozar went around telling Broadway's producers, general managers and agents that Barbra was one of the greatest talents of the decade, but no one listened much."

Rozar says, "I take credit for identifying her as a great talent, and for telling absolutely every agent in this city, '*This* is the most exciting singer alive. She's phenomenal. Come and see her.' " For while Rozar was now overseeing and making decisions about the direction of Barbra's career, he was intent on attracting a reputable agent who could get her actual club bookings. Among those he attracted was Irvin Arthur.

In the James Gavin book *Intimate Nights,* Streisand acquaintance Ben Bagley, producer of Off-Broadway revues, contends that Arthur rejected Barbra as a client. He quotes Arthur as having said, "She's so ugly no one could use her on anything but the radio, and no one wants radio singers these days." In fact, however, Arthur *did* become Barbra's first agent, and he dismisses the quote attributed to him as "totally inaccurate."

Arthur contends that he landed Streisand as a client "by default." It seems that all of the major New York agencies at the time had rejected her. Arthur recalls, "What happened was that they were very shortsighted. Her appearance kind of turned them off. But I had no doubt at all that she was going to be a star. She was one of the first people I booked that I *knew* was going to be a major star. I later booked Bette Midler, Lily Tomlin, and I had something to do with Whoopi Goldberg."

"I signed Barbra to an agency contract," says Arthur, who was working at the time for the Associated Booking Corporation. "I went to her after the show, and we went to a little coffee shop next door to the Bon Soir and talked." Barbra would later quip, "I hired my first agent because he took me out for dinner. A few years ago, I could be bought for an avocado."

"I had her come in to the office, and she signed all these papers," Arthur continues. "At the time, we were just a personal appearance agency. She signed a contract for three years with a three-year option.

Arthur quickly found out that Barbra was not to be just another client. Her nightly phone calls at 11:30 P.M. were indication enough of that.

Typically, she called to inquire whether he had arranged any appointments for her in Manhattan the following day. If he had, that gave her a reason *not* to go back to Brooklyn for the night. "She never wanted to go back to Brooklyn," Arthur recalls. Sometimes, she called to say, "I want-ya to know where I'm gonna be tomorrow, so you can call me." Arthur had a time explaining the late night calls to his sleepy-eyed wife. "My wife used to say, 'So, who's this dame calling you every night?' Arthur recalls with a laugh. "And I would say, 'Just a *star*.'"

For the months of March and April, 1961, Irvin Arthur booked his "star" on a tour, albeit a second-rate one. "I had a circuit of little clubs that sat fifty to sixty people each, and I'd put these female singers from New York on this tour. They would only get $200, $250 a week, which wasn't such a bad salary, really. It was low, but it was enough that they could live on. Hotels weren't so expensive then."

The tour was to take Barbra to the Caucus Club in Detroit, the Backroom in Cleveland, and the Crystal Palace in St. Louis.

In Detroit, the club's owner, Lester Guber, fell in love with Barbra and sought to extend her engagement. He telephoned Billy Weinberger owner of the Backroom in Cleveland, saying, "Hey, listen. Can you postpone your engagement with Barbra Streisand? I think I have a winner here."

Weinberger, who had a $200-a-week contract for Barbra's services, agreed to waive her commitment to appear in his club. His reason? It seems that his brother had seen Barbra's show in Detroit and had informed him that she wasn't *that* good, that she wore "schlumpy" dresses, and that she had a big nose.

In later years, Weinberger would become president of Caesars World, and the CEO of Bally's. But he would never forget the time he had—and lost—Streisand for a mere $200 a week. "Whenever we see each other," Irvin Arthur relates, "he says to me, 'You've *gotta* get me a copy of that $200 contract with Streisand. Nobody believes the story!'"

While she was in Detroit, two major events happened in Barbra's career. First, her manager Marty Erlichman began his long association with her. He had seen her a few months before at the Bon Soir, when he had gone to check out the act of his friend, comedian Phil Leeds. Barbra had been the opening act. That night would have a profound impact on both of their lives. After the show, he approached her and asked if she had representation. She responded that she did, although she was becoming increasingly dissatisfied with Ted Rozar.

First of all, Rozar was not delivering any of the major jobs that he had promised her. Second, according to Barbra, he made the mistake of urging her to have surgery on her nose.

"That was absolutely untrue," insists Rozar. "I did ask her, *once,* 'Would you like to have an operation? If you do, I'll lend you the money to do it.' That was it. And she said, 'No. I like my nose.' "

Furthermore, she was unhappy that Rozar refused to accompany her on the tour. "I had a wife and two kids," he explains. "I wouldn't go on the road with her, and she wanted me to. She wanted someone who would always be there, and act more as a personal assistant than as a manager. I was a manager in title, but to manage Barbra, there was a whole lot more of hand-holding."

Barbra grew to dislike Rozar and resented the commissions she was contractually obligated to pay him. "I loved Barbra," says Rozar, "but there *was* a personality conflict. We were two strong personalities that clashed. She wanted things the way Barbra wanted them, which was totally justified. But Ted wanted to live Ted's life. I wanted to manage Barbra more as an attorney would." And, Rozar adds, "I was twenty-two, she was nineteen. We were still both feeling our way."

Back in Detroit, Barbra picked up the hotel telephone and called a startled Marty Erlichman in San Francisco. She had had it with Rozar, she told him, and she wanted Erlichman to represent her, *without compensation.* Even more surprising, Erlichman agreed. The immediate problem at hand was that, contrary to Irvin Arthur's recollection that she was making $200 a week at the Caucus Club, she was actually getting $150, unlike the other singers on the circuit. She informed Erlichman that she wanted the standard $200, *plus* free dinners. Erlichman, who was practically broke himself, flew to Detroit at his own expense.

Upon his arrival, he went to the club and negotiated a new deal for Barbra. The club's owner agreed to pay her $175 a week, *without* the free dinners. Erlichman told him, behind Barbra's back, that he would pay the $25 balance out of his own pocket, *if* the club would throw in the free meals. Stunned, the owner scratched his head and pondered aloud, "Let me get this straight. You flew here at your own expense so you could pay me twenty-five dollars, and you're not even her manager? You must really believe this girl is going to be a star." Says Erlichman, "I sure as hell did."

"Barbra is the girl the guys never look at twice," Erlichman would say of her appeal, "and when she sings about that—about being like an invisible woman—people break their necks trying to protect her." Including, of course, himself.

At the time, Erlichman, a quiet, stocky man from the Bronx, had only one client, an Irish folksinging group known as The Clancy Brothers. There had been others before him who believed in Barbra Streisand's talent, but there had been no one who was willing to stake his reputation, his livelihood, and his future on it.

"Barbra called me once," says Irvin Arthur, "and said, 'This guy, this Marty Erlichman, is hanging around me all the time. He wants to be my manager. He believes in me so much, he will do it for a year without getting paid.' I said, 'Well, he's a nice guy, and he thinks you're fantastic. What have you got to lose?' "

There was a clause in Barbra's contract with Ted Rozar that gave either of them the right to cancel the agreement with ninety days' written notice. One night, Rozar, Barbra, and her accompanist, Peter Daniels, went to a coffee shop on the corner of Sixty-eighth and Lexington. Barbra was abrupt. "I want to end my contract," she informed Rozar. "Why?" he asked. "Well," she stumbled, "you and I have these, these 'personality conflicts.' " And then, accompanied by Daniels, she got up from the table and walked out. Rozar never heard from her again.

There was some dispute over money. Barbra told friends that she had to pay Rozar off to get out of the contract. Irvin Arthur concurs, saying, "Associated Talent paid him six hundred dollars to go away." Rozar, however, denies this claim, saying that he was paid only the commission owed him for the bookings that had already been negotiated.

While in Detroit, Barbra received an invitation to perform on "The Jack Paar Show," which later became "The Tonight Show." Up until then, her biggest audience had been the hundred or so people who crammed into the Bon Soir. Ironically, it was through Ted Rozar that Barbra was asked to appear. Guest-hosting the show that week was Orson Bean, Rozar's number one client. It was Wednesday, April 5, 1961. Barbra was given permission to interrupt her engagement at the Caucus Club, and she boarded a commercial airline headed back to New York City. It was the first plane ride of her life.

"The Jack Paar Show" was *the* premier late night television program at the time. Broadcast from the NBC Studios, the show aired from 11:15 P.M. to 1:00 A.M. Also booked on that night's program were Gore Vidal and, to Barbra's relief, the very supportive Phyllis Diller. Perhaps it was for Phyllis's benefit that Barbra wore a regulation cocktail dress as one of her two changes on the show.

"This girl is a young girl that I saw down at a nightclub called the Bon

Soir when she was there a couple months ago," Bean informed his audience. "She's never been, to the best of my knowledge, on network television before. She has the most charming manner and the most charming voice. She's flown in from Detroit to be with us tonight . . . and her name is Barbra Streisand."

After she completed "A Sleepin' Bee," which showcased the same upper range and startling clarity that won her the contest at The Lion, Barbra joined Diller and Bean on the panel. Barbra, who had been terrified backstage, sat beside Bean on the couch. She crossed her legs. She laughed. She shared a few whispered words with Diller.

Viewers were astonished by the contrast between the singer and her persona. Her singing voice had been so pure, so ethereal, so mature. Without a song to sing, however, she was just a gangling girl, only two years out of high school. It was an endearing contradiction. She was so fresh, so awkward, so full of breathless abandon. There was exhilaration on her face, and in her voice.

"This is *so* exciting!" she enthused as she looked around the set, "I just can't tell you! All these people! And the cameras! And the lights! . . . Oh!"

Such was Barbra Streisand's first appearance in the living rooms of millions of homes all across America. It wouldn't, of course, be her last.

Eight

Distant Voices, Other Lives

*A*mong other things, the tour gave Barbra a glimpse of the American heartland. It was her first venture away from the East Coast, and it was liberating. It opened her eyes to her own emerging creative powers. There had been no Barry Dennen to lean on for artistic direction. She had to rely on her own instincts, and they usually proved to be right. Novice though she was, she found that she knew more than the club owners, managers, and musicians with whom she came in contact. Once more, she learned that she liked being in control. If she wanted to change the sequence of her songs, or alter the lighting, there was no one to object. Her first taste of that *kind* of power was at once intoxicating and revelatory.

Furthermore, she liked the idea that in her new surroundings, no one knew anything about her, except what she herself divulged. To her audiences in Detroit, she contended that she had been raised in Brooklyn but had been born in Turkey—and they believed her. She also insisted that her name had been spelled "Barbra" since birth. It was her way of presenting herself as different, predestined. Just as she had in childhood, she was *remaking* herself, and, away from her friends, there was no one to stop her.

Neil Wolfe was the pianist at the Caucus Club in Detroit. During Barbra's engagement there, the two became quite close. Wolfe, who had seen second-rate singers on the circuit come and go, was bowled over by Barbra's obvious talent. Although he declined to discuss his personal relationship with her, Wolfe offered this assessment of her act, and her ability:

"She had great pitch, great taste, and great knowledge of music. From what I understood, Barbra used to go around to various composers and they gave her music. When she came into Detroit, she said, 'This is what I'm going to open with, and this is what I'm going to do next.' She did all the songs that were later on her first album."

When asked if he was aware that it had actually been Barry Dennen, and not Barbra, who had conceived and directed the show, Wolfe replies, "As far as I was concerned, Barbra put everything [in the act] together herself. I never knew of anyone helping her." Which, of course, was exactly how Barbra wanted it.

Upon her return to New York, she was decidedly cool toward Dennen. She had, after all, already learned what she could from him. He was no longer of much use to her, although she still occasionally called him for advice. Besides, she now had Marty Erlichman's sturdy shoulder to lean on. Dennen had his own acting career and his own aspirations to be concerned about. Erlichman, however, had only his belief in her—and The Clancy Brothers, but not for long. In time, Barbra would require—and demand—all of his energies. Interestingly, Barbra now also had Neil Wolfe, the pianist, who followed her back to New York, and who got a job working for Erlichman in the small Streisand office.

There were no streamers, no trumpets, no parades to herald Barbra's return from St. Louis. She hoped, particularly after her successful appearance on the Paar program, to have numerous Broadway offers at her disposal. Instead, she went back to the Bon Soir, where she opened for Renée Taylor on May 9, 1961. Interestingly, on the same night, a competing performer opened at the nearby Village Vanguard. His name was Lenny Bruce.

"I'm a very young performer," Barbra told one of her first interviewers, fumbling for the right words. "I don't know where I am, who I am, don't know what I am, yet." She also said that she wanted to act, which, of course, was of no particular surprise to anyone who knew her. She added that she wanted to manage a repertory company and that she one day intended to direct operas, which, she said, "could be the greatest theatrical experience ever!"

During her engagement at the Bon Soir, Barbra was invited back for her second appearance with Orson Bean on "The Jack Paar Show." *TV*

Guide mentioned her in its listing as "Barbara Strysand."

Savvily cognizant of the power of talk show television, she pursued it with a vengeance. She started hounding Joe Franklin's production office at West Forty-second Street near Times Square. Franklin had a local television talk show that aired twice a day, mornings and late evenings, five times a week. He was *not,* however, initially impressed.

"She looked like a young witch-vamp," Franklin recalled. "I was all set to actually wonder how much she'd charge to haunt a house." Still, Barbra, nineteen, persisted with repeated visits to his office. Finally, at the urging of Frank Campana, an early supporter of Barbra's at Columbia Records, Franklin listened to tapes of her singing voice. "As soon as I heard her sing," said Franklin, "my intuition told me that the kid had a terrific set of pipes and a natural style. She was a new, fresh talent. And despite her looks—or lack of them—she would someday have to be reckoned with as a great star. So I started putting her on my TV show."

"I had her on the panel with Rudy Vallee a couple of times," Franklin remembers. "He used to tell her, 'You'll never make it in show business.' I felt sorry for the kid." Franklin also gave her food and money, although he was careful not to offend her considerable and transparent sense of pride.

But it would be on another local television talk show that Barbra would hit her stride. "PM East" aired late at night, Monday through Friday, on Channel 5. It was hosted by Mike Wallace. In October 1961, she made several appearances, and, in short order, she became the show's semiresident eccentric. People began tuning in, hoping to see that "kooky girl singer from Brooklyn." Most viewers were discovering her for the first time, and they rubbed their sleepy eyes in astonished disbelief. Others were devotees from the Ben Soir, and they enthusiastically spread the word.

Robert Richards recalls those late night appearances. "The Mike Wallace show was a little black-and-white show that came on very late at night. Barbra struck up a very strange relationship with Mike. By this time, she was really leaning heavily into that persona of the young kooky girl. Her appearances were very much looked forward to, much the same way that Joan Rivers's first appearances as the hostess of the Carson show were." He adds that gay bars would offer two-for-one drinks the nights Barbra appeared.

When asked what separated Barbra from the usual roundup of talk show guests, Richards responds, "She was homely. She was frank. She was talking in a more candid way about dating and about rejection."

Wallace gave her license to talk, and talk she did. Since she had already done a national network show, she felt the local show was beneath her. "PM East," she told friends, was just a little, low-budget "Tonight Show" wannabe.

"When they called me to go on the show," she later related, "I said to myself, 'What's the big deal? I should go out and buy a dress special for this show? It's not even one of those fancy network shows.' So I'd go like I didn't give a damn. I'd look uglier than I was."

Actually, she did not *try* to look unattractive. After attaining stardom, however, she wanted people to think that she had, and so she conjured up some revisionist personal history. It was another one of her ploys. She tried to make her detractors think that the joke had been on them all along.

On "PM East," she said whatever popped into her constantly churning mind. Before she could articulate one thought, another, on an entirely different subject, would pop into her head, and the two would collide in passing, usually leaving Wallace dumbfounded and confused.

There was always an edge to her appearances. No one knew what was going to come out of her ample mouth—not the audience, not the host, and not even Streisand herself. Once, she began a tirade against the evils of milk. Another time, she condemned the foolishness of Zen Buddhism. Barbra and Wallace developed an adversarial rapport. On one show, Wallace implied that Barbra should be grateful for the exposure the program gave her to the town's producers. "Now let's be honest," Barbra replied. *"Those* people don't watch television, not the ones that do the hiring. A show like this just gets the public interested in paying the minimum to see me at places like the Bon Soir."

On another show, fellow guest Burt Lancaster got up and walked out in protest over Wallace's line of questioning. Barbra informed her host that Lancaster had been right to depart. At another point, she turned to Wallace and pronounced, "You know, I *used* to like you," provoking laughter from Wallace's crew. "No, this is the truth," she continued. "I really like what he does. A lot of people *don't,"* she added, provoking more laughter from the crew. "It's the truth. I like the fact that you're provoking," she informed her host. "Just don't provoke *me!"*

To some, her appearances became grating. She was *trying* too hard. Her efforts at being outrageous were increasingly transparent. On one show, fellow guests Richard Rodgers and Diahann Carroll ignored her. Years later, Rodgers would insist he was an ardent admirer, but Barbra never forgot the earlier snub.

"I scare you, don't I?" she challenged agent-turned-producer David Susskind on one of her more memorable appearances on the show. "I'm so far out, I'm in," she pronounced. Bob Schulenberg recalls the circumstances of that particular show:

"I wasn't there [in the studio]," Schulenberg says, "I was watching at home. Barbra more or less socked it to David Susskind. It was a show about old success and young success. There was David Susskind and Anthony Quinn and Mickey Rooney, all of whom were doing *Requiem for a Heavyweight.* To contrast the older, successful show business talents, they brought Barbra out as a young talent. So she came out to meet these people, who were all sitting in these 'Tonight Show' kind of chairs. When she was introduced to Anthony Quinn, she said, 'How do you do?' To Mickey Rooney, she said, 'I loved you in those movies with Judy Garland!' And then she coldly shook hands with David Susskind and said, 'You're an *agent!*' "

As producer of *Requiem for a Heavyweight,* Susskind wanted to put his agenting days behind him. Bob Schulenberg continues, "So he says, 'I *was* an agent.' And Barbra said, 'Well, that's what I mean.' Mike Wallace was just ready to *seize* on something. Barbra was saying how hard it was for her to get a break. And then she said, 'I had an appointment to see David Susskind, so I went to his office. But when I got there, I was told I couldn't see him. I just waited and waited and waited.' She was sitting there next to David Susskind and she turned and said to him, '*You* wouldn't see me. I had an appointment to see you, and you wouldn't see me. That's what agents are like?" Schulenberg recalls thinking, "Oh, Barbra, you've really done it now. You've really killed yourself now."

Typical of her, Barbra befriended Donald and John Softness, press agents for "PM East," and talked them into doing her own publicity, free of charge. "I think a lot of people helped her because she probably demanded it," John Softness relates. "I don't know what she's like today, but back then, she was an *assertive* young woman. I guess it was her talent [that attracted us]. It must've been her talent. She certainly wasn't all that good-natured."

He adds, "She goes through brick walls. She talks fast. She does everything fast. For example, we once walked into our office and there was a note there for her. She read the note, grabbed a piece of paper, and within sixty seconds, she had written a reply. That's the way she did everything. She did everything very, very fast, and very directly, and very aggressively. I never thought of it as energy—I thought of it as 'I've gotta get the work done, get it over with, finish it.' She was smart enough to be able to do these things and do them fast. I imagine that there's a softer side to her," says John, "a more relaxed side, but I never saw it."

Looking for work, Barbra gave several impromptu performances at various clubs around town. Sometimes, she would stop at Gatsby's on West Forty-eighth Street, where Neil Wolfe had gotten a night job. She would sidle up to him on the piano bench and sing a few numbers. On occasion, she would drop by the Ninth Circle or the Showplace, where a young Cass Elliott had a pre–Mamas and the Papas job checking coats. Donald Softness fondly remembers another of Barbra's impromptu performances:

"There was a little place called Mimi's, which was a little hole-in-the-wall Italian restaurant on the corner of Third Avenue and Fifty-third Street. On Friday nights, they would have a showgirl from Broadway, a girl from the chorus or something, who would come in and sing. I would go there with Barbra and we would sit at a table and Mimi [the male owner of the restaurant] would come over and say, 'Ask Barbra to sing.' And I'd say, 'Barbra, sing.' And Barbra would say, 'I don't wanna sing.' The reason that she never wanted to sing was that she wasn't getting paid. She didn't want to sing for nothing.

"But one day," Don continues, "she was going to sing 'Moon River' on the Mike Wallace show, and she bought the sheet music. That night, we went to Mimi's and Mimi came over and said, 'Ask Barbra to sing.' So I said, 'Barbra, sing. You could sing "Moon River." ' So she said, 'Oh, all right.' And she went up there to Jack [the pianist], and told him her key. She was, like, one in a long line of girls who would go up there and sing. Usually what happened was that the people at their tables would turn around and look at the singer for a second, and then go back to their conversations.

"Well, Barbra went up there, and she looked like she almost always did in those days, like something the cat dragged in. Her hair was unkempt and she had no makeup on. She was wearing old jeans and a disgusting old blouse. She looked like a very young girl from I don't know where. But as soon as she sang the first refrain of 'Moon River,' there was a hush. *Everybody* turned around. There wasn't a sound in the place. I had chills running up and down me, and I said to myself, 'This has *got* to be one of the greatest singing stars in pop music history!' "

Sometimes, she got all gussied up and did the town with Bob Schulenberg. Sometimes, they went out twisting at the Peppermint Lounge. It was she who taught him how to twist. Says Schulenberg, "Barbra was *into* it."

Without a job, Barbra braved another succession of closed Broadway doors. She was also rejected during this period by Julius Monk at the Upstairs at the Downstairs, and by Herbert Jacoby, owner of the Blue Angel, the city's most prestigious cabaret. Jacoby dismissed Barbra as too unpolished for his posh, uptown club with its well-heeled, upscale clientele. He subsequently had a change of heart and signed her for an engagement later in the year.

Unable to secure anything better in the interim, Barbra accepted a booking in Winnipeg, Canada, in July. Reported one of the local critics, "Barbra Streisand has a semi-Oriental look and a singing manner all her own. Miss Streisand is the type of singer you'd expect to find in the Blue Angel or San Francisco's Hungry i. That's why Winnipeggers may find her rather strange. But she seems to grow on you after you settle down to listen."

To the Canadian press, Barbra repeated her assertion that she had been raised in Brooklyn and born in Burma. It was a biography she would take with her when she returned to New York.

After months of auditioning for various producers, who generally dismissed her as too unattractive, and too "unique" (read *too weird*), Barbra landed a part in an Off-Broadway musical comedy revue entitled *Another Evening With Harry Stoones,* for which unique and weird were practically prerequisites. She composed the following partially fictionalized mini-autobiography for the production's Showbill:

> Born in Rangoon, Burma, a graduate of the Yeshiva of Brooklyn and Erasmus Hall High School—Barbra Streisand has had remarkable success in her short professional career. Although she is making her off-Broadway debut, Barbra caused Dorothy Kilgallen to refer to her in her column as a "rising new star" for her singing at the Bon Soir. She has also been on the "Jack Paar Show" two times and Mike Wallace's "PM East" twice [she would end up appearing on many more] as a straight singer. She has also sung in Canada, Detroit and St. Louis and in January will go to New Orleans, Miami and Chicago to work—although she thinks [she's going there] to ride horses."

Harry Stoones would present Barbra in her musical theater introduction to New York City audiences. She was simply one of several promising young talents involved in the production. The show was written and composed by a twenty-five-year-old newcomer by the name of Jeff Harris. *Harry Stoones* was designed to showcase the talents of its performers, in much the same way that *New Faces of '52* had done almost ten years before. It planned to do so, however, with irreverence.

Even the title of the show was a spoof. "At that time in New York," relates Jeff Harris, "there were a lot of shows like *An Evening With Marlene Dietrich, An Evening With Yves Montand, An Evening With X, Y, Z.* So we called our show *An Evening With Harry Stoones.*" Actually, there was no actor or character named Harry Stoones in the show. Nor was there even *mention* of a Harry Stoones in the show. Furthermore, Act 1 of the show was entitled "The Civil War." The second act was entitled "The Roaring Twenties." Actually, the show had nothing to do with either period, and neither was ever mentioned in either act. It was that *kind* of show."

"The show was really ahead of its time," contends Glenn Jordan, who had to bill himself "G. Adam Jordan," because another theater director shared his name. (Jordan, today an Emmy-winning television director of note, has numerous credits including the acclaimed *Sarah Plain and Tall.*) "It wasn't like anything else at that time. It was more like 'Laugh-In,' which was done years later."

"The auditions were very extensive," says Harris, "because, with a revue, the whole trick is getting the right people. We needed people who were multifaceted. They all had to sing, they all had to be able to move, and they all had to do comedy. We had one star in the show, Diana Sands, who had been on Broadway in *A Raisin in the Sun.* I had gone to school with her at the High School of Performing Arts. She was our big gun. We also had Dom DeLuise, whom I had also gone to school with. He had done some off-Broadway stuff, but he was not yet *Dom DeLuise* by any means. We also had Sheila Copelan, whom I had also gone to school with.

"In the nature of the material," continues Harris, "there was some stuff that wasn't as comedic as some of the other stuff. That material eventually went to Susan Belink, who ended up singing [opera] at the Metropolitan. The more comedic stuff, the sketch stuff, went to the remaining girls."

One of the remaining girls, of course, would be Barbra. Numerous other aspiring young singers/actresses/comediennes had auditioned for her slot (there weren't actually roles, per se) in the show. Glenn Jordan distinctly recalls Barbra's August 1961 audition:

"Jeff Hunter, the agent, sent her in to us. We had been seeing people for a very long time, most of whom were not very good, and most of whom sang the same songs. We were getting kind of jaded," Jordan admits. "And then Barbra came in and auditioned." Although he didn't recognize her at the time, Jordan had previously seen Barbra at work. He had attended a director's workshop at Curt Conway's studio and sat in on a dramatic scene performed by Conway's students. One of the performers was Barbra Streisand. Says Jordan, "I was *not* impressed."

In August 1961, Barbra appeared for her audition, singing two songs, "I Stayed Too Long at the Fair" and "A Sleepin' Bee." Glenn Jordan recalls, "She was as good, I think, as she ever got. I still remember the way she used her hands. She had these beautiful hands, and wonderful nails, and she used them very expressively when she sang."

Impressed as he was, Jordan decided against casting Barbra in the show. Contrary to her own self-perception, Jordan viewed Barbra as a singer, albeit a remarkable one, *not* an actress. Besides, they already had a straight singer for the show, Susan Belink.

"I remember calling her," Jordan relates, "to say how sorry we were that we weren't going to be using her. I told her how talented I thought she was. You didn't have to be smart to know how good she was."

The rejection did not deter Barbra, who continued to audition for other shows, including *Bravo Giovanni,* which she lost to Michelle Lee, and *Greenwich Village U.S.A.,* an off-Broadway musical coproduced by Burke McHugh, her early supporter from The Lion. "Barbra called me up one day," recalls McHugh, "and asked me if she could audition for the show. I said, 'Are you kidding? Come on down! Come today!' So she came down to audition, but my partners didn't like her. She never said anything about it, but I think she held it against me that she didn't get the part."

Meanwhile, Glenn Jordan, the director, and Jeff Harris, the writer, continued to audition other girls for *Harry Stoones.* But, as Jordan relates, "I remember saying to Jeff, 'I can't get *that girl* out of mind.'" Jordan summoned Barbra for another audition. The finalists for her slot in the show included two other performers who would later gain recognition themselves, Linda Lavin and Louise Lasser. Others who auditioned for other parts in the revue included Barry Newman, John Voight, and Barbra's former costar, Joan Rivers.

At her second audition, which took place on September 1, 1961, Barbra again sang "I Stayed Too Long at the Fair." "I wrote 'perfect,' 'wonderful,' in my notes," relates Jordan. After she finished singing, Glenn Jordan turned to Jeff Harris and said, "She's so good that I think we *have* to use her." Jordan adds, "One of my guiding principles is, 'When in doubt—go with the talent.' " Harris agreed, and Barbra was cast in the production.

"What happened," Jordan relates, "was that we changed the whole configuration of the revue so that she would have more songs to do. I think that 'Jersey' was added for her, and so was 'I'm in Love With Harold Mengert' [a.k.a. 'Value']."

One of the sketches didn't even require that Barbra speak. It simply called for her to take dictation from her boss, late one night. At the end of the sketch, her boss, beginning to see her in a new light, asks her to take off her glasses. She complies, but as she does, her skirt drops to the floor.

Another, "Big Barry," was set in boys' and girls' high school locker rooms. It cast Barbra as Nancy, the homely one among a trio of girls. In it, she had nothing to do but quietly sit while the other two girls, described by Jordan as "the big sexpots of the school," boasted about their many arduous suitors. They derided Barbra for her lack of good looks and for never being asked out on dates.

"In their locker room, the boys are talking about how 'I fucked this one and that one,' " Jeff Harris says, "and in *their* locker room, the girls are waxing eloquent. Barbra was the misfit, the little ugly one." Over in the boys' locker room, Kenny Adams, as Barry, was her skinny, unjock-like counterpart. At the end of the sketch, they met centerstage in the corridor. Barbra had one line: 'Barry—I'm *pregnant*." Jordan recalls "It was kind of an elaborate setup for that one joke, but it always did very well."

It was the first time Barbra would exploit her lack of good looks in a production to elicit audience sympathy. As she sat in that girls' locker room and suffered the verbal taunting of her cosmetically superior peers, Barbra was embraced by the audience. And they cheered when, at the punchline, it was *she* who got the guy—and his baby. It was something that Barbra would refine, and exploit, throughout her career.

Harris recalls another of Barbra's moments in the show. "She sang a song called 'I've Got the Blues,' in which almost the *entire* lyric was 'I've Got the Blues.' She sings, 'I've got the blues.' Then, 'Boy, do I have the blues.' Then, 'Wow, do I have the blues.' Then, 'Oh gee, do I have the blues.' It just builds and builds until it reaches this terrific height of emotion. At the end, she goes, 'I've got the blues, I've got the blues, I've got the blues, I've got the blues, *I've got the blues!*' And then she takes this deep breath and she says"—Harris laughs—" 'Now I feel better.' "

Another of Barbra's songs was a play in itself entitled "Jersey." It told of the plight of a woman who loves a man who has moved to New Jersey. "She starts singing about the horrors of Jersey," recalls Harris, "and the song sort of goes from a standard form song into an almost African-like chant. Then it comes to its crescendo when she makes the decision that she is going to go and find him. She ends by saying, 'I won't yell, I won't scream, I won't squawk, for it's better to die together in Jersey—than be single in New York.'

"What I found," says Harris, "was that Barbra and I, in a certain way, spoke the same language. Although there was five or six years between us in age, we both came from Brooklyn. Now, in my ear, 'squawk' and 'York' rhymed. And in Barbra's ear, 'squawk' and 'York' rhymed."

One of Barbra's primary problems presented itself early into rehearsals. It was something she would be criticized for throughout her short theatrical career. She either wouldn't, or couldn't do something—whether it be a scene or a song—the same way twice. This, particularly in an ensemble, was problematic.

Glenn Jordan says, "I remember that she told Abba Bogin [the musical director] that, at bar eight, she would be *there*—that she might get there each time in a different way, but that he shouldn't worry, because she would get there."

Despite her lack of discipline, however, Jordan adds, "Her musicianship was excellent. "I think she was less secure with her acting scenes than she was in her musical scenes. Her talent as a singer was full-blown, but her talent as a stage performer wasn't."

Abba Bogin concurs with Glenn Jordan's assessment. "I don't think that she was terribly disciplined," he relates. "One had to treat her almost like a kid in an amateur show, at times. You had to explain to her that if she didn't do certain things a certain way with some sort of consistency, that it was impossible for anybody who she was working with to work around her."

"It was a hideous amount of work," relates Jordan of the three-to-four-week rehearsal schedule. "We rehearsed *forever,* and it got more and more difficult. The actors got more and more edgy about whether any of it was working."

Jeff Harris contends that the problems with the show had nothing to do with the material. "The problem," he says, "was Glenn. It was his first professional job, and I think it overwhelmed him to some degree. So," says Harris, "I replaced him as director, and we had two weeks of previews that hadn't been scheduled."

It was purely my decision," says Jordan of his being replaced on the show. "I was the producer. It wasn't a question of firing the director. I could've closed the show right then if I had wanted to."

Despite the lengthy rehearsal and preview periods, Barbra wouldn't make any lasting friendships during the production. Nor would she even socialize with members of the company outside of the theater. Abba Bogin recalls, "Everybody would kind of agree that Barbra [offstage] was a very strange, introverted girl." Bogin further describes Barbra as being "difficult to work with," because, in addition to her lack of discipline, she constantly wanted to do things *her* way. She was "self-centered," and wasn't about to let anything stand in the way of her stardom, which she was absolutely certain was imminent.

She earned a paltry $37.50 a week and still didn't even have a steady place to live. With her traveling cot in tow, she lived all over the city. Her cousin Harvey Streisand had sublet an apartment on Eighteenth Street, and he let her sleep there four nights a week. On Friday nights, she slept in Peter Daniels's rehearsal studio on Eighth Avenue. The rest of the time, she parked her cot wherever she could. It was a tenuous situation for a nineteen-year-old girl, fraught with inherent drama.

Her apartment-keyring juggling act fell apart when the owner of the Eighteenth Street apartment made an unexpected visit and found Barbra, and not the original tenant, inhabiting his home. "One day she called me," Don Softness recalls, "and she said, 'I'm in trouble—I'm being kicked out of my apartment.' I said, 'What's the trouble, Barbra?' and she said, '*Well,* this man comes back, and he's been away a year, and he's upset that I'm living here. He's throwing me out! Can you come over and help me?' So I said, 'Okay, I'll be right over.'"

What Softness found upon his arrival was the apartment's owner in an animated fit of hysterics. It seems that he worked as a dance instructor aboard a cruise ship, and while away, his tenant had sublet the apartment to someone else, who had sublet it to someone else. And when he came back, there was Barbra, who had redecorated the place entirely with her own particular flair for thrift-shop antichic. "This is *my* apartment! the owner ranted. "*I* decorated it. Look what she did! Look what she did!"

Citing her youth and vulnerability, Softness pleaded that Barbra be allowed to sleep there that night. Having made his point, often, and at the top of his lungs, the owner began to calm down. "Okay," he agreed as he gave Barbra back the key. A fraction of a second later, however, Barbra flung the key back in the astonished owner's face. "I won't stay here another night!" she declared. "Don, I'm moving out right now! I want to move out right this minute! Help me move out!"

And so the two of them ran up and down the four flights of stairs some twenty times, carting, among other things, Barbra's lamps, posters, feather boas, and ratty old fur coats. They loaded them into Softness's convertible, the top of which had to be put down to accommodate Barbra's belongings. "Today," muses Don Softness, "Barbra Streisand has God knows how many houses all over the world. That night, I had all of her earthly possessions in my Pontiac convertible."

They sat in the open-topped car, in the near-freezing weather, and pondered her immediate future. "Where to, Barbra?" Softness asked. "I don't know," she answered. Minutes passed. And then Softness came up with what seemed a perfectly sensible idea. "I'll take you home to your mother in Brooklyn," he volunteered. Barbra turned to look at him and said, "No. I'll go anywhere *except* home to Brooklyn."

Finally, Softness said to her, "Come on, you can spend the night at my office. *But,*" he stipulated, "you can only stay there for one night." Barbra, still distraught, mumbled, "Okay."

She would live in the Softness office for months. Located on East Fifty-third Street, between Second and Third avenues, the office had a full kitchen and a couple of bathrooms. Barbra slept on a couch. According to her standards of the time, the accommodations were luxurious, and she paid no rent. She was obliged to keep the place clean and honor a restricted schedule. She had to be out before the office opened in the morning, and she could not return home until it closed in the early evening.

"By the time we got to work in the morning," recalls John Softness, "you couldn't tell she had been there. Except," he adds with a laugh, "there was all this great kosher food and stuff in the refrigerator. She used to go home on the weekends and her mother would give her food."

Whenever Diana Kind visited the office she was appalled at her daughter's makeshift living conditions. "She used to bring Barbra apples and Doxee clam chowder," Don Softness remembers. "She would come in briefly, bring the food, and leave. Barbra wasn't anxious to spend time with her mother. I never knew why."

After two weeks of arduous previews, *Another Evening With Harry Stoones* opened at the Gramercy Arts Theatre on Saturday, October 21, 1961. The show commenced with what was described as "the *Reader's Digest* version of 'The Star-Spangled Banner.'" The entire cast then rushed onto the stage, waved to the bewildered audience, and enthusiastically sang a number called "Bye, Goodbye and Thanks." The cast then took a bow and rushed off the stage as it blacked out. At first, those in the audience didn't know quite what to make of the opening or of the early sketches, and shifted uncomfortably in their seats. As the show progressed, however, the audience seemed to settle back and appreciate the creative absurdity of the onstage proceedings.

An opening night glitch involved the *Showbill* program. "We were always changing the order of the numbers," recalls Glenn Jordan, "so a new program had to be printed for opening night. They made a mistake, and Barbra's name was printed *smaller* than the others. It was purely a mistake. At intermission, a friend of mine, who was an actor and a director, said to me, 'You know, the one I really love is that girl whose name is smaller than everyone else's.'"

Jordan's friend was not the only one impressed. "During rehearsals," recalls Jeff Harris, "Sheila Copelan, who was probably the funniest woman that ever lived, came up to me and said, 'This show will be remembered because Barbra Streisand is in it.' It turned out," says Harris, laughing, "that what people remember *Harry Stoones* for is that Barbra Streisand was in it."

The opening night cast party was held at the Riverside Drive home of Jeff Harris. He recalls, "Everybody was supposed to bring something, which'll give you an idea of everybody's finances." Everyone showed up at the party, except for Barbra. Then, at two A.M., after everyone had left, there was a knock on Harris's door. It was Barbra. She was carrying a loaf of bread.

When the unenthusiastic daily reviews appeared, *Harry Stoones* was laid unceremoniously to rest. The magazine reviews, which appeared the following week, would be generally favorable. They would also be too late to salvage the show. And so, after five weeks of rehearsal, two weeks of previews, and one single, solitary performance, *Another Evening With Harry Stoones* opened and closed on the same night.

For years after Barbra Streisand became a star, people would tell Jeff

Harris that they had seen—and loved—*Harry Stoones.* Says Harris, with a trace of wistful laughter, "If all the people that told me they had seen the show had actually bought tickets, we'd *still* be running.

One week after *Harry Stoones* closed, Abba Bogin took Barbra to audition for producer Leonard Sillman, who was then in the final stages of casting *New Faces of 1962.* After listening to her sing, Sillman turned to Bogin and pronounced, "This girl is going to be an enormous star. But what the hell can I do with her? I've already got somebody just like her."

The girl "just like her" was Marian Mercer, later a Tony winner for *Promises, Promises* and Wanda Jeter on the television soap opera spoof "Mary Hartman, Mary Hartman." Upon rejecting Barbra Streisand on that day in 1961, Abba Bogin recalls that Leonard Sillman turned to him and pronounced, "I know I'm gonna be sorry."

Barbra, however, had no time to mourn. Her proverbial big break was right around the corner.

Nine

New Face of 1963

*S*he entered the theater and trudged onto the stage, wearing a coat of many colors. Made of tattered fur, it resembled the hide of a neglected horse, splotched with browns, yellows, and whites. She wore a pair of dirty tennis shoes. Her face was contorted into a frown. Her hair, a studied disaster. She carried a red plastic briefcase in one hand, a brown paper bag filled with turkey sandwiches in the other. It was the day after Thanksgiving, 1961. She was nineteen years old.

VOICE FROM THE THEATER. NAME?

BARBRA.　Barbra Streisand. With only two *a*'s. In the first name. I mean, I figured that third *a* in the middle—who needs it? Whaddya want me to do?

[*Laughter is heard emerging from the seats, where the director (Arthur Laurents), the composer (Harold Rome), and the playwright (Jerome Weidman), among others, are seated. "Oh boy, we're in for a good one!" they kid one another with knowing glances.*]

BARBRA.　What are you all? Dead or somethin'? I said, whaddya want me to do?

VOICE.　Can you sing?

BARBRA.　Can I sing? If I couldn't sing, would I have the nerve to come out here in a thing like this coat?

[*More laughter.*]

VOICE.　Okay, sing.

BARBRA　[*Glaring into the overhead work light*]. Sing! Even a juke-

105

box you don't just say, "Sing." You gotta first punch a button with the name of a song on it. *What* should I sing?

VOICE.   Anything you want.

Such was the prelude to the audition that would summon Barbra
Streisand's arrival on Broadway. The show was *I Can Get It for You
Wholesale.* One minute, she was a walking, talking joke, a calamity. The
next minute, she opened her mouth to sing and she was a comic genius.
Once again, the impact upon her audience, jaded professionals all, was
devastating.

She would later contend that she had been tired, having stayed up late
the night before, and walked into the audition with an "I could care less"
attitude. In fact, her appearance was a calculated ploy, and everyone in
the theater lapped it up, playing a gullible Dean Martin to her shrewd
Jerry Lewis.

Well, not quite everyone. May Muth, a seasoned stage manager of
some thirty-six Broadway shows, recalls, "There were a lot of people
there to audition. And I said to everyone, 'You have to stay out here in
the foyer and wait your turn. Take off your hats and coats, and I'll let you
know who's next.' "

It was Muth's job to expedite the process. To get them in and get them
out. "Be sure to have your music ready," she told them. And everyone
dutifully complied. Everyone, that is, except Barbra. When it came to be
her turn, she walked across the stage, still wearing her coat. And as she
fumbled for her sheet music, the entire contents of her carrying case
spilled out onto the stage.

The tactic, of course, helped set her apart from the other auditioners.
It also gave her more stage time, as she comically scrambled to retrieve
the runaway papers. "I must say," says Muth, "that I got dirty looks from
the front of the theater. Miss Streisand just made a nice entrance for herself at my expense."

First, Barbra sang "Value," also known as "I'm in Love With Harold
Mengert," from *Another Evening With Harry Stoones.* "If there was ever
a better audition song than 'I'm in Love With Harold Mengert' for a
show called *I Can Get It for You Wholesale,* I don't know what it is," says
its composer, Jeff Harris. The song had just the right mix of irreverence
and brashness that the *Wholesale* creators were looking for in the minor
part of the secretary, Miss Marmelstein.

When Barbra finished the song, a voice beckoned from the theater.
"Have you got a ballad?" To which Barbra boomed back, "Oh, have I

got a ballad for you!" And then she launched into the opening bars of Arlen's "A Sleepin' Bee," and they were transfixed.

When she finished, the voices from the theater huddled in hushed conversation. Recalls Ashley Feinstein, Arthur Laurents's assistant, "Everyone turned and looked at each other and said, 'She's so young, but she's *so* brilliant.' " They knew then that they wanted her for the show. They also wanted to have a little fun. "More!" they shouted from their seats. "We want to hear more!" they pleaded.

They brought her back for another audition. And then another. "There were a few other people up for the part," says Harold Rome, the producer, "but no one came near to Barbra. We had her come back four times. On the fourth audition, we told her, which we never do [on the spot], that she had the job."

Several nights later, May Muth, who was dining with some friends at the Brasserie, recalls running into Barbra on the street. Muth relates, "And coming out of the place was *this girl.* She turned around and said, 'Oh, hi.' And I said, 'Oh, hi.' And she said, 'So, I hear you're gonna be with *my* show.' " Muth is still amused by the encounter.

Her show was actually a musical adaptation of a play by Jerome Weidman, which had been adapted from his 1937 novel of the same name. It was the story of Harry Bogen, a garment industry worker who rises to the top of his profession through cunning and ambition. It was sort of a *How to Succeed in Seventh Avenue Business Without Really Trying,* mixed with a Jewish *Pal Joey.* The role of the secretary, Miss Marmelstein, was originally intended for an older actress. However, its creators were sufficiently impressed with Streisand to alter their conception. The role was also incidental. As Weidman related, "In our original script, she was, like the desk, just another piece of furniture."

That was, of course, *before* Barbra's post–Thanksgiving Day appearance at the St. James. Actually, the original script provided the character with one musical number, a throwaway comic interlude entitled "Miss Marmelstein." In rehearsals, it immediately became something more. In Barbra's interpretation, it was a savage, funny, endearing, biting, and pathetic indictment of men in general by ugly girls—secretaries, in particular—everywhere.

Rome and Weidman soon realized that Barbra was being underused. It wasn't enough to have her pushing papers and answering telephones and servicing other characters with the standard secretarial business. They had to give her more, otherwise she would throw the entire production out of balance.

"When you have a talent that large on stage," explained Weidman, "you just can't let her wander around. You have to give her something to do or she'll kill you. She'll steal scenes, make up business, throw people off cues." She was so good, in fact, that they had her take the lead in three other songs (including "What Are They Doing to Us Now?" which she sang while her bankrupt boss's office was being stripped of its possessions).

Still, her role was clearly subordinate to those of the intended stars—Elliott Gould as the loathsome, charming Harry Bogen, Lillian Roth as his mother, Harold Lang as his partner, Marilyn Cooper as his girlfriend, and Sheree North as his plaything.

On the very first day of rehearsals, the entire cast assembled to read the script for the director and the playwright. Generally, such read-throughs are an intimate, introductory period in a production, in which everyone is usually a little nervous, highly respectful, extremely hopeful, and on their very best behavior. Barbra joined the rest of the cast, who were seated in a semicircle. As the day progressed, she rarely looked up. She scribbled furiously in her notebook as her fellow actors read their lines and as Weidman and Laurents made their follow-up comments. Her scribbling, which was observed by Weidman, among others, was interrupted only when it came time for her own reading.

At the end of the session, Weidman watched as Barbra engaged David Powers, the show's press agent, in an animated discussion. Curious, Weidman approached the pair and was astonished by what he found. "Get a load of this," Powers told the playwright. "Look what this dame gives me." Apparently, Powers had asked the actors in the company to provide him with their bios for the show's *Playbill*, and Barbra had complied. Weidman accepted her notebook from Powers and read the opening lines, "Born in Madagascar and raised in Rangoon. . . ."

When both Weidman and Powers objected to the creative license she had taken, Barbra walked away, retorting as she departed, "Whaddid I do? Sign a contract I gotta be born in Brooklyn? Who asked for it?"

Jerome Weidman was dumbfounded. There before him had stood a nineteen-year-old girl cast in her first Broadway show. She had spent her first day of rehearsal not taking notes but composing her biography, and a fictional bio at that, for a *Playbill* that wouldn't be published for nearly three months.

A week later, one of the stage managers sounded his whistle, signaling the end of a ten-minute rehearsal break. All of the actors but one dutifully returned to the stage. While cries of "Where's Barbra?!" beckoned from the theater, the actress in question stood unperturbed in a phone booth in the lobby, discussing a matter totally unrelated to the production. When the stage manager finally located her, he bellowed angrily, *"Barbra!* For God's sake, get on stage! You're holding up the entire rehearsal!"

"Just one minute," she replied. "Be right there." However, as the stage manager returned to the theater, she dropped yet another dime in the coin slot and made another phone call, this one long distance. When she finally returned to the stage, she was greeted by the considerable wrath of director Laurents. Barbra bowed her head and bit her bottom lip.

She would keep the company waiting a total of *thirty-six* times during the production. Finally, Actors Equity officially reprimanded her. Still she showed up late. To Barbra, tardiness was an act of defiance, an "I don't give a damn" shrug.

As the *Wholesale* company moved to Philadelphia, and then to Boston, for out-of-town tryouts, the relationship between Barbra and director Laurents became increasingly strained. Ashley Feinstein recalls, "She was doing these strange things in this very conventional show, and it started upsetting people. A lot of people thought she was getting out-of-hand. She was hard to control because she would say, 'I wanna do it *this* way!' Everybody else, Lillian Roth and all those people, were seasoned professionals. Even Marilyn Cooper was very, very professional. So was Elliott. So was *everybody* else except Barbra.

"She was not obnoxious or demanding or anything like that," explains Feinstein. "That was just the way she was. She was an untrained, raw, brilliant talent. And that, maybe, scared a lot of these old professionals.

"One thing I remember is Arthur saying to her, 'You're getting a jazz inflection in this song, and this is a legit Broadway show.' Maybe he was right. No, he *was* right. She was in a Broadway show, not a nightclub. He was trying to get her to be a part of a company, and she didn't know how to do it.

"Another thing I remember," continues Feinstein, "is that Arthur wanted Barbra to do certain movements. One time he wanted her to kick up her heels. There was a certain point that she was supposed to imitate two showroom shop girls. It wasn't so much that Barbra didn't want to do it, but it wasn't natural to her, and she couldn't do it. And Arthur said to me, '*You* take her, Ashley, and try to get her to do that step.' And I remember taking her for *hours*—and by that time she and I were quite friendly—and I would imitate the kick and say, 'Arthur just wants you to do *that,* Barbra.' And she would sort of try to do it. Now, this brilliant person, whom I was absolutely in awe of, was just this clumsy thing who didn't want to do this kick because she didn't *feel* it. Part of it was a lack of discipline. But I think the major part was that she didn't feel it."

A particular point of contention concerned, of all things, a swivel chair. Barbra wanted to sing "Miss Marmelstein," the secretary's lament, while sitting in a swivel chair. Laurents wanted her to stand. Instead of accepting the director's command, as most any novice actor would have, Barbra demanded, "Why can't I use the chair?" After all, she argued, the real Miss Marmelsteins of the world practically *lived* in such chairs. It made the number more realistic, she reasoned, and also served as a potentially humorous prop. Besides, she was less nervous sitting than standing. Still, Laurents objected, and on the last day of run-throughs, the day before the opening in Philadelphia, Barbra was forced to do the number without her chair. But no one could force her to do it.

After the run-through, the actors congregated in the back of the theater to brave the critical comments of their director. When he came to Barbra, Laurents chided her for her obviously lackadaisical effort. "She *was* a little bit not so good in that run-through," relates Ashley Feinstein. "And when the run-through was over, Arthur really *laid into* her. He said, 'You walked through it! You weren't any good!' And all that stuff. Arthur was saying to her that she was childish in wanting to have it her own way, not so much with the chair, but her whole performance. She wasn't giving enough in that run-through. He thought that she was being petulant."

Barbra responded, stubbornly, by arguing that the number would've been more effective with the chair, which, of course, further infuriated Laurents. She was undisciplined, he said. Unprofessional. *Who* did she think she was?

As Laurents concluded his public condemnation of her after that final flawed run-through in Philadelphia, Barbra slumped further down into her seat. She bowed her head. Her bangs fell down her forehead and covered her eyes. If they couldn't see her, after all, they couldn't hurt her.

After the tongue-lashing, the severity of which left other members of the company embarrassed and slightly stunned, Jerome Weidman approached Barbra to offer his condolences. "I'm sorry, kid," he said, gently. Barbra raised her head, revealing not the tears that Weidman expected but a look of inquisition.

"Listen, Jerry," she started, as she showed him a sketch of the apartment floor plan she had apparently been drawing during Laurents's diatribe, "Where the hell would *you* put the studio couch, huh?"

It wasn't that she wasn't hurt by the public lynching, she just didn't want anyone to see the scars. At another point during the production, Laurents *would* provoke Barbra to cry. Later, she would contend that the tears had been faked. Not only did she not want anyone to see her vulnerability, she didn't want anyone to know that they had that kind of power over her. She was still the homesick little girl in summer camp who insisted to those who teased her that she had a loose tear duct that couldn't be controlled.

"She was a skinny flibbertigibbet with no discipline and no technique," assessed the show's producer, David Merrick. "All she had was this enormous talent."

Nevertheless, Merrick wanted Barbra fired in Philadelphia. According to Ashley Feinstein, "Merrick didn't like Barbra. He thought that she was too ugly and messy and strange. He would stand in the back of the theater and say things like, 'This crazy-looking, ugly thing.' He thought that we should go along with someone like Elizabeth Wilson [who also auditioned for the part]. He just never *got* Barbra Streisand."

Barbra would have been fired from the show if not for the strenuous objections of Harold Rome, the composer, Jerome Weidman, the author, and even Arthur Laurents, the director.

As for the apartment floor plan and that irksome studio couch, Barbra had finally found an apartment of her own back in Manhattan. Located at 1157 Third Avenue at Sixty-sixth Street, the tiny third-floor flat sat atop a fish restaurant named Oscar's Salt of the Sea. The smell of cooked fish drifted into the hallways and the apartment. Mornings were particularly fishy. Still, despite having an acute sense of smell—she is known to correctly identify a brand of perfume at thirty paces—Barbra didn't seem to mind. The rent was only $67.20 a month. Besides, she was thrilled to retire her traveling cot and have an apartment of her own. It gave her an address and identity. She didn't even care that the only window looked out onto a black brick wall, or that the bathtub she had found had to be placed in the kitchen. She rationalized that she could snack and bathe simultaneously. When the tub wasn't in use, Barbra placed a board over it, on which she piled her dishes. More formal meals were eaten in the living room, her table a sewing machine.

She designed her home in cheap, thrift shop decor. Feather boas lounged about. *Empty* picture frames hung from the walls. A discarded dentist's cabinet was used to store shoe buckles. She filled an apothecary jar with assorted beauty marks. Two Victorian cabinets with glass shelves, purchased from Renée Taylor's Foyniture Limited Store on Eighty-third Street, were used to store Barbra's treasured collections. And folding screens added both privacy and ambience. Even before she had money, she wanted to design her surroundings.

The bathroom was a tourist attraction. Jeff Harris recalls, "The whole apartment smelled of fresh fish. And, when you went to the bathroom, you wanted to spend an hour in there. Instead of wallpaper, Barbra had made this collage of all sorts of things from newspapers: faces, words, phrases, pieces of an ad. It was unbelievable."

She shared the apartment with a giant rat she dubbed "Gonzola," who lived primarily in the kitchen. Soon, a man would be added to complete her portrait of domestic bliss. He wouldn't, of course, be just *any* man. He would be the star of her show.

Elliott Gould, a former graveyard-shift elevator operator, was promoted to *I Can Get It for You Wholesale* from the choruses of *Rumple; Say, Darling;* and *Irma La Douce.* Born Elliott I. Goldstein on August 29, 1938, he had been performing as a tap dancer since childhood. *Wholesale* was his first shot at stardom. It was a shot that he almost didn't get.

"I was dead-on, right-on-the-money right for the part, although I did not know my ass from my elbow," Elliott explained. "I could sing and dance, but I did not know how to act. I did not know how to let go of myself and still communicate anything that was thought. I auditioned again and I was told that I had *no* chance to get the part."

He was rescued, however, by actress Barbara Harris, who read opposite him at yet another audition. "She was so beautiful and real," Elliott reflected, "that it brought something out in me . . . just enough to get the part." Ironically, Harris, who had been auditioning for the part of his girlfriend, was *not* cast in the show. Still, she was revered by Elliott and envied by Barbra, and her name would be a sensitive subject in the Gould household in the years to come.

After she sang at one of *her* auditions, Barbra peered into the darkened theater. The director, composer, and writer of the show were present. So were some of the actors who had already been cast. "Hey! I just got my own telephone!" she bellowed. "Call me," she said, to no one in particular. "Even if I don't get the job, somebody call me!" She then announced her phone number to anyone who was interested. Later, after she returned home, her telephone rang. "This is Elliott Gould," the caller informed her. "You were brilliant today." And then he hung up. Barbra was sufficiently intrigued.

The next time they saw one another, Elliott offered her a cigar. It was a dare, of course. Barbra had been parading around the theater like, in Elliott's words, "the weirdo of all times." He was testing her limits. Barbra took the cigar, studied it for a moment, and then smoked it with aplomb.

Weeks later, they went to see a horror movie about giant caterpillars that devoured automobiles. After the movie, they had dinner at a Chinese restaurant. As they walked home, at about two o'clock in the morning, it started to snow. They walked around the Rockefeller Center skating rink. The walk turned into a run, a chase, a snowball fight. At one point, Elliott approached Barbra and tenderly brushed her face with the snow. And then he touched her lips with his own. It was their first kiss. It was, as Barbra would enthuse, "Like out of a movie."

A couple of weeks later, they had their first fight. Barbra stormed off and locked herself in her apartment over the fish restaurant. Elliott, distraught, wandered about the city. He stopped at one phone booth and then another. But every time he called, Barbra picked up the receiver, then hung it up. It was a variation of a scene that Barbra would play years later with Robert Redford in *The Way We Were*. Finally, defeated, Elliott returned home to his apartment and went to bed. Then, at four A.M., there was a knock at his door. Standing there in her nightgown was Barbra, her face streaming with tears.

But it was on the road during tryouts that their romance really took hold. Away from home, they both let down their guard enough to let the other in. Certainly, at that point in their lives, they each needed the comfort that comes in the arms of another. They were both on the brink of success in the theater. Particularly Gould. At twenty-three, he was the star of a potential hit Broadway show. Much of the show's success depended upon the effectiveness of his performance. It was an awesome responsibility.

But it was primarily Elliott who looked after Barbra. First, he had been attracted to her talent. Later, he was afraid of, and then entertained by, her eccentricity. But it was her beguiling contradictions that ultimately made him fall in love with her. To others in the *Wholesale* company, Barbra was brash and brazen. As he got to know her, however, Elliott learned that she wore her bravado as a defense. He discovered that she was a frightened, sensitive, terribly insecure young woman who had been emotionally abused in childhood. "She needs to be protected," he would say. "She's a very fragile little girl." Of their romance, he confided, "I had this desire to make her feel secure." He would add, "I found her absolutely *exquisite.*"

Barbra had spent a good deal of her nineteen years embodying the quintessential ugly duckling. No one was more aware of her cosmetic disadvantages than she. Suddenly, however, reflected in the glow of Elliott's eyes, she was the swan. For Barbra, winning, and then retaining, Elliott's love was an all-consuming effort. It's easy to understand her concern. In addition to being the star of the show, Elliott was a six-foot-three-inch, two-hundred-pound, strapping hulk of a man. He had enormous brown eyes and a cleft in his chin. His hair fell in curls upon his forehead and down the back of his neck. His chest was matted with hair. He was an oversized teddy bear, sensitive and shy, and yet he exuded masculinity. Barbra constantly worried that he would be lured away by one of the other, prettier girls in the show.

"Before Barbra came along," relates Ashley Feinstein, "all of the girls in the cast, all of the chorus girls, were in love with Elliott. There was this one girl in the chorus named Luba Lisa, who was this tall [six feet], gorgeous, beautiful showgirl with these *legs.* And she and Elliott went out together. So when Elliott and Barbra first started going out, I was surprised that he would like Barbra after having gone out with Luba Lisa."

There was little effort to keep their budding romance a secret from the rest of the company. "We were out-of-town, pre-Broadway," relates May Muth. "It was an early morning rehearsal, and Barbra was late. So I had my assistant call her up at the hotel, and she wasn't there. I said, 'Something must've happened to Barbra, because she still isn't here, and she isn't at the hotel. Where could she be?' And Elliott—God bless him. Elliott was all right. He said, 'Oh, you might ring *my* room and see if she's asleep again.' So that was the first clue we got of that romance."

"I first noticed their affair when we went out on tour," recalls Wilma Curley, who played one of the models in the show. Later, she would replace Sheree North in the costarring role of Martha Mills. "One of them, I forget which one, had the bedroom next to mine. I had my child with me in my room, and I remember that their bed used to bang up against the wall. The headboards of our beds shared a wall, and their bed would bang all night."

According to Wilma Curley, members of the *Wholesale* company were not envious of the romance, as has been previously characterized;

they were bemused. "They would play all kinds of stupid, childish games. They would do things like go out to dinner and throw food at each other. Spaghetti. And if you were at the table, you got it too. And sometimes, Elliott would lock her out in the hall—with no clothes on."

During tryouts in Boston, Elliott and Barbra teamed with Ashley Feinstein for some sightseeing. They went to Filene's Basement, where Barbra bought a long wool dress, regularly priced at $100, for $12.50. They attended a jazz club called Storyville, where Barbra was lured to the stage to sing. Mostly, though, they wandered.

"We would walk down the streets of Boston," recalls Feinstein, "and Elliott was just adorably funny with people. He would stop people on the street and tell them jokes. He was *so* open, more so than Barbra. Barbra would just sort of go along with it. But they were both really free spirits. I loved being with them."

Still, some members of the company couldn't understand what Elliott saw in Barbra. According to Curley, it was Barbra who pursued Elliott. She went after him, followed him. She was always the instigator. When asked if Barbra's intentions were really that obvious, Curley is emphatic. *"Yes sir,* she was gonna marry the star."

Another thing bonding the fledgling romance, was that they were both in peril of losing their jobs. With Barbra, it was because of her flagrant lack of discipline. With Elliott, it was another matter altogether. "They tried to fire Elliott because he *perspired,"* confides Wilma Curley. "He perspired *buckets!"* The show required that he wear an array of fashionable dress suits, which he invariably, and visibly, stained. "He would turn onstage," recalls Curley, "and the sweat would just come pouring off him. They tried pills and deodorants and all this garbage, but nothing worked. While we were on tour, they kept bringing people in to audition to replace him."

One of the actors brought in to audition for the role was Michael Callan, later star of television's "Occasional Wife." In fact, Callan very nearly replaced Elliott, and probably would have if not for the tearful objection of Nora Kaye Ross. Ross, a ballet dancer, was wife of choreographer and later director Herbert Ross who staged the musical numbers for *I Can Get It for You Wholesale.* It seems that Mrs. Ross had taken a strong liking to Elliott during rehearsals, and she pleaded his case to David Merrick.

"They finally ended up keeping him," Wilma Curley relates, "but ev-

erybody in the show had a towel in their hand, or a napkin, or a tissue."
She adds, with a laugh, "Whenever you saw Elliott, you said, 'Hello,'
and you patted him down. It was funny."

I Can Get It for You Wholesale opened at the Shubert Theatre on Broadway on March 22, 1962.

It was a successful though unspectacular debut. Elliott Gould gave an admirable, although exceedingly *wet,* performance. His reviews, like those for the show, were mixed. Wrote Richard Watts, Jr., of the *New York Post,* "I thought it provided as uningratiating an evening as you could well find. The main trouble with *Wholesale* is not that its central figure's ethics are nonexistent but that, in Elliott Gould's realistic performance, he is so uninteresting and unattractive. Yet he is apparently supposed to have a charm that was not visible to me last night."

Walter Kerr of the *New York Herald Tribune* was more encouraging. "Momma, momma, momma, what a good, solid show. . . . Any hesitations? Very few. Heel Elliott Gould performs his chores splendidly; but they are, either in the writing or the playing, less complex and less fascinating than the behavior of the folk he does in."

It would *not,* suffice to say, be the star-making role Elliott Gould had been hoping for. The reception accorded his girlfriend, however, was another matter altogether.

The night before the Philadelphia opening, an exasperated Arthur Laurents finally conceded. "Do it in your goddamned chair!" What he really meant to say was, "It's *your* funeral." At that evening's performance, Barbra's "Miss Marmelstein" number stopped the show, and the "to sit or not to sit" question was settled, though not without some bitter resentment.

Opening night on Broadway, Act 2, Scene 2, Barbra and her beloved rolling chair were literally pushed out onto the Shubert stage. When she hit her mark, she planted her pumps and locked her knees together. The chair came to a halt. She heaved a heavy sigh of relief, and the audience giggled. They were with her from the start. She was a wallflower on wheels. Her dress was high-necked and sexless, her bones awry. Her hair sat atop her head in a beehive, a pencil piercing her bun. She screwed her face into a soulful grimace and frowned into the darkened theater.

And then she opened her mouth and unleashed her secretarial wail. Oh, *why* was it always "Miss Marmelstein?" she complained. "Take a letter, Miss Marmelstein?" "Answer the phone, Miss Marmelstein." "Get me some coffee, Miss Marmelstein." Everyone wanted a piece of her—except, unfortunately, *that* piece. Why was it always "Miss Marmelstein?" she groused, casting her eyes upward in an exasperated appeal to heaven. Why couldn't they call her "coochy coo," or "baby doll," or "sweetie pie"? At least, she bemoaned, they could do her the favor of calling her by her first name—even if it was Yetta.

Streisand's Yetta Tessye Marmelstein was instantly vulnerable and defiant, funny and touching, pathetic and heroic. She was the underdog finally having her day; the loser finally having her proverbial moment in the spotlight, if not the sun. And she was all of that and more in the confines of a three-minute song.

Just as she had on the road, Barbra stopped the show opening night on Broadway. As she completed the number, the audience jumped to its feet in ovation. They didn't know who she was or, really, *what* she was. They didn't even know if she could sing a straight song. They only knew that she had been able to project through the footlights and communicate directly to them. And they also knew that, one day soon, in some other show, she was going to be a star.

"I saw her opening night in *Wholesale*," recalls Barbra's friend Don Softness over thirty years later, and still with a measure of awe, "and she literally stopped the show. People were on their feet screaming and yelling for five minutes. It was eerie. It was electrifying. She was this mousy little girl who had this great big stage presence. The opening night audience in New York was a sophisticated one, and there was no doubt in their mind that they were seeing show business history in the making."

With her chair in tow, Barbra walked off the stage in triumph. But it wasn't the wildly enthusiastic shouts of approval that she heard resounding in her ears, it was the words of Arthur Laurents: "Do it in your goddamned chair," he had said. She smiled, slightly, briefly, with self-satisfaction. From that moment on, she would never forget, nor would she ever let anyone else forget, the power of her instinct.

Ten

The Revenge of Yetta Tessye Marmelstein

*I*nstead of rejoicing in her success, Streisand was consumed by a conflicting emotion. "I can't tell you how I felt stopping that show," she would say. "I felt *guilty.*"

Guilty because she had, even if inadvertently, stolen the show from her beloved Elliott. *Wholesale* was meant to be *his* show, not hers. Once she had taken it, she couldn't give it back.

A minidrama unfolded at the opening night party at Sardi's. Everyone wondered how Gould would grapple with the greater success of his girlfriend. The two walked into Sardi's arm-in-arm, sharing the limelight and the applause. They would not play out the drama, at least not in public.

"I couldn't find one [character] to whom I could give either affection or admiration," complained John Chapman in his review for the New York *Daily News.* "Well, I guess there was *one*—but she is just a minor mouse in the story. She's a harried, frantic, put-upon, homely frump of a secretary, and she is hilariously played by a 19-year-old newcomer to Broadway, Barbra Streisand."

Wrote Howard Taubman of the *New York Times,* "The evening's find" is Barbra Streisand, a girl with an oafish expression, a loud irascible voice and an arpeggiated laugh. Miss Streisand is a natural comedienne, and Mr. Rome has given her a brash, amusing song, 'Miss Marmelstein,' to lament her secretarial fate."

118

Norman Nadel of the *New York World-Telegram* enthused, "Brooklyn's Erasmus Hall High School should call a half-day holiday to celebrate the success of its spectacular alumna, 19-year-old Barbra Streisand."

According to Bob Schulenberg, Barbra was not only guilty but embarrassed by her success. It had come too easily. "When she did 'Miss Marmelstein,'" he relates, "there were 'Bravos!' from the audience. After the show, she said to me, 'I really wish you wouldn't have done that.' I said, 'Done what?' She said, 'It's really embarrassing when you yell "Bravo."' And I said, 'Barbra, that was not me yelling "Bravo."' And she said, 'It wasn't you?' And I said, 'No. It was a whole bunch of people.'"

Schulenberg adds, "When people told him how exquisite his music was, Mozart once said, 'If you could only hear how it sounds in my head.' And that's Barbra. It really is. She's never good enough."

Despite her guilt and embarrassment, Barbra continued to ruffle feathers backstage. "After I got good notices," she would later contend, "there was some resentment around some people who were sore. I want to do things the way *I* feel, and I don't care if other people disagree with me." She would add, "They say I'm fresh, mostly because I won't take their advice."

One of the people she wouldn't listen to was Lillian Roth. Roth's troubled life had been chronicled in her autobiography and in the 1955 Susan Hayward picture, *I'll Cry Tomorrow*. Now fifty-two, she was attempting a comeback with *I Can Get It for You Wholesale*. Her efforts, however, were overshadowed, as was everything else in the production, by Barbra's performance. Still, Roth tried to take Barbra under her wing and was pushed away. "I didn't want her to help me," Barbra would say, "I wanted to do things on my own."

"I've worked with Lauren Bacall, Bette Davis, Anthony Newley, Sammy Davis, Jr., and other big stars," says May Muth, "and Barbra was a bad child. We liked each other, but she was a naughty kid. She was late most of the time, and she was a little incorrigible. I think I scared her a little bit. *Not* by threatening her, but by being firm with her. I excused her at the time because she was young."

"Barbra was a pain in the ass," Wilma Curley declares. "Eventually, when I took over Sheree's role in the show, I was actually starring over Barbra. She would come into my dressing room and take my makeup."

When asked how she knew it was Barbra, Curley replies, "You just *knew.* Then, when you'd ask Barbra about it, she'd say, 'I *had* to, Wilma, I *needed* it.' "

The Tony nominations were announced just two weeks after the show's opening. Barbra received the only nomination of the entire production. Competing against her in the category of Best Featured or Supporting Actress in a Musical were Elizabeth Allen, *The Gay Life;* Phyllis Newman, *Subways Are for Sleeping;* and Barbara Harris, Elliott's old audition costar, for her performance in *From the Second City.* Other young actresses who created a stir on the Broadway stage that year were Elizabeth Ashley, who would win a Tony for her work in *Take Her, She's Mine;* Sandy Dennis in *A Thousand Clowns;* and Faye Dunaway in *A Man for All Seasons.*

Five days after her twentieth birthday, on April 29, 1962, Barbra sat in the ballroom at the Waldorf-Astoria and politely applauded as winner Phyllis Newman walked toward the podium in triumph. She would have to content herself with the New York Drama Critics Circle Award, and in the years to come, she would derive a measure of satisfaction in comparing her career to Newman's. She would do the same with Barbara Harris.

As spring turned into summer, it was largely Barbra's turn as "Miss Marmelstein" that kept *Wholesale* running. In the eyes of some, she flaunted it. May Muth, recalls, "One night she came over to me and she said, 'I have the prettiest legs in the show.' And I said, 'Oh my God, Barbra!' because we had some very pretty, attractive dancers in the show. I said, 'No you don't.' And she said, 'Who has better?' And I said, 'I do.' And she did a double take and she said, 'Well, you're not *in* the show.' "

After the show had been running for a while, Barbra was informed that her understudy, Elly Stone, was going to be hospitalized for a few days. It wasn't Stone's health, however, that was weighing on Barbra's mind. "Well, you know I realize that if Elly is in the hospital, and *I* get sick," she told May Muth, *"there won't be a show."*

Bemused, May Muth responded, "Oh, Barbra, you're wrong! *I've* been rehearsing every day since I heard Elly was going into the hospital."

"You?" Barbra asked, incredulous.

"Yes," Muth said. "Of course, I can't compete with you, but the show would *not* be closed for the evening, I can tell you that."

And as Barbra turned to leave, Muth took one last shot, "And Barbra, do me a favor. When Elly's in the hospital—*stay home one night!*"

Barbra Streisand's eighth-grade graduation yearbook photo, taken in 1955.

Barbra's high school graduation photo, January 1959. She wanted *out* so badly that her bones nearly jumped out of her skin.

Ascending meteor, 1961. (Photo by Avery Willard. Courtesy of Glenn Jordan)

If a girl isn't pretty like a Miss Atlantic City, 1961. (Photo by Avery Willard. Courtesy of Glenn Jordan)

With Sheila Copelan, Diana Sands, and Susan Belink. Just one of the girls. (Photo by Avery Willard. Courtesy of Glenn Jordan)

Comics and Indians: Cavorting with Dom DeLuise and Sheila in *Another Evening with Harry Stoones.* (Photo by Avery Willard. Courtesy of Glenn Jordan)

The *Showbill* for *Another Evening with Harry Stoones.* Note that Barbra's name was accidentally set in less prominent type than the rest of the cast.

SHOWBILL

"Another evening with Harry Stoones"

GRAMERCY ARTS

stenod productions, inc.

presents

another evening with harry stoones

a new musical revue

sketches, music and lyrics by

jeff harris

with

diana sands

| sheila copelan | ben keller |
| dom de luise | kenny adams |

virgil curry

susan belink

barbra streisand

musical direction and arrangements by	*choreography by*
abba bogin	joe milan
scenery and lighting by	*costumes designed and executed by*
robert e. darling	ruth wagner

entire production directed by
g. adam jordan

PART ONE—THE CIVIL WAR

Carnival in Capri	ENTIRE CAST
To Belong	KENNY
Communication	
Waiter	DOM
Lulu	DIANA
Jose	BEN
Cook	KENNY
Ballad to the International	
Business Machine Building	VIRGIL
You Won't Believe Me	SHEILA
The Wrong Plan	DIANA
Ballet	
Wendy	BARBRA
Michael	KENNY
Nana	DOM
Peter Pan	HARRIET ALL
Bang!	SUSAN
Don't Laugh at Me	VIRGIL & DIANA
Museum Piece	DOM

Barbra's handwritten notes for her *Harry Stoones* program biography.

Superpublicist Dick Falk telling his neophyte client which camera to look into. (Courtesy of Dick Falk)

Bursting with youth, "The New Belter" triumphs on "The Judy Garland Show," 1963 (The Richard Gordon Collection)

At least partially at Barbra's request, Sydney Chaplin was replaced in the Broadway production of *Funny Girl* by Johnny Desmond (pictured here). (The Richard Gordon Collection)

Barbra and Elliott's marriage certificate. Note the spelling of Barbra's name. (Author's collection)

STATE OF NEVADA, ss.
COUNTY OF ORMSBY

CERTIFICATE OF MARRIAGE
Ormsby County, Nevada

N° 108303

I hereby Certify that on the ____13TH____ day of ____SEPTEMBER____ in the year of our Lord one thousand nine hundred and ____SIXTY THREE____ at ____CARSON CITY____ in said County, I, the undersigned, a ____JUSTICE OF THE PEACE.____

did join in the Holy Bonds of Matrimony according to the laws of this State ____ELLIOTT GOULD____, a resident of ____NEW YORK CITY____ in the County of ____NEW YORK____ State of ____NEW YORK____ and ____BARBARA JOAN STREISAND____ a resident of ____NEW YORK CITY____ in the County of ____NEW YORK____ State of ____NEW YORK____ in the presence of ____MARTIN ERLICHMAN____ a resident of ____NEW YORK CITY____ County of ____NEW YORK____ State of ____NEW YORK____ and ____MARTIN BREGMAN____ a resident of ____NEW YORK CITY____ County of ____NEW YORK____ State of ____NEW YORK____ who have subscribed their names hereto as witnesses.

} Witnesses

TO BE RECORDED BY PARTY PERFORMING MARRIAGE

Backstage in her paisley-gone-crazy dressing room at the Winter Garden Theater, 1964-65. (The Richard Gordon Collection)

With Elliott and four-month-old Jason Emanuel. Her arrival in Los Angeles to make the film version of *Funny Girl* in May 1967 was heralded like no other since Vivian Leigh arrived in town to make *Gone With the Wind* nearly thirty years before. (Columbia Pictures. From the Richard Gordon Collection)

In *Funny Girl*, arguably the most auspicious debut in motion picture history. (Columbia Pictures. From the Richard Gordon Collection)

A makeup test for *Funny Girl*. During the shooting,
Barbra was extremely insecure about her looks.
(Columbia Pictures. Courtesy of Cinema Collectors)

Captivated by the continental charm
of Omar Sharif. Note the misspelling
of Sharif's name on his chair.
(Columbia Pictures. The Richard
Gordon Collection)

With mentor Ray Stark. A love-hate
relationship. (Columbia Pictures. The
Richard Gordon Collection)

With Jason on the set.
Hello, gorgeous.
(Courtesy of Cinema
Collectors)

Not seeing eye-to-eye
with Anne Francis,
the co-star who would
be virtually cut out of
the picture. (Columbia
Pictures. The Richard
Gordon Collection)

With Harry Stradling, the man
she learned to trust. It was
Stradling who taught Barbra
about the motion picture camera.
20th Century-Fox. The Richard
Gordon Collection)

With Walter Matthau in
Dolly. The clash of the
co-starring titans. (20th
Century-Fox. The Richard
Gordon Collection)

Hansel and Gretel. Behind the
public smiles, a fairytale ends.
(The Richard Gordon Collection)

She had acclaim, but not yet fame. She was making a name for herself, but not yet money, at least not much. Her weekly salary was raised from a paltry $150 to $200, the same amount Elliott was being paid.

"When I met her," says well-known veteran Broadway press agent Richard Falk, "she didn't have stockings. She was practically starving." Barbra wanted publicity to capitalize on her success in *Wholesale,* and the Softness brothers didn't have the necessary show business connections. So, at the behest of Don Softness, Falk joined the Streisand team for $25 a week.

According to Falk, Barbra would've done *anything* to become a star, and craved the publicity she would later come to hate. Certainly, his efforts on her behalf were paying off. He got her a succession of appearances on "The Joe Franklin Show" and made her name a fairly common sight in the top newspaper columns of the city.

"She was a strange character," says Falk, "a wild dame. To me, she was not all there. No matter when I talked to her, she was always a little off-center. She was an embarrassment, almost. She was not a pretty woman. And she fought with so many people at that time.

"No one's ever *really* interviewed Barbra," Falk says. "Because, if they had, she probably would've spit at them when they asked her a foolish question. She was really a wild character. I remember once when she came up to my office on Times Square. There was a men's room, and, with a piece of chalk, she crossed out the 'Men's Room' sign and wrote 'Shithouse.' She was very filthy, like she didn't bathe. Also, her dress. And the way she talked. I didn't mind that she was wild. As a press agent, you get all kinds of crazy people who want to make it, and they think that nothing will stop them."

According to Dick Falk, who names Norman Mailer and Salvador Dali among his former clients, it was he who dropped Barbra. "I was at my peak then, handling a lot of big people, and, after about six months at $25 a week, I was getting tired of working for her. Besides, Marty Erlichman was doing everything for her."

She may not have fired Richard Falk, but she *did* drop the Softness brothers, her onetime close friends and charitable landlords. She no longer had much use for them. She had her own apartment, and she had befriended one of the *Wholesale* publicists. He was more aggressive and better connected than the Softnesses. Besides, like Marty Erlichman, he was reportedly willing to represent Barbra without a binding contract. His name was Lee Solters, and they would remain together for thirty years.

Although she wanted to be thought of as an actress, not a singer, it upset Barbra that her singing voice was being dismissed in favor of her comic performance. Just as she had been in Eli Rill's acting class, Barbra was uncomfortable being laughed at. To reestablish that she could sing a straight song, she returned to the Bon Soir on May 22, 1962. After taking her curtain bows at the Shubert, she would run outside, hail a cab, and be whisked to the club, where she was invariably late for her performance.

One week after her opening at the Bon Soir, on May 29, Barbra stunned viewers of the television program "The Garry Moore Show" with her audacious rendition of "Happy Days Are Here Again," the Milton Ager–Jack Yellen political convention anthem.

She had rehearsed the song by day at the Bon Soir. "She came in one Monday," Tiger Haynes, leader of The Three Flames, recalls, "and Peter Daniels got out the music that we were gonna rehearse that afternoon. One of the arrangements he gave us was 'Happy Days Are Here Again.' And I said to him, 'Peter, what the *fuck* is she gonna sing *that* for?' Well, after we went through it, I realized why she was singing that song."

Every week, "The Garry Moore Show" featured a segment entitled "That Wonderful Year." The week of Barbra's appearance, the featured year was 1929. It was the year of the crippling stock market crash, and the beginning of the Great Depression. As her contribution to the theme, Barbra was given "Happy Days Are Here Again," which had been published that same year. At first, in rehearsals, Barbra sang the song as it was written. As she continued to struggle with it, Ken Welch, one of the show's writers, suggested slowing down the arrangement. Suddenly, the song was transformed. It was no longer a sunny, political pep song, but a dark, biting tirade. The pathos, hidden for decades in the lyrics, suddenly became painfully clear. Shivers went up and down the spines of everyone on the set. Carol Burnett, a "Garry Moore Show" regular, watched from the sidelines and listened with awe.

Bob Schulenberg recalls Barbra's performance on the Tuesday evening program. "She came into a bar dressed in evening clothes, beautiful sequins, furs, covered in jewels. And the waiter [played by Bob Harris, father of actor Ed Harris] says to her, 'What would you like?' And she says, 'Brandy.' So he brings her the brandy, gives her the bill, and says, 'two dollars,' or whatever it was. And Barbra pantomimed opening her purse and finding no money. So she took off her ring, and she put it on the plate. And then the music started to play and she started to sing, 'Happy days are here again . . .'

"When it got to the second chorus, the waiter came back and took her glass. He brought her another brandy, and she took off her bracelet. And then she sang the second chorus. It was a very strong piece. It was very effective staging."

In fact, there is probably no better single example than her work on "Happy Days" of Streisand acting out the lyrics of a song. It was as if she had taken "The Star-Spangled Banner" and given it new meaning by turning it into her own personal drama. She began with a simple, sweet rendering, and ended seething with sarcasm and bitterness.

On July 16, Barbra moved uptown for a summer run at the Blue Angel. She had actually made her debut at the Angel the previous November, just days before her first audition for *Wholesale.* The difference was, in November, she was the opening act for comic Pat Harrington, Jr., later the building super on television's "One Day at a Time". Eight months later, after her success on Broadway, she was the headliner.

Named after the Dietrich picture, the Blue Angel was *the* premier cabaret in the city. A red carpet rolled out of its entrance at 152 East Fifty-fifth Street, summoning the city's elite. Distinguished out-of-town visitors also figured in the club's clientele. One was Jack Kennedy, who usually showed up when he was in town.

The front room lounge was decorated in black: black bar, black booths, black patent leather walls. The back room, however, was long and narrow and a study in pink: pink rosettes on the walls, pink leather banquettes, a rose-colored carpet. The stage was tiny, and performers were lit by a single, immobile spotlight. It was a tough room to play. Blue Angel acts represented the class of the cabaret circuit. Dorothy Loudon, Pearl Bailey, Carol Burnett, Harry Belafonte, and later Woody Allen, were hits at the club. The Angel's co-owner, Herbert Jacoby, also made some monumental mistakes, reportedly firing Sarah Vaughan, and telling Lena Horne to get out of the business.

For Barbra, Angel audiences represented something of a challenge. First of all, they were more conservative than those at the Bon Soir, and she didn't know how some of her more eclectic material ("Who's Afraid of the Big Bad Wolf?" "I'm in Love With Harold Mengert") would go over. Second, there was no gay bar at the Angel, and gay men still represented her most enthusiastic following. Granted, gay men *did* patronize the Blue Angel, they were just more discreet about their sexuality and less demonstrative in their approval of a performer.

For her engagement, Barbra opened with a number from *The Fantasticks,* "Much More," followed by "My Honey's Lovin' Arms" and Harold Arlen's "Right as the Rain." Added to her repertoire were Leonard Bernstein's "Songs for Children" and Arlen's "Down With Love."

Her success at the Blue Angel, which was considerable, would mean a great deal to Streisand's career. Marty Erlichman had been working on getting Barbra a record deal, and she needed a venue where she could be seen. If industry representatives only knew her in *Wholesale,* she would have been quickly dismissed as a comic. If they saw her at the Bon Soir, she would have been perceived as "too Village." It is understandable, therefore, that Herbert Jacoby felt he was giving Barbra a break by allowing her into his club.

"Herbert was alarmed about her because she was not grateful," Ben Bagley told James Gavin, for his book *Intimate Nights.* "He could be very generous when he believed in someone, like Carol Burnett. He thought she was very sincere. But nothing impressed Barbra."

In addition to reestablishing that she could sing a straight song, Barbra had other motivations for returning to the club scene. One, of course, was money. Another was boredom. She was also tired of playing the virgin frump every night at the Shubert. At the Blue Angel, she would discard the sexless, high-necked dress she wore as Miss Marmelstein, get gussied up, and let down her hair. For her engagement, Barbra also traded in her flashy, anything-for-a-shock garb of club performances past for a simple black cocktail dress.

She had one other motivation. At the Blue Angel, she could sing the songs she wanted to sing, and she could sing them the *way* she wanted to sing them.

While she had become bored and discontented with *Wholesale,* she was blissfully happy with the show's leading man. Elliott, or "Elly," as Barbra referred to him, would reflect upon this time as the most loving of their union. "I must admit that my happiest memories I have of Barbra," he related, "are when we were living together before we were married. We were very dependent on each other then."

After the show, they would play pokerino at the penny arcades and feast on midnight horror flicks and meals at all-night Chinese restaurants. Or they would go home, lock the door of their apartment over Oscar's Salt of the Sea, and play board games, watch television, and dine on frozen fried-chicken dinners and coffee ice cream bricks.

They recognized each other's *lack* of a childhood, and were intent on making up for it. Both had been born in Brooklyn to mothers whose love was misguided. Elliott's parents were both alive, but unhappily married. "By the time I was three, I knew my parents didn't understand one another," he would say, "but they stayed together for twenty-seven years."

His mother, Lucille, vented her frustrations by becoming the quintessential stage mother. Elliott wanted to be a baseball player, but she sent him to tap class. His mother enrolled him in the Professional Children's School, and had him tap-dancing in the Jewish temples of Brooklyn. She also had him working for the Bonnie Kid Modeling Agency.

"She says she wasn't a typical stage mother," Elliott would later quip, "but she was. 'Rose's Turn' [the stage mother's anthem from the musical *Gypsy*] could have been 'Lucille's Choice,' no doubt about it."

Lucille Goldstein's obsession left her son with a serious sense of inferiority. He didn't believe he was as talented as some of the other kids in school, which made him feel like he was letting his mother down. He also did not think he was as handsome as some of the other boys at Bonnie Kid. His eyes weren't blue. His hair was too thick and too curly. He looked into the mirror and wished he were fifties movie heartthrob Jeffrey Hunter, or Robert Wagner, anyone but Elliott Goldstein. Barbra, of course, knew all about looking into mirrors and not liking what she saw.

In her eyes, he was a combination of Bogart, Michelangelo's statue of David, and an American Jean-Paul Belmondo. He saw her as a combination of Sophia Loren and Y. A. Tittle, his two favorite people. They dubbed each other "Hansel" and "Gretel." And the world outside was the wicked, blood-hungry witch.

Back at the Shubert, Barbra divorced herself from *Wholesale,* counting the days until its demise. Her performances were lackluster, but no one seemed to notice or care. Barbra's disdain for her fans took hold during the show's run. She was disturbed that they didn't know when she gave a good performance. Sometimes, she gave only what she could get away with. And still the ovations continued.

Backstage, she entertained herself between numbers by reading *Mad* magazine and working on songs for her nightclub act. For, other than Elliott and Ashley Feinstein, she would make no real friends during the production. "I appreciated her talent," says Harold Rome, "but we weren't friends. She is very difficult to get close to. She is absorbed in herself."

While the rest of the *Wholesale* company worked on each evening's performance, Barbra planned what she would be doing *months* into the future. In her dressing room, she not only rehearsed songs for her nightclub act, she worked on songs for the record album that she knew she would soon do.

Barbra left explicit instructions with the theater management that no visitors were to be allowed backstage to see her. She *did* consent to see her old friends from Erasmus Hall, Diane Lemm and Judy Jacobson. "Right after the performance, we walked to the backstage door," recalls Lemm, "and we yelled up, 'Barbra, it's us—Diane and Judy.' And she yelled, 'I'm coming, I'm coming!' And she came flying down those stairs and we hugged and kissed. I said, 'Barbra, you were wonderful. We can't believe how famous you've become!' And the first thing she said to me, 'Ah, your nails—they're still gorgeous! I love your nails! I haven't had time to do mine.' I was in awe. We talked a few more minutes, and then I said, 'Barbra, do me a favor.' And she said, 'What?' And I said, 'Please sign my *Playbill.* I want your autograph.' And she said, 'I don't have to give *you* an autograph. You're my friend.' "

One person that she refused to see, under any circumstances, was her mother. Diana Kind *was* present for the opening night performance of *Wholesale,* but had not been impressed. "I don't think she understood what I was trying to do," Barbra related to a reporter. Tensions between mother and daughter had only gotten worse since Barbra's success. Diana didn't approve of her daughter "living in sin" with Elliott. It was 1962 and respectable young people didn't do such things, at least not out in the open, and not without shame, and not in an apartment that reeked of seafood.

As *Wholesale* crawled to its close on December 9, 1962, after a respectable nine-month run, Barbra Streisand heaved a giant sigh of relief. She had endured the torture; the prison sentence was over. She had places to go and bigger fish to fry. For while she had been miserably toiling onstage at the Shubert, Marty Erlichman had been negotiating a lucrative concert tour for her to begin in March. More important, after a year and a half of dogged effort, Barbra was finally signed to a recording contract. And it wasn't with just any label. It was with *the* label: Columbia. The home of Johnny Mathis and Tony Bennett. There were offers from Broadway and Hollywood. There were offers for club dates from every part of the country and then some. It was Yetta Tessye Marmelstein's revenge. Everyone wanted a piece of her—including *that* piece.

Eleven

Getting Her Act Together
(Or Trying to)
And Taking It on the Road

*I*n the entire rock era, only *four* artists have surpassed Barbra Streisand on *Billboard*'s album charts: The Beatles, Elvis Presley, Frank Sinatra, and The Rolling Stones—and she seems likely to eclipse Sinatra and the Stones. In retrospect, it seems inconceivable that she would have had difficulty landing a record deal. But such was the case from the spring of 1961 until the fall of 1962. Marty Erlichman carted Barbra, and/or her tapes, to one record company executive after another. He begged, pleaded, *kvetched*. He lured them to see her perform at the Bon Soir and the Blue Angel and plied them with complimentary drinks. When that too failed, he concentrated his efforts on attracting the A&R (artists and repertoire) representatives and the lower-level label executives. She was "too Brooklyn," they told him, "too Broadway," "too Jewish," "too special," "too eccentric," and "too unattractive." She had a nasal delivery and she sang songs that were "too old" and "too obscure." And she had a style and persona that were "too homosexual" in their appeal.

What they wanted was *recycled* talent. Another Patti Page, Brenda Lee, or Connie Francis. And they wanted it all wrapped in a petite package, preferably with flashing dimples and pinup beauty potential. Streisand, however, wasn't another *anyone,* and she certainly wasn't going to sell any records on her sex appeal. She was an original, but the executives couldn't see beyond the keys of their rapidly calculating adding machines to recognize it.

In 1961, Barbra recorded an audition demo of ten songs for RCA. The material was derived from her repertoire at the Bon Soir. However, RCA rejected her in favor of another nineteen-year-old, named Ann-Margret. Like Barbra, Ann-Margret had a penchant for singing old standards. Her first RCA album, *And Here She Is: Ann-Margret,* included "Chicago," "Teach Me Tonight," and "More Than You Know," the last a song Barbra would later record. Unlike Barbra, Ann-Margret oozed vast amounts of undeniable sex appeal. She would also beat Barbra to the box office, becoming a major movie star with the release of the 1963 musical, *Bye Bye Birdie.* Barbra regarded Ann-Margret as something of a rival and, over the years, would follow her career with interest.

Still without a recording contract, Barbra's next venture on vinyl was the original cast recording of *I Can Get It for You Wholesale.* She showed up at Columbia Records' Thirtieth Street studio to record the album on April 1, 1962. Studio time was limited. The atmosphere, tense. Still, the jaded studio engineers were overwhelmed when Barbra stood up to the microphone to sing. Even the show's cast members were taken aback, despite having heard her for months in rehearsals. Just as something inexplicable happened whenever Greta Garbo or Marilyn Monroe stepped in front of a motion picture camera—director Billy Wilder deemed it "voltage"—something *transcendental* occurred that day in the studio when Barbra's voice was projected into a microphone.

"There were no microphones during rehearsal of the show," relates cast member Stanley Simmonds. "And when we recorded the cast record, we were *astounded.* When the record was played back, we could all hear what she had. Everybody knew then that she had something special. Her voice recorded like a million bucks."

Still, Goddard Lieberson, president of Columbia ("God" to those in the industry), was not convinced. In fact, when Harold Rome prepared the twenty-fifth anniversary recording of *Pins and Needles,* the 1930s International Ladies' Garment Workers' Union revue, he was told by the company that he could *not* hire Streisand. At Rome's insistence, however, she recorded six of the songs from the show, including the touching "Nobody Makes a Pass at Me," which was kind of a sisterly companion to her "Miss Marmelstein" number in *Wholesale.* It was about a young woman who conscientiously, and unsuccessfully, tries to bolster her sex appeal through any means available. The public persona of Streisand as the homely, lovable, but unloved loser was beginning to take hold.

"She's nineteen years old, for heaven's sake!" exulted Harold Rome, surprised by her understanding of dated material. "She's not a history student. She doesn't know a thing about the period, and yet she gets into the songs as if she'd been born to them. I don't know where it's coming from."

Barbra shrugged her shoulders, as if to say, "I can't explain it." In fact she had actually telephoned her old friend Barry Dennen and had studied the period intensively in his apartment.

After her unqualified success in *Wholesale,* and after being singled out in the reviews for both the *Wholesale* and *Pins and Needles* albums, the record companies finally began to give Barbra the serious consideration she obviously deserved. Ahmet Ertegun, president of Atlantic Records, wanted to sign her. So did Alan Livingston at Capitol. But Marty Erlichman held out for Columbia, the class of the industry. Finally, in September 1962, Erlichman received a phone call from Lieberson. He had seen Barbra perform at the Blue Angel and had a change of heart. "Look, it takes a big man to admit a mistake," the president of Columbia told Erlichman, "and I believe I made a mistake. I would like to record Barbra."

She signed her contract with the company on October 1, 1962. Although Columbia had the right *not* to renew it at the end of each year, the contract called for a five-year commitment on Barbra's part. Columbia paid her a relatively small advance of $20,000, enormous by *her* standards, and a minimal royalty based on sales. The concessions that the label granted to Barbra were complete creative control and a "record and release" provision which, essentially, forced the company to release whatever finished product she provided. Columbia also agreed to release *two* Streisand albums in the first year. Erlichman insisted upon this demand in order to give his client two chances of sales success before the end of the one-year option period.

On October 16, 1962, Barbra returned to Columbia's Thirtieth Street studio and, working with an orchestra and twenty-four-year-old producer Mike Berniker, recorded "Happy Days Are Here Again" as a single, with a "B" side of "When the Sun Comes Out." Two weeks later, on November 2, the single was released without fanfare. Columbia refused to promote it and pressed only five hundred copies. Inevitably, the single bombed.

"I remember it was a yellow-label 45," recalls Ashley Feinstein. "I was alone with Barbra at her fish store apartment, and she put it on. I remember her minimalizing it, but it was astounding. Tears were coming out of my eyes."

One reason Columbia failed to get behind the record was that God-dard Lieberson and the company brass did not like its ending. They felt the final note—"Happy Days Are Here A-*GAIN!*"—sounded like a shriek. Through producer Mike Berniker, the company asked her to re-vise the ending, and Barbra, wielding her contractual "creative control" clause, refused. The song was going to be recorded the way *she* deemed fit.

Later that month, on November 19, Barbra's version of John Kander and Fred Ebb's "My Coloring Book," with a flip side of "Lover, Come Back to Me" was released and fared little better than the first single, de-spite her performance of both of them on the December 16 edition of "The Ed Sullivan Show."

The Columbia sales department had no faith in Barbra or her appeal. She didn't sing on beat, and she didn't show cleavage. Men wouldn't *want* her. Women wouldn't want to be *like* her. How could the salespeo-ple market her when they themselves didn't believe in, or even know how to define, her appeal? Moreover, she was *not* a singer who could spit out top-ten singles. Streisand was then, and would essentially always be, an artist of meticulously crafted albums.

Huddling with Marty Erlichman, Barbra decided that the best way to capture her appeal was to record a live album. And so, on November 5, 1962, Columbia trucked its recording equipment to the Bon Soir. For the rest of the week, Barbra's performances were recorded. The songs included "Keepin' Out of Mischief Now," "I Hate Music," "Nobody's Heart (Belongs to Me)," "Value" (a.k.a. "I'm in Love With Harold Mengert"), "Cry Me a River," "Who's Afraid of the Big Bad Wolf?" "I Had Myself a True Love," and "Lover, Come Back to Me."

Recalls Tiger Haynes, leader of The Three Flames, "Columbia Rec-ords hired the Bon Soir. They had the candles and the tablecloths and the audience and the whole thing. It was Avril Pollard [on bass], myself, and Peter Daniels on the piano. They hired a drummer for the record, but I don't remember his name."

Variety reported in its November 14 edition: "Columbia Records brought its engineering crew down to this Greenwich Village cellar Monday to record an album. . . . Miss Streisand's stint is well worth pre-serving and the LP should serve as an excellent launching pad for her new career as a Columbia discer."

However, the would-be live album, which was to be titled *Barbra Streisand at the Bon Soir,* was pronounced dead *before* arrival. Barbra, who had creative control, was dissatisfied with the results, and the album was scrapped. With a live recording, she had to sacrifice some control to the elements, which, ultimately, she opted against doing.

On January 23, 1963, she entered Columbia's Studio A at 799 Seventh Avenue. She would take a mere three days to record the eleven songs that would comprise her first official album. It was recorded with a mere fraction of an orchestra and a minimal budget of approximately $18,000. She was, after all, an unproven product who had blown company money on an ill-fated live recording.

The subsequent sessions produced a concept album, telling the story of a young woman's odyssey *backwards*. It began with "Cry Me a River," the bitter, highly emotional story of jilted love, and ended with "A Sleepin' Bee," the hopeful, plaintive tale of newfound love. It was an impressive package that effectively encapsulated her club repertoire at the time. One moment she was sexy, the next moment she was childlike; she was quietly reflective, then she seemed to border on hysteria; she was whimsical, and then she was filled with feminist longing. It was a dazzling exercise in versatility.

There were a few missteps. "A Taste of Honey" was jarringly out of place, and both "Come to the Supermarket in Old Peking" and "Who's Afraid of the Big Bad Wolf?" worked better as performance pieces than on record. The Columbia brass balked at the inclusion of that last number, but Barbra insisted, and prevailed. The other songs, effective in varying degrees, were "Soon It's Gonna Rain," "My Honey's Loving Arms," "I'll Tell the Man in the Street," "Keepin' Out of Mischief Now," and "Much More."

The response to the record within the company was sharply divided. Some were wildly enthusiastic, others revulsed. Mostly, though, there was a great deal of uncertainty about its commercial appeal. And so it was with trepidation that the presumptuously titled debut, *The Barbra Streisand Album,* was released on February 25, 1963.

Just two years before, Barbra's debut concert tour had been a shoddy, $200-a-week affair that had little purpose other than providing pocket change and experience. In contrast, her 1963 tour was designed to promote the release of her album, and the accommodations were strictly first-class. The clubs themselves improved in quality and prestige. And her fees *jumped* to $2,500 to $7,500 per week.

The promotional tour actually began with a return to the Blue Angel in January. The engagement was intended to be a tryout. It became something much more. New Yorkers who knew her only as Miss Marmelstein were stunned by her versatility. And while the town was in the throes of a crippling newspaper strike, the national critics tripped over their penny loafers and wing tips and sang her virtues with abandon.

"Last week at Manhattan's Blue Angel," observed a critic for *Time* magazine, "she squirmed onto a stool and let her coltish legs dangle, ankles flapping. She twisted bony fingers through her hair and blessed her audience with a tired smile. Then she sang—and at the first note, her voice erased all the gawkiness of her presence onstage."

Robert Ruark, in his syndicated column, was even more enthusiastic, extolling, "Her nose is more evocative of moose than muse, and her eyes at best could be called Nilotic only by way of mascara, but about 2 A.M., when she sings 'Any Place I Hang My Hat Is Home,' she's beautiful, even if home is only Brooklyn. Her name is Barbra Streisand. She is 20 years old, she has a three-octave promiscuity of range, she packs more personal dynamic power than anybody I can recall since Libby Holman or Helen Morgan. She can sing as loud as Ethel Merman and as persuasively as Lena or Ella. . . . She is the hottest thing to hit the entertainment field since Lena Horne erupted, and she will be around 50 years from now if good songs are still written to be sung by good singers."

It was with this powerful, critical alliance that Barbra embarked on her tour. The club dates themselves were orchestrated by Marty Erlichman, in conjunction with Joe Glaser, president of Associated Booking. When Barbra's agent, Irvin Arthur, left the company to handle a new folk singer by the name of Bob Dylan, her representation was assumed by Glaser, legendary in the business for his revered clientele, which included Louis Armstrong, Billie Holiday, Dizzy Gillespie, Duke Ellington, and Lionel Hampton.

Barbra had never been particularly fond of Irvin Arthur, but she *did* seem to like Joe Glaser. "He was a little gruff," Arthur says, "but she felt comfortable with him. He was a very nice guy, and she was very loyal to him."

Barbra promoted her album, and her tour, with a March 5, 1963, appearance on "The Tonight Show Starring Johnny Carson." Carson had taken over the reins of "The Tonight Show" on October 2, 1962. Two nights later, Barbra made her first appearance with Carson on the show. Thereafter, in an emphatic display of his support, Carson had Barbra back on the show once a month, *every* month, for five months, ending with the March 5 appearance.

The tour commenced in mid-March in the Eden Roc Hotel's Cafe Pompeii in Miami. Barbra was booked on a curious, ill-advised bill in which she shared the marquee—"Two Great Stars the Critics Are Rav-

ing About!"—with slick Italian baritone Sergio Franchi. A trio of singing, dancing comics known as the Mambo Aces appeared in between
their acts. It was hardly Barbra's kind of fare. She was disturbed, too, by
the club's elderly clientele, which seemed to dole out its reserved applause.

Following the Miami gig, which concluded on March 27, Barbra commenced a three-week stand at the prestigious Hungry i in San Francisco.
Her booking at the renowned nightclub had an interesting, typically
Streisandian, history. She was actually introduced to Enrico Banducci,
the club's owner, one day in early 1962, *before* her success in *Wholesale*.
Making her usual rounds, Barbra barged in on Irvin Arthur at his Associated Booking office in New York, where she found Banducci. "Got
nothing for you today, Barbra," Arthur informed her, dismissively.
"From you, who wants anything?" Barbra retorted in response. Then,
nodding toward Banducci, she said, "I understand that *moron with the
beret* owns the Hungry i." As Banducci shifted uncomfortably in his
seat, Barbra began a tirade about the plight of the fledgling performer,
just as she had done to David Susskind on "PM East." "You nightclub
owners are all alike," she went on. "You're going to be down on your
scabby knees, *begging* me for a contract before the year is out, *idiot!*"

To his credit, Banducci was not repelled by Barbra, as Susskind had
been. "She was easily the kookiest and most arresting-looking kid I'd
ever seen," he would say later. Barbra's performance that day in Arthur's
office was an *act*. She desperately wanted the job, and, unable to beg in
her own behalf, she donned an armor of bravado and *became* someone
else.

"I was scared to death," she would later confess. "But since I really
didn't want to be a singer anyway, I decided to approach it as an actress." Banducci was sufficiently impressed, and when Barbra became
available after *Wholesale* closed, she was booked into his club.

"I am really shy—no, honest," Barbra revealed to a skeptical San
Francisco reporter during her engagement in the city. "Outwardly, no,
because my shyness makes me aggressive or defensive, whichever way
you like to put it." In Streisand's case, being "shy" and being "aggressive" are not necessarily contradictory. Her aggressiveness is often
rooted in her shyness.

San Francisco's introduction to Streisand was a stunning success. Unlike the club in Miami, the Hungry i offered her the perfect venue for her
brand of intimate theatrics. Lines formed around the door and down the

street. Led by its effusive gay population, San Franciscans were smitten. "Once in a lifetime, if you are lucky," raved critic Owen Hiddleson, "you are able to witness the birth of a new star in the entertainment world. . . . The new star? Barbra Streisand, 21-year-old blues [he didn't know how else to classify her] singer from Brooklyn. Miss Streisand is a solid personality who has the talent to become one of the all-time singing greats in show business."

Barbra's run at the Hungry i created a buzz that quickly spread throughout California, and beyond. She became *hip*. It was the day of The Kingston Trio, but, if you didn't know Streisand, you didn't exist. Incidentally, during those weeks at the Hungry i, no one paid much attention, Barbra included, to the young performer who shared the bill with her. His name was Woody Allen.

In April, Barbra ventured to the Midwest, where she appeared at Mister Kelley's on Rush Street in Chicago on a bill with comic Jackie Vernon and spent a week cohosting Mike Douglas's television talk show in Cleveland. The Douglas appearance would *not* help sales of "Happy Days Are Here Again," which Columbia rereleased as a single—it wouldn't even crack the *Billboard* top forty. But it did wonders to boost sales of her album, which had been accorded rave reviews in the weeks after its release. Douglas, certainly, was an enthusiastic fan, and over the course of the week, he had her sing every song from the album. "I'm sure our show helped get the ball rolling," Douglas related. "We gave her the first significant, prolonged, national TV exposure."

For Barbra, nights in Cleveland were depressing ones, spent performing in a dreary club called the Chateau. Despite her appearances on the Douglas show, Cleveland residents didn't quite know what to make of Streisand, and her shows were played to rooms that were only half full. One night, two of the men who *did* show up, both drunk, started to heckle her from the audience. They were commenting, rather cruelly, about her lack of conventional good looks. Barbra tried to ignore them. When that didn't work, she attempted to dismiss them with a joke.

Finally, Marty Erlichman, her unlikely but nonetheless chivalrous hero, rushed to her rescue, as he always did. He marched over to the hecklers' table and threatened them with physical retaliation. Eventually, the two men were escorted outside by the club's burly bouncers, and Barbra, visibly shaken, continued with her show.

Still, she returned to New York with a good deal of optimism. On May 4, 1963, *The Barbra Streisand Album* entered the *Billboard* top-forty-albums chart. In the weeks that followed, it would peak at number eight. The record's endurance proved even more impressive, remaining in the top forty for *seventy-eight* weeks, one of the longest runs for a solo artist in the entire rock era.

On Mother's Day, Sunday, May 12, Barbra made an appearance on the final "Dinah Shore Show." In it, Shore passed the proverbial torch, introducing four newcomers, one of whom was Barbra. She sang "Cry Me a River" and "Happy Days Are Here Again." Rick du Brow, then writing for United Press International, was ebullient in his praise. "I doubt if there is any young act anywhere," he enthused, "more positively astounding than Miss Barbra Streisand. Miss Streisand is a comedienne, but she is quickly becoming known as a torch singer who acts within her songs more extraordinarily than anyone since Lena Horne. . . . Miss Streisand is attractively awkward, a little bit of Fanny Brice and Alice Ghostley and Carol Burnett, with a dash of Mort Sahl. She is a different kind of mama."

The night after the show aired, Barbra opened at the Basin Street East on East Forty-eighth Street in Manhattan. Benny Goodman and his band shared the bill with her. For Barbra, the new surroundings offered her the opportunity to add to her rapidly expanding group of devotees.

During the engagement, Barbra received a warm, congratulatory note from one of her childhood favorites. "You are marvelous," the note read, "more than you realize." It was from Audrey Hepburn.

The continual praise and affirmation helped Barbra gain confidence as a performer, particularly in her rapport with her audience. "Hey, Barbra," one patron yelled out from his seat, "aren't you from Brooklyn?" Without missing a beat, Barbra deadpanned, "Aren't we *all* from Brooklyn, some time or other?"

One night, she burst into the opening bars of the title song from *The Sound of Music,* one of the shows from which she had been rejected. "The hills are alive," she sang in her best Mary Martin impersonation, "and they're pretty *frightening!*"

On another occasion, it was not Rodgers and Hammerstein who were the target of her tongue-in-cheek venom, but the sacred St. Nick. "You better watch out," she sang, "you better not cry. You better not pout, I'm telling you why, Santa Claus is *dead!*"

Some felt it was not confidence but bravado that she exhibited with reckless and tasteless abandon. "They tell me I'll eventually win everything," she told writer Pete Hamill. "The Emmy for TV, the Grammy for records, the Tony on Broadway and the Oscar for movies. It would be beautiful to win all those awards, to be rich, to have my name on marquees all over the world. And I guess a lot of those things will happen to me. I kind of *feel* they will. It could be good or it could be bad, but I'm living my life one day at a time. And I don't see why it shouldn't always be fun. Do you?"

But she really was not having much fun. Daydreaming atop the roof of the Vanderveer projects, the teenage Barbra had always imagined that happiness would accompany fame, that one would not exist without the other. Instead, the increasingly famous twenty-one-year-old found herself still depressed, fraught with tension, and overcome with the pressure of living up to expectations, of being as good as everyone had touted her to be, of maintaining her *own* impossible standards.

"If you maintain a standard of work in order not to get knocked down for not maintaining a standard of work," she said at the time, "then you get knocked down for being a prima donna. Now that I'm accepted on a mass level, I'm starting to get torn down." Indicative of her growing disdain for her audience, she added, "People always want a scene stealer. That's democracy! Most people don't really know when I'm good or bad, that's the sickest part of it."

As she continued her Basin Street East engagement, rumors about Barbra circulated in the local press. One item claimed the cabaret's management wanted to sign her to a five-year contract. Another suggested producer George Abbott planned to star her in a Broadway musical. And then it was rumored she had become pregnant, inspired in part by the fact that Barbra, always strikingly thin, even emaciated, had started to sport a slightly protruding stomach. She also began to wear baggy clothing, even on stage. One of her preferred performance outfits of the period was a four-dollar high-waisted gingham tent dress. Barbra, of course, denied the rumor, saying of those who were spreading it, "Maybe they know something that I don't."

In March, early into her tour, Barbra and Elliott began telling everyone, including their friends and the press, that they had secretly married. The would-be wedding supposedly took place in Miami. "I'm an old married woman," Barbra said whenever she was asked, and even when she wasn't. Elliott concurred. "It was like we shook on it. [We said] 'Let's get married'—glop! So we did!" It's easy to rationalize their lies. Living together out of wedlock was still frowned upon by a pre-flower-power society.

In March 1963, Elliott flew to London, where he was preparing to open in a West End production of Leonard Bernstein, Betty Comden, and Adolph Green's *On the Town,* a revival of the hit 1944 musical comedy, which was subsequently adapted into a 1949 motion picture starring Gene Kelly and Frank Sinatra. In February, director Joe Layton had approached both Barbra and Elliott and asked them to be in the show, with Elliott as Ozzie the sailor, and Barbra as Hildy, the outspoken lady cab driver, a role originated by Nancy Walker. Elliott accepted, and wanted Barbra to join him. He argued it was their chance to pursue their careers without interrupting their idyllic, Hansel-and-Gretel existence.

Barbra felt torn. Her heart tugged her toward Elliott. Her ambition, however, pulled her in another direction. Before Elliott, there had been Marty Erlichman, and there was perhaps no one whose advice Barbra valued more. Erlichman drilled into her head that everything she had ever wanted was right around the corner. *Why* would she risk it all to take a secondary part in a *revival,* to be staged across the Atlantic, in another country, that could very well flop and close in weeks? Besides, he argued, she *had* to go out on the lucrative tour he had arranged to promote her album.

The matter came to a head one night at Sardi's. Angry words were exchanged between Elliott and Marty. Elliott shouted that Marty was interfering with *his* relationship. Erlichman yelled back that Elliott was interfering with *his* client. Barbra sat between them. They pressed her from either side, "Well, what do *you* want to do?"

Finally, Barbra raised her head and looked at Elliott. "I'll go with you to London," she said quietly.

There was a pause. Touched, Elliott shifted gears. "You made the right decision to be with me," he told her. "But you wouldn't be happy with me there. What you *have* to do is pursue your career."

In early May 1963, while Elliott was in London, Barbra had been invited to perform before President John Kennedy at the annual White House correspondents' dinner. "She looked forward to *that* enormously," recalls Ashley Feinstein. It was, after all, the closest America would ever come to a Royal Command Performance. It was also something, at long last, that perceptibly impressed her mother, an ardent Kennedy admirer.

Merv Griffin had been chosen to host the show. His agent, Murray Schwartz, would coordinate the evening's entertainment. Upon seeing the proposed lineup, Griffin balked at Barbra's inclusion. Griffin was then, as he always has been, a proponent of old-fashioned Hollywood glamor. He was *not* a Streisand fan. In fact, he had even rejected her as a guest on his popular television talk show.

To support his objection, Griffin told Schwartz that Kennedy liked bathing beauties and would have little interest in Barbra. Schwartz, however, persisted, and on May 23, the night of the event, Barbra performed, among other numbers, "Happy Days Are Here Again." Suffice it to say, she stole the show.

Following the performance, Griffin, Barbra, and the other entertainers on the bill, Edie Adams, Marty Brill, and Julius Monk among them, stood in a reception line to meet the president. Prior to the show, they had all been briefed as to the proper protocol. They were to be introduced to the president, shake his hand, and then allow him to move rapidly through the line. They were explicitly instructed *not* to detain him.

When Kennedy came to Barbra, she curtsied. Her knees went weak in his presence. There were few celebrities with whom Barbra was enamored, but John Fitzgerald Kennedy was one of them. She then whipped out a pen, held out her program, and boldly asked, "Mr. President, may I have your autograph?" Merv Griffin, looking on, was aghast.

As Kennedy signed Barbra's program on her pianist's bended back, Barbra told him that her mother was an ardent fan of his.

"How long have you been singing?" he asked politely.

"About as long as you've been president," she quipped in response.

When Kennedy handed Barbra the signed program, she expressed her appreciation. "Thanks," she cooed. "You're a doll."

The following morning at breakfast, Griffin, perturbed, approached Barbra. "Barbra, did you *have* to stop the president for an autograph?" he asked.

"I wanted it," she responded.

"Well, did he write an inscription?" Griffin queried.

"Yes," Barbra retorted. " 'Fuck you. The President.' "

Barbra would never forgive Griffin for his reproach, or for having rejected her for his show.

In the weeks that followed, rumors circulated back in New York that Barbra was going around town, mocking the president's Boston accent. When asked about it by a reporter, Barbra expressed genuine, albeit overstated, concern. "He's a great-looking, magnificent-looking man. I'd *never* say that. I'll write the president a letter," she told the reporter. "He must know the truth!"

The continuing sales success of *The Barbra Streisand Album* bolstered Barbra's assessment of her commercial potential. Over 100,000 units were sold in the first year of its release. It would eventually reach the 500,000 units sold plateau, and be certified gold by the Recording Industry Association of America.

"All the people who sing my kind of songs sell only to 'in' type audiences, and sell about 400 copies," she said, in mocking reference to all of the would-be experts who had repeatedly minimized her appeal. "Four of the tunes in the first album were not even in tempo. I just sang ad lib. They told me you couldn't *sell* that kind of thing. I said that was the only way I wanted to do it. . . . It's a wild kind of thing. It proves my point that anything that's truly real, musically genuine, is commercial. Hip people dig it, but the people in Arkansas dig it too." She added, "Why are da Vinci and van Gogh famous all over the world? You don't compromise with quality."

On June 9, Barbra made another appearance on "The Ed Sullivan Show." Upon arriving at the studio earlier that day, Barbra was turned away by the security guard, who mistook her for an autograph-seeking teenager. Eventually she convinced him of her credentials and was allowed into the theater.

A little over two weeks later, on June 25, she appeared on the premiere episode of a CBS musical variety program entitled "The Keefe Brasselle Show." Brasselle (who'd played Eddie Cantor in the film about the famed entertainer) was being pushed by the network at the time as the next *big thing* on the small screen. The hype, however, would fail to be realized. The series would run for only a single summer season, and Barbra's stirring rendition of "Soon It's Gonna Rain" provided the show with its only real highlight.

After fulfilling her various bookings, Barbra crossed the Atlantic to be with Elliott in London. *On the Town* had opened on May 26 at the Prince of Wales Theatre to disappointing reviews and subsequently tepid box office. It was a difficult time for Elliott. Not only was his career a failure, his girlfriend was in the midst of a phenomenally successful year.

Bob Schulenberg, who had been living in Europe, went to visit the couple and was almost immediately aware of Elliott's distress. "I went from France to Oxford, England, to see them," Schulenberg recalls. "It was very tense. I realized that Elliott had his own issues with Barbra that were very difficult for him. He was supposed to have been the discovery in *I Can Get It for You Wholesale*—and he wasn't. He couldn't get *arrested.* You had to try and include him in the conversation.

"But Elliott wasn't interested in talking with me. I realized that I had a history with Barbra that Elliott didn't have. And he didn't necessarily know *what* my relationship with her had been. I'd spend the day with Barbra while Elliott would be rehearsing, and then we'd have dinner at a

Chinese restaurant. I'd try to make light conversation, but I'd end up retreating into my sketchbook, doing my drawings."

For Schulenberg, it was an awkward situation. He was supposed to be the guest, and yet he was virtually ignored by the host, who was lost in *his* own impossible situation. And Barbra did nothing to assuage the tension between the two men. Instead, when the three of them were together, she virtually ignored Schulenberg and carried on her conversations with Elliott as if they were alone.

Says Schulenberg, "She has this low-rent attitude, of going on talking as if no one else is there. If somebody comes over, it's 'Hey, *they* know where it is, let *them* get it if they want it.' My uncle married a woman and whenever we'd go over to their house my mother was always offended that the woman never offered us iced tea or something. The woman's attitude was, 'If you want iced tea, ask me for it and I'll give you some.' With Barbra and Elliott, if you wanted it, you had to ask for it."

After a few weeks together, Barbra and Elliott were again forced apart so that she could fulfill a commitment to Liberace. The flamboyant pianist had seen Barbra perform at the Bon Soir. He saw her again when both were booked on the same "Ed Sullivan Show," and was convinced that he wanted her as the opening act for his upcoming tour. However, Liberace's manager, Seymour Heller, balked, arguing that Barbra would not be accepted in the Midwest. Liberace conceded the argument, and the matter was forgotten until he saw Barbra again at the Basin Street East.

This time, Liberace told Heller, "I'm going to take her to Las Vegas no matter what you say." He was planning a four-week return engagement at the Riviera Hotel, where he hadn't played for five years, and he wanted only the best. To Heller he added, "At least the crowd there will be hip enough to appreciate her."

If Barbra's pairing with Sergio Franchi in Miami had been ill inspired, her teaming with Liberace, at least on paper, seemed destined for disaster. Liberace was the personification of Vegas flash and schmaltz. His audiences were generally an older, middle-of-the-road crowd, hungry for a feast of sequins and glamour. Arguably, he couldn't have selected a more inappropriate opening act. Barbra's stage persona was unpolished, the presentation of her material cutting-edge, and her act itself utterly uncluttered and without frills—just a singer on an almost barren stage. As for her look, it was decidedly antiglamour, take-me-in-my-gingham, the antithesis of everything Liberace represented.

Obviously she was out of her element. On opening night, July 2, 1963, the Vegas audience accorded her applause that was barely civil. Instead of warming up the audience, her designated job, Barbra left Liberace with a cold stage and a frigid, frustrated crowd. When she flopped again during the second show, the Riviera management threatened to have her fired. Instead, Liberace called a meeting in his suite. "Here's what we're gonna do," he pronounced. "*I'll* open the show with a fast number, and then I'll introduce Barbra as my discovery. Big hit in New York and all that. Then she'll come on and they gotta like her because she has my seal of approval. Okay?"

Privately, Liberace also gently suggested to Barbra, "Maybe you should make your wardrobe a little snazzier." She retorted, "Like yours?"

Liberace commanded, and his subjects dutifully obeyed. The following evening's performance was far more successful than the opening, and the Riviera management went so far as to sign Streisand to a long-term contract. It was an agreement Barbra would come to regret. She disliked Vegas audiences in general, and resented the high-rolling, cigar-smoking husbands and their bewigged, bejeweled wives in particular. She also resented the clatter and the clicking glasses that continued uninterrupted during her sets. Streisand was used to an absolute hush when she sang. She could never quite accept that Vegas, perhaps the loudest of all American towns, is quiet for no one. The only thing that she found of interest about the city itself was its scarcity of clocks and its unapologetic disregard for time.

But it was the Cocoanut Grove at the Ambassador Hotel in Los Angeles that provided Barbra with her most important club dates of the year. The legendary Grove was the hangout of the Hollywood elite. Upon its hallowed floor, in decades past, Bette Davis had danced, Joan Crawford had pranced, and many a star had been gloriously wined, dined, and romanced. Like many other New York theater people, both Barbra and Elliott looked down upon Hollywood with disdain as purveying more tinsel than talent. But deep down, she desperately craved its acceptance. Performing before a Grove audience represented, at least to some extent, the fulfillment of her childhood dream.

She said at the time, "I can remember, and not too long ago, when I was on the other side of the entertainment fence looking in. You know what I mean? It wasn't that long ago when I was sitting in a candy store in Brooklyn eating ice cream and reading movie magazines. Now all of a sudden I'm appearing before those very stars—and I'm now one of them."

On opening night, August 21, 1963, Barbra kept the star-filled audience waiting for over an hour. And this was a crowd *not* used to being kept waiting, particularly not by a comparative nobody who had yet to prove, at least to them, that the talent merited the hype. Barbra's Hollywood reputation for being difficult started that very night. When she finally did take the stage, after an inappropriate medley honoring Hawaii by pianist Pierson Thal and his orchestra, Barbra faced a restless, even hostile crowd. "Go ahead," they seemed to say, "show us what you've got."

She peered out into the glittering audience and assumed an air of nonchalance. She looked one way and then the other, showcasing the lines of her irregular profile. "If I had known there were going to be so many stars here tonight," she quipped, "I woulda had my nose fixed." They laughed, and when she began to sing, they forgave.

Louella Parsons was there, along with her perpetually behatted rival, Hedda Hopper. Songwriter Sammy Cahn, who sat next to Hedda, had a transistor radio plugged into his ear. During the show, he infuriated those sitting near him (not to mention Barbra) by barking out the score of the Dodgers baseball game. At one point, in the middle of Barbra's stirring "Bewitched, Bothered and Bewildered," Cahn stood up and cried out, "The Dodgers won! Sixteenth inning! 2 to 1!"

John Huston, aged fifty-seven, spent much of the night lusting after seventeen-year-old Sue Lyon, who had recently caused a sensation in Hollywood with *Lolita.* Natalie Wood and Robert Wagner provoked whispers by sitting in different corners of the room. They had recently separated, and both were with new partners, Arthur Loew, Jr., and Marion Donen, respectively.

Other celebrities present included Kirk Douglas, Henry Fonda, Elizabeth Ashley, George Peppard, Roddy McDowall, Tammy Grimes, Ray Milland, and Edward G. Robinson.

Before the end of the night, as Barbra held the last notes of "Happy Days Are Here Again," her final song, the Hollywood contingent at the Grove was on its feet, at her feet, cheering. They shouted for an encore. Barbra walked off the stage and didn't bother to look back.

Wrote the critic for the *Los Angeles Herald-Examiner,* "After months of hearing exciting reports from the East and Las Vegas about Barbra Streisand, local play spot devotees finally have the opportunity to see and hear for themselves . . . [and she] completely captivated the opening night audience."

The Hollywood Reporter concurred, "Miss Streisand completely captured the jam-packed, celebrity-studded audience at Wednesday's opening, an event which, veteran Grove-goers said, surpassed any other premiere there in recent history."

During the run of the record-breaking engagement (it was completely sold out for the entire three weeks), Barbra caused an uproar among the Ambassador Hotel staff. One day, she couldn't find her shoes, and after a frantic search of her suite proved futile, she picked up the telephone. "This is Barbra Streisand," she tersely informed the hotel operator.

"Who?" the operator queried.

"*Who?*" Barbra retorted, mimicking the operator's voice. "Barbra Streisand. I want to speak to the housekeeper."

Moments passed while the call was transferred. When someone from the housekeeping department finally got on the line, Barbra provided the reason for her distress. "My *shoes* are missing," she said. Then, accusingly, "Has someone taken them out?"

Barbra was eventually convinced that her shoes had *not* been confiscated by the hotel staff. She decided to make one last search of the suite. Moments later, one of her visitors announced that he had found the missing shoes. They had been hidden in the sheets in her bed. Apparently, Barbra had fallen asleep while still wearing her shoes, and they had become disengaged during a night of tossing and turning.

At the backstage postperformance parties thrown in her honor, Barbra often could not be found. One night, columnist Sidney Skolsky mistakenly identified producer Tony Bill's girlfriend as Barbra. He thanked *her* for the show, kissed *her* on the cheek, and made his departure. It was not until later that he learned of his faux pas.

Barbra *did* give a flurry of interviews to the local press. Typically, she requested that the interviews take place at a restaurant. That way, she could capitalize on the situation and indulge in a free meal. One interviewer was astounded to watch her consume, in a single setting, a shrimp salad, a pair of pork chops, *and* a steak.

She talked about her ambivalence toward her celebrity. "It's getting kind of scary to me, you know," she told Skolsky, after he finally tracked her down. "People who don't have success hate success, you know? See, when I was the second act, it was interesting to move. But now, if they pay to see *me,* all the fun's gone. It's all kind of mixed up, you know? I guess I'll have to adjust to it."

To another reporter, during another meal: "Just think, one year ago this month I was earning $400 weekly, and making $108 per week a few months before that. Today, I am turning down offers up to $15,000."

To still another reporter she groused, "Designers tell me I have one of the greatest figures they've ever seen. But no one writes about me in terms of looking good. They just say 'This is the girl that's ugly, but very talented.'"

Her sessions with the Hollywood press were clearly an exercise in altering and refining her public image. She had been hurt when several national magazines mocked the way she spoke and suggested that she was not very intelligent. "She's great when she sings," they seemed to be saying, "if only she didn't talk." Subsequently, Barbra began to make a concerted effort to talk better, slower, and in more complete sentences. She also tried to lose her distinct Brooklynese and peppered her conversations with allusions to her aspiring intellect. "I read a lot of philosophy so I can get some new questions to ask myself," she told one reporter. "I'm always wondering why."

When not dining with reporters, she was being courted by Hollywood agents and executives who saw dollar signs in her presence. The management team of Freddie Fields and David Begelman, who represented Judy Garland, among others, were eager to add her to their roster.

One week after her Grove opening, the *Hollywood Reporter* related: "La Scala [a Beverly Hills restaurant] looked like a smoke-filled room Monday night. Barbra Streisand was being courted by Creative Management ménage (Freddie Fields, Polly Bergen, Phil Silvers and a Gaggle of Bright Young Men)."

Begelman and Fields didn't stop at providing Barbra with free meals. "They used to shower her with a Rolls Royce to take her where she wanted to go," Irvin Arthur says. "And when her contract expired with Associated, she signed with the agency they created called CMA, which was later ICM."

Instrumental in the decision, made by Barbra in tandem with Marty Erlichman, was that CMA was *not* limited to representing only singers and performers, as was Associated Booking. It also had a division devoted to motion pictures, which, even as early as the fall of 1963, was clearly on Streisand's mind.

She concluded her triumphant stand at the Cocoanut Grove on September 8. At the closing night party, actor Tony Franciosa expressed the sentiment of many in the room when he prophesied, succinctly, and without the puffed-up overstatement usually associated with such Hollywood gatherings, "Ten years from now," he said, "you'll remember her tonight."

Twelve

Going With the Kid

$\mathcal{T}$he man who choreographed Streisand's wildly successful introduction to Hollywood was someone who would figure very prominently in her life for years to come. His name was Ray Stark. At the time, Stark was mounting a full-scale Broadway musical biography of his deceased mother-in-law. After much deliberation, and over a year of auditions, he had selected the relative newcomer Streisand as his star. The Cocoanut Grove engagement gave him the opportunity to introduce her to his Hollywood peers, as well as eliciting interest in the musical itself and, if successful, its inevitable screen adaptation. The subject of the production was Fanny Brice. Its title, *Funny Girl.*

Stark knew all about *stars.* As an agent in the 1950s, he represented, among others, Lana Turner, Ava Gardner, and Marilyn Monroe. Merely representing talent and collecting his 10 percent commission dissatisfied him, and he longed to pocket the *real* money and get into motion picture production. In 1957, Stark formed Seven Arts Productions with Eliot Hyman and set about acquiring properties for the screen, among them, *The Nun's Story, Anatomy of a Murder, The World of Suzie Wong,* and *West Side Story.* The project closest to his heart, however, was to film his mother-in-law's life story. He commissioned Isobel Lennart, screenwriter of *Love Me or Leave Me,* the musical biography of singer Ruth Etting, to develop a screenplay.

The Fanny Brice story had been filmed before, thinly disguised in 1939 as *Rose of Washington Square.* Alice Faye was the star. Claiming that she had been slandered, Fanny Brice sued. Eventually, the dispute was settled out of court. In 1948, Stark commissioned a screenplay by

145

Ben Hecht that was deemed unacceptable by Brice herself. Henry and Phoebe Ephron attempted a revision, but that too was rejected. Shortly after Fanny's death in 1951, a biography by Norman Katkov entitled *The Fabulous Fanny* was published which incorporated material from her unfinished memoirs. Despite its title, the book presented Fanny in a not altogether flattering light. The book so disturbed his wife, Brice's daughter, Fran, that Stark allegedly paid Katkov's publisher fifty thousand dollars to have it taken off the market and its plates destroyed.

Stark wanted the story told in a sanitized version which eulogized Brice and was sanctioned by her family. Given this restriction, Isobel Lennart continued work on her screenplay, which she first entitled *Fanny* and then *My Man*. Stark showed a completed draft dated October 20, 1960, to Hollywood studio executives, but found little interest in the property. About a year later, stage director Vincent J. Donehue read the script, then structured as a straight drama, at Isobel Lennart's home in Malibu. Convinced of its potential, he phoned Mary Martin, still enjoying the success of *The Sound of Music*. When Martin agreed to play Brice, the project suddenly became bankable as a big Broadway musical.

Stark was willing to alter his vision. He still intended to make his movie; he was simply facing reality and rerouting its course. He would unveil his pet project on Broadway and *make* Hollywood take notice. The tinsel-town bigwigs, after all, were not exactly known for their vision. Sometimes, they had to be hit, pounded, and clobbered over the head with, well, a *hit*.

Inexperienced in the theater, Stark shrewdly took as his partner Broadway impressario David Merrick. He also elicited the services of Stephen Sondheim, the gifted young lyricist of *West Side Story,* and composer Jule Styne, fresh from *Subways Are for Sleeping* and the enormously successful *Gypsy.*

Negotiations proceeded, egos clashed. Sondheim dropped out. So too did Donehue. Exit one director, enter *the* director. Ray Stark was a man of impeccable taste. For his mother-in-law, only the best would do. And in the musical theater, there was no one better than Jerome Robbins. *Peter Pan, Bells Are Ringing, West Side Story,* and *Gypsy* were all testaments to his brilliance as a director and choreographer. With Robbins's involvement, the production gained considerable prestige. It would need it.

The consensus among many was that Stark's project was an exercise in stroking his wife's vanity. Citing problems with the book, Mary Martin withdrew her name, support, and drawing power, opting instead to venture in a show called *Jennie*. It would flop. Finding another Fanny would be a long, arduous, process.

And so the search continued. The covey of would-be Fannys included Eydie Gorme, Shirley MacLaine, and Georgia Brown. For a time, it was thought that Gorme, a promising recording artist on the Columbia label, would be given the part.

But Fran Stark, who had considerable say over who played her mother, picked Anne Bancroft. Bancroft was a beautiful, dignified dramatic actress who had stunned Broadway with her portrayal of Annie Sullivan in *The Miracle Worker*. And while she was not a *great* singer (neither was Brice), she could carry a tune and, more important, a show.

Championed by Jerry Robbins, another top contender was Carol Burnett, who had made a name for herself in a variety of television shows and on Broadway in *Once Upon a Mattress*. Like Bancroft, Burnett could generate enthusiastic interest in the show and command a considerable advance at the box office.

Jule Styne, discontented with either choice, wanted a *singer* to perform his score. He had seen Barbra in David Merrick's *I Can Get It for You Wholesale*. Although he was not fond of her *personally*, Merrick thought Barbra was right for the part. At Merrick's behest, Styne saw her at the Bon Soir. He had the advantage of being able to compare contending would-be Fannys with the real thing. He had played the piano for Brice in 1930 at a gambling club in Chicago and got to know her. And so, with Merrick at his side, Styne took word of Streisand to Stark, who scratched his head at the familiarity of the name.

Over the years, many people have taken credit for having first brought Barbra Streisand to Ray Stark's attention. Producer Billy Rose, one of Brice's husbands, went to see *I Can Get It for You Wholesale*. After the performance, Rose ventured backstage and informed Barbra, "If ever they do the story of Fanny, you are the girl to do it." Rose then proffered his opinion to Stark.

A similar recommendation came from Broadway columnist Radie Harris, who met Stark at a dinner party at the Beverly Hills home of Kirk Douglas. "I know the perfect actress for you," Harris told Stark upon hearing of his proposed project. "She *is* Fanny Brice."

"Who is this paragon?" Stark inquired, to which Harris answered, "Her name is Barbra Streisand."

Determined, Jule Styne lured the Starks to the Bon Soir to see and hear his discovery. Fran Stark, taken aback by Barbra's still-careless appearance and persona, was appalled. "There is no way *she* will play my mother," she said, adding, "Mother was a comic, but she was never a nut."

Nevertheless, Barbra was called for an audition. And then another. And then another. Aware of the magnitude of the opportunity, Barbra telephoned Allan Miller, her former acting coach. Miller had been her adviser, friend, surrogate father. With their bond instantly revived, Miller agreed to coach Barbra through the auditions. "She was told that her chief competition was Carol Burnett and Anne Bancroft," Miller recalls, "which was pretty heavy duty for a nineteen-year-old [sic] kid. I didn't have any perspective except what she told me Jerome Robbins said was the next requirement. She was too shrill. We worked on getting her unshrill. She wasn't emotional enough. We worked on getting her more emotional. She wasn't mature enough. We worked on getting her more mature."

Fanny had to age in the show from a teenage virgin to a worldly middle-aged woman. To get her to accomplish this feat, Miller taught Barbra to curb her mannerisms and penchant for gesticulation and to do only what was required for any given task. As a student, Barbra was more than willing to explore and experiment. "She was gorgeous to work with," Miller says. "Gorgeous."

Still, the Starks seemed intent on Bancroft. The actress, however, had second thoughts. She had just starred in, and would win an Oscar for, her performance in the film version of *The Miracle Worker*. She now had a lofty reputation to uphold. How could she risk it by portraying an off-center comic? Worse, a comic who *sings*. Moreover, Bancroft had thought that she could talk-sing her way through the show. Jule Styne, however, had other ideas. Still campaigning for Streisand, he handed Bancroft a complicated score that only an accomplished singer could handle without embarrassment.

While Bancroft vacillated, Burnett almost signed for the part, but finally backed out because she didn't have the Jewish ethnicity she felt essential for the character. Upon declining, Carol extolled the virtues of her former rivals. "[Hire] Anne Bancroft if you want a star," she advised Stark, "and Barbra Streisand if you want to *make* a star. You need a nice Jewish girl like that." In retrospect, it was a good thing Burnett decided against doing the show. Shortly thereafter, she announced that she was pregnant with her first child.

Understandably rattled, and displeased with the evolution of the script, Anne Bancroft bowed out. For Robbins and Stark, their big decision was made for them, or so it would seem. Still, they were uncertain of

Streisand. Yes, she had been a standout in a small part in an otherwise mediocre show. Yes, she could sing. But could she carry, curtain-to-curtain, a major, full-scale production? Moreover, could she *act?*

And so she was brought back for *another* audition. And yet another. There would be *seven* in all. For the final audition, Barbra showed up late. Robbins, justifiably, was livid. "Forty minutes we've been sitting here waiting for you," he barked in greeting. A warning followed. "You better be worth it."

Always one to thrive on obstacles, Barbra performed the monologue she had rehearsed with Allan Miller the night before with a ferocity that astounded those watching. When she finished, there was applause. There was laughter. There was relief. "As far as I'm concerned," Robbins enthused, "you *are* Fanny Brice."

Stark, too, was finally convinced. Allan Miller quotes the producer telling Marty Erlichman, "Look, with Bancroft we had a major actress. She can't sing, and she's not that funny, and we had a million-dollar advance. With Burnett we had a major star talent. She can sing, and she's funny, but she can't act, and we had a two-million-dollar advance. With this kid, we've got *no* advance. But, she can sing, she can act, she can do the whole thing. And if she makes it for us, she's worth five million. *We go with the kid.*"

And so, Barbra was Fanny. Or Fanny was Barbra. In the months that followed, the identities of the two women would blur.

Still hoping for the best, and with his wife holding her tongue, Ray Stark announced to the press on July 25, 1963, that twenty-one-year-old Barbra Streisand had been cast in his much-anticipated Broadway-bound musical biography of Fanny Brice. At the time, Barbra was still toiling with Liberace at the Riviera, in the city with no clocks. "I can hardly wait," she enthused when asked for a response to the announcement. "It's going to be a whole new *me!*"

Thirteen

Two Stars Passing in Flight

$\mathcal{B}$ut there was still unfinished business with the *old* Barbra. Before rehearsals could start on the Fanny Brice musical, she had to fulfill previously contracted personal appearances. After closing at the Cocoanut Grove, she joined Liberace again for an engagement at Harrah's Tahoe. Before, after, and in between her sets, and in various states of dress and undress, Barbra worked on the score with Jule Styne, who had flown in from New York. Accompanying Styne was lyricist Bob Merrill, who had replaced Stephen Sondheim months before. Styne and Merrill had previously collaborated on the seasonal television classic, "Mr. Magoo's Christmas Carol."

When not working on her nightclub act or on the Styne and Merrill score, Barbra squeezed in time for Elliott Gould. The debacle of *On the Town* behind him, Elliott returned to the United States with his confidence shaken. He almost hadn't returned at all, at least not with his bones and/or limbs intact. He had spent his breaks from *On the Town* gambling away his sorrows, with money that he did *not* have. He ended up with a debt of five hundred dollars and had to boyishly charm his way out of the country with the earnest promise that, once he crossed the Atlantic, the money would be forthcoming.

Elliott's reunion with Barbra was filled with ambivalence. They still loved one another. But something had changed in the few short months of their separation. They were Hansel and Gretel no more. Now, it was

150

only Barbra. Everyone else in her life would be relegated to the support-ing cast. Elliott arrived in Los Angeles near the end of her Cocoanut Grove engagement. It was his twenty-fifth birthday. At the hotel coffee shop, Barbra conspired with the waitress, who brought Elliott a piece of cake with a lone candle in its center. "Go ahead," Barbra encouraged, "make a wish."

"I want the Dodgers to win the pennant!" Elliott declared as he blew out the candle. Of course, he wanted much more. For starters, he wanted to be alone with his girlfriend. Instead, she was invariably sur-rounded by agents, managers, reporters, producers, Hollywood stars, fans, and hangers-on. Elliott was nauseated by the pumped-up artifice and parasitic interplay. He was also consumed by envy and wracked by insecurity.

And so they got married. It made perfect sense. They wanted to hold on to their fantasy. Marriage, he hoped, would somehow pull in the reins, not so much on Barbra herself, but on the madness that engulfed her. As for Barbra, the world was exploding around her, and Elliott had been her rock and anchor. Besides, to Barbra, he was still the prize, with the mane of curls on his head and the cleft in his chin.

Recalled one of their friends, "Here was a girl from Brooklyn who never had the guys chasing her, never went steady, and who really felt ugly inside. And then a big, handsome, virile guy falls in love and marries her."

On September 13, 1963, at the end of her stint with Liberace in Tahoe, Barbra, twenty-one, and Elliott, twenty-five, drove to nearby Carson City, where they exchanged vows.

Barbra wore a hopeful smile and a modest cotton suit. Accompanying them were Barbra's two Marty's—Erlichman and Bregman—her manag-ing bookends. Bregman was added to the expanding entourage as her "business manager" (as opposed to Erlichman, who was her "personal manager") after she started commanding huge sums of money. So, she now had two managers, two agents, a contingent of press agents, one producer, one accompanist/arranger, and an entire record company at her disposal. And, after the "ceremony," she added a husband. There was no press, no spectacle. Not even an announcement. After all, as far as almost everyone knew, Barbra and Elliott Gould had been married for at least six months. Interestingly, Barbra signed the marriage license ap-plication "Barbara Joan Streisand."

For Diana Kind, back in Brooklyn, it was a glorious day. At long last, her eldest daughter was a respectable "Sadie, Sadie, Married Lady." As a wedding gift, she would present Barbra with the $750 she had been saving for years. The money, Diana had envisioned, would give Barbra a good start in married life. Instead, daughter thanked mother, put the money in the bank, and collected annual interest. After all, she didn't really need the money. She never would.

Recording of *The Second Barbra Streisand Album* started on June 3, and, considering that Columbia again allotted her only a few days of studio time, the results were astounding. In many ways, the album surpassed the first. Gone were the gimmicky selections such as "Who's Afraid of the Big, Bad Wolf?" Like its predecessor, it is full of compelling stories and vivid characterizations. Side 1, with the exception of "Who Will Buy?" from *Oliver,* is all Harold Arlen. From the sexy, defiant opening, "Any Place I Hang My Hat Is Home," to the wildly shifting, ultimately dazzling, "Down With Love" (with its hint of "That Ol' Black Magic"), to the rousing "When the Sun Comes Out."

Side 2 opens with "Gotta Move," the album's only new composition. Written by Peter Matz for Streisand's club act, the song captures her manic energy and seeming passion for *motion*. The album concludes with a stunning rendition of Arlen's "Like a Straw in the Wind," which blends effortlessly into the opening lyrics from "Any Place I Hang My Hat."

Granted, like the first album, there were a few flaws. The high drama is occasionally overwrought, notably on "I Don't Care Much," and occasionally shrill, particularly the ending of "Lover, Come Back to Me." Still, these are minor and, in a way, welcome imperfections. The album presents Streisand in her purest form.

At least by her standards, Barbra had been cooperative while recording the first album, deferring to the studio experience of producer Mike Berniker and technician Frank Laico. She was much more assertive on the second album. "Why do we need this?" "Can we change this?" "Can we add a little of that?" Her virtual bombardment of questions, suggestions, and complaints were seen by some as intrusive, and at one point, an exasperated Laico walked out of the studio and threatened to abandon the project. He *was* cajoled back, but that didn't preclude Barbra from continuing to express her opinions.

The Second Barbra Streisand Album, released three weeks before her marriage to Elliott, rocketed straight up the charts, unlike the slow but steady ascent of her debut. The album bolted into the *Billboard* top ten, an amazing feat given that Barbra had yet to have a hit single. It would spend three weeks in the number two position, second only to something called *My Son, the Nut* by a singing comic of the period named Allan Sherman. Keeping Streisand out of the prestigious number one position was Sherman's wildly popular hit single "Hello Mudduh, Hello Fadduh!"

The stunning success of the second album, according to a *Cash Box* article of the period, seemed "to indicate that the Streisand name could be the biggest to hit show business since Elvis Presley."

To promote the album, Barbra returned to network television. Following her Grove engagement, she had been offered, with the exception of "The Andy Williams Show" (Williams himself turned her down, saying she wasn't a big enough name), virtually every variety show on the air. Skelton. Sullivan. Paar. Carson. She chose "Chrysler Presents a Bob Hope Special," which aired on September 27. She had met Hope in the "old days," when both were in Florida.

"We were in Palm Beach doing a cancer benefit," recalls Dolores, Hope's wife. "Usually those things are attended by older people who only stay for half the show. By the second half, everybody has gone home. When Bob introduced Barbra that night, nobody had ever heard of her. Yet when she got up on the stool and sang, *everybody* came back for the second half. We were told that that had never happened at that theater before. Today, I think she is incredible, but I wasn't too impressed with her at that time. Bob raved about her right away. He knew she was going to be a big star."

Historically, Barbra's most important appearance of the period occurred on "The Judy Garland Show." Garland had been present at Barbra's closing night performance at the Grove. She wanted to personally check out the new singer whom some reviewers had been lauding, rather audaciously in Judy's view, as "the New Garland." Early into Barbra's performance, however, Garland was stunned. "I'm *never* going to open my mouth again!" she uttered with awe.

The same, sad story. Two stars passing in flight. One on the way up. One on the way down. Only it didn't work out that way. Garland was too much of a competitor. She wasn't about to concede defeat to anyone until a few years later, in 1969, when she died of an accidental overdose of sleeping pills. But on that Friday night taping of the show that bore her name, she planted her feet on the stage, belted out her soul, and summoned all the old Garland magic she could command. It was a triumphant performance. And Streisand was every bit her equal. Their voices soared, by themselves and together in harmony.

It was Garland's inspired idea to combine her "Get Happy" with Streisand's "Happy Days Are Here Again." When taped, the electricity exploded off the stage. The chemistry between the two women, sisters in spirit, was astounding. And when viewers tuned in on October 20, they watched one of the truly great hours in the history of network television.

Judy clutched Barbra's hand during their duet, offering support, and seeking the same. She was both enthralled by and terrified of the new young singer who, if reviewers were to be believed, threatened to take her long-held place.

The two spoofed their supposed rivalry. After Barbra finished a rousing performance of "Down With Love," Garland exclaimed, "You're thrilling. Absolutely *thrilling.*" She added in jest, "We've got all your albums at home, you know. And you're so good—that I hate you. I really *hate* you, you're so good!"

To which Barbra laughed and replied, "Oh, Judy, that's so sweet of you, thank you. You're so great—that I've been *hating* you for *years!*"

The only unpleasantness between the two ladies took place behind the scenes, when the show's director, Norman Jewison, had to trim Barbra's act to accommodate the appearance of another formidable guest, Ethel Merman. Barbra was livid, but her anger was directed more at Jewison than at Garland.

Barbra approached the show with her characteristic confidence and nonchalance. Ashley Feinstein recalls, "I remember when she did 'The Judy Garland Show.' It wasn't that she lacked respect, but she was just so offhand about Judy Garland. *Judy Garland!*" In truth Streisand was in awe of Garland. She just didn't want anyone to know it.

After the taping, Barbra backed out of her commitment to appear on a Bing Crosby special. She also had Marty Erlichman cancel all such future television guest appearances. She had, after all, done the *Judy Garland* show. It would never get any better than that, at least not as a guest star on somebody else's program.

Barbra and Elliott, the newlyweds, had no real honeymoon. Bill Harrah provided them with a house in which they could rest, recuperate, and get reacquainted. Playacting in her new role, and in a spasm of domesticity, Barbra invaded the kitchen with characteristic abandon. Among her ambitious undertakings, the baking of a cake. Unfortunately, the cake proved to be inedible. It seems that during the process, Barbra had run out of sugar—and used flour instead.

With Elliott in tow, Barbra taped "The Judy Garland Show" on October 4, 1963. The following night, she performed at the Hollywood Bowl, on a bill with Sammy Davis, Jr. While in Los Angeles, the Goulds stayed at the Beverly Hills Hotel and squeezed in a few carefree moments frolicking in the hotel pool. When time permitted, Barbra would loiter in the hotel lobby, hoping to be recognized.

Sandra Lee Stuart, author of *The Pink Palace,* a history of the hotel, relates one incident in particular: "With all the demureness of Ethel Merman belting 'Everything's coming up roses,' Streisand announced to the bellman, the desk clerks, most of the lobby, and some of the Polo Lounge, that her rooms were to be watched at all times because she was afraid someone might steal her diamonds, which she couldn't, y'know, put in the hotel safe, because things disappear from the safes."

What the hotel employees didn't know, however (nor, apparently, did Stuart), was that Barbra and Elliott were simply having some fun at their expense. Still, she *was* far from the reclusive, hands-over-the-face anti-star she would become. Being recognized as a celebrity in the *Beverly Hills Hotel* proved both a novelty and a rush.

Before leaving town, producer Sam Goldwyn, Jr., met with Barbra and offered her the starring role in his new picture *The Young Lovers.* Barbra declined the offer, citing her commitment to Broadway.

Back in New York, Barbra and Elliott decided to move out of their fish-reeking railroad flat, with its oddly wallpapered bathroom and its rodent named Gonzola. Actually, the decision to move had been Barbra's. But while she had the inclination, and the money, she didn't have the time (there were more concert dates to fulfill). And so it was Elliott, accompanied by Ashley Feinstein, who went searching for their new home. "Barbra said, 'Take a Polaroid and take pictures and send them to me,' " recalls Feinstein. The quarters they found, on the twenty-sixth and twenty-seventh floors of 320 Central Park West, befitted a Broadway queen.

Upon seeing it, Barbra was enthralled with the grandeur of the large penthouse duplex with its elegant, winding stairway ("I can make an entrance, you know what I mean?") and its cultured history (it had once belonged to Lorenz Hart). For Barbra, there would be no more slumming or sitting atop tenement building roofs. As she walked around the massive expanse of her fifty-five-foot balcony, she took in the sights. Central Park. The Empire State Building. Both the Hudson and the East River. And, with a stretch of the imagination, the corner of Nostrand and Newkirk. The world, or so it seemed, was at her feet.

On November 22, 1963, while riding in a convertible through the streets of Dallas, John F. Kennedy was shot and killed. Like the rest of the nation, Barbra was stunned. "You're a doll," she had playfully told him only six months before. That day, Elliott, again accompanied by Feinstein, went to a singing lesson. In a cab on the way back to the apartment, they passed Barbra, in another cab, on her way to an appointment. The two cabs stopped, and the three friends convened in the street. Feinstein doesn't remember what was said. He remembers only that, later in the day, they reunited in the apartment and shared their grief. "Barbra," Feinstein recalls, "was absolutely destroyed."

By late November, Barbra was deeply engrossed in learning both the script and score of her forthcoming show. Official rehearsals with the entire company began shortly thereafter. In the preceding months, there had been numerous changes in the show. Foremost, Jerome Robbins was no longer involved. Around the same time that Barbra's casting was publicly disclosed, Robbins backed out of the production, citing differences with the producer.

Undaunted, Ray Stark turned to a series of experienced talents, among them, Joshua Logan *(South Pacific),* who later recalled in his autobiography, "A man I hardly knew named Ray Stark called me [and] asked me to consider an idea that he had of doing the story of his wife's mother and father—Fanny Brice and the gambler Nicky Arnstein. The thought of trying to capture Fanny Brice with someone less talented seemed unimaginable. I actually felt sorry for him for having such an impossible idea." It was the popularly held belief of the day.

Bob Fosse, the wildly talented young director and choreographer of *Redhead* and *Little Me,* disagreed. Fosse had previously worked on shows with Styne, saw promise in the material, and, after several meetings with Stark, signed on as director.

But it was a tenuous arrangement at best. The New York theater community is close-knit. Stark was a novice, an outsider not to be trusted. Similarly, Fosse was a virtual unknown to the powers of Hollywood, Stark included. Consequently, they approached one another with trepidation.

Fosse also angered Styne by suggesting that "People," one of the songs from the show's score, be eliminated. Fosse thought the song made no sense and had no place in the context of the show. Styne, taken aback by what he perceived to be Fosse's arrogance, said, "Listen, kid. The reason she is singing this song is because this song is going to be fucking *number one* on the hit parade!"

But it was Stark's distrust that finally provoked Fosse, after four months, to part with the show. Reportedly, Stark, in the throes of uncertainty, went behind Fosse's back and asked about his directorial competence. When he learned what Stark had done, Fosse walked out the door and into another show that better appreciated his abilities. Another opportunity for Fosse and Streisand to work together would present itself some years later, but, again, it would not be realized.

It was to sometime screenwriter, sometime movie director Garson Kanin that the beleaguered Ray Stark turned next. Unlike his predecessors, Kanin was decidedly a *Hollywood* person, someone with whom Stark felt much more comfortable. Moreover, Kanin had known Fanny Brice and, more important, had a clear understanding of Stark's vision. What he *didn't* have was much experience as a stage director, particularly as a director of musicals. His one major foray into the field had been on another Styne musical, *Do Re Mi*. Stark hired Carol Haney as his choreographer. She had enough experience for both of them, or so it was believed. But even Garson Kanin and Carol Haney together paled next to Bob Fosse and Jerome Robbins individually.

Isobel Lennart's script was rewritten by everyone who touched it. The bulk of the book concentrated on the courtship, marriage, and separation of Fanny Brice and her second husband, gambler Nicky Arnstein, with Fanny's rise to stardom in the Ziegfeld Follies providing a colorful, entertaining backdrop.

Some of the problems with the story were endemic. The journey, after all, is always more interesting than the destination. Translated, in show terms, it meant a strong first act and not much of a second act. Compounding the problem, the real-life Nicky Arnstein was still alive, threatening litigation if slandered.

Thus, not only was the character of Fanny Brice sanitized beyond recognition (even reference to her first marriage was obliterated) at the insistent behest of Fran Stark, so too was the character of Nicky Arnstein. Fortunately, this trifling with truth did only minimal damage to the beginning of the show, because the first act was designed to exploit Fanny's talent and Arnstein's superficial charm. It was the second act, again, that suffered. In that act, the conflict—good girl in love with the wrong guy—needed to develop, explode, and come to satisfying resolution. As written, when Nicky returns to Fanny from Sing Sing—he was convicted of embezzlement—there seems to be no reason why they cannot resume their life together. He lamely informs Fanny, with suave, leading-man urbanity, that he is simply no good for her instead of finally conceding his true nature, that of a no-good philandering heel and con artist.

Furthermore, Ray Stark could not use any of the original Brice material, which was either unavailable or deemed too dated. To the great disappointment of many, and to Fran Stark in particular, the legal rights to "My Man," Brice's musical signature, were tied up and the song was unavailable for use in the show. In life, Fanny had performed the song on Broadway just after Nick was sent away to prison. With everyone aware of her personal tragedy, Fanny's audience wept in sympathy. The song was thought to be pivotal to the musical biography of her life, and its loss dealt a blow to the Starks and sent Merrill and Styne scrambling to come up with a suitable replacement.

Another perceived loss was David Merrick's defection. In a power struggle over the show's creative reins, tension escalated between Stark and Merrick, and Merrick, perhaps the most prolific of all Broadway producers, added his name to the show's remarkable and expanding list of theatrical heavyweights who had come and gone.

David Merrick's departure nearly closed the show before it began. It seems that Merrick and not Stark had signed Barbra to her contract. When Merrick left, his contract went with him. Without a contract, Stark had no Streisand and, probably, no show. When she learned of this situation, Barbra and her managers engaged in a little renegotiation hardball. She *was* willing to sign another contract with Stark, but on her terms. She wanted a substantial increase in her weekly salary, a chauffeured limousine to take her to and from performances, the services of her own personal hairdresser, and daily complimentary meals for two. Stark, a shrewd businessman himself, failed to capitulate and called Barbra's bluff. She ended up getting a minimal salary increase, to a reported five thousand dollars a week, and little else.

With "My Man" excised from the score, the show was in need of a new title. Isobel Lennart suggested her original screenplay title of *Fanny,* but there had been Harold Rome's 1954 Broadway hit of the same name, with Ezio Pinza. *The Fanny Brice Story* was another possibility, but it was deemed that not enough ticket buyers would remember Fanny Brice. Besides, it was slightly pretentious and suggested serious drama (à la *The Story of Louis Pasteur*) instead of musical comedy. Before making his final exit from the show, it was David Merrick who bestowed the production with the simple, unserious title that would eventually light up marquees all over the world.

Fourteen

Under the Hot Glare of an Awaiting Marquee

Funny Girl went into rehearsals at the Winter Garden Theater with a sense of history and a good deal of uncertainty. In December 1936, twenty-seven years before, Fanny Brice had made her final New York appearance in the Ziegfeld Follies on the very same stage. Playing Nicky Arnstein was Sydney Chaplin. Besides being the son of the famed Charlie Chaplin, Sydney was a musical comedy leading man of some note (he had previously starred in Jule Styne's *Bells Are Ringing* and *Subways Are for Sleeping*). As for the uncertainty, it was hardly a secret within the company that the show had a troubled book, an inexperienced producer as well as a Broadway director with only one other musical to his credit, and a singer who had yet to prove she could develop and sustain a characterization. Barbra showed up late on the first day, smacking her chewing gum and affecting her trademark nonchalance.

Eager to jump right in, Kanin handed Barbra one of the songs from the score. She took the gum out of her mouth, placed it in the palm of Kanin's hand, and sang. It was the old trick from the Streisand repertoire, faking a jab with the left, and delivering a knockout blow with the right.

But while such gimmicks were effective in a nightclub act, or even in an audition, they would not sustain a Broadway show. Ashley Feinstein attended an early run-through of the show, accompanied by Barbra's *Wholesale* director, Arthur Laurents. "We were sitting next to Garson

159

Kanin and [his wife] Ruth Gordon," Feinstein relates, "and Arthur thought that Barbra wasn't so great in the show." The fact of the matter was that, for all her cocky bravado, Barbra had no experience and no technique as an actress. What she *did* have, innately, was a stunning singing voice, good stage presence, remarkably expressive hands, and impeccable comic timing.

It became very clear, at least to Barbra herself, that those innate gifts would *not* be enough. "It's a great opportunity for an actress," she said. "[Fanny] goes from a kid who believes in herself, trying to make it as an actress, to a woman who has a great love affair, and marries, and has children, and then it all falls apart. Very sad. It has everything. Comedy, acting, singing, dancing." Barbra added, "She's a *woman* onstage."

And so, of her own volition, Barbra decided to again solicit the help of Allan Miller. She did so with reluctance. After Miller, months before, had given her enormous help through her multiple auditions, she had never bothered to call him back.

Allan Miller's eventual contributions to Barbra's performance in *Funny Girl* would be considerable. They would also be, for the most part, unheralded.

"Too many people want to perpetuate the myth," Miller explains. "The myth that Barbra was just this glowing, flowing creature who arose from the half-shell. In singing terms, that was true. But, it wasn't true in acting terms. And it would have helped an awful lot of young people who were such admirers of hers to know that she had to work her ass off every day, every night, for thirteen weeks and more to get to that performance in *Funny Girl*."

It was Barbra's manager Marty Erlichman who summoned Miller. "I had read about the production being put together with Garson Kanin," Miller recalls, "and I was pretty miffed that I had not heard a word from Barbra. Then, on the tenth day of rehearsal—it was a few days before Christmas—Marty Erlichman called me up and said, 'Hi, Allan. You know, Barbra's really missed you a lot.' I remember covering the phone and yelling to my wife, 'They're calling! They're calling! *Goddamnit*, they're calling!'

"Barbra used to call every once in a while for a quick fix," Miller continues. "With 'Miss Marmelstein,' she would call up at two o'clock in the morning and say, 'Listen, y'know, *this thing* isn't working anymore. What should I do?' And I would give her a coaching session over the phone. So when Marty called, I figured she wanted a very quick something before they went out of town [for tryouts], and I had sworn that I wasn't gonna do that.

"So Marty went on and on. And then he said, 'I've gotta tell you the truth. There seems to be only one person who seems to know how to really get her to work her best. And the show is in trouble now, and Barbra wanted to know, you know, if you could come down and take a look.' And I said, 'Take a look, and then what?' And he said, 'Well, you know, uh, then we'll make an arrangement.' And I said, 'Okay, when?' And he said," Miller recalls with a laugh, " 'Well, can you come down tonight?'

"So, I went over there and they were already in *run-throughs!* For a major musical, ten days into rehearsal, it was a travesty. The show was in shambles. The whole damn thing was an utter mess.

"Afterwards, Barbra, Marty, myself, and I forget who else—I think Elliott—went to a Chinese restaurant and ordered a bunch of food. Then we continued in her apartment while I kept going over detail after detail after detail after detail as to what I thought needed to be done with the show. Barbra was saying, 'Oh, yes! Yes, right! Yes!' And she'd say, 'What about this or that?' And I'd say what I thought about that. And she'd say, 'Yeah, right. Okay, right.' This went on for three hours, at the end of which she said, 'I've *gotta* have you help me on this. I'm gonna call Ray Stark and let him know that I need your help, and we'll make an arrangement. Okay?' And she gave me a big hug and a kiss good night, and off I went.

"The next day, Marty called me up and said, 'Ray said, "Okay, if you need him, fine, *but don't tell anybody.* I don't want Garson to be upset. You have to introduce him as your cousin, or whatever." ' He made it very clear that I was not to say anything or do anything that would throw attention to the fact that I was there to coach her. And then Marty offered me a [financial] deal which was the worst deal that I could possibly imagine. Finally, after going back and forth twice with Marty, he expressed to me that Barbra felt very—'Well, she'll tell you,' he said, and then she got on the phone and said, 'Y'know, I feel funny, uh, talking money with you. I mean, you're like my father. It's like paying my father.' I said, 'Well, Barbra, even daddies have to eat.' And she said, 'Whatever. Whatever you need.' But, she *hated* what I asked for [and eventually got].

"So I started coming in to see what I could do," Miller continues. "When I was brought into the theater, Barbra would introduce me as her 'lawyer-cousin from California.' And I remember Jule Styne and some of the chorus people coming over and saying to me, 'So, what do you think of show business?'

"We had our first actual rehearsal using the ladies' room of the theater. Sydney Chaplin's wife, a beautiful dancer named Noelle, stood guard outside the rest room door while I rehearsed with both Barbra and Sydney. That didn't go on for very long. They decided that it was better that I work exclusively with Barbra, because if anything happened, they didn't want any reverberations about it. But Sydney was a sweetheart."

Barbra, apparently, thought so too. At least early in the run-throughs and during out-of-town tryouts. In fact, the rumor was that Chaplin and the still-newlywed Barbra, only four months into her marriage, were seeing each other. Chaplin, although also married, was known around town as quite a ladies' man. Broadway columnist Radie Harris later reported, "Sydney had the same irresistible fascination for women that Nicky [Arnstein] had. Judy Holliday had gone bonkers about Sydney when he was her leading man in *Bells Are Ringing*. She really hoped there would be wedding bells. Kay Kendall was 'mad about the boy.' So was Joan Collins. Now along came Barbra, and she flipped too. In the pre-Broadway tryout, the backstage gossip, where all the best leaks come from, was that when Barbra sang 'People who need people are the luckiest people in the world,' she was singing her heart out to Chaplin."

When a friend of Barbra's saw the show during the out-of-town tryouts, he was exposed to the purported affair firsthand. It seems that when he opened Barbra's dressing room door, she and Chaplin jumped rather hurriedly off the sofa. Says the friend, "They looked like lovers caught in the act."

Royce Wallace, the actress who played Fanny's dresser-maid-confidante, was probably the cast member with whom Barbra felt closest. Of the alleged affair with Chaplin, she says, "That was the rumor, it was. I know he *adored* her." Wallace adds that sightings of Chaplin's wife during the production were scarce, and that Chaplin "was always [acting] like a bachelor. Everybody had their eyes open and saw little things [between Barbra and Chaplin]. They used to go out to dinner, supposedly to talk about the show."

As Barbra packed her bags for the out-of-town tryouts in Boston, she was given a morale boost by winning what was described at the time as her first major award. She accepted her prize in a ceremony in the Embassy Room of the Hotel Gotham on December 27. It was presented to her by the editors of *Cue* magazine, in recognition of the quality and sales of her first two albums, as well as the nightclub and television appearances she had made throughout 1963. Upon accepting the award,

Barbra stepped to the microphone and quipped, "It was very nice of the editors of *Cue* magazine to get me out an hour before rehearsal was over."

The award was for the "Entertainer of the Year." Barbra had yet to *star* on Broadway, in movies, or in television. She was twenty-one years old.

The whispers started in Boston. They were hushed at first, but in the weeks that followed, they grew to a roar that hovered over the production: *Funny Girl* was a disaster. Says Lee Allen, who was later cast as Eddie Ryan, Fanny's friend, "In Boston, the word was out that this show was never gonna make it to New York."

In retrospect, it's easy to understand the dismay. *Time* magazine would refer to it as "one of the most fussed-over, reworked, overmanaged, multi-directed Broadway productions ever." All the signs of a flop were there, and they were not without foundation. "We all knew that the show was a turkey as it stood," says Buzz Miller, the company's principal dancer.

Not surprisingly, the book continued to frustrate everyone involved. John Patrick, who wrote Ray Stark's *The World of Suzie Wong,* and later Norman Krasna, were brought in to "doctor" the script. Early in the Boston run, the show was *not* structured in flashback, as it later would be, nor did it provide Barbra's Fanny with her now memorable opening line, "Hello, gorgeous." As for the second act, Nick goes on trial and is sentenced to jail. At the same time, Fanny announces that she is going to have another baby. After Nick is taken away and imprisoned, Fanny launches into the "My Man" replacement, "The Music I Dance To," later altered to "[His Is] The Music That Makes Me Dance." Time passes and Nick returns from jail, only to tell Fanny that he is leaving her. She slaps him as he makes his way out the door. More time passes. Fanny has her baby and her divorce. Finally, she returns to Ziegfeld and the Broadway stage and sings the finale, which was then a reprise of "People."

The show ran for almost *four* hours, with Act 2, in particular, an interminable drag. On opening night at the Shubert Theater in Boston, an embarrassing exodus of ticket buyers left well before the closing curtain. Some departed to catch the last train home. Others were simply bored.

"It *was* pretty bad," recalls Luther Henderson, the show's dance orchestrator. "It just wasn't making it. It wasn't coming over. We were getting no reaction."

The following morning, Kanin, Lennart, Styne, and Merrill met in an attempt to salvage the production. At *that* night's performance, *Funny Girl* was trimmed a full twenty minutes.

Numbers were juggled, and the cuts continued. Slashed from the entire show was the role of Georgia, the prettiest of the Ziegfeld girls and the show's second female lead. There were those in the company who believed that it was the best part in the musical. As one of the actors says, "She [Georgia] was the only character you cared about."

The rest of the company said their goodbyes to Allyn McLerie, the actress who played the part, as she returned to New York, devastated by the abrupt dismissal. "Allyn was a terrific girl," recalls Buzz Miller. "Everybody loved her."

No one was spared. "I had a number with Sydney called 'Temporary Arrangement,' Buzz Miller recalls. "It was a soft-shoe, and Sydney freaked because he couldn't dance. So my big song-and-dance number went out the window. It lasted one performance."

Songs were written, dances were devised, sets were constructed, and costumes were designed—all for production numbers that were trashed and tossed by the wayside. Reportedly, thirty thousand dollars worth of sets alone were thrown away while the show was revised on the road.

Meanwhile, Styne and Merrill composed songs at a furious pace, and discarded them with equal abandon. They would end up writing at least twice as many songs as were finally used. Among those rejected during out-of-town tryouts were "Absent Minded Me" and "Funny Girl" (*not* the title song later used in the film), both of which were eventually included on Barbra's *People* album.

Some members of the company believed that Barbra was partially responsible for the show's failings. "She was *not* coming across," contends one of the actors. "The audience didn't like her." It was Ruth Gordon, Kanin's wife, who came up with the one-line critique that circulated backstage. "Barbra is great," Gordon said, "but she is not yet good."

Part of the problem was due to her projection. As Barbra would herself later acknowledge, "I *never* played to the balcony. I always played to the best seat in the theater."

In fact, early into the rehearsals, Ray Stark had wanted to fire Barbra for, among other reasons, her lack of projection. The matter was resolved by tucking a battery-operated microphone into her bra. It was a humiliating affront to her pride to have to artificially amplify her voice. Furthermore, legend has it that during a performance, strange, muffled voices, audible to those in the front row, began emerging out of the talking brassiere. It seems that the sensitive device was picking up signals from a local police radio.

But it was not her lack of projection that posed Barbra's biggest problem. It was her lack of *characterization*. "There was no character work whatsoever," attests Allan Miller, who accompanied Barbra on the road. "There was no difference between the way she behaved with her first dancing partner, from the way she behaved with her family, from the way she behaved with Nicky Arnstein. And with each singing number, she would stand there like she was at a microphone in a nightclub. She was very stiff, very static. There was nothing wrong with her singing voice. She sang beautifully. And there was nothing wrong with her acting instrument, except that the director and/or Barbra was unable to bring the character to life.

"I'll give you a for-instance," Miller goes on. "One of the first things I talked to her about was the kind of behavior that she has on the street. Fanny doesn't know anything about boy-girl relationships. She's only been with this one guy [Eddie Ryan] as a dancing partner. So I suggested that she treat him like she was a fellow boy, that she be tomboyish, and that there be little punches, digs, and kicks [between them]. Also, that she have ways of saying things that were much more *street* than how she would later say them.

"In the scene where she has her first success at this seedy little nightclub," Miller recalls, "I said to Barbra, 'By opening night, how long do you think you've been *living* in those dancing shoes?' And she said, 'I probably didn't take them off.' And I said, 'That's right. What do you think your feet feel like right now?' And she said, 'Oh my God! They're *swollen!*' So after doing the number in the scene, she went into her dressing room, whipped those shoes off, and started to massage her feet. It wasn't in the lines. She had no lines about her feet. But it was so unexpected, it was funny.

"Then I said to Barbra, 'Well, how are you gonna walk out of the restaurant?' She said, 'Whaddya mean?' I said, 'Well, your feet are killing you.' And she said, 'Yeah . . . ?' And I said, 'So . . . ?' And then she said, 'Well, I guess I'll have to crawl.' And I said, 'That's right. And what are you gonna do with your dancing shoes?'

"So, in the scene, after this great night, she's walking on the floor on all fours, with her shoes hanging around her neck, and then there's this guy [Nicky Arnstein] standing in front of her. She sees only his legs. She looks up and there's this gorgeous-looking guy and she says, 'Gorgeous.'

So I said to Barbra, 'How do you think you're gonna account for the fact that you're down crawling on your hands and knees?' And she said, 'Uh . . . ?' And I said, 'Well, you better pretend that you're making believe you're a dog or something.' So the next time they did the scene, Barbra bumps into the guy's legs, looks up, and barks, 'ruff-ruff' and the guy cracks up. And *then* Barbra says, 'Gorgeous.' So, you have this behavior, based on real things, that simply wasn't in the performance before we started working together.

"Without literally being there to say, 'Move here, move there,' I staged almost 85 percent of what Barbra did in the show," Miller contends. He is quick to add, "I have to amend that to say, *'We* [Barbra and I] staged 85 percent of her performance in the show.' "

When asked how Garson Kanin (he was, after all, the director) felt about the outside contributions, Miller replies, "He knew by then that she was working with somebody. And he said to her, 'Sweetheart, whatever the good things are that you are doing up there, *I'll* get credit for. So go ahead.' I think he deeply appreciated some of the stuff that she was bringing in. But," says Miller, "I never had any discussion with him. I never had any meeting with him. As a matter of fact, he even insisted that I couldn't even come into the theater until *after* he had been seated."

Miller's contributions were not limited to the straight scenes. "They were going to throw the song 'People,' out of the show," Miller recalls. "I didn't work on the songs with Barbra until after the first two weeks. I concentrated only on her relationships and her behavior with various people in acting terms. Then I said, 'Hey, listen, we've gotta start working on some of these songs.' And she said, 'Whatsa matter?' I said, 'You're standing there like you're at a microphone in a nightclub. There's no behavior.' And she said, 'Well, so, like what song?' And I said, 'Well, like "People." ' " And she said, 'Oh, well, that song's not working.' I said, 'Of course it's not working.' "

Much to the ire of Jule Styne, who was still convinced that he had a blockbuster record on his hands, there *was* talk about cutting "People" from the show. It was too static, and it didn't seem to make much sense in the context of the rest of the show. Preceding the number, Fanny's mother is hosting a block party to celebrate her daughter's first stage success. Outside on the street, Fanny finds herself alone for the first time with Nicky Arnstein, and she launches into the introduction to, and opening bars of, the song about people needing people. But *where* were all the people?

Allan Miller continues. "So I said to her, 'What happened to all of these people at the party?' She said, 'They went home. The party was over.' I said, 'No, the party just began.' And she said, 'Oh, yeah. . . . So?' So I said, *'Why* did all the those neighborhood mothers go home so early in the party? What happened?' She said, 'Well, nothing happened.' And then she went, *'Oh!* He . . . he?' And I said, *'Yes!* Prince Charming. This beautiful-looking rich guy comes walking into your party, right? And then all these mothers very quickly said, 'Hello, hello, hello,' and then left. So where are they now?' And Barbra looked up at the windows. And I said, 'That's right. That's where they are. They're watching every move that you make. So how are you going to *behave* now that you know they're all up there watching you alone with this guy?' She said, 'Yeah, yeah, right, right.' I said, 'Use the stoop, go up the steps, lean over the railing. Behave like the kid on the block for a little while. Use the chalk thing that they use for a street game [hopscotch], walk along the line for a while *until* you get to the section of the song where it's about two people, two very special people. And then forget about *them* and make it about just the two of you.

"Barbra was very daring, and she was eager to get these things tried out onstage," Miller says. "She had no time to practice it with the orchestra, but she put it in the show the next night. It nearly killed the orchestra conductor, Milton Rosenstock, who had his baton poised for the regular way [the number was performed]. Then all of a sudden, Barbra turns around and is walking up and down these chalk marks and then going up the stoop and singing! And he had a quick race to try to get the orchestra to catch up with her. She was doing it almost a cappella at that point. And the audience got it right away. They started giggling at her antics. And Sydney Chaplin, who had never seen her do this, was awestruck. He just stared at her, because he didn't know what the heck she was gonna do next. Neither did Milton Rosenstock, who had to keep following her because Barbra didn't turn around to look at him.

"Then, in the middle of the song, she turned it into this 'two people' thing. She was leaning over the railing of the stoop, like a kid on the block, but she couldn't keep from expressing some of her romantic yearnings toward this guy. When she finished singing, he took off his hat and bowed to her like she was the lady of his dreams. And the audience was on their feet. And the roar of approval for keeping the number in the show was written that night."

For the record, others contend that the number remained in jeopardy until the show opened a few weeks later in Philadelphia, when the single, which Barbra had recorded back in New York at Styne's incessant urging, began to get airplay on the local radio stations. Nevertheless, there is no doubt that the "behavior" incorporated by Barbra, devised in tandem with Miller, added greatly to the number's eventual success and popularity.

Still, the company's management did not accept Barbra's radical changes without at least some semblance of struggle. Styne reportedly groused that the new staging detracted from his lyrics. And Milton Rosenstock, an old pro who was used to doing things in the conventional way, bemoaned that he had to work overtime to keep up with his decidedly unconventional young star.

"That night, after the show," Miller says, "Milton comes back into Barbra's dressing room. He was a very nice man and a terrifically experienced and able conductor. He knocks on her door—I was inside with her—and she says, 'Come on in.' He says, 'Sweetheart, can I just talk to you?' He was drenched in perspiration. She says, 'Sure.' And he says, 'Barbra, do you know how many people are in this orchestra?' She says, 'No, why? What are you getting at?' He says, 'There are about forty. Do you know what their average age is?' She says, 'What are you trying to tell me?' He says, 'They're all in their forties and fifties, and do you know what they've been doing all of their adult lives?' She says, 'No, I give up. *What?*' And he says, *'They've been waiting to play for you.* Now, *how* can they play for you if *I* don't know what you're going to do?'

"Barbra really listened to him, because she liked him a lot," Miller adds. "But she says, 'Milton, can I ask *you* something?' And he says, 'Sure. Of course. I haven't upset you?' And she says, 'No, no. I just want to ask you something.' And he says, 'What?' She says, 'What do you do most of the time out there, you know, in between numbers? Do you go away?' He says, 'Of course not. I'm right there.' She says, 'So, you watch the whole show?' He says, 'Of course.' She says, 'So, *you* see *me* all the time?' He says, 'Yeah, of course.' She says, 'So? *Why can't you play when I sing?*' And he says, 'Okay, okay. I'm sorry, I'm sorry. I didn't mean to upset you.'

"And Barbra says, 'You didn't upset me. I'm just wondering. You're there [in the orchestra pit]. You see me. I have to turn around and find you. It's dark, and I'm busy working onstage. Why can't you just play when I sing?' And he says, 'Okay. You're right.' And he backed out apologizing.

"The next night, he came *storming* back into the dressing room, all aglow. He looked ten years younger. And he says, 'You were absolutely right! Why can't I follow what you're doing? There's no reason! You sing! You do whatever you want to do! I'll get that orchestra to play!' "

There was a similar problem with another one of the numbers. Barbra took to regularly improvising the melody of "Sadie, Sadie, Married Lady," Styne and Merrill's tribute to Jewish brides everywhere. In this song, the chorus accompanied Barbra, and when she improvised, the chorus was thrown out of whack.

One night, after the performance, Marvin Hamlisch, the show's young assistant vocal arranger, decided to confront Barbra, of whom he was in awe. "I got up my courage and went to see Barbra in her dressing room," Hamlisch later recalled. "I may have overstepped my bounds here, but I couldn't help telling her that by altering the song, she was throwing off the music of the chorus.

"Barbra looked at me as though she had just landed on Plymouth Rock and I had just crawled out from under it. 'Marvin,' she said, 'what are these people [the audience] paying money to hear—your vocal arrangements?' "

It was the same problem she had had on *Harry Stoones,* and again on *Wholesale.* She either wouldn't or couldn't do a song the same way night after night. But, instead of arrogance or boredom, *Funny Girl*'s dance orchestrator, Luther Henderson, who has, in his time, worked with a good many stars, suggests another possible reason for Barbra's seeming impertinence.

"In the theater, we *do* expect to have things done the same way each time," Henderson says. "This is one of the reasons that jazz music, or the *essence* of jazz music, is sometimes difficult [to adapt to the theater], because its existence depends on individual performance and individual interpretation. I think that that's what Barbra does. She has, and gives, that kind of adrenaline [found in jazz music]. And, not surprisingly, she doesn't seem to have a way of doing it if she's constrained to doing it exactly the same way each time.

"Gregory Hines [with whom Henderson had just finished working— on *Jelly's Last Jam*—at the time of this writing] has the kind of discipline that he *can* do eight shows a week the same with no changes. He understands the demands of the theater and is willing to deal with them and is willing to obey them to a certain extent. And when you write for a person like that, you have to write with little patches of leeway and say [to them], 'I'll give you four bars here. Go for yourself!'

"Barbra Streisand is a jazz singer," Henderson continues, "quite apart, quite different from Julie Andrews, who is also fantastic. Quite different from Mary Martin. You would expect that she might even do a little Ella Fitzgerald scat if she dared, you know?"

Costs were mounting. The clock was ticking. The pressures of producing a major Broadway musical were beginning to take their toll. The show, it seemed, was in a perpetual state of disarray. Stark delayed the New York opening. In try-outs, first in Boston, then in Philadelphia, infighting was the order of the increasingly long days. Nerves were frayed, angry words exchanged. Director Garson Kanin fought with librettist Isobel Lennart. Lennart fought with writer John Patrick. Choreographer Carol Haney fought with composer Jule Styne. Styne fought with Kanin. Kanin fought long-distance with producer Ray Stark. Stark made regular "drop-in" visits from Puerto Vallarta (where he was shooting *The Night of the Iguana* with Richard Burton, Deborah Kerr and Ava Gardner) to assess the show's progress and do his fighting in person.

"It got really strange there," recalls cast member Royce Wallace, who played Fanny's dresser and maid. "There was a lot of bickering in the upper echelon over what was right and *who* was right. You could feel that they were not all in it together. We [the actors] sat around quite a bit, and they'd go in a room and try to get things together. Then they'd come out, and we'd say, 'Okay, maybe *now* we're going to work.' But then we'd start to do something, and they would just go back into the room again. [For most of the actors] it was a lot of sitting around."

While others wilted, under the hot glare of an awaiting marquee, Barbra Streisand thrived. Bombarded with a deluge of constant rewrites, restaging, and new and revised songs to learn, she excelled. By opening night on Broadway, the final scene alone would undergo *forty-two* rewrites. And the one she ended up playing on opening night was a revision she had learned earlier that same day. These were the conditions, haphazard though they may be, that allowed her the constant change and exploration she craved.

Not that she always agreed with the changes. Upon reading a revision, Barbra reacted immediately, instinctively. Sometimes she did so with enthusiasm; other times, with violent opposition. When her opinions were overruled, she often responded with stubborn petulance. She wanted to do things the way she wanted. But she was always bold, never afraid to venture forth and try anything. The challenge, in and of itself, was intoxicating.

As for the backstage infighting, Barbra shrugged it off. It was all, in her view, a prerequisite part of the creative process. Let the best man—or woman—stand and take his or her bows during the curtain calls. Her spirited sparring was directed primarily at Kanin.

"They argued quite a bit," relates Royce Wallace. It was, mind you, nothing personal. Anyone or anything was fair game, all in the name of putting on a good show.

As dance orchestrator Luther Henderson asserts, "Find me a theater piece that's really a great piece, in which there has *not* been a power struggle. There's got to be one. There's no way for a strong director and a strong actor or actress not to clash."

By all accounts, Streisand worked tirelessly. Her commitment to the show was absolute. "She hardly ever complained about anything," Allan Miller says. "She just took everything they threw at her, including more and more songs and longer and longer rehearsals. She had a slightly sore throat one time, but she sang right through it. She was nothing but game the whole time."

Garson Kanin, on the other hand, was not faring quite so well. "I don't think he knew what he was doing," Buzz Miller contends. Another dancer, Blair Hammond, concurs. "Unfortunately," Hammond says, "we had someone directing who really didn't know very much about directing a musical."

Royce Wallace adds in explanation, "I think he was overwhelmed by Barbra. She was a strong lady." Allan Miller is more charitable than the others. "Garson Kanin is a superb director for certain things, but he just didn't seem to get going with this one. Nobody knows why, including me."

And so, reportedly at Barbra's request, Ray Stark made the decision to oust Kanin from the show when it moved from Boston to Philadelphia, where it would play at the Forrest and Erlanger theaters. His replacement was Jerome Robbins.

"Robbins had obviously heard how terrific Barbra was getting to be in the show," Allan Miller says, "and was talked into coming to take a look. Later, he admitted to me that if he hadn't seen how much she had done with the part, he wouldn't have come back at all."

Even so, Robbins did not come cheaply. He reportedly demanded, and got, the then substantial sum of one thousand dollars per day. He also requested a "Directed by" credit. Kanin, however, refused to relinquish his credit. He had, after all, expended an enormous amount of time and energy on the show and had gotten it into presentable shape. Negotiations went back and forth until all parties finally agreed that

Robbins would receive a "Production Supervised by" credit. With that problem resolved, Robbins's return would bring the show full circle, and into its hectic homestretch.

The new director's intentions rapidly became apparent. "Accentuate the positive," or so the song suggests. It was a premise which Robbins vigorously advocated, with "the positive" in this case being Barbra, Barbra, and more Barbra. It mattered little that the show had become less true to its subject. Robbins tightened and trimmed what and where he could, while anything that didn't serve his star was reworked or eliminated.

"He tightened the show and cut my number to ribbons," relates Buzz Miller, the company's principal dancer. "I played in a number called 'Cornet Man,' and he changed it entirely, because it was not good for Barbra. It was completely revised so she didn't look like she was standing there with egg on her face. See, Barbra was not really a dancer. She clapped her hands and stomped her feet. The number was a tour de force for myself, but it was wrong for the show. I understood it, but I hated it."

More of Streisand meant less of everyone else. Naturally, there were some in the company who were none too happy about it. Danny Meehan, as Eddie Ryan, the second male lead, became distraught when his showcase solo was axed. It was a pivotal number which established Eddie's more than friendly feelings for Fanny.

"It's a song I would have *loved* to have done," exclaims Lee Allen, who later took over the role. "It's an embarrassing moment for Eddie. Fanny's mother is using him as a model, and he's got this dress on. He's standing up on a chair, and she is pinning him up. Fanny walks in on the scene, and she treats him like, you know, just an ordinary guy. She doesn't realize how badly he feels about her. She leaves and he's standing there with egg on his face. He just sits down on that same chair that he's been standing on, in that ridiculous dress, and he starts to sing the song. The title says it all. It was called 'I'd Be Good for Her.' "

But the actor most devastated by the incessant cuts was Sydney Chaplin, who watched helplessly as his role of Nicky Arnstein was reduced to a one-dimensional character. The second-act trial, which helped to establish his torment and hence his supposed motivation for leaving Fanny, was cut. So too was the one song which enabled him to elicit sympathy from the audience.

Marc Jordan, who played Mr. Renaldi in the show, recalls, "Sydney had one gorgeous song that I really loved. I was sorry to see it go. It was a song that he sang to the baby in the cradle. It was a lullaby with a bitter [edge] because it ended up referring to the baby's father as 'Mr. Fanny Brice.' "

In fact, *all* of Chaplin's second-act songs would eventually be excised from the show.

But Chaplin, like the other victims of the cuts, tried to remain silent and retain his composure for the sake of the show. "There were rumblings," relates Buzz Miller, "that 'this is working for Barbra. And if it works for her, it works for all of us.' "

And the roles continued to blur.

Was it Brice, or was it Barbra? After a while, no one was really quite sure. Despite her claims to the contrary, Barbra had in fact listened to the old Brice recordings. She further researched the part, again despite her claims to the contrary, by studying Brice's papers, to which she had been given access. During her preparations, Barbra delighted in discovering similarities between herself and her subject. It seemed to indicate that she was destined to play the part.

"The show is fate," she exclaimed. "The play is really about me. It simply happened to happen before to Fanny Brice." She added, "I'm so much like the person it's incredible. Little, silly things. We both love the color white. We both grew up in Brooklyn, had typical mothers concerned about food and health and trying to marry us off. The way we work [is the same]. *I* choose my music, my clothes, everything. People tell me things. I couldn't listen to anybody. I had to do it myself. And here it is in the play. It's incredible. It's scary." Laughing, she added, "I'm waiting for Nicky Arnstein."

Jule Styne noted, "Fanny and Barbra have this in common: You root for them, you think each is playing straight at you. You think each is beautiful, although neither is or was."

Aware of his distinguished success, Barbra took to Robbins immediately. It didn't hurt, of course, that she agreed with his general premise: that *Funny Girl* would stand—or fall—on the basis of her performance.

As the weeks passed and the tryouts in Philadelphia progressed, Robbins became increasingly intent on pumping yet even more of Barbra into the show.

"The 'injecting of Barbra,' " recalls Allan Miller, "was done in every scene. There was marked behavior that came from she and I working things out for the role. These became key things [mannerisms, phrasings, attitudes] that people would later say about Barbra Streisand. But,"

Miller adds, "she created these things for this part."

Perhaps the best example was achieved with the "You Are Woman, I Am Man" number in which Nicky Arnstein seduces Fanny in his private dining room–turned–bedroom. It is significant to note that at that time, not only was the number Sydney Chaplin's, it was also, given the many cuts his character had suffered, his *only* remaining solo in the show.

Previously, the song had been played as a straight seduction scene, with Chaplin exuding all the masculine charm he could muster. However, the number wasn't going over with the audience. Frankly, they wanted Barbra, not Chaplin, and they resented the distraction. To his credit, Robbins recognized the problem. The solution, however, was another matter. *How* does one go about handing the stage over to Barbra in what was designed to be Chaplin's big moment?

"When I saw the number on the tenth day of rehearsal," recalls Allan Miller, "Barbra just kind of stood there. Sydney said his things, Barbra said her things, and she tried to behave a little nervously, a little uncomfortably, and that was it! So, what I said to Barbra was, 'How does this girl know anything about romantic behavior? Where would she have seen any? Her family?' And I said, 'No. So, where would she see any?' And Barbra said, 'The movies?' And I said, 'That's *exactly* where she would see it! So *who* would she try to be like in the movies?' And Barbra said, 'Well, uh . . .' And I said, 'Well, she was known as a comedienne, right? So who are the ones who make fun of romance in the movies?' And Barbra said, 'Well, I don't know. Marie Dressler and W. C. Fields?' And I said, 'Exactly.' So Barbra made a list of eight or ten different movie stars that she, Fanny Brice, would have seen and liked. And so when she did the scene, she would go from Mae West to Marie Dressler to W. C. Fields to Greta Garbo, the whole gamut of them [Miller laughs], without deciding which one should stay there. It was there in the way she would try to drink the drink. In the way she would try to light the cigarette. In the way she would try to sit down. And," Miller adds, "the scene became just *blazingly* alive when she did it onstage."

The audience loved it. Almost overnight, Chaplin's romantic seduction scene had turned into Barbra's *comic* seduction scene. Robbins wanted to take it even further. "He insisted that Robert Merrill and Jule Styne expand the song," Allan Miller recalls, "and incorporate [into the lyrics] some of these crazy, zany things that Barbra was doing. The whole phrase of 'Would a convent take a Jewish girl' was *not* in the original version."

In its final revised form, the number became a duet which had Fanny unsuccessfully feigning sophistication ("A bit of pâté? I drink it all day") while fighting off Arnstein's advances and her own amorous urgings. The scene elicited the biggest laughs in the entire show. For Sydney Chaplin, it was the final and ultimate insult. For Barbra, it was another in a long line of victories.

On the road, with her guard down, she also had something of a personal breakthrough. With the help of Allan Miller, she had accomplished what many had thought she couldn't. She had developed and sustained a characterization. But according to Miller, she was still lacking what he terms an "emotional density."

One night, after a particularly arduous day, Barbra returned to her hotel suite and collapsed on the sofa. She was physically exhausted, and with good reason. The out-of-town tryouts were extended week after week as the show endured an onslaught of changes in preparation for its Broadway debut. The New York opening, in fact, would be postponed a total of *six* times, leading many in the industry to suspect that the show was in serious trouble.

On this particular night, Allan Miller showed up at Barbra's suite for his usual postperformance coaching session. Sensing an opportunity, he gently veered the usual conversation into a discussion of Barbra's family, about which she had previously been reticent. Was she looking forward to her mother being at her New York opening? Miller asked with an innocence that belied his true motivation. Too tired to protest what she considered to be the personal nature of the question, Barbra responded in the negative. Miller then unloaded the bomb. Would she have liked her father to be there? Would she have liked him to be able to see and hear, and appreciate, who and what his daughter had become?

Barbra nearly bolted off the sofa. Miller continued, "You know you've dreamt of what your father would have been like. What your life would have been like if he were alive and here to see you. . . ."

Barbra broke down in tears. It was one of the few times she had allowed herself such an overt expression over her father. Mastering the moment, Miller then asked her to sing one of the songs from the score, right there in the room. There was a catch. He wanted her to sing the song expressly for her father. Barbra was reluctant, but, wiping the tears from her face, she did as she was directed. After she finished, Miller took her hands in his and asked her to take it one step further. He asked her to dedicate her next performance of the show, her entire performance, to her father.

The following night, Barbra delivered what Miller hails as "the most glorious performance she ever gave. There was never a performance that matched that one. It was a major, major accomplishment for her, because up until that time, the emotional depths that she was capable of were pretty well hidden."

At that performance, Barbra looked out into the theater and imagined the face she had seen in photographs. Suddenly, he was *there,* watching her from the audience. During the course of the show, he listened. He laughed. He cried. But mostly he just watched as his only daughter poured forth her heart and captured an entire audience. Barbra would never forget that performance. Nor would she ever forget the imagined look in her father's eyes as they beamed back at her from the fourth row. They were kind, sensitive, intelligent. And that night, at that performance, they were aglow with pride.

Fifteen

Hello, Gorgeous

*S*he crosses the stage with a weary gait. With her mouth in a tight grimace and her joyless countenance, she appears to be an embittered woman who has traded in her life for a dream that did not deliver. Catching a glimpse of herself in her dressing room mirror, she speaks her opening half-line, "Hello, gorgeous," with undisguised sarcasm. Then she sheds the leopard coat she has been wearing, and as she does, she also removes the symbolism it conjures, and the story shifts into a flashback. Suddenly, she becomes an expressive, seemingly much younger woman, full of vigor and life and unabashed idealism. It is a remarkable transformation.

Such was the first part of the brilliantly conceived three-tiered introduction to Broadway audiences of Barbra Streisand as Fanny Brice. In the second part, the succinctly titled "If a Girl Isn't Pretty" is sung by Fanny's mother. She is accompanied by a group of cackling neighborhood Jewish ladies, all of whom denounce Fanny's show business aspirations. Their message is clear, as they sing with self-loathing, "If a girl isn't pretty, like a Miss Atlantic City," and if her "incidentals" are no more substantial than "two lentils," then her dreams of stardom are no more than delusions and should be discouraged. The words, of course, resonated with meaning for Barbra, echoing as they did those of her own mother. Onstage, the song provoked its share of laughs, but it also accomplished much more. It drew the audience into Fanny's corner by providing a glimpse of the formidable obstacles in her path. After uttering only a few words, and before singing a single note, Barbra's Fanny had already been established as the homely underdog and had won over the sympathy of the audience.

When she started to sing her first song, the final part of the elaborate introduction, the audience braced itself, hoping that she wouldn't be *too* bad. After all, if her own mother didn't have any faith in her, how could she be any good? With Barbra as Fanny, however, not only was she good, she was *stunning,* Oh-my-God-look-at-her good, and the audience was sent reeling and thrown for a loop. The song "I'm the Greatest Star," is certainly one of the shrewdest, most evocative, most effective introductory songs ever written for a potential new star. And although she sang it with a self-deprecating humor, there could be no doubt that Barbra, and Fanny, wholeheartedly believed in the title lyrics. Moreover, by the time she finished the song, lentils or no lentils, the audience was on its feet, believing in them too.

It was a dazzling introduction to the show, to Fanny, and most especially, to Barbra Streisand. And while there were additional moments, and individual songs ("Don't Rain on My Parade" and "The Music That Makes Me Dance"), of equal brilliance, on the night of March 26, 1964, at the Winter Garden theater, a major Broadway star was born with her very first song in the very first act of her very first starring role.

The show was a spectacular success, but an underrated score aside, there was no longer any internal struggle or doubt: *Funny Girl was* Barbra Streisand. In 1953, on that same Winter Garden stage, Rosalind Russell had taken Broadway by storm in *Wonderful Town.* Angela Lansbury would do the same in 1966 with *Mame.* But it is quite possible that in its entire history, the Winter Garden has never seen such an electrifying individual success as the one achieved by Barbra Streisand in *Funny Girl. Life* magazine would call it "unquestionably the single biggest personal triumph show business has seen in years." Even a raise in ticket prices couldn't keep audiences away. The price for a ticket to the show was $9.90, considerably more the previous $8.80. It was thought by many that the increase would signal the demise of the Broadway stage. Instead, the Winter Garden management had to add thirty-seven seats to the theater to accommodate the demand.

The opening night ovation for Barbra Streisand rocked the theater. Enthralled first-nighters refused to file dutifully into the street. They shouted, screamed, stomped. The girl who had begged for shards of approval from her mother and stepfather now had the exultant validation of an entire standing-room-only crowd. But not even an astounding *twenty-three* curtain calls could bring a sustained smile to her face. She was too overwhelmed by the crush of her now adoring public.

Backstage, she was literally mobbed, pushed, shoved, pulled, and tugged. She couldn't breathe, let alone reflect upon her success. The faces that pushed their way in her direction were a blur, and the voices that inevitably followed were lost in the relentless din. There were a few notable exceptions. Elliott gave her a hug and a kiss and took his seat in a corner. Ethel Merman bolted her way backstage and belted out her congratulations. And Lee Strasberg, who had previously rejected her as a member of his studio, bestowed upon Barbra what was for him the highest of praise. "Actually," he told her, "you were quite good."

At the postcelebration party at the Rainbow Room, the mayhem continued, with flashbulbs popping from every direction. Microphones were stuck into her face, her neck, her chest. And a sea of fans thrust pieces of paper into her hands, asking for her signature for aunts named Agnes. She was so deluged with demands for her signature, her smile, her eye contact, her snappy retort, that she could barely comprehend that it was Bette Davis, Angela Lansbury, and Sophie Tucker, among others, who were extolling her praises and clamoring for her company.

She would remember only fragments of what should have been the night of her life. She would vividly recall, however, her discussion with Fanny's former husband, Billy Rose, one of the guests at the party. "I understand I was married to you once," she teased upon greeting him. "How was I?"

Rose was quick to respond. "Great," he quipped, "for the first five years."

He then proceeded to inform Barbra that despite his earlier endorsement of her suitability for the part, she had proven him wrong. "No one in the world," he told her, "can play Fanny Brice."

The reviewers, for the most part, vehemently disagreed.

New York Times critic Howard Taubman found that "Miss Streisand is well on her way to becoming a splendid entertainer in her own right, and in *Funny Girl* she goes as far as any performer can toward recalling the laughter and joy that were Fanny Brice . . . Fanny and Barbra make the evening."

"If New York were Paris," wrote the critic for *Time*, "Broadway could temporarily consider renaming itself the Rue Streisand. Some stars merely brighten up a marquee: Barbra Streisand sets an entire theater ablaze."

Cue was even more euphoric, "Magnificent, sublime, radiant, extraordinary, electric—what puny little adjectives to describe Barbra Streisand. After all, she is merely the most talented performer on the musical comedy stage in the 1960's."

But such words were of little consolation to Barbra. It was almost as if they were all describing someone else. She would choose instead to instill greater importance in the few negative lines in otherwise positive reviews. Norman Nadel's comments in the *New York World-Telegram* were particularly disturbing. *"Funny Girl* comes up just this side of great," he praised. To Barbra's ire, he added, "A little more heart, a little more zing, *a little more Fanny Brice (correction: a lot more Fanny Brice)* and you'd have a bell-ringer in the musical which opened last night at the Winter Garden."

And even when a review was not necessarily intended to be negative, she would take it as such. "Everybody knew that Barbra Streisand would be a star," reported the *New York Herald Tribune*'s influential critic Walter Kerr, "and so she is."

Instead of basking in the afterglow of her triumph, Barbra, suspicious by nature, looked nervously over her shoulder for the impending doom that was bound to follow. Someone, she suspected, would try to take it all away. Perhaps that is why she chose not to express openly even some remote semblance of happiness over her success. She may have been afraid that if she did, she would be cursed and it would all vanish in midsentence.

The very day after her Broadway opening, she complained, "Now that I'm supposed to be a success, I'm worried about the responsibility. People will no longer be coming to see a new talent they've heard about. I now have to live up to their concept of a great success. I'm not the underdog, the homely kid from Brooklyn they can root for anymore. I'm fair game."

Those last three little words would be the hardest for her to accept. Arguably, she never has.

Without the arduous daily changes in the show to occupy both her mind and her time, Barbra turned to the business of decorating the luxurious penthouse apartment she shared with Elliott. She desired stately elegance, or so she informed her interior designer, Charles Murray, but she wanted it imprinted with her own unique, still-childlike persona. She was a dichotomy, even in her interior design. The showpiece in the place was an ornate three-hundred-year-old four-poster bed, which she had elevated on a platform like some shrine to the art of seduction. The bed was draped and skirted with olive-gold damask and enclosed with damask curtains hung from brass rods, to resemble, as Barbra described it, "a train berth." Not bad for the girl who had never had a real bed of her own, or for the young woman who, only a few years before, was sleeping on a portable army cot. Confounding the overall ambience of the room was the addition of a bedside mini-refrigerator stocked with Breyer's coffee ice cream bricks. To Barbra, success did not mean happiness. It meant indulging her late night cravings without having to get out of bed.

And so she entered the world of interior design with abandon and a thick wad of cash. "Sure, it's expensive," she told columnist Earl Wilson. "Everything good is expensive." She shopped, studied, shopped some more. And she learned everything she could about styles, periods, patterns, colors, fabrics, and the differences between Frank Lloyd Wright and Gustav Stickley. Predicted Charles Murray of his prodigious protégée, "Someday, she will be a great lady with great collections."

Her debut as a designer would eventually produce a pale mauve entranceway, a paisley kitchen, a formal dining room, a red patent leather bathroom, a burgundy-colored den with a grand piano (atop which lay a shawl, and on top of that, a childhood photo of herself), gold records and nude portraits on the walls, and *six* chandeliers hanging throughout, including one in the bathroom. It was the latter, in particular, along with the extravagant bed, that prompted visitors to comment, sometimes snidely and always behind her back, that the great new star had become at least slightly self-impressed and more than a little pretentious.

The sentiment was further fueled when Barbra purchased a Rolls Royce and, to accompany it, a uniformed chauffeur. But the car broke down or blew up, depending on the story, and the Goulds replaced it with an only slightly less ostentatious 1961 cream-colored Bentley. They also dismissed the chauffeur, although Elliott, for a laugh, occasionally donned the chauffeur's hat.

Befitting a star of her newfound stature, Barbra also hired a personal secretary, and a cook-maid named Mary, whose culinary specialty consisted of a fillet of sole stuffed with salmon, baked in sour cream, and topped with almonds. Often, though, the Goulds ate out. While Barbra's taste in other things was becoming decidedly rich—she offered one guest to her home a taste of caviar, informing the visitor that it cost forty-two dollars a pound—she still loved her take-out Chinese and her fast-food burgers. To her delight, during the run of *Funny Girl,* an all-night White Tower opened up on Forty-sixth Street, and sometimes, after a performance, Elliott would collect Barbra in the Bentley and they would dine on burgers and fries.

Sometimes, to vary the routine, they would go instead to Snacktime on Thirty-fourth Street for Nathan's hot dogs and corn on the cob, or to a little hideaway on Second Avenue for some late-night lemon sherbert. Usually, Barbra insisted on waiting for Elliott in the car, and when he returned, food in hand, they would feast to their belly's content in the backseat. Barbra had come to *loathe* being recognized, particularly when eating. Her most dreaded expression in the entire English language had become, without question, "Listen, I hate to bother you, but . . ."

"The other night I was dying to go to Leone's," Barbra confided at the time to Liz Smith. "You know, they sit you down at a table with a big hunk of cheese and fruit and raw vegetables and breadsticks. But I hadda go there on the night of a festival. The place was jammed, and even though the food was great—listen, they brought us hot chestnuts after, which flipped me—people kept coming up in a stream all through dinner and saying that same thing over and over: 'Listen, I hate to bother you, but will you sign this?' I wanted to say to them, 'If you hate to bother me, why do you? Why don't you just admit that you know you're bothering me and don't care?' To be disturbed when you're trying to eat—that's awful."

She added, "I do dig the steak Diane and chocolate soufflé at [the] '21' [Club], and who would bother you there? In that place, everybody is somebody."

With the exception of Garbo, there was possibly no other star so obviously uncomfortable in her suit of fame. The origins in part had to do with the breed of fan she had attracted. With *Funny Girl,* Barbra expanded her base of diehard fans from, largely, gay white men, to a broader segment of the population: the outsiders. Like it or not, and she *didn't,* she had become the face, and the voice, of the disenfranchised. Some would brand them societal losers. Barbra herself would refer to the more ardent among them as "the crazies."

She genuinely feared these fans, and tried to avoid them at all costs. Instead of making her nightly exits out of the theater from the side stage door, where her most avid admirers congregated, Barbra usually departed through the house, out the main lobby door.

"She was very, very uncomfortable with fans," recalls Blair Hammond. "She just couldn't deal with it. It wasn't in her personality."

One night, she was picked up by Ashley Feinstein, and together, they ventured out the ominous side exit. "There were people outside of the stage door," Feinstein recalls, "and I could see that Barbra was terrified. She wasn't the type to say, 'I'm scared,' but she clearly was. She clutched my hand."

She was particularly disturbed by the fawning and the fanatical. If they "loved" her so much, she reasoned, they could easily, on a whim, hate her with equal ardor. One day, she stood on a rain-soaked Manhattan street, hailing a cab. When the taxi approached, a teenage boy darted out of nowhere and threw his jacket at her feet, covering a puddle she was about to step in. Barbra was both stunned and embarrassed for the boy, and for herself.

"Please, please, pick up your coat," she told the boy. "You shouldn't do that for me. Don't do that for anyone."

Actually, she had difficulty accepting any blatantly overt sign of affection from her fans. On the night of her twenty-second birthday, April 24, 1964, she showed up for work as usual. It had been a depressing day, since Elliott was out of town. During her curtain call after the performance, the audience of 1,524 stood up and, accompanied by the orchestra, serenaded her to a chorus of "Happy Birthday." Instead of being appreciative or in some way moved, Barbra was baffled.

"What does it mean when people applaud?" she pondered. "I don't know how to respond. Should I give 'em money? Say thank you? Lift my dress? The *lack* of applause—that I can respond to. It tears me up!"

The Third Barbra Streisand Album was released on February 10, 1964, and although it would reach the number five position on the *Billboard* charts, its sales proved disappointing, particularly when compared to her previous release. The relatively modest sales were due to the fact that Barbra's album had been forced to compete against the original-cast recording of *Funny Girl*. The latter, released by Capitol Records, would debut in the *Billboard* top forty on May 2. Columbia had first option on the album and passed. It turned out to be a humiliating error in judgment. The *Funny Girl* album would peak in the number two position, where it would remain for three weeks. It was kept out of the top spot, as was most every other musical release that year, by a badly coiffed quartet from Britain known as The Beatles. Their appeal, which would reduce young women everywhere to shrieking, squealing hysterics, would be lost on Barbra.

Already bored with her routine of eight performances a week, Barbra busied herself with a flurry of projects, appearances, and awards to graciously accept or politely concede. She dabbled in Italian and took piano lessons from Shirley Rhoads, who had been recommended to her by Leonard Bernstein. She appeared on the covers of *Time* and *Life,* the latter heralding her as a "Great New Star." She traded barbs with Arlene Francis and Dorothy Kilgallen during a guest appearance on the television quiz show "What's My Line?" which aired on April 12.

And, nominated in three categories, she appeared at the Grammy Awards ceremony on the night of May 12. "Happy Days Are Here Again" would lose in the Record of the Year category to Henry Mancini's "The Days of Wine and Roses." Barbra would be victorious, however, as the recording artist who had given the year's best vocal performance by a woman. She would also win the recording industry's most prestigous prize, the Best Album of the Year, for her debut release, *The Barbra Streisand Album.*

She was less successful with two of the other major entertainment awards programs. On May 25, she was up for an Emmy for her stunning guest appearance on "The Judy Garland Show." Competing against her were Danny Kaye, Burr Tillstrom, Andy Williams, and Garland herself. Kaye, star of "The Danny Kaye Show," was named the winner, and Barbra complained, quite correctly, that she should have been nominated in a separate category. "It was silly," she said, "to put me up against the people who had a weekly show."

The night before, the entire theater community, dressed in its mid-1960s finery, convened at the New York Hilton for the Eighteenth Annual Tony Awards. *Funny Girl* was well represented with eight nominations, including those for Best Musical and Best Actress–Musical Star. The ceremony meant a great deal to Barbra, who had been envisioning her walk to the winner's podium for years. Competing against her were Carol Channing for *Hello, Dolly!,* Beatrice Lillie for *High Spirits,* and Inga Swenson for *110 in the Shade.*

It was generally thought that it was a two-way race between Barbra and Channing. When Channing was announced as the winner, Barbra, crushed, feigned indifference. Ironically, Ray Stark would lose Producer of the Year honors to David Merrick, for his work on *Dolly.* In fact, that night, *Hello, Dolly!* would slay everything in sight, a feat Barbra would file away for future reference. For while Carol Channing was clearing off a shelf for her shiny new statuette, Barbra had her eyes fixed on a much bigger prize.

As spring turned to summer, Streisand continued with her eight-performance-a-week commitment while simultaneously working on *the next thing.* "I remember she had a quick-change room right off the stage," recalls dancer Blair Hammond, "and she always had lyrics pasted up on her mirror. *Not* lyrics from the show, but lyrics for all the new things she was doing. So whenever she was changing, she was also studying."

One appearance she studied for was her outdoor concert at the Forest Hills Tennis Stadium. For Barbra, aged twenty-two, the concert had a great deal of significance. Forest Hills, after all, had been *the* Beverly Hills utopia of her Brooklyn childhood. It was where all of her childhood friends, and enemies, for that matter, had moved when their families struck it rich. To Barbra, Forest Hills represented, as it always would, the girls who could afford to wear real cashmere to school. The concert was her opportunity to *show* those people, some of whom had snubbed her years before, just how far she had come.

It was the night of July 12, 1964. The winds were strong, the sky overcast. It had been raining earlier in the day, and it was thought that Barbra might cancel the concert at the last moment. Instead, wearing a billowy gown of purples, blues, and greens ("my nightgown," as she referred to it), she walked out onto the stage to the thunderous applause of fifteen thousand people.

At first, the conditions were diverting. She wrestled with the wires of her microphone. Her dress whirled in the wind. The stool she was sitting on nearly toppled. The audience sensed her distance.

"Come closer, Barbra!" they chanted.

"How can I come closer?" she wailed. "If I walk on the wet grass, I might electrocute myself!"

Most of the *Funny Girl* company was in attendance. "One day Barbra came backstage," recalls Blair Hammond, "and said, 'Look, if I have to work, you've gotta be there.' The concert was on a Sunday, our night off. I thought it was really a great gesture on her part. These were tickets that had been sold out for weeks in advance."

Lightning streaked the sky, but the rain held its fury, and the Forest Hills concert would be a great success. So much so that a repeat performance was scheduled for later in the *Funny Girl* run.

Another reason for doing the concert was that Barbra wanted to try out new material for an upcoming album. After over four months of release, "People" had finally cracked the *Billboard* top-forty-singles chart on May 23, 1964, and had risen all the way to the number five position. With the single a hit, Barbra's first, and with the Capitol original-cast-recording album also climbing the charts, Columbia pressed Barbra for a *People* album of their own. The album was recorded in late July, two weeks after the Forest Hills concert, and was released in September. Arguably less adventurous than her earlier efforts, it was also, with its luxuriant vocals, less strident and ultimately more commercial. In other words, she was trading in her particular brand of overemotionalism, her trademark *geshreying,* for a more middle-of-the-road sound.

People bolted onto the *Billboard* album charts and, on October 31, shot up to the number one position, where it remained for five weeks. It was Barbra's first number one album, no small feat given that the industry was still in the height of the British invasion. In fact, the album Barbra replaced in the number one slot was the Beatles' *A Hard Day's Night.*

Back at the Winter Garden, Barbra wrestled with overcoming the mundane. Typically, she gave herself nightly doses of adrenaline by altering her performances, a little ad-libbing here, a little change of inflection there. This lack of consistency infuriated a few of the performers who shared scenes with her. Others understood that she was the *star* (unlike the situation on *Wholesale*) and if she wanted to take a few liberties with the material, she was entitled.

Lee Allen, who played the part of Eddie Ryan, Fanny's platonic friend, relates, "She would try to give different readings, different meanings to certain readings, that had no bearing on the play as a whole. For example, rather than the nonchalant approach that she had toward me onstage [as the script intended], there were times when she came across like she was flirting with me."

But Allen was uncertain whether it was Fanny or *Barbra* who was flirting with him. Either way, his interest was piqued. "It became much more interesting [to play it that way]," Allen says, "I mean, to me as a man. I thought, you know, 'She's coming on to me.' So I asked her about it one time offstage, and she said, 'Well, you know, it helps me to [change things]. I can't keep doing the same thing, with the same feelings all the time.' I said, 'Say no more.' Because I understood. You can't work like a machine."

Sometimes, in the name of spontaneity, she pushed the improvisational skills of her coworkers to the limit. "I had a scene that started out with me and Sydney," Marc Jordan, who played Mr. Renaldi, recalls. "I was pouring and drinking a martini, and Barbra was supposed to come in and interrupt at a certain point in something I was saying. But one night, she *didn't* interrupt me. So I started creating a story. It was *two minutes* before she finally came onstage. Afterwards, I remember saying to her, 'Where the hell were you?!' And she said, 'I was only about ten seconds late, but you were making so much sense that I thought they gave you new sides [lines] and they forgot to tell me.'"

Rationalization aside, odds are that Barbra was tempting fate and inserting a spark into the scene.

There were other light moments. "My fly was open onstage one night," Jordan recalls, "and Ray Stark, who was out in Beverly Hills, heard about it from Barbra or somebody, because he sent me a telegram saying, "I hear a new personality almost emerged in last night's performance. You almost pulled a boner. Keep a stiff upper, and fly right."

Recalls Jordan, with a laugh, "I immediately sent him a telegram saying, 'I thought it was time that the show business world saw what I had to offer.' "

The boredom was also allayed by the excitement that typically attended the visiting VIPs. After having well passed the one-hundredth-show mark, Barbra was accused by some of giving perfunctory, "walk-through" performances. Still, she could always "get it up," so to speak, when the situation merited. "Certain nights," relates Lee Allen, "whenever somebody big, I mean real big—who could be good for Barbra [and her career]—was in the audience, she would give a *magnificent* performance."

Allen adds that some nights, when they were onstage together, Barbra would whisper to him. "She'd say, 'Can you see who's sitting in my house seats?' And I'd say, 'Why? Who's supposed to be there?' And she'd say, 'Well, I heard that *Brando* is in town and that he asked for my seats.' And I'd look into the audience and I'd say, 'Well, it looks like it *could* be Brando.' "

According to Allen, the stage managers learned how to motivate (and manipulate) Barbra by making up some of the celebrity visitations. "They would feed her a little line," Allen recalls, " 'You know who's in the audience tonight, Barbra?' Or, 'So-and-so is coming tonight, Barbra.' "

Of the numerous stars who went backstage to her dressing room, there were only a few who made a favorable impression on Barbra. One was Frank Sinatra, although she seemed to feel uncomfortable in his presence. After a few minutes of the standard "You are so good" "No, *you* are" brand of repartee, she found that she didn't have much to say to him. For Barbra, it was a recurring problem.

Another star who impressed her was Ava Gardner. To Barbra, the onetime Mrs. Sinatra represented the quintessential *movie star* of her childhood past. "I don't remember Barbra being impressed with anybody," relates Ashley Feinstein, "except Ava Gardner."

Gardner had been invited to see *Funny Girl* after shooting *The Night of the Iguana* for Ray Stark. Afterward, Gardner ventured backstage and raved about Barbra's performance.

The two women developed something of a rapport, and the conversation veered to interior design. Barbra invited Gardner to see what she had done with her penthouse apartment. That night, at Barbra's invitation, Ashley Feinstein and Arthur Laurents also showed up at the apartment.

"When we walked into the apartment," Feinstein recalls, *"there* was Ava Gardner. Barbra was like, 'Oh, here's my friend Ava.' " Says Feinstein, "But, as much as Barbra was impressed with Ava Gardner, Ava Gardner was more impressed with Barbra."

Vice President Hubert Humphrey also appeared backstage, perhaps to discuss Barbra's appearance at Lyndon Johnson's Inaugural Eve celebration. The event took place on Monday, January 18, 1965, and has the distinction of shutting down two Broadway shows. Both *Funny Girl* and *Hello, Dolly!* took the night off so that Barbra and Carol Channing, respectively, could participate in the proceedings. The rest of the truly stellar lineup included Dame Margot Fonteyn, Rudolf Nureyev, Alfred Hitchcock, Julie Andrews, Carol Burnett, Harry Belafonte, Bobby Darin, Woody Allen, Johnny Carson, and Ann-Margret.

For Barbra, the evening turned into a fiasco. The show's lighting man missed one of his cues, which threw off her entire performance. Subsequently, she was *not* the consensus standout of the evening, a status to which she was now quite accustomed. Backstage, she was livid, yelling at the show's director, Richard Adler, and threatening to have the lighting guy fired.

Moreover, for Barbra, despite all of her external fury, the whole evening had an underlying sadness. Why she agreed to participate in it at all is a question. She was not particularly a fan of Johnson's and she was still bemoaning the loss of her beloved Kennedy. Johnson, in Barbra's view, was, after all, only a stand-in for the real thing.

Backstage on Broadway, visiting celebrities continued to find their way into Barbra's now elaborately decorated dressing room, with its paisley walls, paisley Louis XV day bed, and a glaringly out-of-place crystal chandelier.

Upon meeting Marcello Mastroianni, Barbra, still enamored with all things Italian, pronounced, "Wow! He's real!"

Joe Namath also made a memorable backstage appearance, causing excitement among the show's chorus girls, and a few of the boys, too. Barbra found Namath sexy, but she was utterly unimpressed with tales of his football heroics. Twenty-two at the time, Namath was awaiting word on whether his gimpy right leg had disqualified him from induction into the army and a place called Vietnam.

Hollywood agent Marty Ingels, husband of Shirley Jones, also paid Barbra a backstage visit and presented her with a rather unconventional, and completely unintended, gift. It seems that, while singing her praises, Ingels's false teeth shot out of his mouth with the speed of a bullet and landed smack into Barbra's hair.

Another incident occurred the night Andy Williams showed up. Refusing to forgive or forget that Williams had rejected her as a guest on his NBC television show, Barbra gave the singer a decidedly frigid shoulder upon their introduction. "You know," she is said to have told Williams, "I hate all boy singers. I really hate 'em. But of all the ones I've heard, I hate you the worst."

Her audacity, perhaps, stemmed from the fact that she no longer needed Williams. On June 22, 1964, after months of negotiations, CBS announced that it had signed Barbra for a series of her own television variety specials. The network's founder and president, William Paley and James Aubrey, respectively, had been at the studio taping of Barbra's appearance on "The Judy Garland Show." At the time, both CBS and NBC were vying for her video services. The Garland show, however, convinced the CBS executives to sign Streisand at any cost.

What she wanted and got was complete creative control (something the network fought to the end), and a much hyped five million dollars to do one special a year for a ten-year period. Actually, the initial phase of the contract was for three specials to be delivered by the end of 1966, with an option for the rest of the term.

"We know the talent is there," said Mike Dann, the network's vice president in charge of programming. "We know it is the most explosive, the most dynamic talent to come along in a decade." He added that the acquisition was "the most important thing that has happened to CBS in many years."

What they *didn't* know, however, was what they were going to do with her once they got her, or how she would fit into their roster of stars, which already included Carol Burnett, Mary Tyler Moore, and Lucille Ball. It was thought she might try to duplicate the intimate appeal of Danny Kaye, who simply sat atop a stool and talked to his audience, but no one was quite sure.

Upon signing her contract, Barbra sighed and shrugged her shoulders. "It's okay, I guess," she stated publicly. "But you can live just as well on

$50,000 as on $300,000, you know what I mean? I mean how many cars can you have?"

Actually, she was more impressed with the additional zeroes that were being thrown in her direction than she let on. Blair Hammond recalls the day that the terms of the contract were settled:

"It was during a Wednesday matinee. Marty Erlichman was [backstage] in a meeting. I remember that we saw him in the wings. Barbra went off on one of her quick changes, and when she came back she was beaming. She said, 'Oh my God! I just got a great contract! Guess what? I'm getting a thousand dollars a second!'"

Rehearsals for the first of the specials began in January 1965. From the outset, there was some disagreement between Barbra and the network over the format. Given that she was not a household name outside of New York, the network wanted her surrounded with big-name guest stars. Barbra refused. The special was to be *hers,* a one-woman show.

"Guest stars?" Barbra said with distaste. "Why didn't I want guest stars? It's that idle, silly talk that you have to indulge in on TV shows. It doesn't interest me. I want to do something vital. Something important. Like wow! I'm trusting my creative instinct."

Rehearsals were scheduled for Barbra's non-matinee days. Just as she had during out-of-town tryouts for *Funny Girl,* Barbra amazed director Dwight Hemion, and choreographer Joe Layton (Elliott's old *On the Town* boss), with her seemingly indefatigable energy. She impressed them, too, with her ability.

"Noel Coward was an extraordinary talent," says the show's producer, Richard Lewine. "Rex Harrison was an extraordinary talent. Mary Martin was an extraordinary talent. And Barbra Streisand was an extraordinary talent. She had an impeccable ear for music, for how the orchestra sounded—and for everything else."

Lewine further relates that Barbra had no problem adapting to the new medium; not surprising, given her numerous television guest appearances over the previous four years. Says Lewine, "She was a showwoman. She knew how to perform."

He adds, "I had done a great many specials before that, and I've had plenty of difficulties in my years of doing television, but *not* on that particular show. My relationship with Barbra was most pleasant. Dwight, Joe, and I had nothing but admiration for her talent."

The special itself was to be divided into three distinct acts, which meant three separate, and expensive, taping sessions (139 musicians were required for one sequence alone). On Sunday, March 21, on Barbra's day off from the Winter Garden, CBS unloaded its multitude of equipment at the door of Bergdorf Goodman, the luxurious Fifth Avenue department store, where one of the sessions was to be shot. Barbra had given two performances of *Funny Girl* on Saturday, went home, slept a few hours, and was ready to appear before the CBS cameras at noon on Sunday. The taping lasted well into early Monday morning, which didn't preclude her returning to the Winter Garden that same evening for another performance of *Funny Girl.* Two more sessions, one a musical fantasy sequence, and the other a traditional concert, during which she sang *both* "The Music That Makes Me Dance" and "My Man," were taped at CBS's Studio 50 in New York on April 12 and 14.

Opposite "Big Valley," and preempting "Green Acres," and "The Dick Van Dyke Show," CBS unveiled "My Name Is Barbra" at 9:00 P.M. on Wednesday, April 28, 1965. It was a critical smash, the likes of which have rarely been experienced in television history. Among the few shows with which it can be ranked are "An Evening With Fred Astaire" (1958), "Julie and Carol at Carnegie Hall" (1962), "Liza With a Z" (1972), and "Baryshnikov on Broadway" (1980).

Time called it "the most enchanting, tingling TV hour of the season." The *Hollywood Reporter* hailed it as "a smash triumph for Barbra Streisand."

Critic Rick du Brow, of United Press International, was eulogistic: "Miss Barbra Streisand, 23, of Brooklyn, last night starred in her first television special, and the result was a pinnacle moment of American show business, in any form, in any period. . . . She may well be the most supremely talented and complete popular entertainer that this country has ever produced. She simply dwarfs such contemporary stars as Julie Andrews, Elizabeth Taylor, Judy Garland and Carol Burnett."

Equally important to Barbra was the fact that the show became a hit in the Nielsen ratings. Prior to its airing, she predicted, with characteristic pessimism, "The men in suspenders will never watch it." She would, of course, be wrong. Not only did the men in suspenders tune in, so too did the men in military uniform, who listened to the show as it was broadcast on the Armed Forces Radio Network. It was also televised in seventeen countries.

Following Barbra's success, CBS took out a newspaper ad (which was directed at the difficult-to-impress Barbra more than anyone else) claiming that over thirty million people had tuned in, "more people," the ad proclaimed, "than this 23-year-old enchantress could hope to please if she continued to play the Winter Garden until she collected Social Security at 65."

That the network executives spent time and money computing these figures at all boggles the mind. But their point was made.

Television was an absolute revelation to Streisand. Unlike the theater, it offered her the opportunity for her brand of perfectionism. She could do things again and again until she deemed them acceptable. She also found that she could just as well do without a formal audience, with whom she was becoming increasingly discontent.

"I've switched my opinions," she said. "You have technicians [in television]. They're jaded; so if they like it, you know it works."

Moreover, unlike the theater, television was *permanent.* Then and now, Barbra Streisand is nothing if not a *worker,* but unlike, say, a construction worker, she didn't have the satisfaction of a finished building to show for her sweat. All she had was the faint echoes of an audience's applause, and she rapidly learned that was *not* enough for her. Television gave her something more substantial, more tangible, more enduring for her labor, even if it was only a piece of tape.

Barbra accomplished something else with that first special. In one night, in one *hour,* she managed to change her image. She was no longer the unkempt kook, the walking, talking thrift-shop grab bag. Instead, suddenly, she had become a seeming sophisticate, a chic trendsetter. Her hair had been chopped off and recoiffed to resemble, not the Beatles as was thought at the time, but Nureyev. Barbra had met the dancer at Johnson's inaugural gala, where she marveled at his hairstyle almost as much as his dancing. She then had her stylist, Fred Glaser, cut it accordingly. Despite its origin, the cut would be dubbed "the Streisand Look," and after the television special aired, hairstylists all around the country were besieged with requests to emulate it.

And it wasn't just her hair that was being appropriated. Just as there would be a rash of Madonna-wannabes twenty years later, in 1965, the hills—and other, more urban locales—were alive with not only the sound of Streisand, but the manner, walk, talk, dress, and *nose* of Streisand.

A joke began circulating within the beauty industry. "A woman came in and asked me for 'the Barbra Streisand Look,' " said one hairdresser to another, "so I hit her in the nose with my hairbrush."

But the laughter was now laced with equal measures of envy. For in the nine-minute Bergdorf Goodman sequence (which some wags dubbed "Breakfast at Bergdorf's"), Barbra was the very height of high fashion in hats by Halston, furs by the store's famous resident designer, Emeric Partos, and a $15,000 Somali leopard coat. Moreover, she adopted the extravagant new look for her personal wardrobe as well, cooing to reporters, "I used to hate mink, but now I appreciate it for its solidarity."

Actually, she had grown up *dreaming* of a fur coat, of getting her hands on, and her body draped in, the glamour she saw projected on the movie screen. And now, in the closet of her penthouse apartment on Central Park West, she had it for herself, "it" being not one, but *ten* fur outfits and eight fur hats. She had a fur for entertaining at home, a fur for lunching out, a fur for making head-turning entrances.

She had a $12,000 full-length skunk coat with sleeves that could be snapped on and off; a jaguar suit, tailored like a man's business suit, made from her own design by Reiss & Fabrizio; a black mink cape lined with the maroon fabric that she had used to upholster a couch in the entrance-way of her apartment; a Russian broadtail ("It's the most beautiful fur—but terribly perishable and I hardly wear it because it's so cold"); and a full-length cape of seal, bordered with silver fox, designed by Jacques Kaplan. She wore it with a matching silver fox hat. It was Barbra's favorite outfit. It captured, she was fond of saying, "the elegance of the thirties."

Taking her new role of trendsetter seriously, Barbra's fashion whims changed with the blink of a sequined eyelash. Shortly after the airing of the television special, she announced that her love affair with fur—or rather, with "total fur"—was over. Further, she declared that she was going to cut up her fur coats and turn them into cuffs. "A cloth coat with sable cuffs would be delicious," she said.

She also took to advising the fashion unfortunates. "A boa can be a great look if it's kept simple," she declared, sounding a good deal like her old friend Bob Schulenberg in the process, "like with gray flannel and a hairdo very tight and slim. Curls and boas don't go."

She appeared in fashion magazines and modeled the latest in knitwear by Rudi Gernreich. The transformation was complete, but not everyone was happy about it. The furs, the chandeliers, the Bentley. It was all too much, too fast, and it reeked of pretense, of a nouveau riche who was working overtime to be something she wasn't. The most disturbed were the admirers who had embraced her on "PM East," when she was just an awkward, unrefined young woman who said and sang whatever she pleased.

"It was like she was rebelling for all of us," said one. "Now it's like, here she comes with all her wigs and jewels, and a lot of us feel betrayed."

And so began the Barbra backlash. *"Who* does she think she is?" they asked one another as they sadly shook their heads from side to side.

The answer, sadly, was that even she didn't know.

Sixteen

Her Name Is Barbra

*S*he was creating distances. A distance between herself and her fans. A distance between herself and her past. During the run of *Funny Girl,* people who had known Barbra when she was struggling and in need of their help, found themselves being given the increasingly infamous Streisand snub. Some of them took it personally, while others quietly eased themselves out of her life, choosing to believe that she was simply "too busy" to maintain their friendship. Of course, there was more to it than that. Reported one former friend, "She has cut out anyone who could conceivably suggest that she didn't do it all herself."

Among those dismissed was Elaine Sobel, who had met Barbra when the two were struggling young actresses. Elaine had opened her heart, and her cramped studio apartment, to the teenage Barbra and her portable cot. "She took advantage of me," recalled Sobel, who worked as a waitress at the Russian Tea Room while Barbra lit up Broadway. "I liked her deeply and she knew it. We would spend hours talking until the early morning, but it was invariably about her problems. I had troubles, too, but she never took much interest in them."

Sobel added, "It hurts to talk this way about someone you were once close to, but I feel strongly about it. I am proud of Barbra's achievement, but I resent the way she has brushed me and others out of her life."

Rick Sommers was another aspiring actor who worked as a waiter to support himself and his four children. Sommers said, "Keep in mind that Barbra is successful and we are failures, and what has happened between her and us is an old story. Still, we loved her and it hurts. Barbra used me, but it was with my full awareness. She was terribly naive and quite frightened, but she had a voracious appetite for knowledge. I was

194

her father-director and confidante, and we had a close relationship. But as she attained success, her need for me diminished and she gradually eased me out of her life. It saddened me, but it was all part of the game."

Sommers went on, "Barbra needs unabashed, open love from the whole world. At one time, only I and a few others gave it. But we have come to realize that she is so starved for it that she is incapable of returning it. Barbra is incapable of loving anyone but herself."

Burke McHugh gave Barbra her first professional singing job at The Lion, and personally escorted her to the Bon Soir and encouraged the owners there to hire her. McHugh also found himself unceremoniously excommunicated. He recalls, nearly thirty years later, "When *Funny Girl* came to Boston [where he was living at the time], I called up the box office and I said, 'Do you know where Barbra's staying? I'm a good friend of hers.' And she said, 'Yes, we do.' And they gave me the name of the hotel. So I called the hotel because I wanted to ask her to get me tickets so that I could take Mrs. Hilda Coppage, who had been one of Barbra's judges at The Lion, to see the show. Barbra wasn't in, so I left a message. But she never called back. Never, never, *never.* So, I called the box office and made the reservations myself."

McHugh continues, "Another one of the actresses in the show was a very close friend of mine, and I went to see her after the show in her dressing room. And she said to me, 'Naturally, you're gonna go see Barbra, aren't you?' And I said, 'No, I don't think so.' I told her about the ticket situation. And she said, 'Burke McHugh, you go in there and see her or I'll never speak to you again.' So I knocked on Barbra's door and went in and she said, 'Oh my Lord, why didn't you let me know you were coming?' I said, 'Well, I called your hotel and left a message for you.' She thought about it for a minute and then she said, 'I thought that that message asking for tickets was from *Women's Wear Daily.*' " McHugh adds, "She's a rascal, you know. A rascal." He has not heard from her since.

Barry Dennen, Barbra's onetime lover and mentor, was also rejected. Still struggling as an actor, Dennen could afford to attend only a few of Barbra's nightclub performances. She never provided him with a complimentary ticket. He was surprised, therefore, when he was invited to see *Funny Girl* as her guest. Following the performance, Dennen went backstage, only to discover the *real* reason for Barbra's uncharacteristic overture. After an exchange of superficial greetings, she asked about the audio tapes that Dennen had made of her voice nearly four years before in his apartment.

"Do you still have them?" Barbra asked.

Dennen responded that he did.

"I'd like to have them back," she said.

Dennen, refused, claiming they had sentimental value. He offered to let Barbra listen to the tapes whenever she wanted, but it was clear to him that because of his refusal, his meeting with Barbra, and his friendship with her as well, had come to an end.

Bob Schulenberg, who had given Barbra her Cleopatraesque eyes, and who had introduced her to her first real sense of sophistication, was also eased out of her life during this period. He is uncertain as to the precise reasons why. However, he theorizes Barbra did not want to surround herself with friends who had known her before her success. He also believes that Barbra no longer sought his friendship in order to appease Elliott, who had become increasingly insecure with *his* role in her life.

Schulenberg recalls, "When I came back from Europe, Barbra was the star of *Funny Girl.* I felt close enough to her that she was the first person I saw when I got back to New York. I went that afternoon to visit with her at her apartment on Central Park West. She showed me around the penthouse. Elliott wasn't there. I was in her bedroom while she was getting ready for a Bill Blass fashion show that she had to be at. We were just talking. She was resting and having tea and getting herself together. And then Elliott called and said, 'Barbra, I'll be over for you.' And then I said to Barbra, 'I think I'd better leave, because it would just be better for you if the reason you're late is not because I'm here, you know?' And she said, 'Yeah.' She got it. I didn't have to say anything else. And so I left as Elliott arrived, and it was just, 'Hi, Bob,' 'Hello, Elliott, nice to see you.' "

Schulenberg is not certain why Elliott would have felt uncomfortable that he had been Barbra's friend. "My conceit would say that I had an influence over Barbra, telling her what to do. And *she* told Elliott what to do, so it was like two against one. I don't know whether she would have ever told him about what I had done for her, but there were certainly remnants of my influence over her."

Schulenberg adds, "There was a tremendous jealousy [with Elliott]." When asked if Elliott might have thought that he and Barbra had once had an *intimate* relationship, Schulenberg surmises, "I think there was a jealousy on *every* issue, every kind of a fantasy possible." In fact, Schulenberg says, "I think I might have played a surrogate brother role to her."

All Schulenberg knows for sure is that he simply stopped hearing from Barbra, his onetime very close friend. "I saw Elliott about eight years ago on a movie set," Schulenberg says, "and he could not have been kinder.

He said, 'Does Barbra know you're in town?' And I said, 'Oh my God, Elliott. I don't know if she'd want to hear from me.' Anyway, Elliott took me into his dressing room and dialed her number. I got a machine. I said, 'This is Bob Schulenberg. I'm calling for Barbra. I'm calling from Elliott's dressing room. Elliott dialed the number.' I wanted her to know that's how I got the number. 'I'm just calling to say hello, and I hope all is well.' I never heard anything back from her. I didn't get a note. I didn't get anything."

Don Softness was another of Barbra's friends who did not like Elliott. Presumably, the dislike was mutual. "I was never a fan of Elliott's," Softness says. "To me, he didn't even count." As for Barbra, who had been his friend and a nonpaying tenant in his office-turned-apartment, he says, "She got very successful and we sort of drifted apart. It was just one of those things." When asked if Barbra ever, in any way, reciprocated, or at least acknowledged the help of himself and his brother, John Softness says, simply, "No." He adds, "She *did* say 'Hello' to me once in the lobby of the Plaza, But I don't know if she really remembered who I was. That was fifteen years ago."

Terry Leong, who used to design and manufacture Barbra's clothing when she had no money, also joined the ranks of the friends abandoned by Barbra. "I *thought* we were friends," says Leong, more wistful than embittered. "We were very, very close when she didn't have very much. That sort of changed when she got into *Funny Girl.* By the time she was mingling with *name* people during *Funny Girl,* she really didn't have too much time for me. She also had all of these designers who were dying to do clothes for her. So she went with the new designers."

"To this day," recalls Ashley Feinstein, one of the friends Barbra and Elliott shared, "I don't know why I'm still not friendly with Barbra, because we never had any fight or anything."

Harold Rome, who was instrumental in hiring Barbra for her first Broadway show, and who wrote the song that arguably launched her career, is ambivalent on the subject of Streisand. After her success in *Funny Girl* and with records, Rome sent her a collection of his songs she might wish to consider recording for her albums. When she did not respond, Rome phoned her. A secretary answered.

"Who's calling?" she asked.

"Harold Rome," he replied.

The secretary asked Rome to wait while she passed on word of his call to Barbra. But it was the secretary and not Barbra who came back on the line.

"What is your business with Miss Streisand?" the secretary inquired.

Rome was too shocked to answer. He hung up the phone, grumbling under his breath about being too old and too rich to have to put up with such egotistical nonsense.

When asked if there was ever any sign of gratitude for his contributions to her career, Rome responds, with a laugh, "Not that I remember. She *did* take my wife and me out to lunch, but that's about it. She's a tough girl, but she's one hell of a performer."

On another occasion, Rome assessed, "In show business, the word gratitude is spelled with a very small *g.*"

Allan Miller had been Barbra's surrogate father and teacher, and had spent thirteen weeks on the road with her, developing her characterization and coaching her performance in *Funny Girl.* He had taken her to live in his home when she had no place else to go. He also found himself excised from her life.

Miller says, "After opening night, I was persona non grata with Barbra. In essence, she was the primary force in trying to remove all aspects of her life prior to *Funny Girl* that would suggest that she hadn't done it all herself. She didn't want anyone to know that she had been helped. That's why I was kept such a secret. About six weeks after the show opened, I put an ad in the trade papers because I had been away for thirteen weeks and a lot of people had wondered where I'd gone. I wanted the theater community at large in New York to know where I'd been. I thought it was a pretty damn terrific experience and a credit to have for myself. So I put a little ad in the trades that said something to the effect that 'Allan Miller is resuming classes.' And in rather small print, it said, 'recent coach to Barbra Streisand in *Funny Girl.*'

"Well, about two or three days after the ad started running, I got a call from Barbra's secretary, who said, 'Hi, Mr. Miller? Uh, Barbra would like to talk to you.' And I knew immediately what it was about. And, sure enough, she gets on the phone and says, 'Hi, Listen'—no big greetings or 'How's your wife? or 'How are the kids?' or anything—just 'Listen, you know, *this ad* you put in the paper has really upset me! I don't understand. Why would you do such a thing? Why are you doing this now about *Funny Girl?*' She was furious. I said, 'Barbra, I had been out of town, I had been away. Nobody knew where I was.' She said, 'Yeah, but you didn't have to *use* me as a *credit!*' I was really a little taken aback by the ferocity of the attack, even though I wasn't really surprised by it."

Miller went on, "She said something about how upsetting this 'damned thing' was, and she'd like me to take the 'damned thing' out of the paper, and I said, 'Barbra, let me tell you something, okay? If we made a list of all of the things that I have done negatively to you, and all of the positive things I have done *for* you, and we compared them to the list of positive and negative things you have done towards me or to people that I care about, whose *positive* list do you think would be a lot longer?'

"And she said, 'Allan, I just want you to pull that *thing* out of the paper!' And I said, 'Okay, Let me tell you this in clear, no uncertain terms. I was intending to run this ad only these two times.' And she said, 'Oh.' And I said, 'I had no intention of making this a consistent part of my advertising, because I don't feel the need to. But now that you're *ordering* me to take it out of the paper, I'm not going to tell you what I'm going to do. You'll just have to read the trades and see.' And I hung up on her. And that," says Miller, "was essentially the last time I spoke with her for quite some time."

When asked why he wasn't more surprised by Barbra's sudden attack and subsequent betrayal, Miller says, "Because she had cut off so many other former friends by that time. She had cut off almost every single other person that I was familiar with who had given her some of these apartments to stay at, and stuff like that. She had cut them all off. So, I had seen her do this to a good number of people. I just never dreamt that she would do it to me."

Over a year into the run of *Funny Girl,* Barbra wasn't making many new friends, either. "She didn't communicate with the kids too much," recalls cast member Royce Wallace. "In fact, the kids kind of complained. They were always saying, 'Royce, you're *always* with her. She always talks to you.' They thought that I was the only one that she was friendly to. She didn't take the time to be friendly with the others."

In an effort to allay the increasing backstage tension between Barbra and the rest of the company, Royce Wallace conspired with Elliott to organize a surprise twenty-third birthday party in Barbra's honor. The purpose of the celebration was to give the rest of the company an opportunity to become better acquainted with Barbra. Instead, the press somehow learned about the party, and what was meant to be an intimate gathering turned into a media *event.* Besieged by reporters, Barbra had neither the opportunity nor the inclination to develop new friendships with her coworkers.

The only thing of note that happened at the party was that Barbra was presented with a gift she would come to treasure. Interestingly, Barbra thought, and perhaps still thinks, that the present was a token of affection from the *Funny Girl* company. Instead, it was actually from the owner of the bar.

"He had one of those carts that sells hot dogs," recalls Royce Wallace, "and he said to Barbra, 'So, you want a hot dog?' And she said, 'Yes.' But instead of a hot dog, he gave her a dog. She just assumed that the dog [whom she named Sadie] was from us because we were the ones who gave her the party."

Barbra certainly had little affinity for her understudy, another Erasmus High graduate, Lainie Kazan. Kazan, more conventionally attractive than Barbra, was initially hired as one of the chorus girls for the "His Love Makes Me Beautiful" pregnant bride number performed by the Ziegfeld Follies. Possessing a big, belting voice, Kazan worked her way up to understudying the star role. Unfortunately for Kazan, Barbra was in strapping good health and had no intention of ever letting her go on. Then, on February 3, 1965, after playing approximately 350 performances without incident, Barbra came down with a viral infection.

Recalls dancer Blair Hammond, "I think it was the first time that the Asian flu went around, and she was advised to take time off."

Still, Barbra insisted on going on for the matinee. Just before showtime, however, her condition worsened. Legend has it that she fainted backstage. Whether true or not, she *was* sent home to her three-hundred-year-old bed, while Lainie hurriedly dressed up in her Fanny Brice regalia. All would have ended there, if not for the backstage plotting straight out of *All About Eve.*

"We were all absolutely astounded," says Hammond. It seems that in between her matinee and evening performances, the enterprising Lainie got on the telephone and, heralding herself as a new star to be born, cajoled the city's critics to attend that evening's performance.

That's where Kazan's Eve Harrington–Margo Channing scenario took an unexpected detour. "Lainie was just *not Funny Girl,*" says Blair Hammond. "She was totally miscast. Vocally, she could never compete with Barbra's voice for the kind of songs that were in the show."

But while her reviews were hardly ecstatic, they were *not* unkind. Which is more than can be said for her treatment by Barbra, who made a rapid recovery from her illness and returned for the Thursday night performance. Even though the perceived threat from Kazan had not been realized as planned, Barbra acted as though it had. From then on, she was decidedly cold, if not antagonistic, toward her understudy.

The relationship between the two women was further aggravated because Lainie had been having an affair with Peter Daniels, the show's rehearsal pianist and assistant conductor, who also happened to be *Bar-bra's* longtime personal musical director. The affair became serious, and the two would later marry. To Barbra, the liaison was an act of betrayal, and Daniels was ousted from her life, both professionally and personally.

As for Lainie, her life in the show became intolerable and shortly thereafter, she was "encouraged" to quit, which she did. Her replacement, Linda Gerard, was reportedly handpicked by Barbra. In *her* contract, Gerard had a clause which stipulated that—in the event that she was to go onstage in place of Barbra—she could *not* notify the press. If she did, that in itself would be sufficient grounds for termination.

Other than conductor Milt Rosenstock, Royce Wallace, Grace Davidson (her dresser), her hairdresser, and a few others, Barbra was strictly business with the *Funny Girl* company. Even those that she favored were kept at a distance, both emotionally and physically. "She had an aversion to people touching her," recalls Blair Hammond. "You could never hug her. She hated that. *Hated* it."

She avoided contact of all kinds. "Barbra never looked at anybody in the eye," relates Buzz Miller. "Sydney Chaplin even told me that she wouldn't look at him onstage. She was always looking over his shoulder."

Miller adds, "She was always nice enough to me, but very aloof. She just went straight ahead, and looked right through you. We figured that she was just that way. She certainly never went out of her way to be nice to anyone that I ever saw."

The argument can be made that Streisand is simply a woman who doesn't have the proclivities and/or resources for the social niceties. She is always extremely focused, to the exclusion of all others, on the *work* at hand. As such, she characteristically shuns socializing with most of her coworkers. Chitchat and small talk are not a part of her vocabulary. This gives many the impression that she thinks she's too good for them. Some take it personally. "The chorus girls were always bitching that Barbra wasn't schmoozing with them," recalls Blair Hammond. "They were the professional chorus girls who had been around *forever,* who wore too much makeup and were *dying* to get a husband."

Those who performed their jobs well, and who understood and respected Barbra's *distance,* had a better chance of getting along with her. One of those who did was Lee Allen, Eddie Ryan in the show, who recalled, "I had a good *working* relationship with her. I don't think that too many people got that close to Barbra. But I think that she felt secure with me. She knew that I would hold up my end. She could bounce off of me very easily on the stage. A couple of times, little things happened during a performance. Maybe an ad-lib, a slip, a miscalculation. And I was there for her, and she was there for me."

"She *was* distant," says Blair Hammond, "but I think that it was just in her nature. She was protecting herself. She was a very private person. People used to say, 'Oh, she never pays any attention to me backstage.' This is nonsense. She *wasn't* chatty. She was always too busy with the show to sit and chat. And she was learning. The show rode on her shoulders, which was a great deal of responsibility. She was only twenty-three at the time.

"I got along with her because I had enormous respect for her," Hammond continues. "And, I *never* crossed that line of familiarity with her. With certain big stars, it's different. Mary Martin, for example. With Mary Martin, you can sit in her dressing room, and you schmooze with her, and it'll be like you've known her all of your life. [With] Barbra, it's just not that way."

Then there is her reputation for being so-called "difficult." Even those who only admire Streisand acknowledge that she is not "easy" to work with, "easy" meaning *compliant.*

"She was a wonderful person," declares Royce Wallace, "and we got to be good friends. But she was a little—how should I say it—she had her own views on what should be done. And if she didn't like something, she was very vocal about it."

In addition to having her own views, she also possessed an insatiable appetite for knowledge. She explored every angle, just as she had in childhood. "But tell me *why"* is a common Streisand "demand." Naturally, this characteristic exasperates many of her coworkers, who want to get on with the work that needs to be done. "She'll drive you bats with too much analysis," Ray Stark explained. "It's not arrogance, but doubt. She is like a barracuda. She devours every piece of intelligence to the bone."

Being "difficult" also means not knowing when to stop. Barbra will do things over and over until she deems them right, without regard to other people's money or, more important, to the people themselves with whom she is working: *their* time, *their* schedules, *their* families that are waiting for them at home. She operates, too, without regard to the notion of human limitations in general.

"She can repeat something one hundred times, until it's *exactly* the way that she wants it," says Sid Ramin, who, in addition to being the orchestrator of *I Can Get It for You Wholesale,* also worked with Barbra in the recording studio on one of her albums. "Most people don't have that kind of stick-to-itiveness. I think a lot of it is exasperation. Like, '*What* can she want? *What* is she looking for?'"

She calls it "perfectionism."

While Barbra never asks anyone to work harder, or put in longer hours, than she herself is willing to do, it is also true, though she seemingly fails to realize it, that she is often making a *hundred* times as much money as the men and women with whom she works. She is being proportionately compensated for her time and her monumental effort; they are not. Nor is she terribly patient with her coworkers.

"I think she gets irked easily," says Ramin. "She's just so fast. But she was always extremely cordial to me. I know that she has a reputation for being difficult, and I'm sure that she *is* difficult, but every time I've worked with her, she has been on her best behavior. However, I've heard stories, and I've seen for myself, that she's very fussy."

In addition to her impatience, she can be very undiplomatic. She doesn't know *how* to ask for things. She just does, and often, and in language that is frequently terse.

Talk to the people who have worked with Streisand and they will tell you that she *is* demanding. She *is* inflexible. And she is a woman of little tact. She literally *takes* whatever it is that she wants. But the perception that this is the result of some kind of a star trip gone haywire is incorrect. She was *always* that way. When she wanted the makeup she couldn't afford to buy as a teenager, she shoplifted it from a Brooklyn five-and-dime.

During the run of *Funny Girl,* the same motivation prompted her into the habit of walking into Saks Fifth Avenue, "buying" an outfit, wearing it once to some important public function, and then returning it the next day. She took whatever she could.

Wilma Curley, one of the costars of *Wholesale,* recalls an incident that happened during the *Funny Girl* run. "I was shopping on Fifth Avenue. It was a snowy, icky, rainy day. I think it was Christmas. I was carrying some bags, and a bike, which was folded up, for my children. I decided to walk over to Saks to get a taxi. There was slush all over the street. Finally, as I was opening the door, I heard a voice behind me, and *she* rushed right past me and got into *my* cab! It was Barbra. And I thought, 'My God! She's still taking my shit!'"

Curley laughs. "I grabbed the door and I said, 'Out!' And she said, 'Oh, Wilma! Listen, Elliott was supposed to pick me up and he's late. I *have* to have the cab!' And then," says Curley, "the cab took off."

She doesn't recognize boundaries. Backstage at the Winter Garden, she got into the habit of issuing notes to the members of the cast and crew, complaining that they were not performing their jobs properly. She might have been right, too, but that was beside the point. She was the star of the show. She was *not,* however, the director or the producer.

"Those notes should have come from the director," says Lee Allen. "They should have come from the stage managers."

Sydney Chaplin became the principal recipient of Barbra's infamous notes. His relationship with her had long since soured. Chaplin, understandably, was upset over the extensive cuts that had been made in his part, all of which favored Barbra.

Chaplin complained with surprising candor, "I'm sort of nobody, a straight man for Barbra Streisand. I'm a guy in white tails, a snob. The audience doesn't root for me. And you can't write a good part when the character doesn't *want* something. What can you hope for Arnstein, that he doesn't ruffle his white shirt?"

Though no fault of Barbra's, it had been an emasculating process for Chaplin. Barbra's notes represented the proverbial salt upon the wound. Frequently, before stunned onlookers, the two stars would engage in verbal slugfests. Flying four-letter words, especially from Chaplin, were hurled across the Winter Garden stage with spirited conviction.

"They would accuse each other of stealing scenes," Lee Allen recalls. "And, you know, 'You could've done it this way, you could've done it that way.' I think that Chaplin did not like the fact that he was getting notes from Barbra. I'm sure of it. What would happen is that Barbra might have yelled at him about something during a blackout or as they were leaving the scene. Then, at the end of that performance or the following day, he would get a note from Barbra."

Barbra wanted Chaplin fired. But he had an ironclad run-of-the-play contract, and he refused to be bullied out of the show. Finally, at Barbra's behest, Ray Stark negotiated Chaplin's departure. Chaplin, whose last performance was on Saturday, June 19, 1965, insisted on receiving his full salary, every week, reportedly through the run of the show. He was replaced, for a short period, by his understudy, George Reeder, until a permanent replacement, Johnny Desmond, of whom Barbra approved, was cast.

Certainly, jealousy factored in the less-than-flattering Streisand reputation that was emerging. *Funny Girl* made her a Broadway *star,* arguably, at the expense of Sydney Chaplin, Danny Meehan, and others whose roles were drastically cut to serve *her* performance.

"They took scenes away from everybody but Barbra," Lee Allen recalls. "And no matter what she did, she did it right. No matter what they threw in her path, she was doing it and excelling in it."

Furthermore, at the time of the show's opening, she was only twenty-two years old, and it was resented by some in the company, many of whom were old pros, that she had been given so much, so soon. Her success only underscored *their* failures, *their* unrealized dreams.

Barbra may have lost the Tony award to Carol Channing, to the delight of some in the *Funny Girl* company, but in 1965 she won the Grammy for the second year in a row, for having given the Best Vocal Performance, Female, for her recording of "People." (Barbra was also nominated in the Album of the Year [*People*], and Best Record of the Year ["People"] categories, both of which she lost to Stan Getz, the latter for his recording of "The Girl From Ipanema.") And on September 12, 1965, at the New York Hilton, her first television special, "My Name Is Barbra," was accorded *five* Emmy Awards, including those for Outstanding Program Achievement and Outstanding Individual Achievement. But the acclaim, the awards, and the fame, only further provoked the backstage sniping at the Winter Garden. "Everybody was always saying," relates Buzz Miller, "She's gotten all of this, now she should go out and learn how to *act!*"

Blair Hammond offers another explanation for her unpopularity with some in the company, and, in a broader sense, one of the reasons for her unflattering reputation. "I must say," says Hammond, "I don't feel that Barbra had any *ego* problem whatsoever. I think that she was very confident [in her work]. And unfortunately, I think that people who were less confident misinterpreted this as 'ego.' She wasn't in any way arrogant. Perhaps she had an overabundance of confidence on the surface to mask those fears that we all have."

Certainly, part of the reason for Barbra's reputation of temperamental termagant had to do with her increasingly bad relationship with the press. Typically, she dismissed most reporters with a curt, "I can only give you five minutes." Angered at the rebuff, some reporters sought and attained their retribution through the power of their pens.

As for Barbra, she bristled at any sign of criticism. In this way, she took after her mother, who had become notorious within the New York newspaper community. It seems that whenever a columnist, reporter, or reviewer wrote something negative about her daughter, Diana Kind would send a furiously scribbled letter of protest to the culprit, which she would typically sign "Barbra Streisand's Mother." Once, Diana was provoked to issue one of her letters when a columnist merely quipped that Barbra's conspicuously long fingernails were of the "Fu Manchu" variety.

It was a matter of embarrassment to Barbra. In fact, nearly everything Diana Kind did embarrassed her daughter. She never really fit into Barbra's old fantasy life in Brooklyn, and she certainly did not belong in Barbra's grand new life of fur coats, chandeliers, and penthouse apartments. Nor, could she find acceptance with Barbra's new group of sophisticated, sometimes famous, friends and acquaintances. Undeterred, Diana would leave early from her job in Brooklyn, take the train to Manhattan, trudge up the stage door stairs, and show up unexpectedly in Barbra's dressing room. Invariably, she would be toting, for her daughter's consumption, a carton of chicken soup and some little surprise for dessert. Barbra was enraged by these uninvited visits, which she viewed as an intrusion on her privacy. Eventually, she told her mother to nix the chicken soup act. She was old enough and rich enough to feed herself. Besides, she told her mother, she preferred take-out Chinese.

Still, for once, Diana Kind *finally* saw in her eldest daughter what others had been seeing for four years: Not only was she a talent, she was a *star.*

"One of the big thrills of my life," she would later say of Barbra, "was seeing her open in Philadelphia in *Funny Girl.* I got so excited that I had to walk to the back of the theater. I met a lady there that I knew and she introduced me to all these people who congratulated me."

She basked in the reflected glow of her daughter's success, even if from the back row. Of seeing her daughter onstage in *Funny Girl,* Diana Kind, would say, "That was really—I could never announce it as I could feel it—as though my chest was hurting."

Understandably, Barbra's husband was having a much more difficult time grappling with her success than was her mother. While his wife earned tens of thousands of dollars just by stretching her vocal chords, Elliott, humiliated, stood in the unemployment line to collect his weekly fifty-dollar check. While she became engrossed in her television specials to be produced and her record albums to be recorded, he was occupied with his small-time gambling and his three-man basketball games, usually played in a neighborhood schoolyard. And while she still commanded nightly standing ovations at the Winter Garden, he cavorted in the stands at *Madison Square* Garden, cheering on the New York Knicks.

"To say I love Barbra," Elliott related at the time, "that's obvious." Otherwise, I couldn't have stood it. I know the traps, I know the wounds, and I've decided it's worth it to wage the battle."

He would add, "I have to be above it [Barbra's fame], because if I'm in it, I'm going to get stomped to death."

What he *didn't* acknowledge—perhaps it was not dishonesty, but denial—is that he was *losing* the battle. His ego, or what remained of it, was braving a brutal workover.

While *everything* seemed to go right for his wife, everything Elliott touched seemed to go wrong. He appeared with Carol Burnett in a television special of *Once Upon a Mattress* and was hardly noticed. He seemed destined to stand in the shadows of seemingly more talented actresses. He worked behind the scenes to stage a nightclub act for Anna Maria Alberghetti, who had recently starred on Broadway in *Carnival*. He took singing and dancing lessons and worked on a nightclub act for himself, but never got a booking.

Grasping, he ventured to Jamaica to make a movie called *The Confession* with Ginger Rogers, Ray Milland, and Barbara Eden. In a glorified bit role, he played a mute, and exercised a repertoire of ridiculous expressions until the end of the picture, when he squealed out the news of his sudden, miraculous cure. Fortunately for Elliott, the film was an absolute disaster and didn't get a theatrical release until 1971, when it opened—and closed very quickly—under the title of *Quick, Let's Get Married*, a.k.a. *Seven Different Ways*. The only thing of note about the picture is that it was the last to be directed by William Dieterle, who had seen far better days (*The Life of Emile Zola*, *The Hunchback of Notre Dame*, *Portrait of Jennie*).

For Elliott, back in New York, accompanying his wife in public was a devastating experience. He seemed to be one small step above a hired escort. Publicly, Barbra clung to the notion that Elliott was the American Belmondo. Privately, however, in the confines of their elaborate, frequently redecorated apartment, *her* apartment, she found herself confronted with an increasingly unavoidable fact. She was married to a man for whom she was rapidly losing respect. He *was* talented, that she knew and never doubted. But he didn't seem to have her ambition, her tenacity, her commitment.

Worse, the whole "Mr. Streisand" business was getting to him. In the beginning, Elliott tried to laugh it all off. In time, however, it took its toll. "The strain," says Ashley Feinstein, "Was just so present."

Elliott was increasingly insecure, full of self-doubt, *weak*. And, at that point in her life, Barbra had little interest in, attraction to, and patience for, a man whom she perceived as being weak. She supported Elliott financially, which he hated, but not emotionally.

Elliott would later say of his wife, "Barbra's favorite subject is Barbra. It bugs me a lot, and I get bored by it sometimes. Here is a girl who is a major star, who makes a fortune, but who is unhappy. It is a pain to hear her complain constantly."

She was almost completely self-absorbed. There could have been a war going on (there *was* a war going on); there could have been a revolution going on (there *was* a revolution going on), and as long as it didn't affect *her* records, *her* television specials, *her* nightly performances at the Winter Garden, odds are, she wouldn't have taken notice. The argument can be made that, as much as Elliott was *there* for her, she was incapable of being there for him; she was not, at that point in her life, emotionally equipped to be there for *anyone.*

Instead of bolstering her husband's self-worth, she tore him down. They both pushed those buttons that only people who had been as close as they had, even knew existed.

Elliott later revealed, "I used to be apologetic and feel guilty about expressing my problems in front of Barbra. I thought it showed a weakness in my sex and in me." He added, in a dig at Barbra, "The woman should understand and not hit the nerve of the man's problem to keep him off balance. A couple should understand each other's faults."

Wallowing in self-doubt, Elliott subordinated himself to his wife, catering to *her* needs, giving her everything he had, including his self-respect.

Despite public claims to the contrary, Barbra was fully aware of the situation and all of its *A Star Is Born* ramifications. Elliott, the star of *I Can Get It for You Wholesale,* had been eclipsed by his wife ever since.

"He's a lovely human being," Barbra had reflected as *Funny Girl* first went into rehearsals, "very compassionate and sweet."

Still, even she couldn't resist the irony. "In the play—it's funny, isn't it?—I was the ugly secretary. And now it's just sort of turned around."

There would be moments of realization too. "He does it so great with me, but I can't begin to do it for him."

The whole synergy of their relationship was dependent upon one basic premise: Despite all of her bravado, Elliott had seen in Barbra a fragile young woman, a delicate creature who needed to be taken care of; and she saw in him a strapping specimen of man who could and would be responsible for her. Barbra needed Elliott. It wasn't supposed to be the other way around. "Barbra mistrusts anyone who needs anything from her," Elliott would say later.

They tried to work it out. They formed two production companies, making a show of solidarity by dubbing them with an equally billed amalgam of their two names, Barbell and Ellbar Productions. In the name of their joint ventures, Elliott worked at developing projects for television, one of which was a half-hour series of award-winning documentaries. However, the network executives, whom Elliott would refer to as "a bunch of fucking pigs," made themselves perfectly clear. They were *not* interested in Elliott's shows unless Barbra was to star in them.

Meanwhile, he continued to audition on Broadway. For a while, it looked as though he might finally have a hit show on his hands. There was a good deal of talk that he was to costar in a stage musical version of *Roman Holiday,* the 1953 William Wyler picture starring Audrey Hepburn and Gregory Peck. However, the project never materialized, and Elliott continued his search for a show and, in a larger sense, his self-respect.

Another shot at success came with *Drat! The Cat!* which costarred Joey Heatherton, who would be replaced by Lesley Ann Warren prior to its opening. "I really fought for that job," Elliott recalled. "It took three months of auditions and pain for me to land it. They tried very hard to find someone else [it had been intended for Alan Alda], but they couldn't."

The Goulds invested a good deal of their hopes, and a bit of *her* money, into the production. Their hopes, however, were dashed upon the show's opening at the Martin Beck Theater in October 1965. The show was panned by the critics (those who were able to get their reviews published—the city was in the throes of another newspaper strike), and the producers posted a closing notice after a six-day run.

Ironically, despite all of her good intentions, Barbra seemed to only chip away at Elliott's already bedraggled ego. The press made snide comments that she had bankrolled much of *Drat!* just to give her husband something to do. Furthermore, one of Elliott's solos in the show was a number called *"She* Touched Me." Barbra liked the song, and prior to the show's opening, she decided to record it as a single in the hopes that it would help ticket sales. Unfortunately, the show closed, and the song, under the title *"He* Touched Me," became a mild success for Barbra. Today, the song that was once Elliott's is primarily remembered because it was recorded by his wife.

Elliott was devastated by the abrupt closing and almost unanimous dismissal of the show. "After *Drat! The Cat!*" he confessed, "I grew up. I cried for a week, because I couldn't bear its closing."

Elliott went into analysis. So too did Barbra. Despite all of her wealth, fame, and the constant validation of her abilities, she was terribly unhappy. Her marriage was falling apart, but it went beyond that. She had attained stardom at the young age of twenty-two—the same age, incidentally, as Brando when he skyrocketed to fame on the Broadway stage in *A Streetcar Named Desire*—but it went beyond that too. Her problems extended back to her childhood.

Growing up, survival to Barbra had meant *getting out* of whatever she was in. Having a destination: Fame, Success, Adulation, Wealth. Now that she had all of that, she found that the void that promised to miraculously vanish was still there, gnawing at her. Without her dreams to cling to, she was forced, perhaps for the first time in her life, to face her reality.

She envied those who still had their dreams.

One day, during the run of *Funny Girl,* she attended a rehearsal of the Royal Ballet. "Sitting in the audience," she related, "I envied—not the exquisite grace of Dame Margot Fonteyn—but any one of the girls in the corps de ballet who dream at night of someday becoming the prima ballerina."

There were other deep-seated problems too. She wanted to be attractive to men, and yet, with the echoes of Louis Kind's voice in her ears, she was convinced that she was not. Given the early death of her father, which she perceived as abandonment, and the emotional abuse of her stepfather, she viewed most men with distrust.

She was filled with self-loathing. She was unhappy with her history. She was unhappy with her face. She was even unhappy with her ethnicity. One of the reasons she surrounded herself with such extravagant opulence was that she thought it made her less Jewish.

"I wanted to be gentile," she would later confess. "When I first became successful, I wanted to have the things that all gentiles have . . . like great art. I always thought that having French furniture and art was gentile."

She was also unhappy and embarrassed by her lack of higher education. Because she could sing, she found herself thrust into the company of some of the most highly developed minds in the country.

"I'm constantly depressed at my lack of knowledge," she recalled. "Things that I want to know so badly and don't. So I read ten books at a time and never finish one, because I want to know so much. Then I get depressed by my ignorance and don't read at all."

Some found her striving charming, while others mocked her awkward efforts at intelligence and respectability.

She didn't belong back in Brooklyn, but she didn't seem to fit into the world of celebrities, either. She tried to join in with other personages, but she couldn't. She attended a New Year's Eve party with Ashley Feinstein and spent much of the night huddled in a corner. "Barbra was very shy being with a lot of people," says Feinstein. Among the celebrity guests was Lena Horne, with whom Barbra had frequently been compared. "She was very, very impressed with Lena Horne," says Feinstein.

Nonetheless, after a few minutes, Barbra found that she had nothing to say to Horne. It was the same when she was introduced to Brando at a benefit. He had been her childhood idol, and yet, because of her fear and insecurity and her enormous expectations of Brando, she found herself at a loss for words.

At a party Joshua Logan hosted for Princess Margaret in his Manhattan apartment in the fall of 1965, Barbra was again confronted with her own social inadequacies. Sammy Davis, Jr., entertained the glittering assemblage. So too did Rosalind Russell. Barbra arrived late and hid out in the back of the room, feasting on all the free food. At the request of the guest of honor, Logan and a parade of others asked Barbra to sing. She refused. Her days of singing for her supper were over.

Upon being introduced to the princess, who was flanked in the receiving line by actress May Britt and singer Tommy Steele, Barbra decided not to go with the standard form of royal address. "She is not *my* Royal Highness," she would later explain. Instead, Barbra opted for a simple "Hullo," which visibly took the usually self-contained princess aback for half a second. Margaret then regained her royal composure and told Barbra that she was a fan and that she had all of her records. Not knowing what else to say, Barbra responded with a hardly appreciative "Yeah?" which translated to some as a rather insulting "So what?"

Trying to buffer the situation, May Britt asked Barbra why she had been late in arriving. Barbra shot back, "Because I got screwed up!"

Tommy Steele went white. The princess was aghast. Making a bad situation worse, Barbra babbled on. "So," she said to Margaret, nodding at Steele, "You two know each other from London, huh?"

"I have performed for *Her Majesty* and [for] *Princess* Margaret too," Steele replied.

"Yeah," said Barbra, "that's what I mean."

Even when she met non-celebrities in a similar social situation, Barbra appeared to be uncomfortable. Part of the problem involved articulating her own name. "I can't say, 'I'm Barbra Streisand,' " she explained. "It's a hard thing to say your own name, you know? I'm either very direct or I can't function. Around people I don't know, I'm totally at a loss."

She wanted to be well liked, but she had a difficult time approaching people. They, in turn, were too nervous to meet her, and would usually walk by without uttering a word. "I know I should realize that person may be nervous [about making the first move]," Barbra says. "Instead, I think he can't bear to look at me."

Compounding her problems, she felt that everyone wanted to take a piece of her. While some of these feelings were undoubtedly justified, much of her concern bordered on the paranoid. She believed so strongly that she was being exploited by Trans World Airlines, for example, that she took the company to court. It seems that to promote its in-flight stereo system, TWA had taken out a billboard and produced an NBC television commercial which simply proclaimed, "Barbra Streisand sings on TWA." For that "unlawful" use of her name, Barbra sought a $2.25 million settlement. Her suit claimed that the ads caused her to be "greatly distressed and humiliated" and had exposed her to "public ridicule and contempt." She further characterized the ads as being TWA's "parasitical commercial activities." The case was settled out of court in 1968. It provides a glimpse into Barbra's insecurity with both herself and her stardom.

She was always vacillating between doubt, despair, and determination, approaching life with jerky start-and-stop movements. There would be an advance. Then a retreat. Then another advance. One minute, she exuded confidence, sometimes with teeth bared; the next minute, she was terrified and, like a wounded puppy, retreated into a corner.

Performing onstage had been her one solace, her one safe place where she felt whole and completely comfortable in her skin. But during the run of *Funny Girl,* even that feeling began to change. Every night at about five P.M., she would experience a wrenching pain in her stomach that wouldn't let up until the curtain rose. With each performance, she felt that she was on trial, that she was being judged. Her senses were keenly attuned to each audience. She saw every yawn and heard every cough. Her fans had become the enemy. She was convinced they were all against her.

"Most of them come thinking, 'Nah, she can't be that great,' " Barbra confided. "It makes me feel they're the monster and I'm their victim."

She wasn't just another successful performer waiting for the other shoe to drop, she was Marie Antoinette waiting for the sharp blade of the guillotine.

Desperately, she longed for the end of her nightly trek to the Winter Garden. Months before, she had threatened to break her contract, which she ultimately decided against. Instead, she simply marked off the days on her wall calendar, not unlike a prisoner awaiting her release.

On Saturday night, December 25, 1965, Barbra Streisand, at the age of twenty-three, gave her final Broadway performance of *Funny Girl*. When singing "People," she *felt* the meaning of the lyrics for the very first time. She broke down onstage, overwhelmed by her conflicting emotions. During her curtain calls, the audience serenaded her with "Auld Lang Syne." After the performance, there were no big goodbyes, no celebratory send-off. Just a gold-plated bagel she received from Elliott.

It was a stab at good humor by her husband. But it was also an appropriate parting gift. For, despite all of her success, she was still the outsider looking in, still the bagel on a plateful of onion rolls. Instead of filling the void and delivering all the answers as she had expected, the immense fame that came with *Funny Girl* left Streisand with a series of additional, more-difficult-to-ask questions. Questions like, "How can all these people profess to like me so much when I don't even like myself?"

"When I am not performing," Barbra would say a few months later, "I don't think I have that definite a personality." She would add, sadly, and with great poignance, "I think maybe I have nothing."

Seventeen

Slowing Down for the Crossings

"Tell the audience to go away. I hate them. I hate them." The words of denouncement, delivered to Marty Erlichman, were Barbra's. The occasion was the taping of her second television special, 1966.

The unwitting audience in the television studio just sat in their seats, patiently waiting for the taping to continue. Barbra had already sung five songs when director Dwight Hemion asked her to redo two of them. Barbra agreed, but wanted the audience—an assorted group culled from her local fan clubs—removed from the studio. When working, and certainly when not, she hated, then as now, being watched and judged, particularly by people whose presence could not be considered as essential. Thirty minutes passed as Hemion and Erlichman pleaded with her, explaining all the while that the audience was necessary for, among other reasons, the show's sound continuity. Barbra eventually capitulated and walked back onto the stage. She smiled at the audience as they gave her another resounding reception. "Thank you for staying," she said, sounding suitably sincere. And they cheered some more.

In accordance with her theory that "they're all out to get me," she was determined to make the second show better than the first, hence stalling their imminent attack. After the taping of each number, she flung herself down in an oversized chair.

"She watched the playback with incredible precision," relates Ray Diffen, the show's costume designer, "and if she didn't like it [which almost invariably was the case], she did it again, and again, and again."

214

At one point, a concerned Erlichman cautioned, "You'll be hoarse tomorrow."

Barbra, perturbed, replied, "I sang twenty-five songs a night eight times a week in *Funny Girl.* I won't be hoarse."

Like her first special, "Color Me Barbra" was a one-woman show structured in three acts, only this time in color (hence the title), which was then still in its television infancy. As with its predecessor, the final act (the one for which she had wanted the audience banished) was a straightforward concert sequence. The rest of the show was a much more elaborate undertaking.

Filling in for Bergdorf Goodman was the show-business-friendly Philadelphia Museum of Art, where *Rocky* and *Dressed to Kill,* among others, would later be filmed. Barbra had wanted to shoot the museum sequence at the Metropolitan Museum of Art in New York, but was refused access. The concept had Barbra transcending the two-dimensional and *becoming* the subjects depicted in the museum's paintings.

The primary problem in Philadelphia was the lack of time and, given that, the general insanity of television production. With the financing for the special coming directly out of the Ellbar Productions pocket, everything was tightly scheduled to save money. Moreover, the museum had allotted the TV crew only a single night of shooting. After prerecording the music most of the previous evening—the session, scheduled for 7:00 to 10:00 P.M., did not end until 4:00 A.M.—Barbra arrived at the museum at noon on a Saturday in late January. The taping was scheduled to begin at 6:00 P.M. and last until 10:00 A.M. the following morning.

It was instant chaos. Once shooting began, two of the company's three new Marconi color cameras broke down. Without available replacements (television color was *that* new), the crew had to make do with the remaining one. This, of course, took a good deal of additional time. Barbra watched over the lighting, the sets, the sound controls, the costumes, *everything.* She had trouble, as she always would, relinquishing control. The incompetence of others infuriated her. "You have to do 90 percent of everything yourself," she would say. "You really do."

There were problems, too, in maneuvering the lumbersome equipment and the twenty-five man crew around the pricey, sometimes priceless, works of art, which were guarded by a zealous security staff.

In between takes, an extremely tense Barbra popped pretzels, potato chips, and peppermint sour balls into her mouth. She sat hunched in a corner and fretted over the mass confusion, the slow progress of the shooting, the ticking of the clock. Elliott was at her side, holding her hand and rubbing her back. Diana Kind, who was by now living in Manhattan, also made the trip, although it is unlikely that her presence was in any way soothing to anyone there, least of all her daughter.

Barbra's teenage fans congregated outside at the gate, hoping to catch a glimpse of their idol, whom they perceived as "one of us." They came bearing gifts—a "Welcome Barb" banner and a pot of chicken soup, both intended as tokens of affection. "Get rid of the creeps," Barbra is said to have commanded one of the guards. "These jerks follow me everywhere. Sometimes, they get my autograph three or four times in one night. Whaddaya think they do with all them autographs?"

Despite the tension, Barbra seemed to get along well enough with her coworkers. "I adored her," says Ray Diffen. "I adored her talent. I adored her energy. We would show her samples of fabrics, which she would just ooh and aah over. I respected her, too, which was strange, because she was only a kid. And I could *see* that she had taste.

"She *did* take over dealing with the sound people," Diffen continues, "and the lighting people, and the makeup people, and the wig people. And she *did* preempt an awful lot of people, but she didn't offend me, and I just thought she was worth everything we gave her."

When asked about the interviews in which she claimed that it was *she* who actually designed the costumes for the show, Diffen says without guile, "I suppose you *could* say that she designed the clothes. She likes to say that." He adds, "I don't have any feelings about her diminishing me as an artist." And, "She *did* do little drawings for me."

Shooting extended through the night and into the morning, and it was glaringly apparent to all that more time should have been scheduled. Marty Erlichman negotiated with the museum management, begrudgingly doling out the dollars as he spoke. The company was granted an extension. Shooting continued all day Sunday and finally wrapped, after some thirty-six consecutive hours, at 6:00 A.M. on Monday morning.

The pressure continued when the company returned to New York. The second act, a circus sequence, was designed to show ringmistress Barbra at play, frolicking with an assortment of animals, exotic and otherwise, as she sang them a medley of carefully selected songs, not unlike some kind of pre–Doctor Dolittle in clown-suit drag. For Barbra, however, the shooting, which would last a grueling thirty-two hours, was anything but fun. A lion broke out of its cage, and she trembled. A monkey nearly devoured her finger, and she screamed. And a penguin, conditioned to the Artic cold, expired under the hot studio lights, and she cried.

The only new friend she would make during the taping was an anteater by the name of Izzy. Given the comparison of their profiles, Barbra felt a special affinity for the animal, who returned the affection as the two nuzzled noses. Quipped Barbra, "He must be Jewish."

At another point, Barbra, exhausted and exasperated, exploded on the set. "Too many people not connected with the show!" she shrieked. "Too many people staring at me."

It was with this pressure, and in this frame of mind, that she had met the press back in Philadelphia. *Why* the press had been invited to attend the taping at all is a question. Of course, the show wanted ratings, but at what expense? Interviews are generally designed to present a star at his or her most appealing. Very few stars are shown to advantage while under the kind of duress that plagued Streisand during the taping of this intense production. Disaster was imminent. After keeping the invited members of the press waiting for over three hours, Barbra finally showed up at the designated location. Making no real apologies, and chomping on a banana, her garbled words of greeting were hardly conciliatory. "Okay," she informed her guests, "ya got twenty minutes. Whaddaya wanna know?"

The reporters proceeded to ask their predetermined questions, but their pens were already dipped in poison.

Most lethal were the words of Rex Reed, a hotshot young writer from the *New York Times* who was making a name for himself with his often provocative style. His feature article on the behind-the-scenes production of "Color Me Barbra" would brazenly take public the stories about Barbra as being brash, egotistical, and inconsiderate, that theretofore had only been whispered behind closed doors.

Upon reading the piece by Reed, which was published to coincide with the special's airing, Barbra was shocked, then enraged. She would never again speak to Reed, growing angry at the mere mention of his name. More important, her relationship with the press in general would never again be the same.

Oddly, Barbra seemed to feel betrayed. She seemed to believe that Reed, as an invited guest to the taping, had had some sort of obligation to secrecy. That he was there to continue the propagation of her rigorously cultivated image, not destroy it. She was angered most by her loss of control. Unlike virtually everything else in her career, she had no command over Reed's writing or over the impact of his words. She failed to accept the fact that Reed, a reporter, had a primary obligation to his readers to write about what he saw. And, through no fault of his, what he saw was *not* pretty. But then, it can be argued, shooting a television show, or making a movie, for that matter, rarely is.

If Rex Reed was guilty of anything, it was not betrayal but cynicism. His tone was decidedly bitchy and, arguably, failed to provide a fair context for the events that occurred. He did not seem to take seriously the very real and arduous effort that Barbra had undertaken or the enormous pressure that she was under. She was, after all, a twenty-three-year-old woman-child who was shouldering, virtually on her own, an extremely ambitious, hugely expensive television spectacular. And she was doing so without sleep. Flashes of temperament, moments of anxiety, and assorted indiscretions were all bound to happen. They just should *not* have happened under the narrowed eye of a reporter with a notepad. Particularly not one with a flair for venom. Particularly not one who worked for the influential *New York Times.*

On March 30, 1966, "Color Me Barbra" excelled in the television ratings and received extremely favorable reviews. Highlights of the hour included "Free Again" (sung entirely in French) in the museum sequence, and her old Harold Arlen standby from the Bon Soir, "Any Place I Hang My Hat," in the concert sequence.

Unlike the case with the first special, there were dissenting opinions of note. *Time* called it "over-cute, overwrought, and suffocatingly overproduced." It added, "If anything, the show proved that one full hour of Streisand's peculiarly nasal voice is about 45 minutes too much." The review concluded, "Streisand's talent is considerable, but it is getting lost in a myth."

During the first week of February, Barbra set off on a much-needed vacation. Typically she found a way of having the trip partially subsidized. She had just completed the taping of her second television special and had already planned the third. The newly stylish, gentile-wannabe Barbra had a desire to attend the unveiling of the spring fashion collections in Paris, so naturally she decided that the focus of her special would revolve around that season's couturier designs. Chemstrand, the sponsor of her specials, agreed not only to finance the trip but to pay for the designer fashions, which would be selected by Barbra and worn on the special to be taped later in the year.

The theme, of course, was calculated to further her status as a fashion trendsetter in the international field. Ironically, while young women all over America wanted to be Barbra, Barbra secretly wanted to be Jacqueline Kennedy, with all of her breeding, beauty, and sophistication. And she was, it seemed, on her way to accomplishing just that. Only weeks before, Barbra had been named one of the Ten Best-Dressed Women in America. That year, Jackie Kennedy was taken off the list and bumped up into the Fashion Hall of Fame, a claim shared only by Mrs. William Paley. For Barbra, who placed eighth, it was her premier appearance on the list. She said, "Now I hope people will stop calling me 'kooky.' " And of her growing influence on the fashion world, she quipped, "Two years ago I started wearing fox. Now everybody I know wears fox."

On the flight to Paris, Barbra, twenty-three, entertained herself with a curious diversion. She became fixated on the idea of her own death. She envisioned herself as a 1960s distaff version of James Dean, who had died in a car crash at the age of twenty-four in 1955. Dean's death came only weeks before the release of *Rebel Without a Cause*. After the picture opened, he was elevated, albeit posthumously, into superstardom. Barbra imagined the newspaper headlines telling of *her* death in a plane crash. She wondered what kind of coverage *she* would merit. And she wondered, too, about the millions of viewers who would watch "Color Me Barbra" (which was nearly two months away from airing) on their television sets, knowing all the while that she had died a tragic death.

The trip was an elaborate affair, arranged and organized by Joan Glynn, then the vice president of marketing at the advertising agency which handled the Chemstrand account.

"The point of the trip," says Glynn, "was to buy clothes in Paris, because there was no ready-to-wear then. It was only couture. I had been going to the collections for years. I knew who the people were there. I knew who had to be contacted. So we went off to Paris after all of the negotiations. I preceded Barbra by a couple of weeks to arrange everything.

"She flew over with an entourage of six people, including Elliott Gould, Lee Solters, and Marty Erlichman, her constant mentor. We stayed at the only [acceptable] hotel you could go to at that time, which was the Plaza Athenée. Barbra had almost a whole floor. We negotiated an extra dimension to the trip, which was that *Life* magazine would follow her around. Diana Lurie was the writer. Also, I made a deal with *Vogue* to do a cover story."

The couturiers almost immediately began courting the new and unlikely style-setter. They wanted not only the association of her fame and all of its attendant publicity, but also the lucrative account to do the clothes for the special.

"We were immediately solicited by gifts, flowers, and champagne by all the members of the couture," Glynn recalls. "Cardin sent out an entourage to meet her at the airport. It was extraordinary. She went right to Cardin's house from the airport. The place was filled with all of Paris, all of the top people. Jeanne Moreau was there. It was a social party to welcome her to Paris. It was also at this party that I first saw anyone doing drugs in my life.

"We saw the collections," Glynn continues, "and viewed the shows. We wanted what was called the *place d'honneur,* the place of honor, which was normally given to the Duchess of Windsor. The next row behind that was for the major press. The row behind that was for the big key stores worldwide. It was all very precise. And there was a woman there with a list, who was like a tiger at the gates. You had to check in. Barbra *got* the *place d'honneur.* She didn't know what it was, but I told her that she should have it. I really fought for it."

With that settled, the unveiling of the new spring collections of 1966 began. Chanel showed suits. Grès showed a tent-shaped evening gown, which Barbra critiqued with, "You'd never be able to tell what was going on under there!" And Yves Saint Laurent presented exaggerated sailor suits and transparent organza dresses. After viewing the Cardin collection (over two decades before Sharon Stone would make it fashionable), Barbra decried, "What's this new thing about not wearing underwear? Those girls didn't have a *thing* on under their dresses. I could see right through. I was embarrassed."

Barbra, who fancied herself as the arbiter of good taste at the time, was unimpressed. Publicly, she stated, "Nice, but not for me." Privately, she declared, "It stinks!"

Some felt the same about the outfits *she* wore. She made it a point to tell anyone who listened that she had personally designed the jaguar suit she was wearing, with its masculine shirt and tie, and its matching homburg hat. She further informed whoever asked that it had been made for her by a Manhattan furrier for $3,500. Most of the women who attended the collections—including Marlene Dietrich, Elsa Martinelli, and rows of assorted countesses—dressed in conservative suits so as not to take attention away from the designers being showcased. In contrast, Barbra's outfit was considered positively scandalous, and it hogged a good deal of the attention, and the focus of most of the cameras. It virtually screamed for attention and had even the pantyless models ogling from the stage.

"Cardin was most cordial," recalls Joan Glynn, "and wanted it [the account] badly. There were a lot of paparazzi outside of the Cardin salon. He had alerted them [of Barbra's attendance]. She was over an hour late. The shows were on the second floor in this beautiful salon. I must have gone up and down those stairs thirty times, asking, 'Are the cars here yet?' 'Are the cars here yet?' And they would say, 'The cars are not here, madame.'

"The entire trip," continues Glynn, "was kind of a series of 'How late can Barbra be.' We would be an hour late for something and I would have to go inside and say, 'Barbra, we absolutely *have* to go in ten minutes.' And she would say, 'But I'm not ready.' And I would say, 'But you look *wonnnnnderful.* I've never seen anybody look better in my life!'

"She had a Marilyn Monroe complex," conjectures Glynn. "If you're important, they've *got* to wait for you. She would *always* be late. Maybe she was frightened. Maybe she was putting on her face for the third time, like Monroe used to do. We never knew. All we knew was that she was always more than an hour late for everything. This led to a lot of problems. At the shows, I would almost have to throw myself across five or six seats to hold them for her, because they would want to release the seats to other very important people. 'She's not coming, madame,' they would say to me. 'Yes, she *is* coming,' I would answer."

When asked what it was like to work with Barbra amidst the seemingly glamorous backdrop of Parisian haute couture, Glynn suggests that it was something of a challenge. "Her demands were, 'I *can't* get there at *that* time,' and 'I *can't* be ready,' and [when something went wrong] '*Fix it.*' It was very trying because I was working with people [in the fashion world] who were used to being the king or queen. They didn't understand [the way Barbra operated]."

According to Glynn, despite her newly recognized flair for fashion, Barbra was totally ignorant when it came to the world of couture. "She was always saying, 'Tell me again. *Who* are the great designers?' And, 'Are we getting the *right* designers? Are we getting *it?*'" She was also uncertain about her own appearance and conduct, asking Glynn, "How do I look?" and "Am I doing the right things?"

At the Chanel showing, Barbra was granted a rare audience with Chanel. Glynn recalls, "Chanel sat at the head of a long, curving staircase, and she went like that [motioned us over with the crook of her finger], so we went plowing up the stairs. It was momentous because, at that point in her life, she very seldom entertained anyone. Barbra could not speak French, but she could *mimic* French, and she had this great ear. So she was able to fake French and communicate with Chanel. Actually," recounts a bemused Glynn, "Chanel knew how to speak English, but she wasn't going to say so. Barbra talked to her for half an hour, but we didn't choose Chanel. The deal was no good. She was very tightfisted."

The Dior show was delayed to accommodate Barbra's late arrival. "They held the show in a couple of places," Joan Glynn recalls. "They knew there was money in it. I had already told them that if we chose their house, we would buy twelve to fourteen pieces of merchandise."

Back at the Dior salon, the Duchess of Windsor, among others, waited for the ever tardy girl from Brooklyn. "No wonder the duchess looked so grouchy," Barbra would later comment. The account would eventually go to Dior. "It was then," says Glynn, "the finest French house." Barbra selected nine outfits to wear on the special.

According to published reports of the period, the clothes cost an estimated $20,000. However Joan Glynn says the actual price tag was much higher.

"I kept having to redo the budget because it kept escalating. I was there for a month, and Barbra was there for two weeks. I had to keep defending the budget because I was the one who kept signing the bills. The clothes alone were $150,000. The entire trip cost about $200,000, which was extraordinary for that time."

While in Paris, there was one thing in particular that Barbra wanted to do, Glynn recalls. "She wanted to see the court of Versailles, so I arranged for us to do two things at Versailles. One was a private tour of the whole castle. In addition to that, they opened up something that had never before been opened up for anybody, and that was the little theater that Marie Antoinette had created within Versailles. It was there that she used to stage her own little private performances and shows. Barbra went up onto the stage, walked across it, and pirouetted around. She thought that was the best thing since lox. *That* was a terrific moment.

"The other wonderful evening I remember with Barbra was when Ray Stark arranged for her to have dinner at Maxim's. He had flown in for this night. I think dinner was set for nine o'clock. As usual, I arrived early. The table at the center was for Barbra, Elliott, Marty Erlichman, Ray Stark, and his wife, Fran. I was at the next table. It was *very* elegant. Again, Barbra was an hour or so late. I was pacing outside because *Life* magazine wanted to be sure to get her as she walked into the entrance. When she finally did arrive, she looked, for the first time, like Nefertiti. She had her head wrapped in a white turban with a big jewel. She was dressed all in white, and was wearing some jewelry that looked terrific and must have been borrowed. I guess she realized the value of Ray

Stark, so she came out looking like *that."* Glynn adds, "I never saw her looking that good before."

After the clothes were purchased and the fittings at Dior completed, Barbra and Elliott embarked on a three-week tour of Rome, Marseilles, Nice, and Florence. At the airport in Paris, Joan Glynn bade Barbra farewell. The two women promised to see one another when the special was shot. "It was like a Japanese goodbye," Glynn says. "We were all bowing and waving." Glynn remained in Paris a few extra days for "damage control." She explains, "I had to apologize to all the designers."

The primary reason that Barbra had *not* walked out on her *Funny Girl* contract at the Winter Garden was also the reason that she agreed, albeit begrudgingly, to reprise her performance at the Prince of Wales Theatre in London: She wanted to do the picture, and Ray Stark had made himself perfectly clear. No London, no Hollywood. Stark insisted that Barbra play the show in Europe because he believed it would bolster the eventual foreign distribution sales and box office of the film.

And so she deplaned from Pan American flight 100 at London's Heathrow Airport on March 20, 1966. She was accompanied by her hairdresser, her secretary, and Marty Erlichman. The press agent who had been hired to represent Barbra sent a limo and a note which explained the reason for his absence: her arrival happened to coincide with his wedding. Despite the groom's other plans, Barbra reportedly summoned him to her hotel room that night to discuss the publicity campaign for her show.

While the poor put-upon press agent failed to appear at the airport to greet Barbra, Elliott *was* there. He had arrived in London weeks before to find suitable living quarters for his wife. However, the current tenant of the house he eventually found, Cary Grant, was not quite ready to make his exit. Thus, the Goulds had to content themselves in the interim with a suite at the Savoy.

Months before, Elliott, at Barbra's behest, had been offered the part of Nicky Arnstein in the London show. He had wanted the role when it was cast for the Broadway production, but had not even succeeded in getting a reading. Perhaps sensing a backlash—everyone would have sniped that it was his wife's influence that got him the job—he decided against doing the show in London, despite the likelihood that he could have played the part, and played it well. "I'm more talented than all of the guys who ever played Nicky put together," Gould would later say with no effort at mock modesty.

With the departure of the chivalrous Mr. Grant, the Goulds moved into their temporary new home in the fashionable Ennismore Gardens. Inspired by the refinement of her new surroundings, Barbra, just as she had been doing all of her life, remade herself again. Now, not only was she a gentile, she became a *British* gentile, with some imagined lineage to the royal family. "Shall we go to the drawing room?" she playfully drawled to the visitors of her luxurious flat. The question was usually followed not by an answer but by Barbra's "You will have tea, of course." To guest Sheilah Graham, she announced, "This morning I decided I'd have avocado sandwiches at teatime—isn't it wild?" And, "I've always wanted to have tea and cakes."

Visitors to the house would also learn that it cost $1,600 a month to rent, a figure that seemed to greatly impress Barbra, and that the house came equipped with a butler and a cook but *not* a shower.

Her accommodations at the Prince of Wales theater were far less lavish. Reportedly, upon entering her dressing room for the first time, Barbra scanned the surroundings, did an abrupt about-face, and walked out. Her manager is said to have then informed the theater management that his client would not return until they provided her with a dressing room more befitting a star of her stature. Furthermore, she reportedly demanded that no one be allowed to dress on the same floor, and that a back staircase be reserved for her use alone.

When the dressing room flap was resolved (heads are said to have rolled, walls are said to have come down, and a completely new set of furniture is said to have been moved in), rehearsals commenced at the Prince of Wales, and all of Barbra's attention turned back to work. She had little interest in reprising Fanny Brice, but her fear of failure superseded all her reservations. In fact, she pumped up her enthusiasm by convincing herself that British audiences and critics would be tougher to please than those on Broadway. "They're more serious about theater here," she cautioned members of the company. Moreover, her arrival in London had been treated in the British press like the second coming of fish-and-chips. Barbra feared that these expectations were too impossibly high for her to meet.

With the same "I'll show you" drive that motivated her out of Brooklyn years before, she became a woman with a mission. If she didn't take over the directorial duties of Lawrence Kasha, later one of the creative talents behind "Knots Landing," she certainly shared in them. She didn't like the lighting, or the music, or the sound. Hidden microphones were planted all over the stage, and they had a tendency to pick up the heavy breathing of Michael Craig, who had been cast, with her approval, as Nicky Arnstein.

Accompanying Barbra from the Broadway production were Kay Medford and Lee Allen. "I didn't think I was going to spend as much time in the show as I did," says Allen of his involvement in *Funny Girl.* "Part of that was because of Barbra. She asked me to stay on when I was going to leave the show [during its Broadway run]. And she asked me to go with her to London."

When asked about the problems the show was having during its preparations at the Prince of Wales, Allen responds, "She *was* giving them a hard time in London. She did not like the conductor there, and she did not like the way the orchestra was sounding." Barbra had the conductor fired, and at her insistence, Milton Rosenstock was flown in from New York to take over during rehearsals.

"There was difficulty in the sound system as well," Allen relates. "And Barbra had her own sound man come in from New York."

"She was always a do-it-yourself type," he says. "With Barbra, it was, 'If you don't do it, *I'll* get it done.' Or, 'I don't like the sound of the orchestra. What are we gonna do about it?' And if the director said, 'I don't know,' she would say, 'Well then, damn it, *I* know!' And she would call the people that she could depend on. I always felt," adds Allen, "that Barbra was like a locomotive going at full speed and she didn't slow down for the crossings."

Her efforts apparently paid off. Upon its opening on April 13, 1966, the show received mixed reviews, but Barbra herself was accorded exultant praise, and, later, Great Britain's *Variety* Poll Award as Best Foreign Actress.

Still, she was disappointed with her six-curtain-call opening. She had become accustomed to ovations of the stomping, cheering, wolf-whistling sort. Instead, the British sat in their seats and offered proper, polite applause.

Following the performance, Barbra complained, "I don't think it was electric out there. They were so quiet I only felt the things that were going wrong."

Among the luminaries present that evening were David Merrick, Elsa Martinelli, Rex Harrison, John Huston, Peter Sellers, Leslie Caron, and Warren Beatty.

Contrary to previous published reports, Barbra did *not* feud with her British costars. She *did* keep her distance, which was understood and accepted. She even seemed to develop an affinity, strictly platonic, for

Michael Craig, in whose health she took an interest. He had, it seems, fainted onstage during one of the performances.

One week before *Funny Girl* opened in London it was announced that extensive negotiations had been concluded and that Barbra would embark upon a five-week, twenty-city tour of the United States later in the year. Comic Alan King and his partner, Walter A. Hyman, would sponsor the tour. They agreed to pay Barbra a $50,000 fee for *each* of her twenty performances, or a flat $1 million for the entire five weeks. The compensation was said to be the highest ever given a performer for a concert date, with Frank Sinatra's $45,000 being the previous largest amount. Moreover, her forty-six-page contract also guaranteed that she would have final approval of the concert locations and the ticket prices to be charged, that she would not have to fly more than two and a half hours a day, *and* that she be granted a $500-a-week budget for fresh flowers. The agreement also stipulated that the salaries of Barbra's thirty-five-man orchestra were to be paid by the tour's sponsors, in contrast to Sinatra, who had to pay for *his* accompaniment, the Oscar Peterson trio, out of his own pocket.

Barbra's management, and Barbra herself, for that matter, publicly made much ado about the lucrative, "unprecedented" deal. Later, she would insist that it was the height of vulgarity to talk publicly about money. But before she learned that particular lesson in show business etiquette, she flaunted the fabulous figures that she did, and would, earn.

When asked to name the highest-paid performer in the world, Barbra replied, without batting an eye, "I am." When asked about the Beatles, she insisted, *"I'm* paid more. I get as much for me, one person, as all four of the Beatles."

To further support her case, she flaunted the $1 million fee she was to be paid for her five-week tour. "That's as much as Elizabeth Taylor receives," Barbra boasted, "but she has to spend three to five months on a picture to make it."

And then the roof fell in. Or rather, the stomach protruded *out.* On April 18, 1966, just five days after the show's opening in London, Barbra announced that she was pregnant with her first child, with a due date of December. In making the announcement, Barbra acknowledged that most of her previously scheduled commitments throughout the year would have to be canceled, including all but four of the dates for her planned million-dollar tour. The press came up with headlines like BARBRA IS EXPECTING MILLION DOLLAR BABY! and BARBRA AWAITS MILLION

DOLLAR BABY! Putting a price tag on her pregnancy became a matter of considerable irritation to Barbra. "Why do they have to always talk about *money?*" she would ask.

In addition to the canceled concert dates, Barbra also backed out of the couture-influenced television special for Chemstrand. All the work, time, and money that had gone into the Parisian trip and shopping expedition had been for naught. It made no sense to postpone the special until the following year, because by then the expensive Dior fashions which had been purchased would already be out of style.

Barbra, nevertheless, insisted upon keeping the clothes. Joan Glynn recalls, "Part of our contract with her was that she would get the clothes *after* the show. But Barbra said, 'I get the clothes *anyway.*' Did she ever wear the clothes? I don't know. Did she give them to her sister or to friends? I don't know. I know only that she kept them."

Barbra informed director Lawrence Kasha that her dance numbers in *Funny Girl,* as well as her more rigorous stage movements, would have to be curtailed. She also told the stunned Prince of Wales management that she would be cutting back on her performances. She refused to do the Wednesday matinees and, to the horror of the backers, the Saturday evening shows. "When she discovered she was pregnant," Lee Allen says, "it was a very good excuse for her not to do the matinee, and to cut down to only one show a day." He adds that it also gave her an incontrovertible reason not to extend her run in the show, which Ray Stark and others had been cajoling her to do. "She didn't like London," Lee Allen says. "She couldn't wait to get out of there."

Barbra loved the idea of her pregnancy and, fortunately, did not have the expectant mother's ritual of morning sickness to curb her joy. One week after her announcement, she was already wrestling with knitting needles in the creation—or rather, the *attempted* creation—of a pink wool baby blanket. "My kid's going to have the wildest blanket," she proclaimed, "I'm making it out of all kinds of pink." But she would prove to be too impatient for knitting, and the knitting of the blanket was taken over by her dresser. It would finally emerge, in the end, with patches of pink, orange, and burgundy.

When asked about prospective names for her child, Barbra delighted in her choices and her theories behind them. "If it's a girl," she said, "Samantha. You've got to think of the personality of your child. Samantha has possibilities. If she turns out to be a tomboy, her friends can call her Sam. You've got to think of things like that. Or she can be Samantha, exotic or dignified as the case may be." She added, "Yes, I like a two-way name like that.

"Now, if it's a boy, I'll call him Jason Emanuel. Emanuel was my father's name [Jason, for the record, was reportedly selected in honor of artist Jason Monet, who had been befriended by the Goulds in London]. I like the same sound . . . the—what do you call it . . . alliteration. Jason Emanuel Gould. I thought about calling him Gideon but at school they might give him a nickname like Giddy. I can't allow that. Gabriel was another candidate."

Some speculated at the time, even several members of the company, that Barbra had known about her pregnancy *before* the *Funny Girl* opening. In fact, she had been, in the circle of her intimates, among the last to know. Elliott had conspired with her physician to keep the news from her until the show opened. She had, it was reasoned, enough on her mind and her shoulders until then. Following her six curtain calls, Elliott kissed her, congratulated her on her performance, and then again on her impending motherhood.

The Savoy Hotel had been the setting for the conception. Elliott had had it all planned out in his mind. A baby was to be his gift to his wife. He thought a child would bring Barbra down from the stratosphere and return her to real life, jolt her out of her self-absorption, and put her in touch with her inherent womanhood. Ultimately, he hoped, it would also inspire her to give up her career. That night at the Savoy, after a little amorous cajoling by Elliott, Barbra relented, not really believing that anything would come of it.

Once told, she was stunned, then filled with uncertainty. "But what about . . . ?" became her most frequently employed expression. But once she warmed to the idea, Barbra began viewing her pregnancy as a welcome time-out from her life. She was tired of being a slave to her schedule, and, facing a lineup of formidable commitments, pregnancy was her out.

"This pregnancy is a God-given thing," she declared, "and the timing couldn't have been better." And, sounding very much like an echo of Elliott, she said, "It's the only thing that's going to give me roots again." She would add, "I get so self-involved, too focused on my own problems. But when I think of what's growing inside me, it's a miracle, the height of creativity for any woman. I used to dream about having a child, but it just didn't seem possible that it could happen to me."

After some nine hundred performances in London, New York, Philadelphia, and Boston, Barbra gave her final stage appearance in *Funny Girl* on Saturday, July 16, 1966. Plans to carry on the show with Lisa Shane, her understudy, were canceled when no one bought a ticket at the box office. Actually, the news should not have come as too great a shock to Shane or to the theater management. When Barbra had missed a performance on April 28, due to the flu, *four hundred* people stormed out of the theater and demanded their money back. Those who remained vigorously booed and jeered poor Lisa Shane, who, through some inner resource, made it through the performance.

Barbra returned to New York on July 17. Almost immediately, the four-months-pregnant (and *showing*) Barbra set about plans for her abbreviated tour. First, she attended a Columbia sales convention at the Sahara Hotel in Las Vegas, where she sang a couple of songs from *Color Me Barbra*, the soundtrack recording of her television special.

On July 30, she flew via chartered Aero Commander jet to Newport, Rhode Island, for her scheduled appearance at the Newport Music Festival. Referring to her obviously pregnant appearance, and again setting herself up as the underdog, Barbra self-deprecatingly told the audience, "Thank you for coming to see such a schlepp." And then she sang twenty songs over a ninety-minute period. For her encores, she did "Happy Days Are Here Again" and, despite the summer heat, "Silent Night." The latter, an inspired choice, was rearranged (not unlike the way "Happy Days" had been) and made her own. It was selected in part because she had recorded it while in London and had plans to include it on a forthcoming album of Christmas songs.

The Newport concert grossed $121,000, far exceeding the festival's prior high of $80,000, set by Frank Sinatra the previous year. Barbra felt a strange, and very real, competition with Sinatra, and took particular delight in breaking his record. Still, Sinatra clearly had the advantage. His television special "Frank Sinatra: A Man and His Music" bested "Color Me Barbra" at that year's Emmys *and* Grammys.

On August 2, Barbra played the John F. Kennedy Stadium in Philadelphia, which was followed by the Atlanta Stadium in Atlanta on August 6, and Soldier Field in Chicago on August 9. And then, promising the King-Hyman team that she would make up for her canceled dates with a twenty-seven-city tour in 1967, Barbra flew back to New York to rest and recuperate at a rented beach house at Sands Point on Long Island Sound.

The vacation didn't last long. In September, she resumed the recording of her French album, *Je m'appelle Barbra*, which had been almost a year in the making. It was fairly common for stars of the day to record foreign-language albums, and Barbra, who wanted to expand her international sales base *and* further cultivate her image, proved to be no exception. Despite not speaking the language, she decided to record in French, because she deemed it the "classiest" of all languages. Furthermore, she had met French composer Michel Legrand when she was looking for a musical director to replace Peter Daniels, and the two hit it off exceptionally well. Their relationship would be turbulent but productive, culminating with their collaboration years later on *Yentl.*

Back in 1965, on many nights after a performance of *Funny Girl,* Legrand would meet Barbra on the practically barren Winter Garden stage—he at the piano, she at the microphone. For hours, they would exchange and explore their musical ideas. "She was prodigiously happy," Legrand later related. "Some nights we laughed so much together." Some speculated that the two were having an affair, and they very well may have been. Certainly, Elliott was none too pleased when she would return home to their three-hundred-year-old bed at 5:00 A.M.

Likely, it was Legrand's influence that had Barbra singing in French. But despite their apparent affection for one another, all was not harmonious when the two ventured into the recording studio for *Je m'appelle Barbra.* When Barbra insisted upon *twenty-eight* takes for the recording of "Autumn Leaves," Legrand became exasperated. "The woman," he would later say, "is not very flexible."

Of her reputed temperament, Legrand recalled, "I watched her during certain rehearsals becoming incredibly angry because someone had forgotten to put out his cigarette or because she had seen someone in a corner somewhere whose presence she didn't feel was necessary." He added, "An angry Barbra is all of a sudden a usually courteous and delicate woman seized with fury and capable of the most foul vocabulary. . . . [She is] the epitome of charm and politeness on one side and on the other a sort of Brooklyn nag, aggressive, intolerant, enraged."

Je m'appelle Barbra was released in October 1966, and although it sold well enough for a bilingual recording, it performed disappointingly according to Streisand standards, becoming the first of her albums not to go gold. The album would, however, provide a footnote. It included Barbra's first musical composition, "Ma Première Chanson," with lyrics by Eddy Marnay, which was published by her Emanuel Corporation.

In the last months of her pregnancy, Barbra was, for one of the first and few times in her life, truly, uninhibitedly happy. She could relax without worrying about a performance, and hence a judgment. She could eat without worrying about her figure. She could sit still and let herself go, without feeling unproductive. Pregnancy was, in its way, her ultimate idea of nirvana; accomplishing something great without having to deal with the outside world. The creation—all of it—was taking place inside of her, literally. She concerned herself, mostly, with her natural childbirth lessons (Elliott oversaw her breathing exercises) and thoughtful dissertations on how her child, who she was certain would be a girl, would be raised.

"I don't want a child who has nothing but toys from F.A.O. Schwartz," she told Gloria Steinem. "Kids like simple things to play with: a piece of paper, a walnut shell. They should be dirty and basic when they want to be. I don't want to make her a kid brought up by the book."

She stressed, too, that her child would be given generous, open expressions of love, and have the presence of *both* parents, unlike her own experience.

On December 29, 1966, at 3:00 P.M., Jason Emanuel Gould, seven pounds, twelve ounces, made his bleary-eyed entrance into the world at Mount Sinai Hospital in New York. Barbra had been determined to undergo natural childbirth, but it had been ruled out at the last minute by her doctor, who discovered that Jason was a "breech baby," meaning that he was positioned head up in her womb. He was born, after nine difficult hours of labor, by way of Caesarean section. For Barbra, the delivery was a moment of pure, absolute accomplishment. "My son," she would say, "what a marvelous phrase, 'my son.'"

Jason Emanuel would start out life with something of an identity crisis. Visitors at the observation window had a hard time spotting him among all the other newborns. There was no trace of a "Streisand" or a "Gould" identification tag in sight. What *was* there reflected not only his mother's sense of irony and humor but also her sentimentality. It seems that the tag on Jason's bed had been labeled with an alias. It read, "Angelina Scarangella."

Eighteen

Rolling Out the (Blood) Red Carpet

She threw herself into motherhood as if it were another project to be conquered. She took Jason's photograph every Thursday, the day of his birth, to document his progress. She marveled over his physical features, doting on his every rounded shape, his every dimpled crevice.

"He has his father's cleft, which is absolutely beautiful," she exclaimed.

"You mean a cleft in his chin?" a visitor asked.

"Where else do you have a cleft?" she shot back, combative, even in the lingering afterglow of childbirth.

She tape-recorded each giggle and gurgle. She bestowed him with endearing nicknames, "Jacy" and "Little Frog" among them. She bathed him in his little yellow tub. She set up a nursery off the kitchen of her penthouse apartment. She paid for an electronic surveillance system to be installed in his room so that she could hear his waking cry. She fed him his meals, frequently snatching a spoonful for herself. "Mmm, I love baby food!" she proclaimed in between bites of strained applesauce. She even delighted in his bodily functions. "Isn't he a gas?" she gushed when her persistent back-patting produced the desired audible burp.

She was intent on *not* making her own mother's mistakes. It vexed her greatly when someone would comment, "I hope that he has your voice." Although probably intended as a compliment, she would snap back with an emphatic *"Why?"* Her child would have the freedom to become whoever and whatever he wanted. She had no interest in pushing him into show business, or away from it, for that matter, unless he was so inclined. Her son would follow his *own* course, with selective parenting to guide him, and a good deal of encouragement to reinforce him.

She was remaking herself the model enlightened mother. "It's a whole new me," she exclaimed. "A normal me." Elliott had hoped that Jason's arrival would make Barbra less self-absorbed. Instead, she simply became absorbed with another, theretofore undiscovered, facet of herself. It wasn't so much about Jason, it was—like almost everything else in her narrowly focused world—about *her.* "If I were a queen," she declared, "they would never find fault. I produced an heir."

With, of course, a little help from her husband. "The first thing I want for the baby is two brothers and two sisters," Elliott announced, perhaps a bit hopefully. "The reason to be married is to have children."

However, his dream of Barbra giving up her career to stay home and bake cookies for their kids was his own macho fantasy. It was not in Barbra's nature to accept limitations in general, and she certainly did *not* intend to give up her career, particularly not at that point in her life. After Jason's delivery, and following several months of intensive mothering, she was more than ready to move on to another project. And what a project it turned out to be.

When her run as Fanny Brice came to an end on Broadway, and after she signed to reprise the role in London, Ray Stark announced that Barbra would indeed make her film debut in the Hollywood version of *Funny Girl.* Contrary to rational thought, her casting was *not* a foregone conclusion. Columbia wanted to buy the rights to the picture, but they did *not* want Streisand as its star. She was too unattractive. Too untested. Too Jewish. Too Brooklyn. Basically, the same old arguments Barbra had been hearing and disproving for years. Instead, Columbia sought an established movie star. They wanted Shirley MacLaine.

Ray Stark was adamant. He *knew* the material, and he certainly knew Barbra's capabilities better than any Hollywood executive. Stark remained firm in his resolve, and Columbia eventually acquiesced. Privately, Barbra was both ecstatic and terrified over the prospect. Publicly, she complained, "I'll have a problem in Hollywood with the hours. I don't get up before twelve-thirty in the afternoon, and I can't leave the house before two."

On December 17, 1965, Mike Frankovich, Columbia Pictures' vice president in charge of production, announced that the studio had signed the picture. Although the purchase price of the deal was not revealed, the move clearly represented a major acquisition for Columbia, along with *The Taming of the Shrew,* the studio's other big investment, which would showcase Elizabeth Taylor and Richard Burton, then quite possibly the biggest stars in the world. Concurrently, Ray Stark announced that *his* company, Seven-Arts, would have no claim on Columbia's ownership of the property, and that he would simultaneously mount a screen version of *The Man Who Would Be King* (a project he would later abandon).

The first person seriously considered by Stark to direct the film was Gene Kelly. Though she didn't have any official say in the matter, Stark sought Barbra's input in the selection. He was simply concerned about providing her with a director with whom she could work. She approved of Kelly, and of George Roy Hill, who had directed the engaging 1964 comedy, *The World of Henry Orient.* Hill would also direct two less-than-successful pictures, *Hawaii* (in which a young actress by the name of Bette Midler had a bit part, 1966), and *Thoroughly Modern Millie* (1967).

Eventually, Stark decided to go with a director proficient in dramas but not in musicals. After all, the weakest element of the stage version of *Funny Girl* had been the development of the relationship between Fanny Brice and Nicky Arnstein.

On July 27, 1966, Stark announced that he had signed Sidney Lumet as his director. Barbra was impressed. After all, Lumet's work to that point had included *Twelve Angry Men* (1957) with Henry Fonda, *Long Day's Journey Into Night* (1962) with Katharine Hepburn, and *The Pawnbroker* (1965) with Rod Steiger, all prestigious dramatic pictures.

Lumet went to work on the script, collaborating with several writers, including Sidney Buchman, a Hollywood veteran whose credits included *Mr. Smith Goes to Washington* (1939). Buchman's *Funny Girl* script dated September 25, 1966, was *not* structured in flashback, nor did it open with Fanny's now legendary line of "Hello, gorgeous." Instead, it began with her query to Eddie Ryan, "You think beautiful girls are going to stay in style forever?" and ended with her singing, "Nicky Arnstein, Nicky Arnstein—I'll never see him again." A revised draft later changed the opening again, this time to Mrs. Strakosh's singing of "If a Girl Isn't Pretty." A typical example of Hollywood excess, the final shooting script would revert back to the flashback structure of the stage version, and to the "Hello, gorgeous" opening.

Unlike most producers on most pictures, Ray Stark was passionately involved with every move related to the evolution of *Funny Girl.* It is uncertain whether Stark became disenchanted with Lumet, or whether Lumet tired of Stark staring over his shoulder. When asked to elaborate on the schism between himself and Stark, Lumet would only say, "The matter is now in the hands of my lawyer." Sidney Lumet departed from the production on January 16, 1967, two weeks after the birth of Jason Emanuel.

Stark scrambled around for a replacement. In addition, he almost had to find another *studio,* since Columbia, uncertain about Streisand and leery of the budget, began to waver. Moreover, Stark was anxious to get started. With Lumet directing, the picture was to have started shooting in March. Originally, it was supposed to have started in January, but was postponed because of Barbra's pregnancy.

Columbia and Stark resolved their problems—it was agreed that the budget would not exceed $8.5 million—and someone at the studio suggested William Wyler as the film's director. Two years before, Wyler had made the acclaimed picture *The Collector* for the same studio. At first, Stark was reticent. He feared that Wyler, given his reputation for autonomy, would try to wrest complete control of the picture.

After the two met, however, Stark gave the legendary director his enthusiastic endorsement. After all, if he truly wanted to improve the dramatic elements of the *Funny Girl* material, who better to do it than Wyler, who had directed *Ben-Hur* (1959), *The Heiress* (1949), *The Best Years of Our Lives* (1946), and *Wuthering Heights* (1939), the last regarded by many as the finest romance picture ever made in Hollywood.

Columbia did have several concerns regarding Wyler. He was sixty-five at the time and deaf in one ear. Not a good sign for a man being considered to direct a multimillion-dollar *musical.* And perhaps the most important concern about Wyler was that he had never before directed a musical.

The official story of his signing (made public on March 19, 1967) had Wyler agreeing to do the picture with three stipulations: first, the movie would be credited as "A William Wyler–Ray Stark Production"; second, his work had to be completed in time for him to shoot *Patton* at Twentieth Century-Fox, which was then cast with Burt Lancaster and Jimmy Stewart. (Because of health reasons, Franklin J. Schaffner, not Wyler, would eventually direct; George C. Scott and Karl Malden would star.) It is possible that Wyler's third and final stipulation actually came from Columbia and Stark. Wyler insisted, according to public statements released by the studio, that choreographer Herb Ross, who had recently staged the dances for *Doctor Dolittle* and who had worked with Barbra on *I Can Get It for You Wholesale,* be given free rein over the musical numbers in the picture. In other words—although it wasn't termed or credited in this way—he would serve as Wyler's codirector. To save Wyler, who was revered in Hollywood as an industry treasure, any embarrassment, they may have made it appear that the idea originated with him. Giving added credence to this scenario, Ray Stark and Columbia would repeat a similar version of it years later when they hired John Huston, another filmmaker inexperienced in musicals, to direct a movie version of another hit Broadway musical, *Annie.*

Whatever the case, "Wyler's" stipulations were agreed to by Columbia, and he was signed to direct the picture.

And so, *Funny Girl* went into preproduction during the spring of 1967, with an aging, half-deaf director making his first musical (albeit with the added insurance of a younger all-hearing Herb Ross), a protective producer also making *his* first movie musical, and, a headstrong twenty-five-year-old performer making her first motion picture of *any* genre.

Barbra's arrival in Hollywood on May 2, 1967, was heralded like no other in motion picture history. Still, despite the fanfare and genuine curiosity about her, it was dislike at first sight. "I could *feel* my unwelcomeness," she later said.

Timing, certainly, did not serve as her ally. The very week of her arrival, Twentieth Century-Fox announced that Barbra, and not the beloved Carol Channing, who had originated the role on Broadway, would portray Dolly Levi in the film version of *Hello, Dolly!* The casting caused an uproar in Hollywood of the "Who does she think she is?" variety. The town has held Barbra responsible for the slight of Channing ever since.

At a time when big-name actresses were complaining about the scarcity of roles, *Dolly* brought Barbra's tally to *three* major studio productions with a cumulative price tag of $35 million—*without her ever having stepped in front of a motion picture camera.* Moreover, almost as if her good fortune were being flaunted, the studios announced that she would be making at least $250,000 for *Funny Girl,* an estimated $1 million for *Hello, Dolly!* and $350,000 for *On a Clear Day You Can See Forever.*

It's interesting to consider what might have happened had Shirley MacLaine, or some other Hollywood name, been cast over Barbra in *Funny Girl.* A Hollywood star "taking" a role originated by someone else on Broadway was not an unusual occurrence. Still, a great deal of controversy resulted when Audrey Hepburn was cast over Julie Andrews in the screen version of *My Fair Lady*. If Barbra had been similarly slighted, it is likely, as was the case with Andrews, that Barbra would have been eulogized and revered upon her eventual arrival in Hollywood.

Still, Barbra, without much effort, could have charmed her detractors with her self-deprecating humor and her distinct Brooklynese. Instead, she sensed the hostility and retreated. If she had been an actor in the thirties or forties, she would have been groomed by the studio system to deal with her emerging stardom and all of the difficulties and intricacies entailed. Instead, in the Hollywood of 1967, Streisand was left to her own instincts, and what they told her to do was run for cover and lash out when cornered.

She made other mistakes too. She rented, perhaps without regard to the "I want to be alone" irony of it all, the old Greta Garbo house in Beverly Hills. When asked why she selected that particular house, Barbra told a reporter, "It has class, style—something very unusual for Hollywood." She was barely off the plane and she was already putting the town, and its people, down. "People are so self-concerned in Hollywood," she exclaimed, "such utter self-concentration. It's boring." She added, "I wouldn't want to raise my son here, in a town where people are judged by the size of their swimming pools."

And then there was the party which introduced her to Hollywood. It took place in the late afternoon hours of Sunday, May 14, at the lavish home of Ray and Fran Stark. The garden of the Starks' home was covered with a decorative plastic tent, a status symbol at such Hollywood events. Inside, guests found an all-girl band, a sumptuous buffet table, and a virtual who's who of Hollywood high society: John and Pilar Wayne, Rosalind Russell, Marlon Brando with Mrs. Louis Jourdan, Merle Oberon, Nancy Sinatra with producer Ross Hunter, Ginger Rogers, Robert Mitchum, Steve McQueen, Natalie Wood, Jimmy Stewart, Donna Reed, Bea Lillie, Vittorio de Sica, and William Wyler, among others.

Barbra arrived at the party an hour and a half late. That's not "fashionably late," it's an affront, at least that's the way it was perceived by many of the guests. What they didn't know, however, was the reason for her lateness. She had spent hours getting dressed, and undressed, trying on one outfit after another. She was nervous about what she believed was the inadequacy of her appearance, particularly given the caliber of the star-studded gathering, at which she was to be the center of attention. And so, when she finally did walk into the Starks' entrance hall, wearing a short, dark gray dress, she joked about the afternoon sun. "What's the idea," she quipped to Ray Stark, "of starting me off in this terrible lighting?"

By the time the story circulated around town, it had Barbra stalking into the Stark home and demanding that the lighting be changed—or else.

Much was made, too, of her purported snobbishness. After a few strained attempts at mingling, and a disconcerting five-minute meeting with Brando, Barbra retreated into a more private room and carried on her conversations one-on-one. This led some to charge, "She thinks she's too good for us." Others even accused her of acting like a queen, granting a select few a private audience.

"I was at that party," says David Dworski, Ray Stark's assistant on *Funny Girl,* "and Barbra was probably scared shitless. Everybody who was *anybody* was invited to that thing. It was *Hollywood.* Everybody knew each other. Everybody had been in business with each other or in bed with each other. And here Barbra was, and she didn't know anybody."

Her early Hollywood socializing was kept to a minimum, and even then, marred. Under the impression that it was to be an intimate dinner party, Barbra accepted an invitation to Rock Hudson's Beverly Hills home. Upon arriving, however, she found both reporters and photographers. After making a brief appearance and exchanging a few words with her host, she spun around on her heels and left.

The stories of her social atrocities multiplied. For those in Hollywood, repeating and even believing the escapades served as sweet vengeance for Barbra's obvious disdain for their city. She didn't like their boring, "self-centered" personas and their oversized swimming pools? Well, they didn't like her one-minute-aloof, the next-minute-aggressive, New York attitude, and her oversized ego.

If only they had known that when she gazed into the mirror, she wished that she looked like *them.* "My face? I never worried about it," she lied, publicly putting on a brave front. "Funny thing about my face," she continued, "it has always photographed well [another lie]—always. Besides, most of the stars who made it have unusual faces—Claudette Colbert, Marlon Brando, Humphrey Bogart."

In an age when Elizabeth Taylor, Faye Dunaway, Ann-Margret, Jane Fonda, Katharine Ross, Julie Andrews, Candice Bergen, and Raquel Welch were defining the standards of female beauty in the movies, Barbra, with her unconventional face and her comparatively flat chest, was terrified that she wouldn't measure up.

Columbia, too, became concerned about her appearance. So too were Ray Stark, William Wyler, and Herb Ross, although they did not say so publicly. While she had been a star on Broadway and on vinyl, and had managed to look attractive on television (which had surprised even her friends), the question remained: How would she look under the critical eye of a motion picture camera? And how would her face photograph with every flaw magnified on a twenty-foot projection screen?

Barbra was so uncertain over this prospect that she had one of her television specials blown up to motion picture proportions. She was pleased with the results, but they did little to appease her detractors at the studio. Both Columbia and Stark wanted her to submit to a screen test, "just to be sure." Reportedly, Stark offered her tens of thousands of dollars to do the test and Barbra refused. In fact, amid much secrecy—Barbra would deny it to this day—she *did* finally consent to such a test.

Herb Ross recalled, "We were all very unsure that Barbra would succeed with a film audience, as indeed she has, because, at the time the movie was made, her very special qualities were still relatively unfamiliar and certainly nobody in the history of film had ever had that particular combination of—what Barbra did. So, we did a very, very careful screen test of her. And once we saw her on the screen—and I was the one who did that test—we knew that she was able to project on film as well as she projected on stage. In fact, the medium was even more flattering to her than the stage."

Barbra began musical rehearsals for *Funny Girl* on May 4, 1967, over two months before the actual filming. Concurrently, as is the custom on Hollywood musicals, the picture was "prescored." Under the command of Walter Scharf, the film's musical director, all of the songs were prerecorded on and off from early May through the first week of August.

At that time in Hollywood, musical numbers were typically prerecorded on vinyl, and when the picture was shot on a soundstage, the album was placed on a phonograph and the actors lip-synched to their prerecorded voices.

But early into the proceedings, it became clear that Barbra wanted to do things a dozen different ways. Each night at the Winter Garden, she had been given the freedom to alter her interpretation of a song. At the Goldwyn Studios, however, where the prerecording was done, she had a hard time locking onto just *one* interpretation that could be frozen on vinyl.

Picking up on this idiosyncrasy, Scharf devised a new technique, used frequently thereafter. Instead of prerecording the numbers on vinyl, he prerecorded on tape. He also recorded the numbers, complete with vocals and orchestra, on one primary track; and on another track, he recorded just the orchestra. This technique allowed the actors, Barbra in particular, the luxury of changing, and presumably improving upon, their vocal interpretations long after the completion of the prescoring process. It was a technique which would greatly enhance Barbra's eventual performance in the finished picture.

Rehearsals were extensive, lasting twelve weeks. Barbra spent much of the period working with Herb Ross on the musical numbers. She impressed everyone with her professionalism, coming earlier, and leaving later, than anyone else. She even loitered around the studio when her presence *wasn't* necessary, just to watch Ross audition, and then rehearse, some of the dancers and bit players.

Rewarding her efforts, Stark gave Barbra a three-day weekend to relax. She used the time *not* to rest from the arduous *Funny Girl* rehearsals and prescoring sessions, but to host a television special and, in the lexicon of the day, a "happening."

On Friday afternoon, June 16, 1967, she flew into New York and headed straight for Central Park, where rehearsals were in progress. "We had been having a problem with rain," Bob Scheerer, the show's director, relates. "Everybody was scared to death that it was not going to be able to go on. And Marty [Erlichman] kept bitching because he couldn't get any insurance against *mud.*"

Because of the rain, the already abbreviated rehearsal period ended early, around midnight. Director Scheerer would not even hear two thirds of Barbra's numbers until she actually performed them the following night.

The highlight of the rehearsals came on Saturday afternoon. Several hundred people had congregated in the park and stood at the foot of the stage. When Barbra launched into the opening bars of "Second Hand Rose," the entire group began to sing along with her. Pleasantly startled, and perhaps aware of their presence for the first time, Barbra stopped singing and listened as the group, engaged in a little role reversal, sang the song back to her.

"Her jaw was on her chest," Scheerer recalls. "We all just stood there and watched this entire crowd sing. Barbra tried to re-create it that night, but it was nothing like that afternoon. That afternoon was the most thrilling thing you've ever heard in your life."

"She was a *doll,*" Scheerer says of Barbra, who seemed amenable and open to suggestions.

"It was a one-shot deal," Scheerer explains. "She couldn't sit around and look at it and think about it. She had to just *do* it. It was quite different from her other television specials. I had the same thing happen with Sinatra. Everybody said, 'Oh, wait till the other shoe falls.' Well, it never fell. I've had a couple of rotten experiences with people, but not with Barbra."

Imero Fiorentino concurs. He had the difficult task of directing the show's lighting design. "I found her to be extremely cooperative," Fiorentino recalls. "She was very lovely, not temperamental at all." In fact, Fiorentino received only one unusual request, and it came from Marty Erlichman. "He told me, 'I want you to light all the trees in Central Park that surround the area.' And I said, 'Well, that's a *mammoth* job. To do that, we would have to ship the equipment in from Detroit, from Canada, wherever. And the cost would be phenomenal.' So he said, 'Well, go ahead and find out how much it costs.'

"So I did, and of course it *was* phenomenal. When I came back to a preproduction meeting about a week later, I gave him the cost and everybody had an attack. And then he said, 'Well, how much for *three* trees?' And I said, 'Which three do you want?' "

On Saturday night, June 17, after less than two days of rehearsal, Barbra, twenty-five, stepped onto the elaborate Plexiglas stage that had been erected in the ninety-three-acre Sheep Meadow section of Central Park. A clear, brilliant sky, with its illuminating half-moon, shimmered above her. A striking formation of rocks and three illuminated trees stood behind her. Her hair, her own and then some, was piled high atop her head. She wore a floor-length pink chiffon gown that flapped in the cool summer wind. And then she proceeded to sing nearly three dozen songs over a two-and-a-half-hour period.

It was then the largest crowd ever assembled in Central Park. The audience of 135,000 people—only 75,000 had turned out for Leonard Bernstein and the New York Philharmonic the previous summer—included Manhattan grandmothers and teenagers, Wall Street executives and Greenwich Villiage gays. Also well in evidence with their colorful garb and Flower Power buttons, were representatives of the new cultural revolution which was sweeping the country. They called themselves hippies, and they filled the night air with their talk of "love, peace, and happiness" and with the pungent aroma from their oddly shaped cigarettes.

Thousands were reportedly turned away at the park entrance, and they loitered in the streets. Others, who lived in the neighborhood, stayed at home and opened their windows. And motorists, stuck in bumper-to-bumper traffic on the streets surrounding the park, shut off their car radios and stopped honking their horns.

Eight mammoth towers obstructed the view of the audience in the park. They were strung with high-powered lights. Six television cameras (with their red indicator lights turned off; Scheerer didn't want Barbra to know which camera to look into) recorded the event for posterity.

The free concert was hyped as Barbra's homecoming, her way of paying back the hometown fans. Actually, it was a shrewd multimedia assault. Not only would the one-shot concert produce a television special for CBS-TV, it would also result in an album for Columbia Records and help to promote *Funny Girl* for Columbia Pictures.

What *wasn't* captured on camera or seen by the audience that night was Barbra's genuine fear of being so publicly *exposed*. Bob Scheerer recalls, "She was *terrified* that the spotlights would make her a target for a crazy [person] in the audience. As a matter of fact, my ex-wife had to give her a little bit of a push to get her onstage."

Scheerer didn't know, nor did anyone involved in the production, with the likely exception of Marty Erlichman, that prior to the start of the concert, Barbra had received a death threat, allegedly from a member of the Palestinian Liberation Organization. It was, after all, less than two weeks after the Arab-Israeli Six-Day War, and Barbra was a highly visible Jew.

If she canceled the performance at that late stage, a mob scene undoubtedly would ensue. And so she went on, albeit forty-five minutes late. But when she faced the audience, she did not see the mass adoration of 135,000 fans, she saw only the one potential assassin lurking somewhere in the night. And so she moved all over the stage, flinging her pink chiffon in this direction and that, thinking that if a sniper was indeed in the audience, she would at least make him hit a *moving* target.

That night, she forgot the lyrics to some of her songs, but the crowd seemed not to care. They screamed and applauded and strained to catch a glimpse of the famous Streisand face amid all that billowy chiffon.

There were to be no gunshots fired in her direction, and the concert was judged a resounding, even historic success. The only backstage dramas occurred at intermission. Marty Erlichman marched over to where Imero Fiorentino was taking his break.

"Where are my trees?" he demanded. "I paid money for those trees, and I don't see them!"

Fiorentino explained to Erlichman that the trees were indeed lit as planned. Scheerer had elected not to include the illuminated leaves in the frame of his camera. Erlichman then marched over to Scheerer, and as a result, says Fiorentino, "If you look at the second half of the show, you'll see the trees."

Another drama of sorts involved Scheerer, a CBS executive, and a 120-foot runwaylike ramp. "I had a ramp that I asked for," Scheerer says. "Halfway through the show, one of the CBS executives came up to me and said, 'When are you gonna get to the ramp? When are you gonna get to the ramp?' And I said, 'Hold on, hold on. I'll use it.'" Finally, much to the relief of the worrisome executive, and as Barbra held the final notes of her final song, Scheerer ordered that his camera pull back and reveal the ramp.

Not surprisingly, while orderly, the massive crowd had been irresponsible with its trash. The day after the concert, Rheingold Beer, the show's sponsor, had to pay an additional three thousand dollars to the city for the cleanup, which took three days and thirty men. "I guess if they had enough garbage pails for 135,000 people," Barbra said, "there wouldn't have been enough room for the people." Found in the debris were discarded blankets, empty beer bottles, and one black pleated skirt.

While she *would* give a few more performances over the next five years, Barbra would never again perform live without feeling the unmitigated terror she experienced that night in Central Park. Her fears were validated two weeks later, on July 9, during her concert at the Hollywood Bowl. Guards spotted a potential assassin brandishing a .45. He was promptly arrested, and the show continued uninterrupted. Still, Barbra's very real fear of performing live, provoked largely by her bicoastal Central Park and Hollywood Bowl concerts, is something which she has never really resolved.

Nineteen

Lights, Camera, Perfectionism

*I*n the year 1967, Hollywood found itself weathering the last great big-budget musicals. Among the numerous musical pictures in various stages of development were *Funny Girl* and *Oliver!* at Columbia, *Camelot* and *Finian's Rainbow* at Warner Brothers, *Star!* and *Hello, Dolly!* at Fox, *Sweet Charity* at Universal, and *On a Clear Day You Can See Forever* and *Paint Your Wagon* at Paramount. They were all, of course, trying to approximate the enormous success of *The Sound of Music,* which had been released two years before.

The *Funny Girl* company traveled from Los Angeles to Newark, New Jersey, on Monday, July 10, 1967. Accompanying Barbra, twenty-five, were Elliott, twenty-eight, Jason, seven-and-a-half-months, his nurse, and Grace Davidson, Barbra's wardrobe woman. Location shooting began the following day at New Jersey Central in Jersey City, which was substituting in the picture for the Baltimore train platform and concourse.

In her entrance in the sequence, Barbra wanted to emerge from the train in a great puff of smoke, as Garbo had done decades before in one of her pictures. It was Barbra's first scene in her first movie, and already she was making suggestions and overstepping boundaries that were deeply rooted in Hollywood tradition. William Wyler listened to her suggestion and promptly dismissed it. The scene was shot as planned.

From Jersey, the company moved to New York, where the "Don't

Rain on My Parade" number was to be shot in New York Harbor and in the Battery. Herb Ross would direct the sequence, which was meant to take place in the winter of 1915. The scene called for Barbra to exert a good deal of physical energy. Wearing high heels and an ankle-length wool dress in the heat of a New York summer, she had to run thirty yards, repeatedly, along Pier 36 and the East River, carrying a suitcase in one hand, and a makeup case and a bunch of yellow roses in the other. "When friends ask me what I did in the movie of *Funny Girl*," she said, catching her breath, "I'll tell them I was a porter, the only porter in history to wear a sable hat."

"My back hurts," she moaned to Ross. "My feet hurt. You better get it *right* this time." Ross said nothing in response, but mumbled something under his breath about Barbra *not* being the "athletic type."

"Now, now," consoled Ray Stark, who was observing the action. "You're young and healthy and strong."

"Whaddaya mean?" Barbra shot back. "I'm a working mother!"

She complained, too, about the thorns from the roses. And to a visitor on the set she groused, "They gave me a chair with my name on it. So, when do I get to use it?"

When Ross announced that he was ready for yet another take, Barbra picked up her suitcase, her makeup case, and her irksome bunch of yellow roses and scowled at Ray Stark. "Boy," she said, "am I gonna sue you!"

Such was Barbra's anything-*but*-glamorous introduction to filmmaking. Shooting the sequence itself proved complicated. The number called for a helicopter to swoop down on Barbra as she leaned out of a moving train's window, and then again as she stood aboard a tugboat while it passed the Statue of Liberty, all in synchronization with the prerecorded track. Devised by Ross, it was a dazzling dance sequence without dance, a choreography of land, air, and water, an audacious undertaking for a novice filmmaker. The sequence provided the picture with one of its true highlights.

After nine days of location work, the company returned to Hollywood, where principal photography started at Columbia's Gower Studios on Monday, August 7. To accommodate Barbra, who loathed the early morning calls, Wyler adjusted the shooting schedule to begin daily at 10:00 A.M. and last until 7:00 P.M. Barbra was thrilled, noting that Frank Sinatra was the only other actor in Hollywood who had been given this kind of accommodation.

The more difficult musical numbers were shot first. Much to the chagrin of Jule Styne, several were dropped from the score: "Cornet Man," "Who Are You Now?" "Who Taught Her Everything She Knows," and "The Music That Makes Me Dance" included. They were replaced by numbers including "Funny Girl" (*not* the same song deleted from the Broadway score), "Roller Skate Rag" (which *had* been dropped from the show), and "I'd Rather Be Blue," a Fanny Brice song from a later period.

Another new number parodied "Swan Lake" and had Barbra dressed as a prima ballerina complete with a tutu and a crown. The scene called for her to fly through the air and descend into a moonlit castle courtyard to find a gang of leotard-clad men about to shoot her beloved swans.

Expert Peter Foy, who had flown Mary Martin across the stage in *Peter Pan,* was imported from Britain to oversee the flying sequence. For Barbra, it was a trying experience. First of all, she had to put up with the discomfort of the leather straps and braces that were hidden inside of her ballet panties. Second, in between takes on Columbia's Stage 8, she had to wait suspended in the air in the 100-plus degree heat. Third, the flurry of flying activity had a tendency to tilt her tiara off-center. She complained, too, that the feathers on her tutu were too long. And that the rhinestones which adorned her false eyelashes were too close to her eyelids. "What's the matter with her *now*" became a commonly overheard expression among the crew members down below.

The shooting of "Swan Lake," formerly known as "You Gotta Have a Swan," took an inordinate amount of time and put the production behind schedule from the start. Still, Barbra derived a good deal of satisfaction from the sequence. Unlike most of the songs in the show, it was unknown material and provided her with a fresh challenge. Furthermore, it took her back to the age of five when she was a student in Miss Marsh's dance class in Brooklyn. The number, in a way, fulfilled her dream of becoming a prima ballerina, in spite of all of her mother's gloomy prognostications of broken bones. As such, she took the dancing in "Swan Lake" seriously, perhaps too much so, given that the number was meant to be comical.

Filming the "His Love Makes Me Beautiful" pregnant-bride number also proved problematic. Deriving its inspiration from Busby Berkeley as well as from Ziegfeld, it was designed as an elaborate production number which showcased the leggy beauty of the thirty-eight women who had been cast, largely out of Las Vegas showrooms, as Ziegfeld Girls.

Batteries died. Lights flickered out. The Ziegfeld Girls were crushed under the weight of their elaborate headdresses. The budget also caused problems. Herb Ross wanted Florenz Ziegfeld production values at

F. W. Woolworth prices—not an easy accomplishment.

One day, while the number was being shot, a few of the *real* Ziegfeld Girls visited the soundstage. Upon observing the bouquets of white plastic lilies and the cellophane set, one of them shrieked, *"Cellophane! Ziegfeld would roll over in his grave!"*

In between takes, Barbra leaned against a slant board so she wouldn't muss her wedding gown, which was made from yards of satin, lace, and net. Inserted under her dress and over her belly was the pillow that made her appear pregnant. Despite her awkward standing position, Barbra calmed her nerves and eased her boredom by playing gin rummy, Scrabble, and Perquacky. She liked the latter two games because they helped her expand her vocabulary. Her longtime friend Cis Corman served as her most frequent opponent. At Barbra's behest, Corman had been cast in the picture as one of the Ziegfeld Girls.

Initially, Barbra was frustrated by the constant waiting on the set and the jerky starts and stops of Hollywood filmmaking. She experienced other problems adapting to the new medium. Just as she had difficulty "locking in" which interpretation of a song to use during the prescoring sessions, she had trouble deciding which interpretations, facial expressions, and vocal inflections to use when shooting a straight scene. She had, after all, played the role some nine hundred times and could call on a repertoire of interpretations.

To film critic Charles Champlin, who visited the set, she said, "There are seven ways to do a thing, do a scene, say a line, and you do it the fifth way and then you look at it, and you know the third way or the fourth way would have been better. But," she added in reference to the out-of-town tryouts for Broadway shows, "[in film] there's no New Haven and no Philadelphia. You do it and it's done."

The permanence of film scared her. And while she wasn't afraid of the camera, she *was* extremely respectful of it. Unlike theater audiences, the camera could tell when she was giving her best performance and, more important, when she wasn't. The camera never lied. If anything, it only magnified the flaws.

Contrary to a frequently repeated rumor, Barbra did *not* insist upon the placement of a mirror on or above the camera. Rather, she *did* design her own portable makeup table. It was built on a grip's stand like a tripod, and had a light coming from behind it. There were wheels on the bottom of it so that it could be transported from set to set. Barbra would never walk out to do a scene without first checking herself out in the mirror.

To others on the set, the primitive invention was a nuisance. Barbra would use the device on her later pictures as well, and one of her makeup artists recalls, "The guys on the crew would always say, 'Why don't you get that *piece of shit* out of here? It's in the way all the time!' " He adds, "Which it was. But, it was something that Barbra wanted to use."

Like Garbo, she also did her own makeup. "When she first got to the studio, she came to see me," says Ben Lane, who had worked on Garbo's *Camille* (1936) and who was the director of the Columbia makeup department. "Barbra asked me if I minded if she did her makeup herself, and I said, 'Fine.' I talked to her about what she was doing wrong and what she was doing right. The only problem that we had with her was that when she first started she had that straight ["Cleopatra"] line across her eye, and I had to tell her to take that off.* To me, if anyone can do a better job with their own makeup, that's good enough for me."

Other makeup artists under Lane's authority *were* disturbed when Barbra insisted on doing it her way. The two men assigned to her, both experienced professionals, felt humiliated in their relegated positions as Barbra's lackeys. "They just carried her makeup case," Lane recalls. Actually, they had other duties as well. They held the makeup tray for Barbra as she applied her own makeup, and they passed and cleaned her brushes on request.

Vivienne Walker, a highly respected hairstylist on big period pictures, *Cleopatra* included, came from England to head the hairdressing department on *Funny Girl*. Gertrude Wheeler, who has since passed away, served as Barbra's personal hairstylist.

Vivienne Walker recalls, "Gertrude was a wonderful hairstylist and a very composed, competent middle-aged lady. But it was Barbra who designed her own hairstyles. She *told* you how she wanted her wigs done." And she did so, according to Walker, in terms that were not always pleasant. "Gertrude Wheeler was in *tears* many a morning, and she used to come out at the end of the day like a blithering idiot." Barbra's treatment of Wheeler so disturbed her that she wanted to quit. "We *made* her keep her job," Walker says. "We made her go back. But there was never any friendship there between Barbra Streisand and Gertrude Wheeler."

Actually Barbra's behavior on *Funny Girl* was really no different than it had always been. She knew what she wanted, and she knew how she wanted it done. She had been the same way when the Broadway version

---

*If you look closely at the picture, you'll notice that Barbra *is* wearing the so-called Cleopatra line in the "Don't Rain on My Parade" number, which was shot in the first week of shooting. She does not wear it thereafter until late in the picture, by which time she had the power to get away with it.

of the show was in its planning stages. Upon meeting Irene Sharaff, a famous costume designer, who was to do the costumes for the show and, later, the movie, Barbra reportedly scanned Sharaff's sketches and rattled off a litany of appraisals. "I don't like that," "I like that," "I don't like that."

"I was at that first meeting between Barbra and Irene Sharaff," designer Ray Diffen recalls. "It took place at my shop. Barbra came in with two bags of shoes and antique clothing which she had collected. She had a very clear idea of what she wanted Fanny Brice to look like, despite the fact that Sharaff was one of the most distinguished designers there was. In other words, right from the word go, Barbra wanted to be in charge of every aspect of selling herself." Diffen adds, "And I think she was the best person to do it."

Back on the set of the picture, Barbra drove the company to distraction with details related to her appearance, over which she constantly fretted. "I think she was *very* insecure about her looks," Libby Dean, a spectator on the set, says. "She told me that she liked doing her own makeup because she couldn't stand for anyone to touch her face. I told her how gorgeous she looked in her costumes for *Funny Girl,* and she said that she hated every one of them."

She took forever to decide what pair of earrings to wear in one scene, and just as long to settle on the length of her hair ribbon in another scene. For the scene in which she flashes the diamond ring given to her by Nicky Arnstein, she spent *hours* picking out the actual ring while everyone waited for her decision. She wanted a ring that Fanny Brice herself would have worn, not too gaudy, but obviously expensive. She also kept everyone waiting during the shooting of the "Roller Skate Rag" number. She insisted on tying the shoestrings on her skates into pretty, neat little bows, despite the fact that they were *not* going to be seen on camera.

Such things, Barbra argued—even if it was only a certain piece of fabric on one of her forty-three costumes—*affected* her performance. And because the movie, to a very large extent, depended on her performance, the shooting frequently revolved around such details that were meaningless to everyone but Barbra.

She called it perfectionism. Many others called it a nuisance or worse. Naturally, this kind of indulgence caused a good deal of resentment in some in the company. Many were old pros, brought up in the studio system wherein a movie was made in five *weeks,* not five months, and discipline and economy were the law. If Barbra's credo was perfectionism, theirs was professionalism, and the two were not always compatible.

On the set, everyone addressed her with, "Yes, Miss Streisand," "No, Miss Streisand," which was also resented by some because it was all being directed at a twenty-five-year-old making her very first movie. But because she was so obviously talented, her detractors within the company could do little except attack her reputation.

Stories from the set began to appear in the press, including several that called Barbra, among other things, "a full-fledged girl monster." Instead of giving her side, and still burning from the scathing piece by Rex Reed, Barbra refused to talk to reporters. Consequently, the columnists became even more hostile.

Although she didn't have the technical vocabulary to express it, Barbra knew how she wanted to look on-camera and thought nothing of sharing those desires with cinematographer Harry Stradling. She went so far as to ask Stradling to adjust his lighting, explaining, "I *feel* things like lights. I *know* a light should be two inches to the left." It wasn't totally sensory or intuitive. She had, after all, spent countless hours in front of countless mirrors, studying every bump, bone, and pore on her face. She wasn't about to entrust *her* face, and the presentation of it, to a total stranger, even if that stranger was Harry Stradling.

Sixty years old at the time, Stradling was a Hollywood pro well acquainted with movie star egos, fragile, inflated, and otherwise. His credits included *Pygmalion* (1938), *The Picture of Dorian Gray* (1944), which won him his first Academy Award, *A Streetcar Named Desire* (1951), *My Fair Lady* (1964), which won him his second, and *Who's Afraid of Virginia Woolf?* (1966).

Early into the shooting, Stradling reportedly became so exasperated with Barbra's barrage of requests, suggestions, and questions that he threatened to walk off the picture. Eventually, the two developed a friendly, even close, working relationship.

Essential to their understanding, Barbra learned to trust Stradling. She asked the cameraman to shoot her from the left side of her face (her nose looks smaller from the left), and for the most part, he did. When filming Barbra, he also placed a sliding diffusion glass over the lens of his camera. Typically, the device is used in Hollywood on older stars to prevent their wrinkles from showing. What director Gene Saks and cinematographer Philip Lathrop did with the sixty-plus-year-old Lucille Ball in *Mame* (1974) is an extreme example. In Barbra's case, it was used to soften her features and make her look more feminine. Stradling said of Barbra, "She has youth, but she's a difficult girl to photograph."

Barbra also entrusted Harry Stradling with her slightly crossed eyes. Lee Allen, who replayed his role of Eddie Ryan in the picture, recalls, "Barbra has an eye that gives her a little problem when she's tired. It goes a little bit wayward. The cameraman knew it. And so, a couple of times when we were shooting, Harry would yell for the cut instead of Willie [Wyler]. He would say, 'Barbra, you're tired. Take five.' "

At one point, Barbra suggested that a certain sequence be shot using the "grainy look" prevalent in some European films which were then creating a stir in Hollywood. Stradling was more amused than offended by the suggestion, which some might have interpreted as interference, if not impertinence. "Okay, Barbra," he said, "I'll go ahead and shoot the picture like we usually do—and afterwards we'll scratch up the film for your 'grainy look.' "

Over the years, it has been repeatedly said that Barbra and Stradling did not get along. So too has the story that she gave the master cameraman *orders* on how she should be lit and photographed. Stradling died in 1970, and no matter what Barbra has said since in her defense, the stories persist. However, according to those closest to the production, this version of what happened distorted the facts.

Marshall Schlom, the film's script supervisor, says, "Her relationship with Harry Stradling was extraordinary. *He* is the one who taught her how you make pictures. Barbra respected him highly."

According to David Dworski, Ray Stark's assistant on the picture, "Harry Stradling was a New York guy [born in Great Britain] who had learned his craft in Paris. He spoke French with this wonderful New York accent. And he took the time to explain *lenses* to Barbra. I mean, anything that you've heard to the contrary about Harry being told what to do by Barbra is horseshit! She would say to him, 'What does this lens do? How does this light affect me? What happens here?' And he was a very gentle guy who was at the top of his form and experience, and he *showed* her. She sat behind the camera, and she saw what this or that lens did."

Makeup director Ben Lane remembers, "Harry Stradling was a very calm cameraman. He was one of the best in the business, and, to me, he photographed Barbra better than she's ever looked. He knew which side to photograph, and where to put the lights and everything. He was very careful about everything, and he had complete control of the situation. I was very, very close to Harry, and he and Barbra liked each other. I remember they bet each other about the Academy Award. They talked about splitting it if either of them won."

Barbra Streisand's desire to direct pictures was born on the set of

Funny Girl, under the tutelage of Harry Stradling. She was curious about everything, and once Stradling understood her sincerity (and her insecurity), he happily answered her questions.

Others seemed intimidated by her relentless quest for knowledge. Lee Allen recalls, "I remember the first month that we were out there [in Hollywood], Stark said to me, 'I can't *believe* this girl. She's more interested in the things that take place *off*-camera.' What he didn't know, of course, was that she was going to be a producer and a director." Allen adds, "She scared him."

Stark was irritated by what he viewed to be Barbra's extracurricular interests. She was being paid to do *one* job, not five, and her inquisitive dabbling, general fussiness, and pursuit of so-called perfection slowed the production and cost both Stark and Columbia money.

So, when Stark learned that Barbra was being shown the rushes, he became irate. Typically, when viewing the footage of the previous day's shooting, Barbra would wince at something in either her appearance or performance and would insist upon shooting it again. Naturally, this additional filming would cost both time and money. Consequently, Stark banned Barbra from watching the rushes. She retaliated, reportedly, by walking off the set. Thereafter, she was always allowed access to the previous day's shoot.

While working on *Funny Girl,* Barbra also had late night telephone discussions with producer Ernest Lehman regarding the development of *Hello, Dolly!* The calls would last for hours at a time and would concern such matters as whether Barbra could insert the word "the" before the word "them" in the script; and whether she could change the word "particularly" to the word "especially," because the former had a tendency to trip on her tongue. When he learned of these conversations, Ray Stark commented to columnist Joyce Haber, "I *used* to talk to her for an hour every night, after I was in bed. But not anymore, and my wife says it's a very healthy thing [that I don't]."

Barbra bristled at Stark's public putdown. On his part, like others before him, Stark was both hurt and appalled by Barbra's apparent lack of gratitude. After all, he was the man who had made her a star.

But beyond the issue of gratitude, there is also the question of sexism, and the Hollywood of 1967 was decidedly, inarguably sexist. Before feminism was in vogue, Barbra Streisand took responsibility for her own career, her own artistry. Determined to master the medium of film, she asked questions of everyone, about everything. She understood that knowledge equaled empowerment, even then. Without regard to her personal popularity with her coworkers, she knocked down barriers and entered areas theretofore generally reserved for men.

She refused to be concerned only about her looks, as was expected of actresses and starlets of the period. She would not do what the studio, the producer, the director told her, without some kind of an explanation. She also insisted on expressing *her* ideas, giving *her* suggestions. She wasn't doing it in the name of feminism, she was doing it in the name of Barbra Streisand. But the two, it can be argued, went hand in hand.

Just as her relationship with Harry Stradling started off under strained conditions, so too did Barbra's relationship with William Wyler. "I don't know if Barbra remembers this," Lee Allen recalls, "but on the first day all of us reported in like we were supposed to. That is, all of us except for William Wyler. When he finally walked in, an hour late, Barbra stood up and made an announcement. She said, 'If this [lateness] is going to continue, tomorrow *I'm* gonna be an hour late.' In other words, she was saying, '*I'm* in charge here.'"

She also got off on the wrong foot with Wyler by bombarding him with suggestions as to how the film should be developed. It wasn't that she disrespected the legendary director, or that she did not know *who* he was, as was reported in the press at the time. She was well aware of his three Oscars and his fifteen nominations. She fought against being intimidated by becoming aggressive, a common Streisand trait.

In retrospect, her viewpoint was perfectly understandable. She had a hard time accepting that Wyler, or anyone else for that matter, knew the material better than she did.

"It's rare for a newcomer to come in with a lot of stuff already in hand," David Dworski says. "Don't forget, she *knew* this part. This was not a role that she had to create for the screen. She knew the ins and outs of those lines. She also had an ally in the late Isobel Lennart, who wrote the part and virtually tailored it for Barbra. She knew what was and was not gonna work."

Stories circulated that Barbra treated Wyler like a "butler" and that she took over the direction of the picture. "Don't be too hard on Barbra," the joke went, "she's directing her first picture."

Early in their relationship, tension *did* exist between her and Wyler. But the contention that Barbra ran roughshod over a bedraggled Wyler is not true. For the most part, they held each other in mutual respect.

Moreover, Wyler was no pushover. In his over forty-year Hollywood career, he had a reputation for being tough, particularly on actors. "There's only one prima donna on my pictures," Wyler was quoted as saying, "and that's me." Actors were known to shudder in his presence and walk off his sets in shame or fury, only to return subdued and respectful. He was, after all, worth the abuse. Bette Davis, Charlton Heston, Greer Garson, Audrey Hepburn, Walter Brennan, Fredric March, and Olivia de Havilland were just some of the actors to win Oscars under his direction. After warring with Wyler on *The Little Foxes* (1941), Bette Davis vowed that it would be their final picture together. Nevertheless, she would always cite Wyler as the finest director she had ever worked with.

Granted, the Wyler of 1967 was a good deal mellower than the Wyler of 1937, but he was still a formidable force. So, for the most part, any talk of Barbra walking all over Wyler was made by people with their own agendas. The fact is that when Wyler acquiesced to Barbra's suggestions (and there *were* occasions that he did so), it was because he agreed with her that they served the picture well.

Furthermore, even before they started working together, Wyler was a Streisand fan. In fact, the primary reason he agreed to direct *Funny Girl* in the first place was that he saw Barbra in the 1966 London version of the show and considered her *the* musical talent of her time. He sought to capture both her appeal and her ability on film, despite her nontraditional movie-star appearance. So, much of his efforts were concentrated on presenting Barbra to her best advantage. Afterwards, Wyler said, "I wouldn't have made the picture without her."

As much as he admired her ability, Wyler would acknowledge that Barbra was not the most easygoing actor with whom he had worked. "She was a bit obstreperous in the beginning," he recalled. "But things were ironed out when she discovered some of us knew what we are doing."

He added, "She fusses over things, she's terribly concerned about how she looks, with the photography, the camera, the makeup, the wardrobe, the way she moves, reads a line. She'd tell the cameraman that one of the lights was out, way up on the scaffold. If the light that was supposed to be on her was out, *she* saw it. She's not easy, but she's difficult in the best sense of the word. The same way I'm difficult. I don't just expect obedience."

In many ways, Barbra reminded Wyler of Bette Davis, with whom he had made three pictures (*Jezebel, The Letter,* and *The Little Foxes*), and whom he had almost married. Like Bette, Barbra *loved* experimenting with her work. She was indefatigable and eager to attempt different ways of doing things. She was an actor who did not accept limitations in herself, or in her coworkers. She was also an actor who had to be *convinced* of a director's ability. She didn't trust blindly. Finally, also like Bette, her work consumed her.

"She's so wrapped up in her work," Wyler recalled. "Sometimes too much, I mean too much for her own good, for her own life, I think. She's completely involved. She's got no other life besides her work."

Typically, Wyler would view the action on the set in a chair positioned directly under the lens of the camera. "When they were shooting close-ups," Lee Allen recalls, "Willie would be right *there.*" To compensate for his difficulty in hearing, Wyler wore an earplug which allowed him to listen, not to the dialogue on the set, but to the dialogue as it was actually being recorded. Unfortunately, his proximity to the action caused a few, albeit minor, problems. "If Barbra did something funny," Lee Allen fondly recalls, "Willie would start to laugh out loud, and then you'd hear the sound man yell, 'Cut! I hear laughter from Willie!' " Allen adds, "Barbra always made Willie laugh."

Wyler's style of directing actors was, in a way, *not* to direct them. He refused to dissect a scene or demonstrate what he wanted. Wyler would know what he wanted, or didn't want, when he saw it. Generally, he would begin by letting his actors perform in whatever way *they* wished to do. In this regard, Barbra was probably spoiled by Wyler. Some of her directors that followed him would tell her, even show her, what it was that they envisioned in a scene, without first giving her the opportunity to show them what *she* had in mind.

After watching his actors do a scene, Wyler would typically tell them, "Do this," "Don't do that," "Try this." Sometimes, he wouldn't even do that much. Lee Allen recalls, "He'd say, 'Hey, Lee—uhm, listen, I got an idea. You know when you walk in?' And I'd say, 'Yes, yes.' And he'd say, 'Umm, try it again.' So I'd do it again and he'd say, 'Lee, come over here. *This* time when you walk in, try something else.' So you were left wondering. And you'd keep going and going and then he'd say, 'Okay, print Takes 5 and 17.' And you stop and think and you say to yourself, 'Well, okay, this guy *does* have all of those little statues on his mantel.' "

Wyler was never the type of director to heap effusive praise on an actor after a take. To Wyler, moving his camera into another position was praise enough. Naturally, this failure to express enthusiasm greatly distressed Barbra, who needed the constant feedback of her director. It also further fueled her insecurity.

Wyler related, "She would come on the set in the morning, after we had shot take after take on a scene the previous afternoon, and say, 'You know that scene yesterday? I can do it better today.' I would have to say, 'No, no, Barbra, we've got it.' "

Their interplay took other forms. Lee Allen remembers, "Barbra would say, 'Willie, let me try it this way.' I know that she did that quite a few times. And finally, after doing it four or five times, Willie would say, 'Okay, Barbra, do one your way now.' "

"She had to be convinced that what we were doing was the best possible way," Wyler later explained. "Sometimes, she would argue for her way. If I was set on my way, that's the way we did it. She was not difficult in that sense. She was very cooperative."

Still, there were some on the set who could not understand what they perceived to be the pandering to this self-indulgent newcomer. "Willie Wyler was very strong, and he was tough," Vivienne Walker remembers, "but Barbra usually got her way. She had everybody by the short and curly. Every day used to be a battle of wills on the set. Barbra would say, 'I want to do it again.' Willie would say, 'No. That was fine.' And she would say, 'But I want to do it again.' Barbra always wanted to do it again and again. And Willie would say, 'All right, darling, one more.' They all sort of 'darlinged' her and patted her on the back, but nobody really liked her."

Contrary to Walker's assessment, both William Wyler and Harry Stradling, among others in the *Funny Girl* company, seemed to have had genuine affection for Barbra. But she did remain characteristically aloof with most members of the cast and crew, Wyler included. "She doesn't go out of her way [to be friendly]," he assessed. "It's not her manner to be especially gracious. It's just not in her makeup; that's not the girl."

One company member with whom Barbra definitely did *not* get along was Anne Francis. Cast in the second female lead of Georgia, Fanny Brice's friend and the most beautiful of all the Ziegfeld Girls, Francis, at age thirty-seven, came to the picture with one hit television series, and nearly twenty years of Hollywood dues-paying, behind her.

"I waited for months for the right picture to follow my 'Honey West' series," Francis said. "I didn't want just any part. This [role of Georgia] seemed ideal when they told me about it."

Early into the shooting, Francis found that her part was being methodically, and mercilessly, cut, despite the fact that her work was being generally well received. She started out with three strong scenes, including an alcoholic breakdown sequence which was reduced, in Francis's words, to "a view of my back on a couch." All of her numbers with the Ziegfeld Girls were eliminated, and her lyrics in the song "Sadie, Sadie" were also edited out of the picture. In the end, Francis was left with, again in her own words, "two minutes of voice-over in a New Jersey railroad station."

Francis clearly blamed Barbra. "Every day, Barbra would see the rushes," Francis reported, "and the next day my part was cut or something else was cut. Barbra ran the whole show."

Unlike her nemesis, who was too consumed with the work to engage in such pleasantries, Francis was friendly to, and popular with, the members of the crew, who rallied to her support. "Annie Francis was a wonderful girl," recalls Vivienne Walker, "a hell of a trouper. But she was absolutely miserable. Barbra treated her abominably. If Barbra saw that Anne Francis's costumes were nice, she would see to it that she couldn't wear them. And Anne Francis was also not allowed to wear certain hairstyles that were too flattering."

In her defense, Barbra would claim that she didn't have the power to make those decisions, especially those regarding what should and should not be cut out of the picture.

Still, Vivienne Walker insists, "Barbra had all the power in the world. She had the power to have Annie Francis not wear her beautiful wardrobe that was designed for her. Nobody else stopped that but Barbra."

Prior to the film's release, Anne Francis contacted Ray Stark and asked that her name be removed from the credits. Stark refused. A joke later circulated around Hollywood. "Have you seen Anne Francis in *Funny Girl?*"

"Anne Francis was in *Funny Girl?*" came the response. "Who did she play? Barbra Streisand's *mother?*"

There were others in the company to allegedly suffer at Barbra's behest. Vivienne Walker relates, "A lot of girls in the show were from Vegas, and they gave up jobs there to do the film. And there was this one girl who was *absolutely* luscious and beautiful. One day, I happened to be sitting in front of Barbra and Willie Wyler during the rushes. And she said to him, 'You see that girl? Have her *fired*. She's too pretty.' And the girl was fired! I heard that myself. *This* is why Barbra gained that reputation.

"What I saw her do to other people angered me so much that I couldn't tolerate her," Walker continues. "When the picture finished, she gave me a complete set of her records. So I sent them back. I didn't *want* her records. She sent them *back* to me. I sent them back again. We played volleyball. Finally, the third time, she kept them. I will never forgive Barbra for those two girls, Annie Francis and the girl who got fired.

"But she was a brilliant woman," Walker concedes. "You've got to admire her. It's like having a child. You might love her as a child, but as a person you hate her. I admire her talents, but as a person, I can't stand her."

For the record, another source contends that the showgirl in question was not fired, but moved from Barbra's proximity and pushed into the background. Furthermore, there is no indisputable proof that it was *Barbra* who had Anne Francis cut out of the picture. It is likely that in her conferences with Wyler, Barbra described what had been cut out of the show in its pre-Broadway stages, and that one of the first things to go had been the part of Georgia, then played by Allyn McLerie. So while Barbra may have made the suggestion to cut Francis out of the picture, the final decision ultimately belonged to William Wyler and Ray Stark.

And, in retrospect, it was a necessary decision. The film was too long. *Everything,* every character, every song, that didn't directly serve Barbra had to be cut from the picture. As was the case with the Broadway show, *Funny Girl* the movie would stand—or fall—on Barbra Streisand.

Twenty

Middle East Accord, West Coast Wrap

$\mathscr{A}$mong the members of the *Funny Girl* company, Barbra became closest to Omar Sharif, letting down her guard, and her dress, despite the fact that they were both married. Initially, Sharif wasn't even considered for the part of Nicky Arnstein. Barbra had wanted Marlon Brando or Gregory Peck, both of whom turned down the role. Frank Sinatra was another top contender, but Ray Stark reportedly decided that he was too old and wanted too much money. Besides, Stark sought "a young Cary Grant" with "a touch of evil." He also wanted someone who looked good in, and was comfortable wearing, a tuxedo.

Just before Barbra arrived in Los Angeles for rehearsals, it was announced that David Janssen, who had recently completed his starring role in the highly successful television series "The Fugitive," was set for the part. What happened next is a mystery, except that a few days after Barbra arrived in Los Angeles in early May 1967, Janssen was no longer involved in the picture. Perhaps the two of them met and didn't hit it off on a personal level. Or perhaps they were photographed together and were unable to generate the prerequisite chemistry. Whatever the case, Janssen was dismissed from consideration and the search for Nicky Arnstein resumed.

Upon spotting him in the Columbia Pictures cafeteria, William Wyler suggested to Ray Stark that the part be cast with Omar Sharif. He certainly had the credentials, if not the ethnicity. Egyptian-born Sharif was introduced to American audiences in the 1962 picture *Lawrence of Ara-*

bia. He set many a female libido ablaze in the 1965 blockbuster *Dr. Zhivago.* He looked suitably dapper in a tuxedo and was a gambler by nature, as well as a champion cardplayer.

Upon meeting Barbra, Sharif, aged thirty-five, swarthy and sensual, exuded all the considerable continental charm he could summon. In their test together, sparks flew. It was a case of two opposites coming together, one complementing the other. It was Prince Charming turning the ugly duckling into a swan. She made him seem more attainable. He made her more vulnerable and beautiful. It was the same thing Redford would perfect with Barbra a few years later in *The Way We Were.*

Shortly after Sharif signed his contract to do *Funny Girl,* the Arabs and Israelis embarked upon their Six-Day War. Nothing much was made of the connection between the war and the casting of Barbra and Omar until photographs of them together were published all over the world. The photos showed the two embracing during an on-the-set rehearsal, with Omar nibbling on Barbra's neck and Barbra lying across Omar's lap. "Middle East Crisis Ignored in Hollywood" was a typical bold-letter caption that accompanied the photos.

Ray Stark and Columbia panicked. Urgent meetings were called. Columbia wanted Sharif removed from the production, which was being financed, in large part, with Jewish money. Hollywood has a large Jewish population and strong pro-Israeli sentiment. The studio wasn't making a political statement; it merely feared the financial and public relations repercussions that could have arisen from Sharif's participation.

Barbra's mother, Diana Kind, reportedly declared, "My daughter is not going to work with any Egyptian!" Barbra herself was reticent on the controversy. She was afraid of a backlash from the Jewish community if she lent her support to Sharif.

It was William Wyler, also Jewish, who rushed to Sharif's rescue. "We're in America, the land of freedom," Wyler said, "and you're ready to make yourselves guilty of the same things we're against? Not hiring an actor because he's Egyptian is outrageous. If Omar doesn't make the film, *I* don't make it either!" It was then and only then that Barbra also lent her endorsement to her leading man.

Columbia backed off, and Sharif was allowed to stay in the picture. The matter ended there, in large part because the war, short-lived, was won by Israel.

Ray Stark rearranged his shooting schedule to allow Sharif to complete work on the western *Mackenna's Gold,* another Columbia picture. He completed his work on the film on September 27 and, without a break, segued directly into *Funny Girl* on September 28.

Sharif first saw Barbra Streisand as an ugly woman. Not generally attracted to ambitious, aggressive women, he is repelled by feminists. For Sharif, it is vital that he feels *needed* by a woman.

But he *was* enamored of Barbra's talent, and in time he discovered that her hard exterior was only a façade. She was, he learned, an extremely insecure and fragile young woman who needed to be told she was beautiful. Sharif told her she was beautiful. And in time, he came to believe it.

"Barbra's villa served as our trysting place," he later reported. "At the time, my own villa housed my family. We spent our evenings, our weekends at her place."

He added, "We led the very simple life of people in love. . . . We used to cook. When I'd used up all my Italian recipes—notably, ones for various pasta dishes which I can cook and season quite well—Barbra would heat TV dinners. . . . We seldom went anywhere for supper."

But they *did* make a mistake by going out together to a fashion show at a place called The Factory. On another occasion, they were seen cuddling at a Los Angeles restaurant. When word reached Elliott in New York, he became furious. He called Barbra, who predictably blamed the stories on Hollywood jealousy. As for the fashion show, she told her placated husband that she accompanied Sharif because, in her words, "the ticket would have cost me $250."

Thereafter, they continued their affair with more discretion. Sharif's friend and Barbra's girlhood idol, Gregory Peck, was one of the few who were privy to their relationship. William Wyler was another. When later asked about the compatability of his two costars, Wyler replied, "If all Jews and Arabs got on like Barbra and Sharif, there would never be a war."

The affair lasted for the duration of the picture. It was Sharif who broke it off. He was, after all, used to these short-term, run-of-the-play romances. Sophia Loren, Julie Christie, Anouk Aimée, and Barbara Parkins, Sharif's costars, could each attest to his love-them-and-leave-them ways.

"I have so many women," he would say, "because I don't have one."

Attracting women has never been a problem for Sharif. Once, in a hotel room in Dallas, he was confronted with a gun-toting woman who ordered him to take off his clothes. Once naked, she ordered him to have sex with her. "I would love to, madame, but, as you can see," Sharif said, referring to his unaroused male member, "it's not possible at the moment."

"Getting women, interesting women, is hard work," Sharif would say after the completion of *Funny Girl,* "Getting rid of them is [the charm]."

Barbra was *not* one to be easily dismissed. After all, she usually got whatever it was that she set her mind on. Furthermore, unlike Sharif, she was not accustomed to such Hollywood romances in which the passion in a relationship is compressed into the short and intense time frame of a movie's shooting schedule.

On December 1, 1967, principal photography of *Funny Girl* was completed. The entire cast was set to go home, sleep, take a vacation. However, after viewing that day's rushes, as well as footage that had been previously shot, Barbra insisted on reshooting the "My Man" number, which had been filmed in September. She was convinced that her performance of the song had been too polished, too contrived, not authentically or sufficiently dramatic.

And not only did she want to redo the number, she insisted on doing it without the prerecorded playback. She wanted to perform the song live, which was highly unusual for a big-budget musical. She had had a hard time lip-synching on the picture, and because much of "My Man" was shot in close-up, it showed. Moreover, she argued, concentrating on lip-synching had kept her from concentrating instead on the meaning and emotion of the song.

William Wyler agreed. Herb Ross, who directed the number, was willing. And Ray Stark, weighing the cost of an additional day of shooting, conceded. The number, after all, was important to Stark. It was at his wife Fran's insistence that the song was in the picture at all. Barbra, composer Jule Styne, musical director Walter Scharf, and others wished to retain "The Music That Makes Me Dance" from the Broadway show. But the Starks were adamant. "My Man" was a song irrevocably linked with Fanny Brice, whom the picture, after all, was supposed to be about.

The reshoot took place the following day. Omar Sharif, who had already said his goodbyes to Barbra, was in the process of packing his suitcases when the telephone rang. It was the studio. Would he return to the set? Barbra, he was told, was asking for him.

The idea for staging the number, reportedly, had been Barbra's. She was dressed in all black and was to be shot against a black and therefore invisible curtain. Only her hair, face, neck, and hands were to be seen.

Preceding the number in the picture was the final breakup scene between Fanny and Nick. Fanny tells him that she will remember all the good things he has done for her. Nick replies by asking what he has ever done for her that she couldn't have done for herself. Fanny tells him that he gave her a blue marble egg and that "you even made me feel sort of beautiful."

In real life, it was actually *Elliott* who had given Barbra the blue marble egg, but it was Sharif who had made her feel beautiful. Upon Omar's arrival on the set, he and Barbra went behind the black curtain and played out their farewell scene in private. The words belonged to their characters, but the sentiment was theirs. "You even made me feel sort of beautiful," she tells him. He fixes her with his brown-eyed gaze and says, in parting, "You *are* beautiful."

Tears welled in her eyes. Barbra lifted the curtain and proceeded to perform thirteen wrenching takes of "My Man." The *real* reason she wanted to reshoot the number was that she could do it using the pain of her broken romance with Sharif. The emotion was no longer contrived. The drama of the song, and her relationship with Sharif, for that matter, had been wrung out and played for all it was worth. The song, the romance, and the picture had come to an end.

At the *Funny Girl* wrap party, Barbra stood in a corner, where she kept to herself. "I stayed for twenty minutes," Anne Francis related. "It was embarrassing. Barbra didn't speak to me or anyone else." Still, the gathering was not completely without sentiment. The cast and crew, presumably with a few exceptions, serenaded Barbra with a rewritten version of "I'd Rather Be Blue." She presented William Wyler with an antique eighteenth-century gold watch inscribed, "To make up for lost time." Wyler's gifts to Barbra were also symbolic and presented in jest: a director's megaphone with the Directors Guild of America insignia, and a symphony conductor's telescoping baton.

As for Ray Stark, he presented Barbra with a ten-minute short on the making of *Funny Girl.* Its end credits touted, "Produced and Directed by Barbra Streisand." Ironically, he meant it as a joke.

Twenty-one

Clash of Costarring Titans

$\mathcal{T}$he verdict on Barbra Streisand's motion picture debut would have to wait ten months for the release of *Funny Girl*. In the interim, she had places to go, people to see, battles to be fought.

Barbra returned to New York for the holidays. Elliott was completing the shooting of *The Night They Raided Minsky's* for director William Friedkin. Conveniently "forgetting" about the debacle of *The Confession,* Gould would cite *Minsky's* as his picture debut. His reunion with Barbra was short and strained. Her mind, after all, was in Hollywood, and her heart was overseas.

One day, a man named Valentine Sherry paid Barbra a visit in her Manhattan penthouse. He had a short story he wanted Barbra to read. He told her he thought it would make a good movie. The story? "Yentl, the Yeshiva Boy" by Isaac Bashevis Singer. Barbra read the story and was electrified. Her response was immediate, instinctive. It made her think of her own father, and the relationship she might have had with him had he lived. Forget Fanny Brice and musical comedy. *This* was the kind of story she wanted to tell, the kind of movie she wanted to make.

Barbra phoned her manager, Marty Erlichman, and her agent, David Begelman, and excitedly sent them copies of the story. She presented additional copies to friends and acquaintances. Confronted with her eager requests for a response, most told her that the story was moving, but that it would not make a movie. After all, since when did Hollywood see as commercial a story about a girl who pretends to be a boy so that she can study the Talmud? Undaunted, Barbra purchased the film rights and made herself a vow: *Yentl, the Yeshiva Boy* was a movie she *would* make. It was January 1968.

Later that month, Barbra, accompanied by Elliott, flew to Europe for a vacation. While there, she had a brief rendevous with Omar Sharif, who was in Vienna and Rome making *Mayerling.* However, her efforts at rekindling their affair were gently rebuffed. Given his history, Sharif was most likely smitten with his *new* costar, the exquisite Catherine Deneuve. Or, he may have fallen for the elder, but still comely, Ava Gardner, who also starred in the picture—as his mother!

Back in Hollywood, Barbra found herself in a particularly nasty feud with her mentor and father figure, Ray Stark. On December 28, 1967, Stark had filed suit against Barbra in Superior Court in Los Angeles. The basis for the suit concerned their 1965 contract, which called for Barbra to make multiple pictures for Stark's company, Rastar. Barbra had reportedly wanted to commit to do only one picture, *Funny Girl.* Stark, however, insisted on *four,* and Barbra eventually capitulated.

In November 1967, while *Funny Girl* was still shooting, Stark submitted two film properties, both intended musicals, for Barbra's consideration. One was *Wait Till the Sun Shines, Nellie* by Audrey Gellen Maas. The other was *Two for the Seesaw,* a 1958 Broadway play by William Gibson which starred Henry Fonda and Anne Bancroft and would later inspire the 1973 Michael Bennett musical, *Seesaw.*

According to court documents, Barbra had ten days to consider the properties before responding to Rastar. Upon receiving the submissions, Barbra, through her attorney Richard Roemer, reported that she would indeed consider the material if she was granted script *and* director approval. However, a few days later, Barbra rejected both properties outright, claiming that they had been somehow improperly submitted. Her real reason for declining them, of course, was that Barbra had read, and didn't care for, either property. She aspired, after all, *not* to do musical comedy, but to be Sarah Bernhardt, and play Medea, Hedda Gabler, and Yentl, the Yeshiva boy.

Stark took the rejection as a personal affront. "I love Barbra Streisand as an actress," he was quoted as saying, "but I wouldn't want her for my mother-in-law."

In a way, Barbra had become his daughter and protégée. After all he had done for her, how dare *she* question *his* taste and story sense? Stark saw a way of getting even and seized it. Barbra's contract to do the picture version of *Funny Girl* gave Stark, in writing, *exclusive* use of Barbra's services from May 4, 1967, until the completion of production.

Barbra either forgot or ignored this exclusivity clause when she performed her Hollywood Bowl and Central Park concerts that summer. Or perhaps she had managed to wrangle verbal consent from Stark and had assumed that that would be enough. Compounding the situation, the Central Park concert was being produced as a special for CBS television and as an album for Columbia Records. Stark's suit not only sought to block the airing and release of the special and the album, it also demanded that he be paid all of the proceeds Barbra received (and would receive) from the two concerts *and* everything related to them. In other words, Stark wanted, and was perhaps legally entitled to, a good deal of Barbra's money.

For the next several months, attorneys for the mentor and his protégée played verbal volleyball. Finally, an agreement was reached and the lawsuit was dismissed. Barbra could retain her earnings, which Stark really didn't want. In return, Barbra *would* fulfill the remainder of her four-picture contract with the producer, beginning not with *Wait Till the Sun Shines, Nellie* or *Two for the Seesaw,* but with the film version of the 1965 play *The Owl and the Pussycat.*

Yentl, the Yeshiva Boy would have to wait. Meanwhile, Barbra still had other, even more pressing commitments to fulfill.

Based on the 1955 Thornton Wilder play, *The Matchmaker,* which was in turn based on Wilder's 1938 play, *The Merchant of Yonkers,* David Merrick's musical production of *Hello, Dolly!* opened at the St. James Theatre on January 16, 1964. The rather flimsy plot and infectious easy-to-hum score by Jerry Herman concerned the vacuous exploits of marital matchmaker Dolly Levi, who, after years of being a widow, sets her sights on successful businessman Horace Vandergelder. The show would win an unprecedented *ten* Tony Awards and would go on to become one of the most successful Broadway musicals in the history of the American theater.

As such, the film rights to the property did not come cheaply. Richard Zanuck, executive vice president in charge of production at Twentieth Century-Fox, announced the studio's purchase of the musical on March 9, 1965. The agreement called for Fox to pay Merrick two million dollars *plus* a whopping 25 percent of the box office gross. In addition, Fox also had to disburse "a substantial consideration" to Paramount because it owned the rights to Wilder's *The Matchmaker,* which it filmed in 1958. In *addition,* Zanuck and Fox had to agree that the film version of *Dolly* would not be released while the show itself still ran on Broadway, with June of 1970 being the earliest possible release date.

Casting of the film version of *Hello, Dolly!* is the stuff of which colorful Hollywood folklore is made. Thornton Wilder described his Dolly Levi as being a woman of "uncertain age." This was generally translated as meaning a woman of middle age, not old, but not young, either, and historically, the part was cast as such. Jane Cowl was fifty-four years old when she starred in *The Merchant of Yonkers*. Ruth Gordon was fifty-nine when she performed in *The Matchmaker* on Broadway. And Shirley Booth was fifty-one when she did the film of the same title.

Hello, Dolly! was originally written for Ethel Merman, who was fifty-six in 1964. When Merman rejected the part, it was cast with Carol Channing, who, at the age of forty-three, was considered a bit young to play Dolly Levi. But play it she did, and well, winning a Tony award in the process. When Channing tired of the part she had made her own, she was replaced by a succession of actresses including Ginger Rogers and Martha Raye, both of whom were well into their fifties, as were Mary Martin, Betty Grable, Eve Arden, and Dorothy Lamour, all of whom played the part in road companies of the show.

So, naturally, when Richard Zanuck announced on May 8, 1967, that *twenty-five-year-old* Barbra Streisand would play the part in the film version, more than a few eyebrows were raised. The skepticism in some quarters intermingled with contempt, given Twentieth Century-Fox's blatant rebuff of the beloved Carol Channing. If any of the other *name* actresses who had been considered—Elizabeth Taylor (who wanted to do a musical), Doris Day, Julie Andrews, and Shirley MacLaine, among them—had been cast instead of Barbra, at least it could have been rationalized that Fox wanted to go with an established movie star. But to cast another Hollywood newcomer in the role made the insult to Channing that much more grievous.

Channing was, for countless thousands of theatergoers, the very essence of the bighearted, bigger-than-life Dolly. Summing up the sentiment of many, Richard Coe of the *Washington Post* wrote on May 11, 1967: "Would you believe Barbra Streisand for the screen's *Hello, Dolly!*?! Well, that's the knuckleheaded fact. . . . With all due respect to young Miss Streisand, the mournful Nefertiti is clearly not the outgoing, zestful Irishwoman whose vitality brightens Thornton Wilder's mature, life-loving Dolly Gallagher-Levi. The perversity of not choosing to get Carol Channing's musical-comedy classic on film is hard to fathom."

It wasn't that Channing hadn't campaigned for the part. "I was angling for it like crazy," she said. "That's why I did *Thoroughly Modern Millie,* with the idea that if it came out well enough I would get *Dolly.*"

She added, "I was doing *Hello, Dolly!* at Expo '67 at the time, and when they announced the star for the movie—on that great day—I had the feeling I was Mark Twain and had just died and become an observer at my funeral." Making a bad situation worse, she had learned the news in the pages of that morning's edition of *Daily Variety.*

On that fateful day, Thornton Wilder sent Carol Channing telegrams, one after the other, all day, each offering her his condolences. Julie Andrews, who had been through a similar experience when Audrey Hepburn was cast over her in the film version of *My Fair Lady,* also sent her a telegram, which read, "Don't worry, Carol. You'll get your *Mary Poppins.*" But as time would prove, she never did. *Hello, Dolly!* was her one real shot at movie stardom, and she wasn't given the opportunity.

Ernest Lehman, the film's producer, dismissed the controversy, saying, "I am wary of the whole subject of Carol Channing. I would say I prefer her onstage to on film."

While it wasn't Barbra's fault that she was cast over Channing, many resented her, nonetheless. Certainly, she could have been more diplomatic in her handling of the situation. Even in her grief, Channing promptly sent Barbra a dozen yellow roses. Barbra offered no reciprocal gesture to Channing. Instead, she publicly dismissed the Broadway version of *Dolly* as "a piece of fluff." As for the controversy over her casting, Barbra remarked, "I guess Carol can do any movie she wants to that year and get an Oscar for it."

Barbra also publicly denounced her detractors, saying, "It's so ridiculous and boring. They can cast anyone they want in a picture. I can't help it if I get the part. I don't know whether I'm right for the part or not. I haven't even read the script. If they pick the wrong person for a part, that's their problem. Everybody wants to be a casting director."

"The only thing she hasn't learned," Ray Stark said of Barbra, "is tact."

A joke made the rounds on both coasts: "Did you hear that Katharine Hepburn [then in her early sixties] will be playing Coco Chanel on Broadway?"

"Yes," came the answer, "and I hear Barbra Streisand will star in the movie version."

Adding to the anti-Streisand sentiment was the news that she would receive a flat $750,000 for her performance. When added to her other interests in the picture—her profit participation and her interest in the soundtrack—she stood to earn $1 million, this in a day when the median family income was $8,000 a year. Her salary for the picture was hyped as being the largest ever paid to a performer who had yet to appear in a movie.

Other stories filtered out of the Twentieth Century-Fox lot that had Barbra receiving a block-long dressing room trailer that was elegantly appointed in art nouveau and rose-colored brocade.

Still more stories claimed she had wrested all kinds of additional concessions from her bosses, which Barbra's own comments seemed to substantiate. "I'm not doing it [the film] yet," Barbra reported in August, three months after the announcement of her signing. "They've picked *me* for the part. But there are some things still to be worked out."

Barbra's public comments and generally defiant attitude were, understandably, disturbing to Zanuck and Lehman, the latter fresh from the spectacular successes of *The Sound of Music,* which he wrote, and *Who's Afraid of Virginia Woolf?,* which he wrote and produced.

After reading Barbra's comments, Lehman contacted Zanuck and expressed his concern. "We expected this," Zanuck reported back. In reference to the seemingly bad press, he added, "When you put a 'hot' dame in a controversial part—this makes good copy for the nuts. If we make a good picture, all of this is yesterday's toilet paper."

Of more concern to both men were the horror stories they had begun to hear from across town on the Columbia lot. One report said that *Funny Girl* was "dangerously behind schedule" and that Barbra's "sensitivities" were the primary reason for the delay. Her insistence on repeated takes, takes which had been "adjudged okay by William Wyler," was said to have cost the studio $200,000. The report referred to it as "the Streisand 'attitude' toward picture-making."

One report leaked to the press in the fall of 1967 contended that Fox was "taking a look at Streisand's 'temperament record' at Columbia." Also, efforts might be made in an attempt to settle what was termed Barbra's "ironbound" contract.

"Barbra Streisand will never make *Hello, Dolly!*" went one rumor. "She won't finish editing *Funny Girl* in time."

For a time, Lehman thought seriously about recasting the picture with Doris Day. He also considered caving in to the pro-Channing sentiment. Other Dolly scenarios danced around in his head.

In his Dolly deliberations, Lehman had to consider that whoever was cast, she would have to meld with the rest of the actors. He had already hired mostly very young actors and actresses in an attempt to make Barbra's Dolly seem comparatively mature.

The script had also been tailored for a younger Dolly. "We've created a new Dolly Levi," Gene Kelly later related. Kelly had been selected, with Barbra's approval, to direct the production. Fox agreed, in part, because of the success it was then having with Kelly's comedy *A Guide for the Married Man.*

"[Dolly is now] a very young widow," Kelly continued. "Her husband's death has been recent, she's more in love with his memory. This has meant all the people [in the cast] had to be younger. To get young players with experience I literally interviewed 1,000 to 2,000 people."

Such being the case, Kelly and Lehman began secretly testing younger actresses for the part of Dolly, just in case. Among them: Phyllis Newman, thirty-two, tested on December 12, 1967; Yvette Mimieux, twenty-eight, on December 28; and Ann-Margret, twenty-six, on January 3, 1968.

Nevertheless, after a great deal of drama and deliberation, it was Barbra who reported to the studio for wardrobe measurements on February 13, 1968. She also discussed the costume sketches with designer Irene Sharaff. Just as they had on *Funny Girl,* the two women would come to odds on several occasions.

"Irene is a wonderful designer," recalls Barbara Westerland, the star's wardrobe lady on the picture. "She does her research and she wants [her costumes] to be historically correct. Barbra, however, wants something that looks attractive on her."

In the months to come, Barbra fussed continuously over her costumes, less sequins here, more feathers there. Courtney Haslam, who worked in the studio's wardrobe department, reported that Barbra was "making changes out of the ordinary" in "practically all" of her costumes. She was particularly disturbed by her array of hats, and she made considerable changes in them throughout the production. "She insisted on wearing broad-brimmed hats," reports Barbara Westerland, "which weren't really in period."

Something that *was* in period was the leg-of-mutton sleeve, in which the upper portion of a sleeve is large and puffed out and then tapers down to the elbow. Sharaff designed most of her female costumes with the sleeve. Barbra, however, didn't like the way she looked in the dresses with the sleeve and refused to wear them. Thus, in the picture, all of the actresses wear dresses with the sleeve except for Barbra.

"They [the executives at Fox] had heard about the problems [with Barbra] at Columbia," Westerland recalls, "and they wanted a smoothly running production, so they said, 'Give her what she wants.' "

Partially to improve her increasingly unfavorable reputation, but mostly just for the thrill of it, Barbra agreed to be a presenter at that year's Academy Award ceremony, staged at the Santa Monica Civic Auditorium on April 10, 1968.

Upon Barbra's announcement of the winner in the Best Song category, "Talk to the Animals" from *Doctor Dolittle,* there were audible gasps of "Oh, *no!*" emanating from the audience. The song, it was thought by many, was a lightweight diversion, hardly meriting an Oscar. Sammy Davis, Jr., clad in a Nehru dinner jacket and a strand of love beads, accepted the award for the absent songwriter, Leslie Bricusse.

As for Barbra, she made her Oscar debut wearing a low-cut dress, a choker around her neck, and an ill-advised coiffure of high-piled ringlets, which was described by the press as her "Bob Dylan do."

Shortly after the ceremony, Ray Stark commented, "I thought she was disappointing on the televised Oscar Awards. She is right to demand careful lighting. The ABC-TV show was unkind."

Barbra was greatly disturbed by Stark's comments, and by the generally unfavorable response to her appearance. Still, she learned a valuable lesson. For her future public appearances, at the risk of seeming intrusive, she would try to better control the way she was lit and photographed.

She was also getting a new softer, period look for *Dolly.* "In 1890," Ernest Lehman reported, "respectable women did not use makeup. The term 'painted woman' was, of course, a euphemism for 'harlot.' "

Although she would again *apply* her own makeup, her look was designed by Dan Striepeke, head of the Fox makeup department. Striepeke recalls, "The whole thing that we were trying to create between Ernie Lehman, Gene Kelly, and myself was a John Singer Sargent type of look, the way he painted his ladies of that era. They were very milk white. That was the whole tenor of the makeup on that film. I worked very closely with Harry Stradling and the lab. We did extensive testing, and were very successful at it."

Her makeup was softened, particularly around the eyes, and her wigs, fashioned in a Gibson style, were to be, in Striepeke's words, a "delicate golden red" to set off "the beauty of her blue eyes." Of his working relationship, Striepeke says, "Barbara and I worked very closely together. She's the perfect pro, as far as I'm concerned."

Murray Spivack, an old Hollywood professional, was hired as a sound man and music mixer on the picture. His introduction to Barbra provides a glimpse at how one might best collaborate with her. According to Spivack, it's all in the *approach*.

"She came into the theater where I was doing another job, *Doctor Dolittle,* I think. She had made a picture at Columbia and I had heard that she was dissatisfied with the quality they were getting on her voice. So much so that for *Funny Girl* she had her own microphone sent from New York. So I introduced myself to her and said, 'When you get settled here [on the lot], if you don't mind, I'd like to make a test of your voice with a number of microphones to see which microphone best suits your voice."

"*That,*" adds Spivack, "made a hit with her."

"I had no problem at all with Barbra because the approach was proper," he continues. When asked to compare Barbra to Bette Davis, with whom he worked on *All About Eve* in 1950, Spivack says, "I think Bette was actually rougher than Barbra. They had minds of their own. They couldn't be persuaded. And I admired them both for that."

In preproduction, Barbra demonstrated a mostly unheralded side of herself. She wrote an "urgent" note to Ernest Lehman and asked him to give one of her friends a job. His name was Howard Jeffrey. Coincidentally, one of Howard's friends, Marvin Laird, also worked on the picture as the dance arranger. "I think Howard died about four years ago," Laird says. "He was one of Barbra's best friends. He was made one of [choreographer] Michael Kidd's assistants. Howard's best friend was Mart Crowley, who was Barbra's secretary. Later, Mart wrote *The Boys in the Band,* and it was Howard who was the basis for "Harold" in the play.

"He was divine," Crowley relates. "He wasn't nearly as unattractive as Leonard Frey [the actor who played him in *The Boys in the Band*] portrayed him to be. Howard was a rather good-looking guy. Just the way Jack Cole was with Marilyn Monroe, Rita Hayworth, and Betty Grable, Howard was one of those guys who was really symbiotic with big female movie stars. They adored him."

Barbra met Howard during the shooting of *Funny Girl,* on which he worked as Herb Ross's assistant. The two became close friends, and on most of her subsequent musical pictures, Barbra got Howard a job. "He just worshiped her," Crowley conveys. "Howard really adored talent for one thing, and she felt tremendously secure with him."

"Because Barbra was close to Howard, and I was close to Howard," Marvin Laird relates, "we all sort of hung out a little bit. She was campy and silly, and I remember a lot of times when she was laughing." He adds, "I found her extremely gracious. She was always the hardest-working person around. My biggest impression occurred when I watched her in the prerecording sessions. It was just a great thrill to see someone whose instincts were so dead-on. She trusts her own musicality better than she trusts anybody else's."

The picture was initially budgeted by Lehman at $10 million, substantial, but not alarmingly so. By the time it went into production, *Hello, Dolly!* had leapt into the $17–$20 million range, and by the time of its release in 1969, it would escalate to $24 million, making it, to that point, the most expensive movie musical in the history of motion pictures.

The film's "New York Street" set, built on the Fox lot, cost the production nearly $2 million alone. Lehman, in an attempt to justify its extravagance, would say, "I think this New York street will become a new Disneyland. I think it will be kept here [on the Fox lot]." Sure enough, the set would stand long after the completion of the picture and would be used in other films, including *The Great White Hope* (1970), *Up the Sandbox* (1972), and *Nickelodeon* (1976). It would suffer $150,000 in damages in a 1977 fire.

For another sequence, a massive parade outside of the Fox lot on Pico Boulevard, three thousand extras, and 106 horses had to be paid for and fed for a whole week.

Principal photography started on April 15, 1968, on Fox's Stage 16. Included in the illustrious company were members of the famed old Arthur Freed unit from Metro-Goldwyn-Mayer, director Kelly, associate producer Roger Edens, choreographer Michael Kidd, and orchestrator Lennie Hayton. At Barbra's request, Harry Stradling was the cinematographer.

Everyone seemed cordial enough, as is usually the case early in a film's production. Kelly graced the proceedings with liberal doses of charm and good humor. When a carpenter on the set started pounding away with a hammer during a musical number, Kelly cried out, "If we *must* have hammering, please keep it on beat!"

When not fussing with her costumes, or over sixteen-month-old Jason

Emanuel, an occasional visitor to her *Dolly* trailer, Barbra was entertained with stories by her stand-in, Marie Rhodes, about Marlon Brando. Marie's husband, Phil, had been Brando's longtime makeup man, and Marie herself had worked as Brando's stand-in.

But beneath the surface congeniality, there was a definite pall over the production. Early into the shooting, Barbra began to have serious doubts about her decision to do the picture. She was playing a part she really didn't want, at the expense of someone else, Channing, who emphatically *did*. The doubts had actually started a few weeks after she signed for the role. She had not been prepared for the pro-Channing public outcry, and she began to worry whether she was in fact suitable for the part. She was terrified of failing, of proving her critics right. In the middle of the night, Lehman and/or Kelly found themselves jolted out of bed by the sound of Barbra's panic-stricken voice. Her words varied, but her message was always the same: *"What the hell am I doing in this picture?!"*

Lehman and Kelly constantly reassured her as best they could. They told her again and again that there was no reason why she couldn't play the part, and that, all controversy aside, Dolly Levi was a woman of "uncertain age." Barbra would cling fervently to that phrase.

Early into the production, it was obvious that she couldn't get a grasp on the character. Unlike the movie role of Fanny Brice, for which she had Allan Miller's thirteen weeks of intensive coaching and some nine hundred "practice" performances onstage, Dolly Levi presented Barbra with a completely new and virtually impossible challenge. Optimism aside, she *was* too young for the part. Moreover, she didn't have Dolly's maturity, confidence, or warmth. She tried to compensate for it by being colorful, but only succeeded in appearing brash. She attempted to eliminate any sign of her own ethnicity, but only succeeded in becoming bland and "white-bread." She slipped in and out of character and accents almost as often as she changed costumes. One moment she was Fanny Brice, the next, Mae West, and the next, Barbra Streisand.

Ernest Lehman, however, could not see or hear beyond Barbra's voice. Her rendition of "Before the Parade Passes By" knocked him out. Barbra held the last note of the song for an astounding, almost ridiculous length of time. Much was made by Lehman, composer Jerry Herman, and others of the fact that it was the longest note ever recorded on film.

"Wait till you hear what she does with the score!" Lehman exclaimed to everyone who would listen. "When I heard her singing *that* song, it was goose-pimple time. It was history."

What he meant, of course, was the title song. As a surprise to filmgoers, Lehman arranged to have Louis Armstrong perform the number with Barbra. Armstrong, who had not been in the Broadway show, had had a smash hit record with the song in 1964.

When she learned of Armstrong's involvement in the picture, Barbra objected strenuously. She argued that an appearance by Armstrong would smack of sensationalism and would cheapen the production. On this point, she was overriden. Her objections, it was thought, had more to do with ego and wanting the number for herself than anything else. When he showed up on the set, Armstrong surprised everyone with his slender appearance, having lost twenty-eight pounds in preparation for the picture.

The number itself was shot on Fox's Stage 14. The elaborate Harmonia Gardens set, with its sweeping red-carpeted stairway, cost the production $375,000. Twice during rehearsals, Barbra tripped over the two-and-a-half-foot train of her $8,000 gold gown, which was heavily beaded and weighed some forty pounds. Other times, it was the dancers who got caught up in it. A fight ensued between Irene Sharaff and Michael Kidd over which was to be changed—the train or the choreography. Says Marvin Laird, "Irene Sharaff was constantly struggling for every train that she had designed."

Practicality won out, and the troublesome train was disposed of. But close examination of the picture reveals that the train was still intact when Barbra makes her entrance in the scene. It is only later, when the dancing begins, that the train mysteriously disappears. The filmmakers, of course, were hoping that no one would notice the discrepancy.

It was an extremely difficult number to shoot, particularly given the strenuous, but brilliantly conceived, dance steps of choreographer Michael Kidd. "There was a funny moment during the filming of that number," Marvin Laird recalls. "A lot of it took place on this big staircase, and Michael had the guys doing a couple of steps that were rather tricky. And we had a couple of the dancers injure themselves, and they were sidelined on crutches. And Sheilah, Michael's assistant, who is now his wife, had injured herself, and she was in a wheelchair. And just the day before Michael had hurt himself, and he was on crutches. And in walks this interviewer from *Time* magazine or something, and when he was introduced to the choreographer and the assistant choreographer, the set looked like a medical supply factory."

The number signaled Dolly's return to Harmonia Gardens after a *fourteen-year* absence, since the days when she used to frequent it on the arm of her husband. Given that Barbra celebrated her twenty-sixth birthday during the making of the picture, a little elementary arithmetic shows that she must have been twelve when last seen at Harmonia Gardens. Nevertheless, Dolly Levi was a woman of "uncertain age," Barbra tried to remind herself, and the production plodded forward.

She blamed her lack of characterization, in large part, on the direction— or lack thereof, in her view—of Gene Kelly. "He was not really much of an actor's director," Marvin Laird relates. "He was more concerned with geography, with where to put his camera, than how to get a performance out of somebody. [As an actor] you had to bring it with you." He adds, "I think that Kelly felt over his head, quite frankly."

Kelly, Barbra complained, was also lacking in vision. Early into the shooting, she asked him how he saw the film in cinematic terms. "He didn't have any answer at all," Barbra later said. "I couldn't understand it, because there were so many possibilities. I thought it could have been a wild film."

Given his legendary status in Hollywood musicals, Kelly expected that newcomer Barbra would respect him on that basis alone. He was wrong. Although Kelly has chosen to put a happy face on the relationship he had with Barbra during the making of the picture, the two were far from friends. In fact, according to Ernest Lehman, "They were just not meant to communicate on this earth."

The same could have been said for Barbra and her costar. Barbra, it should be said, was at a disadvantage from the start. Walter Matthau, cast as Horace Vandergelder, her irascible love interest, had a hit picture in current release. The film, *A Guide for the Married Man,* had been directed by Gene Kelly. Thus, Kelly and Matthau had a previous relationship and a close bond. Matthau was secure with his director and with his career. At the age of forty-seven, Matthau had already made scores of pictures, and just days before *Dolly* went into production, he had won a Best Supporting Actor Oscar for his performance in the Billy Wilder picture *The Fortune Cookie.*

Not so Barbra, who was terribly insecure about *Dolly* and who nervously awaited the release of *Funny Girl.* In contrast to her first picture, she had not been given the right to approve (or disapprove) her costar in *Dolly.* She disliked Matthau immediately. The two had met once before in 1965, briefly, backstage in Piper Laurie's dressing room. Laurie had been appearing on Broadway in a revival of *The Glass Menagerie,* and Barbra was paying her a visit when Matthau poked his head in the door.

He paid his respects to Laurie and then, glancing at Barbra, pronounced, "You must be Barbara Harris. You ought to get that nose fixed."

Unlike Omar Sharif, who had courted her favor with batted brown eyes and sweet nothings whispered in her ear, Matthau's style was coarse, abrupt. During the shooting of *Dolly,* he would, for the most part, treat Barbra with gruff indifference. It can be argued that Matthau was disturbed by the general deference shown to Barbra on the set and at the studio, or by the fact that, despite his undeniably impressive track record, his salary of $500,000, while substantial, was a good deal less than Barbra's.

One day, off the set, Matthau approached Jason, who was playing at Barbra's side, and began talking baby talk to him. Barbra, who didn't approve of baby talk, said nothing. "The only way to bring up kids," Matthau pronounced, snorting, "is to talk baby talk to 'em and beat 'em." Barbra bristled. She stood up and announced that she was going to take Jason for a ride in the car. Fully aware that he had rattled Barbra, Matthau continued his assault. "Gonna make poo-poo in the car, Jason?" he asked with a conspiratorial grin. Barbra scooped a terrified Jason up in her arms and marched off, mumbling under her breath.

On at least one other occasion, Matthau arrived on the set drenched with perspiration after one of his jogs. He was wearing a sweat suit. "I don't have anything on under this," he told Barbra. "Doesn't that excite you?"

Their big blowup would not occur until they left Los Angeles. On April 1, 1968, a production crew of forty went to Garrison, New York, to transform, at considerable expense, the town into a replica of Yonkers, 1890. In early June, Barbra, Matthau, and the rest of the company traveled to the converted town for several weeks of location shooting.

The New York heat was sweltering. The heavy period costumes and wigs exacerbated the discomfort of the cast. The heavy Garrison rains further aggravated the situation. The downpour slowed, and at times halted, the production and added $200,000 to the already astronomical budget.

Tempers were bound to flare, and they did.

Tensions between Barbra and Matthau came to a boil on Thursday, June 6. Matthau, who had been stricken with migraines and stomach pains for weeks, was, frankly, sickened by the experience of working with Barbra. Her constant call for retakes exasperated him. He had no tolerance for the way she, in his view, overstepped her bounds as an actor and "suggested" to Kelly how something should be done. And he was upset with Kelly, who constantly tried to placate Barbra when, Matthau, thought, she should have been put in her place.

He had been appalled one day back at the studio when he overheard her telling Lennie Hayton, the film's much-experienced musical director, that the flutes were coming in too soon and that the violins were too fast.

He was irate when she went to Kelly complaining about the way he, Matthau, fed her her lines. Not only that, she proceeded to describe to Kelly *how* she wanted Matthau to give her the lines.

On the day of their fight in Garrison, Barbra reportedly kept making suggestions to Kelly as to how Matthau should deliver his lines. She also had an idea for a bit of business for a scene which took place in a wagon. Matthau finally exploded. "Stop directing the fucking picture!" he screamed. Barbra was at first shocked. Recovering, she lashed back and said that Matthau was just jealous of her because she was more talented than he.

"Cool it, baby," Matthau retorted. "You may be the singer in this picture, but I'm the *actor.*"

The verbal slugfest continued. He called her a "pipsqueak" and "Miss Ptomaine" and told her that she didn't have the talent of "a butterfly's fart." She called him "old sewermouth," and at one point during the production, reportedly marched up to him and presented him with a bar of soap. He told her that she might become a competent actress instead of a "freak attraction" if she learned her trade properly. She reportedly snapped back, "The title of this film is *not* 'Hello, Walter,' " or words to that effect.

And then Matthau delivered the knockout blow. "Nobody in this company likes you," he informed her. Barbra, starting to cry, walked off the set. "Okay, baby. Go ahead," Matthau called after her, "but remember, Betty Hutton thought she was indispensable, too."

"The fight took place outside of Vandergelder's feed store, which was beside the Hudson," recalls Barbara Westerland. "I remember that Barbra went back to her dressing room, which [in Garrison] was not a dressing room, it was an actual house. It was about four houses away from the feed store."

Of Matthau's charge that Barbra was overstepping her bounds, Westerland proffers, "She has this quality about herself to see things in a particular way. I can't fault her for that. I mean, maybe she should *not* have been doing it, but she usually turned out being right."

Shooting was delayed from 3:20 P.M. until 4:50 P.M., while Matthau cooled off and Barbra regained her composure. Thereafter, for the duration of the production, the two stars would make an effort at civility, and for the most part succeeded. They took their complaints to their director. She complained that she was not getting enough close-ups; he complained that she was stepping on his lines.

Their mutual dislike for each other would last well after the shooting of the picture. Years later, Matthau would tell a reporter: "I'm the number ten [box office] attraction, right under Streisand. Can you imagine being under Barbra Streisand? Get me a bag, I may throw up."

And when asked if he would ever work on another picture with Barbra, Matthau responded, "I'd love to work with Barbra Streisand again, in something appropriate. Perhaps *Macbeth.*"

The presence of eighteen-month-old Jason Emanuel provided a lighter note. Marvin Laird, the dance arranger, recalls, "The first time I really got close to Barbra, was when we were shooting in Garrison. We were supposed to have been there for a week and a half, but it rained all the time. Jason was a *real* pistol. He knew *all* of Barbra's dance steps. He used to stand on the side of the set and watch her, especially during 'Sunday Clothes.' He knew *every* move that she made, and he would stand there and do them.

"He was an adorable little cherub of a kid," Laird continues, "and Barbra was as good a mother as she could be under the circumstances. I mean, when you're being fussed over by twenty people from wardrobe and hair and all kinds of things. And you have to spend most of your day on a slant board because the gown that you're working in can't be sat in. You can't exactly pick up your child and lug him around and be a real mommy. But Barbra was real affectionate with him. He had his nanny there, of course."

On July 4, 1968, after shooting in Garrison, Cold Springs, and West Point, New York, the bedraggled company returned to Los Angeles, Barbra included, on three chartered planes. Shooting resumed at Fox the following day. Before leaving Garrison, Barbra confided to a reporter, "I'm afraid they [the public] may think I'm some kind of monster. I don't want people to think I am a terrible human being. I'm not."

It continued, for the most part, to be a hot, humid, unhappy production. Harry Stradling, his health shaky to begin with, had to take a week off to rest before the completion of the picture. His relationship with Barbra continued to be one of trust and mutual respect.

Gene Kelly attempted to keep his stars appeased with his cheerful countenance, but problems, as on most pictures, persisted. Even composer Jerry Herman was brought in for a scolding. Herman, it seems, had been commissioned by Richard Zanuck to write an original ballad for Barbra to sing in the picture. Everyone was pleased with the song Herman delivered, "Love Is Only Love," until Angela Lansbury innocently informed Zanuck, in casual conversation, that the song was *not* an original at all, but a reject from the score of *Mame*. Zanuck was furious and berated the diminutive composer.

The two things Barbra liked about the production were (1) her paycheck, and (2) the days when her presence wasn't required on the set, in contrast to *Funny Girl,* in which she appeared in practically every shot. She also seemed to feel that *Dolly* signaled the end of one chapter in her career, her "last big 'voice' picture."

Barbra completed her principal photography on the film on Friday, August 16. Matthau's "suggestions" aside, she continued to supply Kelly with her input throughout the production. For the "Before the Parade Passes By" number, Kelly shot Barbra in close-up as she held her long final note. Barbra wanted Kelly's camera to zoom out, leaving her a small figure lost in the massive parade. Kelly finally relented and shot a final take Barbra's way. It is *that* shot that is in the picture.

Barbra finished her looping sessions on August 23. The production continued without her for another two weeks until it finally halted, after a grueling 121 shooting days. Surprisingly, despite the large scope and massive budget, the production was very well organized, much to the credit of Ernest Lehman, and was completed without serious incident. Still, for many, the experience would leave a bitter aftertaste.

"There were things going on that were terrible," Lehman later reported to Gene Kelly's biographer Clive Hirschhorn. "The intrigues, the bitterness, the backbiting, the deceits, the misery, the gloom. Most unpleasant." He added, in a commentary on the filmmaking process in general, "It's quite amazing what people go through to make something entertaining for others."

Hello, gorgeous, II.
(Courtesy of Cinema
Collectors)

In the land of the giants. Playing
herself as an eight-year-old in
On a Clear Day. (Paramount
Pictures. The Richard Gordon
Collection)

Letting her fingers do the talking. Barbra making a point on the *Clear Day*
set as director Vincente Minnelli (far left) and Alan Jay Lerner (center)
listen intently. (Paramount Pictures. The Richard Gordon Collection)

Before the fall of the skyscraper hairdo. (The Richard Gordon Collection)

A director is born. Barbra behind the camera on the set of *The Owl and the Pussycat.* (Columbia Pictures. The Richard Gordon Collection)

More image-changing. Barbra does Ann-Margret in *The Owl and the Pussycat.* (Columbia Pictures. The Richard Gordon Collection)

True grit: The old Hollywood and the new. (The Richard Gordon Collection)

With Liza Minnelli, the new belter, 1970. (Courtesy of Cinema Collectors)

With Ryan O'Neal: Love story on and off the screen. (Warner Brothers. Courtesy of Cinema Collectors)

In a tender moment with *What's Up, Doc?* director Peter Bogdanovich. (Warner Brothers. Courtesy of Cinema Collectors)

Up the Sandbox. A woman behind bars. (First Artists. The Richard Gordon Collection)

With O'Neal and Bogdanovich. A Hollywood love triangle? (Warner Brothers. The Richard Gordon Collection)

Streisand and Redford:
Intersecting icons.
(Columbia Pictures.
The Richard Gordon
Collection)

On the set of *For Pete's Sake*, with the portable makeup table she
designed. (Columbia Pictures. The Richard Gordon Collection)

A woman in love, 1975. (Courtesy of Cinema Collectors)

With Jon Peters, part boxer and part beautician; part businessman and part aesthete; part macho tough-guy and part sensitive little boy. (Courtesy of Cinema Collectors)

Blurring the lines between male and female roles. (Warner Brothers. Courtesy of Cinema Collectors)

Peters to Kristofferson: "You owe my old lady an apology." (Courtesy of Cinema Collectors)

Twenty-two

Shattered Hopes, Realized Dreams

"*N*ow it's on to Chicago, and let's win there!" announced Robert F. Kennedy, his words reverberating through the Ambassador Hotel in Los Angeles. Minutes later, he was gunned down by a lone assassin. It was June 5, 1968. He died the following day, the same day as Barbra's showdown with Walter Matthau in Garrison, New York. Two months before Kennedy's murder, Martin Luther King, Jr., was shot and killed in Memphis.

Political, racial, campus, and social unrest filled the streets and flowed into the American consciousness. Hollywood, like the rest of the country, found itself in a state of shock. Unable to stand by in apathy, a faction of the entertainment community mobilized its resources in an effort which culminated at the Hollywood Bowl on July 26, 1968. Billed as "The Entertainment Event of the Year," 18,000 people came to raise money for King's Poor People's Campaign.

The show was hosted by Bill Cosby, and its star appearance was reserved for Barbra Streisand. She took the stage wearing a dress of green chiffon and enthralled the audience with her voice as it filled the summer night's air. Given her frightening concert experiences the previous year, she had not wanted to perform in public. It was, however, something that she *had* to do. The distinction between the two is a recurring theme in the Streisand career.

The show raised a reported $140,000 for the Poor People's Campaign and was a forerunner to "We Are the World," Live Aid, and a host of other such future expressions of Hollywood humanity.

281

With the impending release of *Funny Girl,* Barbra had other career concerns as well. She worried about her fourth CBS television special, "A Happening in Central Park." Her previous special, "The Belle of 14th Street," which was taped for four consecutive days beginning on April 26, 1967, flopped with the critics and in the ratings when it aired during the production of *Funny Girl* on October 11, 1967. In retrospect, the reasons for its failure are obvious: The show was misguided and pretentious in concept, and overproduced in execution. At the time, however, it was feared that, after her first two successful specials, Barbra's appeal had diminished, that the television viewing public had tired of her brand of three-acts-in-a-song theatrics.

She need not have worried. "A Happening in Central Park," the concept of which epitomized simplicity—Barbra standing on a stage, under the stars, singing—would receive excellent reviews and win its time slot for the network. It aired on September 15, 1968, to coincide with and promote the long-awaited release of *Funny Girl,* three days later.

Barbra worried to the end. She pleaded with William Wyler and Ray Stark to keep her beloved "Swan Lake" number entirely intact. She argued, however, to no avail. The picture, at 155 minutes, was already far too long.

Upon seeing Columbia's proposed ads for the movie, Barbra telephoned Ray Stark, irate. "They're vulgar," she informed him. And while she had him on the line, she could not resist telling him about the elaborate dressing room trailer that she had been provided during *Dolly,* in contrast to her trailer on *Funny Girl,* which she deemed "tacky." She also told him that the people involved with *Dolly* respected her suggestions, unlike, in her view, her experience at Columbia.

Ray Stark previewed *Funny Girl* not in or around Los Angeles, as was customary, but in Milwaukee and Dallas. He wanted to see how the Jewishness of the picture would play in more conservative Middle America. In Milwaukee, the preview cards produced 334 "Excellent" and 52 "Good" ratings and only a handful of cards marked "Fair" or "Poor." In Dallas, the preview produced similar overwhelmingly positive results. And the personal ratings for Barbra's performance even exceeded those for the picture itself.

"People" was cited as the best song in the score, with "My Man" a close second. *Not* liked by many was Omar Sharif, whom some thought miscast. Some disliked his accent and thought his appearance too swarthy. "Swan Lake" was the least favorite number in the score, and several viewers complained about Barbra's speaking voice and her fingernails.

Backed with a $1.6 million promotional campaign, and the largest box office advance in history, *Funny Girl* premiered at the Criterion Theatre in New York on Wednesday, September 18, 1968. With Elliott on her arm, Barbra attended the event wearing a filmy Scaasi gown with cape, and her hair piled high atop her head.

Following the screening, she and twelve hundred invited guests attended the massive tent-party held in the middle of Times Square on the site of the old Astor Hotel. The party would be described as "the largest outdoor celebrity circus New York has ever seen." Barbra arrived late and departed early. She passed on the midnight supper, and on the alcohol, downing soft drinks instead. As Marty Erlichman confided to one of the guests, "I guarantee you, right now she'd rather be in a diner." The celebrity guests included Johnny Carson, Rod Steiger, George Segal, and Senator Jacob Javits, among others. The senator caused a mild uproar when he discovered a few grains of rice in his coffee.

The picture premiered in Hollywood at the famed Egyptian Theater (the site of Hollywood's very first movie premiere, the 1921 *Robin Hood* with Douglas Fairbanks, Sr.) on October 9. At intermission, Edward G. Robinson walked around the lobby in an apparent daze, muttering, "She is *everybody*. She is *everybody*."

Again, the postscreening dinner party was held in a tent across the street from the theater, the interior decorated like the Lower East Side of Manhattan. Barbra wore a red satin Scaasi suit with a matching pillbox hat. She arrived late, but surprised all by *staying* late. Still, a bit of her thunder was snatched by Ursula Andress. Andress, on the arm of Jean-Paul Belmondo, the French Elliott Gould, set the paparazzi afire by bulging out of a low-cut mini. Here the celebrity VIPs included Gene Kelly, Garson Kanin, Bob Fosse, Raquel Welch, Natalie Wood, Nancy Sinatra, Vincente Minnelli, Jack Warner, and a positively exalted Ray Stark, who predicted that the picture would make more than $100 million. Said Stark, "The guys go for the first half and the dames go for the second!"

On both coasts, the reviews for *Funny Girl* were mixed but mostly positive. And for Barbra, no less than a coronation seemed in order. Her reviews were euphoric in their praise. James Bacon of the *Los Angeles Herald-Examiner* raved that her performance "must rank her among the great superstars of the movies." Joseph Morgenstern of *Newsweek* heralded her appearance as "the most accomplished, original and enjoyable musical-comedy performance that has ever been captured on film."

Hollywood, which had not witnessed this kind of spectacular debut in decades, if ever, worshipped on bended knee at Barbra's feet. Said Walter Scharf, *Funny Girl*'s musical director, "In all the years, and I've done 200 and somewhat films, I have *never* met a greater talent in my life than this girl. She will go down in history."

Her January 17, 1969, appearance at the Paris premiere of the picture, with Maurice Chevalier as her escort, caused a riot. Some 150 photographers from five countries pushed themselves at her from every direction as she struggled to climb the steps of the Paris Opera. At one point, they managed to break down the security lines, storm the theater, and snap pictures of her as she sank self-consciously into her seat. While in the city, Barbra stayed with Sargent Shriver, the United States ambassador to France, and his wife, Eunice Shriver. Eunice, of course, was the sister of John and Robert Kennedy, and the mother of Maria, who would later become a noted television journalist in her own right.

The Royal European Premiere in London, staged two nights before in Leicester Square, had been a far more dignified affair. At the postscreening dinner party with H.R.H. Princess Margaret, Barbra, dressed in mink, did not sit with Margaret (perhaps she wanted to avoid another blunder in royal etiquette) but with Marty Erlichman. Upon being reintroduced to the princess, Barbra was again tongue-tied, and Omar Sharif had to come to her rescue. "I see that your costar is helping you out again," Margaret laughed. Also in attendance were Ray Stark, William Wyler, David Frost, Cecil Beaton, British producer Lionel Chetwynd and his wife, and Cis Corman, Barbra's best friend.

Elliott Gould was nowhere to be found, which was just as well. Barbra had her sights set on one of the other guests, and it wasn't Sharif. It was the forty-eight-year-old prime minister of Canada, Pierre Elliott Trudeau. Their attraction was immediate. Barbra was enamored with the power and self-confidence exuded by Trudeau. He was charmed by her humor. But their attraction seemed a passing one. He had a country to run, and she had business to attend to, both personal *and* professional.

In October 1968, Barbra had begun conferences and rehearsals at Paramount for her new picture, Alan Jay Lerner and Burton Lane's *On a Clear Day You Can See Forever*. She was cast in the film after it was offered to and rejected by Audrey Hepburn. The picture gave her the role of Daisy Gamble, an insecure neurotic whose psychic abilities include, but are in no way limited to, growing flowers with the mere sound of her voice, sort of a botanical, distaff Doctor Dolittle. Wanting to be "cured" of smoking, she goes to a psychiatrist, Dr. Marc Chabot. While under hypnosis, she regresses into one of her past-life incarnations, Lady

Melinda Tentrees, a nineteenth-century Englishwoman. At first fascinated by his discovery, Chabot becomes infatuated with his subject.

Paramount purchased the film rights to the Broadway musical for $750,000. The announcement of the deal was made on April 25, 1966. At the time, the moderately successful show was still playing on Broadway, with Barbara Harris in the leading role. The picture was budgeted at less than half of the $20 million the studio was risking on the musical *Paint Your Wagon.*

Vincente Minnelli was approached to direct, largely because he had turned Alan Jay Lerner and Frederick Loewe's *Gigi* into an enormous, Oscar-winning hit back in 1959. Moreover, Barbra, who had approval over the matter, met with Minnelli and gave her consent. She too was a fan of Minnelli's work on *Gigi.* Minnelli signed for the picture, despite the fact that he had not set foot on a soundstage in five years and had not made a musical in ten.

The casting of Barbra's costar was problematic. Initially, Richard Harris, then King Arthur in the film version of *Camelot,* was slated to star. Harris, however, backed out. At Barbra's recommendation, and indicative of her dogged persistence, both Gregory Peck and Frank Sinatra were approached, and again they both declined. The part eventually went to Yves Montand, who had yet to expand his European appeal to American audiences.

In its translation to the screen, the story was updated to reflect the changing times, and a thirty-two-year-old actor by the name of Jack Nicholson was cast as Barbra's hippie stepbrother. He was scheduled to have one solo musical number, "Who Is There Among Us Who Knows?" Barbra, however, decided that she wanted to join him on the number, so Nicholson's solo was turned into a duet. Still, he harbored no resentment for his costar, later saying, "Streisand treated me great, man." He would add, "She tried to help me in scenes, you know? She was always telling me things to do."

At that time, Nicholson was known, if at all, as a biker in Roger Corman pictures. By the time of *On a Clear Day*'s release, however, he would gain fame as a counterculture icon in *Easy Rider.* Still, he failed to impress his coworkers in *On a Clear Day,* delivering his lines, no matter how many takes, with the exact same expression and movement, and the exact same flat, nasal monotone.

Montand would come off even worse. His scenes with Barbra were supposed to crackle with the heated electricity that often comes with the meeting of two opposites. However, Montand is *too* stoic in his beagle-eyed blandness. To compensate, Barbra overacts. His musical numbers are also embarrassing, particularly "Come Back to Me." The beginning is shot atop the Pan Am Building in New York and Minnelli seems to have lifted the scene right out of Herb Ross's "Don't Rain on My Parade" tugboat sequence in *Funny Girl.*

As the picture got underway, Barbra received a request to appear for a deposition in a Los Angeles courtroom. With her first flush of movie fame came international adulation, the promise of great wealth, and a flock of people staking their claim. Among them was one of Barbra's "managing bookends," Martin Bregman. For undisclosed reasons, she had fired Bregman in 1967, during the production of *Funny Girl.*

The breach-of-contract suit, filed in New York in December 1968, also named Marty Erlichman, Elliott Gould, and Richard Roemer, Barbra's attorney, as defendants. The suit sought 5 percent of Barbra's earnings, or, according to Bregman's accounting, $1.15 million. The case dragged out for a couple of years. It was eventually dismissed without going to trial. But to Barbra, it proved that her paranoia had some basis in reality. The only business associate she really trusted was Marty Erlichman. "All the others love money," she said at the time of the Bregman suit, "but Marty loves me."

To publicize the launching of *On a Clear Day,* Paramount hosted a "Come as the Person You Would Like to Have Been in a Previous Life" reincarnation ball, an appropriate motif given the picture's theme of past incarnations. Raquel Welch attended as Katharine Hepburn. Omar Sharif went as Che Guevara (whom he'd just played in the film *Che!*). Barbra, the last to arrive, was Colette.

After eight weeks of rehearsals, beginning in late October, *On a Clear Day* started to film on January 6, 1969, despite the fact that producer Howard Koch allowed Barbra a ten-day "vacation" beginning January 10 to attend the European premieres of *Funny Girl.* The picture was scheduled for an eighty-two-day shoot, with 80 percent of it to be filmed in Los Angeles, 15 percent in New York, and 5 percent in England. George IV's Royal Pavilion at Brighton would serve as the stage for the film's banquet sequence.

In contrast to Gene Kelly on *Dolly,* Barbra found a collaborative spirit in Vincente Minnelli. And unlike Wyler, Minnelli was a quiet, unassuming man, with no real ego of his own. He was greatly enamored of Barbra's ability and fully encouraged her ideas. Curiously, however, reports of their rapport would not be mentioned by a press hungry for discord.

Barbra did *not* get along with Montand, but there were no real clashes to speak of. Their mutual dislike was reserved and masked behind a guise of professional politeness. When asked, years later, how he had liked Barbra on a personal level, Montand replied, tellingly, that she was a wonderful singer. He refrained from saying more, adding only that she wasn't there to defend herself and that he didn't want to be too nasty.

Still, it was a set without strife. Barbra spent her free time with her friend Howard Jeffrey, for whom she had obtained a job as the film's choreographer. She also indulged her cravings by having some of her meals flown in from Pearl's, her favorite Chinese restaurant in New York.

And for the most part, she enjoyed what she had to do in the picture, particularly the fantasy aspects of the flashback sequences. One of the scenes called for her to play herself as an eight-year-old. To better create the effect, Paramount enlarged all of the sets and enlisted the services of several seven-foot-tall actors and the tallest horse they could find.

Barbra also got on well with Cecil Beaton, the noted British photographer and designer. Beaton, who had worked with Minnelli on *Gigi*, designed Barbra's period costumes for the picture. According to designer Ray Diffen, who worked with Beaton on *Coco* with Katharine Hepburn, "We talked about Barbra and he adored her. Which was very strange, because he was such an uptight aesthetic type that one wouldn't have thought they would have gotten on. I guess it was because she had such wonderful taste."

But even Beaton would acknowledge that working with Barbra had been a trying experience. "She'll never accept anything until she's convinced in her own mind that it's 100 percent right for her. She'll never just say, 'Oh, I suppose that's all right, let's go out to dinner.' It's a constant battle of attrition with her and her taste, which is very exhausting."

The Paramount publicity department also suffered through Barbra's quest for perfection. When reviewing proposed publicity photographs of herself, Barbra's eye was, as it always is, invariably harsh. Most photos ended up in her "kill" pile. Those she deemed acceptable were sent off to the retoucher's lab. On *On a Clear Day*, Barbra ran up an historic retouching bill of twenty-five thousand dollars.

With the film falling behind schedule, producer Howard Koch began negotiations with Barbra's representatives to extend her contract. However, he could not afford to pay her more money. Barbra's terms, agreed upon by Koch, were simple. At the start of the picture, she had ordered from Paramount a large, elaborately decorated trailer, not unlike the one she had been presented at Fox. Barbra agreed to work the overtime if she was given the following: the trailer and all of its furnishings, all of her wardrobe, including the expensive Cecil Beaton creations, and some stained glass windows from the set.

During shooting of the picture, Minnelli learned that his third wife, Denise, was leaving him for another man. His personal problems would mount with a June 22, 1969, phone call from his daughter, Liza, informing him that his ex-wife Judy Garland had died that day from an accidental overdose of drugs. Ironically, at the time of the call, he was viewing footage of Streisand, hailed by many as "the Next Garland."

After the final day of shooting, in early June, Barbra presented her director with an antique silver coffee service. Noting that Minnelli did not take sugar in his morning coffee, Barbra left out the sugar container. Inscribed on the coffeepot were the words "To Vincente, whom I adore"; on the creamer, "You're the cream in my coffee."

But while she left the picture on good terms with Minnelli, Barbra was greatly displeased with Paramount's postproduction decision to chop some fifteen minutes out of the director's cut. The final cut of the film, Barbra argued, was *not* the picture she or Minnelli wanted to make. Among the excised scenes: Barbra's rooftop duet with Larry Blyden, "Wait Till We're Sixty-five"; Barbra's "ESP," in which she got to sing in multiple languages; and "Who Is There Among Us Who Knows?" Nicholson's solo-turned-duet with Barbra.

With three pictures to her credit, Barbra became increasingly dissatisfied with her station in Hollywood as an actress. She had power, but it was begrudged. She got her way because she was the "demanding star" who had to be appeased, or else. It wasn't because her ideas were necessarily better than her bosses', even though sometimes they were. The power she possessed bred contempt. Barbra, however, refused to be confined to its inherent limitations.

In early 1969, at the age of twenty-six, she began serious negotiations with Paul Newman, forty-three, and Sidney Poitier, forty-four, to form their own production company in an effort to wrest more control over her pictures. At the time, Poitier and Newman rated first and second at the box office, and Barbra, with her first picture only a few months into release, was clearly on the rise.

Forming one's own production company in Hollywood was nothing new—the combined forces of three of the biggest stars in the business *was,* with United Artists, founded in 1919 by Mary Pickford, Douglas Fairbanks, Charlie Chaplin and D. W. Griffith being the only other comparable venture. At the time of UA's formation, Richard Rowland, head of Metro, said with disdain, "So, the lunatics have taken charge of the asylum."

The idea was that each partner—Streisand, Poitier, and Newman—would make a total of three pictures for the proposed company. Each would select their own individual projects, which were not to exceed $3 million in budget, except for musicals, which would have a cap of $5 million. Each would then see them through development, production, and editing. The all-important final cut on their pictures would belong to *them.*

In return for their services, they would not be paid an upfront salary, which would certainly help keep the budgets down, but they *would* receive between 25 percent and 33⅓ percent of the picture's gross. The stakes, obviously, would be high. They could either become exceedingly rich or earn nothing except a considerable blow to their egos, their reputations and their bank accounts. As such, they would put themselves on the line only for those pictures in which they had great personal belief.

With *Variety* heralding the venture as "an undeniable threat to the uneasy status quo in Hollywood filmmaking," the First Artists Production Company was officially born on June 11, 1969. Later, Steve McQueen and Dustin Hoffman would join the powerful triumvirate.

"I know that my new associates have the same desire for artistic individuality and total commitment," Barbra said upon signing the incorporation papers. "This company will fill that need for each individual and at the same time we'll have a teamwork situation based on mutual respect and understanding."

While Barbra was forging new relationships, she was ending, or at least redefining, an old one. In October 1968, while she was in rehearsals and prescoring for *On a Clear Day,* Elliott arrived in Hollywood to begin work on a new picture. *The Night They Raided Minsky's* would be released the following month to critical, if not box office, success. His new film was to be *The Piano Sport* for MGM. However, its development was abruptly, and inexplicably, called to a halt in preproduction. Fortunately, Elliott was paid his salary in full and was promptly cast in another picture, for Columbia. It was to be a daring undertaking for Hollywood, exploring the subject of marital swingers on one level, and societal sexual mores on another. It was called *Bob and Carol and Ted and Alice.*

While in Los Angeles, Elliott lived, of course, with Barbra in her rented home in Holmby Hills, which was owned by writer George Axelrod. It was their first extended period of togetherness in months. It was, they hoped, their chance to rekindle their passion and reestablish some sense of their us-against-the-world existence, which, after all, was the foundation of their relationship.

Over the past four years, they had certainly struggled to simplify the complexities and resolve the more dysfunctional aspects of their union. Both had gone into analysis. And, for a period during the early shooting of *Funny Girl,* Elliott had even abandoned his own career to manage Barbra's. "I have had to juggle some perplexing facts," he said at the time. "We have seven corporations. I'm Barbra's husband and I'm the one to be responsible. Should I continue working in my craft, or try to call the shots on my wife's career?"

The arrangement had ended in a fight, and Elliott returned to New York to make *Minsky's,* while Barbra remained in Hollywood. Perhaps it was spite, or a sense of abandonment, that prompted Barbra to become involved with Omar Sharif. Upon learning of the affair, Elliott was humiliated. It was, like other aspects of their relationship (primarily, the issue of the female as provider), an affront to his masculinity. It was also the ultimate betrayal. Their relationship, it can be argued, never fully recovered.

But their problems went far deeper than infidelity. Faced with the enormity of his wife's fame, Elliott crawled into a shell, suppressing his own ideas, feelings, and beliefs, all in favor of Barbra's. Everything in their relationship revolved around *her.* In the eyes of the world, he was nonexistent, except as her escort and all-around hand-holder. Far worse, he bought into it. But through analysis, Elliott learned that it was okay for him to stop apologizing for his wife's triumphs and his own lack of success.

He could also express disdain over aspects of her personality without fear of his comments being construed as jealousy and/or envy. He was tired of Barbra's apparent inability to be happy. And he could not abide her constant concern about her image, and her need for the validation of others, when *his* words (and her own thoughts) of reassurance should have sufficed. "Barbra lives her life worrying about what people think of her," he said, "not only how she performs but how she looks."

He was tired, too, of having to prove and reprove himself, and of having to constantly regain her trust. "One side of Barbra needed me," Elliott confided. "The other was disdainful of men—and competitive toward them. Barbra has ambivalent feelings about men. She wants to be attractive to them, but is afraid she isn't. She has a problem she can't reconcile, that men are no good and can't be trusted."

Jason was supposed to have "solidified" their marriage—of course, too great a burden for *any* child. Instead, while their love for him was immense ("My one great creation," she would say), he had given Barbra and Elliott one more thing to fight about. "My wife is a typical Jewish mother, full of worry," Elliott said. "If Jason sneezes, she falls apart." Elliott argued that Jason should be allowed to get dirty, trip, fall, fight. In Barbra's household, however, Jason was always well primped and protected. He was taken care of by Barbra's secretary, or by Barbra's cook, Grace Maddrell, or by Barbra's dresser, Grace Davidson, or by his own nanny, a Scottish woman by the name of Barbara Howden.

This was another point of contention between Barbra and Elliott. He wanted her to be more a part of Jason's life. She wanted to be a mother *and* a movie star, and was determined to excel at both. It was not about Jason, but what so many of their differences centered on: her *career.* They might have made their marriage work if only she wasn't *so* talented. "I'm much happier in my career than she is in hers," Elliott said during production of *The Night They Raided Minsky's.* "I'd rather she was a housewife than a great big star—but she has this enormous talent."

A final blow to their marriage came on Monday night, October 28, 1968. The Goulds had gone out for dinner with friends. As they left the restaurant, they were blinded by the incessant, popping flash of paparazzi photo-fire. One photographer, Anthony Rizzo, was particularly persistent. Barbra, terrified by what she considered an assault, covered her face with one of her hands, and with the other, guided herself along the edge of the wall for support.

The confrontation that followed would end up in a Los Angeles courtroom. According to Barbra's August 7, 1969, deposition, when Rizzo continued to snap away in her direction, she pleaded, angrily, "Haven't you had enough?"

He retorted, "If *you* were polite, you would stop. If you were polite, like everybody else, you would stop and let us take your picture."

Barbra continued to retreat, mumbling under her breath. "Tell them to go away!" she pleaded of her husband. Rizzo continued his photographic pursuit. Finally, Elliott lunged toward the photographer. Barbra and her friend, a Mrs. Leff, ran frantically toward the car in the parking lot.

For Elliott, the moments that followed were the culmination of years of unvented frustration. He wanted to provide for and protect his wife. Given that he couldn't do the former, he settled for the latter, if even with his fists, if only against a photographer's camera.

According to the court complaint, Elliott "violently assaulted and struck plaintiff in and about the neck, shoulders and body." The attack, according to Rizzo, had been unprovoked. The case would not go to trial until June 26, 1972, at which time Judge Parks Stillwell ruled against Elliott in the amount of $6,501.

Elliott pleaded his innocence to the end. "I didn't hit him," he protested to a reporter. "I didn't push him. I sort of *put* him against a car. I can't tell you how I pleaded with those guys to stop taking pictures because Barbra was uptight."

In his case, Rizzo had initially contended that Barbra had "instigated, urged and directed Mr. Gould to take whatever action he deemed necessary to prevent the photographers and the plaintiff from taking further pictures." The claim, however, was rejected by the judge, and Elliott was named the sole defendant.

When asked in her deposition how she felt when Elliott, her conquering hero, had returned to the car, Barbra said, "Well, I was very nervous, upset, and I was—oh, many things. I know I felt very proud of him in a way that he was insulted for me at this man's insulting me and that he reacted as my protector. I felt very good about that."

She was then asked, "To that extent, you approved of it, then?"

She responded, "Yes."

On one level, perhaps. On another, Barbra was furious with Elliott for having turned the occasion into a public scene. It would, she told him, only prove a further strain to her relationship with the press and do damage to her already tarnished public persona.

On February 12, 1969, Barbra released news of their separation through Lee Solters, her press representative since the days of *I Can Get It for You Wholesale.* Competing for space in the press was the breakup of another Hollywood couple, Jill St. John and Jack Jones.

Upon hearing the news back in New York, their friend Ashley Feinstein remembers being saddened. "After *Funny Girl* opened on Broadway, there was a picture of Barbra and Elliott in *Newsweek* or *Time.* They were in a swimming pool, and she had her hand over his face. They looked *so* adorable. And I remember sometimes when we would go out together, they would look *just* like they did in that photograph. I really believe that they were very much in love with each other. I was hoping that they would work it out." Feinstein adds, "I liked them together."

With the announcement of their separation, they also vowed to continue working on their relationship, even if from a distance. They avoided talk of a permanent split. Divorce, to both, meant admitting defeat. Barbra talked about how they would continue their business relationship, and how Elliott would not only become a big star but an "important producer" as well.

Those early months of 1969 proved tumultuous for Barbra. In February, around the same time she made her separation from Elliott public, she was named one of five nominees for a Best Actress Oscar. She faced formidable competition: Katharine Hepburn for her work in *The Lion in Winter,* Patricia Neal for *The Subject Was Roses,* Vanessa Redgrave for *Isadora,* and Joanne Woodward for *Rachel, Rachel.*

It was to be one of the most competitive Best Actress Oscar races in the Academy's history. Hype aside, there were *five* outstanding performances that year. Any one of them could have won. The Golden Globe awards, often an Oscar indicator of sorts, went to Joanne Woodward for drama, and to Barbra for musical and/or comedy. This seemed to bode well for Woodward. Drama is perceived by most as the more important genre, and the winner in the Golden Globe drama category is usually considered to have the edge on Oscar. In addition, despite her residence in Connecticut, Woodward was well regarded in Hollywood. Moreover, for her performance in the low-budget *Rachel, Rachel,* directed by her husband, Paul Newman, she had waived her fee, suggesting artistic commitment, something else which undoubtedly appealed to the voting members of the Academy.

Woodward also won the New York Film Critics Award. The only actress to rival her in the other prestigious critics' polls was Swedish newcomer and non-Oscar-nominated Liv Ullmann for her performances in *Shame* and *Hour of the Wolf.*

Sentiment, however, was on the side of veteran Patricia Neal, who had suffered a stroke that left her semiparalyzed in 1965. Her performance in *The Subject Was Roses,* a Pulitzer Prize–winning play, signaled a highly regarded comeback. With an Oscar win, tears would surely flow, and the Academy is a sucker for an emotional acceptance speech.

Katharine Hepburn had several things going for her. First, her superb rendering of Eleanor of Aquitaine. Second, the sympathy felt for her over the recent passing of Spencer Tracy. And third, *The Lion in Winter,* extremely well thought of in the industry, was the favorite in the Best Picture category.

Vanessa Redgrave's performance in *Isadora* was widely acclaimed, but several factors made her a long shot. First of all, the picture did not become a box-office success. Second, her vigorously expressed antiwar activism was bound to alienate the more conservative wing of the Academy. And third, her announcement that she was pregnant out of wedlock by Franco Nero, her costar in *Camelot.* It was 1968 and unmarried, pregnant female stars were still expected to have quick marriages or quiet abortions.

Scandalous among the nominations was the omission of Newman in the Best Director category, despite the fact that *Rachel* was up in the Best Picture category. Even more appalling was the omission in the Best Picture category of Stanley Kubrik's *2001: A Space Odyssey* in favor of the Columbia musicals *Oliver!* and *Funny Girl.* The latter received a total of eight nominations.

As for Barbra, few argued that she had turned in a spectacular performance. In addition, she had the backing not only of Columbia, but also of Fox and Paramount. Each had a stake in a Streisand win. In addition, Hollywood typically loves to trumpet the arrival of a remarkable young newcomer almost as much as it loves heralding a career-capping performance by a seasoned old-timer.

Weighted against all of these positive factors was the dubious perception of her in the industry. Word of her questionable behavior on the *Funny Girl* and *Hello, Dolly!* sets had already become well ingrained in the minds of the community. Awarding her the Oscar, it was thought by some, would only encourage an ego which had already run rampant. She needed to be taken down a notch or two, humbled, and an internationally televised defeat in front of millions of viewers would be a start.

"I've made up my mind just not to think about the Awards," Barbra told columnist Dorothy Manners. "I can't afford to shiver and shake until the verdict is in. But somehow I can't believe I'm going to get it. It's the Jewishness in me, I guess, the pessimism. It's so close under my skin, that old feeling, 'I can't win. Not me.' "

With her previous Oscar appearance a disaster, Barbra was particularly concerned about the way she looked. She wanted to look good, glamorous, sexy, but she also wished for more. She wanted her appearance to in some way convey an "I don't give a damn either way" kind of irreverence, even though she *did* care, greatly. Her favorite designer of the period, Arnold Scaasi, came up with a solution: a transparent, pajamalike pantsuit made of black tulle and clear sequins with a white collar and sleeves and greatly flared bell-bottom legs. It was glamorous, displayed a generous amount of flesh, and showed that she didn't take herself too seriously, even though, of course, she did.

Until the day of the ceremony, Barbra couldn't decide what to wear. It was a choice between the Scaasi creation and two other more conventional designs. She modeled them before the mirror, one after another, and once completed, repeated the cycle. She asked for the advice of anyone and everyone. That afternoon, *On a Clear Day* was called to an early halt so that she could get ready. After completing her last take, she took producer Howard Koch by the hand and led him into her dressing room. She then modeled each of the outfits before his appraising eyes. He picked the Scaasi.

Monday night, April 14, 1969. The Dorothy Chandler Pavilion in Los Angeles. Elliott, at Barbra's request, sat at her side. He wore a tuxedo, looked terribly self-conscious, and was flying high on marijuana. When the television camera panned over the audience and settled on the two of them sitting together, Elliott tugged twice on his earlobe. It was his signal to let one of his friends back home know that he was stoned.

As Ingrid Bergman read the nominated names, Barbra sat clutching Elliott's hand. Woodward, Neal, and Redgrave were also in the audience. Hepburn was not. Bergman opened the envelope and pronounced, "The winner is . . . It's a *tie!*" The audience gasped in shock. The only tie in Oscar history had been between Wallace Beery and Fredric March in 1931–32. "The winners," Bergman continued, recovering, "are Katharine Hepburn for *The Lion in Winter* and Barbra Streisand in *Funny Girl!*"

Barbra, stunned, barely moved. Anthony Harvey, accepting for Hepburn, whom he had directed in *Lion,* leaned over in his seat and suggested to Barbra that they walk to the podium together. As she navigated her way up the few steps to the stage, Barbra tripped on the bell-bottom flair of her pantsuit and momentarily stumbled. When the television lights hit the backside of her outfit, the audience got a clear and ample view of her near-naked, sequin-covered derriere.

When Harvey finished his brief speech in the Great Kate's behalf, Barbra stepped to the podium. She paused. Then, studying the statuette she had been dreaming about since childhood, she gushed, ebullient, "Hello, gorgeous!" The audience *got* it. Not only was she addressing her new inanimate acquisition by repeating a line from her movie, she was talking to—and about—herself. *This* was her arrival.

"I'm very honored to be in such magnificent company as Katharine Hepburn," she continued with obvious sincerity. "Gee whiz, it's kind of a wild feeling. Sitting there tonight, I was thinking that the first script of *Funny Girl* was written when I was only eleven years old. Thank God it took so long to get it right, you know?" After proceeding to thank Ray Stark, Jule Styne, Bob Merrill, Isobel Lennart, Herb Ross, Harry Stradling, and William Wyler, Barbra concluded her speech with the following:

"Somebody once said to me, asked me if I was happy and I said, 'Are you kidding? I'd be miserable if I was happy. And I'd like to thank all the members of the Academy for making me *really* miserable. Thank you."

Clutching Oscar, she walked backstage and then froze in her tracks, terrified. She was expected in the press room to pose for photographs and field mostly inane questions of the "Well, how do you feel *now?*" variety. It would take her fifteen minutes to summon her courage. Finally, she took a deep breath, raised her head, and entered the room.

"Barbra! Barbra! How do you feel now? Barbra! Barbra . . . !"

Twenty-three

Private Portraits, Public Failures

*O*n April 21, 1969, one week after watching his "ugly" stepdaughter receive the Academy Award in front of millions of viewers, Louis Kind, aged seventy-five, died in Brooklyn. In a way, he had been partially responsible for her success, though not in the way he believed. It was his mistreatment of her that had instilled in Barbra much of her "I'll show you" spirit. Upon hearing the news of his passing, Barbra was neither happy nor sad. She felt nothing.

It was around this same time that Kind's natural daughter, Roslyn Kind, nineteen, began to pursue a singing career of her own. Eight years old at the time Barbra moved away from home, Roslyn never really got to know her older half sister. In lieu of a relationship, Roslyn became her biggest fan. During the run of *Funny Girl* on Broadway, she served as the president of the Barbra Streisand Fan Club. For a high school essay, she decided to write a *book* about her sister's rise to stardom on the Broadway stage. Handwritten, and equipped with illustrations drawn by a friend, Debbie Choy, it was titled, ironically, *A Star Is Born.* The opening chapter began:

As her parents glanced adoringly at her in the cradle, little did they know that one day their little girl would have her name in lights.

It all started on the school platform in P.S. 89 in Brooklyn, where Barbra attended classes until the eighth grade. She had volunteered to sing in the school Christmas show.

Barbra wasn't much to look at, being as skinny as she was and you couldn't say she was a beauty!

Roslyn stood in the back of the Winter Garden Theater and watched her sister in *Funny Girl* until every move, every inflection, became ingrained into her memory. She saw the play some *forty* times. Back in Brooklyn, she would listen to the original cast album day and night, and she would stand in front of the bathroom mirror and impersonate her sister.

Her voice was good too. She became the best Barbra Streisand impersonator in the world. Even Diana Kind was impressed. After having done everything in her power to *prevent* Barbra from pursuing a career in show business, Diana now encouraged Roslyn to follow suit. After all, if lightning could strike the family tree once, why not twice or even *three* times? Diana herself began taking singing lessons twice a week and entertained thoughts of her own professional career. As she told her daughters, "Don't forget, you got it from *me*. You didn't fall out of a tree."

Unfortunately for Roslyn, she was almost *twice* Barbra's weight. At the opening night party for *Funny Girl* held in the Rainbow Room, a reporter approached Roslyn and asked, "Aren't you Barbra Streisand's *aunt?*" Roslyn, thirteen, went back home to Brooklyn that night and cried. And then she pigged out. As she would later explain, "After all, I weighed 189 pounds, so a few more didn't matter."

Ted Brooks, the manager of Barbra's music publishing company heard the voice, and saw through the fat. He signed up as Roslyn's manager and described her as having the same four-octave range and "more power, more depth in her lower tones, more 'belt' to a song" than that of her famous sister. Roslyn, to Barbra's aggravation, added, "I don't have [my sister's] nasal quality or her vibrato."

"My main problem," Roslyn said, "was being an ardent fan of my sister's style. I had her down too pat. But that wouldn't do. We spent a whole year trying to find a style of my own." Meanwhile, she lost weight.

The story goes that Brooks took her to RCA and signed her to a $100,000 recording contract even though the company did not know Roslyn was Barbra's half sister. Unfortunately, very few people heard Roslyn's 1968 album, *Give Me You*. Promoted as Barbra's sister, Roslyn *did* get an appearance on "The Ed Sullivan Show." She also managed a two-week engagement at the Hungry i in San Francisco, where Barbra had triumphed six years before. "Why all the attention?" *Newsweek* asked, then answered "Mostly because Roslyn Kind, eighteen, happens to be Barbra Streisand's half-sister."

While she may have had her sister's voice (or a reasonable facsimile), she did not have her tenacity. "I'm not bold like Barbra," Roslyn said. "I can't go up to people and say, 'Hello, my name is Roslyn. Would you like to hear me sing?' I'm too shy to move away from home. My manager says I could never hold my own with a landlord."

Her contact with her sister was minimal. In 1969, while Barbra was in Los Angeles making *On a Clear Day You Can See Forever*, Roslyn was in the same city for a few days doing interviews. The two sisters never got together. Not only was Barbra displeased with the defection of Ted Brooks from her staff, she was not happy about the public comments made by Brooks and by Roslyn.

Although both would undoubtedly deny it, there is, and always has been, an underlying uneasiness between the two half sisters. Roslyn, after all, had been the "beauty" to Barbra's "beast." Roslyn had been the golden child to Barbra's skinny little *marink*. Roslyn had received the praise; Barbra, the broom. The resentment has always been present, beneath the surface, behind the smiles of posed family portraits.

Three days after she won her Oscar, Barbra was on an airplane bound for New York, where she was to do location shooting for *On a Clear Day*. As she settled back into her first-class seat, she was stunned when the film's cast and crew, passengers on the flight, launched into the opening bars of "Happy Birthday." The idea of staging a surprise party aloft had been the inspiration of the film's producer, Howard Koch. Along with their customary service of coffee, tea, and milk, the flight attendants served catered Chinese from Pearl's in New York, followed by ice cream from Barbra's favorite confectionery in Los Angeles. The birthday girl was in heaven—or close to it. It was April 24, 1969. She was twenty-seven years old.

Precocious from the start, Jason Emanuel would begin school before his third birthday. One day, while he was at home watching television, a clip of *Funny Girl* came on the air. The clip showed Barbra on the tugboat belting out "Don't Rain on My Parade." Upset by what he perceived to be her neglect, Jason stormed over to where Barbra was working. "Mommy, you're on TV singing in a boat," he stated. "I *saw* you. Why didn't you take *me* on the boat with you?"

Elliott, who was back working in Hollywood, would fly to New York for weekends to be with Jason. For Elliott, this was the hardest part of the separation, *visiting* his child. "It's unnatural to visit your son," he would say, "and it's unnatural for any child of that age to see that Mommy and Daddy don't have a relationship."

On Memorial Day weekend, 1969, Elliott and Barbra took Jason to see his first movie. It was not *Funny Girl,* or even *Chitty Chitty Bang Bang.* It was Arthur Hiller's *Popi,* which told the story of poverty in the ghetto.

He was an unusual child. Exceptionally bright. Spirited. Creative. The first word of Jason's that Ashley Feinstein recalls hearing was not "Mommy" or "Daddy"—it was *"hat,"* most likely due to the time he spent on set of *Hello, Dolly!*

On May 16, 1969, the Friars Club of New York honored Barbra as the Entertainer of the Year. The club had so honored only one other woman in its entire history, Sophie Tucker. The highlight of the ceremony, which took place in the Grand Ballroom of the Waldorf-Astoria, occurred when Barbra was serenaded by composers Harold Arlen, Jerry Herman, Jule Styne, Richard Rodgers, Harold Rome, Cy Coleman, and Burton Lane.

William Wyler, then directing another picture, was unable to attend. He sent a note: "As your co-director on *Funny Girl* I became so accustomed to relying on your suggestions as to how the picture should be made that I am very much at a loss now that I must go it alone again. Congratulations. 'Entertainer of the Year' is an honor you have earned, and along with it, in my opinion, 'Director of the Year.' "

Seated at the front table were Cis Corman and her husband, psychoanalyst Harvey Corman. During the proceedings, Dr. Corman leaned over to columnist Sidney Skolsky and confided that Barbra's great talent consisted of her ability to hide her fear.

Diana Kind, Barbra's mother, also sat in front of the dais. She was an easy, obvious target for Don Rickles. Fixing her with a mock stare from the podium, Rickles quipped, "It's 110 degrees in this room, so why are you wearing mink? We all *know* you're Jewish!"

In 1969, Kirk Kerkorian was completing plans to open his massive, $60 million International Hotel in Las Vegas. With 1,519 rooms and thirty floors, it was to be the largest resort hotel and casino in the world. Its swimming pool alone was the second-largest man-made body of water in the state of Nevada.

The hotel's general manager, Alex Shoofey, wanted Elvis Presley to make his live-performance comeback by opening the hotel showroom. Presley's manager, Colonel Tom Parker, refused. Elvis *would* make his comeback, but he wouldn't *open* the hotel. "Absolutely not," Parker stated. "It's much too risky. Let somebody else stick his neck out."

Sticking *her* neck out on the July 2 opening was Barbra Streisand. With the hotel still in a state of construction and confusion, and without sets, singers, dancers, flashy lighting, or even an opening act, Barbra simply stood on the stage under a tall cluster of curls and sang.

She was an unequivocal flop. Her characteristically acute instinct had failed her. She had mistaken Las Vegas for New York City. Only this time, she was the headliner, not some protégée of Liberace. She had failed to live up to enormous expectations, and the hotel's billing of "The Most Exciting Star in the World." Despite her opening number, "I've Got Plenty of Nothing," which was *meant* to be funny, she failed to prove that she was worth the much-hyped salary she was purportedly getting. For the four-week engagement, Barbra reportedly received $125,000 a week; she was also allowed to purchase a hefty share of hotel stock at an inexpensive price.

Prior to appearing onstage, she became angry at the hotel management because they had failed to send out all the press invitations and had even neglected to invite Richard Zanuck, the head of Twentieth Century-Fox, as Barbra had requested. She also *loathed* the decor, particularly the life-size replicas of George and Martha Washington which adorned either side of the stage.

But it wasn't anger or aesthetic distaste that marred the opening. It wasn't even that she sang badly, which she didn't. It was, in addition to some miscalculation in format, sheer terror. The International stage was mammoth, and the room itself, the Showroom Internationale, was cavernous, impersonal. Without an opening act, Barbra needed to warm the room with familiar songs. She also needed to establish a rapport with her audience. She didn't. Instead, defying convention, her material was eclectic, and she didn't say a word to the audience until she had sung five songs.

"I was aloof on opening night because I was in a state of shock," she told *Los Angeles Times* critic Charles Champlin. "You could feel the hostility of that opening night audience, all the gamblers who were there because they're important to the hotel, all the actors who resent the fact that you're doing things they think they should be doing. It's total fear time up there. I don't enjoy performing before a bunch of strangers. I don't care about pleasing a group. Some performers get a thrill out of winning over a cold audience—I talked to Elvis about it last night. He does—I don't. It turns me off."

To make matters worse, the hotel charged each guest fifteen dollars and required a three-drink minimum at a stiff, for then, five dollars a drink. When one customer complained to the cocktail waitress, he was told, *"She* gets a million. It's got to come from someplace, doesn't it?"

One night, preparing for his own opening, Elvis watched the show from the back of the balcony. At one point, he turned to the guy sitting with him and pronounced, "She sucks!" After the show, he went to Barbra's dressing room and showered her with praise.

"This place isn't even built yet!" she complained to the once and future King. "I wouldn't be surprised if some night while I'm out there working, some schmuck doesn't walk by with a ladder on his shoulder!"

Reportedly, Elvis also asked her, "What did you see in Elliott Gould?" Before she could answer, he added, "I could never stand him." Barbra, who doesn't like this kind of familiarity, particularly not from virtual strangers, replied that Elliott was the father of her son. With that, the subject was closed.

Word went out that the first week of her engagement was a fiasco and a bore, except for a few notable highlights, like the night that Rita Hayworth showed up and belted a photographer with her handbag.

Artie Butler, a music arranger and conductor who worked with Barbra on a couple of her films, happened to be in Vegas at the time of the engagement. He recalls, "Marty Erlichman invited me to see the show. I remember as I was walking in, they were still hanging up the chandelier."

When asked to assess Barbra's performance, Butler, despite being an ardent admirer of her musicality, says, "To be real honest, I felt that Barbra wasn't 'into it.' I don't think live performing was her strong point. Peggy Lee was performing downstairs in the lounge. And after Barbra's show, I remember everybody getting up and going to see Peggy Lee. Now, *she* got standing ovations. There you're talking about a live performer."

Barbra improved somewhat during the course of the four-week run. She changed some of her material, and even managed to joke to her audience about the hotel's unfinished condition. One night, she stopped singing in the middle of "Jingle Bells"—singing "Jingle Bells" in the middle of summer was in itself a bit aberrant for conservative Vegas audiences—to observe a flurry of white flakes falling from the ceiling.

"That's not snow," Barbra nervously informed her audience, "That's *plaster!"*

Still, she couldn't wait to complete her engagement and, just as she had done on Broadway, marked off her performances on a big wall calendar hung prominently in her dressing room. She closed, to her great relief, on July 30.

But while she didn't seem to fit in with the older, Vegas audiences, she no longer belonged to the younger ones either, as evidenced by her alarming drop-off in record sales. Over the past three years, the American music scene had *drastically* changed. In 1966, the top-selling artists in the country included Frank Sinatra, Simon and Garfunkel, The Beatles, Petula Clark, and Herb Alpert and the Tijuana Brass. By 1969, those names had been replaced by a very different group of performers: Led Zeppelin, Creedence Clearwater Revival, Blind Faith, Blood, Sweat and Tears, and Sly and the Family Stone. The music scene had been almost totally taken over by these and other (young) men who had an apparent aversion to shaving, bathing, and getting their hair cut. Barbra herself was appalled by them.

Since "People" in mid-1964, every Streisand single released by Columbia flopped upon release. "Second Hand Rose," which peaked at number thirty-two, was the only one to even make the *Billboard* top-forty pop chart. Far more distressing was her decline in album sales. *Je m' appelle Barbra, Simply Streisand, Funny Girl* (the movie soundtrack), and *A Happening in Central Park* all sold far below expectations.

It was quite a fall indeed, given that, between April 1963 and April 1966, *eight* Streisand albums made the top ten *and* were certified gold. Furthermore, five of them were nominated for the Album of the Year Grammy. She had also swept the Best-Selling Female Vocalist award from the National Association of Record Merchandisers (NARM) for four straight years, a streak which ended in 1967.

It was the age of Woodstock, *Hair,* and "Aquarius," and Barbra, though only twenty-seven, seemed desperately out of step, behind the times, ancient beyond her years. "She began to lose touch," Clive Davis, the head of Columbia Records, later said. "She became interested in motion pictures and was no longer close to the world of music—which was changing fast."

Confronted with her sales figures, Davis paid Barbra a visit on the set of *Hello, Dolly!* and expressed his concern. She argued for her individuality, her instincts, her creative control. She claimed that he was trying to "commercialize" her. "Your album sales will continue to decline unless something changes," he warned her. His parting words, "You have to contemporize your image."

She argued, but she *listened.* Moreover, artistic integrity aside, she complied. What resulted was *What About Today?* an album of contemporary songs by contemporary songwriters. Released in September 1969, the album did only mediocre business and peaked at number thirty-one on the charts. Robert Christgau wrote in the *New York Times,* "Not only is Miss Streisand's emoting wasted on such dull material, it is shown up as an arbitrary exercise." Nonetheless, Barbra was now determined to "contemporize" her image, whatever the cost. She would have far more success on her next such effort.

Following her split with Elliott, Barbra was reintroduced to the world of dating. Among her flings was Charles Evans, the millionaire brother of Paramount Pictures producer Robert Evans. Another was Warren Beatty. Involved with actress Julie Christie at the time, Beatty met Barbra at an industry party. The two huddled in a corner for hours. He had seen *Funny Girl,* was a fan, and wanted to add Barbra to his notoriously long list of sexual conquests. He told her that she was beautiful. She, at first, was awed by his beauty. She was also quite flattered that *he* was interested in *her.* "Imagine," she reportedly told a friend, "Warren Beatty flipping over me?" For Barbra, this Hollywood stuff was getting quite heady.

One Friday night when Julie Christie was out of town, Barbra was Warren's guest in his penthouse suite at the Beverly Wilshire Hotel. He had chilled champagne, dinner, soft music. The two then proceed to play out the "You Are Woman, I Am Man" sequence from *Funny Girl.* Two days later, Christie returned to Los Angeles, and Barbra's brief "affair" with Beatty was over.

Her relationship with Canadian prime minister Pierre Trudeau was more meaningful. In November 1969, Trudeau, fifty, flew into New York for a series of weekend dates with Barbra. On Friday night, they dined at Casa Brasil, an intimate East Side eatery, then danced at Raffles, a private discoteque. On Sunday, they went to the Polish Lab Theater. On Saturday, presumably, they stayed in at Barbra's Central Park West apartment. Asked how long he had known Barbra, Trudeau responded, "Not long enough." The two would share an inside joke. Whenever someone would ask about their relationship, Trudeau was supposed to point at the offending questioner and command, "Arrest that man!"

On January 28, 1970, Trudeau flew Barbra to Canada to be his guest at the National Arts Center party which marked the anniversary of Manitoba's centennial. They arrived at the event separately. Upon Barbra's arrival, Trudeau leapt out of his limo, dodged past the Royal Canadian Mounted Police, and personally opened her car door. Barbra would later say of the experience, "It happened to be overwhelming."

She was later his guest at the House of Commons. She sat in the visitor's gallery and watched Trudeau's every move. He watched her too. At one point in the proceedings, one member of the Tory opposition testily quipped, "I should like to ask a question of the Prime Minister—*if* he can take his eyes and his mind off the visitor's gallery."

Trudeau showed her the sights of Ottawa and treated her to an evening of ballet and buffalo burgers. She was also his guest for a romantic, candlelit dinner at 24 Sussex Drive, the prime minister's mansion.

Barbra was absolutely enamored of Trudeau. Despite his own accomplishments, he wanted to talk only of her. He loved Chinese food and was intense, funny, charming, and shamelessly flirtatious. Unlike Elliott, he was also secure with himself, and exuded power. For Barbra, it was an intoxicating combination. She fantasized about a life with him, as Canada's first lady. She had it all figured out in her mind. She would campaign and make speeches for him, promote his causes, as well as her own, *and* make movies in Canada.

But it was not to be. Trudeau was looking for a wife, but Barbra, at that point in her life and career, was far too self-involved to become subordinate to any one man, particularly one who came attached to a country. Moreover, he was devoutly Catholic, and Barbra was reluctant to convert. His religion also gave him serious reservations about certain aspects of her lifestyle and some of her beliefs.

At the same time he was dating Barbra, Trudeau, whether she knew it or not, saw other women as well, among them a professor of French literature named Madeleine Gobeil. He also called on a pretty young woman by the name of Margaret Sinclair. Throughout Barbra's trip to Canada, Trudeau continued to phone Margaret, who would hang up on him, shouting, "Go back to your American actress!"

Margaret Sinclair would later became Mrs. Pierre Trudeau, first lady of Canada, and Barbra had to content herself with life on the twenty-sixth floor in New York.

She wanted out of her apartment. Memories of Elliott, and of their life together, permeated every room. She found a co-op that she liked at 1021 Park Avenue between Eighty-fifth and Eighty-sixth streets. Barbra offered a more-than-reasonable $200,000 for the place, but was inexplicably turned down. A little probing by a London newspaper revealed the reason. According to a representative of the building's board of directors, she was "not suitable." Further probing defined the term to mean that she was an actress, and not a respectable actress of the theater but a "Hollywood type." Barbra was convinced that she was also rejected, at least in part, because she was Jewish.

It was the second time in a year that her application to purchase an apartment had been turned down. Outraged, Barbra contemplated a move out of Manhattan. She would not live, she vowed to whoever would listen, in a city that didn't want her. What happened next showed her that she was right.

At considerable expense, Twentieth Century-Fox finally convinced David Merrick to allow the release of *Hello, Dolly!* despite the fact that the stage version was still running. Besides the money, Merrick consented because the show had already surpassed *My Fair Lady*'s record on Broadway of 2,717 performances.

The picture premiered on December 16, 1969, at the Rivoli in New York. What transpired that night was a scene out of Nathanael West's *The Day of the Locust.* In freezing weather, one thousand fans gathered outside the theater to get a glimpse of their beloved Barbra. When she arrived in her chauffeur-driven Mercedes-Benz limousine, the crowd transformed itself into an unruly mob. They ambushed her car and rocked it from side to side. Barbra, trapped, was mortified.

The police stormed through the crowd, flinging bodies off the car. They also had to push screaming fans away from the red-carpeted entrance. It would take the police fifteen minutes just to get a pale and visibly shaken Barbra out of her Mercedes and into the theater. Enroute, she was clutched and clawed at, and she nearly toppled over on several occasions.

The police barely managed to escort her into the theater when security lines collapsed. Some fans and photographers pushed their way into the lobby. In Barbra's defense, Marty Erlichman got into a slugfest with one wire-service photographer, and they ended up wrestling in the aisles. Four-letter words were spewed back and forth. The photographer punched Erlichman in the cheek, drawing blood, when security finally intervened.

All of this happened *before* the start of the movie, which was delayed to accommodate Barbra's arrival. Finally, after an hour of waiting, Darryl F. Zanuck himself stood up from his seat and bellowed, "Start the picture!"

He might have wished that he hadn't. *Hello, Dolly!* was a colossal flop. It received mostly unfavorable reviews. Pauline Kael wrote, "It really is hard to believe that people have gone to all this staggeringly unimaginative effort." The movie would earn fifteen million dollars at the box office, a loss of nine million dollars.

Not only did *Hello, Dolly!* signal the demise of the old-fashioned, big-budget Hollywood musical, it also provided Barbra Streisand with the biggest flop of her career.

Ironically, Carol Channing, who attended the disastrous New York premiere, came to Barbra's defense. Sort of. "Barbra has a characterization [in the picture]," Carol reported, "but at least it's not *mine.* When Marilyn Monroe got my part for the movie *Gentlemen Prefer Blondes,* she sat in the orchestra, third row center for eighteen nights, studying all my gestures. She did them on-screen. That really hurt. This didn't." Of Barbra's performance, Channing expressed what many believed, "I thought she did the best job she could do."

What Channing meant to say, of course, was that she never should have played the part in the first place.

Twenty-four

The Fall of the Skyscraper Hairdo

*I*t was to be the end of the billowy chiffon and the skyscraper hairdos. Barbra Streisand was twenty-seven, and yet the perception of her was hopelessly *unhip*. By virtue of her succession of period pictures, Vegas-type engagements, and ridiculously long and accomplished résumé, she was viewed as a card-carrying member of the Establishment. She was at that awkward stage: too young to play Dolly Levi, too old to play a woman of her own age. The time had come for Streisand to let down her hair, take off her clothes, and rejoin her own generation.

The role of Doris Wilgus—part-time hooker, part-time model, and the feline half of Bill Manhoff's Broadway comedy, *The Owl and the Pussycat*—seemed like a good start.

The part had been played on Broadway by Diana Sands, a black actress with whom Barbra had appeared in the 1961 revue *Another Evening with Harry Stoones*. Barbra had seen the play in London and liked it. When Ray Stark filed a lawsuit against her in late 1967, Barbra resolved the dispute in part by agreeing to do another picture for him. What she wanted was *Pussycat*. Her obstacle was Elizabeth Taylor.

Stark had intended the project for Taylor as a welcome change of pace after her explosively dramatic emoting in Edward Albee's *Who's Afraid of Virginia Woolf?* Her intended costar, in the part originated by Alan Alda, was *Rod* Taylor. When Rod Taylor was eliminated from consideration, William Holden stepped into the proposed scenario.

For whatever reason, the project as originally designed by Stark did

308

not come to pass, and in November 1968, two months after the release of *Funny Girl,* it was announced that it would be Barbra, and not Elizabeth Taylor, who would star in the picture. Eyebrows were raised almost immediately. *Barbra Streisand* as a sexy hooker? Herb Ross, the film's director, would later bristle at any such skepticism. "She was the perfect casting for *The Owl and the Pussycat,"* he said. "Indeed, the whole project was conceived for her."

Given that the play had been cast with an interracial couple, Barbra's first impulse was to reverse the skin color of the protagonists and have Sidney Poitier, one of her partners in First Artists, play the part of Felix Sherman. The Oscar-winning Poitier was a major box-office star at the time. But, for reasons of her own, Barbra backed away from the idea of making on-screen love to a black man. She wanted an image adjustment, but this, she feared, was too much.

Publicly, she rationalized her view, or attempted to, by saying, "What I felt was wrong with the play as it was done on Broadway and in London was that it was played by a Negro girl, but with no reference to the problem . . . which is silly."

Apparently, she believed that the subject of racial discrimination would have to be addressed in the script for the casting to be viable. "Great! Oh, it's a step forward!," she went on, not without a little sarcasm. "We'll have a Negro play the white and you'll see we're all equal!" Which, of course, was the point. The fact that one of the characters is black was *incidental* to the story—no expository production needed to be made of it. Barbra had a perfect opportunity to make a social statement of significant importance, and she backed down.

Nonetheless, *The Owl and the Pussycat* started shooting in a small studio rented from Twentieth Century-Fox on West Fifty-sixth Street in Manhattan on October 6, 1969. With locations including Central Park, Doubleday, Riker's Restaurant, and New York's Club 45, it is, to this date, Barbra's only picture shot entirely in New York City.

The dressing rooms at the rented Fox studio hardly befitted a star of Barbra's stature, so John Robert Lloyd, the film's production designer, was asked to do something about it. "I was in a *very* busy period," he recalls, "and the producers came to me and said, 'Would you redo her dressing room?' They told me that she had caused a great deal of consternation on her last film, *Hello, Dolly!* She was trying to be obstinate or something and had caused them thousands and thousands of dollars redecorating her dressing room. I think she was just taking spite out on somebody, because that didn't happen with us.

"So I just stripped out her dressing room," Lloyd continues, "mirrored it completely, put in thick white carpeting, and all kinds of funny things—beanbag chairs, things that were faddish. And I made her a special dressing room table with those three-fold dressing mirrors with lights around them like the old-fashioned dressing rooms used to have. And I put a star on the door. Her people said to me, 'Oh, she is never gonna go for *this.*' But I brought her in and she was happy as a child. It wasn't much, but I think she was pleased that someone had given her the thought."

She would have an early showdown with Ray Stark. Before signing to do the picture, Barbra made it clear to her mentor that this was to be her first *non*singing part, no singing in the picture, no singing over the titles, no singing, period. She wanted to get away from her association with musicals and be acknowledged for the first time as a straight actress.

Stark contended that a Streisand picture without a Streisand song would lose money at the box office. He announced to the press that he was revising the part of Doris from part-time hooker/part-time model to part-time hooker/part-time *folk* singer. It was, after all, 1969. Stark reasoned, this way Barbra would have the opportunity to sing a couple of songs in the picture.

She was livid. She *liked* the idea that Doris was a part-time model, which she thought would help to dispel the perception that she was unattractive. Moreover, she was furious that Stark put her in the position of coming off like the temperamental ("No, I *refuse* to sing!") star, when that had been their agreement from the beginning.

Early on, the picture flirted with the idea of an X rating, which was becoming somewhat fashionable in Hollywood with the success of *Midnight Cowboy.* George Segal, who had created a sensation in *Who's Afraid of Virginia Woolf?* a few years before, was cast as Felix Sherman. The part called for him to do a full-frontal nude scene witnessed by Barbra's Doris. The scene was shot, but in the picture's final cut, Segal's male member was totally obscured by a carefully placed set piece.

While the shooting of Segal's nude scene was awkwardly embarrassing for everyone involved, the shooting of Barbra's *topless* scene was fraught with tension. It would take director Herb Ross an hour to get her to discard her bathrobe. "She only calls me 'Herbie' when she's uptight," Ross recalled. "Otherwise I'm Herbert. For that scene, as soon as I heard 'Herbie, I gotta talk to you,' I knew she had big reservations even though I thought we'd worked them all out. She got me into a corner and said, 'Herbie, I can't. I've got goose bumps and they'll show. Herbie, I just can't. What will my mother think?' "

While Ross patiently tried to coax Barbra out of her robe, Segal, waiting for her in the bed, fell asleep. Finally, in a moment of daring, she exclaimed, "Oh, what the hell. I'll do it once!" She tossed off her bathrobe and crossed the set bare-breasted. Relieved to get it over with, Ross yelled, "Cut and print! Beautiful." But Barbra, to the shock and laughter of everyone present, asked for *another* take. She went back to her starting position and completed her first nude scene on celluloid.

But she would insist that the scene be cut. Instead of claiming reasons of modesty or her mother's disapproval, she rationalized that the nudity ruined the comedy of the next scene. "The producer and the director are both pleading with me to put it back in the film," she said, "but I won't. It's out and it stays out."

Barbra insisted on being given the film negative of the nude takes, which she was. What she *didn't* get, however, was *all* of the prints that had been made. In 1979, several frames would be blown up and published in *High Society* magazine. Barbra filed a lawsuit to block the publication and succeeded, in a way. She had sought five million dollars in damages. Instead, the judge in the case ordered that publisher Gloria Leonard send out telegrams to her five hundred wholesalers asking that they tear the pictures out of the magazines, which at the time were either on or enroute to, the stands. In her suit Barbra sought to have the issue's table of contents changed as well. Originally, it read, "Class Act, Class Ass: Barbra Streisand Nude." Interestingly, the only thing Barbra wanted deleted was the word "Nude."

One day, back on the *Pussycat* set, Diana Kind, on vacation from her job as a school secretary in New York, paid Barbra a surprise visit and was appalled by what she found. Barbra was dressed at the time in Doris's sheer, skimpy, custom-designed negligee. Shaking her head from side to side, Diana proclaimed, "I'm really shocked at all these things an actress has to do today."

Perhaps it was because of her mother that Barbra had one of the lines in the script changed. Initially, at one point, she was to exclaim, "Fuck off!" Barbra had the line revised to "Up yours!" Either way, it would jolt Streisand audiences out of their G-rated complacency. So too would Doris's line of "I may be a prostitute but I am not promiscuous."

It's unfortunate that Barbra didn't use her influence to change some of the other, even more offensive lines in the script, as adapted by Buck Henry. In the first ten minutes of the picture, she used a series of antigay slurs—"fairy," "fag," "queer," and "fruit" among them. Given Barbra's experience around and friendships with gay men, her derisive attitude toward them in this picture is both startling and disturbing. Furthermore, there is no reason why Doris should assume that Felix is gay in the first place, except for her general view that he is despicable, an assumption which, of course, smacks of homophobia. It is also not made clear when and why she realizes that he is *not* gay.

During the production, cinematographer Harry Stradling became ill and had to be replaced with Andrew Laszlo (*The Night They Raided Minsky's,* 1968). Stradling returned to Los Angeles, where he died from a heart attack on February 14, 1970, at age sixty-two. For Barbra, it was a profound loss. *The Owl and the Pussycat* was their fourth picture together. "She had the greatest cameraman that ever worked in the industry in Harry Stradling, Sr.," ventured Jack Solomon, a veteran sound man who worked on four pictures with Barbra, including *Funny Girl* and *Hello, Dolly!* "She had a lot of respect for him. She loved him. She used to call him Uncle Harry."

During breaks from shooting, Barbra relaxed by engaging in her latest passion: painting. Recalls production designer John Robert Lloyd, "She was very interested in becoming a painter, so we set up a little studio outside of her dressing room to keep her amused. Inside the studio were canvases that were almost like paint-by-number. We did layouts on them in pencil so that she could practically paint them in.

"She was interested in [artist] Frank Stella at the time, Barbra was not a serious artist, but she liked to pretend. What she really liked was the fact that certain artists got big prices for their paintings. I think that's what her interest was. Frank Stella was getting these *huge* prices for what she considered were things *she* could do." Lloyd adds with a laugh, "I think she was serious about wanting to make money in that easy a way."

Lloyd is baffled when asked about his personal working relationship with Barbra, and her unfavorable reputation within the industry. "I think that she is very cooperative. I never understood any of that talk. She is *not* to be fooled with. You don't give her a glad hand and a false smile. She doesn't go for that. She is very sincere herself, and very, very shrewd. She sees right through any sham. There's no fakery about Barbra, ever. If they try to save money and say, 'Oh, Barbra, that was perfect,' she would say, 'That was *not* perfect. I can do it better! I'm gonna reshoot that tomorrow.' They try to talk her out of it, and she hates that."

The Owl and the Pussycat completed principal photography on January 19, 1970. Around the same time, Barbra was presented the Golden Globe award as the World Film Favorite, Female. It's a distinction she would duplicate the following year as well.

Although she did not receive a Best Actress Oscar nomination for *Hello, Dolly!* (it wasn't really expected), Barbra attended the Academy Award ceremonies on April 7, 1970, to present the Best Actor award. Immediately after arriving at the podium, she asked for the winning envelope, explaining, "Just in case I forget to ask for it later." She opened it, read it, laughed, and clutched it to her chest. "I'm not going to tell you," she teased the audience. But, of course, she did. The winner was John Wayne for his performance as a one-eyed geriatric gunslinger in *True Grit.*

Upon receiving his statuette from Barbra, Wayne whispered in her ear, "Beginner's luck." He then told the audience, "Wow. If I had known that, I would have put that eyepatch on thirty-five years earlier."

The following day, fellow Best Actor nominee Richard Burton wrote in his journal: "John Wayne won the Oscar as predicted. We went to the party afterwards and sat with George Cukor and the [Greogry] Pecks and the Chandlers [owners of the *Los Angeles Times*] but were surrounded by scores of photographers, who, to my delight, took very little notice of anybody else, including the winners. Barbra Streisand, who fancies herself a big star, was totally eclipsed."

In the months after completing *Pussycat,* her fourth picture in succession, Barbra went on a domestic sabbatical, resting, recuperating, redecorating. She shopped, saw friends, and spent time with Jason, who at three and a half was beginning to sound like his mother. One day, Barbra pointed out a girl, saying, "Isn't she cute? She looks French." Jason retorted, "Yeah, cute. Like French toast."

On another occasion, Barbra took Jason to a Sunday matinee performance of the Joffrey Ballet. At intermission, autograph hounds descended to Row G, where Barbra and Jason were sitting. While his mother cowered, Jason stood to his feet and authoritatively declared, "No autographs today! No autographs today!"

On March 31, 1970, Barbra purchased a five-story townhouse at 49 East Eightieth Street at a cost of $420,000. But by the time the deal went through, she was ready to sell it. She wanted a home that was more horizontal than vertical and could not seem to get comfortable in her new surroundings. She would sell it, soon thereafter, at a substantial loss. She returned to her Central Park penthouse and later purchased a large house in the Holmby Hills section of Los Angeles, both of which she owns to this day.

She went to the theater and the movies. Reflecting the cultural rebellion of the country, Hollywood had undergone massive changes since Barbra's arrival there in May 1967, but she had been too busy studying lighting and camera angles and getting in and out of her cumbersome period costumes to pay much attention. Now was her time to catch up: *Easy Rider, Midnight Cowboy,* and *They Shoot Horses, Don't They?*, among others, had revolutionized the industry with a less glamorous, grittier style of picturemaking targeted toward a younger, hipper, more socially conscious audience.

On a Clear Day You Can See Forever was glaringly outdated by comparison, and Barbra knew it. The Vincente Minnelli musical was released in June 1970 to mixed reviews and only modest business. If she had not already undergone an extensive image overhaul in *The Owl and the Pussycat,* Barbra would have had great reason for concern. As evidenced in *On a Clear Day,* she was beginning to resemble an overcoiffed, overcostumed dinosaur on the verge of cinematic extinction.

Ironically, the actor who seemed to best reflect the rapidly changing values and mores of the late sixties and early seventies was Barbra's estranged husband, Elliott Gould. Nominated for a Best Supporting Actor Oscar for *Bob & Carol & Ted & Alice* (1969), Elliott had finally broken through with success of his own. *Time* magazine hailed him as "the urban Don Quioxte." The acclaim was vindication for the years spent in his famous partner's shadow. When later asked when it was that he had attained his manhood, Elliott would be compelled to cite the day he was nominated for his Oscar.

After *Bob & Carol,* in rapid succession came *M*A*S*H, Getting Straight,* and *I Love My Wife.* "I'm the hottest thing in Hollywood right now," Elliott boasted, obviously reveling in his own success. "Four movies in one year—that's not bad, right? I always knew there were things going on in me, that I had something to express." In September 1970, the phenomenal year of Elliott Gould—which, ironically, just so happened to coincide with his separation from Barbra—reached its apex when he was named Star of the Year by the National Association of Theater Owners (NATO).

On December 13, 1970, after first fulfilling a commitment at the Riviera, Barbra returned for a two-week engagement at the International Hotel, which would be renamed the Las Vegas Hilton. It wasn't that she wanted to perform live, she *had* to, given her 1969 contract with the hotel.

"She *hated* being in Vegas," relates Wayne Bernath, entertainment editor for the *Las Vegas Sun*. "She was so uptight about having to perform live that to unwind she would go to a bar called the Atomic Lounge, which was a blue-collar bar built in the fifties. Barbra used to stay at the Hilton when she performed here, but she couldn't walk in the lobby without being mobbed. So she and a few friends would play pool at the Atomic Lounge until the sun came up. Barbra could unwind there and was never bothered by the other patrons. She was quite a pool shark, from what I hear."

Compared to her last, less-than-successful Las Vegas engagement, Barbra's performance was perceptibly more relaxed and, consequently, more effective. The principal reason for the improvement had nothing to do with the addition of an opening act, or even a change in repertoire, but was a soothing high that came from the inhalation of a funny-looking cigarette. In an effort to abate her sheer terror of performing, Barbra had started to smoke marijuana, both off and *on* the stage.

"I'd take out a joint and light it," she later acknowledged. "First, just faking it. Then I started lighting live joints, passing them around to the band, you know? It was *great*. It relieved all of my tensions." She ended up with what she described as "the greatest supply of grass ever." It seems that the other acts on the Vegas Strip started to hear about Barbra's penchant for smoking pot and kept replenishing her quality supply as a token of their admiration.

Actually, the onstage smoking-a-joint bit was just that, a *bit,* a contrivance, a special effect. Granted, it did relieve Barbra's fear. In part, it was also a calculated effort to alter her public image. The campaign included her giving an interview to *Rolling Stone*. "Look, I'm considered this kind of institution thing," Barbra said in what was then, arguably, the hippest of all publications. "But I ask you," she posed, "twenty-eight—is that old? Is twenty-eight all that old?"

Another vital step in the modernization of Barbra was the continued updating and commercialization of her recordings. At the request of Clive Davis, president of Columbia Records, she scrapped *The Singer,* an album she was recording, in favor of a more contemporary project featuring the work of Laura Nyro, Randy Newman, Joni Mitchell, and other new, young songwriters.

In mid-December 1970, Barbra's recording of Nyro's uptempo pop song "Stoney End" entered the *Billboard* top forty. She had recorded it with a great deal of reluctance. It required that she sing on the beat, a practice she loathed. Moreover, she was utterly unconvinced of its appeal. To her great surprise, it would go all the way to number six on the charts, becoming her biggest selling single since "People," a full six years before. The album of the same title would make the *Billboard* top-forty albums chart in late February 1971. It would peak at number ten and would eventually go platinum, a major accomplishment, particularly considering that Barbra's previous album, the soundtrack to *On a Clear Day You Can See Forever,* had peaked at number 108.

The Owl and the Pussycat, Barbra Streisand's first "small" movie, first nonmusical, and first straight comedy, was nationally released on November 20, 1970. The advertisements for the PG-rated picture featured the *new* Barbra, her hair loose and down past her shoulders, wearing Doris's scandalous, semisheer negligee. The accompanying copy added further titillation: *"The Owl and the Pussycat* Is No Longer a Story for Children."* In a further attempt at drawing the younger ticket buyers, the film's soundtrack boasted songs by Blood, Sweat and Tears, one of the most popular rock groups of the day.

The multimedia, multitiered campaign proved a success. Audiences began to reconsider Barbra Streisand. For the first time in her career, and perhaps for the first time in her life, she was perceived as a strikingly attractive, vibrantly sexual, "with-it" *young* woman. Moreover, the picture received mostly favorable reviews and would go on to earn some $11.5 million in North American rentals, making it one of the most successful pictures of the year, behind only *Ryan's Daughter, Summer of '42, Little Big Man,* and, the year's blockbuster, *Love Story.*

Twenty-five

Bringing Up Barbra

$\mathcal{B}$ased on the page-turning, tear-wringing, and oh-so-slight novel by Erich Segal, *Love Story* would go on to become one of the biggest-grossing pictures to that time. It would also catapult its fresh-faced young actors, Ali MacGraw and Ryan O'Neal, into major movie stardom. O'Neal had spent five years as Rodney Harrington, the resident stud in a prime time town called "Peyton Place." Of his tenure on the show, O'Neal would quip with self-deprecating humor, "My principal function in the script was to get everybody pregnant."

His *own* love story was a complicated one. Divorced from actress Joanna Moore, mother of his children, Tatum and Griffin, Ryan married actress Leigh Taylor-Young, who acted with him in "Peyton Place." Known in Hollywood more for his accomplishments in the bedroom than on the soundstage (at least at that point in his career), O'Neal had a pretty face, a good build, and a cocksure bravado that women found irresistible. Among his conquests were Anouk Aimée, Ursula Andress, and Barbara Parkins, the latter another "Peyton Place" costar.

Around the same time that he started dating Barbra Streisand, O'Neal separated from Leigh Taylor-Young, who took their young son, Patrick, and moved to New Mexico. At first, Barbra and Ryan were discreet about the nature of their relationship. In time, they began making public appearances hand in hand. On June 18, 1971, they attended the premiere of Ryan's picture *The Wild Rovers.*

As a couple, they also went to a dinner party hosted by Ingrid and Jerry Orbach for fashion designer Valentino, who was gaining fame as the couturier of choice of Jacqueline Onassis. Barbra attended the function wearing a figure-clinging red pantsuit with a red headband. When asked if it was "a Valentino," she quipped, "No. It's a somebody else." Ryan *was* in Valentino, right down to his belt, which sported a prominent gold *V* on its buckle.

They appeared to have a complementary relationship. He was secure where she was not, and vice versa. Ryan was insecure about his ability as an actor; Barbra was insecure about her looks. Having Hollywood's golden boy of the moment on her arm, and in her bed, gratified her fragile sense of self.

She also liked his enthusiasm for life and envied his sunny, California countenance. She was attracted by his masculinity and the fact that he was an ex-amateur boxer who wasn't shy to use his fists. Ryan was more comfortable in his sexuality than Barbra, and he helped her to loosen up.

Moreover, Ryan had grown up in the movie business and knew it inside and out. He helped Barbra better understand some of its none-too-pretty machinations; to learn to adjust, relax, and not take everything quite so personally.

They were bound, too, by their aspirations. Together, they worked to expand their vocabulary, using the book *It Pays to Increase Your Word Power* as their guide. In bed, behind closed doors, they quizzed one another on the spelling and definition of this word and that.

They were also striving for something more in their careers. Neither was really being taken seriously as actors and each commiserated with the other. They discussed how their images had confined them, and how they were misunderstood. They talked about the serious ideas that were going on in their heads, and about the statements that they wanted to make in their work.

Which is precisely the basis for Barbra's loathing of *What's Up, Doc?* "What is it about?" she would ask rhetorically. "I'll tell you what it's about—*nothing!*"

The origins of the picture belong in the pages of Hollywood folklore. The project actually got its start with Barbra's not-quite-yet-ex-husband, Elliott Gould. With his partner Jack Brodsky, Elliott produced and starred in *Little Murders* for Twentieth Century Fox. As their second effort, they mounted *A Glimpse of Tiger* from an original screenplay by Herman Raucher.

The Warner Brothers picture had begun principal photography in New York on February 26, 1971. During the first week of shooting, Elliott had what was referred to as an emotional breakdown. He reportedly fought with director Anthony Harvey, and came close to striking his female costar, Kim Darby. Executives from Warners shut down the production. The film, or rather the nonfilm, signaled Elliott Gould's rapid fall from grace. He *would* go on to make other pictures, but his reputation in Hollywood was, for ten years, tarnished, if not destroyed.

The project then reverted back to Warners, which announced its plans to convert the story into a picture for Barbra. John Calley, Warner Brothers' production chief, asked Peter Bogdanovich, a promising young director who had just completed a film called *The Last Picture Show*, to take over the production. Barbra had seen a screening of the film, which would go on to garner great acclaim, and was much impressed.

Upon reading *Tiger*, however, Bogdanovich backed out. "I read the script and I didn't want to do it," he said, "but I told him [Calley] I'd love to do a picture with Barbra." Bogdanovich was a big fan of the screwball comedies of the thirties, and in Barbra he saw the perfect heroine to revive the genre. "That's the way I saw Barbra," he added, "sort of a Carole Lombard."

Barbra, however, perceived herself as a dramatic actress of great depth. She had little interest in what she viewed to be cardboard comedy. But she liked the idea of working with Bogdanovich. The advance word on *Picture Show* was that it would launch the director as the industry's new boy genius. More than that, she wanted to work, and be, with Ryan. *A Glimpse of Tiger* was to have costarred the two of them, and Barbra was still determined that they do something together.

Bogdanovich, however, *didn't* want Ryan. With Barbra's pleading, and at the urging of agent Sue Mengers, who represented all three of them, he screened *Love Story*, met with O'Neal, and eventually consented to casting him.

Surprisingly, Barbra signed her contract *without* script approval. Perhaps she was so enamored with O'Neal that she forgot to take notice. Or perhaps she put too much trust in Mengers, who negotiated the deal. Or perhaps she was just blinded by the fact that the contract provided her with a fat 10 percent interest in the picture. It also gave her various bonuses, including having her house painted inside and out, having her pick of any of the furniture used in the film, and allowing her to put complimentary gas in her car on the studio lot.

In one of its first official acts, the fledgling production team met at Barbra's Holmby Hills home to watch the Howard Hawks 1938 classic, *Bringing Up Baby*, which provided *What's Up, Doc?* with its inspiration. Between bites of popcorn, personally popped by Barbra, the room was filled with laughter. That is, except from Barbra and Ryan, who sat nervously on the couch, uncertain that they could ever fill the comedic shoes of Katharine Hepburn and Cary Grant.

Bogdanovich hired David Newman and Robert Benton, who had created the brilliant script for *Bonnie and Clyde* (1967), to write the original screenplay. Their first draft was rushed out in two weeks. Bogdanovich, displeased, ordered another. Dissatisfied with their second output, Bogdanovich began looking for another writer. John Calley suggested Buck Henry, who had successfully worked with Barbra on *The Owl and the Pussycat.*

Meanwhile, as another quickie draft was scripted by Henry in Hollywood, a quickie divorce was underway in the Dominican Republic. Barbra and Elliott had finally filed for divorce in a joint petition in Santo Domingo on June 30, 1971. Barbra, preparing for the picture, would not be present in court. Elliott was accompanied by Jenny Bogart, his pregnant teenage companion. Leaving the courtroom, they announced their intention to continue living together out of wedlock because, as they sang out in unison, "We don't believe in marriage!"

Elliott was living the so-called hippie lifestyle in the Greenwich Village apartment he shared with Jenny. His hair was long, he sported a beard, and he was generally unkempt. Stepping into the apartment, visitors were greeted with the pungent aroma of marijuana, which Elliott smoked openly, without apology. A poster on one of his walls proclaimed, "Fuck You." Another one, "Hey, Wanna Suck?"

Of his wife-*not*-to-be, Elliott would say, in apparent reference to Barbra, "She's not ambitious. She's very interested in primitive, organic, simple things, which is something that I never really knew about. It's been a terrific revelation to me to see that she's not very material." He added, "Nothing material is truly significant." As for his now ex-wife, Elliott's feelings were ambivalent. "I am Barbra's friend," he said, "but she can't be my friend. She doesn't understand me." He added, "She's got her own problems."

Molly Gould would be born in November 1971. Elliott and Jenny would break up the following year and then reconcile. Their son, Sam, would be born on January 9, 1973. And despite their lack of faith in the institution, they would get married in Las Vegas in December 1973.

What's Up, Doc? started shooting in San Francisco on August 16, 1971. While on location, Barbra and Ryan stayed together in a suite at the Huntington Hotel on Nob Hill. They were accompanied by Jason. One day, Jason's nanny answered the telephone. On the other end of the line was a professed "admirer" of Barbra's who informed the nanny that he would kidnap Jason unless he was able to express his "deep love" for Barbra, *personally.*

Barbra was terrified for both her son and herself. Ryan stepped in and took charge. He called the hotel security, and assured Barbra that everything would be all right. He was there to be her protector, which further served to bond their relationship. Barbra confided in Ryan about her fear of going out in public.

Actress Sharon Tate's brutal murder by the Charles Manson gang in 1969 had riveted and terrified Hollywood. It would also leave behind lasting repercussions. Ryan O'Neal had been closer to the murder than most, having been friends with Tate's husband, director Roman Polanski, whose child Tate was carrying when slain. Barbra talked to Ryan about her own fear of being murdered, of her becoming another Sharon Tate.

Back on the set, Ryan had a difficult time with the part of Howard Bannister. "I'd never done a comedy before," he said. "Every day was hard. I would go in with butterflies in my stomach. I haven't had that trouble since I started thirteen years ago."

This time, it was Barbra's turn to reassure Ryan. "I was lucky," Ryan acknowledged, "because I have known her a long time, several years, and she is a relaxed friend of mine, a very good friend. And so we went to work almost as a team."

Ryan was further helped by Peter Bogdanovich. A former actor who studied under Stella Adler, he virtually acted out the part, scene by scene, line by line, and Ryan would just have to impersonate him. O'Neal said of his director, "He asked me to do things that were against my instincts as an actor and as a human being and I did them."

Barbra, however, put up a fight. "She doesn't work from a confidence base," Ryan attempted to explain in her defense. "She likes to go into a project thinking it's the worst and then she builds from there." He added, "She thinks very negatively about certain things."

Bogdanovich's directorial style of acting out every part, modeled somewhat on the style of Ernst Lubitsch, infuriated Barbra. At one point, after Bogdanovich demonstrated how he wanted her to read a line, Barbra, appalled, snapped, "Are *you* giving *me* line readings?"

Throughout the filming, Barbra would tell her costar, "Ryan, we're in a piece of shit! I mean, we're *really* in trouble. *I* know what's funny, and *this* isn't funny!"

Typically, when preparing to do a scene, Barbra would ask her director what he wanted her to do. He would tell her or show her, and she would say, "Do you think that's *funny?*"

Unlike Herb Ross, Bogdanovich had little patience with Barbra. He was commanding, almost dictatorial. At one point on the set, he was compelled to put Barbra in her place and ordered, "Sing something!" And she *did.*

"She has a tendency," Bogdanovich later said, "to be insecure about everything except singing. She has this feeling [that] to be a serious actor you really have to *act.*"

While Bogdanovich prepared to shoot the rooftop scene in which Barbra was to sing "As Time Goes By" to Ryan, she was on the phone yelling at Sue Mengers for getting her into the picture. Because cinematographer Laszlo Kovacs wanted to work out the scene's camera angles, Bogdanovich acted as Barbra's stand-in. He climbed up on the piano and proceeded to sing, "You must remember this . . ." to a befuddled Ryan. At the end of the number, presumably as a joke, Bogdanovich leaned over and kissed Ryan, who fell off the piano stool. The crew broke into laughter. Little did Bogdanovich know that Kovacs had shot the entire rehearsal. It would later be used in the film's trailer.

The other song Barbra sang for the picture was the old Cole Porter standard, "You're the Top." It was arranged for the film by Artie Butler, who had known Barbra years before at Erasmus Hall High School.

"She won't admit it," Butler recalls, "but I even went out with Barbra once. She told me it never happened, but I'm sure she just doesn't remember. If my memory serves, we went to a cafeteria called Garfield's and we went to a movie. It was a date. We talked about everything from music to zits.

"There are a lot of people that bad-mouth her," Butler continues. "I guess because she's had temper tantrums. But I've never, ever seen it. When we did 'You're the Top,' I remember her calling me up one night and saying, 'I really *love* that arrangement.' And we talked about the vocals. The song, as finished, was not *one* vocal performance. It was pieced together from a bunch of different tracks.

"It was real tough to do. Barbra is the one that made the choices. She called me up and said, '[We're gonna use] "You're the Top," Track 6; "You're Mahatma Gandhi," Track 7; "Nile," Track 10; or whatever. *She* broke it down. She knew what she was talking about 101 percent."

Butler adds, "I don't think that anybody has a right to get angry when she gets that picky, because you've got to realize who you're dealing with. I got in this business to work with great artists. There are a lot of famous people, but there are very few *great* artists. She's a great artist. There's a big difference."

The picture would present Barbra in yet another altered appearance. Her skin was tanned; her hair, long and straight, and colored with golden highlights. Ryan's influence, and that of his Malibu beach home, were evident.

"She was probably in her best physical form I had ever seen in terms of weight and tone," recalls Don Cash, Jr., her makeup man on five pictures. "When you get into period films, everything is hidden by clothes. In *What's Up, Doc?* she had a cute, sexy little look. She was extremely foxy. I kidded her about it [her figure] once or twice, and she just said, 'Oh, *come on,* Don!' And I said, 'Well, it's just *there,* that's all.' "

She also adopted an extremely natural look for the picture. "We used a very thin base and just a little bit of eye makeup and mascara," Cash says. "Also, very light rouge and very natural lipsticks. That's all that was necessary."

Bogdanovich concurred, "We did it with no makeup, almost none. She thought one of her sides was better than the other, which is not true. I shot her from any angle I wanted, and people say she's gorgeous."

Madeline Kahn, who would make her first real impression with critics and audiences in the picture as Barbra's rival for Ryan's attention, had been reticent about accepting the assignment. "I knew about Streisand cutting Anne Francis out of *Funny Girl,*" Kahn later said, "and I didn't want to do the film." To Kahn's surprise, she ended up liking Barbra, although the two never became close. "I got a glimpse of what it's like to be a really big superstar. I don't think I'd like that."

Meanwhile, the production put a strain on Barbra's relationship with Ryan. To Barbra's distress, Ryan frequently sided with Bogdanovich in her spirited discussions with the director. Actually, Ryan got along so well with Bogdanovich that he would also be in his next picture, *Paper Moon.* Costarring would be Ryan's nine-year-old daughter, Tatum, who would win an Oscar for her performance.

Barbra was certainly none too pleased when Peggy Lipton visited Ryan during a break from her television series, "Mod Squad." To get even, Barbra went out with director Milos Forman, who would, a few years later, receive great acclaim and an Oscar for *One Flew Over the Cuckoo's Nest.* There was also some speculation that she engaged in a brief affair with Bogdanovich. Ryan countered by taking out his former flame, Barbara Parkins.

At one point during the shooting, Ryan suffered a back injury and had to undergo major surgery. But it would not be Barbra who nursed him back to health, nor would it be Barbara Parkins or Peggy Lipton. It was his wife, Leigh Taylor-Young, who had flown back from New Mexico to be at his bedside. The two reconciled, and it would be Leigh, and not Barbra, who accompanied Ryan to the preview of *Doc.* Barbra and Ryan would remain friendly over the years, but the sexual component of their relationship had come to an end.

Bogdanovich was having some difficulty with the very end of the picture. Preview audiences, it seems, were not hearing Ryan's last line because they were laughing too loudly at Barbra's. The scene called for Barbra to bat her eyelashes in rapid succession. It was film critic Judith Crist who made the suggestion to Bogdanovich. "Can't you take out one of Barbra's blinks?" she asked. Bogdanovich, amused, repeated the suggestion to his editor, Verna Fields, adding, "Imagine what Barbra would say to that."

Meanwhile, Barbra continued to be displeased with the picture's development. "She thought that *What's Up, Doc?* was about the worst thing she ever had to do," Bogdanovich acknowledged, adding, "She complained about everything. I just kept laughing, which *threw* her. She'd say, 'This is *terrible,* goddamnit!' "

Barbra's discontent would continue after the picture's release. "I hated it with a passion," she said. "I was embarrassed to do that film. I thought it was infantile humor and not one-sixteenth of the film that it was trying to emulate [*Bringing Up Baby*]. I only agreed to work with Bogdanovich because I had liked *The Last Picture Show* so much. But it was a disappointing experience."

With no faith in its appeal, Barbra sold her 10 percent share of the picture back to the studio, telling its chief, John Calley, "I'll bet ten grand it doesn't [even] gross $5 million." Calley declined the bet because he knew Barbra wouldn't pay him either way. Upon its release, *What's Up, Doc?* would receive mostly positive reviews and gross some *$35 million* at the box office.

As Barbra viewed it, with the inanity of *What's Up, Doc?* behind her, she was free to go on to a new project that meant something to her. But which one would it be? One possibility was a screenplay by W. D. Richter entitled *Bent Jane*. The proposed picture would be directed by Lee Katzin, whose experience was primarily in television, and would have had Barbra, against type, play the part of a woman with a compulsion to kill.

But she was more seriously considering two other projects. One would have fulfilled her long-held passion to portray Sarah Bernhardt, the legendary French stage actress and silent-screen star whose 1915 leg amputation did not preclude her continuing her career. Garbo, in her first starring role, had portrayed Bernhardt in the 1927 silent *The Divine Woman*. In 1969, Barbra was given the opportunity to star on Broadway in *The Divine Sarah*. Booked with film projects, and not terribly anxious to return to the nightly demands of the stage, she declined.

In 1971, however, Barbra began negotiations with British filmmaker Ken Russell to do a film biography of the actress. Russell was much sought after in Hollywood after the unexpected success of *Women in Love*, which won an Oscar for Glenda Jackson. He was eager to do the picture. Barbra had been drawn to Russell not only by *Women in Love* but also by *Deleus,* a documentary he had made for the BBC.

Barbra and Russell came to an agreement to do the picture, and actually concluded the deal. The picture would be coproduced by Russell's company and by Barbra's First Artists. Russell would direct from his own screenplay. Shooting would start in the spring of 1972, with locations in Paris and England. Then, suddenly, after months of negotiations, everything fell apart. Barbra sought changes in Russell's eventual script, and he refused to compromise and do as she wanted. A film biography of Sarah Bernhardt *would* be made, but it would be without the participation of Barbra Streisand *or* Ken Russell. *The Incredible Sarah,* directed by Richard Fleischer and starring Glenda Jackson, was released in 1976.

Another project Barbra considered, and in fact was set to do, was a remake of *The Merry Widow*. The picture had previously been directed by Erich Von Stroheim in 1925 with Mae Murray, by Ernst Lubitsch in 1934 with Jeanette MacDonald, and by Curt Bernhardt in 1952 with Lana Turner. Barbra wanted Ingmar Bergman to direct her version.

She would have numerous phone conversations with the legendary Swedish filmmaker, and the project was scheduled to shoot sometime in 1972. However, Barbra was displeased with the second half of the script, written by Bergman, and she asked for a rewrite. The director, used to unquestioned autonomy on his pictures, refused. Barbra, unwilling to compromise on her instincts, backed out, and the picture was never made.

And so her interests turned to yet another project. For the past couple of years, Hollywood had been trying to find a way of filming the frustrations of the everyday housewife, torn between her love of family and her dreams of a life outside of the kitchen. The most prominent picture of this new subgenre was *Diary of a Mad Housewife* (1970), which was directed by Frank Perry and starred newcomer Carrie Snodgress, who won an Oscar nomination for her performance. It was a film, ironically, that Barbra had been offered and turned down.

After the success of *Mad Housewife*, producers Robert Chartoff and Irwin Winkler outbid producer-director Robert Altman for the film rights to Anne Richardson Roiphe's novel, *Up the Sandbox*. Barbra became interested in the project because she related to the character of Margaret Reynolds, the Waspy oppressed wife of a Columbia University professor and the mother of two children, who fantasizes her way out of her oppressed, mundane upper-middle-class existence. In her fantasies, Margaret ventures to Africa, blows up the Statue of Liberty, challenges Fidel Castro to a debate, and confronts her own mother.

Barbra knew all about fantasies. She had, after all, fantasized her way out of a dreary and abusive Brooklyn childhood.

She also knew about sexism and the resistance that occurred when women balked at playing their predetermined roles, that is, when they refused to fit into society's rigid definition of good, compliant wife and apron-stringed mother. "In making a movie, where all the power is in the hands of men, there's a vicious ego game being played," Barbra contended. As an example, she declared, "When a woman stops to powder her nose, there's impatience—the waiting-for-the-woman-eye-rolling bit. When a male actor stops to comb his hair, that's okay. I feel the sexism all the time.

"I had ideas, and I expressed them," she continued. "But because I was a woman, I was disregarded. There is this prejudice against actresses. They're supposed to look pretty and read their lines, then shut up and go home."

And yet she also strongly believed that women should *not* look for a life outside of the home unless they were so inclined. To the surprise of some, she also seemed ambivalent about the women's liberation movement of the early seventies. She was repelled by the whole idea of bra burning, and she drove diehard feminists to distraction with her public views on the subject. One of Barbra's often-repeated quotes of the period paraphrased Voltaire: "When we demand equality," she warned, "we give up our superiority."

Taken out of context, the quote was disturbing. Barbra's views on the subject were more complex, and actually signaled the direction the movement would eventually take. "Equal job opportunities . . . yes,"

Barbra proclaimed in 1972. "The fight against traditional role playing
... yes. Abortion ... yes. Women should hold the right to say whether or
not they want babies. But there should also be a time for mothering.
Many women today are in conflict with their role in society. They feel
they should be allowed to do more, yet they still have that primal urge of
mothering. Most of all, a woman should be allowed to do what she wants
to do."

For Barbra, reaching thirty became a turning point, which just so happened to coincide with the burgeoning women's movement. "All of a
sudden it was very clear to me that I wasn't a kid anymore," she said,
"that the excuses I'd given myself for not growing up just didn't work. I
felt I no longer had an alternative. I mean, when you're thirty, you're
thirty. And you've got to start being responsible. It's too late to be just a
little girl anymore."

She realized she had spent her young adulthood on, or in pursuit of,
the job. She had allowed her work to become an obsession at the expense of her life. "It was a wonderful way of avoiding myself," she acknowledged. "You work all day and then come home and fall asleep
from sheer exhaustion. No time for thinking, no time to talk. That's that.
But sooner or later your demons come back and haunt you and I found
that very frightening."

The making of *Up the Sandbox* represented Barbra's way of confronting herself and taking responsibility for her life. It reflected her power as
a woman and as an artist. And it meant sticking her neck out, at the risk
of a none-too-pretty public beheading. And yet, it was something that
she *had* to do. When asked for a reason why she was doing the picture,
she answered, simply, "Because I am a woman. Because I wanted to do
something. *What's Up, Doc?* was about nothing. I wanted to do something about something."

Up the Sandbox was to be Barbra's first of three pictures for First Artists. It was also the first film on which she had *official* power. In her newfound position, Barbra's first acts of business were to hire her manager,
Marty Erlichman, as her associate producer, and her friend Cis Corman
as her casting director. For Corman, the assignment would launch a
whole new career. And she would prove to be good at her job, as evidenced by the roster of talent she lined up for *Sandbox*. Among her discoveries who would go on to bigger successes were Paul Benedict ("The
Jeffersons"), Isabel Sanford ("The Jeffersons"), Conrad Bain
("Maude"), Paul Dooley (a character actor in several Robert Altman pictures), Anne Ramsey (the title character in *Throw Momma From the*

Train), and Stockard Channing (*The Fortune,* et al.).

Principal photography started in Los Angeles in March 1972. Consistent with her new, more adult approach to life, Barbra decided to make amends with her staunchest (other than herself) foe: the press. Columnist Dorothy Manners was being given an award by the Publicists Guild, and Barbra agreed to participate in the proceedings. So, during a lunch break from *Sandbox,* she rushed over to the ceremony, presented the award to Manners, and promptly returned to the set. Despite her good intentions, subsequent press reports chastised Barbra for the hastiness of her departure. Barbra, sighing with exasperation, concluded, "With me and the press, it's a case of I'm damned if I do, and damned if I don't."

She faced yet another foe. On June 5, 1972, screenwriter Robert Kaufman and Bobka Productions filed a $100,000 breach-of-contract lawsuit against Barbra. It seems that she had liked one of Kaufman's original story ideas, entitled "Breaking Up," and had commissioned him to develop it into a screenplay. Upon its completion, Barbra had, according to court documents, refused to financially compensate Kaufman for his services. The case was eventually settled out of court, with Barbra, presumably, paying Kaufman some renegotiated, mutually agreeable, fee.

In May, the *Sandbox* company moved to New York, but not before shooting a fantasy sequence at the Biltmore Hotel in Los Angeles in which Margaret confronts Fidel Castro. Gotham locations included Harlem, the Hudson River, and a little playground off of Riverside and 123rd Street. It was at the latter location that Jason Gould, at age five and a half, made his film debut. He is seen in the film pushing, and then riding, a swing, his curly hair blowing in the wind.

An occasional visitor to the set in New York was Congresswoman Bella Abzug, a friend of Barbra's, who campaigned to further the film's call for the equality of women.

Filming in New York was completed on Friday, May 19, 1972. From there, the company was transported all the way to Nairobi to shoot another fantasy sequence. To their surprise, producers Chartoff and Winkler discovered that it was actually cheaper to shoot in Africa ($8,000 per day) than in Los Angeles ($13,000 per day) or New York ($19,000 per day). While there, Barbra picked up a few makeup tips. As she later related, "I asked a native girl to put some of her blue eye makeup on me. She broke a twig from a tree, took a long thread from her husband's skirt, made like a Q-Tip, broke off a piece of soft, blue rock, spit on it, and put that on my eye with the Q-Tip. Now I put all my eye shadow on with a Q-Tip."

Barbra used her power on the picture to help mold some of the characterizations, notably the figure of the meddlesome mother. For Barbra, she was, in many ways, akin to her own mother. Diana Kind had been outraged when she learned that Barbra was going to Africa ("Of all places!"), and worse, that she was taking Jason with her. For Barbra, it was another no-win situation. When she *didn't* take Jason with her on her trips, Diana complained that she was a negligent mother, more concerned with her career than her child.

For years, Barbra attempted to block out her mother's unsolicited counsel on child-rearing, but she was not always successful. Certainly, Barbra's views on the subject were in direct opposition to those of her mother. When asked about her philosophy on raising children, Diana responded with a gleam in her eyes, "Spanking. It saves the psychiatrist's fees. There's a Jewish saying that whenever a child gets spanked, it finally finds it way to the head so the head clears." Prompting shivers from her daughter, she added, "And never give your kid too much praise. In fact, I try to tone them down if I see they have an exaggerated opinion of themselves."

A child of many interests, Jason Emanuel was captivated by archaeology. Before departing on his adventure, he had been briefed on the Leakeys' discoveries in Africa and was thrilled with the prospect of going out on a dig. Using a little maternal psychology of her own, the ever-prepared Barbra packed some chicken bones and planted them into the ground so that her son would be certain to have something to discover. She didn't want Jason to leave Africa disappointed.

It was around this period that Jason started showing flashes of rebellion. He even insisted upon changing his name. "My name is Jason Streisand, my name is Jason Streisand!" he was fond of chanting. Barbra invariably corrected him. "Gould, darling, your name is Jason *Gould.*" Jason, in a compromise, retorted, "My name is Jason Gould *Streisand!*"

After leaving Nairobi at the end of June 1972, Barbra and Jason went to Tel Aviv, Israel, where they were the guests of the Israeli Tourist Office. The day after her arrival, Barbra was the guest of Deputy Prime Minister Ygal Alon. She was escorted all over the country for the duration of her six-day stay. To acknowledge the hospitality of the Israeli people, Barbra made vague promises that she would return to the country later in the year and give two concerts. However, little did anyone know at the time, Barbra had given, as of this writing, the final commercial live performances of her career earlier that year (December 24, 1971, to January 13, 1972) at the Las Vegas Hilton. For Barbra, performing live had not only become something to fear, it had also become "vulgar" and "exhibitionistic."

Back in Los Angeles, postproduction work on *Sandbox* proved arduous. In October, a roll of the film's negative was lost, and a week-long search failed to turn it up. Still, no reshooting was done, because it was deemed that enough material existed in the outtakes to compensate for the loss.

Barbra would return home to her Holmby Hills house every night at around two-thirty A.M. and telephone the director, Irvin Kershner, or the editor, Robert Lawrence, with some additional bit of business she had thought up. Sometimes, it was composer Billy Goldenberg who was the recipient of her late night, early morning calls. Her words of good night, "Hum me the music for tomorrow."

Barbra had great hopes for the picture. In addition to the social and political statements she hoped it would make, she also hoped that it would finally prove her ability as an actress. Said Marty Erlichman, days before the picture's December 21, 1972, release, "When a nice Jewish girl from Brooklyn can play a WASP who fantasizes, you know you've got an actress. Did you know that we did not get one card at any of the previews that objected to casting Barbra as a WASP?"

The eventual critical and box office failure of *Up the Sandbox* came as a devastating blow. Shortly after its release, Barbra took a friend to see the picture at a theater in Westwood. There were four other people in the audience.

For Barbra Streisand, it was a humbling experience, and a hard lesson to learn. Her name and star power were *not* enough. Nor were good intentions, which, as she learned, sometimes came at a price. She also learned that having something to say did not necessarily mean that anyone would want to listen. Over the duration of the decade, Barbra's film projects would be far more commercially motivated than *Up the Sandbox,* and there would be far less talk of her playing Bernhardt or working with Bergman.

She was at a fork in the road, and she decided to go, head first, straight down the middle.

Twenty-six

Intersecting Icons

$\mathscr{W}$ith the success of *The Owl and the Pussycat,* Ray Stark was eager to lure Barbra back to the fold of Rastar, his production company. He sent her a fifty-page treatment for *The Way We Were* by Arthur Laurents, her director ten years before on *I Can Get It for You Wholesale.* She read it, counted the number of potentially good scenes there would be for her to play—there were five—and agreed to do it almost instantly. She told Stark over the phone, "I want *this* to be my next movie."

From an original screenplay by Laurents (which he later adapted into a book), *The Way We Were* spanned in time from the 1930s through and beyond the McCarthy hearings of the 1950s. It tells the story of Katie Morosky, an intense, leftist activist whose politics and passion alienate her from most everyone around her, including, ultimately, the man she loves.

With Barbra signed, Sydney Pollack, who had won acclaim directing Jane Fonda in *They Shoot Horses, Don't They?* (1969), was hired in April 1972. Attention then turned to casting the male lead. If ever a picture consisted of its casting, this was it. The setting involved politics, but this was a love story driven by one central idea: Katie Morosky and Hubbell Gardiner are two polar opposites, powerless in their attraction for one another. In this more than any picture Barbra has made, the chemistry with her leading man would be key.

As written, Hubbell was the quintessential WASP—blond, blue-eyed, fair complected, and golden when tanned. The kind of guy for whom everything, including women, came easily. Dennis Cole met with Barbra only to be rejected. So too was Ken Howard, who auditioned not on a soundstage but on the tennis court.

331

At the prompting of her friends Alan and Marilyn Bergman, Barbra had added tennis to her extracurricular activities. The idea of Barbra Streisand on a tennis court seems incongruous with her persona. Indeed, she would play with flailing arms, poor coordination, and an utter lack of athleticism. Still, that did not prevent her from plunging into the sport with racket-swinging abandon, joining Marilyn Bergman at La Costa to play doubles with Pancho Segura and Jimmy Connors, no less.

Ryan O'Neal was another possible Hubbell Gardiner. Pollack, however, held the opinion that Barbra had walked all over O'Neal in *What's Up, Doc?* "She has a tendency to take over a picture, just by the size of her talent and larger-than-life presence," the director declared. "It's hard for a costar to stay in the same ring with her." Not only did Pollack seek an actor who could hold his own with Barbra, he hoped to get a male star who could bring more depth to the essentially one-dimensional character of Hubbell Gardiner.

He wanted Robert Redford. Months before, Stark had sent the treatment to Redford, who dismissed it as "a piece of junk." Nevertheless, Pollack began what would become a six-month campaign to get him. The two were friends, having appeared together as actors in the 1961 picture *War Hunt,* Redford's film debut. Pollack had also directed Redford in *This Property Is Condemned* (1966) and in the recently completed *Jeremiah Johnson.*

Among other things, Redford objected to Hubbell's vapidity. He was a sex object, a man without conviction or purpose, all the failings Redford despised. Pollack tried to convince him that Hubbell was actually the more interesting of the two characters. A tough argument, but Pollack persisted. The director maintained that Hubbell's struggles were internalized, but still compelling, still valid; Katie's, on the other hand, were obvious and predictable.

Redford vacillated. He would play the part, then he would not. On June 6, 1972, the *Hollywood Reporter* announced that Redford had officially joined the cast. The following day, a retraction was printed saying that the part had yet to be cast, and that Redford would definitely *not* do the picture. Then, on Thursday, June 8, Ray Stark, ready to sign Ryan O'Neal, gave Pollack one hour to either get—or forget—Redford. The deal for Redford to costar in the movie was closed that night at eleven-thirty. In its June 12 edition the following Monday, the *Hollywood Reporter* printed a retraction of the retraction.

Redford still detested the script and the character he was to play. He consented, really, to appease Pollack, who was insistent that he play it. If

Redford had refused, Pollack intended to back out of his own commitment to direct. He felt *that* strongly about Redford's rightness for the role. Also prompting Redford's decision was the faith he had that Pollack would deliver on his promise to revise the script and give Hubbell something substantive to do. Another determining factor was the offer to Redford of a substantial fee (it would be the only time in her career that Barbra's salary was exceeded by her costar's) *and* a profit percentage in the picture.

Arthur Laurents had intended the story to be Katie's and resented that Redford, in his view, was exerting his star power and his friendship with Pollack to slant it more in Hubbell's favor. Laurents refused to compromise and was taken off the project. He would later be brought back, reportedly at Barbra's request. In the interim, *twelve* writers were brought in to do rewrites, including Dalton Trumbo, Francis Coppola, Judith Rascoe, David Rayfiel (whom Barbra dated after her split from Elliott), and Alvin Sargent.

What resulted, among other things, was the addition of the Union Station scene in which Hubbell has the opporturnity to express anger and at least demonstrate some point of view.

Pollack also wanted to begin the picture with Hubbell on the witness stand, testifying before the House Un-American Activities Committee. It was to be the dark side of the fair-haired boy, Prince Charming turned informer. Katie was to be in the hearing room, listening to him as he surrenders to the pressure of the committee. As she listens to him inform on his friends, her memories of Hubbell are triggered: the way he was, the way they had been together. The rest of the picture would then become a series of flashbacks.

Pollack argued that this dramatic structure put the characters in the center of the controversy; that it made the politics of the picture integral to the characters, rather than just having Katie and Hubbell stand on the sidelines, observers to the travesty. It also gave Katie more credibility. Triggering her memories would be Hubbell's politics and his morality, rather than his blond hair and impressive bone structure.

It was a brilliant idea, but Stark rejected it. He did not mind depth, but not at the expense of turning audiences against Hubbell. This was *not* a political story, nor a morality tale. It was the simple, age-old drama: girl loses goy, girl gets goy, girl loses goy.

And so the picture opens with Barbra spotting a practically shimmering Redford sitting at the bar of the El Morocco in naval dress uniform. He is a conquering hero instead of an informant and a heel. He is also asleep; Sleeping Beauty, Hollywood-style. Katie is attractive in a well-put-together kind of way. It is the kind of attractiveness that has been worked at. Seeing Hubbell, she practically drools all over her bright red period lipstick. Her lips part with desire. Her breathing becomes labored. Her *lust* is palpable, the longing of women and gay men everywhere. The audience is drawn in.

The picture then goes into flashback, and Katie, a far cry from the well-turned-out woman of the previous scene, is shown working as a frizzy-headed waitress to pay her way through college. She is forced to serve the richer, prettier girls on campus who snicker at her poverty, as well as her unfortunate coiffure, behind her back. Barbra could relate to Katie's resentment of these girls. They were, after all, the "cashmeres" of Erasmus Hall High School, who moved to Forest Hills. And sitting with those very girls in the coffee shop in which Katie worked was Hubbell. She holds up her head, and sticks out her chin, as she walks to the table to take their order. Even before the end of the opening credits, she has been established as the lovable underdog, and the audience is hooked.

Later, when she slips out of her clothes and joins a naked, drunk, and sleeping Hubbell in *her* bed, she is thrilled just to be beside him. He cuddles up next to her and she practically has an orgasm. Later, when she cries because he doesn't know who she is, our hearts break for her. Never has such unadulterated, seemingly unrequited desire been so effectively portrayed on the screen.

After the two fall in love, and then break up, she says to him, "It's because I'm not attractive enough, isn't it? I know I'm attractive—sort of. But I'm not attractive in the right way, am I?" The scene is all the more effective because of what we know about Streisand. The lines are hers as much as they are Katie's.

When deciding whether to do the picture, Redford had been reluctant to meet with Barbra. She wanted the two of them to get together, to talk. To see if there was any chemistry between them. He put it off, once, and then again. His reluctance to see her is curious. Undoubtedly, he had heard the stories: She was demanding. She was a perfectionist. She was apt to provide her director with unsolicited suggestions. He undoubtedly had also heard of her feud with Matthau and her romance with Sharif.

Barbra began to take personally Redford's refusal to meet with her. Finally, Sydney Pollack interceded and insisted that Redford talk to his costar-to-be. Redford agreed, but only if Pollack accompanied him. The two went to Barbra's house for dinner. At that first meeting, Barbra was mesmerized by Redford's beauty.

With a budget of $5 million, filming began on location in Schenectady, New York, in late September 1972. Union College, one of the oldest in the country, substituted for Cornell University circa 1937 in the picture. Humorously, the film company had an unexpected problem recruiting male extras to "play" students. Given the style of the times, most of the guys were sporting long hair. To entice them into getting haircuts, Columbia representatives offered them fifteen dollars a day plus lunch, and even then, the response was underwhelming.

A young actor, James Woods, had been cast in his film debut as Katie's nerdy political sidekick. On the first day of shooting, Barbra turned to Woods and asked him if he was afraid of her. "Fuck, no," Woods retorted. Barbra was taken aback by the young actor's audacity. He continued. "Honey, when [the director] says action, it is just you and me and the camera. No star, no billing, no credit, no nothing!" Barbra paused. Observers on the set waited for her to blow up. Instead, she turned to director Pollack and pronounced, "I like this guy—he stays in the movie."

Both Barbra and Redford began the shooting with trepidation. Despite the changes that had been made to accommodate him, Redford was still displeased with his character. "What does he *want?*" Redford frequently asked in reference to Hubbell Gardiner. The seemingly unavoidable answer was that he wanted nothing. Which, of course, was the point. As for Barbra, like Laurents, she was concerned that the script was being slanted too far in Redford's direction.

Recalls Don Cash, Jr., Barbra's makeup artist, "The first day on location in Schenectady, I had mentioned to Kaye Pownall [Barbra's longtime hairdresser] how much I loved the script. And she said, 'Well, Don, don't say too much, because from what I pick up, neither one of them likes it that much.' And I said, 'You've got to be kidding. I'm not sure about Redford, but, knowing Barbra like I think I do, this is the *perfect* part for her. If she plays it right, she'll win an Oscar.'"

Pownall shared the story with Barbra. Later that day, while shooting at Union College, Barbra turned to Cash and said, matter-of-factly, "Hey, Don. I understand that I'm gonna get an Oscar."

The truth is, neither Streisand nor Redford knew what they had in *The Way We Were.* Cash says, "You kind of picked up that neither one of them liked it, and that they were both just going through with it." Actually, no one involved in the production could have guessed at its eventual enormous commercial success and enduring popularity.

As was typical of her, Barbra kept mostly to herself during the production. "Barbra finds it very, very difficult to socialize," said Bradford Dillman, the film's second male lead. "She'd see me come on the set and she'd turn this way and that and hem and haw and finally she'd get up the nerve to come over and say, 'Uh . . . how are the children?' She found it hard to share even that common bond of interest." He adds, "You know, she worked so hard, I really wondered if she enjoyed anything. I think I saw her laugh twice during the months we were together."

"With Barbra," relates Cash, "there is always a distance. You have to expect that." But that distance does not preclude acts of kindness. On the day that Barbra shot the scene in which Redford, drunk, shares her bed, Cash's second son was born. A week later, a gift was delivered to his house. It was an expensive baby outfit from a Beverly Hills boutique. Upon opening the accompanying card, Cash was surprised to find that the gift had come from Barbra.

Despite the usual creative differences, Barbra would get along well with Pollack. Unlike some of her other directors, who were more concerned about camera placement than character, Pollack, an actor himself, was greatly interested in his two protagonists. In a way, he fell in love with them. "I think of these two characters as components of a single person," he said. "What I feel is that if Katie had a little more of Hubbell, she'd be better, and if he had a little more of her, he'd be better. They're invaluable to each other."

While there were no fights between Redford and Streisand, each struggled over which character would dominate the story. Barbra fought with Pollack; Pollack fought with Redford. But they were friendly fights, never personal, always about the work.

"It's hard to talk about Sydney Pollack, because you don't know where he's coming from," Don Cash, Jr., says. "You always felt there was something behind everything he did, like a master politician. He would listen to Barbra, where she was coming from, and he would listen to Bob, and where he was coming from. It was a delicate balancing act."

Pollack was certainly nurturing with Barbra. He didn't want her ranting and cavorting all over the place, as she had done in some of her other pictures. He worked to tone her down. Redford helped in this regard too. Through his own acting, he taught Barbra the art of subtlety.

During the shooting, Barbra continued to carry the torch for her co-star. It can be argued that her on-screen lusting for Redford was so nakedly transparent because it required virtually no acting on her part. Redford, however, was a happily married family man with a reputation for keeping his trousers on and his emotions guarded. In time, Barbra's attraction for Redford's looks was supplanted by her admiration for his ability. She became convinced that he was so good that he was stealing the picture from her. Redford, for the record, thought the same of Streisand.

The two got on well, despite the fact that both have reputations for being controlling, and have totally different approaches to their craft. Barbra likes to talk about a scene and dissect it line by line. After working all day on the set, she would typically call Pollack late at night and talk for an hour or two about the following day's work. She would have done the same with Redford, too, but he wouldn't hear of it. Redford just likes to do it.

This difference translated to the set. "She's inquisitive, extraordinarily curious, enthusiastic and a very, very hard worker," Pollack said. "[But] sometimes I'd want to say, 'Will you just relax?'"

Barbra wanted precision; Redford, spontaneity. Barbra likes lengthy rehearsals and multiple takes, and is usually better in the later takes. Redford is better in his early takes. After that, he just gets bored.

For Redford, as much as he may admire her professionally and like her personally, working with Streisand is just that, *work*. It's more work than he likes to put into acting, which probably explains why, despite their talk of "not finding the right project," they have not made a picture together in the twenty-plus years since *The Way We Were*.

In addition to teaching her restraint, Redford and Pollack influenced Barbra in another way as well. During the production, they glowingly talked to her about Sundance, Utah, where both owned property. They spoke about the mountains, the fresh air, the skiing. Redford owned the Sundance Lodge, a ski resort. "Other people have analysis," Redford was fond of saying, "I have Utah."

Later, after completion of shooting, and motivated in large part by the stories of Redford and Pollack, Barbra ventured to Aspen on her first ski vacation. Pollack said, "You must realize what a big step this was for her."

"I went up in that chair lift and knew I'd have to get down," Barbra recalled. "And I thought, That's it, I'll have a heart attack." Within four days, she was skiing down the slopes with liberating assurance. "I was learning so much: what it feels like to fall, that the snow is soft, that you don't get killed, that you survive. It was very exciting for me. I spent that whole year skiing."

One disagreement Barbra had with Pollack concerned her fear that Katie was being made too wimpy, too much the victim. With her growing sense of the women's rights movement and of her own feminism, she worried that too much of Katie's happiness seemed dependent upon Hubbell. And so she asked Pollack to eliminate some of Katie's crying scenes. She also, reportedly, went to Margaret Booth, the film's editor and one of the pioneers of women in film, and asked *her* to trim the tears. Pollack, however, put his foot down, and the tears remained.

Barbra would be extremely upset with Pollack after seeing the final cut of the picture. She would intimate in the succeeding years that if she had had the power on *The Way We Were* that she had on some of her other films, it would have been a better picture.

An interesting aside: Upon meeting Margaret Booth at Ray Stark's house before the start of the picture, Barbra's first words to the much-acclaimed, seventy-year-old editor of Garbo's *Camille* (1936) were, "So, what do you think of *me?*"

Despite Barbra's concern over Katie's tears, *The Way We Were* is a much-underrated, unheralded picture in terms of its portrayals of men, women, and the cause of feminism itself. For one, it provided a twist on the sexual clichés prevalent in decades of Hollywood moviemaking. In this one, it is the *woman* who is propelled by lust, while the man is passive; it is the woman who buys the flowers; it is *she* who takes *him* home; it is *she* who takes advantage of *his* being drunk. She doesn't go too far, of course, because she does have her pride; she teeters between her own inner conflict of desire and decorum. Still, it is the *woman* who offers the age-old line of millions of men, "I promise I won't touch you." Clearly, in *The Way We Were,* it is the woman who is the aggressor and the man who is the object. And it is a revelation.

At the end of the picture, despite her heartbreak over losing Hubbell, it is obvious that Katie will survive. What the film also does, however, is give the impression that a woman cannot have her career *and* a man, a theme that Barbra began playing in *Funny Girl.* It is a theme that would repeat itself in Streisand's film career, and in her life.

At an early screening of the picture which she attended with Alan and Marilyn Bergman, Barbra was transfixed by Redford's performance. "Redford's the best leading man she's ever had," Marilyn recalled, "and she knew it. We sat with her when she first saw the movie. She kept nudging me and saying how great *he* was."

Interestingly, when scoring the last scene, Marvin Hamlisch (Barbra's old rehearsal pianist from the stage version of *Funny Girl*) decided against using the picture's now familiar melody. He reasoned that it had been repeatedly played in other parts of the movie, and that the emotion of the scene was strong enough without the addition of the music. However, after seeing a preview at which the audience did *not* cry at the end, Hamlisch went back to Columbia and asked for a rerecording session with fifty-five musicians. When the studio refused to grant the costly session, Hamlisch decided to pay for it out of his own pocket. He was rewarded when, at the picture's next preview, the tears flowed.

As for the movie's title song, there were actually *two* completely different versions recorded by Barbra. After composing the first version, with which he was enthralled, Hamlisch turned it over to the Bergmans, who had won an Oscar for their lyrics to "The Windmills of Your Mind" from the 1968 picture *The Thomas Crown Affair*.

Upon hearing the result of their collaboration, Barbra issued her verdict: she hated it. "I had to beg her to sing it," Hamlisch later said. She told him that the song was too simple. He replied, "So is 'My Funny Valentine,'" to which Barbra retorted, "I hate 'My Funny Valentine.'"

Barbra insisted upon an entirely different, more complicated song. She loved it upon completion, and asked that it be the version used for the film. "I had heard two versions," recalls Don Cash, Jr., "and to tell you the truth, this was one time I thought Barbra was wrong. Because the first version was the personification of the mood of the film."

Wisely, Sydney Pollack decided to score the picture using both songs under the same scene. Everybody was then asked to vote on the song they liked best. To Hamlisch's great satisfaction, Barbra was outvoted. The song went on to become Barbra's first gold single and the first number one hit of her career. It would also win an Oscar, as would Hamlisch's score. Still, their relationship would never quite recover from the flap over the dueling versions of "The Way We Were."

"I'm afraid to go near her with a new song," Hamlisch would tell Rex Reed in 1977, "She scares me to death."

Upon releasing her album *The Way We Were*, Barbra received a legal letter from Ray Stark. Claiming copyright of the title, Stark threatened to sue unless it was changed, which it eventually was, to *Barbra Streisand*. With the original title still intact, however, the album went straight to the top of the *Billboard* charts and would eventually go platinum. It was Barbra's first number one album since *People*, ten years before. At the same time, the film's soundtrack, also titled *The Way We Were*, made the *Billboard* top twenty. Barbra's comeback as a recording artist was now fully realized.

With ads touting, "Streisand & Redford, Together!" *The Way We Were* opened to blockbuster business at the nation's box offices. Much was made in early reports that it had surpassed the record held by *Love*

Story (1970) at one key New York theater. The film would go on to post some $25,650,000 in domestic rentals alone, almost matching Columbia's all-time record up until then of $26,325,000 set by *Funny Girl.*

It was such a success that some reports from the period credited the picture with saving the studio from sure financial ruin. Nevertheless, that did not prevent Robert Redford and Sydney Pollack from having to file suit against Columbia and Ray Stark to obtain their percentage of the picture, which they estimated in 1976 to be $5.3 million. Not bad, considering that it was a picture Redford had not wanted to make and that Pollack had almost backed out of.

The picture, in combination with *The Sting,* released later the same year, made Robert Redford the biggest movie star in the world. On Oscar night, April 2, 1974, Redford was nominated as the year's Best Actor for his work in *The Sting,* and Barbra, true to Don Cash's prediction on the first day of shooting, was up as Best Actress for *The Way We Were.*

A few months prior to the ceremony, Barbra became embroiled in a behind-the-scenes feud. Academy president Walter Mirisch had asked her to sing "The Way We Were" on the night of the show. Barbra refused. The show's producer, Jack Haley, Jr., asked her to sing it. Again, she refused. Her friends the Bergmans asked her to sing it. Still, she refused. Finally, conceding defeat, Mirisch got Peggy Lee to sing the song instead.

Then, according to Haley, "A week before the show, [Barbra] switches. [She said,] 'I wanna do the song now. Get rid of Peggy Lee.' I said, 'No way.' That boggles the mind. I'm gonna fire Peggy Lee off the show? She canceled a club date in Canada to do it."

Barbra reportedly stormed off, furious with Haley. As she left, she muttered something about not bothering to attend the ceremony at all.

The competition that year was said to be between Barbra and Joanne Woodward, the latter for her performance in *Summer Wishes, Winter Dreams.* Ironically, Woodward was supposed to have been her primary competition in the 1968 balloting as well. Since Barbra had won that competition (along with Katharine Hepburn), it seemed only right that the prize this time should go to Woodward. Ray Stark was in a precarious position because he had produced both pictures. Woodward won the New York Film Critics Award, but seemed to hurt her chances for Oscar when she derided the awards by saying, "The Oscar has become a political gesture, or a business gesture."

That night at the ceremony, Woodward, Marsha Mason *(Cinderella*

Liberty), and Ellen Burstyn *(The Exorcist)* were in the audience as their names were announced. Glenda Jackson, a long shot for her performance in the comedy *A Touch of Class,* didn't bother to attend. And Barbra, despite her earlier threat, *did* show up, but refused to sit in the audience for the benefit of Jack Haley's cameras. Instead, she hid out backstage as the nominees were announced. When Glenda Jackson, who had won the award only three years before for *Women in Love,* was named the surprise winner, Barbra was both stunned and appalled. "I felt I deserved the award," she later said. "I felt [my performance] was the best of those five for the year." She was convinced that she did not win because Hollywood did not like her.

Years later, Glenda Jackson recalled, "Watching it on television here in my hotel suite, I kept telling myself that I ought to turn it off and go to bed. I felt disgusted with myself, as though I were attending a public hanging." She added, "No one should have a chance to see so much desire, so much need for a prize, and so much pain when it was not given."

On November 2, 1973, one week after *The Way We Were* opened to box office success, Barbra's fifth and, to this date, final, network television special aired on CBS. It had been five years since the airing of her Central Park concert, and her television guest appearances in the interim had been sporadic: "Don Rickles' Brooklyn" (September 18, 1968), the Tony Awards (accepting the Star of the Decade award, April 19, 1970), "A World of Love" (December 22, 1970), and "The Burt Bacharach Special" (March 14, 1971).

Taped over an eight-day period in May 1973 at Elstree Studios in London, "Barbra Streisand and Other Musical Instruments" reteamed Barbra with Dwight Hemion, who had directed her first two, highly successful, specials. Like Barbra, Hemion is known within the industry as a perfectionist. One number took *twenty-three* takes to complete. During the taping of another, Barbra snapped, "Dwight, *you* are going to have to adjust to me, I am not going to adjust to you."

Despite the advantageous timing of its air date, "Barbra Streisand and Other Musical Instruments" was overproduced and received mixed reviews and only fair ratings. The following year, Barbra's exclusive contract with CBS expired, and she opted not to renew it. She had tired of television. It was too much work for far too little reward.

For if there were any lingering doubts on the subject, *The Way We Were* had answered them with resounding authority. Barbra Streisand was a *movie star.* She had acted with Redford and more than held her own. Even Diana Kind was finally convinced. She stopped pinching herself, packed her bags, and moved to California.

Barbra, it seemed, had it all. Well, almost. "I was putting up defensive walls," she later related, "relationships were difficult for me. I was so full of fantasy about other people that I turned off anyone who wasn't perfect. What I didn't realize then was how hard it is to accept imperfection in others until you can accept it in yourself."

Like Katie Morosky, she had everything at the fade-out except for the guy. But that too would soon change.

Twenty-seven

The Normal Heart

$\mathcal{H}$e had been summoned to her Holmby Hills home to work on her wig. It was August 1973. Driving his red Ferrari, he raced up Carolwood Drive. This, after all, was a date he had long anticipated. In fact, he had put out the word months before that he would go anywhere, do anything, to get his hands on, and fingers in, Barbra Streisand's hair. He passed through her imposing gates, parked, and practically leapt out of his car.

An hour and a half later, Barbra finally descended her grand staircase, clutching the wig in question. "Don't you *ever* do that again," he ordered in a voice that commanded respect. *"Nobody* keeps me waiting."

His name was Jon Peters. Half Italian, half Cherokee, he was twenty-eight years old, darkly handsome, and reeking of masculinity. He talked with a cocky, street-smart assurance, and walked as if the weight of the world swung between his legs. He was wearing tight blue jeans and no underwear.

"See those gates out there?" Barbra asked of her visitor. Peters nodded, unimpressed, or not showing it if he was. "Are you afraid of them?" she queried. It was one of her informal personality quizzes.

"No," he shot back, "I want a pair of my own."

John Pagano Peters had been a disturbed, trouble-making kid who dropped out of school in the eighth grade. His temper was quick, his mouth foul, and his fists eager to connect. He married at fifteen and became an amateur boxer. Then, with family money (Pagano was a well-known name in the Los Angeles hair industry) and barely out of his teens, he opened his own beauty shop.

Divorced from his wife, Peters, twenty-two, became romantically involved with one of his clients, actress Lesley Ann Warren, who had attained celebrity with a 1966 CBS production of "Cinderella." They married in May 1967, the same month Barbra Streisand arrived in Hollywood to make *Funny Girl.*

The relationship between hairdresser and actress has always been an intimate one, particularly when the former is attractive, heterosexual, and male.

Jon Peters was *not* the inspiration for the 1975 Warren Beatty picture, *Shampoo* (Gene Shacove was), but, other than the fact that he drove a Ferrari and not a motorcycle, he could have been. Through his wife's industry connections, Peters soon found himself the darling of the Beverly Hills wash-and-blow-dry circuit. The celebrity clients he is said to have romanced, in and out of the chair, include Jacqueline Bisset and Leigh Taylor-Young.

Back behind the gates up on Carolwood Drive, Barbra turned around and gave her guest an ample view of her backside. "You've got a great ass," Peters told her, not blinking an eye. For a moment, the compliment stunned her. At first, the reason for her surprise escaped her. And then it hit her. He was not treating her like a *thing,* a commodity, an idol to be revered, or a monster to be feared. His words, and Peters himself, for that matter, reminded her that she was, above all else, a *woman.*

The wig that brought Barbra Streisand and Jon Peters together was to be worn in *For Pete's Sake,* her new picture for Columbia/Rastar. Originally titled *July Pork Bellies,* and then *For Love of Pete,* the picture was being directed by Peter Yates (*Bullitt, John and Mary*). It started shooting in Manhattan on September 24, 1973. While there, Barbra flew Peters to New York and put him up at the Plaza Hotel. The official purpose of his presence was to act as a consultant on her wardrobe. She liked, among other things, his sense of aesthetics. By this time, however, Peters was working on far more than Barbra's wigs and wardrobe, and much of his consulting was taking place in his bed or hers, and in the Jacuzzi at his Malibu ranch.

After the debacle of *Up the Sandbox,* Barbra's decision to do a mindless comedy was understandable despite all of her "What's it about?" protestations on *What's Up, Doc?* If her audience craved crass commercialism, she was now willing to serve it up in heaping portions.

What *is* surprising, however, is her decision to do *this* particular comedy. *For Pete's Sake* was created by Stanley Shapiro and Maurice Richlin, who had written several successful Doris Day vehicles in the late fifties and early sixties. But while their script for Barbra offered her ample opportunities to be alternately brash and charming, it was also blatantly offensive.

The picture's plot, after all, required that her character do *anything* to bolster her husband's business prospects, which included borrowing money from the Mafia, transporting stolen cattle, and selling her body. How Barbra reconciled this message with her own growing feminist values is an unanswered paradox. Troubling, too, is her derisive putdown of a lisping grocery clerk whom she assumes is gay. *"You* keep the Fruit Loops," she tells him, "you'll love them." And, despite her belief in racial equality, she allowed a black maid to be portrayed as lazy and ill-tempered, a characterization which had become unfashionable, if not reprehensible, in the Hollywood of the 1960s, much less the mid-1970s. Since her manager Marty Erlichman produced the picture, she certainly wielded a good deal of power over the production.

For Barbra, the picture was damaging in another way as well. Since *Funny Girl* on Broadway, she had been accused of castrating her male costars by overpowering them with her presence and/or by having their parts cut and minimalized. She was also criticized for selecting weak actors who could be easily dominated, in much the same way that Bette Davis had reduced her male costars, George Brent, for one, to mere props some thirty years before.

The Way We Were had gone a long way to show that Barbra *was* willing to share the screen with a formidable male star in a role that was relatively equal in size to her own, despite all of her behind-the-scenes machinations. What *For Pete's Sake* did, given the meaninglessness of Michael Sarrazin's title role, was to reinforce the perception that she was a scene-stealing megalomaniac.

The picture completed shooting on December 11, 1973. The highlight of the production had been the bull-riding sequence. Workers at the studio gathered to watch the novelty, the *special effect,* of Barbra Streisand trying to commandeer a bull. Artie Butler was on the Warner lot that day. He had composed the film's score, and had written the title song with Mark Lindsay, formerly of the old Paul Revere and the Raiders pop group.

"I was there doing another project," Butler recalls, "and Marty said to me, 'Come back at one-thirty, Barbra's riding the bull.' I remember saying to myself, 'Boy, is that bull going to be *in* for it. He's going to be told that he's running wrong. She's gonna tell him how to run.' I remember making a joke of it, saying, 'She's gonna take the bull by the horns— literally.' "

For Pete's Sake was released on June 26, 1974. It was almost universally panned, and called into question Barbra's much-touted instinct for doing what was "right for her." Her decision to do *For Pete's Sake* was all the more deplorable when one considers the pictures she had turned down in the preceding years. Among them, *Klute* and *Cabaret* (which won 1971 and 1972 Best Actress Oscars for Jane Fonda and Liza Minnelli, respectively), *The Devils,* and *The Exorcist.* She also turned down *They Shoot Horses, Don't They?* because she didn't want to have to do all the dancing required in the script. Jane Fonda ended up getting the part, and it turned her career around. Barbra also declined an opportunity to work with Martin Scorsese on the 1974 picture *Alice Doesn't Live Here Anymore.* She reasoned that the role called for her to be a *bad* nightclub singer, and that, at the age of thirty-one, she was too young to play the mother of a twelve-year-old. Ellen Burstyn went on to play the part and won an Oscar for her performance.

Barbra kept the news of her late night trysts at Jon Peters's Malibu ranch a secret. Even to friends, she acknowledged only that she was seeing a "businessman." On November 1, 1973, Jon and Lesley Ann Peters separated. Lesley Ann would not publicly fault Barbra for the breakup of her marriage, but the fact is that Barbra began her affair with Peters while he was still married. Lesley Ann remained with Christopher, their five-year-old son, at the family home in Encino, California, while Peters moved into his Malibu ranch house.

Slowly, Jon and Barbra began taking their relationship public. For ten days, from December 3 through December 13, he accompanied her nightly to the United-Western recording facility in Hollywood, where she was making her *The Way We Were* album. He was at every session except for one. They had had a fight earlier in the day. That night in the studio, Barbra broke down in tears and, within earshot of the engineers, called Jon on the phone and begged him to forgive her.

He introduced her to his friends at a Christmas party he gave in December at a restaurant on Sunset Boulevard. Those present were not so much surprised by their relationship as they were by the incongruous portrait of Barbra Streisand, demure and head-over-heels in love.

The press began to snicker about Barbra Streisand, thirty-one, and her twenty-eight-year-old "shampoo boy." It was, from the start, an unfair characterization. Jon Peters, after all, was not a mere hairdresser. He *owned* three successful salons in Beverly Hills, Encino, and Woodland Hills, which reportedly brought in a cumulative $100,000 a week. Moreover, even if he *was* "just a hairdresser," that in itself was hardly grounds for the abuse that would be hurled in his direction in the years to come.

They were bonded by the untraditional spellings of their first names. "When I took the 'a' out of Barbara," she later said, "and he took the 'h' out of John, we didn't even know each other. Isn't it amazing how an affectation can bring two people together?" Barbra took this idiosyncrasy as a sign that their togetherness had been predestined.

Furthermore, she always appeared enamored by the paradoxical, and Jon Peters was a walking contradiction. Part boxer and part beautician; part businessman and part aesthete; part macho tough guy and part sensitive little boy. As Barbra would later say with admiration, "Jon is a very macho man. He's got scars all over his hands from fighting, but he's very good at hair and clothes."

She loved his lack of fear. Unlike her, he was unafraid of the mountains, the ocean, the sharks, *and* the Hollywood barracudas. For years, she had been forced to don a suit of calloused toughness and slay her own dragons. With Jon Peters, however, she could strip away her protective layers and return to the free-spirited, thrift-shop-wearing kook of her Greenwich Village period.

She also loved his spontaneity and brazen disregard for polite social graces. One night at a party, he took her outside, propped her on his shoulders, and despite her insistent squeals of protest, refused to let her down. Not only did he resurrect the kook she once was, he also brought out in her the repressed little girl she had never been.

Together, they embarked upon the childhood neither one of them had ever had. Like Barbra, Jon had lost his father at a young age. He told her how, at the age of nine, he had watched his father die in front of his eyes.

He also made her laugh out loud. He got her to embrace the outdoors. They went horseback riding and skiing in Vail. He lured her out of her fairy-tale world of movie sets and recording studios, and back into some semblance of reality. It was with his encouragement that she got her hands dirty. Literally. She planted spices and herbs and created the English garden of her girlhood dreams. She had come a long way from being the girl who was afraid to venture out into the country because she was allergic to the fresh air.

In January 1974, to please Jon, Barbra used her clout and got Teddy Brenner, president of Madison Square Garden, to give her the very last two tickets to the Muhammad Ali–Joe Frazier fight. They were tickets that Brenner had been saving for his own brother-in-law. Jon and Barbra boarded a plane for New York and showed up at the match wearing nearly identical cowboy outfits. From her seat in the front row, Barbra happily told whoever asked that she was there because her boyfriend had wanted to see the fight. She was gently corrected by Jon. *They* were there because they had *both* wanted to see the fight. He was concerned, even then, about giving the impression that he was in any way using his famous girlfriend.

She told friends that she had never been in love "like this" before. She divided her time between Jon's house and her own. Using textured fabrics, pastel colors, and decorative knickknacks from her Carolwood home, Barbra warmed and softened his environment. Gradually, she added furniture. Previously, entertaining at the house had been done primarily in the Jacuzzi. It was, as Peters himself acknowledged, a place where "people took their clothes off."

It was Jon's influence that prompted Barbra to start eating health foods. She still consumed her beloved hot dogs, but she ate them on buns that were made of whole wheat.

She cooked, using the herbs from her garden, and cleaned for him. She washed and blow-dried *his* hair. She let him pick out *her* clothes. Friends worried that she was following him around "like a lovesick puppy dog."

Barbra would later bristle at any suggestion that Peters was the dominant figure in the relationship. But the perception was the result, at least in part, of her own words: "I actually enjoy being subjugated to him," she said. "It's far more important to a man's ego to have a career than it is to a woman's. I don't need to work anymore to feed my ego. I get all the ego nourishment I need from him."

The fact is that Peters had been catered to by women all of his life, and he expected the same from Barbra. He believed that a relationship should be dominated by the male 90 percent of the time, and by the female 10 percent of the time. For Barbra, it was refreshing to let someone else take control and make the decisions. For a while. As their relationship evolved, Peters's ratio of 90/10 would shift: 80/20, 70/30, 60/40, 50/50 . . .

Meanwhile, as much as she dreaded it, the time had come for Barbra to return to work. Among the film projects she had been considering was *Freaky Friday,* based on the Mary Rodgers book about a thirteen-year-old girl in the body of a woman. It was being produced by Marty Erlichman, who intended, with Barbra's involvement, to turn the story into a musical.

Erlichman wanted Barbra to star in another picture, *With or Without Roller Skates,* based on an unpublished novel by George Slavin. The film would have cast Barbra as a nurse who worked in a veterans' hospital, fighting the authorities for the rights of her patients.

Interestingly, Barbra also considered the role of murderess Ruth Snyder, the thirty-two-year-old bleached-blonde housewife who, one night in 1927, crushed in her husband's skull. While in jail, Ruth received 164 offers of marriage from men who begged to be dominated by her. She was sent to the electric chair on the night of January 12, 1928. The following day, the New York *Daily News* published a photograph on its front page that showed Ruth Snyder sitting in the chair as the electrical current was thrown into her body. It was that photo that fascinated Barbra Streisand over thirty-five years later.

But Barbra would seek far safer territory. During several contentious arguments with Ray Stark, she had repeatedly said that she would never reprise the role of Fanny Brice. "When Ray Stark told me he wanted me to make the sequel to *Funny Girl,*" Barbra recalled, "I told him, 'You'll have to drag me into court to do that picture.'"

It was, apparently, an empty threat. The reasons for her eventual capitulation are worth exploring. First, she was anxious to get out of all of her pressing contractual commitments. She sought to spend more time in her garden, and in her newfound domestic bliss with Jon Peters. Moreover, she wanted the projects that she *did* do to reflect a vision that the two of them shared.

Barbra's initial contract with Stark had called for her to make four pictures, which she did (*Funny Girl, The Owl and the Pussycat, The Way We Were,* and *For Pete's Sake*). However, Stark must have coerced her into a fifth picture as a part of the out-of-court settlement of his 1967 lawsuit against her. Either that, or when she signed to do *Funny Girl,* Barbra also agreed to star in a potential sequel above and beyond her four-movie obligation. Whatever the case, as of 1974, she still owed her former mentor one final picture, and she was eager to have it wiped off her slate.

Another factor motivating Barbra's decision to return to her star-launching vehicle was the very clear threat she saw in Liza Minnelli. She had been hearing about Minnelli for years. The year after Barbra lost the Tony Award for *Funny Girl,* Liza, only nineteen, won it for the musical *Flora, the Red Menace.* In Hollywood, Liza won acclaim as a dramatic actress, and received an Oscar nomination, for her performance in *The Sterile Cuckoo* (1969).

With her enormous success in 1972 in *Cabaret,* which won her the Oscar, and "Liza With a Z," which won her the Emmy, Minnelli was being hailed all over Hollywood as the successor to the Streisand throne. She was four years younger than Barbra, who seemed to have lost all interest in the musical genre. Liza added salt to the wound, or appeared to, by entertaining her friends with her humorous impersonations of Streisand singing "People."

But Barbra was not quite ready to step down. She decided to make *Funny Lady,* turning it into her *Cabaret.* John Kander and Fred Ebb, who had composed both *Cabaret* and "Liza With a Z," were hired to compose the music. Jay Presson Allen, who wrote the screenplay for *Cabaret,* would do the same for *Funny Lady.* And although she couldn't entice Bob Fosse (Herb Ross was attached to the project), she *could* get his choreographic style in the picture. She also obtained the services of Ben Vereen in a supporting part. A Fosse protégé, Vereen took a leave of absence from the hit Broadway musical *Pippin,* which Fosse directed, to appear in the film.

On Tuesday, April 2, 1974, Barbra arrived at rehearsals for *Funny Lady* in seemingly good spirits. The night before, up for *The Way We Were,* she had lost the Best Actress Oscar to Glenda Jackson. Noticing Don Cash, Jr., her makeup man on both pictures, she said, "Hey, Don. I thought you said I was gonna get the Oscar?"

Today, Cash relates, "She remembered [the prediction he had made nearly two years before]. She doesn't forget a thing."

Budgeted at $7.5 million, surprisingly less than the original, *Funny Lady* started shooting the first week of April, 1974. For the first sixteen days, the picture was shot on MGM's theater soundstage, before it moved to Burbank Studios in early May for the rest of its fourteen-week schedule.

Two days into the shooting, cinematographer Vilmos Zsigmond was fired. Barbra, it seems, didn't like the way she was being lit. Zsigmond was giving the picture a gritty, realistic look, when Barbra, Stark, and Ross all wanted the glamorous look Harry Stradling had created for the original. Zsigmond, at forty-four, was influenced by the relatively new school of cinema in which a sequence was photographed to convey the mood of an entire scene, in contrast to the studio system veterans, who concentrated more on the look of the players.

Zsigmond's work (*Close Encounters of the Third Kind, The Deer Hunter, Blow Out*) would go on to win great acclaim. He was replaced by James Wong Howe, seventy-five, who had been shooting pictures in

Hollywood since the 1920s. During the production of *Funny Lady,* his final picture before his death in 1976, Howe provided the newly domesticated Barbra with recipes for his favorite Chinese delicacies.

On the Easter weekend of April 13–14, Barbra provided items in the gossip columns by vacationing in Palm Springs *without* Jon Peters, who was back in Encino, working out some difficulty with his family. In Palm Springs, Barbra was the guest of Herbert Allen, Jr., the nephew of multimillionaire Charlie Allen. Her son, Jason, and her longtime friend, Rick Edelstein, accompanied Barbra on the trip. Jason, seven, was taking tennis lessons, while Barbra lounged around the pool at the Racquet Club, reading the script for *Funny Lady.*

As on their previous pictures together, the bickering between Barbra and Ray Stark continued on *Funny Lady.* One scene, shot at the Los Angeles Swim Stadium, called for Barbra, dressed as a clown, to cavort in the pool. "Barbra isn't crazy about this scene," one studio executive said at the time. "It took her fifteen minutes to wriggle her big toe in the water last night." It seems that she didn't like the water temperature. Stark had the temperature heated to 86 degrees. Barbra wanted the pool heated to 92 degrees. Stark refused, saying, "Do you have any idea how many thousands of dollars it would take to heat a million gallons of water?"

Stark also had his disagreements with Barbra's costar, James Caan. It seems that the thrill-seeking Caan had snuck off during the production to participate in a team-roping competition in a Palm Springs rodeo. To Stark's ire, Caan broke his thumb and was forced to wear a cast. He would spend several weeks of the production in a good deal of pain. Herb Ross was able, for the most part, to shoot around Caan's cast, except for the love scenes, which required that the cast be removed.

On another occasion when Caan was missing from the set, Stark drawled, sarcasm dripping, "Have you checked the alligator farms around here? He's probably wrestling one."

The casting of the tall, good-looking Caan as the short, unattractive, Broadway impresario Billy Rose was a stretch, even by Hollywood standards. But Ray Stark was determined to repeat the success of the Streisand-Redford pairing in *The Way We Were.* Among those who had auditioned for the part were Dustin Hoffman, Robert Blake, Richard Dreyfuss, and Robert De Niro. Given his physical inappropriateness for the role, Caan compensated, or tried to, by basing his characterization of Rose on a cross between Peter Falk and Don Rickles.

Despite sexist speculation that she was a pussycat on the *Funny Lady* set because she was being satisfied in bed, Barbra was her typically mal-content self during the production. She simply did not want to make *Funny Lady,* and she thought nothing of letting everyone know it. Jay Presson Allen later recalled, "Figuratively speaking, [Barbra was] es-corted to the set every day by a team of lawyers."

She gave Herb Ross in particular a bad time. In the twenty years since the completion of *Funny Lady,* the two have not worked together. Part of Barbra's disdain undoubtedly had something to do with Jon Peters, who thought that the role of "Ray Stark's mother-in-law," and the pic-ture itself, was the wrong vehicle for Barbra at that point in her career. It aged her, he argued, and would contribute to the perception that she was an outcast from her own generation.

For this and other reasons, vanity among them, Barbra, thirty-two, was reticent to play Fanny at thirty-five and older, as dictated by the script. She did so, but only at the fervent insistence of her director.

As usual, Barbra came to the set with a good many of her own ideas. Jack Solomon, a veteran sound man who worked on *Funny Lady,* as well as three other Streisand pictures, credits Barbra with at least being up-front about her suggestions. "This goddamned business isn't really based on people who will go one-on-one with you," Solomon says. "Peo-ple go behind the scenes and play a lot of politics [to get what they want]."

"But, I worked for John Ford. And if an actor went to John Ford and made a suggestion about a scene, he would not have gotten an answer. Ford would have said, 'What, you're a director? You're gonna cut this picture? What the hell do *you* know?' These people [directors like Ford] were complete bosses." Solomon adds, "Times have changed, and not for the better."

According to Jay Presson Allen, the film's writer, because of Barbra's reservations and insecurities about the part, Herb Ross had to concen-trate his energies on the straight scenes, at the expense of the musical and comedic numbers. "Herbie had to spend an unconscionable amount of rehearsal time with her on the scenes," Allen said.

Of the picture's two big comedic numbers, one was virtually cut out, and the other was used in motion picture wasteland: under the titles. Infuriated at the expense incurred in the shooting of the numbers, Ray Stark and a Columbia executive took out their wrath on Ross. "Herbie took the rap," Allen reported, "but in my opinion, the lady bore consid-erable responsibility."

Perhaps it was because he was rushed on the musical numbers that Ross borrowed not only from Fosse, particularly on the "Clap Hands,

Here Comes Charley" number, but from *himself.* The swooping helicopter shots in "Let's Hear It for Me" are right out of "Don't Rain on My Parade," only here they seem less lyrical, and forced; and instead of traveling in a train, to a taxi, to a tugboat, as she did in *Funny Girl,* Fanny goes from a Rolls-Royce to an airplane. For the latter, a terrified Barbra actually flew over Santa Monica in a 1937 biplane with an open cockpit. When traffic congestion forced the pilot to delay their landing, a panic-stricken Barbra became convinced that she was the victim of an elaborate kidnapping plot.

Also appearing in the picture, reprising his role of Nicky Arnstein, was Omar Sharif. This time, however, his continental charm and batted-brown-eyes act failed to seduce, for it was Barbra who rebuffed Sharif. It is ironic, of course, that in the picture, Fanny, after carrying a torch for him for years, finally realizes that she is no longer in love with Nicky.

It is also worth noting that the whole scenario plays less like biography and more like a scene out of *Gone With the Wind.* Scarlett O'Hara, after years of carrying the torch for Ashley Wilkes, realizes that it is really Rhett Butler whom she loves. After having dreamed about it as a child, Barbra got to play Scarlett after all, albeit in only one scene and decades out of period.

Jon Peters was a frequent visitor on the set, absorbing everything he could about motion picture production and, undoubtedly, keeping his eyes on both Jimmy Caan and Omar Sharif.

Another man in Barbra's life almost made a brief appearance in the picture. While she was shooting a sequence at the Beverly Hills Hotel during the week of June 18, Elliott Gould, accompanied by his girlfriend, Jennifer O'Neill, checked in to the hotel. Complicating the scenario was the presence of Jon Peters, and the fact that Elliott was in the process of ending his marriage to Jennifer Bogart and that O'Neill was still in her first year of marriage to writer Joseph Koster. Despite talk of their own marriage, Elliott's affair with O'Neill would be short-lived. She was soon replaced in his affections by Valerie Perrine, who was then creating a stir in town with her performance in Bob Fosse's *Lenny.*

Filming one of *Funny Lady*'s final scenes, Barbra was unable to cry as dictated by the script. "It's hard, when you're happy, to be asked to produce tears," she confided. "To do that, you have to go looking around inside you for something that hurts. I'm not going to work for a while after this. I've discovered a whole life to live away from show business and this time I like it."

Funny Lady completed shooting on July 9, 1974. As a parting gift, Barbra presented Ray Stark with an antique mirror, suggesting perhaps, in her none-too-subtle way, that he take a good look at himself. Her inscription, reportedly written across the glass in red lipstick, read, "Paid in Full." A second message, engraved on a plaque, revealed her ambivalent feelings for the man who was her mentor, producer, father, and foe. "Even though I sometimes forget to say it, thank you, Ray. Love, Barbra."

With her contract to Stark fulfilled, she was, in a way, the adolescent leaving home. But instead of striking out on her own, Barbra merged forces with Jon Peters. The first item on their agenda was the completion of a record album on which they had been collaborating.

Peters had arrived on the set of *Funny Lady* one day with a gift for Barbra. It was a diamond-and-sapphire butterfly. A week later, he presented her with a one hundred-year-old Indian butterfly. Barbra, it seems, reminded Jon of a butterfly. So it made perfect sense that they would christen their first joint project *ButterFly*.

The concept for the album cover was Jon's. No photo of Barbra, no fancy logo. Just a stick of unwrapped butter with a fly perched on it. The back cover showed a painting of Barbra depicted as some sort of golden goddess of butterflies. It was Jon's personal commentary on Barbra's stardom. The butter was her talent (it had to be *sweet* butter, as he notified the advertising agency who handled the photo shoot); the fly in the ointment represented the press, as well as her parasitic fans; and through it all she was still able to emerge, like the butterfly, resplendent in her glory.

Naturally, the executives at Columbia Records were none too pleased when Barbra informed them that her lover, who didn't have any experience in the recording studio, would produce the album. When Columbia balked, Barbra insisted, wielding the "complete creative control" clause in her contract. "Do they think I would let Jon produce a record if I wasn't absolutely sure he could do it?" she said in her own defense. "I believe in imagination. I believe in taste. These are the important ingredients, and they're all things he has."

The recording of *ButterFly* actually started in March 1974, *before* *Funny Lady* went into production. But it was to be a troubled project which was still ongoing months after the completion of the picture.

After Peters worked on the album for months, Kathy Kasper, a "music contractor," was brought in to survey and repair the damage. She was followed by veteran engineer Al Schmitt, who had worked on the *The Way We Were* album. "They've recorded seven or eight songs for this new LP," Schmitt related. "Columbia played them and they were unhappy with what they heard. . . . This album has a flat, one-dimensional sound." He added, "Peters is a nice guy, but he's not a record producer."

A few days after he was hired, Schmitt was removed from the project. "Essentially," he said, "Peters wants all the money, and I'd be doing all the work." Reportedly, Schmitt's parting words to Peters were, "I've been in this business for twenty-five years. You've been in it for twenty-five minutes."

"I don't even know this Schmitt," Barbra angrily replied in Jon's defense. And, regarding their joint efforts on *ButterFly,* she declared, "This is possibly the best singing I've ever done. It's the most open, the most free, the most happy."

The result of their collaboration was a highly eclectic mix of material, including "Grandma's Hands" by Bill Withers, "Crying Time" by Buck Owens, and "Guava Jelly" by Bob Marley. They were making a statement with the audacious diversity of the material. Just as she had aspired to be an actress when everyone told her she was a singer, just as she had aspired to drama when everyone told her she belonged in musical comedy, Barbra refused to sing only the songs that were expected of her. She would not be confined by the limitations imposed on her by others. The same could be said of Jon Peters, who kept pressing, pushing, sometimes shoving, and always striving, for something *more.* He aspired to be Mike Todd when the world saw him only as Vidal Sassoon—if even that.

Among the songs recorded for *ButterFly,* but not used, were the Billie Holiday standard "God Bless the Child," and "A Quiet Thing," the John Kander–Fred Ebb song which had been sung by Liza Minnelli in the Broadway musical *Flora, the Red Menace.*

Upon its release in October 1974, *ButterFly* was accorded scathingly negative reviews. Robert Kemnitz of the *Los Angeles Herald-Examiner* deemed it Barbra's "all-time recording low."

Even David Bowie, asked to critique Barbra's cover of his "Life on Mars," was compelled to call it "bloody awful." "Sorry, Barb," Bowie declared, "but it was atrocious."

Nevertheless, released on the heels of her smash *The Way We Were* album, *ButterFly* made it to number thirteen on the *Billboard* charts and went gold within three months.

Years later, with perspective and objectivity on her side, Barbra would confess that *ButterFly* was the least favorite of all of her albums.

The conventional wisdom in Hollywood circa 1974–75 was that Jon Peters had some Svengali-like influence over Barbra, affecting her better judgment. "Jon Peters seems to have an absolute iron grip on Barbra," reported columnist Robin Adams Sloan. The theory was given added credence when Barbra, at Jon's urging, decided to separate from Marty Erlichman, her manager, confidante, and close friend of fifteen years.

It had been an agonizing decision for Barbra, and came about only after several passionate fights with Peters. She argued the case for Erlichman's loyalty. She knew that she could trust Marty to be there in the long run. How did she know that the same could be said about Peters? Jon argued the case against Erlichman's judgment. Using the inanity of *For Pete's Sake,* which Marty had talked her into doing, as an example, Jon argued that it was time for Barbra to take more control over her own career.

In a way, Barbra loved her arguments with Jon. She found them stimulating, mind-expanding. He exposed her to the metaphysical, and to the theory that there was no *one* truth, that everyone had their own reality. It was a theory she came to embrace, if not always practice. In time, Barbra started going to Jon's psychoanalyst, and many of their conversations at home began to be peppered with allusions to Gestalt therapy.

Peters was the first man in her life who fought as tenaciously for his position as she did for hers. They battled often, and sometimes in public. They attended a party thrown by David Geffen at the Beverly Wilshire Hotel. Among those present were Mel Gibson, Jane Fonda, Jack Nicholson, Joan Rivers, and Diane Von Furstenberg. Barbra interrupted her fight with Jon to try to buy the diamond ring from Von Furstenberg's finger.

But while she admired his convictions, she also feared his temper. Once, during one of their fights, Jon put his fist clear through a solidly built closet door. On another occasion, he broke his right foot while kicking a photographer who had been trying to get a shot of the two of them together.

In later years, Jon's temper would get him in trouble with the law. There was one occasion in which he pointed a .45 at two landscapers who showed up at his door wanting the money he owed them. And then there was the day of March 5, 1978, when Peters broke through a police roadblock in Malibu. He was trying to get back to the home he shared with Barbra, which had, in recent days, been pummeled by heavy Southern California rains. When Officer Patrick Meister wouldn't allow him into the restricted area because he lacked identification, Peters broke through the roadblock and sped off. Three miles down the road, Meister caught up with him. According to police records, Jon came at him "in an aggressive manner." Purportedly in self-defense, Meister hit Jon on the leg with his baton, pushed him against the car, handcuffed him, and took him to the sheriff's station. Jon made his one phone call, and Barbra, in a panic, came rushing to his aid with the five hundred dollars bail.

"I'm not going to do self-deprecating parts anymore," Barbra stated upon the release of *Funny Lady.* "This is the end of a cycle."

The picture premiered on March 9, 1975, at the Kennedy Center for the Performing Arts in Washington. The screening, preceded by a few songs from Barbra, was to benefit the Joseph P. Kennedy, Jr., Foundation's Special Olympics for the handicapped. Barbra attended the event on the arm of Jon Peters. Also in attendance were President Gerald Ford, with his daughter, Susan, and several members of the Kennedy clan. Family martriarch Rose Kennedy, eighty-five, was also there. She entertained onlookers by marching up to some of the guests, and even the bartender, and feistily pronouncing, "My name is Rose Kennedy and I'm the mother of the former president, Jack."

Following the Washington premiere, Barbra and Jon flew to England for the royal screening. Upon being introduced to Queen Elizabeth, Barbra, reportedly miffed that protocol had precluded Jon from standing beside her in the receiving line, ventured to ask, "Why do women have to wear gloves and not men?"

The Queen replied, "I'll have to think about that one. I suppose it's a tradition."

While in London, Barbra was shopping on old Bond Street when a car pulled up to a jewelry store. Two men jumped out of the car, threw firebombs into the street and attempted to break the store windows with an ax. Barbra hid out in a doorway and watched. "Two men in bowler hats rushed up and hit the thieves with their umbrellas," she later reported, enjoying her new role of eyewitness. "It was like a British film comedy about a bungled burglary. It seemed so funny and happened so quickly. I didn't get scared until that evening."

Funny Lady was released to mixed, mostly negative reviews. Like most sequels, it was compared unfavorably to the original. What it proved, however, was that when showcased in certain vehicles, Barbra Streisand transcended the quality, or lack thereof, of her pictures. Despite being trashed, *For Pete's Sake* had earned an impressive ten million dollars in domestic rentals. Despite being trashed, *Funny Lady* would earn double that amount. Barbra was also named the number one female box-office star by the Quigley Poll in 1973, 1974, *and* 1975. She received the Golden Globe award in 1975 as the World Film Favorite, and also the People's Choice awards that year as the Favorite Movie Actress and Favorite Female Singer.

She could do whatever she wanted to do, or so it seemed. What she chose to do was typically Streisandian. Reeling from the negative reviews of her acting in both *For Pete's Sake* and *Funny Lady,* the biggest female movie star in the world quietly began taking acting lessons at the Actors Studio West in Los Angeles. In her first official assignment in the position, Barbra *directed* herself, and actress Sally Kirkland, in a scene from *Romeo and Juliet.* The scene was performed for Lee Strasberg, visiting from New York, in May 1975. Barbra thought her performance as Juliet, whom she portrayed as a spoiled brat, was the best acting she had ever done. Strasberg was also enthusiastic—that is, as much as he ever got enthusiastic about anything.

She was so taken with her performance, and with her virgin venture into directing, that Barbra called her agent, Sue Mengers, and told her that she wanted to play Juliet in a television special of *Romeo and Juliet.* Naturally, Barbra assumed that all three networks would jump at the chance to get her doing *anything.* As it turned out, they were not so eager. "Who will be playing Romeo?" they asked. "What will she be singing?" they wondered.

And so she set her sights on another project, one that Jon had been developing for her. It wasn't *Romeo and Juliet,* but it *was* a love story. Namely, *theirs.*

Back in mid-1974, during the production of *Funny Lady,* Barbra received an unusual fan letter. Actually, it was a group of fan letters. As part of a class assignment, fifteen first-graders from New Jersey wrote Barbra, each saying, "Dear Miss Streisand: I am in the first grade and we are studying famous people." Using the same wide-lined paper, and in the same large style of print, Barbra wrote back, saying, "Dear Students: I am a famous person studying first graders. Your notes made me very happy. Love, Barbra Streisand."

Twenty-eight

Somewhere Over the Rainbow Road

*J*ohn Gregory Dunne and his wife, Joan Didion, were driving in downtown Honolulu on their way to the airport. As they passed the landmark Aloha Tower, John, inspired, uttered sixteen words: "James Taylor and Carly Simon in a rock and roll version of *A Star Is Born."* Many times over the succeeding months, Dunne and Didion would come to regret that seemingly harmless outburst. They would also remember the time and the day—one P.M., July 1, 1973.

Upon their return to the mainland, Dunne and Didion telephoned their former agent, Dick Shepherd, who had become the head of production at Warner Brothers. Shepherd loved the concept. As it turned out, Warners owned the rights to the property, having made the picture before, in 1954, with Judy Garland and James Mason starring and George Cukor directing. The story had previously been filmed in 1937 with Janet Gaynor and Fredric March. In turn, that version had been partially based on the 1932 RKO picture *What Price Hollywood?*

Despite their various differences, each version explored the same basic premise: one fading, self-destructive male star (a male *director,* in the case of *Hollywood*) helps a struggling young woman to stardom and falls in love with her in the process. Her stardom eclipses his, propelling him to some tragic suicidal death.

To absorb the rock and roll milieu of the proposed new version, Dunne and Didion ventured out onto the road for three weeks, a deafening and seemingly endless series of one-night stands, with the rock groups Jethro Tull and Uriah Heep. Their subsequent first draft, entitled *Rainbow Road,* would take six months to write.

Initially, Dunne and Didion wanted Warren Beatty to direct. Beatty, who had produced *Bonnie and Clyde* (1967), was in the process of writing and producing *Shampoo* (1975). At thirty-seven, he was young and hip enough to relate to the rock and roll world, which Dunne and Didion viewed as a prerequisite. If they were unable to get Beatty, they wanted Mike Nichols. To their chagrin, the script was also sent to Peter Bogdanovich, whose work they regarded with disdain. Moreover, Bogdanovich was interested in the property because his girlfriend, Cybill Shepherd, a part-time singer, hoped to make a musical. She would, too—*At Long Last Love* (1975)—and it would nearly ruin her career, as well as that of Bogdanovich, who directed it.

But it was Mark Rydell who became attached, albeit unofficially, to the project. The director was so enamored with Dunne and Didion's tough, savage depiction of the rock and roll world that he agreed to develop the project on speculation. Rydell submitted the script to agent Sue Mengers at International Creative Management (ICM). She, in turn, submitted it to her number one client, Barbra, who turned it down. As she told Mengers, she had no interest in the world of rock and roll. Besides, she saw no point in a third remake.

Meanwhile, the couple who provided the impetus for the project, Carly Simon and James Taylor, were still vacillating over the script. Following their marriage in November 1972, Taylor's career had steadily declined, while Simon's had skyrocketed with the huge hit, "You're So Vain." In early 1974, the couple began to record together, and it was generally believed that Simon was now carrying her husband. They eventually turned down *Rainbow Road,* reportedly because it too closely resembled their own lives.

Songwriter Kris Kristofferson was approached to play the Norman Maine part, redubbed John Norman Howard in this version. In the 1954 picture, Maine (a role, by the way, turned down by Laurence Olivier, Richard Burton, and Cary Grant before it was accepted by James Mason) was a cultured, civilized actor with a drinking problem. To reflect the times, in the updated version he was a raucous rock star with a drinking—and drug—problem.

Kristofferson had made a series of pictures including *Cisco Pike* (1972), *Blume in Love* (1973), *Pat Garrett and Billy the Kid* (1973), and *Alice Doesn't Live Here Anymore* (1974). Still, despite some good notices, he had yet to achieve movie stardom. Upon reading the *Rainbow*

Road script, Kristofferson expressed enthusiastic interest in the part, but refrained from signing. He wanted to see another draft of the script. He also wanted to find out who would be playing opposite him.

The casting of the female lead of Esther Blodgett was far more problematic, and the time was getting short. Warners wanted the picture made for a 1975 release and had scheduled shooting to begin in September 1974. Unhappy with what was deemed to be his slow progress, the studio ousted Mark Rydell from the production. He was replaced by Jerry Schatzberg, who had previously worked with Didion and Dunne on *Panic in Needle Park* (1971) and was coming off the critical success of Warners' *Scarecrow* (1973), both with Al Pacino. As for Rydell, he would have to wait a few years to do *his* rock and roll picture, *The Rose,* which savagely depicted the story of a *female* star in decline.

Back on *Rainbow Road,* producer John Foreman submitted the script to, among others, Diana Ross, Liza Minnelli, and Cher. Of the three, Cher was the only one with even remote roots in rock. At twenty-eight, she was separating from Sonny Bono, and had just had back-to-back number one records with "Half-Breed" and "Dark Lady." She read the script and became enthralled with the story of two stars passing in flight. Her interest was understandable. After all, she had practically lived the part while married to Bono. To the amusement of many in the industry, Cher desperately wanted to become a movie star, and beyond that, a respectable *actress.* She saw *Rainbow Road* as her opportunity. She agreed to submit herself to one audition after another. As it evolved Cher probably would have been signed if not for the unforeseen hurricane that swept over the production.

In April 1974, while Barbra was working on *Funny Lady* and while Jon Peters was producing *ButterFly,* Peters "discovered" the *Rainbow Road* script and was smitten. With her boyfriend's enthusiasm, Barbra agreed to give the script, now in its second draft, another look. She still wasn't crazy about the rock and roll element of the story. Furthermore she believed that the male character was the stronger of the two parts.

Nevertheless, Barbra agreed to make the picture on the condition that Jon Peters produce it, despite the fact that John Foreman had been acting as the producer on the project for nearly a year. Moreover, not only had Peters never before produced a film, he had not worked, in any capacity, in production. In fact, the only film experience he had ever had, outside of doing Barbra's wigs, was to have worked as an extra in Cecil B. DeMille's *The Ten Commandments* (1956) when he was a child.

Barbra would respond in Jon's defense by pointing out that some of the pioneers of the movie industry had started out as salesmen, and she was right. But what she didn't choose to acknowledge was that these pioneers had also paid their dues. The issue wasn't that Jon had been a hairstylist, or even a successful businessman, but that his relationship with her had catapulted him, without benefit of education or experience, to the position of motion picture producer.

Barbra also insisted that Warner Brothers relinquish control of the picture to her production company, First Artists, and act only as a distributor. In addition, she demanded that Warners relinquish the soundtrack, and all profits from it, to her recording company, Columbia Records. It is quite possible that Barbra made such demands because she still had reservations about the project, and had consented mainly to appease the ebullient Peters.

Furthermore, if *Rainbow Road* did not work out, she still had her choice of projects. Robert Benton and David Newman were writing a script for her entitled *The Gift Shop,* which was being adapted from the suspense novel by Charlotte Armstrong. And Peters was developing another project for her, a comedy, from a screenplay by Joane A. Gil. It was entitled *Suppose They Met* and told the story of a feminist leader who falls in love with a sexist millionaire playboy. The picture was to be produced for Rastar, with a start date of spring 1975.

Seeing mega-dollar signs in a Streisand musical, however, the Warner executives acquiesced to her every demand, and *Rainbow Road* was a "go." One of Jon and Barbra's first acts of business was to redub the picture *A Star Is Born.*

In early July 1974, columnist Joyce Haber announced that Barbra would star in a remake of *A Star Is Born.* A few days later, on the morning of July 8, Haber broke the news that John Foreman had been "kicked upstairs" into an executive producer position and that Jon Peters would produce the picture. Later that day, Lesley Ann Peters filed for a divorce.

Meanwhile, Cher felt betrayed. The part had been all but promised to her. "Barbra Streisand and Jon Peters just walked in and took over the project," Cher fumed soon after the film's release. She was embittered by the fact that the project not only had been taken away from her, but that it had been done so by a rock and roll *outsider.* Cher, who would win a 1987 Best Actress Oscar for *Moonstruck,* declared, "Barbra doesn't know *shit* about rock and roll." Because of the behind-the-scenes machinations on *A Star Is Born,* the relationship between the two women, never close to begin with, was done irreparable damage.

Barbra had met Didion and Dunne several years before at a dinner party given by Sue Mengers. After saying "Hello," and without missing a beat, she proceeded to ask them their views on fidelity in marriage. Several months later, perhaps because of the breakup of her own marriage, Barbra contacted the couple and asked them to write a picture for her about marital infidelity. The proposed project, however, never came to pass.

Didion and Dunne had several meetings with Barbra and Jon during the summer of 1974. Together, they shared a few laughs and a lot of wine, and seemed to get along well enough. At the time, Didion and Dunne were preparing a third draft of the script, supposedly tailored to Barbra's specifications. She asked that the story be softened. It was too harsh, too documentarylike. She wanted "more heart," "more schmaltz," "more love story," and less rock and roll ambience. She also wanted her character, renamed Esther Hoffman in this version, to take on greater importance in the story.

Two weeks after Barbra entered the picture, Dunne and Didion went to their lawyer and to Warners and asked for a release. They did not approve of the version Barbra now insisted they write. Nevertheless, they were told that such a defection would be considered a legal violation of their contract. And so they remained, for the time being.

Upon reading their third draft, however, Barbra and Jon wanted Dunne and Didion removed from the project. They had not delivered the version Barbra had asked them to provide. This time, however, it was Dunne and Didion who threatened a breach-of-contract lawsuit. Jon called a meeting with John Calley, who had replaced Ted Ashley as Warner Brothers' president. Peters told Calley that Barbra, who had yet to sign a contract, was having second thoughts about the project. Peters added that she found the script "unsuitable." Either they—Barbra and Jon—be allowed to develop the project *their* way, with *their* writers, or Barbra would walk away, taking with her her $50 million projected gross.

Buckling under the pressure, Warners signed the project over to First Artists and negotiated a release for Didion and Dunne. The couple would not only retain their screen credit, they were also granted a $125,000 fee and a *huge* 10 percent of the gross. In the long run, for John Gregory Dunne and Joan Didion, those sixteen words uttered in Honolulu would pay off very handsomely.

The script of *A Star Is Born* was then given to novice writer Jonathan Axelrod, stepson of screenwriter George Axelrod, and a friend of Jon

Peters's. His assignment was to carry out the wishes of Barbra and Jon; his top priority, to enhance Barbra's part. Axelrod's solution was to reverse the roles, with the woman becoming the star in decline, and the man the one in ascent.

Not only did this reversal give Barbra the meatier role, it was also closer to the real-life situation between Barbra and Jon. Although Barbra's career was hardly in decline, she *had* "discovered" Jon Peters and launched his career as a film producer. It was *his* star that was being born on this picture, not hers.

Barbra and Jon at first loved the reversal. They later changed their minds, however, and the characters reverted to their original form. Still, they worked with Axelrod in turning *A Star Is Born* into the story of their own romance. "You and Me Against the World" by Helen Reddy was on the radio constantly that summer. It could have been the ballad of Barbra and Jon. Everyone, or so it seemed, was against their succeeding on the picture, and as a couple. Instead of collapsing in the face of the animosity, they *fed* off of it, recycling it into the "I'll show you" drive of Barbra's past.

"The world is waiting to see Barbra's and my story," Peters declared with characteristic immodesty. And so they took their conversations, and fragments of their conversations, and inserted them verbatim into the *A Star Is Born* script. "You've got a great ass," John Norman Howard tells Esther Hoffman on the night of their meeting.

Also included in the script was Barbra's relationship with, as she saw it, a predatory press. "When is it ever enough, goddamn it!" she has Esther snap at the paparazzi. Her feelings on the subject of her fans were also addressed, inserted into the nightclub scene in which she is first heard singing. John Norman Howard innocently walks into the club and is forced into a fistfight by an obnoxious so-called "fan." "With fans like this," John Norman seems to be saying, "who needs stardom?"

It is not an oversight that nowhere in the script is there a positive depiction of a fan or a member of the press. The message seems to be that the only problems between John Norman and Esther (and Jon and Barbra by extension) are caused by the fans and/or the press.

Also included in the script was a glimpse into Barbra's relationship with Elliott Gould, which, after all, was a real-life take on *A Star Is Born.* "I love you, Johnny," Esther tells John Norman, in a scene Barbra had played out with Elliott years before, "but it's not enough, is it?"

With the picture, Jon Peters also wanted to introduce the world to an all new Barbra; the Barbra *he* knew and loved, the *real* Barbra, the intimate Barbra, the sexy Barbra, the braless Barbra, the see-Barbra-in-love

Barbra. He promised to deliver a "beautiful, sensual Barbra—the Barbra I have experienced."

There would be no Fanny Brice wigs, no Bob Mackie costumes. Just Barbra in tight jeans, with gratuitous shots of her derriere. "Jon has a way of seeing me," she confided. "He knows me as a woman, as a sexual being, and I'm tired of being just Funny Girl, a self-deprecating waif."

Meanwhile, Peters was also concerned about the characterization of John Norman, who, after all, was largely based on himself. "[He's] a man I identify with greatly," Peters said. "It touches on the facts of my life—the street fighter and overachiever. The macho thing is very much me. I fought for what I believed in and was not above using violence."

Because he so strongly identified with the character, the film's ending was greatly disturbing to Peters. He didn't want John Norman to have to resort to suicide. It was, in Peters's view, cowardly and unmanly. If he had to die, Jon wanted the character's death to be an accidental one. It was an issue that would gnaw at Peters until the end, and it was one battle he would not, and could not, win. The story dictated that John Norman self-destruct, with the ultimate self-destruction being his own death. When he and his sports car go up in flames (off-camera) at the end of the picture, he is no longer just John Norman Howard, he is James Dean. The crash *may* have been accidental, but the end result was not.

Meanwhile, after feuding with Peters over, among other things, billing (Barbra didn't want his name with hers above the title), the actor who was to play John Norman, Kris Kristofferson, backed out of the production.

There was brief speculation that Jon himself would take over the part. "Can he sing?" everyone asked, aghast. "No," came the response. Peters argued that his voice could be dubbed, or that his inability to sing could somehow be finessed by the director.

The idea, however, was quickly rejected, but not before word was leaked to the gossip columnists, who had a field day with the perceived presumptuousness of Jon Peters. "It has become an impossible scene," a source on the production revealed to Marilyn Beck. "It's a terrible ego thing with Jon Peters."

After feuding with Peters on this and other matters, the director, Jerry Schatzberg, made *his* exit from the production. Perhaps predictably, Jon Peters then announced that *he* would take over the direction. Barbra, initially, liked the idea, or seemed to. In the ensuing months, however, she grew increasingly wary over the idea.

Meanwhile, problems with the script persisted. Jon fired Jonathan Axelrod, with whom he was no longer so friendly. According to Jon, Axelrod had just been acting as *his* screenwriting puppet. It was time, Peters declared, to hire a *real* writer. Enter the husband-and-wife writing team of Bob and Laurie Dillon. The former had recently completed scripting *The French Connection II.* Barbra, for one, was enthusiastic that a woman writer was to be involved.

The Dillons started work in January 1975, and they promptly discarded Axelrod's five months of labor. Instead, they looked to the 1937 script by Dorothy Parker, Alan Campbell, and Robert Carson as their starting point.

Barbra and Jon would be greatly disappointed in the Dillons' script, which was completed in April 1975. The search for a writer who could carry out their vision resumed. All told, *fourteen* writers would come and go at various times in the development of the project, including Jay Presson Allen, Buck Henry, Arthur Laurents, and Alvin Sargent.

Renée Taylor, with whom Barbra had worked nearly fifteen years before at the Bon Soir, was summoned to the Malibu beach house, along with her writing partner and husband, Joseph Bologna. Despite her unsatisfying experience with the Dillons, Barbra still thought that a male-female writing team would give the script the sexual-gender balance she wanted.

"Barbra cooked Chinese for us," Taylor recalls. "And she asked us to write a movie for her. A love story. She and Jon told us about an idea they had. I suggested that we do it another way. Barbra didn't like the way I suggested."

Before making *their* exit, the Bolognas attended Barbra's thirty-third birthday party. Hosted by Jon at the Malibu ranch, the party was catered by a Westwood bakery and featured a menu of Armenian delicacies. Attending along with the Bolognas were Alan and Marilyn Bergman, Diana Kind, and Ryan O'Neal, with his daughter, Tatum, aged twelve, in tow. The precocious Tatum raised a few eyebrows at the party by dressing up for the occasion in a pair of towering high heels.

In June, her divorce final, Lesley Ann Peters again became Lesley Ann Warren. Her settlement gave her physical custody of their son, Christopher (officially, Jon shared joint custody), their house in Encino, as well as all of its contents, their 1970 Mercedes-Benz, and, $1,000 a month in alimony until January 1, 1983. Jon was also required to pay child support of $400 a month until Chris turned twenty-one. And he was obligated to pay for all of his son's schooling and, when needed, his medical and dental care. In addition, he was ordered to take out a life insurance policy in the amount of $100,000, naming Lesley Ann and Christopher as the sole beneficiaries. Later, when asked to describe her relationship with Barbra, Lesley Ann replied, "It's very fragile. I think she's a marvelous lady, but she has reason to be careful of the woman Jon was married to for six years."

As part of the publicity campaign for *Funny Lady,* Barbra was scheduled to appear on "The Tonight Show Starring Johnny Carson" on Wednesday, July 9, 1975. NBC publicized her appearance for a week, as it was to be Barbra's first appearance on the show, or on any television talk show, for that matter, since 1963, when she had been a struggling singer and Carson, giving her a break, had put her on *seven* times in five months.

A week before the show, Marty Erlichman (who was still, at that point, wrestling with Jon Peters over the management of Barbra's career), called the show's producer, Freddie DeCordova. The following is a transcript of the conversation, as recalled by DeCordova:

MARTY: She's worried about the lighting.
FREDDIE: I'll put on a special lighting man just for her.
MARTY: Can she come and see it?
FREDDIE: Yes.
MARTY: She wants a special makeup man and hairdresser.
FREDDIE: Okay.

The day before the show, however, Barbra's representatives informed DeCordova that she would *not* show up as scheduled. Upon being told, Carson was furious. On Tuesday night's show, he announced to his viewers, "I was informed prior to going on the air that we'll have a cancellation tomorrow night. Barbra Streisand will *not* be with us. We don't know why. Nobody has been able to reach her."

He added, "Although she doesn't owe the show anything in particular, we thought it only fair to tell you, so when you tune in, you don't get mad at us. I would rather you get mad at *her.* Streisand will not be here Wednesday night—nor will she be here in the future."

Carson's ban on Barbra was more than temporary tough talk, as the years would prove. It was a grudge he would carry over into his nightclub act in Las Vegas. Onstage at Caesars Palace, Carson quipped, "I was out in the alley playing Frisbee . . . with Barbra Streisand records."

Back at the Malibu ranch, it was decided that Jon Peters would *not* direct *A Star Is Born* after all. When asked why he agreed to be removed from the position, Peters was quoted as saying, "How could I direct her and keep our relationship? I had to decide which was more important, our love or the movie."

As much as she loved him, Barbra did not want, or *trust,* Jon in the position. He was, however, bequeathed a consolation prize: as *Star* continued to crawl through preproduction, he was hired to produce *The Life and Times of Bruce Lee* for Barbra's company, First Artists. Barbra expressed her support by showing up at the Hollywood auditions for the picture, where she was taught a few martial arts moves by Chuck Norris.

Meanwhile, due to legal reasons, the start date on *Star* had to take place on or before January 2, 1976, and, as of July 1975, the picture was still without a director, a writer, and a costar.

With the tension mounting, Barbra and Jon approached a series of directors to take over the project. When asked why *she* didn't grab the directorial reins herself, aspiring director Streisand is said to have responded, "I couldn't just take over as director from Jon, could I? But I couldn't let Jon direct; can you imagine Jon Peters directing?"

Among the directors approached to replace Peters were Bob Fosse, Arthur Hiller, Hal Ashby, Sidney Lumet, and Robert Altman, all of whom turned it down. Altman, who had a major hit on his hands with *Nashville,* released that June, had not forgiven Barbra for her behavior during the screening of one of his pictures. Barbra claims that she had walked out on the screening because the picture was too violent. Altman claims that he *threw* Barbra out of the screening because she was self-absorbed and a "rude bitch."

On August 4, 1975, a surprising announcement came out of the First Artists/Warner Brothers camp: Frank Pierson, aged thirty, had taken over as the writer *and* director of A Star Is Born. Pierson was the screenwriter of the superb *Dog Day Afternoon,* which would be released that October. His previous writing credits included *Cat Ballou* (1965) and *Cool Hand Luke* (1967). His sole feature-directing credit to that point had been an unsuccessful 1970 British picture, *The Looking Glass War.*

Barbra and Jon would later claim their agreement with Pierson called for collaboration; that is, Pierson, as director, would carry out, almost puppetlike, *their* vision of their picture. If true, it's easy to understand why they agreed to sign him. After all, if one of them had *officially* directed, they, as a team, would have been the sole target of all the criticism directed at the picture. Pierson offered them not only a "collaborator" but a front and, if necessary, a potential scapegoat.

Embarking on the project, Pierson announced that he had "sixty pounds of unproducible script" on his hands. He discarded the script by the Dillons and the several drafts by Axelrod and went back to the one he deemed best, the third draft by Dunne and Didion. It had great rock and roll ambience, and a well-developed leading male role in John Norman Howard. What it lacked, however, as Barbra was quick to point out, was a strong love story, and a female role befitting a star of her stature.

Pierson became closely acquainted with the insecurities of his star. At one point, Barbra confronted him. "I don't feel you really want to love me. All my directors have wanted to make me beautiful." She informed him that he was to shoot her from the left, except in comic situations, when it was okay to shoot her from the right. She further instructed that she be shot with a lot of backlight. In fact, Pierson ended up shooting her with *so* much backlight in the picture that Barbra often seems ethereal, even angelic, when she is supposed to be playing a natural, *earthy* young woman.

With Pierson on board, Barbra and Jon concentrated their considerable energies on casting the part of John Norman Howard. They were looking for a male performer who could sing, act, and look appropriately ravaged, while also managing to cause female hearts to flutter. Their other primary prerequisite was that the actor be able to look at Barbra with love in his eyes. Earlier, Barbra had toyed with the idea of Brando, then fifty-one, playing the part. She had always wanted to work with her idol, and there *was* something in his persona that seemed suitably wasted.

Mick Jagger was another possibility, but Barbra feared that he might blow her off the screen in the performance sequences. He was too powerful, too dynamic, to be believed as a rock and roll has-been. Moreover, aesthetically, Barbra didn't like the way they looked together.

In April 1975, Barbra and Jon had flown to Las Vegas to meet with Elvis Presley, who was performing at the time at the Las Vegas Hilton. Barbra told him that she always thought he had been underrated as an actor and that *Star* was his chance to prove her right.

Over the succeeding months, Elvis deliberated over the idea, but in the end he declined. In his entire film career, only once had he shared the screen with a formidable female musical star: Ann-Margret in *Viva Las Vegas* (1964). She stole the picture, and Elvis vowed never to do it again.

And so Barbra and Jon returned to Kris Kristofferson. This time, they offered him billing above the title, and, to their great relief, he accepted.

After all, he was the *perfect* John Norman Howard. Like the character, he knew a little something about drinking, drugs, and self-destructive behavior in general. Once, Kristofferson told his entire audience to "jack off." Furthermore, he looked believable with Barbra, and as a washed-out rock and roll singer.

Kristofferson had also lived with, and had an affair with, Janis Joplin, the godmother of self-destructive rock and roll artists everywhere. While Jon Peters saw himself in the character of John Norman Howard, Kristofferson saw a fusion of Janis Joplin and Jimi Hendrix. Ironically, Kristofferson had also dated Carly Simon, who was the initial coinspiration for the project. He had *also* dated Barbra Streisand, after her breakup with Elliott Gould, much to the jealousy and dismay of Jon Peters. Later, when shooting the film's bathtub scene—which, by the way, seems inadvertently more religious than sexual, given the abundant supply of burning candles—Kris slid into the tub and waited for Barbra—completely naked. When Peters found out, he insisted that Kris put on a flesh-colored bathing suit.

Kristofferson's signing was announced on September 19, 1975. "He will be one of the major stars in movies after this film," predicted Jon Peters, "because the chemistry between Barbra and Kris is absolute magic, both musically and dramatically."

In March 1975, replacing Jack Nitzche *(The Exorcist),* who had replaced record producer Richard Perry, Rupert Holmes was signed as the film's musical director. Previously, he had worked on a couple of songs for Barbra's *Lazy Afternoon* album, on which their relationship had been harmonious. Dazed by the continually changing *A Star Is Born* script, however, Holmes found himself floundering on the score. Finally, after composing a dozen or so songs, most of which Jon, in an outburst of rage, deemed unacceptable, Holmes returned to New York and never returned to the production.

It was now literally three months before shooting, and they still didn't have a score. What they *did* have was one song, "Queen Bee," derived from a conversation Holmes had with Barbra about a beekeeper, and one melody, "Everything," both written by Holmes. There was also a complex melody by Kenny Loggins, which later, with the lyrics of Alan and Marilyn Bergman, became "I Believe in Love."

The picture would include a collaboration between Barbra and Leon Russell entitled "Lost Inside of You." The number came about when Russell, who had met Barbra through Gary Busey, one of the actors in the cast, walked out of the bathroom of the Malibu ranch to find Barbra tinkering on the piano. Loving the melody she was playing (which she had written), Russell improvised a secondary melody and accompanying lyrics. Frank Pierson was so touched by the scene that he later wrote it into the picture.

Still looking for a new musical director, Barbra and Jon summoned Paul Williams to the ranch. "She had recorded a couple of my tunes before, but we had never met until *A Star Is Born*," Williams remembers. "She called me on the phone, but evidently, I wasn't listening. She only wanted *one* song for the end of the picture—a song like 'You and Me Against the World' [which Williams had written]. What *I* had heard, however, and I don't know if it was my own grandiosity or what, was that she wanted me to write *all* the songs for this movie.

"So I went out to meet with Barbra and Jon, and they sat there and just kind of looked at me, because I rambled on for about forty-five minutes, telling them my ideas for the whole score. They asked if they could be excused for a minute because they wanted to talk. So I left the room for a while. When I came back in, they said, 'You're not intimidated by this, are you?' And I said, 'No. No, I'm not. I'm a really good song-writer.' "

Barbra and Jon were impressed with the audacious arrogance of the diminutive Williams. "You've gotta understand," he says, nearly twenty years after that meeting, "I was prepared for such immense power that the way I handled it was by being as quirky and as aggressive as I imag-ined them to be."

Surprisingly, given Barbra's penchant for control, the contract Wil-liams signed to do the picture gave *him* final say over his material. In other words, no one, not even Barbra, could change a lyric without his consent. "The only person who got any latitude with that," Williams re-lates, "was Kris. There were little changes that he made in the melodies and in the lyrics, and I was fine with them. I have so much respect for him. I mean, *Kristofferson!*"

The relationship between the songwriter and his boss started out posi-tively enough, with Barbra telling him, "Whatever you need to be com-fortable to write—let me know."

Williams responded by telling her, "When I'm writing, wherever I'm at, I have to have white wine and macadamia nuts constantly at my fin-gertips." He had meant it as a joke. "The next time I went back to her house," Williams recalls with a smile, "there were these little bowls of macadamia nuts at every table, *everywhere*. She really bent over back-wards."

In retrospect, however, the working relationship was doomed from the start. After all, by the time Williams and Kenny Ascher entered the production, shooting on *A Star Is Born* was to begin in only *ten weeks*. Ten weeks to compose almost an entire motion picture musical score. It was an impossible schedule.

"Kenny and I would go off on our own and write stuff," Williams relates, "and then we'd go back to the house and play it for Barbra. I remember playing her the lyric for one of the tunes. I had the lyrics written down, and I had certain lines that were underlined because I hadn't finished them yet. Anyway, I'd sing her the entire lyric, and she'd say, 'There are two lines that can be better.' Now, she hadn't seen my paper, but they were the *same* two lines as the lines I had underlined and was going to change. Her response was immediate. She didn't have to sit with it. She *knew*. I almost always agreed with her choices on melody and lyric. The only thing we ever disagreed on was 'Morning glory and the midnight sun'—I don't think she ever got that one."

Meanwhile, the weeks raced by. Director Frank Pierson later quoted Williams as having told him, "How can I write when I have to talk with her all the time and nothing ever gets finished because before I finish the damn song she's already asking for changes?"

Today, Williams explains, "There was *so* little time. Every time the phone rang, it was Barbra, and she wanted to know how we were doing, and she wanted to have another meeting. And all of that was time that Kenny and I didn't have time to write. There *was* some tension [between us] about that."

Further aggravating the situation, Barbra would spend her weekends listening to boxes of albums, catching up on the latest sensations in the music industry. On the weekend of October 27, 1975, after Bruce Springsteen appeared simultaneously on the covers of *Time* and *Newsweek*, Barbra picked up a copy of Springsteen's *Born to Run*. That Monday, she told anyone who would listen, "We've gotta have more Springsteen!"

"It seemed like *every* Monday, after she spent the weekend with a bunch of albums, she'd come back with a new approach," Williams said.

Obviously, for Williams and Ascher, the constant changing of musical direction was exasperating, particularly given the lack of time. "One of the elements of working with Barbra was that there was *so* much direction," Williams explains. "There was *so* much input."

Sometimes, the input was appreciated. Recalling the first time he heard Barbra's composition of what became "Evergreen," Williams recalls, "She said, 'I want to play you this melody and see what you think. Maybe it's something we can use.' Because I had never heard anything she had written, there was a place in the small of my spine that went, 'Oh, God, *no!*' But she played this *wonderful* melody. And she was like a little girl. I've never seen her more charming. She was kind of shy. She had been taking guitar lessons, and she was watching her fingers to make sure that she got the chording right.

"This is the love melody!" Williams exclaimed when she finished. "This is it!"

In the succeeding weeks, Barbra continually asked Williams, "When are you gonna write *it?* When are you gonna write it?," meaning, of course, the lyrics to her melody.

Williams told her not to worry, that he already knew what he intended to do with the song. "I'm gonna call it 'Evergreen,' " he told her, "because when I listened to it I went, 'Love ageless and ever, ever green.' " He also told her that he wanted to concentrate on the rest of the score. " 'Evergreen' was the *last* thing that I wrote," Williams says, "and that *totally* pissed her off."

Meanwhile, as the deadline approached, the pressure began to wear on Paul Williams. "There were times that I cried," he recalls. "It was like, *'God,* what have I gotten myself into here? We're *never* gonna get this done.' "

Nerves frayed, Paul got into an argument with Jon Peters that turned physical. Reportedly, Williams was the one who threw a punch. Today, Williams allows only that "Jon and I had our differences. We got a little pushy-shovey. We wrestled around and knocked over some music stands." When asked what motivated the incident, he says, "It was something between Jon and me that we resolved. We were both acting like nine-year-olds, and now we're eleven, so we don't have to talk about it."

He adds, "I saw Jon the other day. It had been a long time. We threw our arms around each other and gave each other a big hug. The last time I saw him, we were screaming at each other."

After the confrontation with Jon Peters, Paul Williams returned to his house and unplugged the telephones. "I had a button that I had installed," Williams says, "that turned off the gates, the bell, and the phones. I *had* to get some silence to write. I think the last thing I said to them was, 'I'm gonna take my songs and go home.' "

For the next three days, sequestered in his home with Kenny Ascher, Paul Williams proceeded to write the music for *A Star Is Born*. Meanwhile, Barbra and Jon panicked. After all, they did not know what was going on. They could not be sure whether Paul had walked off the picture or was merely cooling off. "When we saw them again," Williams recalls, "everything was done."

He adds, "I remember thinking when it was all over that I would never put myself in that kind of bind again. And I don't know if that meant that I'd never work with Streisand again, or it meant that I'd never work in that kind of time frame again. The relief of having it behind me was immense. Doing that movie was one of the hardest things I've ever done in my life."

When asked to describe what Barbra had been like through the process, Williams says, "I think she expects everybody to be as good as she is. I used to tell a joke about how Barbra was working on a *tree*—you know, only God and Barbra Streisand can *make* a tree. She never stopped being Barbra. The Barbra who wanted it, and wanted it right, and wanted it *now*."

Williams also remembers, "She went out of her way to make me comfortable. She treated me really well . . . better than I treated her."

Twenty-nine

The Final Cut

With a six-million-dollar budget, a sixty-day shooting schedule, a producer and an executive producer who had never before produced, and a director with only one feature film to his credit, *A Star Is Born* started production on February 2, 1976.*

For Barbra, the production of the picture gave her the chance to explore the relationships between men and women in general, and her relationship with Jon in particular. The film had come to have an inordinate amount of importance in their personal lives as a couple. If it failed, it would mean not only public vilification but also, in all likelihood, the demise of their relationship. As Frank Pierson quotes Barbra as saying, "If this film goes down the drain, it's all over for Jon and me."

As shooting progressed, Barbra and Jon continued to insert their conversations, their interactions, and even their *bodily fluids* into the script. "Jon and I had a spitting fight the other night," Barbra related during the shoot. "Well, not a fight, but we were in bed, and we were kind of drooling all over each other. And you know, when you're in love, that's a very intimate thing." She added, proudly, "That's in the movie, too."

Some of their furniture and decorative pieces from their Malibu ranch also found a new, albeit temporary, home on the set. Barbra even had the skylights and stained-glass butterfly on the ceiling of their own bedroom duplicated for the movie. She *also* had cinematographer Robert Surtees try to emulate the lighting in their living room.

Perhaps still trying to justify the remake—to herself if no one else— Barbra became convinced that the movie offered her a chance to say

*The mandatory start date of January 2 was legally extended by one month.

something about sexism and add something to the cause of feminism. For her, the story about a male rock and roll singer in decline had became a story about a woman confronting a male society, about a woman seizing her own power. The Paul Williams–Kenny Ascher song "The Woman in the Moon" was particularly significant in this regard. "I'm for women's lib," she said at the time. "Who know's *who's* up there? Why does it always have to be referred to as 'The Man in the Moon?' "

The picture was shot with numerous references to this kind of well-intentioned, if obvious, role reversal. For example, in the bed scene with Kristofferson, Barbra made a point of it to be the one shown taking *her* pants off first. She couldn't understand why movies had always depicted the man as being the first to disrobe. While taking off her belt when shooting the scene, Barbra envisioned herself as the conquering seductress, a female Clint Eastwood. This too came from her relationship with Jon Peters. It was in his bed that she had learned to become sexually aggressive.

In another scene, it was also important to Barbra that *Esther* be the one to propose marriage to John Norman, and that she be costumed in a man's suit at the time. Again, the role reversal was well-intentioned, if obvious.

More significantly, Barbra insisted that Esther *not* offer to end her career to appease John Norman's faltering ego, as had been the case in the previous versions. In addition, she refused to allow Esther to give up her own name at the conclusion of the picture, as was also done in previous versions. Instead, at the finale, and with perfect, politically correct symbolism (and fifteen years before Hillary Rodham Clinton entered the national consciousness), she renames herself Esther Hoffman *Howard.*

Barbra's primary challenge was to enter and assimilate into the alien milieu of rock and roll. During preproduction discussions, Barbra asked Kristofferson if he was ready to stretch as an actor. He responded, "Are *you* ready to *get down?* I'll stretch as far as you get down."

In the film's centerpiece concert sequence at Sun Devil Stadium in Arizona, Barbra addressed the young, beer-drinking, pot-smoking audience of fifty-five thousand with, "Hey, you *motherfuckers!* Are you having a good time?" She was wearing her new, Jon Peters-designed Afro-like hairdo ("Growing up, I always wanted to have curls. Now I have them"), which everyone, including her mother, told her made her look years younger. She then proceeded to inform the crowd that in the picture they were shooting, she would talk dirty *and* smoke grass, prompting, as if on cue, cheers of approval.

At another point during the filming, the crowd's attention was fixated on Barbra, standing on the side of the stage, when it was supposed to be riveted on Kris Kristofferson's double, who was performing motorcycle stunts for the benefit of the churning cameras. Reprimanding the crowd, whose job it was to act as dutiful extras (even though they had each paid $3.50 for admittance), Barbra marched up to the microphone. "You *can't* look at me," she wailed, "You're all supposed to look at the motorcycle. What? You wanna look at me? *Fuck you!*"

The day before the shooting of the concert sequence, in the blistering 100-degree desert heat, Barbra, Kris, and Jon conducted a mass press conference in the middle of the aptly named Sun Devil Stadium. Lunch was catered on the fifty-yard line, and the trio talked with the various members of the press. It wasn't something Barbra *wanted* to do, of course, it was something she did to appease the First Artists and Warners money people back in Hollywood.

The invited press, 150 strong, devoured the free food, drank the free drinks, and listened to the inane promotional quotes that were tossed in their direction. Some were offended by the "I use you, you use me" exploitation that was going on. Others simply accepted the assignment as a three-day, all-expenses-paid vacation. *None* of them expected a spectacular, pyrotechnic display of star-studded temperament, which was, to their voyeuristic delight, exactly what they got.

During rehearsals, Barbra and Kristofferson became engaged in an argument on the stage. Unbeknownst to them, the technicians were checking sound levels at the time, the microphones were on, and their four-letter-word expletives were being broadcast over the stadium sound system. Wiping the sweat from their brows, the visiting scribes furiously scribbled down the exchange for publication and posterity. The subsequent reports revealed a glimpse into the *real* relationships between personalities under fire.

Barbra told Kristofferson how to read one of his lines. Infuriated by what he saw as her repeated breach of protocol, Kristofferson barked, "*Who's* the director?!" which he followed with a barrage of insults.

"Look, you're not doing what I tell you to do," Barbra continued, undeterred. "Listen to me when I talk to you, goddamnit!"

"Fuck off!" Kristofferson replied. "I'll be goddamned if I listen to anything more from you!"

At that point, Jon Peters entered the fray, facing off with Kristofferson. "You owe my lady an apology," he said, half demanding, half threatening. The two pugilists, however, did not come to blows. Instead they promised to postpone their showdown until after the picture's completion. The producer, after all, could not very well mess up the face of his star. At the same time, the star could not very well incapacitate the man who was signing his weekly paychecks.

That day, on the Sun Devil stage, it was Kristofferson who had the last word. "If I need any shit from you," he informed his producer, "I'll squeeze your head!"

It wasn't the first major confrontation between Streisand and Kristofferson. During rehearsals, the two had clashed over the band Kristofferson wanted to use for the picture. Kris was passionate about using members of his own band. Barbra, however, deemed that they were not rock and roll enough. She wanted a tougher, more Springsteen-like sound. Furthermore, Kristofferson objected to the way he and the band were being costumed. Barbra had decided not to hire a costume designer for the picture and had selected the clothes herself.

"Barbra, you are trying to dress us like something that was either dead a long time ago or is dying a slow death in a Vegas lounge," he told her. "I'm not rock and roll, but *that* look sure as hell ain't!"

The argument continued until Kristofferson finally stalked off, shouting, "I ain't trusting my career to the judgment of a Vegas singer and a hairdresser!"

For Kristofferson, it was a difficult shoot, made barely tolerable by downing tequila and beer chasers for breakfast. In addition to his conflicts with Barbra and Jon Peters, he resented Frank Pierson for tolerating what he perceived to be Barbra's directorial interference.

Referring to the mixed signals he was getting from the film's two, sometimes dueling, directors, Kristofferson mused, "Barbra and Frank make me feel like a jackass between two stacks of hay. I don't know which one to go for."

Asked to describe his costar, Kristofferson said, "I'm scared to death of her. The best one-word description of Barbra would be 'formidable.'"

As for the production itself, he commented, "It's the hardest thing I've been through since I jumped out of planes in ranger school." He added that he was writing a song about the experience, entitled "It's Never Gonna Be the Same Again." When asked *what* was never gonna be the same again, Kristofferson replied, "My fucking *head!*"

The company was scheduled to shoot in Arizona for three weeks. Despite the relatively short duration of their stay, Barbra had the furniture moved out of her suite at the Ramada Inn in Tempe and had her own furniture and personal belongings trucked in from Beverly Hills.

Traveling separately, but part of the exodus nonetheless, was nine-year-old Jason Gould. Miserable at the Malibu ranch, Jason, over the telephone, talked his mother into allowing him to join her in Arizona. He was, after all, fascinated by filmmaking. He was six at the time he had directed his first home movie. For one of his films, he coerced his father into playing one of the two leads. Elliott was paid $121 for nine weeks of work. Upon signing their agreement, Elliott gave his son a gift. "I gave him a cigar," the proud father said, "and he knows when we smoke cigars it's business." By the time he was nine, Jason was collaborating on eight-millimeter monster pictures with his seven-year-old friend, and sort-of stepbrother, Christopher Peters.

Meanwhile, relations between Barbra and Frank Pierson grew increasingly strained. He had, as far as she was concerned, breached the unofficial terms of his contract by not strictly adhering to her vision of the film. Streisand and Peters charged that Pierson tried to pacify them by agreeing to do things their way and then going off and doing them the way *he* wanted. Distrusting, suspicious, and unconvinced of his ability, Barbra was constantly peering over Pierson's shoulder, watching his every move, questioning his every directorial decision.

"Listen," she warily told him at one point, "where are the close-ups? There are never any close-ups in this picture. When I worked with Willie Wyler, we had close-ups in every scene."

"When I worked with Willie Wyler . . ." was a common refrain heard by Streisand's directors.

The editor of *A Star Is Born* was Peter Zinner, who had worked on Francis Ford Coppola's tandem masterpieces *The Godfather* (1972) and *The Godfather Part II* (1974), and who would later win an Oscar for Michael Cimino's *The Deer Hunter* (1978). Zinner, who was editing *Star* from a motel room as it was being shot, recalls, "Frank is a very nice guy. Very easygoing. But I know that Barbra was very frustrated. She talked to me about her frustrations. She was upset about the fact that she was not really in control, and my interpretation was that she felt she could do better."

Barbra and Jon had wanted to shoot the desert oasis sequence at their Malibu ranch. Instead, Pierson selected a location in Tucson. In the scene, Barbra wanted to be covered in mud. Pierson objected to the idea, saying that it would be tacky, like "female mud wrestling," and that it didn't belong in the picture. Barbra insisted, however, and prevailed. But when it came time to shoot the scene, someone in the crew replaced the mud with excrement, which was then smeared all over Barbra's white pantsuit. When she objected to the odor, someone told her that it was a preservative which had been mixed into the mud. She *knew* better. To her credit, Barbra took the incident as a joke, or tried to, and laughed it off.

On or around April 15, 1976, the *A Star Is Born* company returned to Los Angeles. A few days later, shortly after midnight, on Lankershim Boulevard in the San Fernando Valley, Esther Hoffman proposed marriage to John Norman Howard, and, without any major physical harm done to the various feuding factions, and to the great relief of everyone involved, the picture wrapped production.

First Artists took out a two-page advertisement in the Hollywood trade papers congratulating Jon Peters for completing *A Star Is Born* "on schedule, on budget and on target—a sure winner!" A combination wrap party and Barbra's thirty-fourth birthday party was thrown at the Mandarin, an expensive Chinese restaurant in Beverly Hills. Four hundred people attended.

But for some, the work was just beginning.

Frank Pierson's contract gave him six weeks to assemble his "director's cut" of the picture. The final cut, however, belonged to Barbra. "She and Frank did not part very well," recalls Peter Zinner. "I knew that she was trying to get rid of Frank and do her own thing. She *couldn't wait* to get her hands on the picture."

"She's very hungry for control," Zinner continues. "She was so good in her field, which was music, that it was almost automatic that she wanted to extend herself. She talked about wanting to direct. She told me about the story of *Yentl.* This picture [*Star*] was what really whetted her appetite for directing. Eventually, she started to feel, 'Why do I need a director? I'll do it myself.' "

After Pierson screened his cut for her, Jon, and a few special guests, Barbra kissed Pierson good night—and goodbye. She spun around on her heels and had a $500,000 editing facility installed at the Malibu ranch. She hired a staff of editors, headed by Peter Zinner, who would, in the succeeding months, work twelve- to fourteen-hour hour days.

"I was cutting in the pool house," Zinner recalls. "I remember that Barbra had a Polish cook, and the woman's husband was the gardener. She cooked meals for us. I know that I gained a lot of weight. I was there *forever.*"

When asked what Barbra wanted to change in Pierson's version, Zinner says, "Primarily, she felt that her character needed more time on the screen. She felt that some of the sequences were too heavy with Kristofferson. I would say that she made major changes, not so much with the story line, but as far as the characters were concerned. Her character became much more pertinent."

When asked to describe the experience of working with Streisand, Zinner is contemplative. "I liked Barbra very much. She's a magnificent specimen of professionalism. *But,*" he adds, "she *is* difficult."

When asked to define "difficult," Zinner elaborates, "She's difficult because she changes her mind. She was never satisfied. We were running short on time and had to get the stuff ready for sound effects and music. When we were getting down to the final cut, Friday would come around and I would run the reel with her and she would say, "Okay, that's *it!*" And I would ask her, 'Are you sure, Barbra?' And she would say, 'I'm sure.' So I'd say, 'Okay, let's shake hands. *No more changes.*' And we'd shake hands.

"And then, Monday morning comes along," Zinner says, able to laugh about the experience seventeen years later, "and she says, 'You know, Peter, there's just one little thing. . . .' "

Just as she had spent her weekends listening to record albums, Barbra now spent her weekends rescreening the previous week's edit. She had apparently learned how to operate the KEM editing equipment, which allowed her to screen, fast-forward, rewind, and freeze-frame the footage. She did *not,* rumors aside, do any of the editing herself. "God knows," Zinner says, "I would have walked out!"

Barbra invited friends over on the weekends to view the edited footage. Among the regulars who came and offered their appraisals were Alan and Marilyn Bergman, Cis Corman, and Sue Mengers. "Her friends influenced her, I think, quite a great deal," Zinner says, "because every time Monday would come around, she'd say, 'There's just one more thing I'd like to do.' And I'd say, 'But we *discussed* that.' And she'd say, 'Well, I know, *but . . .*' She would say that she wanted it changed, so, of course, I had to change it. Our Friday handshake became almost like a joke."

Particularly problematic was the editing of Barbra's seven-and-a-half-minute concert sequence which provides the picture with its finale.

The sequence itself was the inspiration of Paul Williams and Kenny Ascher. Barbra had wanted *one* song, along the lines of "You and Me Against the World." It turned, of course, into something much more.

"Kenny and I both loved the remake of *A Star Is Born* with Judy Garland," Paul Williams relates. " 'With One More Look at You' was totally inspired by James Mason saying to Judy Garland, 'I just want to take another look at you.' I once told James Mason that, and he said, 'Oh, really. I don't even remember that I said that.'

"When Kenny and I wrote 'With One More Look at You,' we had already written 'Watch Closely Now' for Kris," Williams explains, "and it *never* occurred to us to put them together. But we were sitting there and playing, 'I want one more look at you . . .' and all of a sudden, we looked at each other and went, 'Are you watching me now . . .' And I went, 'Oh, *fuck!*' It worked together. It was perfect. It gave her a chance to reprise *his* song! Barbra loved it. I remember it being a home run with her. She actually said"—Williams laughs—" 'That's a nice idea.' "

In postproduction, Barbra had a difficult time deciding how the number should be edited. Frank Pierson had chosen to present it with multiple cuts. Barbra, however, wanted the entire sequence intact, without a single cut. As the days passed, however, she vacillated back and forth. Cut. Uncut. Cut. Uncut . . .

"It was her big number," recalls Peter Zinner. "There were seven or eight cameras on that goddamned thing. We had two previews of the picture to decide which ending to use. The previews were held on the same day in Arizona. In the afternoon, we had the ending with multiple cuts, and in the evening, we had her ending, the one-shot. I felt that the edited version was stronger. The other one was too long. It went overboard. Seven and a half minutes is too much of a load for one person, no matter how good you are.

"Afterwards, we waited for the preview cards," Zinner continues. "Everybody was kind of anxious to see which ending played better. When it was all over, Barbra said, 'Well, Peter, I guess you won.' "

But after the response at the previews changed her mind, Barbra would *again* change her mind and decide to go with her original choice of the unedited version: seven and a half minutes of pure, unadulterated Streisand. It was a risky thing to do, considering the short attention span of most young filmgoers, at whom the picture was to be targeted. As Peter Zinner puts it, "She has a lot of guts, you know?"

Asked to compare Streisand with Francis Ford Coppola, Zinner says, "Francis has a different approach altogether. But as far as prima donnas are concerned, he is one too, of course. And the fact is that he changed a *great* deal from the first *Godfather* to the second. After the huge success of the first, he was quite different—a little more difficult to work with, and a little less accessible. I don't think he likes people around him that have a strong personality. Barbra is the same way. But I didn't feel it as much with her as I did with Francis on the second *Godfather.*

"I admired her a great deal," Zinner concludes. "She's really quite sensitive. She's a remarkable, unique person. Very gifted. She's neurotic, in a way, but of course we all are to a certain extent."

When asked if he would work with her again, Zinner is clear. "Absolutely. But I think she probably ties me in with Frank [Pierson]."

During the summer of 1976, while Barbra was consumed with the editing of her picture, Jason was spending more time with his father. Elliott took Jason on vacation with him to Holland and then London, which was the first concentrated period of time the two had spent alone together in years.

Back in Malibu, when the two returned, Barbra took a break and hosted a little Labor Day party. Diana Kind arrived at the house carrying some spinach pancakes and a sponge cake that she had baked for Barbra. She was pleased to have the opportunity to see Jason. Over the years, Diana was frustrated by her repeatedly thwarted attempts to spend time with her grandson.

"Sometimes these maids don't even let you go upstairs," she said. " 'Oh, you will disturb this, you will disturb that, it is his bathing time, this is suppertime,' you know. You feel like hitting them in the head. But you can't cross them either, when they are adamant about things."

Diana was also pleased to see that Jason was spending more time with his father. That night, as the party fizzled, Elliott took Jason with him to see a baseball game.

Barbra, meanwhile, worked feverishly with Peter Zinner on her picture. Her first cut ran three and a half hours. She eventually whittled it down to an acceptable 140-minute length. "She's in there scoring and looping and dubbing and doing," Jon Peters reported in early November. "Frank Pierson hasn't been around for two or three months, but Barbra's still working sixteen hours a day, seven days a week on this film."

Before severing ties with Pierson, Barbra reportedly confronted him and asked that he share his director's credit with her. He refused. She would have to content herself with her acknowledged (and *deserved,* contrary to rumor) credits of executive producer, star, and contributing composer. She would also be credited on-screen with providing the "musical concepts" for the picture, and the clothes from her closet.

Promotional photographs, in preparation for the film's release, were taken by famed photographer Francesco Scavullo. During the session, perhaps still in her Esther Hoffman Howard character, Barbra was the sexual aggressor with the shirtless Kristofferson. Unhappy with the way things were going, Scavullo took Kristofferson into the back of the studio and told him that he had to become more aggressive with Barbra, that he had to "show her who the man was."

Barbra strained to hear their whispered conversation. When they returned, ready to resume work, Barbra informed the pair, "I heard everything you said—and may the best *man* win!"

Two major publicity events were arranged to promote the film's release. On December 16, Barbra was scheduled to have her handprints and footprints immortalized in cement in the forecourt of the famed Mann's Chinese Theater. At the same time, she was to get her star on the Hollywood Walk of Fame. It was to be the first time in Hollywood history that a star would be presented with both honors at the same time. At the last minute, however, Barbra inexplicably canceled her appearance.

She did not cancel the second event, but she approached it with great trepidation. Given that she was no longer welcome on the Carson show, which was then *the* promotional venue for discerning top-ranking stars, Barbra was convinced by Sue Mengers to do an interview with Barbara Walters. It was for the very first of Walters's now famous television interview specials. Jimmy and Roslyn Carter were to be the other interviewees on the show. Before lending her participation, Barbra demanded—and got—final cut. That very night, after the interview was taped at the Malibu ranch, the footage was replayed for Barbra's approval. Watching it with her on the sofa were Jon Peters, Sue Mengers, and Marty Erlichman (yet to be totally ostracized from Barbra's inner circle), each offering their own critical assessment.

After Barbra's appearance aired on December 14, Barbara Walters vowed never again to give *any* interviewee control over the material. "I did two interviews with Streisand," Walters would later say. "The first time, I nearly went out of my mind. By the second time, I knew her better and I realized there would be a phone call almost every day until the show aired, because she's such a perfectionist. She will worry, literally, about whether these flowers should look like this or whether the buds should be opened."

Warner Brothers had to pry the final cut of *A Star Is Born* out of Barbra's hands. As the finished picture was shipped to movie theaters all over the country, Barbra, like the mother sending her child out into the world for the first time, wrote an accompanying letter to the theater owners. If she could have been there to run the projectors at every theater in every city, she would have. She instructed them on how to care for her picture. "In setting your usual level of sound," she wrote, "please make sure that Reel 1 and Reel 2 are allowed to play *as loud as possible.*" She added, "The color is also at its best at 14½-foot candlepower...."

With her reputation, an enormous sum of money (Barwood Productions was a principal financial backer), and her relationship with Jon Peters all hanging in the balance, Barbra attended the premiere of *A Star Is Born* in Westwood, California, on December 18, 1976.

She was terrified, uncertain whether she had accomplished what she had set out to do. Instead of joining Kristofferson on the red-carpeted walkway which spanned the short distance between the theater and the postscreening party at Dillon's discotheque, Barbra had a limousine drive her to a back entrance of the club. Once there, she was escorted to her own private party, which was held on an entirely separate floor.

The thousands of fans who had congregated outside of the theater, hoping to get a glimpse of their idol, went home disappointed. Meanwhile, at the party, many of the invited guests who had paid a good deal of money for their chance to hobnob with Streisand, seethed when told that *her* party, on *her* floor, was restricted territory. Still, they milled about, chomping on Chinese finger food in their formal disco finery. The invitations had called for them to wear all white, so that the evening's attention could be focused on Barbra, who wore all black. It is ironic, of course, that the star who wanted to be left alone also wanted to stand out. Amusingly, one of the guests who ignored the dress code was the seventy-four-year-old William Wyler. "I don't have a white suit," said Wyler when asked the reason for his rebellion, "but my *underwear* is white."

A Star Is Born would become the biggest-grossing picture of Barba's career. Most of the reviews, however, were scathing. Lambasted, in particular, was Barbra's questionable attempt at passing herself off as a rock singer.

Influential critic Pauline Kael, who had been an ardent Streisand supporter in the past, wrote, "Streisand has got herself into too many false positions: her singing isn't rock, as it's meant to be, but show-biz pop, and we're acutely aware of the Broadway–Las Vegas intonations. The director and the writers, those credited and those uncredited, must be partly responsible, but the sinking feeling one gets from the picture relates largely to her. One is never really comfortable with her, because even when she's singing she isn't fully involved in the music; she's trying to manage our responses."

Using a little profanity, Barbra had been able to momentarily fool fifty-five thousand people at Sun Devil Stadium, but with the close eye of the camera, she was not able to "get down" without the attempt being shown for what it was: a glaring contrivance.

When asked about the criticism over the attempt to turn Streisand into a rock and roll singer, Paul Williams today acknowledges, "We *didn't* write rock and roll for her. Kristofferson was the rocker in the movie. I mean, 'Watch Closely Now' is pure, hard-core rock and roll. I think for Kenny Ascher and I, two middle-aged guys who write songs like 'You and Me Against the World,' we did pretty good. If we had been having this conversation ten years ago," Williams says about the music he wrote for Barbra in the picture, "I probably would have been a lot more defensive about that. I probably would have said, 'It *was* rock and roll!' But I look at it now, and, clearly, it wasn't. I'm *not* a rock and roll writer."

Despite the largely negative critical response, *A Star Is Born* won three Golden Globe awards: Best Picture (Musical/Comedy), Best Actress (Musical/Comedy), and Best Song. Barbra was also named the Top Female Box-Office Star by the Quigley Poll for the fifth consecutive year (1972–76).

In the annual Oscar balloting, however, the picture was totally overlooked in what is generally considered to be the "major" categories. Still, it did receive nominations in the cinematography, sound, and scoring categories. It also received a Best Song nomination for "Evergreen."

Released as a single, "Evergreen" entered the *Billboard* pop chart on January 8, 1977, and bolted to the number one position, where it remained for three weeks. It was, to that date, only the fourth Streisand single to make the *Billboard* top thirty. It was her second number one, and her second single to go gold. Meanwhile, the film's soundtrack proved a smash. With a list price of $8.98, it was then the highest sum ever charged for a pop recording. Nevertheless, it entered the *Billboard* top forty on December 25, 1976, the week after the film's release, and went to number one, where it remained for *six* weeks. It was Barbra's biggest-selling album to date.

With the only remote competition coming from Bill Conti's "Gonna Fly Now" from *Rocky,* "Evergreen" was the favorite to win the Best Song Oscar. In contrast to the situation a few years before with "The Way We Were," Barbra agreed to sing the nominated song on the show. She was introduced by Jane Fonda, who reported, "This is the first time an executive producer has ever been asked to *sing!*'"

Following Barbra's performance, and prior to announcing the winner, Neil Diamond took a moment for some personal commentary. "Before I mention a winner, about three weeks ago I was talking to Barbra, and I said, 'I love your song so much that no matter who wins, I'm gonna read your name.' But I have to cancel out on that, Barbra. So if I call your name out, you actually won. And if I don't call your name out, you wrote a fantastic song [the] first time out. We'll see."

After opening the winning envelope, Diamond smiled and then proclaimed, "The winner is . . . 'Evergreen'!"

"In my wildest dreams," Barbra said in accepting the award, and with obvious sincerity, "I never thought I would win an Oscar for writing a song."

She was accompanied on the stage by Paul Williams, who must have felt diminished by Neil Diamond's commentary. "I remember going up [to the podium]," Williams says, "and I was gonna make a comment about, 'Isn't it nice they gave *me* one too,' but I kept my mouth shut about that, I think." What Williams *did* say was, "I was going to thank all the little people, then I remembered I *am* the little people."

"I was far from sober," Williams candidly recalls. "My guess is that I was *whacked* that night. I certainly was before the night was over. I went to all of the parties. And then I went home and got into the Jacuzzi with a bottle of Dom Perignon, and probably a lot of cocaine, and I stayed there for a bunch of hours."

Williams's comment about winning the Oscar: "It was your basic Midwestern dream come true, you know?"

When asked if there was any joint post-Oscar celebration between himself and Barbra, Williams replies simply, "No."

Today, after spending four years in drug and alcohol abuse recovery programs, Paul Williams is reflective about his experience on *A Star Is Born* in general, and his relationship with Barbra in particular.

"Recovery is a process," he explains, "not an event. But all of a sudden, there was a big flag waving in front of me that said, 'You know what? You need to look at the whole experience of working with Barbara Streisand a little differently.'

"I saw how much of it [the experience] was about me being afraid of living up to what was expected of me. And I responded like most good drunks do. I had another drink, another toot, because I'm also a recovering cocaine addict. I fought my own fear with grandiosity. And it occurred to me that I hadn't been fair to her."

Further explaining his contriteness, Williams cites something he had said at the 1977 Grammy Awards ceremony. "Evergreen" was nominated in four categories. Barbra would win for Best Female Pop Vocal (her fourth win in the category, the last time having been in 1965), and she and Paul Williams were named for having written the best song of the year (in a tie with Joe Brooks, who wrote the Debby Boone hit "You Light Up My Life").

"When we won the Grammy," Williams recalls, "I said, 'I want to thank Barbra for writing a beautiful melody, and Dr. Jack Wallstader for the valium that got me through the whole experience.' The message was that I had to have valium to deal with Barbra Streisand. *That,*" says Williams, "was really unkind."

With time, objectivity, perspective, and not to mention sobriety to help sharpen his insight, Paul Williams has a kinder, gentler view on his experience with Streisand. "She *didn't* do a lot of ego massaging," he says. "There was not, 'Oh, that was wonderful, but there are a couple of lines that can be better.' She would skip the 'Oh, that was wonderful,' but I think that the woman brought out the best in Kenny and me. And I think that, like a lot of people, I responded to the rumors about Streisand before I ever met her. I don't think she's a Mother Teresa, and *yes,* she's tough," he concludes, "but that's how she got to be Barbra Streisand."

Thirty

A Star Is Bored

$\mathcal{B}$urned and burned-out from the long, arduous production and be-hind-the-scenes warring on *A Star Is Born,* Barbra retreated into the laid-back domesticity of life in Malibu. Bank accounts bulging, she also became quite the land baroness. Beginning in October 1974, and using a variation of names (Barbra Gould, Barbra Streisand Gould, Barbra Streisand), she began purchasing the Rancho Topanga property surrounding the Ramirez Canyon ranch she shared with Jon Peters.

Interestingly, she bought the property alone, without the partnership of Peters. Together, they built the first of what became *five* separate houses on the property. When designing and decorating it, the two had so many fights that they decided to build separate, "his and her" homes thereafter. One advantage of having multiple homes: in the aftermath of a fight, they slept not in separate rooms, but in separate *houses.* One was done in art deco, one in Victorian, one in peach-colored California contemporary. Each of the houses was self-contained on two acres of land, with the smallest being 3,500 square feet. "Nothing like it has ever been tried on the kind of scale we're attempting," Peters proclaimed.

The property featured a tennis court, horses (including one named Cupid, which had been presented to Barbra by Jon), riding trails, cats, a lion cub, and a swimming pool. Construction on the pool began on February 4, 1976, and was completed on June 17, at a cost of $10,634. When Barbra refused to pay the bill, the Atlas Swimming Pool Company filed a mechanic's lien against the property.

In June 1977, given the newfound stability in their relationship following the overwhelming, empowering commercial success of *A Star Is Born,* Jon Peters became co-owner of the property.

Protecting their fortress, then valued at around five million dollars, was an eight-foot metal fence with hidden TV scanners and electronic gates. Also present were a full-time bodyguard and a succession of guard dogs, supplied by trainer Michael Kamer. (Once, while waiting in the reception area of Kamer's office, Barbra became unnerved when one of his other clients recognized her. She pounded, in a panic, on his closed office door and asked if she could wait *in* his office.)

Warning signs were posted around the estate, reading, "Danger. Beware: Guard Dogs Trained to Attack." That they were. One menacing Doberman was particularly pugnacious. When photographer Francesco Scavullo visited the compound, he was bitten by the Doberman and had to be rushed to the hospital. At their subsequent photographic session, Barbra was particularly cooperative with Scavullo. The photographer suspected that it was because she was afraid of being sued.

On January 16, 1977, Muriel Harris was invited to the ranch for a meeting. Suddenly, she was attacked by a dog. Screams were heard all over the ranch as efforts were made to separate the visitor from the Doberman. In her subsequent lawsuit, which was settled out of court, Harris charged that the animal "had a vicious nature, disposition, and propensity," and that the "defendants negligently failed to have said dog under restraint or to take any other precautions to prevent the dog from attacking plaintiff." In her suit, Harris sought damages to compensate her for her physical injury, severe shock, pain and suffering, and loss of subsequent income.

Barbra and Jon continued to build and buy homes. On June 7, 1978, they jointly purchased, as tenants-in-common, and at a price of $564,000, a beach house at 72 Malibu Colony Drive.

Later in the year, on November 14, Barbra purchased a $200,000 condominium on Burton Way in Los Angeles. Although she retained title to the property for herself, Barbra allowed her mother, who had been renting a nearby apartment, to move in. Diana Kind, approaching seventy, had, in recent years, been dabbling in an acting career. She took lessons at an adult class at Fairfax High School in West Hollywood. She also got a job as an extra in a movie at Paramount that paid her twenty-five dollars a day plus meals.

Explaining that she hated thrillers, Barbra declined to star in Jon's production of Irvin Kershner's *Eyes of Laura Mars* (1978). Instead, Faye Dunaway played the role of the fashion photographer who is beset with terrifying premonitions of gruesome murders.

During the film's production in New York, a party was given for the three hundred members of the company at Studio 54, then *the* center of the city's nightlife. Refuting rumors that he was having an affair with Dunaway, Jon extolled Barbra at the party. "She's the most exciting woman in the world," he said, "the only woman in the world for me." Barbra greeted Jon's guests, who included Dunaway, Karen Black, and Margaret Trudeau. Jason Gould, aged eleven, was also there, and before the night was over, he cajoled his mom onto the dance floor.

Barbra's respite from moviemaking afforded her more time with her son. Certainly, she was able to do things for and with Jason that she hadn't had time to do before. Her son, she learned, was a big fan of a movie that was making Hollywood history at the time, George Lucas's *Star Wars*.

One day, Barbra called Twentieth Century-Fox licensee Don Post, who was manufacturing four thousand *Star Wars* masks every week at forty dollars each. She wanted to surprise Jason, she told Post, with a Darth Vader helmet. Could he help? Post, stunned that Barbra Streisand herself would make such a call, promptly complied.

Although she had declined to star in the picture, Barbra did agree to sing "Prisoner," the love theme from *Laura Mars*. It would fail, however, to repeat the success of "Evergreen," not even making it into the *Billboard* top twenty. Nonetheless, presumably to the ire of Faye Dunaway, the song was made the centerpiece of the film's marketing campaign.

Barbra also volunteered to sing another movie theme song during this period. She contacted director Richard Brooks and told him that she would sing "Love Comes from Unexpected Places" over the opening titles of *Looking for Mr. Goodbar,* his adaptation of the Judith Rossner novel. Brooks, however, declined. Later, rethinking his position, he contacted Barbra and asked if she would sing the song over the *closing* credits instead. She refused.

Meanwhile, Barbra had a host of other projects she was considering. One was the much-anticipated sequel to *The Way We Were.* Sydney Pollack even had the story worked out in his head, if not on paper: Katie and Hubbell's daughter, Rachel, has grown up and is going to Berkeley. The story is set in the 1960s, and Rachel is a political radical, to Katie's great pride. She is also heavily into drugs, to Katie's consternation. For once admitting that she is unable to handle their daughter alone, Katie gets on the phone and summons Hubbell. He arrives on the scene, and, bonded by their concern for their daughter, the two end up back together.

But for a variety of reasons, including scheduling and script approval (not to mention the kinds of astronomical salaries Streisand and Redford were then commanding), the proposed picture was repeatedly post-poned. In the succeeding years, every time she would run into Pollack, Barbra would ask, "So, when are we going to make this sequel—when I'm sixty-five?"

Later, Pollack, Redford, and Barbra commenced talks about doing a "reunion," as opposed to a sequel, entitled *After Love*. But that too would eventually be dismissed, for similar reasons.

Following the smash, singular sensation of *A Chorus Line* on Broad-way, Michael Bennett was foreseen as "the next big thing" in Holly-wood. He was courted by the studios and flown to the West Coast for a succession of "pitch" meetings. With his choice of properties, he wanted to make a picture called *Roadshow*, which was about a touring produc-tion of the Broadway show *Two for the Seesaw*. As his stars, Bennett wanted Robert Redford and Bette Midler.

Midler, who had created a sensation on Broadway and in records, had yet to star in a movie. Still, in some quarters, she was being hailed as "the next Streisand," particularly after it became apparent that Liza Minnelli would not fulfill her spectacular early screen promise.

The comparisons between Streisand and Midler were obvious. The careers of both had been launched by the gay community in New York City. Both knew and understood that "camp" had nothing to do with summer, sports, or the great outdoors. Both achieved success despite looks that were unconventional. Streisand was more a singer who could be funny; Midler was more a comedienne who could sing. Both started their careers by being defiantly Jewish and defiantly provocative. And those who missed the edge in Streisand's performances were, by the mid-1970s, turning to Bette Midler in droves.

However, Hollywood was leery of Midler. As Michael Bennett was told by an executive at Universal, "She's too ugly." Universal wanted Bennett to make the picture with Barbra. Bennett objected, as did the film's screenwriter, Jerome Kass, who insisted that Barbra was too old for the part, despite the fact that, at thirty-six, she was only two years older than Midler. He added, "You just don't make a movie with Barbra Streisand: *She makes a movie with Barbra Streisand!*"

Still, Universal persisted. Bennett refused, saying that he didn't want to do a movie with Streisand. When Universal issued the final dictum that it would *not* finance a movie with the untested Midler, Michael Ben-nett departed, and the project never materialized.

Around this same time, Barbra, perhaps stuck in a Judy Garland mode, acquired the rights to Irving Berlin's *Annie Get Your Gun,* a 1950 picture Garland started to make before personal problems required that she be replaced by Betty Hutton. The musical of Annie Oakley's life was to have had Barbra singing, among other numbers, "Anything You Can Do (I Can Do Better)," and "There's No Business Like Show Business." The picture was to have been produced by Jon Peters.

Another project that never got made was one that Barbra wanted to direct. As her star, she wanted Sean Connery. For reasons of his own, Connery, like Robert Redford before him, was reluctant to meet Barbra alone. She solved the problem by inviting Connery to dinner at her house, along with his friend and costar *(The Man Who Would Be King)*, Michael Caine. It was only upon his arrival that Caine realized he had only been asked to ensure Connery's presence. He later said, "[Barbra] knew that if I came, so would Sean, but he wouldn't have come on his own."

At the dinner, Barbra made her proposition to the venerable Connery: would he consider starring in a movie that she was directing? Without blinking an eye, Connery answered with an emphatic, "Good God, *no.* Why should I? I've made more pictures than you."

Then, turning the tables on Barbra, Connery queried, "Would *you* be directed by *me?*"

Barbra, crestfallen, replied, "No."

The last word was Connery's. "Well, why on earth would you even ask me the question?"

One Sunday afternoon in 1978, Gary Guthrie, a deejay at WAKY-AM in Louisville, Kentucky, went to the studio, inspired. Then in the process of an amicable divorce from his wife, Guthrie wanted to present her with a parting gift that somehow expressed his feelings. Neil Diamond had recorded a song, "You Don't Bring Me Flowers," which he had cowritten with Alan and Marilyn Bergman for a failed Norman Lear television pilot, "All That Glitters." Barbra was introduced to the song and recorded her own version for inclusion on her *Songbird* album.

Although he liked both, Guthrie felt that something was missing in each version. On that fateful day in the studio, he proceeded to splice together the two separate recordings. Suddenly, the song seemed whole. It was not only an expression of *his* failed marriage, but a lament of men and women everywhere. For the novelty of it, the radio station played the electronic duet on the air the following morning.

Almost immediately, the song was added to the station's rotation. As Guthrie described it, "All of a sudden, the phones started going bananas." Not only were the calls coming from listeners, but from record stores all over the city. There were, in fact, twenty-four thousand requests for the single in stores in the Louisville area alone.

On October 17, 1978, prompted by Gary Guthrie's makeshift production of the song, the two singers were cajoled into a recording studio in Hollywood. Labelmates at Columbia, Barbra and Neil had attended Erasmus Hall High School together. Both sang in the school choir, but they had not known one another.

Jon Peters was at the session, as were Alan and Marilyn Bergman, who showed up at Barbra's request. As the recording proceeded, they made little adjustments here and there in the lyrics of the song. It took seven takes until everyone was satisfied. Portions of each take, with Barbra and Diamond deciding which ones they liked best, were then edited together.

The song entered the *Billboard* top forty on November 4, and leapt into the number one position. Diamond was reportedly miffed that Barbra tacked the duet onto her *Greatest Hits, Volume II* album, which would also top the charts, when *he* was using it on his latest studio album, retitled *You Don't Bring Me Flowers.* After all, he had cowritten the song, so naturally he felt that *his* album should have had the first chance at reaping the benefits of its success.

The script for *Knockout,* a boxing comedy, had been kicking around Hollywood since the mid-1970s. The story concerned a Beverly Hills businesswoman, Hillary Kramer, who has been swindled out of her fortune by her accountant. Her one remaining asset is the contract of a washed-up prizefighter by the name of Eddie "Kid Natural" Scanlon. Determined to make her comeback, and acting as his manager, she forces "The Kid" back into the ring.

As of early 1978, under the new title of *The Main Event,* it was being developed as a project for Diana Ross, whose movie career had floundered since her impressive 1972 debut in *Lady Sings the Blues.* The picture would costar James Caan. When Caan backed out, the script was sent to Sue Mengers, for the consideration of her client Ryan O'Neal.

Through Mengers, Jon Peters, a boxing enthusiast, read the script and liked it. He wanted to produce it, with Barbra as his star. Although she read the script and deemed it mediocre, Peters persisted, and Barbra acquiesced. Diana Ross was out, and Barbra Streisand was in.

Her decision to do the picture was a curious one. How it fit into her emerging consciousness as a woman, as a feminist, and as an artist who wanted to be taken seriously, seems inexplicable, except, of course, on the most superficial level: It's the story of a woman who literally *owns* a man.

Her reasons, obviously, were less noble. Just as she had made *Funny Lady* to fulfill her contract with Ray Stark, she agreed to make *The Main Event* to fulfill her contract with First Artists. Furthermore, after *A Star Is Born,* the thought of making a simple, frivolous, *untaxing* (as much as any project can be untaxing for Streisand) comedy probably appealed to her. And after *Star,* she undoubtedly had enormous trust in the commercial instincts of Jon Peters. *The Main Event* seemed certain to make an enormous sum of money.

With a budget of seven million dollars, the picture started shooting on Monday, October 2, 1978. Howard Zieff *(Hearts of the West, House Calls)* was the director. Zieff, like Frank Pierson before him, had been chosen in large part because he was compliant, willing to discard his own ego and carry out Barbra's vision of the film. For her, it appeared to be the best of both worlds: Just as had been the case on *A Star Is Born,* she could serve as a director without having to assume the full responsibilities of the position. Even Barbra would later acknowledge that Zieff's function, like Pierson's, had been to act as her "middleman."

The picture started to shoot without a completed final draft of the script. The screenwriters, Gail Parent and Andrew Smith, would write and rewrite scenes, with contributions from Barbra, Ryan O'Neal, and Zieff, just before they were played before the cameras.

Reportedly, O'Neal agreed to accept the picture only on the condition that Barbra be his costar. His career in trouble, he needed a hit. He knew that his former girlfriend would deliver at the box office. Besides, he was a former boxer and was enthusiastic about displaying his skills on the screen.

Boxing scenes were filmed at the Main Street Gym in Santa Monica, and on Stage 7 at Hollywood General Studios. One day during rehearsals, Ryan went three rounds with Jon Peters. Contrary to rumor, it was all in fun. With tongue in cheek, they redubbed their picture *Glove Story.*

Given the enormous success of Sylvester Stallone's *Rocky,* Hollywood, always eager to pounce, pummel, and pulverize a trend to box office death, was producing a flurry of boxing pictures—among them, *The Champ* (which Ryan lost to Jon Voight), *Rocky II,* and *The Main Event.* The best of them, Martin Scorsese's *Raging Bull,* was still in the developmental stage and would be released in 1980.

Ever the promoter, Peters wanted to set up a boxing challenge between *The Main Event* company and the *Rocky II* company. The Stallone camp, however, declined.

Barbra worked on the script, on the set (she had the art deco doors from her home transported to the studio), and on her body, with personal trainer Gilda Marx. In *The Main Event,* two years before Jane Fonda discovered a gold mine in workout tapes, Barbra would introduce aerobics to the national consciousness.

Unfortunately, the manner in which the scenes were presented was patently offensive and inherently sexist. Howard Zieff's camera seems to have had some sort of magnetic attraction to Barbra's behind. But he alone can't be faulted. After all, she had final cut on the picture, and the appallingly gratuitous close-ups of her various body parts could have easily been excised.

Barbra also worried about her hair, which was dyed red for the picture. One morning at two A.M., she was overheard outside of a Fat Burger fast-food stand, discussing her hairstyle for the following day's shoot. "Should I wear it up or down?" she inquired of the Warner Brothers executive who was with her. "Jon has lost all professional distance when it comes to my hair."

On December 15, after eight days of location shooting at Cedar Lake near Big Bear, California, the company returned to Los Angeles and wrapped production.

As expected, the film, which premiered in New York on June 22, 1979, was a hit at the box office, grossing over $40 million. It was also attacked by the critics, many of them staunch Streisand supporters. To many, it seemed that she had lost her way. Either that, or she was bored.

Bette Midler, on the other hand, made a stunning film debut a few months later in Mark Rydell's well-received biopic *The Rose,** in which she played a Janis Joplin–like rock star. Her Rose had all of the fire, passion, pathos, and grit that Barbra's Esther Hoffman Howard had lacked. Midler would receive a Best Actress Oscar nomination, largely for her emoting in the straight scenes, and loomed as an even more formidable threat to the Streisand throne.

Brooklyn-born Paul Jabara cowrote with Bob Esty the theme song for *The Main Event,* entitled, "The Main Event/Fight." It entered the *Billboard* chart on July 7, 1979, and peaked in the number three position.

Jabara had written the Oscar-winning disco anthem "Last Dance" for

*Midler's official movie debut was in a bit part in the 1966 picture *Hawaii.*

the 1978 embarrassment *Thank God It's Friday,* in which twenty-three-year-old Debra Winger made her film debut. The song was sung by Donna Summer, who had previously appeared with Jabara, along with Diane Keaton, in the hit Broadway musical *Hair.*

It was Paul Jabara's dream to unite Streisand and Summer in the recording studio. The songwriter, however, could not get them together in the same room. Barbra, reportedly not much of a disco fan, was unfamiliar with Summer's music. After a string of number-one hits—"MacArthur Park," "Hot Stuff," and "Bad Girls"—Donna Summer was the biggest-selling female recording artist of the period.

"Enough Is Enough" was written by Jabara for Barbra's *Wet* album. The LP was to be a concept recording, with the concept, in this case, being that all of the songs had something to do with water. "Enough Is Enough" was rejected by Barbra because it wasn't "wet" enough. Determined, and a diehard Streisand fan, Jabara inserted a new opening line in the song: "It's raining, it's pouring . . ."

Scheming, Jabara asked his friend Donna, who had just returned home from touring, if she would like to accompany him to Barbra's house for lunch. She agreed to go if Barbra approved. Jabara got on the telephone. Jason Gould, aged twelve, answered the phone. "I told him to ask his mother about lunch," Jabara recalled. Jason screamed, "Donna Summer! Donna Summer!" Said Jabara, "Turns out Jason was the biggest Donna fan in the world. So I owe it all to him."

Jabara and Summer drove to the Malibu ranch compound. They *didn't* get lunch, but Jabara did play his revised song for Barbra. Jason developed a rapport with the songwriter, fawned over the visiting queen of disco, loved the song, and urged his mother to do it. Uncertain about the number, but swept up in her son's excitement, Barbra agreed.

"Enough Is Enough" was recorded in a Los Angeles studio in August 1979. Although there *was* some of the usual bickering and insecurity of the "Is her line better than mine?" variety, the dueting "divas" were anything but dueling. Instead, they approached one another, sitting stool by stool, with mutual respect.

"Barbra and Donna were intimidated by [each] other," Jabara related, "and each couldn't understand why the other person should be intimidated."

The two women sang with, and *at,* each other for hours. At one point, Donna was having a hard time holding a certain note as long as Barbra. Out of breath, she lost her balance and fell off her stool.

Retitled "No More Tears (Enough Is Enough)" to better fit into Barbra's wet concept, the song was a smash, with both singers more than holding their own in the end result. It entered the *Billboard* top forty on October 27, 1979, and bolted into the number one position. For Barbra, however, the *real* reward was that Jason, who never seemed to like any of her records, played the song constantly in his bedroom.

On December 14, 1979, Paul Zimmerman, aged thirty-five, was struck by a car while standing at the corner of Ocean Avenue and Colorado Avenue in Santa Monica. It seems that the car collided with a bus, spun out of control, and then plowed into Zimmerman. The driver of the car was Ruth Lozoya, an employee of Barbra and Jon's at the Malibu compound.

Zimmerman was taken to Santa Monica Hospital, where he remained in a coma for nine months before his death. Since Ruth Lozoya did not have automobile insurance, and because she used the car for business purposes (just before the accident, Lozoya used Barbra's credit card to fill the tank with gas), the Zimmerman family turned to Barbra and Jon to help pay Zimmerman's hospital bills. They refused, claiming no responsibility for the accident.

The Zimmerman family then went to the City of Santa Monica, which owned the bus that was involved in the accident. The city, however, told the Zimmermans to contact Barbra and Jon, who continued to absolve themselves of all responsibility.

Without other recourse, the Zimmermans filed a lawsuit seeking damages to help defray the cost of the mounting medical bills. The case, however, would not be resolved until 1985, long after Paul Zimmerman's death. Settled out of court, the City of Santa Monica ended up paying $50,000; Barbra, $30,000; and Jon Peters, $7,500.

It wasn't the first time that one of Streisand's employees had caused her legal problems. Yvonne Paulin was driving Barbra's 1973 Rambler when she got into a crash with William MacNeil, who was permanently disabled as a result of the accident. MacNeil subsequently filed a lawsuit against Barbra, which was also resolved outside of the courtroom.

There were more problems with other employees, and even *would-be* employees. Betty Ann Mendoza met with Barbra on July 28, 1977, and was hired to work as a live-in domestic, beginning on September 1. Consequently, Mendoza quit the job she then held. On August 31, however, one day before she was to start her new job, Mendoza received a phone call from Barbra and was told, without reason, that her services would not be required. When she couldn't get her old job back, Mendoza filed a breach-of-contract lawsuit against Barbra, which, presumably, was also settled out of court.

On February 27, 1980, Barbra made a joint appearance with Neil Diamond on the televised Grammy Awards, staged at the Shrine Auditorium in Los Angeles. Over the phone, Barbra had instructed Diamond as to what they were to do on the show, down to the kiss he was to plant on her hand at the conclusion of their number.

Although the song was shut out in the awards, which were dominated that year by the Doobie Brothers, Barbra and Neil's live performance of "You Don't Bring Me Flowers" stopped the show. Not only did it overshadow the dominance of the Doobie Brothers, it also eclipsed a rare television appearance by Bob Dylan.

There was some talk that Barbra and Diamond would star in a film version of the song. Several scripts were developed, but nothing materialized to Barbra's satisfaction. Diamond went on to start his film career with *The Jazz Singer,* which was critically lambasted upon its 1981 release.

Other film projects that Barbra considered during this period were *Third Time Lucky,* a psychological love story set in England; a project with John Travolta, then still the rage in Hollywood after the back-to-back successes of *Saturday Night Fever* and *Grease;* and, a remake of the 1939 claws-out cat-fight classic, *The Women,* to be produced by Jon Peters, and costarring Faye Dunaway and Raquel Welch.

In the years that followed her heralded 1969 start in show business, nothing much seemed to happen in the career of Roslyn Kind. After the initial novelty of it, and despite her efforts to find her own style, she still came off, according to her critics, like a repackaged copy of her famous sister.

Her record contract canceled, and unable to get further bookings, Roslyn took a job working in a Westwood bakery named, ironically, Butterfly. It was owned by Liz Brooks, wife of Roslyn's manager, Ted. By then, the Brookses had become Roslyn's surrogate parents, and Roslyn, to Diana Kind's great chagrin, had moved in with them.

At the bakery, Roslyn tried to avoid dealing with the customers. Liz Brooks recalls, "She never liked to work the counter, because she thought that that was beneath her." People who found out what Roslyn was doing for a living generally had one of two responses. One was to ridicule her: "Her cakes rise, but her career doesn't," or words to that effect. The other was to ask, with unmasked incredulity, *"Why* hasn't your sister done anything for your career?"

When she had first learned that Ted Brooks wanted to manage Roslyn's career back in 1969, Barbra had had him removed from his position with her music publishing company. Perhaps she was afraid of a possible conflict of interest. Perhaps she was afraid of the competition.

The fact is that, over the years, Barbra has done woefully little to help her sister, perhaps rationalizing that *she* made it on her own, so why shouldn't Roslyn? She did get Roslyn one booking in a nightclub in Las Vegas. After the engagement, in a rare moment of candor, Roslyn went public with her frustration and hurt.

"It was the worst place you've ever seen," she said. "Absolutely no one knew it existed." Of her sister's less-than-benevolent support regarding her career, Roslyn confided, "If only Barbra would say something nice about me when she is asked. I've always worshiped her as a person and a performer, but I feel she is now hurting my chances to succeed."

"Barbra has *never* helped Roslyn Kind," states Richard Gordon, a family friend and a business associate of Roslyn's. "She has never lifted a finger. The truth of the matter is that Barbra Streisand is one of the most powerful women in Hollywood. All it would take is a phone call or two from her to a network executive, to a record company, to a studio. Why can't she even give her sister a small part in one of her movies? Roslyn was an *extra* in *The Main Event.* She was in the aerobics class at the beginning of the movie. She was also an extra in *A Star Is Born.* She sat at Barbra's table during the Grammy Awards scene. But she had *no* lines, and *nothing* to do."

As for the possibility that maybe Roslyn didn't *want* Barbra's help, Gordon dismisses the suggestion as ludicrous. "All that 'I want to make it on my own and be known for me' stuff is bullshit. Roslyn would *love* the help, are you kidding?

"I booked Roslyn into this nightclub in New York called the Grand Finale, which was a hot, *in,* gay, Upper West Side kind of club," Gordon continues. "It was 1977–78. Chita Rivera, Bernadette Peters, Jane Oliver, and Julie Budd all played there. Barbra did not attend the opening night because, she *said,* she didn't want to take the focus away from Roslyn.

"She ended up coming four or five days into the engagement. I was told by Barbra's publicist that I couldn't tell any press people that she was coming, or she wouldn't show. Now, here I am a young publicist right out of college, and I'm being told that I couldn't publicize her appearance. Anyway, Earl Wilson, who was a columnist for the *New York Post,* calls me up and says, 'I hear Barbra Streisand is gonna be there tonight,' and I had to lie.

"Well, Barbra *did* show up that night, but she didn't do it discreetly. She didn't arrive in a cab, she arrived in a *limousine,* dressed to the nines, wearing a turban and a maroon outfit, and looking very much the star. Jason was with her, and Jon Peters came later.

"Roslyn was staying with Tony Chase, who is one of my best friends," Gordon continues. "Tony and Roslyn grew up together as children and had a very close friendship. The three of us were 'The Three Musketeers.' The show was a success, and I got Roslyn on all the television shows. I really think that that period," says Gordon, with a hint of wistfulness, "was the peak of Roslyn's career."

Shortly thereafter, Roslyn dissolved her professional and personal relationship with Ted and Liz Brooks. "She felt that my husband was controlling her personal life," Liz says. "My husband felt that Roslyn should have been more like her sister. Barbra had pursued her career, and that's all she did. Roslyn didn't have Barbra's drive. Teddy always told her that, and Roslyn really didn't like hearing it."

According to Liz, another reason for the breakup also had to do with Barbra. "Roslyn got involved with some friends who told her that she should be on her own. They told her that if she went out on her own, Barbra would help her more." Liz adds, "[But] I don't think she ever did."

When asked why Barbra hasn't, over the years, been more forthcoming in helping her sister, Richard Gordon says, "I'm sure Barbra resented that Roslyn didn't have to struggle in gay clubs. She started with the Sullivan show! She started in the Persian Room at the Plaza hotel, which was a very elegant, chic nightclub. *Stars* performed in that room. Nobody *starts* there."

"And," Gordon adds, "don't forget, Barbra hated Roslyn's father."

With the stupendous success of the *Saturday Night Fever* soundtrack, and *six* number one records in a row, a feat unmatched by Elvis Presley or the Beatles, Barry Gibb and the Bee Gees were the hottest act in the recording industry. As the follow-up to her duets with Neil Diamond and Donna Summer, Barbra shrewdly handpicked the brothers Gibb for her next collaboration.

The subsequent negotiations took *two years* to navigate. The negotiations included Charles Koppelman of the Entertainment Company, a host of executives from Columbia Records, and Robert Stigwood, the Bee Gees' manager. Ultimately, it was decided that Barry Gibb would write and produce an album for Barbra and would retain full publishing rights to the songs (Barbra had requested—and was denied—a cut), full producer's royalties (shared with his partners, Karl Richardson and Albhy Galuten), and half the royalties on his duets with Barbra.

With a deal signed, Gibb brazenly declared that he would make Barbra "more mainstream."

Initially, there was a power struggle over the material. Barbra liked the songs, but wanted changes in some of the lyrics. She likes her lyrics to mean precisely what they say. Gibb, on the other hand, has a tendency to write lyrics that are less literal and more abstract. Compromises were made on both sides, but, considering Gibb's phenomenal track record, it was primarily Barbra who gave in.

All the songs on the album were written or cowritten by Gibb expressly for Barbra, with the exception of "The Love Inside." The musical tracks were recorded at Criteria Recording Studios and Gibb's own Middle Ear Studios in Miami, without Barbra even being present. It is the first and only time in her career that she relinquished that kind of power to one of her collaborators.

Guilty became the biggest selling album of Barbra's career, supplanting the soundtrack to *A Star Is Born*. Breaking into the *Billboard* top forty on October 11, 1980, the album climbed to the number one position, where it remained for three weeks. A smash in the international market as well, it also spawned the hit singles "Woman in Love" (Barbra's first—and only—non-movie-related solo to become number one), "Guilty," and "What Kind of Fool," the latter two being duets with Gibb.

At the Grammy Awards ceremony held at Radio City Music Hall on February 25, 1981, Barbra was nominated in five categories, including Album of the Year, Record of the Year ("Woman in Love"), and Female Pop Vocal Performance. However, the awards were swept that year by Christopher Cross and "Sailing," and Bette Midler was named the year's best female pop singer for her recording of "The Rose," the title song from her hit movie. Barbra and Barry *did* win one award, Best Pop Vocal Performance by a Duo or Group for the single "Guilty."

At the very private postawards party held by Columbia Records at the Four Seasons restaurant, the question was, would Barbra show up as scheduled, given her multiple Grammy losses? As one reporter rather flippantly put it, "Was Babs in a frenzy? Would she show? And if she did, would she make life miserable for everyone?" To the surprise of many, and to the disappointment of some, Barbra *did* appear that night. Moreover, she stayed until 1:40 in the morning, mingled with the other guests, and never stopped smiling.

Meanwhile, back in Hollywood, Gene Hackman was preparing to return to movies following a two year-sabbatical after *Superman.* For his "comeback" vehicle, he turned down *Ordinary People,* which was being directed by Robert Redford, and chose instead to make an offbeat comedy called *Night People,* which was to mark the American directorial debut of Jean-Claude Tramont.

Filming started on April 14, 1980, at Universal. Early into the shoot, studio executives changed the picture's title to *All Night Long.*

On April 24, Barbra celebrated her thirty-eighth birthday by walking into the Right Bank Clothing Company and almost buying out the entire store. Among her purchases: a Basile blazer, a Thierry Mugler T-shirt, a dress, a pair of shorts, and an armload of shoes. All her selections were on sale for half-price. Upon returning to her home, Barbra ripped the designer labels off the items. As she explained, she didn't want to advertise any particular store or designer.

On May 13, Universal announced that Barbra would replace twenty-eight-year-old Lisa Eichhorn in *All Night Long.* The abrupt announcement rocked Hollywood. First of all, what, if anything, had Eichhorn done to be dismissed so disgracefully? Second, *why* would Barbra Streisand agree to play a secondary part in a "small" film? And not a colorful part at that, but that of a San Fernando Valley housewife who falls in love with a drugstore manager.

Despite the fact that the picture had already shot four weeks on a ten-week schedule, Eichhorn had actually only put in one week's worth of work when the announcement was made. The picture shut down production on May 19 for two weeks to "prepare for Barbra's arrival." Translated, it meant that the script, to Gene Hackman's dismay, was being rewritten to accommodate Barbra's demands. Hackman, understandably, feared that Barbra would try to steal *his* picture. "It's mostly my film," he said. "She has five or six good scenes and that's it."

The controversy over Eichhorn's dismissal continued. Had Barbra forced her way in? Tramont said only that "the part was too much of a stretch for Lisa." One source on the set described Eichhorn as having been "very difficult on the set, objecting to things like camera angles as if she were—excuse the pun—a star like Streisand."

Eichhorn defended herself, or attempted to, by saying, in an apparent reference to Barbra, "You know how it is in this business. If you have opinions and you're not earning a million dollars, you're considered difficult. If you *are* earning a million dollars, you're just strong-willed."

Although she didn't know it at the time, and after having shown considerable promise in *Yanks* and *Cutter's Way,* Eichhorn's dismissal from *All Night Long* would seriously hamper the progress of her film career.

Eichhorn and Streisand came face-to-face shortly afterwards in a Beverly Hills coffee shop. "She was just getting ready to leave," Eichhorn recalled, "so I felt I would not be intruding. I said, 'Excuse me, I just wanted to tell you how much I've always admired your work.' She didn't want to know. She looked up at me with a please-go-away look and nodded thanks, rather ungraciously. So I turned and left. She had no idea who I was, of course, not that it would have made any difference."

Eichhorn added, "I suppose it must be tiresome having people come up like that, but it isn't hard to be gracious. I think the only reason I did it was because I saw her in *Funny Girl* when I was at school and that was what determined me to be an actress."

Despite denials to the contrary, the question of how Barbra became involved in the project is a simple one to resolve. For Jean-Claude Tramont, *All Night Long* was both a breakthrough and a gamble. The picture, if a success at the box office, would mean a great deal to his future in Hollywood. Tramont's wife happened to be Barbra's longtime agent and friend, Sue Mengers. When Mengers learned of her husband's on-the-set problems with Eichhorn, she picked up the phone and called her number one client.

Even with the Streisand name on the marquee, however, *All Night Long,* panned by most critics, was a failure at the box office. Budgeted at $14 million, the picture grossed a domestic rental of about $4 million. Many of those involved were tarnished by the experience. Gene Hackman lost out on *Ordinary People,* which went on to win the Best Picture Oscar; Lisa Eichhorn lost the momentum in her career; Jean-Claude Tramont lost his future in Hollywood—the picture would be his first and *last* English-language feature; and Sue Mengers lost Barbra as client. At some point during the production, the two women had a fight. By the time the picture premiered in New York, they were no longer on speaking terms and did their best to avoid one another.

In fact, the only person *not* tarnished by the experience of *All Night Long* was Barbra Streisand. For it wasn't just loyalty or friendship to Mengers that prompted her decision to make the picture, it was, plain and simple, *money.*

Lisa Eichhorn was to have received $250,000, which she was paid despite her dismissal. In contrast, for a mere twenty-four shooting days, Barbra was paid the astronomical sum of $4 million, plus 15 percent of all profits, of which, of course, there would be none. But she, for one, wasn't complaining.

And the money kept rolling in.

Thirty-one

"After Her Father's Death . . ."

> "I want to be something and make something. I don't care what. Acting and singing aren't enough. You can't put your hands on them, they're too ephemeral. I want to make something I can touch. I bought a Singer sewing machine; I want to be able to do something with that."
>
> —Barbra Streisand, 1963, age twenty-one

*B*arbra Streisand was not, by a long shot, the first woman to direct a movie in Hollywood. Lois Weber had directed *Hypocrites* (1915), *Where Are My Children?* (1916), and *The Blot* (1921), and she was only one of several female filmmakers during the silent era. Through the decades, women continued, although in small numbers, to make their presence felt behind the camera. Dorothy Arzner directed *Merrily We Go to Hell, Christopher Strong, Nana,* and *Craig's Wife* in the thirties; Ida Lupino wrote and directed *Outrage, The Bigamist,* and *The Hitch-Hiker,* among others, in the fifties; Stephanie Rothman directed a series of exploitation pictures in the sixties and seventies, including *Student Nurses* (1970) and *Terminal Island* (in which a young, unknown Tom Selleck appeared, 1973); Joan Micklin Silver wrote and directed *Hester Street* and *Head*

Over Heels in the seventies; Claudia Weill directed *Girlfriends* in 1978, and Lee Grant directed *Tell Me a Riddle* in 1980.

But, arguably, none of these pioneering women overcame more obstacles and broke more feminist ground than Barbra Streisand with *Yentl*.

Ever since she first read the Isaac Bashevis Singer story, "Yentl, the Yeshiva Boy" in January 1968, Barbra *knew* that it was a movie she wanted to make. Indeed, no sentence was more compelling to her than the first one that began: "After her father's death . . ."

In an odyssey that would extend sixteen years, Barbra faced a succession of formidable challenges, not the least of which was the unconventional story itself. Set in nineteenth-century Poland, "Yentl, the Yeshiva Boy" tells the tale of a rabbi's daughter whose yearning to learn is so great that she defies Talmudic law and chops off her hair, straps down her bosom, changes her sex and her name to Anshel, and attends a yeshiva. Further complications arise when she falls in love with Avigdor, her male study partner. At Avigdor's insistence, and to prove her manhood, she weds—and beds—Hadass, another *woman*.

The first director attached to the project was the Czech-born Ivan Passer. He eventually backed out, explaining that Barbra was both too famous and too old to play the part. In Singer's story, Yentl was meant to be sixteen, or thereabouts. When she was introduced to the property in 1968, Barbra was twenty-six.

During their first weekend together in 1973, Barbra read the story to Jon Peters, acting out the various parts as she spoke. She told him that it was her dream to turn the story into a movie one day. Peters was enthralled, not so much with Yentl's story, as with Barbra's passionate commitment. He was impressed, too, by the size of her dreams.

But, like Ivan Passer, Peters believed that Barbra was too old to play the part. He also expressed the concern that she was too feminine to be convincing as a male yeshiva student. In time, she came to agree with him. By 1976, the thirty-four-year-old Barbra acknowledged that she was too old to play Yentl. Unwilling to abandon the project, she altered her vision and decided that she would direct the picture, instead.

It was 2:30 in the morning. Jon Peters was awakened by the sight of a grim-faced man wearing a hat and smoking a pipe. Thinking it was an intruder, Peters, blurry-eyed, leapt out of bed. Only then did he realize that the menacing, would-be burglar was his beloved Barbra. Earlier that day, she had gone to Western Costume in Hollywood and rented a boy's yeshiva outfit. With Peters dumbfounded, and her point made, Barbra recommitted herself to the idea of casting herself as Yentl.

And she remained resolute about her intention to direct. Hollywood scoffed behind her back. *"Let her direct"* was the concensus in the studio commissaries. "It's *her* funeral." Some delighted in the idea that Barbra Streisand would finally "get what's coming to her." Others believed that the project itself was ill-advised, and would never get off the developmental ground.

In March 1978, Jon Peters signed a three-year production pact with Orion Pictures. Included in the deal was an undisclosed project to be directed by Barbra Streisand. It was not until over a year later that Barbra officially entered into an agreement with the studio to star in and direct *Yentl.*

At the time, she was operating from a screenplay by Ted Allan, who had received an Oscar nomination for Jan Kadar's 1975 picture, *Lies My Father Told Me.* "Barbra called me because *Lies My Father Told Me* was about me and my grandfather," Allan says. "It was a loving story of a Jewish family. So, she thought that I had a feel for something Jewish."

Barbra would eventually discard almost all of Allan's screenplay. "The script I wrote gave indications of the anti-Semitism in Eastern Europe that drove the Jews to America," Allan relates, "and I don't think that Barbra liked that. She had a different concept."

Barbra described her forthcoming picture as "a realistic fantasy" and "a film with music." She didn't want to call it a "musical," because she thought the term would demean the seriousness of the story. The songs in the score, with music by Michel Legrand and lyrics by Alan and Marilyn Bergman, were not to be handled in the conventional way, either. Allan recalls, "The only thing I think Barbra kept of mine was the idea that Yentl *sing* her thoughts. If anybody denies it, fine. But it was *my* idea."

Initially, the film was to be coproduced by Joan Marshall Ashby, a friend and associate of Barbra's, as well as the wife of director Hal Ashby, and Jon Peters, who was then shooting *Caddyshack* with Chevy Chase in Florida.

Barbra's research for *Yentl* was painstaking, exhaustive, and all-consuming. She spoke with dozens of rabbis, Orthodox, Conservative, and Reform, soliciting their advice. Her approach was disarming and direct. To Chaim Potok, author of the novel *The Chosen,* she blurted out, "I want you to help me. I mean, I want to know what you know as a writer and as a rabbi."

For the most part, she offered nothing in return for the information imparted. To Potok, she agreed to sit for a magazine interview. To a woman by the name of Adele Grubart, she apparently offered nothing at all. Later claiming that she had provided Barbra with a wealth of information on Jewish culture, music, and history, Grubart took her case to the courts, seeking remuneration in the amount of $77,500.

A chosen few, however, were extravagantly compensated. Much of Barbra's research was done in connection with the Hillel Center at UCLA, upon which she bestowed the funds for a Jewish performing arts center, and with Rabbi Daniel Lapin and the Pacific Jewish Center, cofounded by writer Michael Medved, in Venice, California. In the spring of 1981, following a significant financial contribution by Barbra, the Pacific Jewish Center grade school in Santa Monica was, at her request, renamed and rededicated the Emanuel Streisand School. Barbra said at the time, "This is a school of moral and ethical excellence, and we're proud that my father's name, his thoughts, and his life will be a part of it."

Developing *Yentl* forced Barbra to confront her feelings about her father—his life, his work, his beliefs, and his religion. While researching Judaism, something unexpected happened: her own spiritual awakening. She didn't become a "born-again Jew," as was thought by some, and snickered at by others, but for an intensive period of time during the preparation of her picture, Barbra *did* immerse herself in Jewish customs, laws, and principles, particularly as they pertained to women. With enthusiasm, she shared this rediscovery of her cultural and religious heritage with her friends, Marilyn Bergman, among them, and with her son.

Coincidentally, Barbra's research for *Yentl* coincided with Jason Gould's thirteenth birthday. One can assume that if it hadn't been for *Yentl,* Jason would *not* have had a bar mitzvah. Certainly, there was nothing in his upbringing that had recognized traditional observance. If anything, the opposite was true. Barbra believed that some Jewish teachings were limiting.

Recalls Rabbi Lapin, "She met with me, together with Jason's father, Elliott Gould, and said that she wanted a bar mitzvah for her son." Rabbi Lapin was impressed by what he perceived to be Barbra's sincerity. "She could have gone and made it a Hollywood star [kind of] celebration, which was exactly what was expected. Or she could have taken another, more surprising route, and that was to take it very seriously, which is what she did.

"I explained to her that in order for the bar mitzvah to have any meaning, in a deeper sense, for her son, he would have to know and see that it meant something to her, too. And I recommended that, if she was serious about it, she ought to spend the year studying Judaism along with her son, which she did, at no small sacrifice to herself. She studied with me for many, many months. We used to meet once a week. We would cover some of the classical texts and the many philosophical issues that would crop up. She was really quite brilliant."

Conducted by Rabbi Lapin, the services for Jason Gould's bar mitzvah were held on Saturday, January 5, 1980, at the modest Pacific Jewish Center synagogue in Venice. Standing with Jason on the *bima,* were Elliott Gould and *his* father, as was the custom, as Barbra watched with pride from her designated position in the front row.

The party that followed was held at the Malibu ranch compound, upon which three huge art deco tents had been erected. The menu was Hollywood schizophrenic: one table was strictly kosher, the other, gourmet Chinese. Entertainment was provided by Diana Kind, who used the event to make her debut as a singer, before a crowd that included James Caan, Neil Diamond, Ray Stark, and a host of Hollywood powerbrokers.

As work on *Yentl* proceeded, Barbra continued to see Rabbi Lapin, who was made an official consultant on the picture. "Working with Barbra was a wonderful experience," he recalls. "I felt that, compared to many of the Hollywood personalities that I had encountered during my work in Venice, she struck me as being very much more aristocratic, if you know what I mean."

Of the charge leveled at Barbra that her spiritual pursuit was a superficial, thinly disguised attempt to obtain free research for her picture, Rabbi Lapin responds, "She had a very genuine interest in Judaism at the time. I think that *Yentl* was a *consequence* of her Jewish interest, not the cause."

As fate would have it, the very day (October 19, 1980) Barbra submitted her budget, reportedly around $17 million, to Orion Pictures, United Artists released the financially disastrous Michael Cimino picture, *Heaven's Gate,* in New York. Catastrophic in its failure, the film sent the industry reeling. At Orion, where *Yentl* was in development, the proverbial boom was lowered: No More Ego Trips for Star Performers or Star Directors. Unwilling to finance *Yentl* beyond the sum of $10 million, Orion decided to absorb the losses it incurred in development and placed the project in turnaround.

Naturally, it was assumed that the picture would then go to Polygram, where Jon Peters had another production deal, and there was some movement in that direction. By this time, however, Jon and Barbra were having considerable problems in their personal life.

Among other things, Jon was ambivalent about what he perceived to be Barbra's obsessive spiritual pursuits and her relentless determination to make *Yentl,* which seemed to go hand-in-hand. Certainly, he felt that he was being neglected at home, and was none too pleased about the amount of time Barbra spent with Elliott, in preparation for Jason's bar mitzvah. Moreover, he had considerable doubts about *Yentl*'s commercial viability.

Instead of making the movie, Peters wanted Barbra to do a worldwide concert tour. In 1979, British impressario Malcolm Feld had offered her $1 million to perform for two hours in concert at Wembley Stadium. When she turned down that proposal, he doubled the offer to $2 million, plus all expenses, including a chartered Concorde to transport her, her staff, and her friends. Joe encouraged Barbra to accept the offer. He also encouraged her to play Las Vegas.

Barbra refused. As she pointedly told Peters, she would not make any more movies like *The Main Event,* which she had come to loathe. In the future, her pictures would be important ones, she told him, movies with something to say about the human condition, about individual growth, about the relationships between people. Movies like *Yentl.*

At one point during a particularly contentious fight, Peters told Barbra that, without *his* help, *Yentl* would never get made.

His words jolted her back into reality. In truth she *had* become too dependent on Jon Peters. Peters had also given her the "I'll-show-you" impetus she needed to move forward on the project, and with her life. Their split would be gradual but their relationship, if not their friendship, was over by the time Barbra began shooting her movie. In the meantime, she still had to find another studio.

If she needed any more motivation to go ahead with her commitment to *Yentl,* Barbra got it when she was taken to a psychic by her brother, Sheldon. While sitting at the table, the medium spelled out their father's name. The medium then asked if the spirit had a message for Barbra. Spelled out were the words "s-o-r-r-y," "s-i-n-g," and "p-r-o-u-d."

Barbra interpreted the message as being an apology from her father for having left her when she was an infant; an indication he was encouraging her to make *Yentl;* and an expression of his pride in her varied and vast accomplishments.

Swallowing her pride, and with newfound resolve, Barbra assembled an *audition tape* comprised of several songs from the picture's score, and

Super-8 footage that she had shot while doing research and scouting lo-cations in Eastern Europe. To convince studio executives of her believa-bility as a male yeshiva student, Barbra also included in the audition tape shots of herself in costume, and in character. And to allay concerns that she was too old to play a sixteen-year-old regardless of gender, Barbra took out her pen and script, crossed out the "1," replaced it with a "2," and made Yentl twenty-six instead of sixteen.

Even after such elaborate efforts, she was still turned down by every major studio in town. Barbra commented, "I think there are certain peo-ple in this business who get a pleasure out of saying, 'Guess who I turned down today? I turned down Barbra Streisand.' " Barbra was convinced, too, that sexism played a part in her difficulty in placing the project.

Perhaps, but the real problem was not with Streisand, or her gender, but with the property itself. Studio executives couldn't seem to get a handle on the project. As Barbra reported, "First of all, [they didn't like] the title, *Yentl.* They go, '*Yentl,* what's that?' They think it's *Yenta,* something from *Fiddler on the Roof.*"

Even the first studio executive to okay the project at Orion had told Barbra that the title had to be changed. She argued, "This is like being 'Barbra Streisand' and everybody said, 'You better change your name. Change it to Strand, Sands, something the people will remember.' "

At one point, the project was retitled *A Secret Dream.* At another, the title and character names were changed to *Leah,* inspired by playwright Leah Napolin who adapted the story, with Barbra's permission, into a 1975 Broadway play starring Tovah Feldshuh. The character as a male was renamed Leon. But, as Barbra related, "it just wasn't true to the piece. Her name *had* to be Yentl."

Despite one bruising rejection after another, she continued to shop and re-shop *Yentl.* At the same time Barbra considered other projects as well. One was *The Triangle Fire,* based on the novel by Leon Stein, with a script by Naomi Foner. It told the story of the Triangle Factory fire in New York City which took place in 1911 and killed 145 female employ-ees. The tragedy, à la Martin Ritt's *Norma Rae* (starring Sally Field, 1979), resulted in the formation of the International Lady Garment Workers Union. The film would be produced for MGM by Cis Corman and would co-star Jane Fonda.

Another prospective project was entitled *White Hotel,* based on the novel of the same name by D. M. Thomas. The film would have cast Barbra as a cocaine addict and patient of Sigmund Freud.

One part that Barbra wanted desperately was Sophie Zawistowska in the film adaptation of the William Styron novel, *Sophie's Choice.* A number of actresses and actors vied for the main roles. Styron wanted Ursula Andress for the part of Sophie; director Alan J. Pakula wanted Liv Ullmann; and Marthe Keller was another top contender. Vying for the part of Nathan were Dustin Hoffman, Al Pacino, and Robert De Niro. It was, however, Kevin Kline who would later be cast.

Meryl Streep called Pakula and reportedly *begged* for the part of Sophie. Barbra went one better. She phoned Pakula and told him that she would play Sophie *without salary.* All she wanted was a percentage of the movie. But it was not meant to be. Sir Lew Grade, who was involved in the picture's financing, did not like Barbra's looks. Meryl Streep got the part and won an Oscar for her performance.

After losing Woody Allen to Orion, United Artists hoped to entice big star names into the fold, and there was no star more coveted by UA than Barbra Streisand. One project the studio began to develop for her was a musical biography of Sarah Bernhardt. Another was an adaptation of *La Vagabonde,* the autobiographical novel by Colette. UA executive Steven Bach proposed the project to Sydney Pollack, who wanted to make a musical with Barbra. Pollack agreed, if the studio could get Arthur Laurents to write the script and Stephen Sondheim to compose the score. Unfortunately, the studio was unable to get the rights to the novel and the proposed production was scrapped.

Another UA project in development for Barbra was *House of Flowers,* the Harold Arlen–Truman Capote stage musical which contained Barbra's favorite song, "A Sleepin' Bee." UA owned the rights to the property, but it was never developed to Barbra's satisfaction.

It is ironic, of course, that it was United Artists, the bedraggled studio that released *Heaven's Gate,* that would come to the rescue of Barbra's *Yentl.*

UA executive Steven Bach shuddered when initially approached with the idea of Barbra Streisand producing, writing, directing, acting and singing in a picture about a girl who pretends to be a boy so that she can study the Talmud.

Nonetheless, he pitched the idea at a company production meeting in the boardroom of the Occidental Tower in downtown Los Angeles. Everybody, including company president Norbert Auerbach, laughed at the seeming insanity of the idea. As one of the executives put it, "What if she turns out to be the female Michael Cimino?" Talent aside, all agreed that one Cimino was enough and the matter was dismissed. Cimino's *Heaven's Gate,* after all, not only cost the studio its reputation, it also ended up losing $35 *million* of the studio's money.

Shortly thereafter, Bach, in Los Angeles, received a startling phone call from Auerbach in New York. "I'm in love," the company president informed his subordinate, pausing for maximum effect, "with *Yentl.*" Apparently, he had spent the day at Barbra's penthouse apartment in Manhattan. He shared stories with her about his childhood in Prague. She told him about *Yentl,* and even sang him several songs from the score.

Bach tried to protest, to no avail. "No buts," Auerbach interjected. "I think we should do it. Besides, there's someone else already cast, the father in the picture."

"Who?" asked Bach.

"Me," Auerbach replied.

According to Auerbach, Barbra told him that he would be perfect for the part of Yentl's father, and she had promised him the part.

On March 31, 1981, United Artists confirmed that Barbra would direct, produce (without either Joan Marshall Ashby or Jon Peters, but with former Peters associate, Rusty Lemorande), cowrite, and star in *Yentl.* "The picture nobody wanted," Steven Bach later reported, "was ours." Production was slated to start in February 1982.

Steven Bach met with Barbra at the Malibu ranch compound, where she was now living, off and on. She took him on a tour of her art deco house and he was greatly impressed with her visual sense and meticulous attention to detail, down to the color of the soaps in the bathrooms, and the hue *and* period of the clothes in the closets.

He lated disclosed, "Like Auerbach, I fell in love. She is intelligent, funny, professional, obsessive-compulsive, a perfectionist with a soupçon of parsimony, and far more attractive off screen than on. Telephone conversations with her about the script tended to go on rather longer than it took to lay the Atlantic cable and rarely required more than the occasional 'uh-huh' from me to indicate I was still listening. But I liked her, and the force of her personality and common sense persuaded me that if anyone in the world could make *Yentl* work, it was she."

One night in May 1981, while Bette Midler was having a nervous breakdown in Lake Tahoe making *Jinxed* for their studio, Steven Bach, Norbert Auerbach, and a few other UA executives took Barbra out for dinner at Ma Maison in Los Angeles. Everything was going fine until Auerbach started relating the same stories about his childhood in Prague that he had shared with Barbra that day in her Manhattan apartment. Barbra, it seems, made the mistake of commenting that she hadn't known that Auerbach was from Prague. Puzzled, Auerbach responded, "That's why you asked me to play your father (in *Yentl*], remember?"

"My *father?*" Barbra answered, astonished. *"Morris Carnovsky is going to play my father!"*

Actually, Nehemiah Persoff would be cast in the part, but the point was clear: Auerbach had either misinterpreted Barbra's words, or had been deliberately deceived.

Whatever the case, $14.5 million had been promised, the paperwork had been signed, and Barbra had her *Yentl*. But, it came at a substantial price. To seal the deal with United Artists, she had to relinquish script approval, limited casting approval, *and* final cut. She also had to agree that all budget overruns would come out of her own pocket. She would later characterize the agreement by saying, "I had to eat shit."

But, of all the obstacles Barbra had to face in getting her beloved *Yentl* to the screen, the most damaging came not from a Hollywood studio executive, or even from Jon Peters, but from Isaac Bashevis Singer, the author of the story that had entranced her so many years before.

"I sold it [the story] to a poor producer," the Nobel prize–winning Singer related, "and he sold it to Streisand. Now she's found people who fitted the story to her desires. But the actor should adapt to the play— not vice versa." He added, in reference to Barbra's suitability, or lack thereof, for the part he had created, "Even I can't make Barbra Streisand sixteen again."

Defying all odds, with years of preparation, several postponements, and a reported *twenty* versions of the script behind it (including one by Elaine May, and another one by Singer himself), *Yentl* started principal photography at Lee International Studios in Middlesex, England, on April 14, 1982. The first day on the set, Barbra, the fledgling director, took a crew member's hand and found that it was wet with perspiration. "Believe me," she confided in the shaken man, "there's no one more nervous than me. We're all going to make mistakes—especially me."

Less than two weeks later, Barbra celebrated her fortieth birthday. "It was time to put up or shut up," she said of the occasion, and of her undertaking, "I could no longer blame anyone but myself. There is no cop-out on this one."

For the next *seven* months, Barbra would wake up every morning at five, put in a full day of work, and then stay up until 2:00 A.M. planning her shots for the following day.

After interiors were completed in England, the company moved to Czechoslovakia to shoot the exteriors. Barbra had selected the locations after also scouting Poland, Yugoslavia, Hungary, Romania, and Austria. She had been warned by many not to venture into such politically volatile communist territory, and, at one point, Barbra considered substituting Lake Placid, New York, for Eastern Europe. In the end, she confronted her fears and did what she felt was "more true to the piece."

And it would show on the screen. Certainly, one of the most impressive aspects of the film would be the authenticity of its look, feel, and attention to detail. Barbra hired David Watkin, who had shot *Chariots of Fire* (1981), and who would later do *Out of Africa* (1985), as her cinematographer. She had wanted the superb Italian cinematographer Vittorio Storaro, an Oscar winner for *Apocalypse Now* (1979) and *Reds* (1981), but he would have added $250,000 to the budget, money that would have had to come out of her own pocket.

To make herself look more masculine in her scenes as Anshel, Barbra had her face shot from the right. In addition, she surrounded herself with pretty, young male extras with soft eyes and full-lips. In a bit of daring, she also cast some girls as boys for the yeshiva-related crowd scenes.

To make the sequences with Anshel's bride, Hadass, more believable, Barbra made Amy Irving, the actress she cast in the part, as pretty and feminine as possible. "Barbra was always adjusting the lighting or the camera angle to make me look perfect," Irving recalled. "She'd fix my hair ribbons, brush an eyelash off my cheek, paint my lips to match the color of the fruit on the table. I was like her little doll that she could dress up."

For the scene in which Anshel was to kiss Hadass, Streisand, despite encouragement from Irving, refused to rehearse. Then, when it came time to shoot the scene, the two women kissed. Those hoping for even a trace of titillating homoeroticism, however, were disappointed. After the first take, Barbra backed away and pronounced, "It's not so bad. It's like kissing an arm." Irving, who had done her best to be alluring for the scene, was momentarily hurt and offended by the blatant rebuff.

One of the failures of the film was the casting of Avigdor, the object of Yentl/Anshel's desire. Barbra had wanted Richard Gere for the part. She sent an emissary to catch him on Broadway in *Bent,* and the two later met. Although they got along well, Gere turned the part down, reportedly because of reservations over Barbra's multiple job assignments. Barbra then went after Michael Douglas, who also rejected it. John Shea was another contender, but he was eventually passed over. At another point, it looked as if Barbra was going to cast international singing star Enrico Marcias, but that too was not meant to be.

Instead, Barbra cast Mandy Patinkin, who had won a Tony on Broadway for his performance as Che Guevara in *Evita*. The failure of his casting had nothing, really, to do with Patinkin. The fact is that Avigdor and Anshel do *not* interact, physically, like two men. Perhaps that is one reason why there are no homosexual overtones to their scenes. Moreover, Patinkin is such a masculine man that he makes Anshel seem that much more frail and feminine. Barbra should have cast a prettier, slighter, less imposing actor.

Given what little he has to do, Patinkin also seems wasted in the picture. Because he is such a strong presence, the fact that his part is underwritten is only punctuated. Barbra also probably made a mistake in casting an actor known primarily for his singing. Audiences watch the picture, *waiting* for Patinkin to sing. When he never does, it is assumed that Barbra, as the director, and in a fit of egomania, either cut out his songs, or didn't give him any to sing in the first place.

The fact is that, except for the very end, the only singing that takes place in the picture goes on inside of Yentl's head, in her own, internal world. Barbra determined that any other singing would be distracting to the story. What she apparently had not counted on, however, was that audiences would be distracted by Patinkin *not* singing.

Impressive in the picture is the scene in which a group of elderly ladies are gossiping about Yentl's desire to learn the Talmud. One says, "Better she learn how to get a husband." Barbra shot the scene through a rail with bars, which represents, of course, a prison. But, Barbra made the point that it is not a prison that *men* have put them in, it is, as evidenced by their disparaging remarks about Yentl, and about all women in general, a form of *self-imprisonment*. Barbra ends the scene by cutting to a shot of chickens in a cage. It is one of Barbra's most effective moments as a director.

Less inspired is the sailing-to-America finale in which, Yentl, for the first time, is able to come out of her interior world and openly express her feelings in song. Yentl demands, "I am *me*—let me be free!" but the scene is hampered because it calls to mind Herb Ross's "Don't Rain on My Parade" tugboat sequence from *Funny Girl*.

Furthermore, one wonders why Yentl is going to America in the first place. The ending seems incongruous with the rest of the picture, and feels tacked on just so that Yentl, and the story, can have a happy conclusion. Worse, the number itself is awkwardly staged. As Yentl sings, none of the extras on the boat look up at her, as if belting aboard ship were a perfectly natural occurrence.

To be fair, there *were* extenuating conditions involved in the shooting of the sequence. For one, Barbra was directing the action aboard the ship with a helicopter hovering four feet above her head. Terrified, she kept ducking. Moreover, her work was rushed because the helicopter was running out of fuel, and the shooting was taking place far offshore. Further exacerbating the situation, the musical playback was malfunctioning, so when shooting the song, Barbra could not hear her prerecorded voice, or the music itself. To compensate, she took out an old tape recorder, which she takes with her everywhere, and blasted the tape so that she could hear—and sing—Yentl's triumphant finale.

During production, members of the *Yentl* company issued a letter to the press about their producer-director-writer-star, which read, in part, ". . . during the last three months of rehearsal and filming she has completely captivated us all. Though undoubtedly a perfectionist in her dealings with everyone . . . she has shared jokes, chat, and pleasantries each and every day. She appears to have no temperament. . . . We have all worked with directors and stars who are the complete antithesis of Barbra Streisand but whose antics don't reach the newspaper. This letter is entirely unsolicited and is the result of our collected affection."

Barbra's multiple, hyphenated duties of director-producer-writer-star actually made her job, in some ways, easier. "I found that doing more than one job was beneficial," she said. "Each job served the other. Put it this way, there's four less people to disagree [with]. Everyone gets along, you see? The actress doesn't fight with the director, the director doesn't disagree with the producer, the producer doesn't argue with the writer."

Production on *Yentl* wrapped in London in October 1982. In the months that followed, Barbra worked diligently on preparing her director's cut. Steven Spielberg was preparing *Indiana Jones and the Temple of Doom* on the same lot. Spielberg was then involved with, but not yet married to, Amy Irving. Barbra showed Spielberg some of the assembled footage from her film, which prompted speculation that he was helping her out in the editing room. When asked for a response to the rumors, Barbra said, seething, "Do you know how repulsive that is to me? I hate it. It's like they're already taking my film away from me!"

The mini-furor continued when Barbra told a reporter from the *Los Angeles Times* that Spielberg had seen a cut of the picture and advised her "not to change a frame." Barbra was justifiably irate when the newspaper printed only that Spielberg had seen a cut of the film and had offered his "advice."

Actually, it should not have mattered if Spielberg *had* offered Barbra more substantive advice—male filmmakers do it for, and with, one another all the time. The sexist implication in Barbra's case, however, was that a novice, *female* filmmaker needed the help of the successful, male Spielberg.

Making *Yentl,* Barbra was very much aware of the responsibility she had to aspiring women filmmakers in Hollywood. "A man can fail, and nobody says, 'We won't hire any more men,'" she said, "but let a woman fail, and it hurts all women."

When the picture went over $1 million over budget—it would eventually cost $16.2 million—the Completion Bond Company, the bonding outfit insuring the picture, stepped in and ordered that Barbra finish the dubbing of the picture in six weeks. If she didn't, the company threatened that it would take the picture away from her and hire another filmmaker to complete it. Barbra pleaded that she needed at least ten weeks to complete the film, but neither Completion Bond nor United Artists would budge. "Please, we're going to ruin the movie!", she implored repeatedly, "I'm going to die from the pressure!"

Nevertheless, testing the power of her own will, and with an extraordinary effort, Barbra finished the picture in the allotted six weeks. The experience left her both exhilarated and near physical and emotional collapse.

For her work as coscreenwriter on *Yentl,* a credit shared with Jack Rosenthal, Barbra was paid nothing, per her agreement with UA.. For her work as director, she was paid only the Directors Guild of America minimum, $80,000. And she ended up putting half of that back into the picture because she wanted to rescore some of the music, which the studio refused to pay for.

As the picture neared its release date, Frank Yablans and Frank Rothman, the heads of MGM/UA (the two studios had merged) were working at cross-purposes. While Yablans was trying to get Barbra to do more publicity for the picture, Rothman was financially punishing her for having gone over budget. Reportedly, Barbra ended up having to return half of her $3 million acting fee to compensate for her budget overruns.

Amid much fanfare, and with a great deal of anticipation, *Yentl* premiered at the Cinerama Dome theater in Los Angeles on November 16, 1983. To Barbra's great satisfaction, the MGM/UA executives ended up leaving her director's cut intact. Nonetheless, the subsequent reviews were decidedly mixed and wildly varying, with some calling it "a masterpiece," and others, "a bore." Actually, it was something in between. Certainly, it was not the disaster that some had been forecasting and, perhaps, hoping for. It was, in many respects, an accomplished work and a remarkable directorial debut.

One of the criticisms came from Barbra's mother. Diana Kind's problem with the picture had nothing to do with the acting or the script, but with the end credits. Barbra had dedicated the picture to Emanuel Streisand. Diana reprimanded her daughter, "When you dedicate the film to your father, you should also dedicate the film to your mother."

The most devastating review came from the man who had become Barbra's harshest critic, Isaac Bashevis Singer. The writer refused to attend the premiere (he had been invited by Barbra) but saw the picture at a later date. He was appalled by the way Barbra had, in his view, expanded her part at the expense of the other characters.

"The leading actress must make room for others to have their say and exhibit their talents," Singer commented. "No matter who you are, you don't take everything for yourself. I must say that Miss Streisand was exceedingly kind to herself. The result is that Miss Streisand is always present, while poor Yentl is absent."

Singer added, "I did not find artistic merit neither in the adaptation, nor in the directing. I did not think that Miss Streisand was at her best in the part of Yentl. I must say that Miss Tovah Feldshuh, who played Yentl on Broadway, was much better. [Streisand] got much, perhaps too much, advice and information from various rabbis, but rabbis cannot replace a director."

To the great relief of MGM/UA, Streisand proved not to be another Cimino, and *Yentl* proved *not* to be another *Heaven's Gate*. Although hardly a blockbuster, the picture grossed a respectable $40 million in the United States alone.

On February 22, 1984, Jon Peters sold Barbra all of his interest in the Malibu ranch compound, formalizing their breakup which had been several years in the making.

Among the men Barbra dated during her lengthy split with Peters were Israeli multimillionaire Arnon Milchan (who would go on to executive produce pictures including *JFK, Under Siege, Falling Down, Sommersby,* and *Free Willy*), Richard Gere, and her old flame, Pierre Trudeau, who had divorced his wife, Margaret, several years before.

Another boyfriend was millionaire businessman Richard Cohen, ex-husband of Tina Sinatra. Barbra met Cohen in January 1984 at the fortieth birthday party for Kenny Rogers's wife, Marianne. The two dated until late spring.

It was also during this period that Barbra had a "date" with a struggling young female singer from New York. Cis Corman phoned Barbra and told her that she had found a girl whose spirit, ambition, and tenacity, reminded her of the early Barbra. Her name was Madonna Ciccone and she was twenty-five years old. Cis told Barbra that Madonna would be coming to California, and when she did, she wanted them to take her out for dinner.

Upon her arrival, Cis and Barbra brought Madonna to a Chinese restaurant. Barbra was perplexed by, and a little in awe of, the *hungry* creature before her. The newcomer was brash, aggressive, and so nakedly ambitious. Barbra was also astounded when Madonna, unabashedly taking advantage of a free meal, set down her menu and ordered an *entire* fish.

In March, Barbra went on an overseas tour to promote *Yentl*, culminating with the April 1, 1984, premiere in Israel. For Barbra, the highlight of the Israeli trip was the five minutes she spent alone atop the Golan Heights at Mitzpe Gadot. She would later declare, "I don't think of Israel as a foreign country. It is my land also, because we are all Jews."

On April 3, on the Mount Scopus campus of Hebrew University in Jerusalem, Barbra participated in the dedication of the Emanuel Streisand Center for Jewish Studies, which she partially helped to fund.

Later in the year, Barbra was honored with the Scopus Award, presented by the American Friends of the Hebrew University in a black-tie ceremony at the Beverly Hills Hotel. In making the presentation, Vidal Sassoon mistakenly referred to Barbra's film as *"Yenta."* "It's *Yentl*," Barbra corrected. *"Yenta, Yentl,* what's the difference?" Sassoon shot back. The important thing was that the purchase of each table at the ceremony represented a three-year scholarship for an Israeli student. One-hundred-twenty such scholarships were created that night for chosen students to be known as the Emanuel Streisand Scholars.

With a donation of $500,000, she had previously established the Emanuel Streisand Chair of Cardiology at the UCLA School of Medicine in Los Angeles.

Just as she had done with her own, Barbra was putting her father's name all over the map.

In Isaac Bashevis Singer's story, Yentl's father had died before the narrative began. In Barbra's movie, Yentl's father was given life in the first reel. In a sense, it was Barbra's way of giving herself the father she never had; a father who could teach her what he knew; whom she could please and make proud. And when Yentl says *kaddish* for her father at the cemetery* in Yanev, a town outside of Prague, it is also Barbra's way of saying *kaddish* for *her* father. With *Yentl,* she was able to embrace, and then release, and finally, merge identities with, Emanuel Streisand.

In addition to allowing Barbra to find peace with her father's passing, the movie, just as it did for Yentl, gave Barbra Streisand a voice. Actually, she *always* had a voice. The movie provided her with a safe and welcome place for her voice, her ideas, her opinions. After spending her entire career apologizing for her suggestions, Barbra, suddenly, was respected for them.

In becoming a film director, she had finally found a home.

---

*Shooting at an actual cemetery, Barbra had the existing headstones temporarily transported to a hill because she liked the idea of the dead having a view.

Thirty-two

Homecoming

"*I*'m trying to give Jason some of the love I got from my father," Barbra said, as she returned to life high atop Holmby Hills. "Now I've stopped preaching, stopped judging. I tell him what I think or feel, and if he doesn't accept it, that's fine."

Yentl had physically separated Barbra from her son for at least a year; given her obsession with her picture, their time apart was even longer. The mother and child reunion did not take place without difficulty. When Barbra began to work on *Yentl* on a day-and-night basis, Jason was a fourteen-year-old boy. At the time of *Yentl's* release, he was a young man about to turn seventeen.

In June 1984, Barbra reunited with Elliott Gould to watch as Jason received his diploma from Crossroads High School in Santa Monica. Perhaps as a graduation gift, perhaps just as a show of encouragement, Barbra financed and served as executive producer on a movie Jason produced, directed, and edited. It was called *It's Up to You*. Filmed at the Holmby Hills house, the picture starred Jason's grandmother, Diana Kind, his aunt Rozie, and his father. At the time, Elliott was enjoying his first steady job in some time, a half-hour CBS sitcom entitled "E/R."

In late September, Barbra once again stepped before the cameras, *not* for another movie or television appearance, but to make her first music video. With its pounding beat and flashy, quick-cutting images, MTV, introduced in 1981, had swept an entire generation off its feet and changed the face of the recording industry in the process. Barbra, reticent at first to jump on the video bandwagon, eventually capitulated, but did so on her own terms. Instead of the standard, often nonsensical, three-minute clip, her debut venture was a six-minute minifilm which showcased (again), an "all-new, sexy Barbra." Kris Kristofferson appeared as her costar, proving that their four-letter-word-spewing face-off at Sun Devil Stadium was buried and behind them.

The video, however, did little to boost sales of Barbra's single, "Left in the Dark," which failed to even make the *Billboard* top forty. *Emotion,* the album on which the song was included, proved to be Barbra's lowest charting studio album, peaking at number 19, since *What About Today?* in 1969.

By the time she went to London to make another video for another single from the album, Barbra was seriously involved with the new man in her life. His name was Richard Baskin, and he was an heir to the Baskin and Robbins ice cream fortune. At thirty-four, eight years younger than Barbra, Baskin was a composer who had served as musical director on Robert Altman's 1975 picture, *Nashville.* His other film credits include *Buffalo Bill and the Indians* (1976), *Welcome to LA* (1978), and *Honeysuckle Rose* (1980). The two had reportedly met at an industry Christmas party, shortly after the release of *Yentl.* As she was about to leave, Baskin, described as a "quiet type," boldly approached Barbra, told her how much he had liked her film, and began a conversation. She told him how much she loved his family's coffee ice cream, which, one imagines, if one imagines such things at all, she has been receiving on a complimentary basis ever since.

Perhaps motivated by her son's entry into college, or by Yentl's great yearning to *learn,* Barbra returned to school, auditing a class at the University of Southern California (USC) on human sexuality and the role of men and women in society. Typically dressed in dark glasses, a black hat, and plain, dark clothing, Barbra sat in the back of the class. Usually, she was escorted into the classroom after the session began, and was rushed out before it ended, so as to discourage anyone from approaching her. Later, with a substantial (reportedly $300,000) donation, Barbra endowed the school with the Streisand Chair of Intimacy and Sexuality.

Inspired by the obstacles overcome and conquered on *Yentl,* Barbra, forty-two, recommitted herself to the idealism of her youth. She announced her intention to play the great classic roles for women, "Everything from Hedda Gabler to Medea."

She was also still developing *The Triangle Fire,* the project that was to team her with Jane Fonda, as well as another property, a comedy with Goldie Hawn.

Another project Barbra considered was the film adaptation of the Andrew Lloyd Webber musical, *Evita.* The show's producer, Robert Stigwood, initially determined that the film rights would go to Paramount, with Ken Russell directing. Negotiations collapsed, however, when Stigwood refused to accept Russell's choice of leading lady, Liza Minnelli, whose film career had perceptibly deteriorated.

Other actresses considered, without Russell's participation, included Barbra, Bette Midler, Ann-Margret, and Patti LuPone. Some of the more absurd possibilities: Cher, Olivia Newton John, and Marie Osmond. For a while, it looked as though Oliver Stone would direct Meryl Streep in the part. Streep, however, backed out, reportedly concerned over whether she could handle the difficult score.

When Stone met, and didn't get along with the next prospective Eva Peron, Madonna, he dropped out of the project and was replaced by Glenn Gordon Caron ("Moonlighting"). With this package, the Disney studio agreed to make the picture, only to later balk at the escalating budget, said to be around $30 million, and as of this writing, the beleaguered project is still on hold.

Disillusioned by *Emotion,* and her unfulfilling forays into rock—and perhaps emboldened by the unexpected success of *What's New,* Linda Ronstadt's daring album of standards—Barbra decided to return to her musical roots for her next album. She later explained, "I had to stop recording songs that any number of other people could sing as well as, if not better than, I could."

For *The Broadway Album,* Barbra phoned composer Stephen Sondheim in March 1985 and, summoning her nerve, asked him to rewrite three of his songs for her, including his classic "Send in the Clowns" from *A Little Night Music.* She didn't like his last line, "Well, maybe next year," and asked if the song could end instead with "Don't bother, they're here." She also asked if he would write an additional eight-line second bridge for the song. Wanting to work with Streisand, Sondheim complied.

Typical of her inclination to fuse her creative and romantic impulses, Barbra hired Richard Baskin to produce two of the tracks on the album, "Something's Coming" from *West Side Story,* which he also arranged, and "Not While I'm Around" from *Sweeney Todd.* Previously, Baskin had cowritten and coproduced several tracks from Barbra's *Emotion* album.

The Broadway Album also reunited Barbra with her onetime fan, Paul Jabara, who had written her hits, "The Main Event/Fight" and "No More Tears (Enough Is Enough)." For her new album, Jabara agreed to coproduce and coarrange three songs from *The King and I,* "I Have

Dreamed," "We Kiss in a Shadow," and "Something Wonderful."

Upon completion of the work, Barbra allegedly asked Jabara to relinquish his producer's royalties for the songs. He refused. He did the work, he argued, and should share in the proceeds. Nevertheless, in the years that followed, the songwriter reportedly had difficulty collecting his royalty checks from Barbra. In 1992, Jabara, forty-four, died of lymphoma. From his deathbed, he was reportedly still haggling with Barbra over the monies that were owed him.

In spite of Columbia's reservations about the project from inception through recording, *The Broadway Album* was a spectacular critical and commercial success. Entering the *Billboard* top forty on November 30, 1985, the album, without benefit of a hit single, reached the number one position on January 25, 1986, where it remained for three weeks. As of this writing, it is the biggest selling solo album of Barbra Streisand's career.

Film director William Friedkin *(The Night They Raided Minsky's, The French Connection, The Exorcist)* was surprised to receive a call from Barbra asking him to direct the music video for her single, "Somewhere." Curious, Friedkin agreed to meet with her and learned that the reason she selected him was his reputation for making violent pictures. According to Cindy Chvatal, Friedkin's assistant, Barbra wanted the video "to show people blowing each other up. Mushroom clouds. And she wanted riots in South Africa. Her point of view on how the video should be was, 'If you don't protect it, then it's going to go away.' "

To Barbra's surprise, Friedkin rejected her concept. Instead, he envisioned shots of people arriving at Ellis Island, and children playing in pools in Africa. Each tried to convince the other that *their* concept was the best, with Friedkin eventually winning out. As Chvatal later characterized it, "They were having a charm contest." As for the concert portion of the video, it was shot on October 29, 1985, at the Apollo Theatre in New York.

The Broadway Album would bring Barbra her eighth, and to this date, final, Grammy award (Best Pop Vocal Performance Female).* It also reunited her with Peter Matz, who had arranged *The Barbra Streisand Album* in 1963, as well as her other subsequent early recordings. Matz coproduced, coarranged, and conducted nearly half of all of the tracks on *The Broadway Album.*

---

*Upon accepting her award at the February 24, 1987, ceremonies, Barbra acknowledged that she suspected she might win. It was February 24, her lucky number. She had been born on the 24th of April; and it had been 24 years ago that she had won her first Grammy.

The reunion was reportedly marred, however, when Matz, like Jabara, was denied his producer's royalties. When contacted for this book, and asked specifically about his problem collecting the royalties owed him, Matz offered no denial, saying only, "No comment."

Perhaps it was the nostalgia conjured by her vinyl return to Broadway that reunited Barbra with the man who had, twenty-five years before, flown to Detroit to negotiate her a pay hike from $150 to $175 a week *with meals*. Marty Erlichman had worked as Barbra's manager from 1961 through 1976, when Jon Peters officially took over his duties.

In the years that followed, Marty, who had produced pictures including *Coma* (1978) and *Breathless* (1983), had not seen or heard much from his former client and surrogate daughter. But, with Peters being fazed out of her business dealings, the time seemed right for a reunion. While on a skiing vacation in Utah in 1984, Barbra learned through a mutual friend that Marty was also vacationing in the area. She phoned and arranged a meeting. The two recalled old times and made their amends.

With the term of her obligations to Peters legally expired, Erlichman resumed managing Barbra's career at the beginning of 1986. "She and I jumped right into it like there had been no gap," Marty enthusiastically reported, "It's like we were married for sixteen years, and then split; when you get back together you kind of know each other. Age has worked well for both of us in the sense that we can talk more shorthand then we used to."

It was the day of Ronald Reagan's bombing of Libya, but on March 24, 1986, the controversy in Hollywood revolved around the Academy Awards. *The Color Purple* had received *eleven* nominations, but its director, Steven Spielberg had been bypassed in the Best Director category. Barbra agreed to be a presenter on the show, with several conditions. One, she wanted to present, pointedly, the Best Director prize (which her *The Way We Were* director, Sydney Pollack, was the heavy favorite to win for his work on *Out of Africa*); two, she wanted a clip of herself directing *Yentl* included in the introductory montage of directors in action; and, three, she wanted the montage scored with "Putting It Together," one of the Sondheim songs from *The Broadway Album*. If she should make an appearance on the internationally televised Oscars, after all, she might as well get in a plug for her latest project.

"A director is part artist, part politician, part father-confessor, and part Jewish mother," Barbra informed Oscar's audience from the podium. As she opened the winning envelope, and saw the name on the card, she smiled and began to sing, "Memories . . . ," calling attention, of course, to the film she had made with the winner twelve years before. When none of the nominated directors moved from their seats, she shouted out, "Sydney Pollack!"

Avoiding the paparazzi after the ceremony, Barbra snuck into Spago, Wolfgang Puck's designer pizza parlor to the stars, and sat with Jessica Lange, Sam Shepherd, and a very pregnant Meryl Streep.

Barbra and Lange had recently shot a cover for *Life* magazine as "Hollywood's Most Powerful Women." They were joined on the cover by Sally Field, Goldie Hawn, and Jane Fonda. Glaringly absent from the illustrious group was Streep, who turned down the opportunity, reportedly because of her pregnancy. That didn't stop Hawn, however, who was five months pregnant.

The historic session took place at photographer Greg Gorman's house in the Hollywood Hills. Everyone arrived on time, except for Barbra, despite the fact that her Holmby Hills home was only fifteen minutes away. Jessica Lange had even driven in all the way from Santa Fe and managed to arrive at the appointed time. Irritated, Jane Fonda kept checking her watch, wondering aloud as to Barbra's whereabouts. It was one thing to keep the press waiting for an interview, or guests waiting at a party, but to keep Fonda, Lange, Field, and Hawn waiting on their day off was another matter altogether.

Barbra finally arrived, forty-five minutes late. "I never have been a joiner," she said, in a feeble attempt at explanation, "I never even had fun at recess in grade school."

In November 1981, Universal Pictures announced that Mark Rydell would direct the film adaptation of the Tom Topor play, *Nuts*. Rydell, considered a hot property at the time, was on the critically acclaimed and financially successful heels of *The Rose* (1979) and *On Golden Pond* (1981). For his new project, he considered casting Bette Midler. However, her breakdown on the set of *Jinxed* seemed to all but destroy her once promising career in Hollywood. And so Rydell turned to Debra Winger, twenty-six, who was considered by many at the time to be the best young actress in Hollywood.

Nuts is the story of Claudia Draper, a high-priced prostitute who kills one of her clients, she contends, in self-defense. However, the question of her guilt is secondary to the question of her sanity. Her stepfather wants her put away, he says, to avoid the nastiness of a trial. It turns out that he has his own motivations for wanting her discredited and institutionalized.

Central to the plot was the question of "What is *normal?*" It was a question Barbra had been asking, and defying, all of her life. Claudia Draper is a woman who is, above all, misunderstood. She is a woman who is *too* honest. "That's what I love about this character," Barbra later related, "she speaks the truth and she gets in trouble." In Claudia Draper, Barbra saw her truth-speaking, misunderstood self.

Nuts also presented to Barbra the opportunity to deal with child abuse, and, at least on some level, her relationship with her stepfather. There is no indication that Barbra was sexually abused by Louis Kind (as is the scenario in Claudia's case), but, she *was* emotionally abused. There were other characteristics belonging to Claudia's stepfather, Arthur Kirk, which Barbra identified with Kind. It is Kirk who wants Claudia put away in a mental institution to, in essence, shut her up, as her mother stands by and passively watches. Years before, Louis Kind dismissed "crazy" Barbra, tore down her ego, and ignored her presence, as her own mother stood by and passively watched.

Tom Topor adapted his play and wrote the first script, which was followed with drafts by Carol Sobieski, Andy Lewis, and Mark Rydell.

With Barbra displeased with the results, Rydell sent the script to writer Darryl Ponicsan *(Cinderella Liberty, Vision Quest)*, who thought well of the material and wanted to become involved. Ponicsan met with Barbra, who liked both him and his approach. Rydell then went on a vacation in Hawaii, telling Ponicsan that a deal would be finalized upon his return. Enthused, Ponicsan got off the phone with Rydell and telephoned his friend, Alvin Sargent, to share the good news.

Before sharing the new development in his life, Ponicsan asked Sargent what *he* was working on. Sargent replied, *"Nuts."* Ponicsan was floored. Recovering, he proceeded to tell his friend that *he* was also working on *Nuts.* Upon further conversation, the two writers, both well established in the industry, realized that they were each being duped by Rydell. Both had been promised a deal, "after I get back from Hawaii."

Furious, but also bemused by such Hollywood machinations, both men walked out on the project. Ponicsan called Rydell's answering machine and imparted his own brand of *aloha:* "After Hawaii, go directly to hell."

Upon hearing the news, Barbra called Ponicsan and expressed her disappointment over his departure. Unwilling to concede defeat so easily, she asked if the two writers would consider working *together* on the project. Ponicsan, still smarting from the deception, answered with an un-qualified no. Ponicsan then received a phone call from Rydell, who spent forty-five minutes apologizing profusely. A few days later, after reconsidering their position, the two writers agreed to a collaboration.

Meanwhile, the executives at Universal were becoming less enchanted with the project, which, with Debra Winger in the leading role, had been intended as a "small," moderately budgeted picture. With Barbra's involvement, however, the budget escalated well above $20 million, with $5 million alone going for her acting salary, and an additional $500,000 to be spent on her services as producer. For her work collaborating on the screenplay, Barbra waived her fee and her credit.

In September 1985, Universal placed the picture in turnaround, and it was promptly picked up for $575,585 by Warner Brothers.

Poniscan and Sargent turned in the first draft of their script. Barbra loved it. Executives at Warner Brothers, however, did *not*. The two writers went back to work and drafted a second screenplay. This time, both Barbra and Warners were pleased.

The studio, however, was less satisfied with Rydell. Citing what was only described as "major differences with the studio," Mark Rydell either left or was coerced out of the project. Contrary to rumor, Barbra seems to have had little or nothing to do with his departure. Reportedly, the studio had to pay Rydell's fee, $1.8 million, which was subsequently written off in the budget as "abortive costs."

With Rydell out, Barbra began her search for another director with whom she could collaborate. For years, she had been wanting to work with Martin Ritt (*Hud, Sounder, Norma Rae,* et al.), whose pictures she regarded as being suitably serious and distinguished. Barbra phoned him, introduced the project, and sent over the script by messenger.

At their subsequent meeting, Barbra was shocked by Ritt's response. "I'd like to do this movie," he told her, "there's only one thing—I don't know if you could play the part."

"What?!" Barbra responded, stunned. Recovering, she studied Ritt's face for a trace of malevolence and found none. She admired his straightforwardness and apparent lack of intimidation. She was also astute enough to realize that by challenging her in such a way, he provoked her defensiveness, which was precisely what she needed for the part of the cornered, entrapped Claudia Draper.

"Good," Barbra told the director, "you're the one."

To research her role of an incarcerated psychotic patient, Barbra, accompanied by Ritt, and her friend, Cis Corman, the film's coexecutive producer, met with a series of psychoanalysts. She also visited the neuro-psychiatric wing at UCLA, the Mental Health Court in the San Fernando Valley, Elmhurst Hospital in Elmhurst, New York, and Bellevue Hospital in New York City. After meeting with a series of mentally disturbed, schizophrenic female patients, Barbra confided, "I felt totally comfortable with them."

Other locations scouted on Barbra's "field trips," conducted in the spring of 1986, included the Santa Monica Arraignment Court and its lockup holding cells, the Santa Monica Courthouse, the Department of Correction in New York City, and Riker's Island Women's Prison.

Meanwhile, casting the male roles, particularly the lead of Aaron Levinsky, Claudia's beleaguered court-appointed defense attorney, proved problematic. Among the actors who declined the part because, for one, it was clearly secondary to Barbra's role, were Richard Gere, with whom she was still intent on working, Al Pacino, who wanted $5 million *if* he agreed appear in the picture, Robert De Niro, Marlon Brando, Paul Newman, Jeff Bridges, and Robert Duvall. Kevin Kline was pursued until it was reported back that he was "unavailable." Elliott Gould's name was brought up as a possibility, but he promptly turned down the opportunity.

Among the actors who expressed interest in the part, who were eventually bypassed, were Ron Leibman, Alan Arkin, John Malkovich, Sean Penn, Bob Hoskins, and Peter Falk.

Early on, it looked as though Richard Dreyfuss would be cast in the part. In fact, his deal was all but set. But, whether it was over money, or dissatisfaction with the script, Dreyfuss backed out. Or he was nudged out. What *is* known is that during the week of April 14, 1986, Dreyfuss's deal was being negotiated with Warner Brothers. The following week, it was *Dustin Hoffman's* deal, for the same part. For the next two months, it seemed certain, pending a few contractual points, that Hoffman would be playing opposite Barbra in the picture.

By June 16, however, Hoffman was out and Dreyfuss was back in. This time Dreyfuss was signed for a salary of $1.5 million. The following day, Martin Ritt sent Hoffman a letter which read, "Dear Dustin: I am not totally sure of what happened, but I am sorry that we didn't get a chance to work together. I would have liked that. Perhaps another time."

For the crucial part of Claudia's stepfather, Arthur Kirk, actors pursued included George C. Scott, Burt Lancaster, José Ferrer, Robert Mitchum, Kirk Douglas, Richard Widmark, and Gregory Peck. Barbra had been trying to work with Peck ever since she arrived in Hollywood. Ben Gazzara, another candidate, was a favorite of Cis Corman's, but was deemed "too ethnic" for the part. Also considered was Richard Basehart, until it was learned that he was dead.

Eventually, it was Karl Malden who was signed, with Maureen Stapleton cast as Claudia's mother. Cast in the part of the judge was Eli Wallach, one of Barbra's earliest and most ardent supporters from her days at the Bon Soir. It was a superlative cast.

With a direct cost budget of $21,584,000, which escalated to $27,468,000 when considering other costs including studio overhead, *Nuts* commenced principal photography on October 20, 1986. The ensuing production was rife with tension, particularly due to the friction between producer and director. Barbra, particularly after *Yentl,* on which she called all the shots, was not used to being told what to do. As for Ritt, he was not accustomed to giving up final cut to his producer, particularly when it was his star who was his boss.

Moreover, Ritt never amended his initial opinion that Barbra, forty-four, was not the right actress to play Claudia Draper. There were others who agreed. After all, Claudia, as described in the play, was a $500-an-hour call girl capable of "taking your body to heaven and sending your mind south," and of "spoiling you so bad you'll hate every other woman you touch."

Despite the question over her casting, reports emerging from the Warner Brothers lot were that Barbra was delivering a bravura performance that would finally put her with Meryl Streep in the front ranks of America's dramatic actresses.

Production on *Nuts,* which was shot by cinematographer Andrzej Bartkowiak (who had previously filmed the HBO documentary, "Putting It Together: The Making of *The Broadway Album*"), was completed on February 3, 1987.

Ritt had ten weeks, beginning on March 16, to come up with his director's cut. On May 22, he screened his version for Barbra. She made several suggestions, and, per his contract, he was given a second cut, which he screened for her a week later.

On June 1, for a three-week period, Barbra took over the editing of the picture. Over the summer, she then worked on the score, which she had decided to compose herself. She later said, "For some time, I had dreamed of scoring a movie. When I produced *Nuts,* the dream became a reality—after all, who else would hire me . . . or fire me?!" It was her first, and to this date, only such attempt.

Nuts premiered to mixed, though mostly favorable reviews on November 20, 1987. Despite the earlier, wildly enthusiastic prognostications that had come out of the studio, Barbra's performance, certainly one of the finest of her career, was also accorded reviews that were mixed. Some admired her gritty tenacity of her performance, while others could not get beyond the question of her suitability for the role.

Following the film's release, Martin Ritt, though reticent to publicly discuss the subject of Streisand, received letters from friends, of the "I'll bet you had fun" and "it couldn't have been easy" variety. One friend wrote, "I understand from [name deleted] that dealing with Barbra never got any easier, even in postproduction."

Given the reviews, and the somber nature of the story, *Nuts* performed disappointingly at the box office, grossing only an approximate $31 million. Some pointed to the returns as evidence of Barbra's diminishing appeal. "She doesn't have it anymore," they said. Or "She should have stuck to musical comedy." Or "She's lost touch with her audience."

It's ironic, of course, that by the time *Nuts* was released, the number-one female box office star in Hollywood was Bette Midler. With a string of popular hits, including *Down and Out in Beverly Hills, Ruthless People,* and *Outrageous Fortune,* the divine and durable Midler resurrected a career that, only a few years before, had seemed destined to become a Hollywood footnote.

As Barbra completed work on *Nuts* in postproduction during the fall of 1987, after three-and-a-half years of togetherness, Richard Baskin moved out of Barbra's house. "I was surprised [to see him go]," a friend said. "She really liked him a lot. One day he was there, the next he was gone."

It was the day after Christmas 1987. Barbra was at a party in Aspen, Colorado, when Don Johnson, the "Miami Vice" costar who had made pastels, Ray Bans, and stubble the fashion rage for men throughout the land, marched up to her. The two had met briefly once before, at the Grammy Awards ceremony the previous February. Standing at Barbra's side on that occasion had been Richard Baskin.

Back at the party in Aspen, Johnson took Barbra by the arm and led her off to a private place where they could talk. She was exhilarated by his nerve. She later divulged, "If I want to meet people, I have to talk to them first because so many are intimidated by me. So if a guy does make the first move, he is already a step ahead."

With its popularity rapidly diminishing (over a two-year period, the show had slipped from fifth to forty-ninth place in the Nielsen ratings),

Johnson was then actively pursuing a life beyond "Miami Vice." He had just completed work on a modestly budgeted feature film with Susan Sarandon entitled *Sweet Hearts Dance,* directed by Robert Greenwald.

Given his Warren Beattyesque reputation, Johnson surprised his co-workers with his absence of female companions on the set. When questioned about it by Greenwald, Johnson shot back, "I'm putting myself in a state of absolute emotional and physical deprivation, 'cause it's the only way I know to get myself upset enough!"

Boyishly handsome, masculine, and very secure with himself, Johnson exudes both sexuality and charm. "He has enormous charm," Greenwald related. "When he turns it on, he could charm Hitler."

The same could have been said for Jon Peters. In fact, Barbra has a pattern of being attracted to men younger than herself who are confident and at least slightly cocky, sexually aggressive, athletic (Johnson is a fishing, golfing, tennis, skiing, and powerboat racing enthusiast), financially secure, and possessing a power of their own. It is highly unlikely that she would ever become involved with, as other female stars might and *have,* a struggling garage mechanic, bagel maker, or construction worker.

Streisand and Johnson had things in common. Like her, he has a reputation for being controlling, and a perfectionist in his work. They also share a disdain for the press. "What lens are you using?" Johnson once demanded of a photographer from the *Los Angeles Times.* Refusing to do a certain pose, Johnson, sounding a good deal like Streisand, informed the photographer, "This is *not* a flattering angle. I've been in this business a long time, and I can usually tell what looks good." Further dissatisfied with the way things were going, Johnson walked out on the session.

Like herself, and like Claudia Draper, for that matter, Barbra felt that Johnson was misunderstood. His "bad boy" reputation, she argued, was both distorted and undeserved.

Moreover, Barbra is, and always has been, attracted to paradoxes in people, and Don Johnson was a walking, talking, lovemaking paradox. Despite his reputation for being a womanizer, he yearned for domesticity and family life; though he possessed a tough, sometimes swaggering veneer, he was a surprisingly sensitive man, still suffering from the effects of his parents' divorce which happened when he was eleven.

After getting acquainted at the post-Christmas party, Barbra invited Don to her New Year's Eve party, also in Aspen. But, it was Johnson who did the wooing. One of Barbra's friends called Lance Brown, one-half of the colorful, "guess who, don't sue" Hollywood Kids gossip duo, and told him, "You'll never guess who've been seeing each other." According to Brown, Johnson had to pursue her with persistence because Barbra was worried about, among things, their difference in age. Like Richard Baskin, Johnson was nearly eight years Barbra's junior.

Several weeks later, the couple was spotted together at the Conservatory Restaurant in the Mayflower Hotel in New York City. Columnist Liz Smith reported that the two were cozily huddled in a leather booth one minute, and the next minute they had slid from sight under the table.

Around this same time, Don was called back to the set of *Sweet Hearts Dance* to reshoot the film's ending. Johnson phoned director Greenwald and told him that he might be bringing Barbra along. At the last minute, however, she chose to stay home. "I decided there were enough directors on the set as it is," she said. Later, after being shown a rough-cut of the picture, Barbra supplied the director with a few minor suggestions.

On January 22, Barbra and Don took their relationship public by attending the Holmes-Tyson fight at the Atlantic City Convention Center. Not expecting to see the two of them together, and certainly not expecting to find Barbra Streisand at a prizefight, the attending press had a field day. "It was the first time I enjoyed my celebrity," Barbra later reported, "because I wasn't having to apologize to the man for getting all this attention, because he got as much attention as I did."

On February 25, 1988, Barbra was scheduled to make an appearance at the ShoWest Convention in Las Vegas where she was being named the "Female Star of the Decade." She would be late in arriving. When she *did* arrive, on the arm of Don Johnson, pandemonium erupted. Sitting on the dais was Jon Peters, who bolted out of his chair and embraced both of them as they took their seats.

"Sorry I was a little late," Barbra told the conventioneers, "but I was auditioning for a part on "Miami Vice.""

The following day, Barbra, in Miami, made an unbilled, unpaid, walk-on appearance on "Miami Vice." While on the set, a still photographer began snapping candid photographs of Barbra and Don together. Barbra spotted the lensman and said something to Johnson, who marched over to the photographer and physically confiscated the film.

On March 14, the couple attended a surprise birthday party for Quincy Jones. In the weeks that followed, Barbra accompanied Don to Aspen, where he purchased a $1 million home. Indulging what is perhaps her favorite pastime, she enthusiastically became her boyfriend's interior designer.

Meanwhile, Johnson was offered another picture, *Dead-Bang,* which was to be shot on location in Calgary. Barbra didn't care for the action-oriented script, which called for Johnson, a homicide detective, to vomit on a suspect. Nor did she like the idea of being separated from Don for the three-month shooting period. Nevertheless, the picture gave Johnson the opportunity to work with director John Frankenheimer (*The Manchurian Candidate),* and he accepted the assignment.

On April 24, Jon Peters threw a forty-sixth birthday party for Barbra at his home. Don Johnson, shooting *Dead-Bang,* was not there. His ex-wife, however, Patti D'Arbanville, who had appeared with Barbra in *The Main Event* and to whom he was still close, *was* there. In his absence, Don reportedly presented Barbra with a $25,000 Arabian stallion.

Barbra was invited to another party held a few months before, at the home of Pamela Des Barres, a former lover of Johnson's, with whom he was also still close. In her book, *I'm With the Band,* she unabashedly described Johnson as an enormously endowed sex god. Wrote Des Barres, in an excerpt from her journal, "I'm getting off like I haven't in AGES."

Back at Pamela's party, Don was out of town on business at the time, so it was assumed by others that Barbra wouldn't appear. Lance Brown was one of the invited guests in attendance. He recalls, "I remember somebody said, 'You're not gonna believe this, but *Barbra Streisand* is walking into this house!'

"Barbra came to the party as a gesture. She didn't know most of the people there. She was very friendly with Patti D'Arbanville [who was—and is—close to Des Barres]. She stayed the whole night and talked to everybody. She kept going over to the table and sticking her finger into the cake."

Lonely as the weeks passed, Barbra boarded a plane and flew to Calgary to be with Johnson. Coincidentally, her sister, Roslyn Kind, happened to be performing in a production of *Leader of the Pack* in Calgary at the time. "She was being billed as 'Barbra Streisand's Little Sister in *Leader of the Pack,*'" recalls a former friend and business associate of Roslyn's. "Barbra called and said, 'Don and I want to come and see the play, but don't let anybody know we're coming.' Roslyn told only the stage manager, who cleared out the whole top balcony of the theater for Barbra and Don. Their limo drove them up to the theater at the last minute before the show was to start. When they were taken up to their seats, everybody in the theater turned around to look at them. Barbra was furious [with Roslyn]."

At the time, Roslyn was having a difficult time getting even radio or television commercials because she sounded so much like her sister. She was up for one commercial for a tile company, but before the contracts were signed, Roslyn had to first sign a disclaimer saying that, by hiring her, the company was *not* attempting to do, or suggest, a Barbra Streisand impersonation.

Meanwhile, Barbra was obviously smitten. "I'm happy, very happy," she exclaimed. "And I have never been very happy, so it's something I'm learning. It's as if I were a child again." It mattered little that she had said the same kind of thing when she was first going out with Jon Peters, fourteen years before.

Little did Barbra know that while Johnson was in Calgary, he was also going out with a pretty fitness instructor and aspiring actress by the name of Pamela Loubman. "I had met his trainer at the gym," Loubman says. "I had just gotten a part in *Dead-Bang* as Don's wife. So, one day when I was on the set, his trainer introduced me to him."

Johnson was working on getting fit for the movie, and Pamela started accompanying him on his daily jogs. In time, the two were going out to movies together. Then, on Memorial Day weekend, Don invited Pamela to join him at his new home in Aspen. "I *did* date Don Johnson," she says, "and I did go with him to Aspen." Accompanying them on the trip were his trainer, his personal assistant, and his six-year-old-son, Jesse, by Patti D'Arbanville.

"I felt real comfortable with him," Loubman continues. "He's quite a gentleman and he has great respect for women. He's real easy to be with. His personality comes across much more in person that it does on the screen."

As for her relationship with Johnson, Loubman says, "It was casual. There was not the pressure with me as there was with a Barbra Streisand. We had common ground. There was no threat, and we got along well together." She adds, "I didn't expect anything from it. I have no hard feelings whatsoever."

It was Pamela's impression that Johnson's relationship with Barbra was *not* a serious one. "Definitely, there's no question about it. Don thought of himself as a single man."

Following the completion of *Dead-Bang,* back in California, Barbra and Don began work on a musical duet entitled "Till I Loved You." Johnson wanted to establish a recording career for himself. In the fall of 1986, his song "Heartbeat" had made it to the number five position on the *Billboard* pop charts. His album of the same name went gold, despite only peaking at number seventeen on the charts.

When asked why he wanted to become a rock and roll star, Johnson candidly answered, "Because I *can.*"

His relationship with Barbra was seen by some as a ploy on Johnson's part to further his recording career. "I think that he had a very warm regard and admiration for Streisand," recalls freelance entertainment reporter Tony Sands, "but there were also a lot of built-in benefits."

According to reporter Diane Albright, who wrote a book about Johnson, "Don wanted to work on a record with Barbra, to prove to the world that he could sing. He felt that if he could sing with Barbra [and hold his own], everyone would think that he *must* be good, and his singing career would take off."

In May 1988, Don's friend and ex-wife Melanie Griffith checked into a rehabilitation center for alcoholism. The two had met and become sexually involved in 1971 when she was fourteen and he was twenty-two. They later married and divorced, but continued to have a close friendship.

When Melanie was released from the rehab center in July 1988 it was Don Johnson who was waiting for her. The spark between the two reignited. According to Johnson, it was Melanie who pursued him. In the months that followed, the two fell back in love.

It is not known at what point Johnson informed Streisand of his renewed relationship with Griffith. What *is* known is that it was on Barbra's arm that Don attended the September 18, 1988 premiere of *Sweet Hearts Dance.* A few days before, the two went into the recording studio to record "Till I Loved You." Upon its release several weeks later, the single was lambasted by critics and the song failed to make the *Billboard* top twenty.

It was around this time that Johnson, when asked about marriage, told a reporter, "I always have in the back of my mind that eventually I am going to be married again." He added, provocatively, "and I'm encouraged of late."

Naturally, most everyone assumed that he was talking about Barbra as his prospective bride. Actually, however, he was referring to Melanie.

"I think Streisand was a bit shocked [by the news of Johnson's renewed relationship with Griffith]," recalls Tony Sands, "because I think Streisand was much more smitten with Johnson than he was with her."

Although he would contend that the breakup with Barbra was a mutual decision, Don Johnson would later acknowledge that, "Barbra was more willing to stay [in the relationship]. We genuinely tried to make it work. But we'd reached a point where we had to make a commitment or let it go."

In December 1988, around the same time she was being accorded stardom and acclaim for her performance in Mike Nichols' *Working Girl,* Don presented Melanie with a four-carat diamond engagement ring. The two were remarried the following spring. Of Barbra, and of the other women in his life, Johnson would say, "We all consider each other family. Patti's part of the family. Miss Pamela [Des Barres] is part of the family. Barbra is part of the family."

Barbra resumed dating Richard Baskin, and threw herself back into her work. She had wanted to star in the black comedy *The War of the Roses,* but director Danny DeVito went with Kathleen Turner instead. She also sought the female lead in *Frankie and Johnny,* but would eventually be rejected by Garry Marshall in favor of Michelle Pfeiffer.

Another role Barbra considered was Mama Rose in a big screen remake of *Gypsy.* Madonna was to play her daughter, stripper Gypsy Rose Lee. But the proposed production would eventually be developed for television instead, with Bette Midler in the part.

And so she continued to develop her own projects. Among them was a film biography of Margaret Bourke-White. Barbra sent the script to Richard Gere, with whom she *still* hoped to work. She wanted Gere to play the part of Southern writer Erskine Caldwell, with whom Margaret has an affair.

But, it would be another project that Barbra ended up going forth with, one that would take her back to her Brooklyn past and force her to confront the unresolved emotional scars of her own childhood.

The project was Pat Conroy's *The Prince of Tides.*

Thirty-three

Casting Caution to the Tides

Following her sleep-jarring, middle-of-the-night directive to light up her art, and after reaching an accord with Columbia Pictures, Barbra immersed herself with the casting of her new picture.

It came as little surprise to anyone that she should want to direct *The Prince of Tides*. After succeeding on many levels with *Yentl,* a monumental undertaking, there was little that seemed beyond her directorial range. What *was* surprising, however, was that she would choose to *act* in a picture in which she did not have the central role. To some, it was a sign of her artistic, as well as emotional, growth.

The Prince of Tides is the story of Tom Wingo, a South Carolinian shrimperman's son who rushes to Manhattan, to the aid of his suicidal twin sister, Savannah. While there, he is engaged by her therapist, Dr. Susan Lowenstein (Barbra), to unearth and recount the paralyzing secrets they had been suppressing since childhood.

With Robert Redford refusing the role of Tom Wingo and no longer in the realm of her astute and highly charged senses, and with Don Johnson no longer in her bed, Barbra set out on a search to find the man who would be Wingo. Her next choice was a curious one.

She wanted an actor who personified, at least on a superficial level, the quintessential Hollywood leading man, an icon of male sexuality and macho bravado whom she could, with her director's wand and feminine insights, probe and penetrate until she exposed the essence of the man beneath the posturings. She also sought an actor with some of the same

Kristofferson showing Barbra "who the man is." (Warner Brothers)

Diana Kind: A distant relationship with her famous daughter.

Family portrait: With brother, Sheldon Streisand, and sister, Roslyn Kind.
(The Richard Gordon Collection)

The Main Event: Anything but a knockout. (Warner Brothers. Courtesy of Cinema Collectors)

Flaunting (her idea of) her assets. (Warner Brothers. Courtesy of
Cinema Collectors.

The mirror cracked: Yentl becomes Anshel. (MGM/UA)

With Mandy Patinkin: A passion for learning. (MGM/UA. Courtesy of Cinema Collectors)

With Amy Irving: Skirting the homosexual issue. (MGM/UA. Courtesy of Cinema Collectors)

Sharing the spotlight with Don Johnson. (Courtesy of Cinema Collectors)

Blurring the lines:
What is normal?
Who is *Nuts*?
(Warner Brothers)

With Richard Baskin: All the free coffee and ice cream she wants. (Courtesy of Cinema Collectors)

Sharing a kiss with Jesse Jackson at a pro-choice rally in Los Angeles, 1989. (Mark Goins)

Jason Gould with Nick Nolte: The son also rises. (Columbia Pictures)

With Nick Nolte, the man who would be her Wingo. *The Prince of Tides*, 1991. (Columbia Pictures)

Streisand as director: At long last comfortable. (Columbia Pictures)

Quiet reflection, 1970.
(Columbia Pictures.
The Richard Gordon
Collection)

inner qualities as Tom Wingo, the man who expressed pain through laughter and whose wound was his geography. She wanted someone who would not only *act*—that is, hide behind the character he played—but who would also, in certain instances, be *himself* on the screen. It was an ambitious assignment for the actor, who would be called upon to unveil facets of himself he had never before revealed on the screen. Barbra would frequently tell those chosen to be her actors, "It's much more difficult to *be* who you are."

It was, perhaps, too much for Barbra to ask of Warren Beatty. Like Redford, Beatty is a fine actor, but not one who is generally known for unleashing torrents of raw emotion. Instead, he is (or *was,* given his 1991 marriage to Annette Bening) generally regarded as the preeminent Hollywood stud, whose conquests included Streisand herself, while his on-screen persona consisted of a detached reserve, a clenched jaw, a calculated cool. Beatty was indeed interested in playing the part of Tom Wingo, but he was not willing to display the emotional vulnerability Barbra required. For a while, he vacillated on whether to take the part, much to Barbra's frustration. Interestingly, Beatty agreed to star in *Bugsy* for director Barry Levinson, in which he would expand his range and silence his critics by delivering a surprisingly risky, explosive performance. Particularly good would be the scene in which Beatty as Bugsy mercilessly and sadistically humiliates a subordinate. It is a scene in which Beatty bursts forth, exposing a kind of passion he never before dared in front of the camera.

Meanwhile, another potential Tom Wingo emerged. During the shooting of *Q & A,* a 1989 drama about police corruption, the film's producer, Burtt Harris, presented Nick Nolte with Conroy's book. Nolte read it and was immediately taken by the notion of a man who had to deal with the women in his life in order to resolve the traumas of his childhood. "I asked [Harris] what the deal was with this piece," Nolte said, "because I liked the novel a lot. He said 'Barbra Streisand is going to direct it.' " Through Harris, Nolte requested a copy of the script. He then asked Harris to relay to Barbra that he wanted to discuss the project with her. Actually, she already *knew,* as she had asked Harris to casually approach Nolte with the book. Barbra was no fool. After her experiences with Redford and Beatty, she no longer wanted to do the courting. The man who would be her prince would come to *her.*

At that point in his career, Nick Nolte was a respected actor who rarely needed work. However, he was not viewed as a "leading man." For example, leading men do *not* get on their hands and knees, tongue exposed and panting, and devour dog food from a bowl on the floor, as Nolte did in *Down and Out in Beverly Hills* in 1986. He was younger than Redford, but dirtier, scruffier, less slick, and more menacing. In sum, he was Robert De Niro in Robert Redford's body.

Born in Omaha, Nebraska, in 1941, Nicholas King Nolte was the son of Helen and Frank Nolte. His father, a semipro football player turned traveling irrigation-pump salesman, was stationed in the Philippines during World War II when his only son was born. Nick did not even meet his father until he was nearly three years old. The absence of that early bonding, and the pain of never really getting to know his father in later years, left scars that Nolte would bring to *The Prince of Tides*. He suffered, too, when at the age of ten he accidentally impaled himself on a neighbor's white picket fence, mangling his groin. Instead of castrating him, the injury caused young Nick to develop what appeared to be a third testicle. It was a deformity that alienated Nick from his peers and marked his boyhood. Those close to the actor speculate that this child-hood accident of fate subconsciously instilled in Nolte the need to flex his masculinity and flaunt his rebellion.

Years later, when a reporter would ask the middle-aged and well-preserved Nolte if he had had a face-lift, Nolte, never one to play it straight with the press, replied that he hadn't, but that he *had* undergone a "testicle tuck." Nolte quipped to his audience, now rapt with attention, "It makes the penis look larger."

As a teenager, Nolte, a high school athlete, also became a prodigious drinker. He was thrown off the football team, for which he played quarterback, after he was caught drunk and unruly and with a bottle of whiskey stashed in his locker. Eventually, a sports scholarship carried him to Arizona State, where he floundered and eventually flunked out. Before he did, he left his mark, dubious though it was, by selling fake draft cards to interested students. Nolte was arrested, convicted as a felon, and sentenced to five years' probation.

In an effort to better direct his considerable energies, Nick started acting in regional theater, where he would spend years developing what would become his craft. He made the first of several television appearances in a 1969 "Walt Disney's Wonderful World of Color" and was eventually accorded his big break in the 1976 ABC miniseries "Rich Man, Poor Man," in which he costarred opposite Peter Strauss and Susan Blakely. This miniseries was followed by the insipid but popular 1977 feature *The Deep,* in which he costarred opposite Jacqueline Bisset's wet and altogether transparent T-shirt.

Nolte's drinking, carousing, and general excess progressed commensurately with success. Once, he greeted a reporter with a gun and a couple of six-packs of beer. One day, while shooting *The Ultimate Solution of Grace Quigley* (1984), Nolte received a phone call from his irrepressible costar, who chastised him, "I hear you've been dead drunk in every gutter in town, and it has to stop!" The costar was Katharine Hepburn, who, by way of her experience with Spencer Tracy, knew something about alcoholism. Not missing a beat, Nolte retorted, "I *can't* stop. I've got a few more gutters to go."

Nolte's early meetings with Barbra Streisand were peppered with and bonded by references to theories espoused by psychologist John Bradshaw. They had both read and been greatly influenced by Bradshaw's book *Homecoming: Reclaiming and Championing Your Inner Child.* Their meetings eventually evolved into a one-on-one symposium on the state of male-female relationships.

Certainly, in his personal relationships with women, Nolte has had his share of difficulty. He married and divorced actress Sheila Page, and was charged by actress Karen Eklund with a $5 million palimony suit. He engaged in a tempestuous marriage to dancer Sharon Haddad, and allegedly carried on an affair with Debra Winger during the shooting of *Cannery Row,* the 1982 picture that was notable primarily for the $10 million court settlement it netted for Raquel Welch's *non*appearance. In 1983, Nolte met Becky Linger, a doctor's daughter, who became his third wife. By early 1990, their marriage was on the verge of a nervous divorce.

Nolte says, "There haven't been many women who've been able to live with me very long. I'm an extremist."

Streisand was intrigued with the challenges presented by the actor's errant ways with women, and by—as she would tell friends—"his *issues* with women." Could *she* inspire his confidence and trust? Could *she* break down his macho bravado? Would he function well, if at all, with a woman as his boss? She was compelled, too, by the parallel issues between screenplay and actuality, reel and real life, that Nolte would bring to the project.

He was, like Wingo, a son with childhood scars that had gone unheeded, and thus unhealed; he was, like Wingo, a husband whose marriage was about to collapse; and like Wingo, he had yet to learn how to deal with the women in his life. In the movie, Wingo would have to come to trust a female therapist, while behind the camera, Nolte would have to come to trust his female director. Everything ran parallel, interlaced, reflected upon the other, and ultimately connected.

And so Barbra settled her sights on Nolte. However, she had a time convincing studio officials of Nolte's desirability. Nonetheless, when Barbra Streisand is intent on something or someone, she perseveres and she usually prevails. He was the right actor, for the right part, caught at the right window of time in his life.

Only months before, Nolte had given up drinking, and again like Wingo, he was at an emotional crossroads and on the road to self-discovery. He was an artist consumed by pain who needed a canvas to be expressed. As would most good directors, Barbra wanted to capture and, frankly, capitalize upon that pain with her camera, while also providing Nolte with his canvas for catharsis.

"I saw a lot of pain in his work, in his eyes," Barbra would later relate. "In talking to him, he was at a vulnerable place, ready to explore feelings, romantic feelings, sexual feelings, and deep, secretive feelings."

Of the name actors whom she had considered, Nolte was the one who would allow himself to be the most vulnerable. The question in Barbra's mind was whether she could inspire his trust and then command that vulnerability on cue. The question in Nolte's mind was whether he really wanted the part.

Understandably, given her reputation, Nolte felt reticent about working with Streisand. He called Karel Reisz, who had directed him in the 1978 picture *Who'll Stop the Rain,* and asked his advice. He also approached Sidney Lumet, his director on *Q & A,* with the same doubts and the same question. Both urged Nolte to do the picture. Streisand, they said, was not *that* bad, and the role was *that* good. In addition, a hefty paycheck did not hurt. Prior to *Tides,* Nolte reportedly commanded $1.5 to $3 million per picture. There were some who felt that, given his less-than-imposing box office stature, he was overpriced and should reduce his fee. According to longtime industry analyst John Voland, "The buzz around town was, 'Well, Nick is great, but he never "opens" a picture, so why is he getting so much money?' "

Nevertheless, if he was going to expose his soul for *The Prince of Tides,* Nolte would make certain that he was well compensated for it. For his work on the picture, Nolte demanded—and got—an impressive increase in pay—a fat $4 million. Nolte, of course, contends that his agreeing to play Wingo had nothing to do with money. "I decided," Nolte offers, "that this was absolutely the right piece for Barbra to direct."

Nolte claims he had wanted to work with a female director for years.

He had gone so far as to have several discussions with Lee Grant, but the two had been unable to find a mutually agreeable property. "I had a theory that when a male director and a male actor worked together, they get together at an emotional moment in a film that has to be fulfilled and they fulfill it, and that's it. They move on to the next thing. But with a female director you get to that moment, you complete that moment, and the female asks, 'Well, what's the next feeling?' "

Meanwhile, Barbra screened all the Nolte pictures she could obtain and concluded that he had not, in her view, fulfilled his potential. "I looked at all his films, and the love scenes were always truncated. There's never a bedroom scene. . . . He was brilliant in *Q & A*. He's much more comfortable in character roles. I just think when anyone has the potential to be that good, why not push it a little more? I know he's a man, a physical man, a sensual man, so why not incorporate that in the part?"

In a gender-reversing variation on Henry Higgins, she decided to transform Nolte into what many thought he always should have been: a leading man. At her urging, he would lose thirty pounds, wear costumes of her choosing, dye his locks to a golden and Redford-like glow, exploit his natural good looks, and present a screen image that was alternately charming and vulnerable, as well as salable to the masses. He would also consent to do a love scene or two, with his director—to the dismay of some—as his leading lady.

"I thought *I* was the best person for the role," says Barbra Streisand. "Could you think of someone to play it better?"

Nothing would miff her more in the succeeding months than when someone would mention the controversy of her own casting. Beauty parlor bitchery and trivial commentary aside, the controversy was not without some validity. Much of the criticism has its roots in what can only be described as the Star Factor.

In the book, the part of psychiatrist Susan Lowenstein is essentially one of several supporting roles. The character is a little too pat and predictable in her victimization and saintliness to come fully alive on the screen and is hardly a challenging one to play. After all, the character was not intended to be a leading role, nor was it meant to be played by a *star*.

With Streisand as Lowenstein, the entire picture is arguably thrown off balance. It's not so much that her part would be expanded as it would be highlighted. The book is of epic length and spanned decades. Obviously, not everything in it could be crammed into two hours of celluloid. Something had to give. Those who came before her had a problem in adapting the material. They struggled over such fundamental choices as which parts of the book should be featured, which portions should be skimmed, and which should be discarded altogether.

Streisand, however, had no such problems. With herself as costar, every single one of Lowenstein's moments in the book would be retained when translated to the screen. Hers is the only character who would not suffer a single cut in the adaptation—at the expense of other, arguably more essential elements of the book. It would not be at all surprising if Streisand's "artistic differences" with Robert Redford revolved around this very issue.

Barbra would offer as an explanation, "Needless to say, we couldn't bring all 567 pages of the novel to the screen, but I do believe that the essence of the story is here."

The essence, perhaps. The soul, however—good intentions notwith-standing—would be conspicuously absent from Streisand's script. The real title character in *The Prince of Tides* is not Tom Wingo but, rather, his older brother, Luke, a simple man of modest needs who lives his life with startling and enviable clarity, who adores and protects his family and who reigns over his kingdom of shrimp, swamp, and golden South Carolinian marshes with inherent humanity. "None of us suspected it when we were growing up," Pat Conroy has Tom Wingo reflect in his book, "but Luke was the one living the essential life, the only one that mattered." Luke Wingo is one of the most ebullient and heroic charac-ters in Conroy's fiction, and he is certainly the most interesting character in, and the soul of, *The Prince of Tides.* He has, however, been virtually and regrettably excised from Streisand's script.

Like Luke, sister Savannah too would suffer in the adaptation. Melinda Dillon, cast in what materialized as a glorified cameo, would have nothing to do in the picture but look pallid and pained in a hospital psychiatric ward. Furthermore, Tom Wingo's motivation for going to New York to rescue her in the first place is diminished by Streisand's script. The extraordinary closeness of their relationship is never really explored, except to establish that they are twins, as if that were sufficient exposition in itself.

Missing too from the picture would be a passage which probably did more to define the character of Tom Wingo, while also eliciting empathy for his struggle, than any other in the book. It is the sequence in which teacher Wingo learns that one of his female students has been physically abused by her father. Wingo, the warrior, marches to the girl's house and proceeds to pummel the abusive father. Here, we learned, was a man who would fight to protect somebody else's defenseless child, but who could not even address the pain of his own childhood; a man who would fight to protect the rights of a youngster he barely knew, while allowing, to borrow from Bradshaw, the child within himself to die a slow, torturous death.

And then there are the childhood scenes, which would be translated by Barbra sparingly and in flashback. Arguably, the childhood sequences were the best, most vividly told passages in the book. Still, they would be all but eliminated in the film. The story of the majestic porpoise that is rescued from Sea World–like exploitation by Tom, Luke, and Savannah is a classic tale of childhood idealism with enormous visual and heartrending potential. It too would be missing from Streisand's script. Missing also would be the colorful tale of Caesar the Bengal tiger, who saves the Wingo family from a sure and horrific death. Also, the powerful story of the Wingo children's rescue of Benji Washington, a black boy, on the day he integrates Colleton High School. The exclusions, unfortunately, go on.

Perhaps for reasons other than time, the critical rape scene would also be truncated in the adaptation. In an admirable effort to be sensitive to her young actors, it is possible Barbra allowed the scene to be diminished by awkward, tilted camera angles and quick edit cuts. Perhaps in a concerted effort not to sensationalize the scene, she was too delicate in her handling of it. In both the book and the picture, Tom Wingo is shamed and scarred for life when he is sodomized by an intruding thug. In addition, he is rendered impotent to prevent the brutal rapes of his mother and his sister. It is a devastating sequence in the book and in the life of Wingo, the absolute horror of which would not be fully realized in the picture.

Instead, audiences would be treated to languishing shots of Streisand's legs, a scene in which she breaks a fingernail, and twenty minutes of schmaltz in which Streisand and Nolte gaze into one another's eyes in a hopelessly dated montage that recalls those awful television commercials of the 1970s in which a young couple run, in slow motion, into one another's arms. It's a series of sequences which is incongruent with the contemporary and disturbing psychological issues that are the backbone of the story.

Barbra, however, would refuse to acknowledge that the various story choices and cuts she made, almost all of which benefited the character of Lowenstein, had anything to do with directorial favoritism, and would allow only that "there are of course, inherent difficulties in bringing such a widely read and beloved literary property to the screen. People become attached to certain aspects of the book that they love."

True enough on the surface, but if explored further, it can be argued that she imposed her considerable will on, and at the expense of, the material to transform the character of Susan Lowenstein, and the story itself, into a suitable vehicle for Barbra Streisand.

As well as provoking criticism for creating an imbalance to the story, her casting was also disparaged on a more personal level. "When I read the book," Barbra says, "I said, 'Oh my God! Except for the hair color, this is me. This could be me!' "

As her critics would be quick to ask, "Who does she think she's kidding?" Consider Pat Conroy's introduction of Susan Lowenstein: "She was expensively dressed, and lean. Her eyes were dark and unadorned. In the shadows of that room, with Vivaldi fading in sweet echoes, she was breathtakingly beautiful, one of those go-to-hell New York women with the incorruptible carriage of lionesses. Tall and black-haired, she looked as if she had been airbrushed with breeding and good taste."

Later, Wingo tells Lowenstein, "By any measure or by any standard in the world, that is a beautiful face. It's been a pleasure staring at it for the last couple of weeks. . . . [Your husband] is either a homosexual or an idiot. You look fabulous, Lowenstein, and I think it's high time you got some enjoyment out of the fact."

Still later, he tells her, "I can't even consider falling in love with someone as beautiful as you." And finally, he reflects, "Her beauty, dark and carnal and disturbing, stirred me as it always did."

Streisand's looks would not be a factor if they were not so integral to the character of Lowenstein and to the credibility of the story. Lowenstein is a woman who, at least on the surface, has it *all*, a woman who doesn't have to work at being beautiful. It is her beauty and her "world-class body" that initially captivate Tom Wingo, and conflict arises out of his considerable attraction to her face and body, while he is, at the same time, guarded against and not a little afraid of, her perceptive and probing mind.

Privately, even Barbra questioned whether she had the looks to play Lowenstein. She understood the character, and she could certainly act the part, but could she feign not just beauty but that *kind* of beauty? Growing up, Barbra the child was told that she was ugly. It was her half sister, Roslyn, who would be referred to as "the pretty one." Those were words from which Barbra would never quite recover.

Reflecting back on her own childhood with the distance of age and perspective, she would say, "Parents can put you in a role. You're the bad kid, you're the lunatic—like in the book [*Tides*]—he's the fanatic, you're a failure. And you grow up playing out the role—unless you get conscious and say to yourself: 'Hey, I'm not the ugly duckling. . . . I deserve to be happy.' " In assuming the part of Susan Lowenstein, Barbra may have been telling her mother, the world, and, mostly, herself, that she was no longer willing to play, no longer willing to accept, the role of the ugly duckling.

In an unusual move, Streisand the director decided to privately conduct a screen test of Streisand the actress to see, presumably, if Streisand the producer approved of the casting. She enlisted the services of a makeup artist and a cinematographer, attendants in her secret mission.

Paranoid that she would be ridiculed for testing for a part in her own movie, Barbra insisted to others who found out about it that she had not tested to see if she could *play* the part, but rather to see if she could *look* the part, which, of course, was true. She was so uncertain, in fact, that she showed the screen test to Pat Conroy. Conroy himself later admitted that he had seen such a test. He recalls, "When I first met Barbra, she asked me if she looked like the doctor, and I said no. So she said, 'Does *this* look like Lowenstein?' and she flipped this button and this huge image of her comes up on her screen. She had not tested for the part, of course, but she dressed for it and she was in character in the scene. I told her, 'Yeah, that's Lowenstein.' "

There are those who believe that Pat Conroy was more than a little generous with his approval. Granted, Barbra is a striking, attractive, and sometimes even beautiful woman with an ample bosom and a good pair of legs.

But a classic beauty she is not. God's gift to carnal man she is not. Nor is she Sleeping Beauty, who, like Lowenstein, sleepwalks through life until her handsome prince comes along and delivers the fateful kiss that rouses her from slumber. In brief, in physical appearance, Susan Lowenstein—as written by Pat Conroy—she is not.

The argument, of course, can be made—and is certainly not without some validity—that without Streisand in a starring role, the film would never have been budgeted at $25 million, unless, of course, she cast, instead of Nick Nolte, a Harrison Ford or a Kevin Costner (whom she reportedly pursued) as Wingo. Another, less appropriate, alternative would have been to cast a comparable female box office name in the part of Lowenstein. However, the idea of Julia Roberts, Bette Midler, or Cher in the part seems even more farfetched than Streisand. Michelle Pfeiffer could have played the beauty, but not the Jewishness. Whoopi Goldberg could have played it as a comedy, donned in a nun's habit. Meryl Streep could have played Lowenstein, but that's redundant, of course. Meryl Streep could have played Popeye in a picture directed by Pasolini and gotten away with it.

Perhaps even more audacious than her own casting was Barbra's selection of her own son for a supporting though pivotal role. He was not, however, her first choice.

From the time he learned that his mother would direct the picture, Jason Gould, then twenty-three, campaigned to be cast as Lowenstein's troubled son. He had already appeared, in small, insignificant roles, in *The Big Picture* (1989) with Kevin Bacon, *Say Anything* (1989) with John Cusack (1989), and *Listen to Me* (1989) with Kirk Cameron.

Barbra, however, was reticent to cast her son. First of all, she didn't want to be accused of nepotism. Later, referring to the debacle of *The Godfather Part III,* in which Francis Ford Coppola made the crucial mistake of casting his daughter, Sofia, who would be lambasted mercilessly for both her looks and her performance, Barbra acknowledged, "It's just scary to hire one's own son after what's gone on with some other movies with directors hiring their kids."

Furthermore, she realized that in casting Jason in such a prominent role, he would be considered a public figure and would therefore be introduced to the same kind of scrutiny in his personal life that she had been subjected to in hers. Barbra would later confess, "I thought, deep down, Well, it's dangerous. We could both get attacked for this."

And then, of course, there was the part itself as well as Jason's suitability for it.

The character of Bernard Woodruff called for an angry, rebellious, and yet repressed teenager who plays the violin to appease his virtuoso violinist father, while secretly harboring a fantasy to play football. Barbra did not think that her son was traditionally masculine enough for the part. Jason, after all, is on the slight and skinny side, and football was not his favorite pastime. Still, he auditioned for his mother, with and without a football.

Weeks passed, then, as Barbra herself relates, "Jason has never asked me for anything. Jason is not ambitious. He doesn't have a big desire to be famous or anything like that, because, you know, it's complicated being my son and Elliott's son, problems of competition and all that. But here my kid calls up one day and says, 'Mom, about that role, I hear you're getting ready to cast someone else, but what happened? I thought you thought I'd be good for it.' "

Barbra had already cast another actor in the part, Chris O'Donnell, who, unlike her Jason, had been the star quarterback of his high school football team. Pat Conroy recalls, "Barbra showed me this kid that she had cast for the role of her son, a very handsome blond kid. Of course, everyone looks wonderful in Hollywood, but I said, 'That ain't the kid.' So she said, 'I already hired him.' I said, 'That still ain't him.' And she said, 'Look, he's a good athlete.' I said, 'This kid [Bernard] is not a good athlete. That's the point.' So she sort of flipped me through other kids she'd auditioned. She finally came to this one kid. I didn't know it was her son. But he showed a snarling, wonderful teenage quality. I said, '*That's* the kid, right there.' She said, 'But he *can't* play football.' And she had pictures of this kid trying to throw the ball. He certainly wasn't good. He'd never thrown a football. So I said, 'Well, that's what you want, because then you can coach him. You can train him.' "

Barbra's objections, however, persisted. "Jason doesn't *look* like Bernard," she protested, ignoring the fact that she was not exactly a dead ringer for Lowenstein. "Bernard should be a stockier kid," she pointed out.

Conroy, who of course conceived the character and was well acquainted with his physique, corrected her. "No, no, no," he insisted. "He's described in the book as weighing 140 pounds."

Not one to take correction easily, particularly not about her own son, Barbra proceeded to tell Conroy that that being the case, Jason was too small for the part, since he weighed a mere 125 pounds. She confided her concern to the author, "I always think he should eat more—I'm his mother."

Surprisingly perhaps, Barbra Streisand is the quintessential "Jewish mother." She is obsessed with the idea of her son's undernourishment and has been known to make a series of unexpected midday appearances at Jason's various homes, wearing no makeup and a babushka wrapped around her head, and clutching a bowl of chicken soup to her bosom as some sort of maternal offering. She would stay for a few minutes and then depart with a single word of instruction: "Eat!"

Lydia Encinas lived in the same West Hollywood apartment building as Jason. She soon became aware of Barbra's visits. "She pulled up at the door in this big limo. She always had packages with her. You know, things a mother will bring her son. She was very 'Jewish-mother.' You could see her bringing in the chicken soup. She would ring the door downstairs and he would let her in. He was on the second floor and she would just go up the elevator like everyone else. It was a quiet building.

Usually, most people were at work during the day, so she would come when there was nobody around." Following her visit, Barbra would hurry back to the protection of her awaiting limo. Encinas adds, "Obviously, she didn't hang around to talk to people."

To prove her point to Pat Conroy about her son's frailty and thus his inappropriateness for the part of Bernard Woodruff, Barbra picked up the telephone and dialed Jason's number. When he answered at the other end, she blatantly blurted out the purpose of her call: "How much do you weigh?" No doubt startled, Jason, who had been working out at the Sports Connection gym in West Hollywood, answered, "140 pounds. Why?"

Barbra not only had her son's urging and the author's approval, she had her *sign*. Her son weighed in at precisely the same poundage as the character he so desperately wanted to play. Chris O'Donnell, beautiful, blond, and ball-proficient though he may have been, was presumably paid off and quietly dismissed.* "It was," says Barbra, who places great stock in such things, "destiny."

Nevertheless, she would keep the news of Jason's casting a secret for as long as she could. Finally, while the cast and crew packed their bags for two months of location shooting down South, Columbia Pictures announced that Jason Gould would be playing Bernard in *The Prince of Tides*. Putting on a brave face, Barbra clutched her son's hand and braced herself for the worst, as the lions clawed at their cages.

*Chris O'Donnell would later to make a name for himself in *Scent of a Woman*.

Thirty-four

Southern Exposure

*I*n May and June of 1990, about one hundred members of the cast and crew of *The Prince of Tides* descended upon the small town of Beaufort, South Carolina. They came armed with their high-tech razzle-dazzle gadgetry and designer running shoes, with extended-distance walkie-talkies and revered Ray-Ban sunglasses, with scarce and much-sought-after Columbia Pictures security passes and an abundant California attitude. The town of Beaufort—that's "Bew-furt," or "Bew-foot" for foreigners and nonlinguists alike—boasts a population of 9,576 souls. An historic seaport city, it fell to the Yankees shortly after the fall of Fort Sumter in neighboring Charleston, but was spared destruction because of its shipping facilities. In fact, it is likely that the last time the folks in Beaufort experienced such an implosion of foreigners and flurry of frantic activity was during those unfortunate, interminable days of the Civil War.

Still, they cared not. They opened their doors, and, literally, their homes, to these strangers with capped-teeth smiles, and all they asked for in return was a glance . . . at *her.*

Barbra Streisand very nearly bypassed Beaufort as her principal shooting location, despite the fact that it was indeed about Beaufort that Pat Conroy had written so eloquently. At the age of sixteen, Conroy moved to Beaufort with his family. He attended Beaufort High School, where he would later teach English and coach football, like his alter ego Tom Wingo. In the book, Conroy christened his town Colleton, but there was little doubt to anyone familiar with the Lowcountry, as it is called, that he was writing about Beaufort.

Streisand quietly slipped into this Southern town in early February

1990. Her host was Jim McDill, executive director of the Beaufort County Economic Development Board.

"Great God!" McDill amiably thunders when asked how it was that Barbra eventually selected Beaufort as her principal shooting location. "That represents about two and a half months of work that we did. I'm the local liaison between the South Carolina Film Office and this community for film shoots, and I can tell you that the work we put into *The Prince of Tides* was certainly equal to any manufacturing location, or any other business kind of location, that we've ever had in this community.

McDill adds, "The scouting came about when the South Carolina Film Office, under the direction of Isabel Hill, contacted my office and said, 'Jim, these are the locations that we are looking for in your county: We need [Savannah's] apartment, we need ocean vistas, we need shrimp boats,' and so forth. It was up to me and my assistant, Lisa Halopoff, to begin identifying the locations in the script. Then we met for dinner one evening with Miss Streisand, who turned and said to me, 'Well, Jim, why do you think we should shoot in Beaufort?' "

McDill could not have foreseen that the town would be able to use the good publicity in the coming weeks and months. Beaufort is considered a safe, gracious place, where chivalry and old-fashioned family values are still honored. During a seventeen-day period in April and May, three months after McDill first met Barbra, Beaufort would be rocked by scandal and tragedy. A Beaufort County deputy would be killed while escorting a man from a mental health center; a twelve-year-old boy would kill another boy—a playmate friend—and then himself; and a fifteen-year-old boy would gun down his father and his stepmother. Bud Marchant, executive vice president of the Beaufort Chamber of Commerce, would be compelled to pronounce in the wake of the bloodshed, "Right now, regrettably, Beaufort seems to be the murder capital of South Carolina."

Jim McDill did *not* tell "Miss Streisand," as almost everyone involved in the shooting referred to her, that *The Prince of Tides* had been the subject of local controversy. There were some in Beaufort who felt that Conroy's depiction of Southerners was demeaning. The controversy escalated in 1988 when the book was read by students as a class assignment at a South Carolina high school. Outraged, a certain Charleston minister deemed the book to be "raw, filthy, raunchy pornography" that was unfit for the tender eyes and consumption of South Carolinian youth.

That night at dinner, McDill *did* tell Barbra the movie should be shot in Beaufort because it had been written about Beaufort. The town was not asking for anything that didn't already belong to it. Still, when selecting shooting locations for a picture, Hollywood producers, including

Streisand, have a tendency to knock on the door of a collectively star-struck town and say, "Okay, show me what you've got." Subsequently, the town is expected to strut out its best stuff with civic pride, with the hope that its visiting audience will prove appreciative.

For the next two days, McDill took Barbra on a tour of the community and its environs, pointing out the deserted beaches, the historic antebellum homes, the marshes, and next to the Chesapeake Bay, the second-richest estuary system on the eastern seaboard. He described to her the importance of the relationship the community had with the water, the environment, the fishing industry. At one point during the tour, Barbra, who has a peculiar and highly developed sense of smell to begin with, inhaled an awful aroma. Her face contorted.

McDill smiled. "That's the 'pluff mud,' " he offered by way of explanation. "It's the mud that's exposed at low tide. It has a very rich and earthy aroma that some people find offensive, but we know that there's a tremendous value to the pluff mud in terms of the crabs and shrimp and oysters and clams, and therefore we don't find the earthy smell at all offensive. We think of it as just a really good natural fragrance because we have such pure waters in this country."

Barbra nodded, feigned a grin, and held her nose.

"We felt very good after they had left," McDill recalls, "*but* we had received no commitments." Actually, Barbra was also meeting with film officials in North Carolina, where she was given similar tours. Barbra was most apprehensive about Beaufort's lack of movie soundstages or available space that could be converted into soundstages. The town had previously hosted the filmings of Lewis John Carlino's *The Great Santini* (1979) and Lawrence Kasdan's *The Big Chill* (1983), in addition to several movies made for television, but it had never had within its borders a film with the considerable magnitude, budget, and demands of *The Prince of Tides.*

John Williams, a Beaufort resident and a reporter, covered the shooting of the picture, as well as the attendant drama of the city's selection as its principal location. Williams recalls, "Streisand was going to move the production up to Wilmington, North Carolina, where the Carolco studios are. But all of a sudden, I guess over a weekend, Jim McDill and a few other people put together this package of studio space and convinced Streisand that Beaufort would do everything possible to make this an easy and profitable venture."

Williams adds, "This is also a right-to-work state, so they wouldn't have any problems with unions."

When pressed, Jim McDill confesses there had been a problem with securing Beaufort as the chosen location. "One day, a Saturday morning, I got a phone call from Los Angeles. I was mowing the grass. It was Isabel Hill, who was in Los Angeles working to get the film [in Beaufort]. She said, 'Jim, there's a very good chance that this project will go to North Carolina unless we can find them 50,000 square feet of production space in your area, and we need to know by Monday.'

"Hell, this was Saturday morning! So, I got on the phone and I contacted the president of the community college here in Beaufort [the Technical College of the Lowcountry] to inquire about the utilization of a vacant gymnasium. I got a confirmation on the telephone that it would be available to Columbia Pictures *free of charge*. I called the county administrator—we have a 30,000-square-foot warehouse—and the county agreed to vacate the warehouse and make it available to Columbia Pictures, again free of charge. I contacted the South Carolina National Guard, and they agreed to provide their 12,000 square feet of space for just a small maintenance fee. So, in the period of twenty-four hours, this community came up with approximately 50,000 square feet, and it did so, for all intents and purposes, free of charge. I had the letters committing the space signed by ten o'clock, our time, Monday morning. By eight o'clock in the morning Los Angeles time, I was faxing our commitment to Columbia Pictures."

Within a week, Jim McDill received word that Beaufort had been selected as the primary location site for *The Prince of Tides*. "When they saw that kind of community response," McDill says, "and when they realized how much we wanted this picture in Beaufort and that we would go all out to get it, I think that's when the affirmative decision was made."

Among other Beaufort area locations, the Technical College's gym on Ribault Road would serve in the picture as the interior set of the Wingo family's dilapidated home, the setting for, among other things, the childhood rape scene; the county warehouse on Depot Road would house the interior set of the elegant and well-appointed home Dr. Lowenstein shares with her husband and son; and the National Guard Armory on Rodgers Street would house the interior set of Savannah's New York apartment and the interior set of Lowenstein's Manhattan office.

And so the stage was set. With the crash of the tide heard somewhere in the distance, and after two weeks of rehearsals, a reported and astounding *seventy-five* drafts of the script, and four long years in and out of various stages of preproduction, Barbra Streisand finally delivered that most magical of movie commands . . . *"Action!"*

Thirty-five

The Undertow

*I*t was June 18, 1990, when *The Prince of Tides* finally and mercifully went before the cameras. The first scene to be shot was Tom and Savannah's childhood birthday party sequence. In a study of Hollywood film-making organization and preparedness, and, some would add, excess, Barbra had on hand not only one cake for the celebration, but *five* "stand-in" cakes as well, in case the frosting on the first one melted under the hot studio lights. "These were just regular, nine-inch cakes," said Theresa Watson of Beaufort's The Cake Boutique. And when questioned that same day by a curious bystander, she was quick to reply, "Of course you can eat them. They're very good," and, with a trace of discernible pride, "I made the batter myself this morning."

To commemorate opening day, Jon Peters, back in Hollywood, set the town of Beaufort abuzz by sending Barbra twenty *dozen* pink and white roses from Bitty's Flower Shop.

Contrary to her strident reputation, she is, or can be, disarmingly feminine. "She seemed delicate and fragile," says Nancy Rhett, cast in *Tides* as Isabel Newburry. "At one point [during the shooting], she was just like a little girl, and I just wanted to say to her, 'Nobody's gonna bite you. It's okay. It's all right.' Her whole attitude is vulnerable, shy, fragile, little-girl-like."

As production designer, Paul Sylbert worked very closely with Barbra for several months. He reveals, "I think she flirts with the men [in the cast and crew]. One of her weapons as a woman [director] is that she can deal with the men as a woman. She can be charming, and a little intimate sometimes, in a kidding kind of way. Suddenly, she'll be flat-out honest with you and say how frightened, how nervous she is. And of course, what are you going to do? You're going to help her out, protect her."

But, the subject was roses. It is no surprise, then, to those who know her that Barbra typically surrounds herself with pink frills, doilies, and floral patterns. She is also big on fresh-cut flowers. During the two month shooting of *The Prince of Tides* in Beaufort, she had fresh flowers, at considerable cost and presumably paid for out of the picture's megamillion dollar budget, delivered to her rented home *every* day.

Barbra's passion for flowers extended into the shooting as well. In the book, Pat Conroy described Tom Wingo's mother, Lila, as having a particular affinity for gardenias. Determined to preserve the word-for-word authenticity of the book, Barbra sent her foot soldiers on a concerted search for the fragrant and fragile white-petaled flower.

As it turned out, local gardenias had stopped blooming a month before. Furthermore, out-of-state nurseries had only short-stemmed gardenias available for shipping. Lila Wingo's passion for gardenias was of the *long-stemmed* variety, which, of course, was precisely the variety that Barbra was intent on obtaining. The search for the gardenias extended throughout the South, across the country, and beyond.

Finally, after months of exhaustive search, Barbra's staff located a florist who agreed to have the gardenias shipped in, at substantial expense, from South America. Barbra would have her flowers throughout the summer of 1990.

Given her almost microscopic attention to detail, Barbra is a born director. In fact, the sharpness of her eye may be her strongest directorial attribute. Certainly, she sees things that others do not, or if they do, they choose to ignore.

One scene in *Tides* had Nancy Rhett's Isabel Newburry hosting a tea party for her society friends in which the game of mah-jongg was to be played. Before the scene was shot, however, a question suddenly occurred to Barbra.

Rhett recalls, "I was sitting in the makeup truck, and Nick Nolte was on my right, Kate Nelligan [cast in the picture as Lila Wingo] was on my left, and Barbra Streisand was crunched between us standing by my left knee. We were sitting there talking. She looked at me and said, 'Off with the hat,' and my hat came off. And then she said, '*You're* a native. Did the ladies of Beaufort play mah-jongg?' And I wanted to say, 'Yes, and they still do, but it is just the *Jewish* ladies in town who play.' But I thought, No, I better not say that. That doesn't sound polite. So I just said 'No.' 'Bridge?' Barbra asked. And I said, 'Frankly, they probably would be playing Canasta.' The next thing I knew, she practically clicked her fingers and there were two decks of cards." Mah-jongg was out. Canasta was in.

For the same scene, Barbra did a quick study of the set, and with a sixth sense in which she takes great pride, she was certain that something was missing. Rhett recalls, "They had on our set some teacups, little bits of food like we had been eating, and some lemon slices. Barbra looked around and said, 'There is no teapot here.' She had a table brought in. It was put in the corner and a teapot was put on the table.

"Meticulous is hardly the word!" Rhett adds in reference to Barbra's fanatical attention to detail. "The little tag on a tea bag showed and had to be fixed, the lemon had to look *squeezed,* everything had to be perfect. Then, when we broke for lunch, in came 'the Polaroid crew.' There were these three different people, each with a Polaroid camera. One person photographed each of the people [in the scene] front and sideways, to make sure that our costumes and hairdos didn't *shift* during lunch. Another came in and photographed the whole tabletop, so that if something moved, nothing would be different [when we resumed shooting]. And then the third person photographed the room from several different angles. Barbra herself inspected our hairdos, the pins we were wearing, and the buttons we had on our costumes."

In another scene, it was not a missing teapot but a misplaced beer bottle. Barbra arranged and rearranged the bottle around the set until it was placed, in her judgment, to perfection. In yet another scene, it was the placement of a vase that was the cause of concern and delay. In a Streisand picture, there is very little that her hand is not in, on, or around.

For the early, flashback scenes in the picture, Barbra instructed Kate Nelligan to look as "floozy" as possible. Apparently, it took Nelligan, in tandem with the costume and makeup people, several attempts to deliver to Barbra the desired degree of flooziness. One day, Nelligan walked into the makeup trailer for inspection by her director. Nancy Rhett, who was there at the time, relates, "Kate Nelligan, funny as she can be, comes into the room, smacking and chewing gum, flinging her hips, with one hand on her hip. She's wearing this *terrible,* tacky dress, with all the petticoats, and ankle-strapped shoes. She was looking just as trashy as can be, and she says to Barbra, "Well, is *this* floozy enough?""

Barbra was also very exacting about the nuances in Nelligan's accent. As Lila Wingo ages, Barbra wanted Nelligan's accent to also age, intensify, become more Southern, in a subtle kind of way. Says Nelligan of her director, "She is very precise. After all, this is *her* film, these are her choices. She knows quite well what she wants the picture to look like and be like. In explaining this view, she's very clear."

Certainly, she made herself clear to the company's caterer, a Nash-ville-based outfit called TomKats. While the film was still in a flurry of preproduction, Barbra even took the time to consult with the chef about her particular culinary likes and dislikes. She also liked the fact that the company was environmentally friendly and had a policy of recycling all of its paper plates, aluminum cans, and glass bottles. Furthermore, under Streisand's explicit orders, no plastic or Styrofoam could be used during the shoot.

Barbra also did not like or want her film company's catered meals to be too fattening or, more important, too hot or spicy, which just so hap-pened to be the specialty of the chef, George Harvell. Apparently, she was concerned that spicy food, combined with the summer heat, would slow down the productivity of her workers.

Following his work on *Tides,* Harvell moved his catering crew to Mis-sissippi for another film shoot. While there, a member of the new com-pany informed Rupert Adkisson, a TomKats representative, "You are the only caterers that I know of who have ever made it through a whole shoot with Barbra Streisand." Says Adkisson, "Apparently, she'll fire them right in the middle of the shoot." When asked why he thought it was that his company escaped unscathed from Barbra's proverbial wrath, Adkisson replies, "She liked everything we were putting out." He adds, with a hint of conspiracy, "She especially liked our [presumably unspicy] quesadillas."

In preparing her shooting schedule, Barbra and her cinematographer, Stephen Goldblatt (*The Cotton Club,* 1984; *Joe Versus the Volcano,* 1990; *For the Boys,* 1992), spent months studying and pouring over the tedious local tide and moon charts. "We have very dramatic tide changes here," explains one local resident. "If they wanted a scene of water, they had to wait for the tide to come in. In some areas, when the tide goes out, it's mostly marsh and marsh grass." "What she did," says another source, "was get ahold of a tide chart. The South Carolina Coastal Coun-cil prints up a tide chart every year and it tells you high tide's at this time, low tide's at that time." Barbra committed the chart to memory and planned her schedule accordingly.

One scene taken from the book provides yet another glimpse of Bar-bra's particular brand of perfectionism. The scene called for Lila Wingo and her children to go for a walk while the sun and the moon were simul-taneously visible. Although such a phenomenon of nature could have easily been faked for the cameras, Barbra insisted on capturing the real thing, which occurred only three days that summer.

Naturally, Barbra's painstaking attention to detail was not appreciated by everyone, particularly not when it infringed, in the view of some, on the territory of others. Barbra, some would argue, hires the best people she can find and then proceeds to tell them how to do their job. "Yeah, she does," concurs Paul Sylbert, "and then you have to tell her, 'Go fuck yourself.' In one way or another. You manipulate her, although it takes a lot of your energy, and manipulating people is the most boring thing in the world. You do what you have to do to get it [the work] done, that's all. The thing with Barbra is you have to focus her on something—let her obsess on *that,* and then you can get your work done."

With credits such as *One Flew Over the Cuckoo's Nest* (1975), *Heaven Can Wait* (Best Art Direction Oscar winner, 1978), and *Kramer vs. Kramer* (1979) behind him, Paul Sylbert was hired by Barbra as her production designer. Essentially, it was his job to design the overall look of the picture, particularly the sets.

Barbra, of course, considers herself something of an interior design connoisseur. "She's got eight houses," quips Sylbert. "As soon as the eighth one is decorated, the first one starts again."

Conflict, which seems inevitable in retrospect, occurred when Sylbert showed Barbra one of his designed sets for the movie. I don't like it," she flatly and rather ungenerously pronounced.

"Why?" asked Sylbert.

"Because, I just don't like it," Barbra repeated, miffed by the presumption that her word alone was not reason enough.

Sylbert replied, "What you like and don't like has nothing to do with it."

"In a film," Sylbert explains, "there are certain requirements, and they aren't a matter of personal taste. When I design, the client isn't the director. The client is the *character*. I'm not concerned about what the director likes. I'm an expert at what I do, and what others like or dislike has no bearing on it at all."

The set that provoked the rift in the Streisand/Sylbert relationship was the home Lowenstein shares with her husband. "Barbra had a very different concept," Sylbert says. "She wanted that house of hers to be, as she put it, 'formal but comfortable.' She was really thinking of American decorating in the way that rich WASPs live. I had a completely different concept of it. My concept was from the character of Lowenstein and of the husband, Herbert Woodruff. Any man who could dominate *this* woman all those years, cheat on her, put her in a position that she felt ugly, had to be a very strong character. I wanted him to be European. Barbra was right when she cast a European [Jeroen Krabbe]. He was an arrogant, imperious tyrant."

Sylbert continues, "So I made an interior that was very clean, an international style connected very strongly with Europe. I wanted the *severeness* of it. And I wanted the black and white [the floors were black, and the walls white] as a contrast to how rich people deal with black and white as compared with poor people. If you notice in the beginning of the movie, where Nick grows up in the shrimper's cabin, the floor is also black and the walls are also white. But they're a very different black and white."

According to reporter Frank Jarrell, who interviewed Sylbert during the shooting, the situation between Streisand and Sylbert got so tense that Barbra walked onto the set in question and told him that she wanted him to construct it all over again from scratch. He refused, saying that his job was to build sets according to the script and not to accommodate the whims of some interior-designer-wannabe.

Says Jarrell, "Basically, Sylbert said to her, 'Look, if you say that to me again, I'm gonna quit and I'm gonna pull the entire art department.' " That, apparently, was that. Sylbert's set stood as designed with Barbra's permission, albeit begrudged.

"Barbra finally bought my ideas," Sylbert says. "I won *that* battle. How did I win? You've got to be strong with her. There's no other way. And you've got to know *why* you want this, that, and the other thing. I had reasons for everything. She's a good listener and she's not a dummy. If you can tell her why, and if you can show her why, you *can* win the battles."

Barbra would later have to subordinate her ego and acknowledge that Sylbert's vision had been the right one for the picture. "I remember when she saw Lowenstein's apartment in the dailies," Sylbert reflects, savoring the memory. "There were just a few of us there that night. I was standing behind the console where she was sitting, but she didn't know I was there. On the screen, there was a shot of her standing next to the column with Nick. Their backs were to the dining room, where the maid was lighting the candles. [Watching it] Barbra said aloud, '*That's* the *perfect* apartment for them.' The cameraman squeezed my leg because he knew what the battle had been like. It just came out of her. That's the way she works."

Another battleground for a duel between Streisand and Sylbert was the set for Lowenstein's office. "The only instruction she gave me [in designing the set] was in telling me, 'I see myself surrounded by wood,' " relates Sylbert. And so he gave her wood. Rich antique oak, and lots of it. Upon completion of building the set, however, Barbra decided that she wanted the private bathroom adjoining Lowenstein's office to be extended. Sylbert balked. "She wanted to add to the bathroom in her office," he explains. "Now, I usually don't give a shit about the money they [the film's producers] are spending, but I got real mad at her and said, 'Look, all we've had for the last month on this picture is fights over money.' " The proposed bathroom addition, Sylbert attempted to reason, would be a blatant waste of money. "You're never gonna see it [in the shot]!" he argued to deaf ears. Frustrated, Sylbert made the mistake of *yelling* at Streisand. She has never forgiven him. "She got very, very upset that I yelled at her," Sylbert acknowledges. "She was justified, really. And I was justified in getting upset myself at that point because we had been getting a lot of pressure about money."

"The bathroom," says Sylbert, "is an example of Barbra being overly concerned with having the whole thing right. But I knew it was right [as originally built] because Nick [Nolte] could only open the door so far. After all, I'm much more experienced than she is." Nevertheless, Barbra insisted on the bathroom addition, and Sylbert eventually complied. "In fact," Sylbert adds in retrospect, "the bathroom was *never* seen. The original walls that were put up *were* seen. The new walls we put up and decorated were never seen because you couldn't open up the door far enough to see it. We doubled that bathroom for no damn reason."

"Now I understand," says Sylbert with a hint of defiance, "that Barbra is telling everybody in Hollywood what a son-of-a-bitch I am. The next film I did [*Rush*] was with Lili Zanuck, who was a first-time director and a woman. She said to me, 'I would love to hire you, but Barbra has really been bad-mouthing you. She said that you were really mean to her.' Well, Barbra probably remembered that one time that I screamed at her about the bathroom. But Lili and I chatted about it, and she hired me anyway. So it was no skin off my nose."

Back in Beaufort, stories of Barbra's pursuit of perfection as *she* defines it circulated all over the Lowcountry. One popular story involved the local Marine Corps. The planes that flew over the city were affecting not only Barbra's shooting but her sleep as well.

Relates one local resident who asked to remain anonymous, "The rumor was that Barbra Streisand was all upset about the overhead plane traffic. She was *livid*. Unfortunately, the city is right over the major flight zone. Anyway, the story goes that she called up the commanding general of the base and demanded that he reroute his planes because they were making too much noise and were causing her problems."

"I called to track down that rumor," recalls John Williams, a local reporter. "I went all the way to the Marine Corps headquarters in Washington, D.C. But they kind of just laughed and said, 'The Marine Corps doesn't change their flight schedule for *anybody*.' "

So, what happened? "She just had to stop shooting when they flew over," Williams says.

Barbra—a woman not used to conceding much of anything to anyone—would have to abruptly stop shooting her movie in the middle of a shot more than once in the succeeding weeks. During such impasses, she clasped her hands over her ears as the roar of the engines passed overhead. Sometimes she swore, or muttered under her breath, or collapsed her shoulders in exasperation.

"Barbra Streisand might be a good singer, and she might be a good movie lady," John Williams was told by the Marine Corps official in Washington, D.C., "but she doesn't have *that* much power."

"Professionalism" is a big word for Barbra Streisand. "Perspective," it seems, is *not*.

The relationship between the film company and the community, and, more to the point, between Barbra Streisand and the people of South Carolina, started out promisingly enough. Certainly, during her scouting sojourns into the Lowcountry several months before, Barbra uncharacteristically let her guard down. In Beaufort, she paid a visit to Plums Restaurant, a casual, family-owned waterfront café identified by its burgundy awnings and black-and-white checkered floor. On her first visit, Barbra ordered the "diet maintenance special" ($3.75), a turkey sandwich with very little turkey. She was so fond of the sandwich that during the subsequent shooting she would order it by phone for take-out (which would then be picked up by an assistant), despite the fact that the film company had on the set its own costly and distinguished caterer.

On another occasion, Becky Kilby, a saleswoman at the Rhett Gallery in Beaufort, looked up from her paperwork and was stunned to be face-to-face with Barbra Streisand. "She came in at lunchtime," remembers Kilby, "and stayed for about an hour. She was very small, petite."

Adds Nancy Rhett, the gallery's owner, "I looked up and there she was, all her little tiny self. At one point, she had pictures spread out all over the floor in the workroom. She was down on her hands and knees, moving them around to form a grouping. A few minutes later, the UPS man, as he always did, came bursting through the door and had to jump over the pictures. He said, trying to be funny, '*Who* left this mess on the floor?' He's always ribbing my girls who run the gallery. Everybody's always teasing everybody else. And I looked at him very coolly and said, 'Oh, Barbra Streisand.' His knees melted. He was just starstruck."

It was Becky Kilby's impression that Barbra and her male companion, producer Shel Shrager, were in a hurry. There were other customers in the store, which made Barbra uncomfortable. Barbra asked Shrager to ask Kilby if she would mind reopening the shop that night after it closed.

Kilby relates, "To me, she was very nice. She came back at about quarter to six and stayed until eight-thirty or so that night. She talked about the fact that she liked antiques. We mostly talked about the work itself, the antique prints and ways to frame them. She wanted them framed for her New York apartment, the hallway entrance.

"The only time we talked about something other than the work she wanted done," says Nancy Rhett, "was when I told her I had seen her in *Funny Girl* on stage. She had been, to that point, very businesslike, very professional. She's a smart gal, and it shows. She had been concentrating hard on what she was doing, the pictures she was buying. When I told her about *Funny Girl,* it was like all of a sudden somebody pulled a light string and she just turned on and laughed. The difference in personality when you mentioned show business was a complete change. She glowed over that. She just absolutely relished it."

The overtime was apparently worth it. That night, Barbra purchased thirteen or fourteen prints (some of which dated back to 1828 and featured delicate, tiny yellow flowers), which Kilby had shipped to Barbra's penthouse apartment in New York. Barbra also purchased some work by Rhett, who is also an artist, and for whom it was an enormously profitable day and night. Not only did her sales register ring repeatedly, her meeting with Barbra would also lead to her being cast in the picture in the small speaking part of Isabel Newburry, Lila Wingo's dying friend and former foe in the story.

Scouting in Charleston, Barbra was, given her penchant for privacy and solitude, bordering on the gregarious. Accompanied by an entourage that included her personal physical trainer, she dined one evening at the exclusive Chouinard's on Vendue. Following the meal, Barbra accepted an invitation by some of the restaurant's employees to partake in a walking tour of the city—an audacious move for her.

Compared to her relatively accessible demeanor during scouting, Barbra closed up like the proverbial clam once shooting started, surrounding herself with a wall of subordinates, her "people," as they were collectively called. As for the townspeople of Beaufort, Streisand sightings became rare and privileged.

Barbra felt exploited if anyone not directly connected with the making of the movie was given access to a glimpse of her hair, eyes, nose. This is a woman who wants to do what she wants to do in private, all the while hoping that what she does will be hungrily and *publicly* consumed. She feels exploited, too, when she walks into a restaurant, a grocery store, or even across the street and senses that prying eyes are upon her.

Back at the Rhett Gallery, Barbra retreated, almost in an attempt to make herself invisible, when other shoppers entered the store. "She kind of had her hair hanging down," Nancy Rhett relates, "and when people walked in and would see who it was, she'd put her head down and let her hair fall over face, and then she'd sort of back around a partition."

"She is," Rhett reflects, "one of the shyest people I've ever met."

Shyness alone is too simplistic an explanation. To this day, Barbra becomes outraged if someone, even a fan, attempts to take an unauthorized snapshot of her. If, when shooting out at a location for *Tides*, Barbra saw someone point a camera in her direction, she would have one of her assistants confiscate the camera.

One day, while shooting one of the dock scenes, Barbra, through her peripheral vision, spotted a camera aimed in her direction. Livid, she proceeded to direct one of her henchmen to retrieve the offending instrument. It turned out, however, that the spectator was actually carrying a Nintendo game and *not* a camera, and a photo of Barbra Streisand was hardly high on his list of priorities. Apologies were made in proxy, and the shooting proceeded as before.

The no-photo policy remained intact. Confirms Norma Woods, mother of Justen Woods, one of the young actors in the cast, "*That* was one thing that was totally off-limits while we were in Beaufort. She told us that she didn't want to be caught off guard."

Woods adds, with a trace of humor, "She wanted to be *posed.*"

Thirty-six

Guards at the Gate

As shooting progressed, Barbra, wired by stress and wilted by the South Carolinian summer heat, withdrew further from the community, and as she did, her popularity within it declined. She went, or so it seemed to many, into hiding. Even from the outset, upon moving into the white three-story antebellum house located at 509 North Street that belonged to Beth and Gene Grace, who had moved out for the summer, she established certain boundary lines, real and inferred, by having a white canvas tarp hung up across the backyard fence to shelter her from view. This act offended more than a few Beaufortonians.

Among them was Fred Trask, a local resident and homeowner. "I can understand why she would not want to be gawked at," Trask notes. "But, it's also irritating that hometown boys can't get anything done [to their property] without going through all the proper channels, and then somebody like that comes in and gets anything they want done just by snapping their fingers."

When Streisand snaps her fingers, somebody, somewhere, delivers.

But, with what *style* they were snapped. Barbra is renowned not only for her quest for control and perfection but also for her well-manicured set of nails. Upon the picture's release, she would be lambasted for the attention the camera accorded them. The criticism is trivial. However, in *The Prince of Tides,* Barbra *would* offer her audience languishing shots of her long and meticulously attended nails.

The *Los Angeles Times* referred to it as a "nail gaffe." Screenwriter Ellen Shepard opined, "Her nails upstaged her entire performance. It's hard to believe no one suggested that she take the focus off her hands."

Glendale, California, psychotherapist Christine Maginn theorized,

"Women who aren't comfortable with their appearance often fixate on one feature that they like and take special care to call attention to it."

And Beverly Hills manicurist Rando Celli surmised, "She wants us to understand her power and control. Those long, strong nails say, 'Keep your distance.'"

If her nails failed to keep the people away, if her backyard tarp didn't hold the curious at bay, there was also the matter of her dress. While in Beaufort, Barbra wore, almost exclusively (except of course when she was in costume and in front of the cameras), big, baggy clothes that shielded her figure; large, floppy hats that hid not only her hair, but half her face; and huge sunglasses that hid her eyes in the event that the brim of her hat failed to do so. Such was her daily armor.

If that were not enough, Barbra would have her assistant dress in the same or similar attire to act as a decoy. Sometimes, in a tactic taken from the U.S. Secret Service, the diversionary assistant would drive around in Barbra's rented car, a highly visible silver Cadillac Coupe de Ville with a license plate bearing the moniker "LOVE," while Barbra herself was actually in another car in another part of town.

Some evenings after work, if the streets seemed deserted and if she was so inclined, Barbra ventured into the dark and walked her dog through the historic neighborhood that surrounded her rented home. On other nights, the assistant, again dressed like her boss, would do the dog walking. Neighbors peered out their windows and called one another up on the telephone to confer whether it was Barbra Streisand or her double who was at the other end of the leash.

"Sometimes," muses local reporter John Williams, "the assistant would go into a local restaurant, sit down, and order, knowing that the locals were gawking at her." While some Beaufort residents scratched their heads between bites and wondered whether she was the genuine Barbra, others, according to Williams, "headed over to her table asking for autographs."

Meanwhile, the real Streisand was actually across town, dining at another restaurant. Some of the locals were amused by the charade and by the lengths Streisand would go to distance herself from the community. Others, however, were offended or simply perplexed.

A large part of her aloofness stems from fear. "My nightmare," she once told a reporter, tellingly, "is that I'm driving alone and have to go to the hospital. I'd say, 'Please, help me,' and people say, 'Hey, you look like . . .' And I'm *dying* while they wonder if I'm Barbra Streisand."

Maria Swift, a Japanese-massage therapist, lives in neighboring St. Helena's Island. One night, Swift received a phone call that Barbra wanted a massage at 11:00 P.M.

Swift rushed over to Barbra's rented home in Beaufort and upon her arrival was tersely greeted by her new client with, "Hello. Here's the routine I like." Barbra proceeded to instruct Swift to begin the massage at her scalp. It seems that, in addition to relieving stress, a scalp massage is also something of a hair-growth stimulant, and Barbra was reportedly obsessed with the fear that she was going bald. Prior to going to South Carolina, she is said to have made repeated visits to a Beverly Hills hair-health specialist and subsequently resorted to using Minoxidil, a heart medication that has shown some effectiveness in preventing hair loss. The drug is topically applied to the scalp on a daily basis.

From the scalp, Swift worked her way down to Barbra's neck and then proceed south. She did as she was told, and twice during the massage, Barbra fell asleep, a compliment to those in the trade. Still, Barbra was not entirely pleased by Swift's kneading style, and in the following weeks, she auditioned various other local masseuses before she eventually settled for a chiropractor she found on a nearby island.

And then there was Bob Bender, owner of The Shop, which is located half a block from what was Barbra's rented home. During production of the picture, Bender designed a commemorative T-shirt emblazoned with the logo, "I Was at the Filming of *The Prince of Tides*," which he sold in his shop for ten dollars apiece. As a courtesy, Bender sent several of the shirts, free of charge, to Barbra. What he received in response was a letter, charging copyright infringement, from the Columbia Pictures legal department back in Los Angeles. "Talk about beating up on the little guy," Bender said. "I mean, come on, this is ridiculous."

The studio demanded not only that Bender stop selling the T-shirts but also that he turn over all of the "counterfeit merchandise" as well. Instead, Bender, using a little creative license, reprinted the text of Columbia's legal letter on the back of one of his T-shirts and his own rebuttal on the front, and sent it to the studio attorney.

The T-shirt read, in part, "I am not convinced, as of this writing, that my artwork does infringe on the rights of Columbia. . . . Enjoy the shirt, counselor, it's a bona fide, hand-signed original, compliments of The Shop."

Perhaps fearing a public relations backlash, the studio subsequently backed off on its threatened legal action.

In another gesture, Bender spent twenty hours silk-screening by hand a turquoise beach outfit for Barbra to wear during her stay. He sent it to her with a note that read, "Welcome to Beaufort."

"I didn't expect Barbra herself to call and say 'Thank you,'" says Bender, "but her assistant could have." With more sorrow than anger, Bender adds, "I heard nothing."

It would not have taken much for her to appease the people of Beaufort. They wanted to get to know her, even if superficially. But she didn't give them—or herself—the chance.

Nick Nolte, on the other hand, was overwhelmingly embraced by the people of Beaufort. In his unlikely but omnipresent attire of surgical scrub greens, he was a welcome and common sight all over town, biking, jogging, walking. He dined at the local restaurants, played with his four-year-old son Brawley King Nolte in the front yard of his rented home (around the corner from Barbra's), fraternized with his neighbors, and did his own shopping at Wal-Mart.

As resident Evelyn Grayson describes him, "Nick Nolte was like a neighborhood person. He used to eat at a restaurant, Quincy's, where my friend worked. They got to know him real well. We saw him out walking and jogging. You looked out the window and there he was, going around the corner."

To prepare for his role of Tom Wingo, Nolte was granted permission to work for a day as a substitute teacher at Beaufort Academy. He taught English, literature, and moviemaking to an enthralled audience comprised of Tom Horton's ninth- and eleventh-grade students. "What he basically wanted to do," says Horton, "is get into the character of a Southern English teacher. I thought the best thing for him to do was get into the classroom and see how it really feels."

Nolte is infamous in Hollywood for what some would call his obsessive preparation for a picture. To play the bum in *Down and Out in Beverly Hills,* he lived on the streets for days and declined to bathe, much to the chagrin of Bette Midler, his costar; a month before shooting was to commence, Nolte moved into the jungle to acclimate himself to the environment so that he could prepare himself for his role as a soldier in Borneo in *Farewell to the King;* for a drunk scene in *Who'll Stop the Rain,* Nolte downed a pint of Ten High Whiskey for breakfast, and by midafternoon he was sufficiently inebriated to shoot the scene; and to play the corrupt cop in *Q & A*, he added fifty pounds to his girth and six inches to his height.

For *The Prince of Tides*, Nolte lost thirty pounds, went into training and reacquired the body of an athlete, learned basic shrimping techniques, and reacquainted himself—he had played a teacher in the 1984 film *Teachers*—with the classroom. Perhaps his most difficult task, however, was mastering the Lowcountry accent of Tom Wingo. To aid his research and preparation, Nolte had Columbia Pictures hire Wayne Zurenda, an English instructor at the Technical College of the Lowcountry, as his personal tutor. Zurenda conducted numerous coaching sessions with Nolte at the latter's rented home. It was Zurenda's hope that he could prevent Nolte from resorting to the contrived and stereotypical Southern accent that Hollywood has historically portrayed in the movies. He was particularly offended by Vivien Leigh's Scarlett O'Hara. *"That,"* said Zurenda, "was the most phony Southern accent I've ever heard."

Also working on *her* Southern accent was Kate Nelligan. Canadian-born and trained on the British stage, the National Theatre, and the Royal Shakespeare Company, the highly acclaimed Nelligan, once touted as "the next Meryl Streep" had, prior to her arrival in Beaufort, never before set foot in the American South.

Barbra knew that she wanted Nelligan in *Tides* after she saw her on-stage in New York in *Spoils of War.* Barbra initially envisioned Nelligan as Tom Wingo's philandering wife, Sallie. Later, however, Barbra decided that despite the fact that she was actually ten years *younger* than Nick Nolte, Nelligan was better suited to play his mother than his wife.

Initially, Barbra planned to cast two different actresses in the part of Lila Wingo, who aged in the story from her twenties to her early seventies. Nelligan was to play the younger Lila, and Irene Worth was to play the elderly Lila. This approach was eventually shelved, and Barbra opted instead to place her trust in Nelligan's acting ability and Manlio Rocchetti's makeup. For the scenes with elderly Lila, Rocchetti covered Nelligan's face in latex, which he then set with a hairdryer. Not only was her facial discomfort exacerbated by the brutal Beaufort heat, Nelligan's face was also, given the temperature, frequently in danger of melting.

Nelligan perceived Lila not as a villain in the *Mommie Dearest* mold but, rather, as a troubled woman who believed that her life was destined for greater things than it was dealt. "Don't call Lila a bitch," she would later warn those who were quick to judge. She regarded her as "beautiful—human, flawed, and gallant." If Nelligan was a little sensitive on the subject, it might be because she modeled the character not only on Pat Conroy's mother but on her own as well, an alcoholic who passed away in 1974.

To prepare for her role, Kate Nelligan, like Nolte, tape-recorded the dialect and speech patterns of the natives. She asked virtual strangers off the street to read passages from Conroy's book into a microphone. In addition, she wanted to meet women who represented the town's social elite, a class to which Lila Wingo so desperately wished to belong. At her home Ebbtide, located at Burckmyer Beach, a local resident, Marguerite Garrett, hosted a party in Nelligan's honor. Thirty-five of Beaufort's leading ladies, "the upper echelon of Beaufort," as described by resident Mary Lee Morris, were in attendance. Adds Morris, "The same women who are at all the teas—doctors' wives, attorneys' wives."

To her embarrassment, Nelligan underdressed for the occasion, and upon her arrival at the party, she was painfully aware that Southern women of this class regard style of dress with the utmost seriousness. In fact, the woman who escorted Nelligan to the gathering even offered, presumably with some diplomacy, to lend her some jewelry.

More important, Nelligan studied their speech. She later said, "Almost all of the Beaufort women asked me not to make them out as having strong accents." Nelligan added, bemused, "I don't know what to do about the fact that they *do* have them."

Nelligan's unfamiliarity with the South was made all the more obvious by Blythe Danner, cast in the picture as Tom Wingo's wife, Sallie. Danner had previously lived in Beaufort during the shooting of *The Great Santini,* had several friends in town, and was totally at ease in the South. Interestingly, Danner was initially considered by Barbra for the then more prominent part of Savannah, a role that eventually went to Melinda Dillon.

"The idea of reading for Barbra was terrifying initially," Danner relates. "But she was so accessible and human, from the moment you walked in the door, that you forgot about that."

In addition to his daily classes with Nick Nolte, Wayne Zurenda rewrote the entire Wingo script—phonetically. Says Zurenda, "[Nolte] had some of the stereotypical Southern accents the Hollywood dialect people teach. But we got over those quickly. I told him we say 'first' as 'fust,' and when I wrote his part of the script in phonetics, I said 'Beaufort' should be pronounced like 'Beau-foot.' "

Nolte became so engrossed in the speech of Tom Wingo that the walls of an entire room of his rented home were filled with lines excerpted from the script which were phonetically mapped out.

Beaufort Academy teacher Tom Horton later related, "I went up into his room, and on one side of the room was a big poster board that covered the whole wall. On the other side of the room was another, completely covered by color-coded [pages of the script]. He had the whole film divided into emotional beats, with different colors for different emotions."

Recalls John Williams, "It got to the point, as I understand it, that Zurenda read the entire script, Nolte's entire part, into a tape recorder, so that Nolte could always have it with him to remind himself how it should sound." It was to these tapes that Nolte listened while jogging and bicycling around Beaufort.

In addition to teaching Tom Horton's classes at Beaufort Academy, Nolte also addressed the entire student assembly and was engulfed by teenagers requesting that he autograph their recently received yearbooks. Wherever he went, Nolte was usually approached for autographs. Typically, he complied with a smile.

He did more than that for Frank Heflin, a reporter for a newspaper in Columbia, South Carolina. Heflin's editors wanted a big story about the shooting of the movie. However, Streisand had banned her actors from talking to the press.

For two days, Heflin staked out Nolte's rented home, in hopes of catching a private moment with him. Unsuccessful with that approach, and totally blocked from the set by the Columbia Pictures security officers, Heflin decided to attempt a more direct approach: he wrote Nolte a note. "My editors have gone insane," Heflin wrote. "They sent me here to take a picture of Nick Nolte on his bicycle. [I] get hysterical calls in the middle of the night [from my editors]. . . . As much as I detest having to follow you around like a teenager looking for an autograph, such is my lot in life. I have to get a picture for the State newspaper. . . . No B.S.— *North Dallas Forty* was a great movie." Nolte got the note and, in a direct rebuke of Streisand's ban on the press, granted Heflin his story—and his picture.

Such exceptions aside, most of the people of Beaufort and its environs were shut out of the production, and few were happy about it. "We had been promised great things when this film production was coming [to town]," explains John Williams, "because they acknowledged that it was going to be a bit of a hassle, what with closing streets temporarily, and renting different pieces of property, such as the gym at the Technical College. It's not a big school, but it does have eight hundred students or so who need to park in that area to attend class. Suddenly, they were told that they couldn't park anywhere near [the gym]. So the movie was sold to the community as, 'This is going to be a great, fun summer. We're going to have all these stars in our midst—think of the excitement, making a movie right in our home!' "

For Fred Trask, the movie was made a little *too* close to home. Trask not only owns a home near Beaufort, he also owns the island upon which it sits. He is a marsh-spawned native with a great love for the natural beauty of the area. He is particularly fond of the various species of birds, the great blue herons, the snowy egrets, the wood storks, all of which and more have found a haven of sorts on his island of tranquility. That is until Barbra Streisand and *The Prince of Tides* came to town.

It was around two P.M., July 17, 1990. Trask was enjoying a late lunch of fried shrimp and butter beans at his home on the banks of the Beaufort River. "All of a sudden," recalls Trask, "I heard this noise. I didn't know what the devil it was. And then all hell broke loose."

Trask looked up into the sky, and to his great astonishment, and then fury, he saw the great blades of a helicopter hovering over his land, the trees, the birds. As Trask would later relate, "The helicopter swooped into the seething rookery as if it owned the place."

Barbra, who publicly proclaims herself to be environmentally sensitive and correct, directed her cameraman to capture a shot of birds in flight and flurry. As described by Trask, it was the kind of shot that moviegoers have seen thousands of times before, in which a flock of birds scatter, "not in a respectable and orderly fashion, as they might scatter before the approach of a bald eagle, but frantically, hysterically, feathers flying, cowering beneath the wings of a horrifying predator."

Without seeking permission, and without conducting any research on whether any endangered species would be in the vicinity (which there were: about fifty rare and endangered wood storks inhabited the area), Barbra's cameraman and his pilot set about their task. Not content with just one or two takes, they hovered over the treetops and indiscriminately shredded nests with the whirlwind of their helicopter.

"There were these little baby birds in those trees," Fred Trask relates.

"Great blue herons. They had these big nests, and at that time of year, they were giving birth. The little fledgling birds were in the nests at the time and were knocked out of the trees and were killed."

Understandably enraged, Fred Trask jumped into his car, drove to the site, and then followed the helicopter as it made a beeline to the local naval hospital, where Barbra was shooting. However, once there, he was refused admittance by guards ("very, very tough military people") who had been posted at the gate. Finally, after an hour of persistently pleading his case, Trask was allowed to register his complaint to a representative of the film company, and even then it was just to a guy with a clipboard clutched to his chest.

Says Fred Trask of his experience on that day, "There were plenty of casualties among the native population and enough arrogance and hints of egos to fill movie houses throughout the nation. Here I was, living in this town," Trask ruefully summarizes, "and these people just come and take it over."

Barbra's daily ritual in Beaufort had her waking up around six o'clock. At eight A.M., she would leave her rented house from a side door and get into her fully equipped Chieftain Winnebago mobile home, both usually chauffeur-driven. Typically, Barbra would be able to view and edit footage that had been shot the previous day en route to whatever location she was shooting at that morning. The vehicle would be parked as close to the set as possible.

"It gets hotter than hell here in the summer," relates reporter Frank Jarrell, "and they had built almost like a tunnel, an enclosed [air-conditioned] walkway, where her motor home could park, and they would attach the walkway to her motor home door so that she could walk from her motor home to the set—without ever having to go outside." In other words, without ever seeing the sun, and without ever having to be seen.

Another promise made when the film company first came to town was that the movie would be heavily populated with the familiar faces of the people of the Lowcountry. However, all the principal adult roles for the picture had already been cast. According to Tracy Fowler, casting director for Fincannon and Associates of Wilmington, North Carolina, the company was primarily looking for stand-ins and extras. In fact, the script called for very few scenes requiring the presence of extras. One such scene concerned the cocktail party given by Eddie (George Carlin), a mutual friend of Lowenstein's and Wingo's, in his New York apartment; another, the more intimate dinner party in which Nolte as Wingo threatens to fling a Stradivarius over a balcony.

Cattle-call casting notwithstanding, the people who in some way facilitated the production were rewarded with parts, however nominal, in the picture. The huge casting search conducted in downtown Beaufort was, more than anything, part of a public relations campaign to appease the townspeople.

The Prince of Tides did come through with at least one of its promises to the community, and that was casting the picture with the faces of Southern youth. The script called for Tom, Savannah, and Luke Wingo at three stages of flashbacks: at six to seven years of age, nine to eleven years of age, and as teenagers; it also called for actresses to play Tom Wingo's three young daughters.

Casting the children was an exercise in discipline for Barbra. She had to learn to sacrifice, or at least curb, her own dogged personal tastes for what was deemed to be the best interests of the film. "There might have been one kid that I wanted," Barbra would later acknowledge, "but she didn't take to Nick. I couldn't hire her if she was to play his daughter."

"Her personal taste was the problem," asserts Paul Sylbert. "She was casting those two young boys—Nick [Tom] as a young boy and his brother [Luke]. The pretty one was *so* pretty, the reddish-haired kid, that Barbra wanted him to play Nick as a child. I said, 'That's wrong, Barbra.' She said, 'But I like him so much.' I said, 'Barbra, I've told you this one hundred times. It isn't what *you* like or dislike, it's what's *right* for the movie.' And she called me back later and said, 'You remember what you said about liking and disliking? I put him [the redhead] in the part of the other brother and I used the blond boy for Nick.' And I said, 'That's the way it has to be done for the whole movie.' "

Justen Woods of Swainsboro, Georgia, was cast in the part of Tom at the ages of six and seven.

"It concerned us to begin with," concedes Norma Woods, Justen's mother, "that Barbra wasn't used to being around little kids . . . but she was great. Most of the shooting was done in Beaufort. The older children had a lot of scenes there, like the rape scene and all that. Barbra was really good about it. She took our [set of] children on the set so that they could see what was going on, so that they could see the fake blood and all the different effects.

"Barbra interacted with the children a lot. I think it helped that she let them call her Miss Barbra rather than Miss Streisand. There were a couple of times when she'd have to say to them, '*Don't* look at the camera, don't look at the camera.' I know one particular time she really got on Justen for looking into the camera. But she was great. One scene called for Justen to climb a rope up to the tree house. His little hands were getting all red, and so Barbra got behind him and kind of propped him up with her hands to give him a break."

Barbra tried to create an environment in which the kids could be *kids,* so that their innate childlike qualities could be captured on camera and translated onto the screen. This would be one of her triumphs.

Perhaps the single best-directed scene in the entire picture, and a testament to Barbra's attention to detail, was the sequence in which young Tom, Luke, and Savannah Wingo leap off a dock and plunge into the depths. They join forces underwater in almost balletic fashion and then virtually explode out of the water, bursting with renewed life, vigor, and camaraderie.

"For us," relates Norma Woods, "the most difficult scene to shoot was the Charleston [actually, Wadamalaw Island] scene when the children were jumping off the dock. They had to take a lot of precautions because there were alligators in the water. Barbra had the underwater divers go underwater first. She also had a standby helicopter there in case anything went wrong.

"Barbra was in her little paddle boat, directing. She wanted Justen to jump first and for the others to follow. They shot that scene about five times in one day. They had dryers set up out there because each time [they shot], it meant taking off their clothes, putting on other clothes, drying the wet clothes, and then putting them back on. Still, it wasn't any longer than ten minutes between shots, which was real stressful because everyone was in such a hurry.

"We [the parents] were very far removed from everything. We wanted to be able to see our children, but Barbra wanted us in the background. She even snapped at one of the fathers who was helping his daughter, Tiffany [Davis], get dressed. Barbra preferred that one of the costume people help Tiffany get dressed."

The actual underwater sequence in the scene was shot back in California. Columbia flew the three children and their parents to Los Angeles for two weeks in November. For the first week, the children trained with Olympics swimming coach Linda Huey to perfect their underwater swimming techniques. They initially trained at the facility at UCLA, but because of a lack of privacy, they moved to a pool at a private home in Beverly Hills.

"Staying underwater," says Norma Woods, "was the main thing. Justen worked at staying underwater for almost a minute. They also had to learn the formation that Barbra wanted. Justen was trained to go down the deepest and be the point where everybody went down to, because he was the one who went down first. And then they would have to learn how to extend their legs out straight, and try not to float up, all while they are holding hands and trying to stay underwater. The little girl [Tiffany Davis] even ended up having to wear some weights during the filming."

The actual shooting was done in a tank at Columbia Studios in Culver City that had once been used by Esther Williams. Barbra shot the swimming sequence in segments. "One day," Norma Woods recalls, "she shot the children coming out of the water. She had this idea of them *popping* out of the water. On another day, she had them underwater, swimming up and holding hands. Another afternoon was spent doing the face shots. The children were actually being held down on either side [in the tank] by Linda Huey and her assistant. Barbra was directing them with a microphone from an underwater observation window. She would tell them, 'Look to your left,' 'Look ahead,' 'Look to your right,' and would try to get them to blow out bubbles."

Also during that visit to Los Angeles, the three children recorded their voice-overs in what is generally called a "dubbing" or "looping" session. The dubbing was incorporated into the beginning of the movie in the scene in which the children are seen running out of the house. To get the Southern accents that she wanted from the children, Barbra recited their lines with a Southern accent of her own, something, according to Norma Woods, "that she was totally incapable of." To get the spontaneous laughter she wanted from them, Barbra snuck up behind her young actors and tickled them silly as they stood before the microphone.

Prior to shooting the underwater sequence in Los Angeles, Barbra studied the footage that had been previously shot in Beaufort. What she determined, to the embarrassment of the hair and makeup people who should have detected it themselves, was that the children's hair length varied between June and November, and moreover, that they had lost their summer tans. If the discrepancy was disregarded, the discerning filmgoer might have observed that the resulting shots did not match those filmed in Beaufort.

Norma Woods was witness to something she was not supposed to see. She was present in the room when the two makeup artists were applying body makeup on Justen to simulate his lost summer tan. Barbra walked into the room, and, according to Norma, "She really let them have it, really read them out.

"They had gotten body makeup on his costume," Norma confides, "around the neck and all. Barbra wiped it all off and then she put the makeup on herself. I wish we could've gotten a picture of Barbra Streisand putting body makeup on our child. And then she took the scissors and trimmed his hair like she thought it should be. She's one of these people who really has an idea of how things should be, and then she does it herself."

To Norma Woods, Barbra's demeanor was radically different from June to November, from Beaufort to Los Angeles. Upon their arrival at their hotel room in Los Angeles, the Woodses received a bowl of gardenias from Barbra with a note that read, "Welcome to L.A.! Can't wait to see you. Love, Barbra." They were more than a little surprised by the effusiveness of the note.

"In South Carolina," explains Norma, "I think we could sense that she was under a lot of pressure. She maintained a lot of seclusion. She had her entourage around her, and they were the ones who basically communicated with her. When we went to Los Angeles, it was much more pleasant. Most of the strain of getting the movie together was over. I think that most of her stress had been being on the time deadline she was on, and being in the South with the heat and all the gnats. In Los Angeles," recalls Norma, "[Barbra] asked us if it was still hot back home and if the gnats were still out. 'The people were fine,' she told us, 'but I just don't like the area.' She did *not*," Norma Woods reiterates "like the South."

Actually Barbra could not *wait* to get out of Beaufort. When the location work on *Tides* was completed, she packed her bags and fled to the comforts of her air-conditioned New York penthouse without a word to the townspeople.

When asked if Barbra or the film company did anything in particular to thank the accommodating community before they made their exit, John Williams responds with a resounding "Not a damned thing." He adds, "I wasn't around for [the shooting of] *The Great Santini,* but everyone I talked to said it was a wonderful experience. People could stand around and watch the different scenes being shot. Robert Duvall served as the Grand Marshal for a downtown parade during a summertime festival. There was real community involvement, giving something back to the community, letting the people see what was going on."

In an apparent effort to provoke some, even token, act of appreciation from Barbra, the editor of the *Beaufort Gazette* wrote an editorial shortly before the company wrapped up its location work. "One has only to look to the town of Chester, South Carolina, where the movie *Chiefs* was filmed," the editorial read. "The film crew brought excitement to the town, just as the crew for *The Prince of Tides* has brought to Beaufort. The stars and the crew exacted a lot from the town, just as has happened here. They tied up the main traffic arteries through the town with sand and built a part in the middle of the street. People were inconvenienced, but they lived with it. Before they left town, though, Charlton Heston, Wayne Rogers and others repaid the community for their generosity. They participated in poetry readings and book readings to raise money for a new library. Heston, Rogers and others, too, played in softball games to help raise money for local charities and the library. . . ." The editorial went on to suggest that a similar response should be forthcoming from Barbra and her company.

Barbra, however, chose not to respond to the editorial. Instead, she had a studio publicist send a letter in her behalf to the paper. The letter was unsigned, and when the paper could not determine its veracity— calls to Barbra's office went unreturned—it went unpublished.

Other than the economic and tourist benefits typical from most shoots of this type, and a "Thanks to the City of Beaufort" tagged to the ending screen credits, the town and its people would receive little in return for their Southern hospitality. *The Prince of Tides* would not even be premiered in Beaufort. The city *would* get what was deemed an "early screening" before the movie's national release, but neither Barbra nor any of the film's stars would show up for the screening and party. For some, such ingratitude was indicative of Hollywood's use-them-and-lose-them exploitation of smalltown America. For others, Barbra's rejection of Beaufort, and of the South at large, was a stinging slap in the face.

Thirty-seven

Director at Work

*H*onking horns in traffic. Obnoxious cab drivers. Steam emanating from the city street. Impatient Jewish women with pressing doctors' appointments. *This* is Barbra Streisand's New York—or at least it's the New York she introduces us to in *The Prince of Tides.* The sequence, of course, is a cliché, and it illustrates one of Streisand's weaknesses as a film director. Too often, she seems to be inspired not with any real originality or creativity, but rather by films (including some of her own) from her past. The awkwardly shot boat finale from *Yentl,* for example, was lifted out of the (much better staged) ferry boat sequence ("Don't Rain on My Parade") in William Wyler (and Herb Ross's) *Funny Girl.* And the twenty-minute romance sequence that concludes *The Prince of Tides* seems to belong more to Sydney Pollack's *The Way We Were* than to the novel by Pat Conroy. It's not that Streisand doesn't have ideas—she has a plethora of ideas—it's just that her choices are sometimes obvious, unoriginal, and uninspired.

To establish early on that Dr. Susan Lowenstein, despite her rather frosty exterior, is a good sort, and therefore one worth rooting for, she is seen ordering an underling to lower the dosage of Savannah Wingo's medication. Not only do we learn from this self-serving bit of business (which, significantly, was *not* in the book) that Lowenstein is a conscientious doctor, we also glean that she is compassionate. The scene fails to work, however, because Streisand's directorial motivation is all too transparent. See Barbra in charge. See Barbra be caring.

Obvious, too, is her use of voice-overs to tell us what a character feels. It's easy to understand Streisand's attraction to voice-overs. She is, after all, a singer whose songs typically encapsulate tales of drama which she delivers with considerable histrionics. She is also the director of *Yentl,* which, like most musicals, employed song lyrics to express a character's emotions. As Yentl, Barbra even *sang* in voice-over. She uses voice-overs in *The Prince of Tides* the way she would use the lyrics of a song in a musical.

With an actor of the caliber of Nick Nolte, however, she needn't have resorted to such an obvious, shorthand device. Unlike lesser actors, Nolte needs only his face and body to express the inner workings of a character. Streisand's utilization of voice-overs in the picture bespeaks her insecurity with Nolte, with the material, and most of all, with her own direction.

Production designer Paul Sylbert detected another relationship between Streisand's musical background and her work on *Tides.* "I think what happens that never leaves the movie is the way she deals with dialogue. If you really listen to it, it's *lyrics,* it isn't dialogue. Barbra thinks of the dialogue as lyrics. When she does a speech, it has its ups and downs. Musical cadence is where her focus is, and that's fine. In the old days in the theater, that's all anybody ever did. But even that gets worked out when you give the dialogue to Nick Nolte, because he's gonna move it around, he's gonna break up the cadences. When *she* acts, the cadences are more noticeable, because she's basically a singer.

"Take the speech in the hospital where Tom Wingo meets Lowenstein and comes out of his sister's room enraged. Listen to any of the long speeches in the psychiatric sequences. They're treated as lyrics. Not only did I notice it, but one of the editors who worked on a rough cut of the picture told me that he noticed exactly the same thing. He also said that, technically, she didn't know that much about music—and he was right."

Another significant flaw in the picture is Brad Sullivan's characterization of Henry Wingo, Tom, Luke, and Savannah's father. Under Streisand's direction, Henry Wingo is a raging monster, a caricature of the complex patriarch created by Pat Conroy. Barbra's choice to villainize Henry Wingo to the hilt is another example of her tendency toward the obvious. She fared far better with her direction of Kate Nelligan's subtle, textural interpretation of Lila Wingo.

It may be that the inconsistency in Streisand's interpretation of the Wingo parents was rooted in her own upbringing. Louis Kind, Barbra's stepfather, was the Henry Wingo of her childhood. Her relationship with her mother Diana, however, was, and continues to be, full of ambiguity. It is possible that the character of Lila Wingo received more care and development in *Tides* because Barbra herself was more interested in exploring her relationship with her mother rather than her relationship with her stepfather.

Streisand claimed that in her version of *Tides* there was no clear-cut "bad guy." In truth, Henry Wingo is the villain of her movie, just as Louis Kind, in her view, was the villain of her childhood. And, if *Yentl* was an homage to Emanuel Streisand, the natural father whom she never knew, *The Prince of Tides* is, in part, about forgiving and accepting the frailties of her own mother.

For years, Barbra struggled with the animosity she felt for her mother. It gnawed at her. *Why* had she not been her mother's favorite? *Why* had her mother not believed in her? *Why* had her mother subjected her to Louis Kind? With *The Prince of Tides,* and through the relationship between Tom and Lila Wingo, Barbra the artist saw an opportunity to come to terms with her past.

Three weeks into the filming of *Tides,* Diana Kind underwent open-heart surgery in Los Angeles. Barbra refused to play the role of the dutiful daughter and did not postpone the shooting of the picture to be at her mother's bedside during her hospitalization and eventual recovery.

Still, when facing the possible death of a loved one, it is human nature to regard that person with renewed appreciation. With *The Prince of Tides,* Barbra was doing just that with her own mother. Like Lila Wingo, Diana Kind had done her best, pitiable as it may have been, with the cards she had been dealt.

Barbra tried to put her mother's operation in perspective. "My mother had undergone bypass surgery," she would say later. "I was very terrified starting to make this film because I hadn't directed in eight years. When she survived that operation, that was real life and death. The movie took on second place. It wasn't real life and death anymore to me."

Barbra Streisand is positively possessed when she directs a picture. She puts in twenty-plus-hour days and thinks nothing of making midnight phone calls to various associates to discuss the most minute of details. Anyone who complains about her mode of operation is, in her view, less of a professional than she. But while she is demanding of her cast and crew, she is, inarguably, hardest on herself.

Coproducer Shel Shrager told columnist Cindy Adams at the time, "Barbra Streisand is up late editing film, up early checking dailies, and up all day before the cameras. Thirty-five years in this business, I've never seen anyone so good. Some nights she hasn't slept at all. She's awesome in her vitality."

Even Paul Sylbert has to acknowledge, admiringly, "She starts out like a train, very slowly. But when she builds up momentum, she'll go right through the walls. Nothing stops her."

When asked about the interminable length of her working days, Streisand cryptically explained, "That's the way it goes. That's the way it has to be, because something, you know, happens on the set one day and then you have to continue it the next day. Something *real* happened. I've gotta change it, I've gotta rewrite it, I've gotta *do* something."

When she was growing up, the family budget did not allow for Barbra the frivolity of dollhouses, toy furniture, and designer clothing for Barbie. As an adult filmmaker, however, Barbra gets to play the games she missed out on as a child. For *The Prince of Tides,* for example, she commissioned elaborate "dollhouses" to be built which were actually miniature reproductions of the sets. Back at her home in Beverly Hills, she then blocked the action and planned her shots for the picture by maneuvering her Nick Nolte doll, her Barbra Streisand doll, her Kate Nelligan doll, around on the miniature sets.

In preparing her camera setups, Streisand sometimes preshoots a scene on videotape to see how it will appear. She then views the footage and makes whatever adjustments she deems appropriate before filming. She also hires an artist who prepares detailed scene sketches from which she further plans her shots.

It is not lack of preparation or disorganization that causes delay and added work on a Streisand picture. Rather, it is her pursuit of perfection, and, just as significant, her chronic *uncertainty.* If there were to be a single word in the Streisand vocabulary, it would be "Why?" She is, perhaps, unrivaled among filmmakers when it comes to her arsenal of questions about everything and everyone around her, including questions about her own ideas and self. Her mind is devouring. Whether it be about finding the "truth" in a particular scene, or determining if a certain syllable in a certain word in a certain line is given the most effective inflection, she is constantly probing, exploring, striving, questioning.

"She sure asks a lot of questions," says Paul Sylbert. He adds, echoing a sentiment felt by many Streisand coworkers, "She could drive you nuts."

It's quite possible that Streisand's uncertainty is precisely what gives her her dynamic. Some of it, of course, has to do with the fact that she is still a novice film director. Her critics tend to forget that she has only directed, including her contributions to *A Star Is Born,* two and a half pictures.

"She's still learning her job," Sylbert says. "When she walks onto a set, like all people carrying the burden of a film in which she is dead *everything,* she is really rolling the dice. She had to be very nervous. This fear locks her up, and when she's locked, she doesn't really see what's in front of her for a while. It takes time for her to acclimate to a new set or a new place, and little by little, we [trusted members of the crew] kind of turn her in the right direction."

She is known within the industry for asking others their opinions on even the most seemingly insignificant detail regarding a film she is directing. Whether she is swayed by these opinions, of course, is another matter.

On *The Prince of Tides,* Barbra consulted with, among others, acclaimed director James L. Brooks *(Terms of Endearment, Broadcast News).* She showed him a rough cut of the picture and then reportedly barraged him with a series of questions. Brooks thoughtfully responded to each of her queries, but later remarked, "I figured out that she doesn't want your opinions. She [just] wants someone to talk to while she's making up her mind. If you just flap your jaw for a while, you'll supply the background music for where she's going anyway."

It wasn't only James Brooks whose opinion Barbra sought. She also asked everybody and anybody who had seen the picture in its early previews for their advice. When one female fan stopped her on the street and told her how much she had liked the film, Barbra asked the surprised stranger for suggestions on how it could be improved. She is said to have even solicited the advice of her gardener.

Because of her insecurity, Streisand tends to overshoot. In fact, she has become famous in the industry for shooting one scene many different ways, a reflection of the uncertainty of her own ideas. She has herself acknowledged, "I always do every take differently. [Therefore] I have a lot of choices as an editor at the end." These "choices," more than anything, are for self-protection. If an approach to a certain scene doesn't work out one way, she simply reaches into her bag of extra takes and pulls out an alternative version. The editing room is her salvation. While some filmmakers, pumped up with self-confidence and/or ego, roll the dice at every whim while shooting a picture, Streisand is more cautious, more deliberate. To a great extent, she works from a defensive position.

Naturally, not everyone in the *Tides* company was pleased by the extra work called for with Streisand's repeated, sometimes seemingly purposeless, takes. One Beaufort reporter relates, "I went down to the set one day, and one of the guys in the crew was telling me all this stuff about how Barbra was overshooting. He told me how they had been shooting this one scene over and over again because she didn't know what she wanted. He said that they had been shooting in the gym until some *ungodly* hour of the morning."

At one point, Barbra got into a fight with cinematographer Stephen Goldblatt over the way a particular scene, set in the Reese Newburry living room, was to be shot. Goldblatt prearranged the shot, orchestrated the lighting, and directed the placement of his cameras all so that the library, adjacent to the living room, could be seen. After a considerable amount of work had been done, Barbra stepped in and decided that she didn't like the shot. She wanted it photographed from the *opposite* direction. Goldblatt tried to reason with her, explaining that a lot of time, and hence money, had already been spent arranging the shot. Barbra insisted that the scene be shot *her* way.

A verbal battle ensued, with Barbra prevailing. The shot was entirely restaged and relit according to her wishes. When asked for her reason for the change, Streisand responded that she wanted a fish on the wall to be captured in the shot, despite the fact that the fish had already been seen in a previous shot.

Paradoxically, for someone who has the reputation for being difficult to work with, one of Streisand's strengths as a director is her ability to elicit quality performances from her actors. Unlike many other directors, she doesn't just give her actors commands to sit, stand, and speak. She invites them into the creative process. With Nolte, Barbra spent many hours in lengthy analytical discussions, exploring and developing the relationship between Tom Wingo and Susan Lowenstein. She also nurtures her actors, almost in a maternal sense.

"You don't get good performances," Barbra commented in reference to her reputation, "just by being controlling and demanding. I'm a woman. I'm a mother. I know that to get the best out of people, you have to be kind and gentle and nurturing and caring."

Bob Hannah, cast in the picture as Reese Newburry, was surprised by the warmth Streisand projected to her actors. "I didn't know what to expect, because Barbra Streisand is sort of bigger than life in our generation. [But] from the minute I walked in the door of the meeting room, I felt good about it because she was just down to earth and real easy to talk to. We spent a lot of time talking about Southern accents. She invited me to watch the playbacks of the scenes we shot on a video screen, and she was so pleased that she hugged my neck." It is characteristic of Streisand to hug her actors after they have completed a scene.

She is sensitive to her actors partly because she spent years taking orders from directors who dismissed her questions and ignored her suggestions.

Being an actor herself, Streisand has the tendency as a director to act out a scene to illustrate how she wants it to be played. Naturally, some actors are resentful of this technique, while others are knowingly tolerant. A nonprofessional like Nancy Rhett found it to be helpful. For a card-playing scene (which was later edited out of the picture) involving Rhett and three other inexperienced actresses, Streisand had no difficulty conveying what it was that she wanted.

"She came over," Rhett relates, "and started talking to us. She bent down a little bit because we were sitting in our chairs, and what I remember is her fingernails. She talks with her fingers. Actually, she talks with her finger*nails.* She told us how we were to be *so* bitchy and so critical of Kate Nelligan, who was to come in wearing this terrible, tacky gardenia in her hair.

"We were scared to death, but by the time we had finished shooting all of our takes for the day, it was completely natural what Barbra had pulled out of us. I was amazed how she had taken four lumps of clay and molded us into real bitches.

"She would also give us ideas of lines to say. She kept encouraging us, saying things like, 'You've got be *really* mean. Go ahead—be a real *bitch.*' She kept pulling this out of us. She kept encouraging us to get meaner, uglier, bitchier, colder, and snobbier."

Despite various disagreements he had with her over interpretation, Nick Nolte accepted Streisand's introspective, probing style. For the most part, he also was willing to sacrifice his own ego.

"It's been pounded into me from the theater from day one," Nolte explained. "The director is committed to the author; the actors are committed to the director of the author's work. That's the chain of it. Now, there are some actors who don't believe that. They believe that their responsibility is to be interesting, or cute, or mannered, or pretty. They feel they have a direct obligation past the material and directly to the audience, and therefore they have to be entertaining. I don't want to be bigger than the story; I have no interest in that.

"Acting," Nolte summarizes his approach to his craft, "can either be the ultimate ego trip or a selfless act, working in the service of the story."

Interestingly, Nolte's comments could be taken as a cutting commentary on Barbra Streisand the actress. Just ask some of the directors for whom she has worked. This is an actress who has rarely, if ever, been willing to sacrifice her persona and stature for the service of a mere story. As an actor, she is the antithesis of Nolte.

One of the biggest points of contention on the picture between Nolte and Streisand was over the direction of the hallway sex scene. "When we were doing the love scenes at first," related Nolte, "they would just get *hot*. Just start to really work, and she'd cut! The actress would jump and say, 'Wait, wait, *wait*,' and the actress would order the director to cut. And I would say, 'Barbra, why are you cutting it? It's just getting good.' "

"He [Nick] was getting turned on," Barbra related in her defense. "I was embarrassed. Every time it got a little hot, I yelled, 'Cut!' [I thought] where is it [the scene] going to go? Is he going to take off all my clothes and we're going to fuck on the floor?"

Barbra confesses, in retrospect, "The shy actress got in the way of the director. She screwed the director by yelling 'Cut!' I know I should've probably gone on. But you could say that the director was looking and going, 'I don't need any more of this because I'll only use this amount.' But I did get very shy and go, 'Oh my God! How can I be making love to him in the corridor here with my crew watching?' "

There is something very dated, the cinematic equivalent of Muzak, about a Streisand-directed sex scene. There is no real passion, no heat, no sweat. And certainly no *breasts*. One of the takes in *Tides*, either inadvertently or by design, revealed Barbra's breasts on camera. Daring for her, Streisand incorporated the take into the picture for one of its early previews. She later excised it.

"I got a feeling," she rationalized, "that it took people out of the scene. It was like, all of a sudden, *there's Barbra Streisand's breasts*, instead of the emotion of the scene. So I cut it differently. I made it into a two-shot in close-ups."

"I like audiences to use their imagination—like in old-time movies," Streisand says in defense of her love scenes. What she doesn't address, at least not publicly, is that she has a tendency toward schmaltz. Consider the awful love scene in *A Star Is Born* in which she is seduced by Kris Kristofferson in a bathtub filled with bubbles and surrounded by more candles than are found in a Catholic church. It's uncertain whether Streisand's point was to equate sex with Kristofferson to a religious experience or whether candelight simply turns her on. In her love scene with Nolte in *Tides,* Barbra is again surrounded by candles.

Unlike Ellen Barkin, who was every inch Dennis Quaid's sexual equal in *The Big Easy* and Al Pacino's in *Sea of Love,* Streisand directs herself in *Tides* as being the more sexually passive partner. Feminist though she may be, she seems to find it sexy to wither in the arms of a strong man. In a Streisand-directed love scene, everything seems soft, the lights, the music, and sometimes even the focus.

Privately, Streisand herself is aware of her penchant for schmaltz. According to Paul Sylbert, she even quietly asked him to keep a watchful eye on her inclination toward the banal. "She's a very *schmaltzy* singer," says Sylbert. "And I think she's a very schmaltzy director. And I think she's aware of it. She asked me early on—and I don't know if she asked anybody else about this—she asked me to try to make sure that she didn't do too much of that schmaltz."

Even with her own conscious efforts, *The Prince of Tides,* particularly the last twenty minutes, is laden with syrup and soap opera. Sylbert assesses, "I liked it [the picture] a lot until then. That's where Barbra had six different rocking chairs for that scene where she's sitting in Nick Nolte's lap. She had [shot] much more of that little-baby-in-the-lap stuff. I thought the movie should've been over after the therapy, Nick's big breakthrough, the catharsis. The movie was *over.* This little love *thing,* which was very hard to integrate, for me never really got integrated. She treated it too cute. What she was doing was showing Barbra in love, Barbra young again, Barbra this and Barbra that. And it was wrong."

Streisand the director, however, disagreed. She wanted to include more, not less, footage of her romance sequences with Nolte, despite the fact that they comprised only a small portion of the book. Sylbert, among others, tried to talk her out of it, to little avail. Sylbert says, "Barbra has to feel that something is *right* for her. She has intentions with everything she does, and there are times when she is bulletproof, when no matter what you say, it's not going to change. She feels the need to do that schmaltzy stuff, and she does it."

Reportedly, Streisand wanted an *additional* twenty minutes of the romance sequence incorporated into the picture, but finally, begrudgingly, relented on orders from Columbia.

"I know there was about twice as much as was finally used," says Sylbert, "and what they used was too much. Listen, the studio must've talked to her at length to get her to cut out those [additional] twenty minutes."

For Barbra, shooting in New York was far more enjoyable and comfortable—no nagging gnats—than it had been in South Carolina. She even relaxed—a little. For a scene in Greenwich Village that required a traffic jam, Barbra, displeased that her production manager had not hired enough cars, boldly marched up to startled drivers on Sullivan Street and asked for their help.

"Hi, I'm Barbra Streisand," she declared, as if anybody needed to be told. "I'm directing a movie here. Would you mind being in the shot?"

For added assistance, she approached a police officer and, turning on her feminine wiles, pleaded, "Hey, officer, would you do me a favor? I don't have enough cars, and I'd love for them to back up. Would you mind?"

During breaks from shooting, Barbra also surprised the locals by being social, and the paparazzi by being accommodating. She indulged in a filet of lemon sole sautéed in peanut oil at the Oyster Bar; dined at Luma, the chicest natural foods restaurant in the city; visited the showroom of her friend, fashion designer Donna Karan, and raved about the cashmere; and attended a cabaret show at the Blue Angel, where she had performed thirty years before.

Still, the Streisand temperament was not entirely silenced. One day on the set, she reportedly burst into a fit over a toilet in her motor home trailer. It seems that the flush handle on the toilet was located in the wrong place. Barbra, accustomed to the accoutrements of fame, fortune, and the socially correct, was used to simply reaching back and flushing the handle without having to turn around. Her trailer toilet required that she stand up, turn around, and flush the handle. Upon Streisand's command, the offensive, wrong-handled toilet was promptly replaced.

In Central Park, Barbra found it difficult to articulate to her son, Jason, what she wanted from him. Although it may have strengthened their relationship in the long run, Barbra's direction of her son as Bernard, one of the picture's pivotal roles, was not without its difficulties. She carried her apprehension about Jason's suitability for the part into the production. While shooting the football sequence between Jason and Nick Nolte, Barbra called for take after take, either uncertain about exactly what it was that she desired, or unable to give diplomatic expression to it.

One of Jason's line readings, in particular, vexed Barbra. She had him do it again, again, and again. Finally, Jason lashed out in protest.

"What don't you like?!" he snapped.

Barbra, trying to balance her dual role as mother and director, attempted to respond firmly and with reason. She reminded Jason that he had to separate their relationship as mother and child from their relationship as director and actor. She told him that she didn't think his line reading was "believable" and that she wanted him to keep doing it until he got it "right."

Jason stormed off and found solace in the arms and reassuring words of Cis Corman, who had been watching from the sidelines. As he walked away, Barbra called out, "Don't be mad at me as your *goddamned* mother!"

After cooling off, Jason returned to reshoot the scene. Still, he couldn't resist goading his mother, *"Cis* likes my reading."

Barbra, undaunted, shot back, "Yes, but Cis is not the director."

When shooting at Grand Central Station, it was not Jason's line reading that distressed Barbra. It was his *walk.* Moreover, Barbra had been granted only two days, at five hours a day, to shoot the scene. The conventional wisdom, and Barbra's own advisers, told her that it would take at least twenty hours to shoot. The scene called for Jason to play the violin, say goodbye to Nolte, and then walk off to catch his train. Barbra wanted the scene to symbolize Bernard's newfound maturity and confidence. Playing football with Nolte's Wingo had transformed him from an aimless and petulant problem child into a well-adjusted young adult. After shooting take after take of the scene, an exasperated Barbra exploded in front of the cast and crew.

"Walk like a man!" she allegedly demanded of her startled son. "Walk like a *man!"*

When she made the decision to cast Jason in her picture, Barbra feared that as a public figure, he would become subjected to the same kind of scrutiny of his personal life that she had faced in hers. As Barbra labored over *Tides* in postproduction, a tabloid publication fulfilled her worst fears by splashing Jason's photo on its cover. BARBRA WEEPS OVER GAY SON'S WEDDING, the headline pronounced. The accompanying article read, in part, "Jason, 24, married his regular companion, underwear

model David Knight," and went on to chronicle Barbra's purported objection to her son's "wedding" as well as her presumed despondency
over his sexual orientation.

The story was a fabrication. Nevertheless, it sent reverberations
throughout West Hollywood, where Jason lives, and where gossip trav-
els with glee and at the speed of push-button automatic dial. Although
several people affirm the veracity of the story to this day, there is no evidence to give it credence. Furthermore, for the first time since "the
story" broke, David Knight, the exceptionally handsome fashion model
turned actor, spoke publicly for this book. "I don't know Jason," says
Knight, who obviously wants to put the notoriety behind him, "I've
never even met him." When questioned further, Knight relayed his suspicion that the story was conjured up by a former, vengeful acquaintance.

Interestingly, Knight was not the only one linked with Jason. Another
tabloid received a lead that Jason was involved with the son of a celebrity, Griffin O'Neal. The story, however, was deemed too absurd even
by the tabloid, and it went unpublished. What is evident, from these and
other incidents, is that someone, for whatever reason, was out to get
Jason and exploit his newfound public status.

Barbra, who remained loyal and devoted to her son, said, in a statement to the press, "I've just about gotten used to the garbage they've
been writing about me for years, but this is a new low in rag journalism."

To Jason's credit, and by extension to Barbra's, he ended up providing *Tides* with one of its most natural, least affected performances. Barbra, pleased that most of her reservations about casting Jason had gone
unfounded, beamed over his finished work on the picture.

More interesting, perhaps, than Barbra's direction of any other cast
member was her direction of herself. Despite her hyphenated title and
duties on the picture, there was, according to Streisand, an absence of
ego, of conflict of interest. "The star doesn't exist for me," she insists. "I
find it interesting just to throw away the actress."

"I filmed my [Lowenstein's] office scenes last and made me a 'cover
set,'" Streisand declares as evidence of her sacrifice. "When it rained
outside, which it rained a lot, you know, then I'd have to come in and
act. But if I were the star of the show, I'd never allow that, believe me.
When I'm the director, I absolutely shove the actress aside. She gets no
catering from me."

Paul Sylbert, however, disagrees with the contention that Barbra discarded her actress's ego. "You always have to find out what her *real* intention is. I went to New York and the sketch artist, Brook Mason, was there. And I looked at these things and I noticed something about them. They were [sketches of] two sets and two sequences—and they were treated identically. What happened was that after the second shot, Barbra ended up in the *foreground* and everybody else ended up in the background. I said, 'These are the same shot, Barbra—which means that every set will have to be designed for you to do this, with you always in the foreground and everybody else always in the background.' She kind of said, 'Oh, I didn't notice.' "

"Also," Sylbert adds, "everything had to be shot on her good side [the left side of her face]. Do you realize that whole *sets* had to be rotated to her good side?"

Not only does Streisand the director shoot Streisand the actress primarily from her good side, she also favors her with highly flattering shots. In *Tides,* Streisand accords herself languishing shots of her legs and fingernails—presumably her assessment of her own best physical features—that are glaringly gratuitous in the context of the story.

"That's just nonsense." Streisand says in response. "I would shoot me the way I would shoot *any* actress playing the role—the way I would shoot Blythe Danner, the way I would shoot Kate Nelligan. . . . You want to make everything look as beautiful as it can in the movie."

Streisand, however, misses the point. In the picture, she is supposed to be playing a highly regarded psychiatrist, and yet, in her office scenes, her fingernails are given more focus, and thus more importance, than the diplomas and certificates on her wall. Furthermore, the audience should not have to be telegraphed and told that an actress is beautiful. She either is or isn't.

In *Tides,* Streisand makes such a distinct point of telling her audience that she is attractive ("Doesn't Babs look great?" you can almost hear an audience member gasp) that it is distracting to the story. In the cocktail party scene at Eddie's apartment, Barbra is meticulously framed and backlit like some ethereal, golden goddess—hardly the effortless beauty, the "one of those go-to-hell New York women" written about by Pat Conroy.

The scene called for Nolte to discover Streisand's presence in the heavily crowded room. However, the way she is lit, no discovery on Nolte's part is required. She practically glows like a neon billboard.

Certainly, as her own director, Streisand is not as self-involved as she is when she simply acts in a picture. She doesn't have time to be. But as far as throwing the actress away, to borrow her own terminology, that simply isn't true. That, of course, should not come as any surprise. For a quarter of a century, Barbra Streisand has been engulfed by mass, sometimes fanatical, adulation, living in a vacuum created by her own fame. To think that she could shed all semblance of ego on command is unlikely, if not altogether impossible. Still, directing herself, she'll never be as good as she can be until she learns how to make her ego disappear.

With four years of preproduction and four months of shooting behind it, and with yet another year of editing and postproduction in front of it, *The Prince of Tides* completed principal photography in late September, 1990. The company wrap party was to be held at the Crane Club on Amsterdam Avenue in New York City. Overcome with a mixture of relief, exhilaration, and fatigue, Barbra was certainly deserving of a celebration. Her accomplishments on the picture had been enormous.

On the night of the party, however, the festivities were dampered when Barbra created a scene by refusing to enter the Crane Club through its front door. She insisted upon entering the restaurant through an adjacent restaurant on Seventy-ninth Street, which was connected by a secret corridor to the private room where the party was under way.

After boldly confronting and resolving the numerous, sometimes arduous, sometimes acrimonious battles and challenges that presented themselves during the making of *The Prince of Tides,* Barbra Streisand, conquering warrior and champion of her own commitment, was afraid. And just what was it that she was afraid of? She was afraid of being seen. She was afraid of being recognized. She was afraid of being asked for an autograph.

Thirty-eight

Sudden Shock of Light

*I*t was an early Sunday morning. Bob Schulenberg, Barbra's old friend from her days at the Bon Soir, was in his bedroom, radio on, when the telephone rang. "Bob?" queried the voice on the other line. "Yes?" he answered, not recognizing, or really hearing, the caller's voice. She repeated her name. "Excuse me?" said Schulenberg, still unable to make out the name. She tried again. *Still* he couldn't understand her. "Just a second," he finally told her, "let me close the doors and turn down the radio." He then came back on the line, saying, "Hello, again. Who is this?" "Barbra Joan Streisand," the caller responded. "Do you remember me?"

It had been almost twenty-five-years since he had last heard from his once very good friend.

"We immediately started up," Schulenberg recalls. "We talked for three hours. It was like I had never stopped talking with her. She said, '*We* never had a fight, did we?' And I said, 'Not that I know of.' And she said, 'Why did we lose track of each other?' And I said, 'Well, when you married Elliott, I didn't want to intrude. I felt that it was competitive, and Elliott was having a slow start [with his career].' And she said, 'I remember.' She was aware of it. But, there was a little bit of a lack of gracefulness on her part not to have realized that I had made a sacrifice for her.

"When another friend of mine [who is also a friend of Barbra's], heard that I had gotten a call from her," Schulenberg continues, "he said, '*Well,* what did she *want* from you?' "

What Barbra sought was a photograph Schulenberg had taken many years before which captured her and Phyllis Diller together in a moment of repose at the Bon Soir. She wanted to incorporate the photo into a booklet accompanying *Just for the record . . .* (formerly titled *Legacy*), a compact disc box set retrospective of her career to date.

When released in September 1991, with a staggering seventy-dollar price tag, the remarkable, beautifully packaged four-disc box set was accorded mostly favorable reviews, although a number of critics complained that some of the material, including a duet of "You'll Never Know" between the thirteen-year-old Barbra and the about-to-turn forty-six-year-old Barbra bordered on the self-obsessed and the self-congratulatory.

Three years before, Barbra's longtime friend, choreographer Howard Jeffrey, who had worked with her on several of her pictures, passed away. "It got really bad the last six months of his life," relates Howard's best friend, playwright Mart Crowley. "Barbra was very nice to him when he was dying. She used to send food to the house. I never saw her visit, but she may have done so."

In Howard's memory, Barbra dedicated the 1970s disc of *Just for the record . . . ,* "to my friend, Howard Jeffries, who would have liked this record."

"His name was misspelled!" Crowley wails. "It would have driven Howard totally *bonkers.* If anybody ever spelled *her* name B-a-r-b-a-r-a, I'm sure they would hear from her. But, isn't it typical of a movie star to be "best friends" with somebody, and not know how to spell their last name?"

The Prince of Tides was initially scheduled by Columbia Pictures for a September 1991 release. After several wildly enthusiastic previews, however, the studio decided to delay showing the movie, making the film *the* major Columbia release of the lucrative Christmas season. After one such screening, Barbra, waiting anxiously in the editing room, practically leapt upon Shirley MacLaine. "What *didn't* you like?" Barbra pleaded of her friend, who was still adjusting her eyesight to the sudden shock of light. "Tell me what didn't you like?!"

Vanity Fair planned to run its cover story on Barbra in September to coincide with the release of *The Prince of Tides.* When the picture was postponed, Barbra and Columbia requested that publication of the story also be delayed. The magazine refused and ran the piece as scheduled.

As its release date neared, it became obvious that Barbra intended to promote *Tides* more vigorously than she had done for any picture in her career. The modern-day Garbo, who had great and frequently articulated disdain for the press, was suddenly *everywhere*.

For a press junket at the Mark Hotel in New York City, Barbra, through her representatives, informed the participating television shows and stations that all of her video interviews would be shot by *her* camera crew from Columbia Pictures. On-air television reporters would be ushered in, given their eight minutes, if even that amount of time, handed their cassette, and ushered out.

Several days before the scheduled event, Barbra summoned the crew for taped rehearsals. It is, perhaps, the first time in history that a studio has paid for rehearsals of an *interview*. After seeing the footage that had been shot, Barbra, displeased, reportedly had a makeup artist from Los Angeles flown in for the event. Still displeased with the way she looked on camera, she adjusted the lighting a few dozen times, and called for one retake after another. Finally, she reportedly directed the cameraman to put a stocking over the lens.

Bill Harris of Showtime was one of the invited interviewees. "I had spent twelve years interviewing major stars," he reflects, "and I hadn't been this nervous since my first two or three interviews. Barbra was very generous and I was impressed and pleased beyond measure."

Harris was surprised not only by Barbra's warmth, but also by her appearance. "She's much more attractive in person than I thought she would be," he says. "It's really a lovely smile that she has, that funny, crooked smile that we know so well. And when it's directed at you, it's truly disarming and very feminine."

But, the surprising softness of her appearance belied the firmness of her grip, which had tight control over every aspect of the proceedings. "Make no mistake about it," Harris continues, "*she* directed this interview. It was a pre-set interview in that she had the lights on her just the way she wanted, and she had the cameras facing her just at the angle she wanted. And you, the visiting journalist, came in and sat in your designated chair.

"She corrected my pronunciation of her name *on camera*, which is always terrifying. She said, 'Bill, Bill, do you mind if I stop you a minute?' Now, you've only been given eight minutes so every moment is golden. So, the truth is, 'Hell, *yes* I mind if you stop and interrupt me with a question.'

"But, what is one going to say? So, you say, '*Nooooo.*' And then she said, 'Say my name.' And so I said, 'Streizand.' And she said, 'Ah-hah! You see, you're saying it wrong. You're saying Streisand with a *z*, it's actually Streisand with a soft *s*. Say Strei*s*and.' And I said, 'Streisand.'

And she said, 'There, that's it! I tell Jane Fonda the same thing. She *never* gets my name right.' "

When doing an interview on another occasion for "60 Minutes," Barbra literally took over—or attempted to—the direction of the show. "Can I just see the difference if you put that one lightbulb on right there?" she asked the cameraman. "Come in closer on the back camera to sort of simulate the distance . . . ," she continued, pointing out directions as she spoke.

Meanwhile, a perturbed Mike Wallace, who had known Barbra from the days when she was a struggling singer and frequent guest on his show "PM East," tried to gain control of *his* interview and *his* show. "Start the interview," he told the program's director, *"please."*

During the course of the subsequent interview, the two reminisced about their experiences on "PM East," and Wallace startled a visibly shaken Barbra by proclaiming, "You know something? I really didn't like you back thirty years ago."

"That wasn't true," says Donald Softness, who, with his brother John, handled the public relations for "PM East." Mike *did* like her. [Saying] that was just a technique he used with Barbra to get her on edge. You know," Softness adds, "Mike thinks he's the grand inquisitor."

The Prince of Tides premiered in Los Angeles on Wednesday, December 11, 1991. Among those attending were Diana Kind, Jason Gould, Richard Baskin, Kate Nelligan, Blythe Danner, Sean Connery, Goldie Hawn, Tom Hanks, and Jon Peters. The general reaction to the screening was overwhelmingly favorable, with most guests raving about the performance by Nick Nolte. "Come next spring," predicted *The Hollywood Reporter*'s George Christy, "don't be surprised when you hear, 'And the envelope, please . . . the Oscar goes to Nick Nolte for best actor.' "

At the post-screening party, Cis Corman sat on Barbra's right. Sitting on her left was Kevin Costner, along with his wife, Cindy. Costner's assigned placement was far from fortuitous. According to one source, Barbra arranged for the actor-director to sit at her side because she was harboring a major-league crush on him.

Earlier in the year, Barbra had volunteered to present the Best Picture prize at the annual Academy Awards ceremony because she was certain, as was everyone else in town, that Costner would win for *Dances With Wolves.* She wanted, or so the story goes, to be the one to present him with his winning kiss.

In accordance with the film's Southern setting, the food at *The Prince of Tides* post-premiere party, catered by Along Came Mary, included fried chicken, mashed potatoes, country gravy, biscuits, collard greens, soft-shelled crabs, shrimp slaw, corn salad, corn bread, peach shortcake, pecan pie, lemon meringue pie, chocolate cake, and coconut cake.

Two days prior to the event, Barbra reportedly sampled all of the food to be served, and gave her approval to everything *except* the fried chicken. She pronounced that *her* fried chicken was better and promptly proceeded to give her recipe to the startled, but accommodating caterer.

The reviews of the picture, for the most part, were raves. Extolled the critic for *Daily Variety:* "*The Prince of Tides* has a quality not often found in contemporary American movies—passion—and a quality not usually associated with Barbra Streisand—self-effacement. . . . Streisand also puts herself indisputably into the front ranks of directors."

"Streisand is an *outstanding* director," declared Gene Shalit of "The Today Show." "One gauge of her directorial gifts is the superb performances she has drawn from this notable cast."

Exalted Jeffrey Lyons of "Sneak Previews," "A blockbuster, must-see, can't-miss movie. . . . Streisand's direction is intelligent, and Nolte gives the performance of his career."

David Ansen of *Newsweek* was more guarded in his praise. "In the face of *The Prince of Tides'* rampant emotionalism you have three options: unconditional surrender, grit-your-teeth resistance or some heart-wavering combination of the two. . . . Streisand's empathy for the characters is bighearted and contagious. *Prince of Tides* [sic] may be a guilty pleasure, but it's a pleasure nonetheless."

There were others who liked the picture, but found fault with Barbra's performance as Susan Lowenstein. "I saw an *abominable* performance," says Allan Miller, Barbra's former surrogate father and acting coach." I thought it was one of the worst pieces of acting she's ever done. She should have chosen somebody else to do the role because I'm sure she would have directed someone else way better than she directed herself. Barbra did wonderful work, I felt, as a director, but not with her performance. I thought it was mannered. And I hated looking up her legs most of the picture. I thought it took away from the character of the psychiatrist."

Others didn't like the performance *or* the picture. Naming it the second worst film of the year (next to Bruce Willis's $50 million *Hudson Hawk* fiasco), *Rolling Stone* commented, "Director-star Barbra Streisand gives Willis a run for the ego in this turgid dysfunctional-family saga whose plot is as nonsensical as its congratulatory reviews."

There were *no* disputes, however, about the picture's considerable success at the box office. Opening on Christmas Day, *Tides* earned $15.4 million in its first five days, extremely impressive for an adult drama. The only pictures outpacing it were *Hook, Father of the Bride,* and *Beauty and the Beast,* all of which were designed as mass-appeal family fare.

With one clear, incontrovertible swoop, the success of *The Prince of Tides* terminated all talk of Barbra Streisand's "diminishing appeal." The picture would end up grossing over $75 million in North America alone, approximately three times its production budget. The film would also be a hit in the international and home video markets.

A deluxe laserdisc edition, which featured running commentary by Barbra and multiple outtakes (including blooper-like comic material), was also scheduled for release. However, according to Liz Collumb, a representative of the Voyager Company, the disc's would-be distributor, Barbra gave her approval to the product, but as it was going to press, demanded last-minute changes. When Voyager refused to comply, deeming the changes too minor for the added expense, the disc was shelved by Barbra, who had final approval over its release.

Following Don Johnson's storybook return to Melanie Griffith, there was a succession of courting suitors in Barbra's life. Rumored to have joined her list of famous paramours, which already included Omar Sharif, Warren Beatty, Anthony Newly, Pierre Trudeau, Kris Kristofferson, Ryan O'Neal, and Don Johnson, were actors Sam Elliott, Liam Neeson (Julia Roberts's onetime live-in lover), and Clint Eastwood.

The alleged dalliance with Eastwood, then fifty-eight, took place when both were on skiing vacations in Sun Valley, Idaho. Eastwood had recently broken up with longtime girlfriend Sondra Locke, and he called Barbra, forty-seven, and asked her out for a date.

A more significant relationship took place with composer James Newton Howard, eight years Barbra's junior, and the former husband of Rosanna Arquette. True to her pattern, she started to date Howard during the Christmas holidays (as had been the case with Don Johnson and Richard Baskin) in 1990. For Barbra, there seems to be something amorously rousing about the seasonal spirit.

At the time of her burgeoning relationship with Howard, Barbra had already hired John Barry to compose the score for *The Prince of Tides.* Controversy erupted when Barry, generally regarded to be one of the best in the business, was abruptly replaced by Howard *(Pretty Woman, Flatliners).* A spokesman for Columbia dismissed the controversy, saying that Barry had not been *signed* to do the picture.

On January 24, 1991, Barbra arrived at a birthday party for Tri-Star Pictures president Mike Medavoy, held on a Columbia soundstage. Ignoring the other guests, who included Jon Peters and Richard Baskin, Barbra is said to have made a beeline for Don Johnson, who was standing in the middle of the room. According to one observer, the two locked eyes, engaged in what appeared to be *very* friendly conversation, and abruptly left, as "mouths dropped open all over the place."

The seeming sign of reconciliation, however, was dismissed by Lee Solters, Barbra's longtime publicist. Johnson simply escorted Barbra out to her car, according to Solters, as she left the party to meet with Howard. Nevertheless, Melanie Griffith, who undoubtedly heard word of her husband's "reunion" with Barbra, arrived back in Los Angeles from a film shoot the following day.

Barbra's relationship with Howard cooled in the coming weeks, and was well over by the time his work was completed on the picture. Following the affair, Howard promptly went back to his former girlfriend, Sofie Barron.

For Barbra, another pattern seemed to be emerging. Don Johnson left her and returned to his former wife, whom he then remarried; James Newton Howard left her, although which one of them broke off the affair is unclear, and returned to his former girlfriend, whom he then married. In *The Prince of Tides,* Tom Wingo left Susan Lowenstein to return to *his* wife. Barbra, or so it would appear, was taking method acting to a punishing extreme.

She was the heroine who never seemed to get the guy at the fade-out. But, the real question, at least in Hollywood, was whether she would get the *Oscar.*

In its entire history, the Academy of Motion Picture Arts and Sciences had only presented *one* woman with a Best Director Oscar nomination—Lina Wertmuller for her acclaimed 1976 Italian picture, *Seven Beauties.* And, it should be noted, the nomination came in a relatively poor year for movies. In fact, the film that won the Best Picture and Best Director Oscars that year was *Rocky,* generally regarded as one of the weakest winners in Academy history.

Things had changed perceptibly in the Hollywood of 1991. In fact, at least four female directors turned in pictures that were acclaimed enough to be considered Oscar-worthy: Martha Coolidge's *Rambling Rose,* Jodie Foster's *Little Man Tate,* Agnieszka Holland's *Europa Europa,* and Barbra's *The Prince of Tides.* Of the four, Barbra was by far the most likely to receive a nomination. Unlike the other three, admirable though they were, *Tides* was a big, lush, sentimental, picture, the kind the Academy loves to recognize. Moreover, it was a major financial success and had the full backing of its studio.

One week before the release of the nominated names, the *Los Angeles Times* came out with its annual predictions. In the Best Picture category, three films were deemed "sure to be nominated": *The Prince of Tides, Bugsy,* and *The Silence of the Lambs*—in that order. The paper assessed, "With its glossy mainstream romanticism, *Tides* is the most academy-friendly picture around, and most observers consider it the early favorite to actually win the Oscar."

In the Best Director category, Barbra, Barry Levinson *(Bugsy),* and Jonathan Demme *(Lambs)*—again, in that order—were seen as the leading contenders. However, the *Times* acknowledged that "the academy's past indifference to Streisand makes her more of a question mark than she deserves to be."

The *Los Angeles Times* was referring to Barbra's previous snubs by Oscar. Her generally well-regarded performance in *Nuts* was bypassed in the 1987 balloting, despite an expensive ad campaign waged in her behalf. A few years before, provoking even more controversy, she wasn't nominated as Best Actress *or* Best Director for *Yentl,* despite having *won* the Golden Globe award in the latter category.

Still, circumstances were obstensibly different in the 1991 balloting. For one, *The Prince of Tides* was a much bigger popular and critical success than either *Nuts* or *Yentl.* Second, not only did Columbia launch a massive ad campaign in the industry trade papers, but Barbra *participated* in the proceedings, smiling for the cameras, giving interviews, playing the Hollywood game, and being generally amenable.

On January 28, 1992, her Oscar chances were boosted immeasurably when the Directors Guild of America named her one of the five nominees for its annual prize. The DGA awards are generally viewed as a reliable precursor of the Oscar competition.

Also receiving DGA nominations were Jonathan Demme, Barry Levinson, Oliver Stone *(JFK),* and Ridley Scott *(Thelma & Louise).* Barbra, thrilled by the nomination, was only the third woman so honored in the forty-four-year history of the Guild, with Lina Wertmuller (again for *Seven Beauties,* 1976) and Randa Haines *(Children of a Lesser God,* 1986) being the other two.

With the DGA endorsement, the question wasn't whether Barbra would be nominated for the Oscar, it was whether she would *win.* The nomination itself was a given. Or so it was thought.

When the Academy of Motion Picture Arts and Sciences unveiled its list of nominations in the early morning hours of February 19, Jonathan Demme, Barry Levinson, Ridley Scott, and Oliver Stone were all cited as expected. But, pointedly, Streisand was *not*. In her place was twenty-four-year-old African-American filmmaker John Singleton, for his debut work, the modestly budgeted, critically acclaimed, *Boyz N the Hood.*

Barbra's omission was made all the more glaring by the fact that the picture she produced, starred in, cowrote (without credit), *and* directed received *seven* other nominations, third only to *Bugsy* and *JFK*. Among them: Best Picture of the Year.

The omission stunned the industry. How could a movie receive seven nominations, including Best Picture, Best Actor (Nick Nolte), Best Supporting Actress (Kate Nelligan), Best Screenplay Adaptation, and Best Cinematography, and its director, the person primarily responsible for all of its various components, *not* be nominated?

The answers, for there is not just one, are complex. First of all, one has to take a look at the way the nominations are voted upon. There are 4,968 voting members of the motion picture academy, which includes actors, directors, producers, writers, technicians, and publicists. *All* of them get to vote in the Best Picture nomination process.

There are only 281 voting members of the *director's branch* of the Academy. All are feature film directors who, one would assume, know more about the direction of a picture than the Academy at-large. *Only* the director's branch of the Academy gets to vote in the Best Director nomination process.

According to veteran filmmaker Stanley Donen (*Singin' in the Rain, Funny Face),* "The argument that I always hear is that Streisand's film was nominated in seven categories, so how could she be overlooked as a director? The point is that only the directors vote for the director category and they don't know that it's going to get all those nominations. Obviously, the directors didn't think she did as good a job as the others."

Which then brings up the question of *why* Barbra received a Directors Guild of America nomination if her work was not particularly appreciated by her peers, that is, other film directors. In contrast with the relatively small, elite director's branch of the motion picture academy, the DGA has 9,672 voting members. Significantly, the group is comprised not only of film directors, but also includes television directors, commercial directors, assistant directors, and production managers.

Barbra, it seems, is less appreciated (and/or less well liked) by *film* directors, than by the industry at large. This explains why, incredible as it may seem, in Barbra Streisand's twenty-five-year career in Hollywood, only *five* film directors had ever offered her a job in a movie. Of course, she has received innumerable offers from studio heads, producers, agents, and other assorted *money* people, but *not* from directors.

Barbra has suggested that her non-nomination and unfavorable reputation was the result of Hollywood sexism. "A man is commanding, a woman is demanding," she declared in a prepared speech before the Women in Film organization a few months later. "A man is forceful, a woman is pushy. A man is uncompromising, a woman is a ballbreaker. A man is a perfectionist, a woman's a pain in the ass.

"He's assertive, she's aggressive. He strategizes, she manipulates. He shows leadership, she's controlling. He's committed, she's obsessed. He's perservering, she's relentless. He sticks to his guns, she's stubborn.

"If a man wants to get it right, he's looked up to and respected," she continued. "If a woman wants to get it right, she's difficult and impossible. If he acts, produces and directs, he's called a multitalented hyphenate. She's called vain and egotistical.

"It's been said that a man's reach should exceed his grasp. Why can't the same be said for a woman? . . ."

It's a refrain that has been heard over and over throughout Barbra's career.

There is no doubt that sexism exists in Hollywood. No can one doubt that female filmmakers, as well as actresses, are discriminated against by industry producers, executives, and studio heads. According to the Screen Actors Guild, actors earn twice as much money as actresses and, as of 1990, were awarded 71 percent of all feature film roles. And the discrepancy increases with age. Women over forty were cast in less than 9 percent of all film and television roles. All of which makes Barbra's accomplishments with *The Prince of Tides* even more remarkable.

But sexism alone is not sufficient explanation for Barbra's unpopularity within certain factions of the industry. Was it sexism when *The Color Purple* received *eleven* Oscar nominations in 1985 and its director, Steven Spielberg was shut out? Was it sexism when the Best Picture Oscar went to *Driving Miss Daisy* in 1989 and its director, Bruce Beresford wasn't even nominated?

The fact is that the Oscar competition is, in large part, a popularity contest, and the repeated slighting of Barbra Streisand exemplifies that. As Robert Osborne, columnist for *The Hollywood Reporter,* succinctly put it, "[She] conjures up such strong feelings within people, particularly in show business. People [Academy voters] are so impassioned about her one way or the other and they don't look at her with clear judgment."

Jodie Foster, for one, is an actress who has made the transition to directing *without* developing a reputation for being, to appropriate Barbra's terminology, "demanding," "pushy," "a ballbreaker," or "a pain in the ass."

When asked about the comparisons between Streisand and Foster, professional industry analyst Anne Thompson explains, "First of all, Jodie's first movie was a small, independent production. It wasn't a big-budget movie. Secondly, I would say that Jodie is perceived as a 'good girl.' Jodie is someone whom everybody likes and admires and regards as their little sister. She's not someone who is threatening. She doesn't tend to throw her weight around. She's perceived as being easy to work with, cooperative, and collaborative."

"If a man did the same thing I did," Barbra told *Playboy*'s Lawrence Grobel in 1977, "he would be called thorough—while a woman is called a ballbreaker."

"If a man did the same thing I did . . ." is another common Streisand refrain. And, her point is often well founded. However, it is also true that Barry Levinson, for example, would never presume to go on "60 Minutes," or any television show for that matter, and tell the director how to direct. He would not advise the cameraman where to position his lights and/or camera. The fact is that Barbra impulsively oversteps those fine and invisible lines. She has done it her entire life, always pushing. Some people accept her behavior with knowing resignation, "That's just Barbra." Others respect her for it. And others dislike her for it.

Barbra, however, perceives herself as a victim. She has enclosed herself in a foolproof, rubber-made defense shelter. If men do not like her, they are sexist; if women do not like her, they are self-loathing and *anti-woman*.

Clearly, Barbra identifies strongly with Anita Hill (not to mention Joan of Arc), whose hearings before the Senate Judiciary Committee she watched with alternating measures of fascination and horror. "Women are so competitive with each other. It's horrible!" Barbra decried, "Women are not supportive of each other in general. Look at the women who called in about Anita Hill. The number who thought she was lying shocked me. She was the smartest, she was the best looking. She probably had the most style, the most grace, the most opinions. And they're ready to go in there and crucify her. This was a witch-hunt. They were going to burn her at the stake. Somehow, it was like she was accusing [instead of Judge Clarence Thomas] their husbands, or their fathers, or their sons."

Surely, Barbra *has* been wronged, but *she* has also been wrong, something she has never acknowledged, much less apologized for. There are many people in Hollywood with whom she has worked, particularly during her early years, who harbor unhappy, and sometimes painful, memories of the experience.

Theorizes Vivienne Walker, who had served as the head of the hairdressing department on *Funny Girl,* "Barbra didn't get a Best Director Oscar nomination, because the voting is done by your peers. And her peers didn't forget about little Annie Francis, and others like her."

In 1967, Elaine Joyce, a very attractive, twenty-two-year-old actress, was excited to be working on the film version of *Funny Girl.* But, like Anne Francis, Elaine was all but cut out of the picture. Like Francis, she holds Barbra responsible.

Joyce recalls, "She would ask to reshoot things without me in the shot." She adds, "But, I can understand why Barbra wouldn't want the camera to pan from a close-up of me, to a close-up of *her.* She was so insecure about her looks. She was desperate. I mean, movie stars are generally gorgeous people, and here's a woman who felt that she was just awful looking.

"Making that movie was such an unhappy experience for me, and I think it was unhappy for a lot of people. It became a torture. It was really just diabolical what went on. I've never had as unhappy a time on a set or a show since then."

When asked about Oscar's flagrant snubbing of Streisand, Joyce says, "I can only say that I was somebody who worked with her who never wanted to work with her again. There must be legions of people like that. People who didn't understand the problems she had [regarding her insecurity over her looks] just didn't like her. I don't think it is sexism at all. *She* is the reason she has this reputation. She brought it on herself. You don't have a reputation like this if you've been Ann-Margret."

Actually, *not* getting a Best Director Oscar nomination may have been the best thing that could have happened to Barbra in the long run. The seeming unfairness of the snub garnered her vast amounts of sympathy, not only in the industry, but outside it too. Suddenly, it became fashionable to defend her honor. It is, after all, an American tradition: build stars up, tear them down, and—*if* they stick around long enough—build them back up again. Streisand has stuck around long enough.

"I know she's a Grammy legend," Whoopi Goldberg was overheard saying at the Grammy ceremonies one week after the Oscar nominations were announced, "but she's also a great director." Even Madonna complained about the Oscar injustice on a "Saturday Night Live" sketch, in which Barbra herself made a surprise appearance.

The new goodwill directed at Barbra culminated on March 30, 1992, the night of the Oscars. Despite the fact that Nick Nolte was the favorite to win the Best Actor prize, *The Prince of Tides* was shut out in all seven of its nominations.* This, of course, deprived Nolte, or any of the other would-be *Tides* winners, from acknowledging Barbra's directorial accomplishment in their acceptance speeches. Nevertheless, as the evening progressed, Barbra was thrust into the Oscar spotlight when two different groups of presenters singled out her achievements from the podium. On each occasion, the camera cut to Barbra, seated in the audience. Graciously acknowledging the comments, she beamed—*winningly.*

The wave of pro-Streisand sentiment carried over into an elaborate fiftieth birthday party celebration in her honor on Saturday, April 24, 1992.

The party was hosted by Jon Peters. He had come a long way since that day in 1974 when he drove his Ferrari past the gates of Barbra's Holmby Hills home to style her wig. And he had certainly come a long way since the combative days and nights of *A Star Is Born,* when there was so much at stake, and so much to prove.

Paul Williams, who has had a few battles with Peters in the past, today comments, "I think you could drop Jon Peters in the middle of Russia completely naked and, not even speaking the language, he would come marching out of that country a mogul. And I think that if we all knew that about Jon Peters *then,* as we know it now, he would have been treated with a lot more respect."

Staged at his twelve-acre Beverly Hills estate (surrounded by *his* own gates), Jon's $200,000 bash for his former girlfriend was part *Cinderella,* part *Beauty and the Beast,* and part P.T. Barnum. The three hundred guests, among them Frank Sinatra, Meryl Streep, Goldie Hawn, Warren Beatty, Annette Bening, and their one hundred children participated in the festivities. Its theme: "Welcome to Barbra's Magic Castle." Providing the entertainment were magicians, jugglers, stilt-walkers, pup-

---

*The *Silence of the Lambs* won Best Picture, Best Actor (Anthony Hopkins), Best Actress (Jodie Foster), and Best Director (Jonathan Demme). The DGA award also went to Demme.

peteers, a petting zoo, fire-eaters, face painters, and a circus elephant.

Diana Kind was also a guest at the party. Today, at eighty-four, she looks young for her age, but appears frail. She used to get around town on the bus, but, in recent years, she rarely leaves her home. Despite their public claims to the contrary, Barbra and her mother are *not* close. In fact, although they only live five or ten minutes from one another, they rarely even see each other.

"They *don't* have a healthy mother-daughter relationship," relates a family friend who has asked to remain unnamed. "It's a very strange, estranged, separated kind of relationship. They are not at war with each other. But, it's not a loving, mother-daughter, 'Are you okay, Ma?' kind of relationship.

"Diana and Roslyn are both scared of Barbra. They *do* go over to Barbra's house when she has a party for the holidays, but, there might be fifteen to twenty guests and Diana and Roslyn always end up at one end of the table, while Barbra sits at the other end with Cis Corman, Marilyn Bergman, and those people. There's never that communication.

"Barbra and Roslyn are not close *at all.* I don't think Barbra *wants* to be friendly with Roslyn, you know? She has her Marilyn Bergman, and her Cis Corman, and her Donna Karan. Recently, Roslyn was in New York for three months, and she would have liked to have stayed at Barbra's apartment. She asked Barbra if she could, but Barbra never got back to her. So, Roslyn had to rent an apartment. There's bad blood there."

Back in 1984, Diana Kind underwent open-heart surgery. While recuperating, she was invited to stay at Barbra's Holmby Hills home. "But, she drove Barbra crazy," says the family friend. "Barbra and Richard Baskin would be having a romantic evening in the screening room, or in the bedroom, and Diana would just walk in on them. Barbra couldn't stand that. So, Diana went back home."

For the last fifteen years, 'home' for Diana Kind has been a condominium, owned by Barbra, just outside of Beverly Hills. By all accounts, it's a nice, though hardly luxurious place.

"It's in a state of disrepair," confides the family friend. "Roslyn [who has also been living in the condo since the break-up of her 1983 marriage to casting director Randy Stone] has a dog, and the carpet is filthy. There are spots and holes all around. The place also needs a paint job. Barbra hardly *ever* goes there. I said to her, 'Diana, Barbra should see this. This is disgusting. You shouldn't be living like this.'

"Diana lives her life like a lower-middle-class woman," continues the friend with obvious incredulity. "Once, I helped her with the cable on her television. The cable went out, so I called the company and they said, 'Well, she didn't pay her bill.' Finally, I said to her, 'Diana, why don't you just send all of your bills to Barbra's accountants? Let them take care of everything. Your daughter is one of the wealthiest women in the world. She's worth millions and millions of dollars! If you want a car, it doesn't have to be a stretch limo, but if you want a car at your disposal to take you shopping and do errands, or whatever, Barbra will do that for you.'

"But, Diana's feeling was, 'Well, I don't want to bother her. I don't want to be a burden. She's very busy.' "

According to the family friend, Barbra gives her mother $1,000 a month, or thereabouts, and has been giving her the same $1,000 a month since the 1970s. He adds, however, *"Who* in the 1990s can live on two hundred fifty a week?"

"Barbra Streisand is worth—what—*one hundred seventy million dollars?* And her mother does not live *well.* She does not live like some other superstars' mothers might be living. She could be leading the life-style of a woman whose daughter is a multimillionairess. Instead, she lives a very plain, normal lifestyle. She doesn't ask for things. A thousand dollars a month is just *terrible!"*

Attempting to explain Barbra's distance from her mother, the friend says, "Diana and Roslyn have been much, much closer over the years. It's like how you always root for the underdog. To Diana, Roslyn's the underdog."

One night, Barbra attended Michael Caine and Sidney Poitier's joint birthday party held at Tatou, a trendy Beverly Hills restaurant and nightclub. She was accompanied by Peter Weller *(Robocop),* her new boyfriend. Also in attendance, among others, were Oprah Winfrey and Elizabeth Taylor. Caustic comedian Don Rickles provided the entertainment.

Lance Brown, who also attended the event, recalls what followed. "Don Rickles got up to emcee the birthday boys and sort of roasted Michael and Sidney. And then he sort of went off and started dishing people in the audience. When he saw Barbra, he *went into her.* He said, 'Oh, look! There's Barbra Streisand sitting over there playing Garbo. Hello, Barbra.' He said, 'Barbra hates me. The last time I said something about her, she didn't talk to me for years. What could be the worst thing that could happen to me tonight—she won't speak to me for another thirty years?'

According to Brown, Rickles continued his meant-to-be comic assault. "And then he said, 'Barbra, for God's sake. Call your mother. She's old. She needs you. Call Roslyn, your sister. She's broke. She could use some money.'

"Well," says Brown, "he said this in front of all these stars. Barbra had this phony smile on her face the whole time. When Don was done, she went upstairs to the private room. Everybody was *shocked."*

In December 1992, Barbra signed a new, historic, multimedia contract with the Sony Corporation. The deal is said to be bringing her $2 million a year—for the next ten years—just to *develop* film projects for Sony. Furthermore, she is also set to receive $1 million for each Sony Corporation picture she produces, $3 million for each picture she directs, and $6 million plus 15 percent of the gross revenues for each picture in which she acts. Conceivably, given her multihyphenated capabilities, that is well over $10 million dollars per picture.

The new contract will also pay her $5 million for every album she records, plus a *whopping* 42-plus percent royalty rate on the wholesale price of each unit sold.

It is, along with similar multimedia contracts signed by Prince, Madonna, and Michael Jackson, the most lucrative deal in the history of the entertainment industry—not bad for the young woman who used to stash her weekly pay into envelopes marked "miscellaneous," "phone," "laundry," "rent," and "food."

Thirty-nine

A Woman's Reach . . .

*W*illiam Jefferson Clinton was *not* Barbra Streisand's first choice for President in the 1992 elections, nor was he her second. Her first choice was Gov. Mario Cuomo of New York. When he decided against running, she leaned toward Sen. Tom Harkin, but was uncertain of his chances to win. When asked in January whom she would be supporting, Barbra replied, "I can't say yet." She did, however, allow, "I am going to support a Democrat, that's for sure. We've had two presidents who lived in denial—Reagan and Bush, a president who said, 'What recession?' I have to look at a lot of things, like who's pro-choice.' "

Although it would prove, by far, to be her most visible involvement, the election campaign of 1992 was certainly not Barbra Streisand's first foray into presidential politics.

Her initial brush with real political power came in 1963 when, starstruck at the age of twenty-one, she sang for President John Kennedy at the White House Correspondents' Dinner. Her first presidential inauguration came in January 1965 when she sang for Lyndon Johnson.

Still, she knew little about politics, and not much more about the world around her. She had no real ideology but, like her mother, she supported only Democrats. When asked in 1966 for her views on Black Power and the Vietnam War, she admitted her ignorance and confessed that the only thing she read was her own reviews—and *Women's Wear Daily*.

Her ignorance embarrassed her. And so she began doing her homework. In 1968, she supported the presidential campaign of Eugene McCarthy, because of his stand on Vietnam. Like many others of her generation, it was America's involvement in this war that triggered Barbra's first political responses, if not her activism.

"Our foreign policy is very—unreal," she said at the time. "I guess they think they are sticking to the American tradition or something. But all that waste and killing. Maybe we just will have to learn to lose some face. I mean, this is the destruction of the earth we're risking. In a way, it's probably all inevitable. The thing is that, so far, any scientific development exceeds our emotional development."

Around the same time, Barbra made her first philanthropic gesture. She donated, *anonymously,** the then staggering sum of $400,000 to the Emergency Campaign for Israel. It was the largest single anonymous gift given to the campaign.

In 1970, Barbra lent her new and unfurnished townhouse at 49 East Eightieth Street for a fundraising party for lawyer Bella Abzug, who was battling congressional representative Leonard Farbstein for the Democratic party's nomination in the Nineteenth Congressional District. The two women had met in a restaurant when Barbra approached Abzug and told her that she had a young son and wanted to do something "about peace."

Barbra mailed three thousand invitations to the fund-raiser, encouraging recipients to contribute $25 to the cause of sending to Washington a "very special lady. . . . who is dedicated to peace." The invitation promised, "There will be stars of stage, screen and radio!—drinks—canapes, but *no* furniture!!"

In 1971, Daniel Ellsberg, a former government researcher, presented the *New York Times* with a study entitled the "Pentagon Papers" which showed that the U.S. military had been misleading the public about American involvement in Vietnam. The Nixon administration tried to stop publication, which led to a court battle that the newspaper eventually won. Ellsberg himself was indicted in 1971 on charges of conspiracy, theft, and espionage. Barbra was one of several Hollywood celebrities who helped raise money for his defense. The charges against him were eventually dismissed in 1973.

But, it was the 1972 presidential campaign that provided Barbra with her real political awakening. About to turn thirty, she was reassessing her life and taking a serious look at the world around her. She had come to despise Richard Nixon, both the man and his policy, and was looking for a way to vent her disapproval.

---

*When William Wyler learned about this (though not through her), he forgave Barbra for many of the "difficulties" she caused him during the production of *Funny Girl*.

Shirley MacLaine had been campaigning virtually non-stop, state by state, for Sen. George McGovern of South Dakota. "I will unabashedly use my celebrity to try to influence people," MacLaine boldly proclaimed at the time. "I think this is a proper use of power. I mean, what good does my turquoise swimming pool in California do anybody else?"

MacLaine's brother, Warren Beatty, was another ardent McGovern supporter. It was Beatty, Barbra's former lover, who asked her to give a benefit concert for the McGovern campaign.

She was reticent. First of all, she had come to loathe performing in public. Her last live public singing performance had been at the Las Vegas Hilton in a late December 1971–early January 1972 engagement. Second, McGovern supporters were generally younger than Streisand audiences. She didn't know how well she would go over with a predominantly rock and roll audience. Third, sharing the bill with her were to be James Taylor and Carole King, then two of the biggest names in the pop-rock field.

Barbra, eventually, agreed to appear. Controversy ensued when King, through her producer, Lou Adler, requested that *she* be allowed to close the show. After all, her *Tapestry* album was one of the biggest-selling albums of all time, having remained in the number one position for *fifteen* weeks, and her follow-up, *Music,* released in late 1971, also went to number one.

Through Marty Erlichman, Barbra insisted that the closing spot be *hers.* The matter was resolved and the show—with celebrity ushers, Jack Nicholson, Julie Christie, Gene Hackman, and Sally Kellerman showing major financial contributors to their seats—went on as scheduled on April 5, 1972. The King and Taylor portions of the program went over well, as was expected. When Barbra made her entrance, however, there was still some apprehension, both backstage and on, about how she would be received by the young crowd of twenty thousand screaming McGovern supporters who had crammed into the Los Angeles Forum.

She was also terrified by the potential threat of an assassination attempt. By standing centerstage, not only had she become an easy target for a lunatic who didn't like *her,* she now could be shot by a sniper who did not share her *political views.* She was so nervous, in fact, that she had some of the lyrics to some of her songs scribbled out on the stage floor.

"It was a fund-raiser during the height of the California primary," Senator McGovern recalls today. "I had a number of Hollywood people working actively in the campaign, principally, at that time, Warren Beatty. And he spoke to Barbra about doing this fund-raiser."

"I'll tell you frankly there was some mild anxiety that maybe Barbra would be overshadowed by James Taylor and Carole King. But, by the opening set, the opening line, it was clear that it was the same old Barbra Streisand, if not better. I thought it was the best I've ever heard her."

After the show, which raised some $300,000 for McGovern's presidential campaign, Barbra met with the candidate and expressed her views. "She was utterly opposed to the Vietnam War," McGovern recalls. "She thought it was a disaster. That was the transcendent issue at the time. The fact that I was the candidate most sharply defined on the war was enough for her.

"But, she also thought that there needed to be political reform, that there was too much 'business as usual' and not enough in the way of addressing our problems courageously. And I think that she responded to the fact that I had direct answers on most of the questions. I also had a lot of women working on the campaign, and even then she was interested in women's issues—although not nearly as much as she was later on."

George McGovern's loss greatly disillusioned his famous supporter. "I can't understand the Nixon landslide," Barbra said. "Maybe people are afraid of change. It's as if they've grown almost comfortable with corruption. I mean, Nixon is so *obviously* dishonest. His promise to end the war in Vietnam was just par for the course, wasn't it? I don't know, it's all so *self*-destructive." She added, with the kind of pessimistic doom surprising for a thirty-year-old movie star who seemed to have it all, "But then I believe the world is moving toward inevitable self-destruction."

In June 1973, John Dean III issued a list to the Senate Watergate Committee that sent an electrifying jolt through the nation's capital and reverberated westward. Prepared prior to September 1971, it was dubbed the "White House Enemies List." The politicians given the dubious distinction (depending on how one looks at it) of being included were Edward Kennedy, George McGovern, Walter Mondale, Edmund Muskie, Bella Abzug, Shirley Chisholm, Eugene McCarthy, and George Wallace.

The naming of the show business "enemies" seemed even more shocking: Carol Channing, Bill Cosby, Jane Fonda, Joe Namath, Paul Newman, Gregory Peck, Tony Randall, Dick Gregory, and Barbra Streisand.

The idea of being considered an enemy of the White House terrified, and then paralyzed, Barbra. For the next *thirteen* years, she went into political retreat. In 1976, she lent her Beverly Hills home for Bella

Abzug's West Coast fund-raiser, but that had more to do with her friendship with Abzug than anything else. She didn't even read the newspapers. Politics, air pollution, the chemical contamination of food, and the "inevitable destruction" of the world around her, became too depressing to contemplate.

Still, she contributed to the political campaigns of her choice. Surprisingly, in the 1980 presidential election, she supported independent candidate John Anderson instead of supporting Jimmy Carter. At *least* she contributed funds ($1,000) to Anderson, rather than to Carter. Following the general election, she donated another $1,000 to the campaign of Edward Kennedy, to help recover costs lost in his bitter defeat in the primaries to Carter.

Barbra also donated funds to the Senate campaigns of John Culver of Iowa, Elizabeth Holtzman of New York, Birch Bayh of Indiana, and Gary Hart (a Streisand favorite) of Colorado.

In the 1984 elections, Barbra contributed to the presidential primary campaigns of George McGovern and Gary Hart, but not to Walter Mondale. After Mondale's nomination, however, and with his selection of Geraldine Ferraro as his running mate, Barbra donated $10,000 to the Democratic National Committee.

She also contributed to the senate campaigns of Bill Bradley of New Jersey, Tom Harkin of Iowa, Nancy Dick of Colorado, Lloyd Alton Doggett of Texas, James Hunt of North Carolina, Joan Anderson Growe of Minnesota, Margie Hendriksen of Oregon, and Elizabeth Mitchell of Maine.

But, while she privately donated her money to the Democrats—she has *never* supported or contributed funds to a Republican—Barbra opted against lending her name, her fame, and her public endorsement.

And then something happened that changed the course of her life—and the course of the world around her.

"It was April 26, 1986," Marilyn Bergman related. "[Barbra and I] were talking about the disaster at Chernobyl. She called me that morning, and she was absolutely horrified at what happened. The question was, 'What can be done about this?' And the answer was, 'The only thing that I know to do about it is to take back the Senate for the Democrats.' "

In the 1986 senatorial elections, Barbra made donations of $2,000 each ($1,000 in the primary, $1,000 in the general—the maximum amount allowed by law to an individual candidate) to Patrick Leahy of Vermont, Tom Daschle of South Dakota, Alan Cranston of California,

Harriett Woods of Missouri, Barbara Mikulski of Maryland, Tim Wirth of Colorado, Wyche Fowler of Georgia, Bella Abzug of New York, and Mark Green, also of New York. For the latter two, Barbra also appeared at several fund-raisers.

One week after Chernobyl, with renewed political vigor, she gave a speech at a Women in Film ceremony in New York. "Our technology is more advanced than our hearts," she declared. And, in a slap at Ronald Reagan she said, "Violence is too prevalent in television and film, and with a president who thinks *Rambo* is the height of filmmaking, we unfortunately see real life imitating art.

"We need to believe in our own sensibilities and our own power," she continued, preaching on one hand, and reminding herself on the other, "but we need to do more. After this week's major disaster, we as women have a responsibility to put our energy and talent into repairing the universe. As the Talmud says, to mending the broken pieces of the world."

And so she began her political renewal. Bonded by the threat of a downwind blow, Barbra was introduced by Marilyn Bergman into the Hollywood Women's Political Committee, then a struggling group of 190 women that no one in the decidedly sexist political world took seriously. The driving issues of the HWPC were environmental concerns in general, and a woman's right to choose an abortion.

If she was going to become further politically involved, Barbra decided she would do so seriously. She had disdain for Hollywood celebrities who made public statements on the trendy topic of the day, and didn't really know what they were talking about. Moreover, she was well aware that *her* political pursuits would be perceived by many as a pretension and a joke, fodder for the conservative right, as well as the late-night television comics.

The Political Education of Barbra Streisand began before, after, and during dinners at the home of longtime liberal activist Stanley Sheinbaum. At her own home up on Carolwood Drive, she was tutored in nuclear energy by Marvin L. Goldberger, then the president of the California Institute of Technology, and physicist Sidney Drell from Stanford. "She started with very little knowledge," Goldberger reported, "and a great deal of suddenly awakened concern."

Once she was tutored, the issue then became how to best utilize Barbra in the effort to return the Senate to the Democrats in the November 1986 elections. A fund-raising concert was deemed to be the best approach. For Barbra it became a matter of weighing her fear of performing before an audience with her fear of nuclear holocaust.

She recorded the personalized invitations on audio cassette which were then delivered in canisters filled with potpourri. "I could never imagine myself wanting to sing in public again," Barbra said in her recorded message. "But then, I could never imagine Star Wars, contras, apartheid, and nuclear winters in my life, and yet, they are in everybody's life. I feel I must sing again to raise money so that we send people to Washington who will solve problems, not create them."

Despite a phenomenal price tag of $5,000 per couple, the "concert," almost overnight, became the social and political *event* in Hollywood. It had, after all, been six years since Barbra last sang in public (at a benefit honoring Alan and Marilyn Bergman), and *fourteen* years since her last concert.

Sen. George Mitchell, chairman of the Democratic Senatorial Campaign Committee, wanted all of the proceeds from the concert to be funneled into his committee. Barbra, Marilyn Bergman, and the HWPC, refused. They insisted that at least the bulk of the money be given only to those Democrats who espoused views with which *they* agreed. The selected beneficiaries: California's Alan Cranston (who would get the biggest percentage), Patrick Leahy (Vermont), Tim Wirth (Colorado), Harriet Woods (Missouri), Tom Daschle (South Dakota), and Bob Edgar (Virginia).

Leahy upset Barbra, and other members of the HWPC, when he opted against showing up at the concert. "Why take the risk of being seen as too glitzy, six weeks before the election," one of his aides explained. Harriett Woods caused even more uproar. Not only did she not show up at the concert, she also refused to accept the subsequent proceeds. Woods, like Leahy, was not only afraid of being associated with "Hollywood glitz," she also feared being linked with Hollywood *liberalism* in general, and with Jane Fonda, an HWPC member, in particular. Fonda, as is well known in political circles, is often used as a red light ("Hanoi Jane!") button by the conservative right.

Nevertheless, the outdoor concert, staged on Saturday, September 6, 1986, at Barbra's Malibu ranch compound, was a spectacular success. Just as her Central Park concert had been two decades before, it was a historic show business *happening.* Jane Fonda, Bette Midler, Jack Nicholson, Sydney Pollack, Sally Field, Whitney Houston, Bruce Willis, Goldie Hawn, even Walter Matthau, among numerous others, sat under the summer night's stars as Barbra overcame her trepidation and sang, "Somewhere," "Over the Rainbow," "People," "The Way We Were," "Happy Days Are Here Again," "America the Beautiful," and others including "Send in the Clowns," which was rewritten for the occasion. The new lyric? "Send *home* the [Republican] clowns."

The proceeds from the concert exceeded all expectations. "This is more money than women have ever raised in history!" exclaimed an exultant Marilyn Bergman. Some $1.5 million was earned from the price of admission alone, with thirty couples and $150,000 having to be turned away due to a lack of seating space. And, in the November elections, all but one of the candidates (Bob Edgar) who received a portion of the proceeds was elected to the Senate, whose control, to Barbra's great satisfaction, was wrested by the Democrats.

There is no doubt that it was Barbra's fund-raising concert that put the HWPC on the political map. Today, the group is a powerful political-action committee whose support is courted by Democratic candidates throughout the country.

Finally, the concert also affirmed the political awakening, or reawakening, of Barbra Streisand. "By my silence," she told her audience that night, "I was giving consent to the madness of nations,"

And then there were the ancillary proceeds.

Gambling with $250,000 front money, HBO taped the concert, *without* guarantee that it could air the subsequent footage. "Barbra has the right for a few days to look at it," Michael Fuchs, the cable company's chairman and chief executive officer said. If she didn't like the footage that had been shot (and given her usual insistence on perfectionism, the odds could not have seemed favorable), the proposed special was to be scrapped, and HBO would have to write off the $250,000.

However, much to the relief of everyone, Barbra agreed to allow the telecast to proceed—at a considerable price. On top of its $250,000 production costs, HBO paid an undisclosed broadcast fee, which is said to have been substantially more than any of the major networks would have paid.

"Barbra Streisand: One Voice" first aired on December 27, 1986. Excluding the documentaries, "Putting It Together: The Making of *The Broadway Album*" (HBO, 1986) and "Papa Watch Me Fly" (ABC, 1983), the taped concert was Barbra's first and only television special since "Barbra Streisand and Other Musical Instruments" was aired by CBS in November 1973.

CBS/Sony subsequently manufactured a "One Voice" home videocassette, and Columbia Records produced a *One Voice* album, which entered the *Billboard* top forty in May 1987, and went platinum.

All told, Barbra's one-night stand in her own backyard produced ancillary proceeds which have reportedly scaled the *$5 million* mark. Instead of using the money to fund future political campaigns, however, Barbra assembled a board, hired a director, and launched The Streisand Foundation, a nonprofit organization dedicated to civil liberties, disarmament, and environmental concerns. In 1986, through her foundation, Barbra donated $100,000 to the educational arm of the Sierra Club. She also donated $330,000, which was dispersed among a variety of groups, including Human Serve, Citizens Leadership Project, Southwest Voter Registration Project, the National Coalition for Black Voter Participation, and the Forum Institute.

After initially supporting Gary Hart, and then Paul Simon in the presidential campaign of 1988, Barbra jumped on the frontrunner's bandwagon and donated $1,000 to the presidential nominee, Michael Dukakis of Massachusetts.

On Sunday, October 16, 1988, she performed a couple of songs at a HWPC fundraiser for Dukakis at the Beverly Hills estate of Ted Fields. She hobnobbed with Kitty Dukakis, Jesse Jackson, Ann Richards, and Massachusetts senator, John Kerry. Conspicuously absent from the proceedings was the candidate himself who, in an unsuccessful effort at dodging the "liberal" label, was otherwise occupied.

Barbra also made contributions to the 1988 senatorial campaigns of Edward Kennedy of Massachusetts, and Leo McCarthy of California, and to the congressional campaigns of Pat Schroeder of Colorado, Mike Espy of Mississippi, and Anna Eshoo and Gary K. Hart, both of California.

After the Exxon Valdez oil spill in Alaska's Prince William Sound on March 24, 1989, local radio station KCHU presented the nation with live on-the-scene news reports. However, to finance their coverage, the small station had to spend money that had been budgeted to last until June 30. Faced with bankruptcy, the station broadcast a plea for help. One of those listening was Barbra Streisand, who contributed $5,000 to keep the station on the air.

Two months later, The Streisand Foundation donated $250,000 to the Environmental Defense Fund to endow the Barbra Streisand Global Atmospheric Change Chair. She said in making the grant, "I am convinced that with all of our participation, we can obtain real and workable solutions. Each of us must do whatever we can to help repurify and reestablish our respect for the environment."

Meanwhile, the apocalypse she had once predicted suddenly seemed terrifyingly near, at least in Los Angeles. On April 29, 1992, the jury in the Rodney King beating trial returned a verdict which acquitted the police officers tried in the case. Thousands of enraged South Central Los Angeles residents took to the streets. For the next two nights, the city was under siege. People were killed. Businesses were destroyed. The night sky was aglow with terrorist fire.

From her view high atop her gated home in Holmby Hills, Barbra refused to retreat into her world of fear, as she undoubtedly would have done only a few years before. Instead, she sought to do something constructive.

On August 10, she donated $52,500 to various organizations to help rebuild the Los Angeles neighborhoods that had been ravaged during the riots. The groups receiving the funds included the Urban League, the Asian Pacific American Dispute Resolution Center, and the Community Young Gang Services organization. The donation brought her cumulative contribution in the "Rebuild LA" effort to $102,500. Earlier, she had donated $50,000 to the First African Methodist Episcopal [AME] Church.

Reconciling herself to the fact that Tom Harkin, who came closer to sharing her ideology, didn't have a shot in the presidential campaign of 1992, Barbra joined the wave of Hollywood support* firmly entrenched behind Bill Clinton. It wasn't his stand on abortion rights, women's issues, or the environment that swayed her decision. The other democratic candidates—Harkin, Bob Kerrey, Paul Tsongas, and Jerry Brown—had taken positions that she liked as well, if not better.

There were two primary reasons for her support of Clinton, starting with Hillary Rodham Clinton, a potential first lady to whom Barbra could relate. Exceptionally bright and capable, and unapologetic for being so, Hillary was also a mother trying to balance family concerns with the demands of an exacting, high-pressure profession. Moreover, Barbra was impressed with Hillary's commitment to the rights and protection of children.

Second, in Clinton, Barbra sensed someone who could *win.* The Democrats had not elected a president in sixteen years and Barbra, like other Hollywood liberals, kept her eyes on that elusive White House prize. If they could not elect Edward Kennedy, Gary Hart, Walter Mondale, or Michael Dukakis, and if they couldn't even get Mario Cuomo to run, they would settle, albeit grudgingly, for Bill Clinton.

A September 16 HWPC fundraiser at the Ted Field estate raised an

---

*After initially being divided between Clinton and Bob Kerrey, Hollywood shifted en masse behind Clinton. Exceptions included Cher, who threw her support behind Ross Perot.

estimated $1.1 million for the Clinton–Gore ticket. Barbra, who sang a few songs, told the partisan crowd, "Six years ago, I was motivated by the disaster at Chernobyl. Now I'm motivated by the possibility of another disaster: the reelection of George Bush and Dan Quayle."

Clinton himself addressed the Hollywood crowd with his own brand of homespun Southern charm. "Did you see Whoopi Goldberg in *Sister Act?*" he said. "I wanted to be in that choir so bad I could *spit.*"

Barbra met with Clinton during the night and was impressed with both his charisma and his sincerity. Moreover, they were bonded by a shared tragedy. Like her, he had lost his father at a young age. And like her, at least to some degree, he has been overachieving to compensate for it ever since.

Barbra is said to have promised to move to England if George Bush was reelected president. The proposed relocation proved to be unnecessary. On November 3, 1992, by a significant electoral margin, William Jefferson Clinton was elected the forty-second President of the United States. That night, Barbra wired the new president:

"I'm so very excited for you, for me and for the rest of America. Your victory restores my faith in the people of this country."

Two weeks later, Barbra was onstage at the Universal Ampitheatre in Los Angeles to accept an award for her efforts related to AIDS. The Commitment to Life award is presented by AIDS Project Los Angeles (APLA), and may well be the most prestigious award of its kind presented anywhere in the world. Previous recipients of the award include Elizabeth Taylor, Bette Midler, and Madonna.

"Barbra Streisand has continually shown energy, leadership and compassion in battling discrimination and disease throughout her whole life," proclaimed David Wexler, chair of APLA's board of directors, upon making the initial announcement that she was to receive the award. "We are proud to honor her for her work in raising funds and increasing public awareness for a variety of humanitarian causes, including AIDS."

But the proposed presentation of the award to Barbra was not without controversy.

In June 1981 the Centers for Disease Control in Atlanta reported five unusual cases of pneumocystic pneumonia in homosexual men in Los Angeles. Soon, cases were reported in New York. It was called Gay-Related-Immunodeficiency-Disease (GRID). Others just called it "The Gay Cancer."

In the summer of 1985, with the announcement that Rock Hudson was stricken with the illness now called AIDS, Hollywood *finally* began to take notice. Elizabeth Taylor jumped into the issue. Exercising the full weight of her celebrity, she worked to raise funds that would find a cure, care for those afflicted, and educate others to protect themselves from infection. She even confronted, head-on, the homophobia which has plagued America's response to the disease. Taylor's passionate commitment to AIDS awareness is arguably unparalleled by *any* star's involvement with any cause in modern-day Hollywood.

Bette Midler and Madonna also made themselves available for fundraising events related to AIDS. Cher, Joan Rivers, and Liza Minnelli were also publicly supportive.

But, many others, people who should have known better, remained silent. The fact is that AIDS was still perceived as a gay disease and many Hollywood figures didn't want the association. So, they made their contributions quietly—or not at all.

Glaringly absent from the public arena in the fight against AIDS was Barbra Streisand. Many in the gay community began to ask, "Where is Barbra?" The question became a chant. After all, there are many who believe that if any living entertainer had a debt to pay to the gay community, it was Barbra.

Actually, Barbra *had* arranged for part of the proceeds from "Somewhere," her single from *The Broadway Album,* released in late 1985, to go to the American Foundation for AIDS Research (AmFAR). Unfortunately, the single was not a hit. The song received little radio airplay, and the contribution received little press.

She also donated a substantial amount of money to organizations related to pediatric AIDS. This, however, only further fueled the questions over her response. Why were her efforts largely in behalf of *pediatric* AIDS, when tens of thousands of young gay men were dying? Gay men who were suffering from two separate but related diseases: the ravages of a virus, and the homophobia of a society.

To many in the gay community, Barbra's response to AIDS was woefully inadequate. "That's their opinion," she said in her defense when confronted with the controversy by Kevin Sessums in the September 1991 issue of *Vanity Fair.* "I give loads of money. I've given a lot to pediatric AIDS. . . . and all the proceeds from the single 'Somewhere,' from my Broadway album went to AmFAR.* I don't give public appearances;

---

*Actually, reportedly, only half of the proceeds went to AmFAR. The other half went to a Pro-Peace anti-nuclear arms march.

Madonna and Bette Midler like to perform. Elizabeth Taylor has this as her *one* cause."

But, she had already proven that when sufficiently motivated, as with Chernobyl, she *was* willing to perform, and when she performed, she was capable of raising millions of dollars. If Barbra was willing to sing for the threat of a deadly downwind blow, why wasn't she willing to sing for the million Americans infected with HIV? The hundreds of thousands with full-blown AIDS? The 120,000 who had died?

Shortly after publication of the *Vanity Fair* article, Barbra joined the board of directors of Hollywood Supports, an AIDS organization founded by entertainment industry moguls Barry Diller and Sid Sheinberg. She also donated more money to AIDS-related organizations. As of June 1992, The Streisand Foundation had reportedly contributed more than $350,000 to the cause.

Her detractors, however, were quick to point out that she had spent $363,000 in a 1988 auction for a piece of Gustav Stickley furniture. She had also recently purchased a $5.5 million home in Beverly Hills to go along with her $3 million Holmby Hills home, and her $19 million Malibu ranch compound. The point was clear. Though it can hardly be characterized as "feed money," the total sum of Barbra's contributions to AIDS hardly represented a financial sacrifice.

"Elizabeth Taylor is an AIDS activist," declares David Lacaillade, a member of the militant AIDS activist group ACT-UP. "Barbra's support is certainly not an Elizabeth Taylor kind of support." He adds, "You're *not* an AIDS activist when you pin on a red ribbon."

"I wouldn't call it a *lot* [what she has done for AIDS]," says another source, a former employee of APLA, the organization that was honoring Barbra for her efforts. "I don't think it is as much as she could be doing. They gave her the Commitment to Life Award, but she really didn't do anything to get it."

According to this source, who has requested anonymity, it was actually Mayor Tom Bradley of Los Angeles who was supposed to have received the award that year, with industry mogul David Geffen* as the corecipient. "Well, when someone got *Barbra Streisand* [to agree to participate], Mayor Bradley was nixed—even *after* he received the official notice that he was receiving the award! So, what they did to compensate for it was they gave him an honorary award at the APLA walk [another,

---

*In a three-month period in 1992 alone, Geffen donated $1 million to APLA and another million to the Gay Men's Health Crisis in New York.

less glamorous fund-raising event] in September. They basically kicked him out of the Commitment to Life benefit. Why? No one would have paid anything to see him."

Staged at the Universal Ampitheatre on Wednesday, November 18, 1992, the Commitment to Life benefit proved a spectacular success. "As a gay man, I've come a long way to be here tonight," David Geffen confided to the crowd upon being presented with his award. His words reflected his coming to terms with his own sexuality and set the tone for the intimacy, the compassion, and the healing which, that night, lifted the spirit and roused the soul.

Featuring the songs from *West Side Story,* musical highlights of the show included Natalie Cole, Patti LaBelle, and Sheila E's rendition of "America;" Wynonna Judd and Kenny Loggins's "Tonight;" and Elton John's campy "I Feel Pretty," which he performed complete with pearls and a fluttering fan.

Barbra's performance, of course, was reserved for the finale. In a duet with Johnny Mathis, she sang "One Hand, One Heart" and "I Have a Love." Solo, she closed the show with "Somewhere," Leonard Bernstein and Stephen Sondheim's plaintive, yet hopeful, call for tolerance.

That night, perhaps emboldened by the election of Bill Clinton, Barbra Streisand responded to many of the theretofore unanswered questions about her commitment to AIDS, and to the gay and lesbian community in general. Largely because of her involvement, 6,500 people paid $50 to $1,000 per ticket, and that year's Commitment to Life benefit raised *$3.9 million* for APLA, more than three times the amount generated by each of the five such previous events.

But, it wasn't just the money, or her performance, that was meaningful to the gay and lesbian community—and to everyone who believes in the human and civil rights for all people—it was her words:

> Few of us have responded with enough urgency to meet this crisis of catastrophic proportions, certainly not the last two presidents. . . . I will never forgive my fellow actor, Ronald Reagan, for the genocidal denial of the illness' existence, for his refusal to even utter the word "AIDS" for seven years and for blocking adequate funding for research and education which could have saved hundreds of thousands of lives. . . .

She added, in response to the homophobia propagated from the podium at that year's Republican Convention:

A lot of us of different political outlook came together that night. The radical right linked the issues for us and reminded us how much was at stake as they branded the concerns of women, gays, minorities and Democrats as un-American. How dare they call us un-American!

... When Pat Buchanan thundered, and I quote, "We stand with George Bush against the amoral idea that gay and lesbian couples should have the same standing in law as married men and women," I wondered: Who is Pat Buchanan to pronounce anybody's love invalid. ... ?

It was an evening of coming out, coming to terms, and coming together. It was also, in a way, Barbra Streisand's long awaited embracing of, and coming home to, the gay community that discovered her.

Forty

Emancipation

*D*efiantly, she stuck out her long, slender neck. In the 1992 elections, voters of the state of Colorado, arguably swayed by right-wing propaganda, passed into law Amendment 2, which stripped away existing laws protecting gays and lesbians from discrimination in housing and employment. With heartfelt ardor, Barbra called for, or seemed to, a retaliatory boycott of the state.

"There are plenty of us who love the mountains and rivers of that truly beautiful state," she declared in her prepared speech at the APLA Commitment to Life benefit, "but we must now say clearly that the moral climate there is no longer acceptable, and if we're asked to, we must refuse to play where they discriminate."

With reports of Barbra's appeal appearing in headlines in the morning papers, Terry Schleder, a member of Boycott Colorado, a small gay and lesbian grassroots organization in Denver, rejoiced. She says, "We were climbing the Capitol steps to call for this boycott from *inside* the state, when Barbra Streisand's news hit the press. We had *no* idea what was going on. We had had no connection with Barbra, or her office, or anything. We love Barbra, believe me. She really kicked a lot of this off."

But then she seemed to run for cover. On November 25, one week after her speech, Mayor John Bennett of Aspen called a press conference and read a statement from Barbra in which she said, "I have not called for a boycott. The people living in Colorado are contemplating many strategies. I will respect whichever they feel is most effective."

In fact, "the people living in Colorado" were themselves divided on the issue. Even the gay leaders of the state argued over the right course of action. A blanket boycott of the entire state would threaten and possibly destroy local businesses, *including* businesses that were owned by, or friendly to, gays and lesbians.

"We were really disappointed," says Terry Schleder of Barbra's apparent retreat on the issue. "We were wondering, 'Hey, what's going on with this?' "

Among other things, billionaire oilman and movie executive Marvin Davis, part owner of the Aspen Ski Company, was applying pressure on Hollywood to boycott the boycott. And, it so happened that Lee Solters, Barbra's publicist of some thirty years, was also Davis's publicist. Torn between two clients, both wealthy and both powerful, Solters reportedly went to Barbra and talked her into making a qualifying statement, which was read at the Aspen press conference.

Pro-boycott activists felt Barbra had given in. To her credit, she swiftly rectified the matter. On December 11, 1992, at the Century Plaza Hotel in Los Angeles, Senator-elect Barbara Boxer* presented Barbra with the ACLU Bill of Rights award. Her corecipient was Anita Hill. Barbra used the opportunity to clarify and restate her position. As for the confusion, she blamed the media, the well-trampled doormat of the 1992 presidential elections.

"I made some comments that seemed obvious to me," she said, "but which some of the media had some difficulty grasping. I spoke of my concern for a referendum passed in Colorado that deprives gay men and lesbians of their civil rights. If that law were passed against Jews or people of color, the country would be outraged and nobody would question a boycott of that state.

"What I said was 'If we are asked to, we must refuse to play where they discriminate.' I did not EVER back off, back down or back away from my original statement as some of the press reported. So let me clearly state my position tonight: It appears that a boycott is underway in Colorado and I will personally honor it and find some other state to vacation in."

Unfortunately, she picked the wrong one. Rather than spending her winter vacation in Aspen, Barbra, like other celebrities, notably, the Kennedy family, chose to go to *Utah* instead, a state in which sodomy is still against the law.

"There are certainly states where they could go vacation that have gay and lesbian civil rights protections and that don't have antiabortion re-

---

*In a historic election, *two* women from California were elected to the United States Senate in 1992. Accompanying Barbara Boxer to Washington was Dianne Feinstein.

strictions and sodomy laws," Terry Schleder said. *"Why* they're not spending their money in *those* states is pretty hypocritical. Utah is not a friendly or safe state for gays and lesbians at all."

Other Colorado residents resent what they perceive to be the intrusion by Hollywood, and the inconsistencies in Barbra's commitment. "Has someone asked Barbra Streisand to withdraw *The Prince of Tides* from all the video stores in Colorado?" asked Stella Pence, cofounder of the Telluride Film Festival. "When I see that, then I can believe there's some serious commitment here."

Terry White, chairman of the Aspen Gay and Lesbian Community Services Center, which opposes the boycott, also questions Barbra's sincerity. According to White, Barbra has done nothing to fight the law* that prompted the boycott in the first place. "Since she announced her boycott on Colorado," he says, "she has not sent any funds or done anything whatsoever, to my knowledge, to help fight Amendment 2."

Nor has she done anything to help Boycott Colorado. In fact, the struggling grassroots group received no word from her, or any of her representatives. Nevertheless, the boycott is apparently taking its toll. Businesses have pulled out of the state. Cities in other states have barred official travel to the state. Conventions have been relocated. And tourists have chosen alternative vacation sites. Reportedly, $16 million "trackable" dollars have been pulled out of the state. According to Boycott Colorado, the figure is closer to $120 million. Granted, people are probably not boycotting the state *because* of Barbra, but many were made aware of the boycott's existence by her having called attention to it.

There was an unfortunate sidebar to the story. After a thirty-year relationship, Barbra and Lee Solters parted company because of a conflict of interests. According to one insider, it was Solters who informed Barbra that he would no longer be able to represent her.

There is no question that Barbra Streisand has decided to use her political power to change public policy on behalf of the gay community. However, why, given her longtime relative silence on the subject, would she make such an issue in support of gay and lesbian rights? Why would she call for the boycott of an entire state, risking the alienation of its residents, many of whom, Don Johnson among them, are her personal friends? Why would she give up a close, longtime personal and professional relationship with Lee Solters?

Certainly, she is comfortable in the presence of gay men. Throughout

---

*Currently, there is an effort to have the law repealed.

the years, many of her friends have been, and continue to be, gay. In fact, her first lover, Barry Dennen, is today a proud and openly gay man. Moreover, she does believe in human and civil rights for gays and lesbians, as she does for all people. But, there is more to it than that. According to several sources—not that it in *any* way diminishes her contributions—her clarion call has been personal, and *maternal.*

Intelligent, artistic, elusive, and in many ways like his mother, Jason Emanuel Gould moved out of Barbra's house in June 1988 and bought a condominium at 837 West Knoll Drive in the city of West Hollywood. He was twenty-one-years old. Nearly three years later, with financial help from his parents (his down payment was $70,000), he purchased a $345,000 home, also located in West Hollywood. It was sometime between the two moves that Jason *came out* to his mother.

"I didn't detect any great interest in things homosexual from her until the last few years," says a friend of Barbra's. "And I think that must stem directly from the fact that her son is gay. You know, most people are like that. Unless it affects them personally."

A well-connected gay activist from West Hollywood concurs. "I am one hundred percent sure the reason Barbra is supporting gay causes is because Jason came out."

According to another source, an acquaintance of Jason's, Jason told Barbra about his being gay, two or three years ago. To help her adjust to the news, Jason, accompanied by a friend, went to her house and presented Barbra with several books on the subject of homosexuality. Says the source, "She's a very bright woman who likes to read up on everything she doesn't understand."

Reportedly, Barbra then agreed to participate in the APLA Commitment to Life benefit at which she delivered the speech voicing her passionate call for the equal rights of gays and lesbians. It wasn't her son's sexual orientation that prompted Barbra's belief in gay rights, but it was, reportedly, what prompted her into taking action.

Barbra was the first entertainer invited to perform at *President* Clinton's inaugural gala. She had, after all, helped raise more than a million dollars for his campaign. And while she may have been late in endorsing Clinton, once the decision was made, her support was unwavering.

Following her performance at the gala on January 19, 1993, Barbra would be criticized not for her singing, but for her fashion statement. She wore a three-piece pin-striped suit with a skirt slit to the thigh. One prominent newspaper would describe it as "the peekaboo power suit."

She was, however, not the only one singled out for her inaugural-eve attire. Aretha Franklin was also criticized for appearing onstage, in front of a largely liberal, pro-animal rights crowd, wearing—and flaunting—real fur.

While in Washington, Barbra, accompanied by Jason, ran into Sen. Arlen Specter of Pennsylvania in a Capitol Hill elevator. A member of the Senate Judiciary Committee, Specter had interrogated Anita Hill during the Clarence Thomas hearings. The tension in the elevator was palpable. "I don't like the way you treated Anita Hill," Barbra is said to have told Specter, "but what is there to say?"

Specter replied, "After saying that, you've said it all, haven't you?"

In late March, Barbra, along with a contingent of other Hollywood representatives, was invited to the White House for a briefing on the Clinton administration's health-care policy. The group was then asked for their ideas on how to best communicate the policy to the American public. In a separate, private meeting with the president, Barbra discussed AIDS research and funding.

"She was also in town the night of the Gridiron Dinner," recalls *Newsweek* correspondent Eleanor Clift. "It was really funny because that afternoon, somebody from the White House called over and said that Clinton had some 'house guests' and could he bring them to the dinner? Now, that's a very tightly subscribed dinner. Last-minute seats are almost unheard of. Nobody *ever* cancels. But the house guests were Barbra Streisand and the [Mike] Medavoys, and they definitely found room for *them*."

At the Gridiron Dinner, hosted by the Washington Press Corps, Barbra rubbed shoulders and traded barbs with, among others, John McLaughlin, Al Hunt, and Evans and Novak. For Barbra, a devout C-Span, CNN, and Sunday morning political TV–talk show junkie, it was a thrill.

While a house guest of the president, Barbra slept overnight in the family quarters of the White House.

After celebrating her fifty-first birthday at a party given by Donna Karan in New York, Barbra returned to Washington, again at the invitation of her new friend.

It was a triumphant visit. Exuding Hollywood star power with off-the-scale *voltage,* Barbra commanded head-turning, neck-craning commotion everywhere she went. Some of the usually composed male politicians and powerbrokers sought an introduction. Braver men and women introduced themselves. The Washington elite was used to visits from Arnold Schwarzenegger, Charlton Heston, and Gerald ("Major Dad") McRainey. But they were not used to *her*.

"I am *not* a star," Barbra insisted several years before. "Call me an actress, a singer, whatever you want, but *not* a star. I look at pictures of Sophia Loren and Jackie Onassis, and those are stars. They always have a smile in the paper. Me, it's always pictures of my arm over my face, running away, saying leave me alone."

However, suffice it to say, during that first week of May in Washington, she was a *star*.

"In general, Washington is enamored with the glitz of Hollywood because it's such a droll, staid, gray-suit town," observes Mary Matalin, George Bush's former campaign director and current CNBC-TV talk show hostess. "Hollywood needs Washington to give it gravity because they're such perceived featherweights, and Washington needs Hollywood to give it fun and glitz."

In the corridors of power, Streisand spottings were the talk of the day. One night she was attending the White House Correspondents' Dinner, where she had last appeared in 1963 when she sang for President Kennedy. Another night she dined at Citronelle with new Attorney General Janet Reno. And during another night she attended the Democratic Congressional Dinner with Health and Human Services Secretary Donna Shalala. Another night she attended an exclusive Georgetown dinner party and hobnobbed with the city's elite.

She continued to cause a sensation wherever she went. "At the White House Correspondents' Dinner," says Mary Matalin, "you would have thought that the Pope walked in."

"Barbra Streisand and Janet Reno were the two people that you wanted to meet and stand next to," relates Eleanor Clift. I thought that Barbra was very gracious. She clearly did *not* want to talk about herself. She wanted to talk about the stimulus bill. She had all the arguments. She had all the Clinton talking points down. I do believe that she knows what she's talking about, but I don't think that anybody is really focusing on it. You're just standing there thinking, 'I'm talking to Barbra Streisand.' "

While there, she socialized with Colin Powell, the chairman of the Joint Chiefs of Staff. Others watched as they shared a few laughs and, by Barbra's account, six minutes of conversation. "Things are much better now between me and your president," Powell told her, teasingly. He was referring, of course, to the rift he had had with President Clinton over the gays in the military issue.*

It was subsequently reported that Barbra had spent her time with Powell lobbying him not only about gays in the military, but also about the military situation in Bosnia. Barbra denied having spoken to him about either. While it is unlikely that she would have been so presumptuous as to counsel Powell on Bosnia, according to one source, she *did* discuss the gays in the military issue with him.

For the most part, however, they talked about the time they had spent together at the American Academy of Achievement. The year before they had each participated in a three-day conference at which gifted high school students were invited to hear prominent people discuss the reasons for their success.

During her stay in Washington, Barbra attended the House Armed Services Committee hearings on gays in the military. Mostly, though, she played tourist. Treated like a visiting dignitary, she visited the Smithsonian. At the National Archives, she held in her hands George Washington's inaugural address, the Louisiana Purchase Treaty, and the Emancipation Proclamation. She visited the Holocaust Museum, and toured the FBI headquarters. And she looked at Thomas Jefferson's drawings of the Capitol Dome at the Library of Congress. Upon her return to New York, inspired by her visit to Monticello, she decided to redecorate the dining room of her Central Park West penthouse in all white.

Throughout the trip, there was no sign of her legendary aloofness or temperament, except one. When inspecting her suite at the Jefferson Hotel, she reportedly became "quite upset," because she did not like to walk on the cold marble floor of her bathroom. Apprised of her discontent, the hotel management had the bathroom carpeted for the rest of her stay.

The heavily publicized "Ms. Streisand Goes to Washington" story fueled criticism that the newly elected, saxophone-playing president was starstruck. Wrote the *Washington Post*'s Richard Cohen, "The new President's guest log is becoming hard to distinguish from a Valley Girl's autograph book."

Clinton went jogging with Judy Collins. He hosted Richard Dreyfuss,

---

*Barbra agreed with Clinton's initial stand on the issue which was that the ban on gays should be lifted. She signed a petition to that effect, which was also signed by, among others, Richard Gere, Ted Danson, Michael Douglas, Patrick Swayze, Joan Rivers, and Sharon Stone.

Christopher Reeve, John Ritter, and Lindsay Wagner at meetings in the Oval Office. He dined with Paul Newman and Joanne Woodward. He took a break during the Vancouver summit to have tea with Richard Gere, Cindy Crawford, and Sharon Stone.

Suddenly, the relatively harmless criticism of Clinton's celebrity fraternization turned serious. Accusations were leveled that the Hollywood-friendly president was guilty of seeking policy advice from his new friends.

And there was no celebrity who embodied the new political clout of the "Hollywood elite" more than Barbra, or whose power was more resented. Much was made over the fact that she had not attended college, the implication being that she lacked intelligence and therefore should not be taken seriously. It was also assumed, erroneously, and not without apparent sexism, that her interest in political and social issues was a pretension, an entertaining between-pictures diversion prompted by the election of her friend the president.

Bristling at the criticism of her and her profession, Barbra responded, "We have the right as an industry, as people, as professionals, to be taken as seriously as automobile executives. No one would question the president or vice president of General Motors talking to all sorts of people in Washington."

She was right, of course. Why anyone would fuss over Barbra Streisand, or any actor, for that matter, spending a night or two in the White House is beyond reason. Ronald Reagan, after all, went to Washington and spent *eight years* in the White House—and he wasn't even much of an actor.

"Everything in politics is contextual and has to do with timing," Mary Matalin comments. "The context that made the Hollywood [issue] a controversy was the juxtaposition of the way he [Clinton] ran. He ran as a populist. What he ran as was mainstream America, and for the little guy. And the first thing he did when he came to Washington was have all these Hollywood people come in and stay in the Lincoln bedroom.

"The other context of it is that Barbra Streisand epitomizes the kinds of causes that are not part and parcel of middle America's lives. It's not that they reject these causes. It's not that anybody wants to kill whales or bash baby seals. It's that they are issues that have nothing to do with 'It's the economy, stupid.' In that context with that timing, it *did* become a controversy."

Susan Estrich, former campaign manager of Michael Dukakis, and presently a law professor at the University of Southern California, is an

astute observer of the political ins and outs of Washington. "The inauguration was probably over the line, glitz-wise," Estrich says. "And then
you had 'The Haircut.' I think the issue had nothing to do with Hollywood per se, it was a question of whether this president had sort of lost
the pulse. And because of that, his ties to Hollywood became, at least in
the short-run, something of a liability to him.

She adds, "The reality is, when a president is up in the polls, he can do
whatever he wants, and everybody says, 'God, that's smart.' And when
he's down in the polls, anything he does looks stupid. So, this president's
flirtations with Hollywood seemed to be rather charming in January, and
they seemed to be not so charming in June. How they seem six months
from now I think will depend on where he is in the polls."

Certainly, no such similar protest emerged in previous years when
Bob Hope, Charlton Heston, Arnold Schwarzenegger, Bruce Willis, and
half the entire country music industry, descended upon a Republican
White House.

"You've also got a *generational* difference with Clinton," Susan Estrich points out. "I mean, this guy's in his forties. His taste in Hollywood
is gonna be different from Ronald Reagan's taste in Hollywood. In truth,
there was a *shitload* of Hollywood around the Reagan presidency. It was
just a sort of old Neanderthal Hollywood."

Former Sen. George McGovern, who raised the Hollywood-Washing-
ton connection to a new level in his 1972 presidential campaign, is nonetheless wary of the idea of Hollywood influence on matters pertaining to
policy. "I don't think they're [celebrities] any better informed on the
issues than, say, clergymen and teachers and journalists and writers and
others who are anonymous figures. So, I never felt that they were ever a
source of great wisdom on the issues simply because they had famous
names."

"Now, there are *some* of them," the former senator says, "who have
made a study of the public questions and are really very knowledgeable
about it. I think, for example, Robert Redford is an expert on environmental questions. And I think that he is worth listening to on those issues. Warren [Beatty] is a student. He is well read. He's a thoughtful guy
and he's worth listening to on public questions. I also found Burt Lancaster to be an intelligent man."

What then, generally speaking, is the political role for a concerned,
socially conscious, Hollywood celebrity? "Politics needs everything it
can get today that lifts its stature and increases public interest," McGovern adds. "I think that *that's* the chief function that a Hollywood celeb-

rity does—to raise the visibility of political campaigns, and to increase public curiousity and public interest in what's going on."

Susan Estrich concurs. "If you and I go down to testify in Washington, no matter how smart we are, and no matter how much we know about our subject, we won't have cameras following us up the stairs of Capitol Hill. If Barbra comes with us, we will. I think what a celebrity can do is get attention to your issue."

When asked if Hollywood was having too much influence impacting political policy, Susan Estrich replies, "We should be so lucky." She adds, on a more serious note, "I don't know that anybody can point to *any* particular case where anybody's changed their mind [in Washington] or done something different because of Hollywood. If *that* were the case we would have gotten a better deal on gays in the military."*

So, just how much political power *does* Barbra Streisand have? According to Susan Estrich, *a lot.* "Anybody who can decide to open up their mouth and raise millions of dollars—whether it's singing or talking, I don't care—is a serious force. People will pay money to be in the same room with her. And they'll pay more money to be in the room with *her* than they will to be in the room with almost any other politician short of the president or vice president. I would rather have her in a room [supporting an issue] than *any* member of the United States Senate.

"There will always be political wisecrackers who will say, 'Who does she think she is?' But the reality is, they can wisecrack all they want. People are more interested in looking at her, being with her, and hearing from her than they are most politicians. And *that* gives her a starting point that almost nobody in American politics has. The question is how wisely and well she uses it."

The one area of Barbra's life that has remained unfulfilled has been her love life. Like Scarlett O'Hara who loses Rhett Butler ("After all, tomorrow is another day"), and like so many of her own heroines, Barbra somehow seems fated to stand valiantly alone as the end credits roll.

Certainly, she loved Elliott Gould and Jon Peters. She *seemed* to be head-over-heels in love with Don Johnson. And, she seems to love Richard Baskin.

Her relationship with Baskin is a curious, ongoing one. In fact, although they claim to be "former" lovers and "just friends," there are

*And the ban played on. Instead of signing an executive order lifting the ban on gays in the military, Clinton enacted a "Don't Ask, Don't Tell, Don't Pursue" policy which, essentially, allows gays into the military—as long as no one finds out they're gay.

some who believe that they have renewed the romantic aspects of their relationship. At public events, and even at private dinners with friends, Baskin is the man almost invariably at her side, and they appear to be very much the couple. Seemingly, they also have an *understanding,* each giving the other the freedom to date outside of the relationship.

In middle-age, Barbra seems to be reliving, or attempting to, the childhood and young adulthood that she never had. Hence, her attraction to younger men. Don Johnson was eight years younger than she, as was James Newton Howard, and as is Richard Baskin. Recent boyfriend Peter Weller is five years younger than Barbra. And tennis star Andre Agassi is *twenty-eight years* younger than she, *and* four years younger than her son.

The two met in the spring of 1992 when he telephoned her after seeing *The Prince of Tides.* He told her how much he liked, and was moved by, the film. Their rapport was immediate, and they talked for two hours. It's doubtful they talked much about tennis, which Barbra plays, but badly. Their phone conversation was followed, shortly thereafter, by a dinner date.

They took their friendship public at the September 1992 U.S. Open. During the match, one droll television sports commentator said Barbra looked at Andre like "an ice cream cone with a cherry on the top."

"He's very intelligent," she said of her new friend, "very, very sensitive, very evolved—more than his linear years. And he's an extraordinary human being. He plays like a Zen master. It's very in the moment."

In between serves, spectators kept interrupting the match by screaming out her name. Finally, Barbra stood up and left, later explaining, "I didn't want him to be distracted." She *didn't* attend Agassi's next U.S. Open match against Jim Courier. His longtime girlfriend, Wendi Stewart, *did,* setting off rumors of a tempestuous love triangle. Agassi, by the way, lost the match.

Later that month, when Agassi was playing in a tournament in Los Angeles, it was Barbra who cheered him on. Reportedly, the two had a private tennis match of their own, with Andre giving Barbra a little one-on-one instruction.

Then, suddenly, their fledgling "relationship" seemed to cool. Rumor has it that Wendi Stewart forbade Andre to see Barbra, despite all of their talk of just being friends. He apparently listened. When attending the November premiere of the Kevin Costner–Whitney Houston picture, *The Bodyguard,* it was Wendi who was nestled in Andre's arm.

And then came Wimbledon. On the night of June 29, 1993, Barbra decided not to use her complimentary tickets to see Patti LuPone in a preview of Andrew Lloyd Webber's *Sunset Boulevard,* which, ironically, tells the story of an older (but faded) movie star infatuated with a much younger man. Instead, she went out to dinner with Andre.

The following day, Barbra appeared at Centre Court to watch Andre play Pete Sampras in the Wimbledon quarterfinals. Dressed in a military style navy and white pants suit with a white sailor's cap, she was a little taken aback when, upon her arrival, the steward guarding the "Friends' Box" asked her to provide her ticket stub. Not used to having to deal with such formalities, she dug through her purse, retrieved her stub, and took her place beside Agassi's brother, Phil, and his coach, Nick Bollettieri.

During the course of the match, Barbra screamed out Andre's name, jumped up and down, and flailed her arms about, all in an attempt to propel her friend to victory. Despite her efforts, however, Agassi lost the match. Following match point, Barbra was near tears.

Much to the shock of his female fans, Agassi had played the match hairless, at least from the neck down. He had shaven off the hair on his chest, stomach, and legs.

Moreover, Agassi is everything Barbra finds attractive in a man: cocky, yet sensitive; athletic, yet intelligent; secure, yet vulnerable. He is also handsome, much desired by other women, and financially independent. In 1992 alone, Agassi, twenty-three, earned an estimated $11 million.

While Barbra is almost entirely silent on the subject, Agassi has hinted that his relationship with her has gone beyond the friendship stage. "She's my version of a friend," he said of Barbra, adding provocatively, "I've been learning about the sweet mysteries of life, and this is one of them. I'm not sure I can fully explain. Maybe she can't either. But it doesn't matter. We came from completely different worlds, and we collided, and we knew we wanted to be in each other's company right then."

On June 29, 1993, *Back to Broadway,* Barbra's "sequel" to 1985's *The Broadway Album,* rocked the music industry by *debuting* at number one on the *Billboard* charts. In her thirty-year recording career, it is the first Streisand album ever to do so. Selling an estimated 120,000 units in its first week of release, the album bested Janet Jackson's six-week stranglehold on the top position, an astonishing feat for a collection of Broadway show tunes.

The accomplishment is only one of many since Barbra sang for her supper and $50 a week at a Ninth Street nightclub in Greenwich Village. She won two Grammys, including Album of the Year, for her first album; an Emmy for her first television special;* and an Oscar for her first movie. She was also the first female musical composer to win an Oscar, and the first woman to direct, produce, write, and star in a movie since the silent era. Thirty-four of her albums have gone gold, and twenty-one have gone platinum. In fact, her last *eleven* albums have gone platinum, and her last twenty-four have gone gold, an awesome achievement. Since 1964, she has sold a staggering *sixty million* albums.

Although there are no awards to acknowledge such things, Barbra has also succeeded in redefining beauty, not only in Hollywood, but in the American consciousness. She became famous for fulfilling the fantasies of every woman, illustrating that, with a sense of humor and a disarming personality, even the ugly duckling could get the gorgeous guy. It was a message that was liberating to millions of other so-called ugly ducklings, and to women and gay men who perceived themselves as such.

But, with her own emerging feminism, she tired of the self-deprecating role and began to *insist* upon being treated as a beauty. And, somewhere along the way, she *became,* if not beautiful, strikingly attractive, alluring, sexy. The new message, clichéd though it may be, was also liberating: the ugly duckling *can* turn into the swan, and she can do so *without* resorting to cosmetic surgery.

Moreover, in the way she has conducted her life, in her performances before the camera, and in her accomplishments behind the camera, she has furthered the cause of *all* women. As Jaynne C. Keyes, New York governor Mario Cuomo's commissioner for film and television development put it, "She's not knocked on doors and opened them for [women], she's blown them apart for us."

It has been an Anne Frank-remarkable life. And there is, one senses, much more life for Barbra Streisand to live; more injustices to be challenged, more self-exploration to be conducted, and more fears to be confronted and conquered.

For more than a decade, there has been talk of Barbra embarking upon a worldwide tour, one last series of concerts to signal the end of her live (commercial) performance career. She has not gone out on the road, after all, since her pregnancy with Jason truncated her tour of 1966.

There is no doubt that a worldwide Streisand tour would be financially lucrative. Given the inevitable spin-off live recording, the televi-

*One of 5 Emmys presented to "My Name Is Barbra" in the 1964–65 television season.

sion special, and the home video, Barbra, reportedly, would stand to earn $100 million.

But, more than the financial compensation, a tour by Barbra would be the personal triumph of *will* conquering fear. Since the summer camp days of her youth, fear has always been a very large part of her makeup. And her fears have only multiplied through the years. "As she's gotten older," Marty Erlichman says, "I have noticed more fear in her. I don't know where that comes from."

It has not been the obstinance of a studio head, or the sexism of a society, that has provided Barbra with her most formidable obstacle, it has been her own fear.

While waiting for the tour that may or may never take place (and one senses, given her susceptibility to the lure of a challenge, it *will*), Streisand fans will have to content themselves with her recorded performances. Upcoming for her in the studio is an album of movie songs, sort of a bi-coastal companion to her Broadway albums, to be entitled, appropriately enough, *The Hollywood Album.*

As this is being written, she is also planning to finally team with Frank Sinatra to record a duet version of "I've Got a Crush on You." There is, however, a glitch in the negotiations. It seems that Sinatra has already gone into the studio and recorded the song, and he wants Barbra to add her vocal tracks to his. She, however, wants to record the duet the old-fashioned way, each standing at the microphone, side by side, and/or face to face. The mutual admiration that exists between Streisand and Sinatra, arguably *the* two pop vocal talents of the last thirty years, has always been laced with competition, and the power struggle continues to this day.

After the success of *The Prince of Tides,* and the sympathy generated by her having not been nominated for an Oscar, Barbra seems well-poised to *win* a Best Director and/or Best Actress Oscar for her next picture, assuming that it is a success.

The question is *which* picture it will be. She does not make the ultimate commitment to a movie easily. In the ten years since *Yentl,* she has only made *two* films, and both, in some way, reflected some deeply personal aspect of her own life experience. It is very important to her that she do *important* work and leave a meaningful legacy behind her.

As of this writing, Barbra has a full slate of film projects in various stages of development. Among them, *The Mirror Has Two Faces.* With a script by Richard LaGravenese *(The Fisher King)* the story, reportedly dealing with how a mother can negatively impact her adult daughter's self-esteem, presents Barbra with the opportunity to confront her relationship with her own mother.

At one time, acclaimed Italian director Bernardo Bertolucci (*The Conformist, Last Tango in Paris, The Last Emperor*) was scheduled to direct the picture, which came as a welcome surprise to many in the industry. After all, with the exception of Martin Ritt with *Nuts* (who conceded final cut to her—something most great directors would refuse to do), Barbra has not placed herself in the hands of a strong, accomplished director in *twenty* years—since Sydney Pollack directed her in *The Way We Were*. It is no accident that was the movie for which Barbra received her last Best Actress Oscar nomination.

However, Bertolucci has since reportedly dropped out of the project, and, as of this writing, Barbra is set to direct, produce, and star in the picture herself. The film is being developed for Tri-Star, a division of the Sony Corporation. The project unites Barbra with her old beau, Arnon Milchan, who is attached as executive producer.

If it is produced, *The Mirror Has Two Faces* may well present Barbra with a first in her career. To this date, she has yet to share the screen with a formidable actress in a role equal to the one played by her. Reportedly, the *Mirror* script (at least at this stage) calls for the role of the mother to be of equal size and stature to the role of the daughter. Somehow, however, the idea of Barbra sharing the screen in a *Thelma & Louise*–like turn seems unlikely. Previous, much-discussed projects with Jane Fonda and Goldie Hawn were eventually scrapped, presumably, at least in part, because of this very issue.

Another project in development, also for Tri-Star, is *Where or When,* adapted from the novel by Ann Shreve. It's a love story set in New England which would cast Barbra in the part of a married writer who meets up with an old friend. He too is married, which doesn't preclude them from falling in love.

Jeffrey Potter's book, *To a Violent Grave,* is the basis for another Streisand project. From a screenplay by Christopher Cleveland, the story tells of the relationship between Abstract Expressionist painter Jackson Pollock and his wife, artist Lee Krasner. Playing Pollock will be Robert De Niro, with whom Barbra has long wanted to work.

Bringing her politics into her art, Barbra will be serving as coexecutive producer of a made-for-television movie about Col. Margarethe (Greta) Cammermeyer, who was expelled from the army after she acknowledged she was a lesbian. Cammermeyer was the highest ranking woman in the entire armed services when her twenty-six-year career ended in 1989 because of her sexual orientation.

"This is a story that throws light on one of the most important issues of our time," Barbra said when announcing that her production company, Barwood, planned to make the telefilm. In the part of Cammermeyer will be Glenn Close, who will also serve as coexecutive producer.

But, the project that Barbra seems to feel the most passionate about is *The Normal Heart,* which she has had in and out of development for the past eight years. Based on the play by Larry Kramer, it tells the story of the early years of the AIDS crisis and the in-fighting that went on between the founding members of the Gay Men's Health Crisis in New York City. The project is being developed at Columbia, and will cast Barbra as the wheelchair-confined Dr. Emma Brookner, a physician who treats people with AIDS.

At one time, Barbra was to only produce and star in *The Normal Heart,* but she was unable to find a director who, given the subject matter, would agree to doing it. She even approached the eighty-one-year-old Elia Kazan with the idea that he would make a comeback with the picture. He too turned her down. Unable to find someone else, Barbra reportedly plans to direct the film herself. After many false starts, it looks as if the picture may finally get made. As Larry Kramer exuberantly put it earlier this year, "She's revving up!"

She is, possibly, the last great star. There were Katharine Hepburn, Clark Gable, Bette Davis, Cary Grant, Marilyn Monroe, and Humphrey Bogart. Today, despite the rarity of her big-screen appearances, there is Elizabeth Taylor. And, then there is Barbra Streisand.

But, in reviewing Barbra's film performances to date, there are some who are disappointed with her accomplishments as an actress. She seems to hold back, unwilling to sacrifice herself completely to a role, to unleash the emotion stored within. With the exception of her work in *Nuts,* her best performances to date came early in her career in *Funny Girl* and *The Way We Were.*

There has also been regretfully little adventure, with Yentl being an obvious exception, in her choice of roles. And, despite all of her lofty ambitions, she has not played Camille, Medea, Sarah Bernhardt, or Shakespeare's Juliet, as she had once vowed to do. Instead, she chose to play *All Night Long*'s Cheryl Gibbons, *The Main Event*'s Hillary Kramer, and *A Star Is Born*'s Esther Hoffman-Howard.

"Let me put it this way," says Allan Miller, her former acting coach, "What I saw up until the time my relationship with her ended was the makings of a *major* acting—as well as singing—talent. I don't think that that has ever come to pass."

Adds Eli Rill, another of her former acting coaches, "It seems to me, and I say this very cautiously, it always impresses me the natural ability that she has to use the light colors of herself without any strain, whether it's from *Funny Girl* or *The Owl and the Pussycat*. There's no strain, no effort. To this day it seems to me, if I were coaching her, I would say to her, 'Don't strain so hard to be serious. You *are*.'"

Like all of us, Barbra Streisand cannot be defined with one- or two-word platitudes. She is not *just* "difficult." She is not just "demanding." She is not just "a perfectionist." It's not that those are inaccurate terms to describe her, they are just not *all* that she is.

She is tough, but she is also feminine; intimidating, but shy; powerful, but vulnerable; controlling, but insecure; dysfunctional, but also lucid. She is different things to different people; and, sometimes, she is different things to the same person.

"I was surprised by her good side," says Paul Sylbert, her award-winning production designer on *The Prince of Tides*. "From what I'd heard from people who had worked with her, there was nothing good. It was just a horror show. And there were things that I will never forgive her for, but they weren't things done to me, they were done to other people. There's a lot of openness, a certain amount of sweetness, and sincerity. And there is a malleability, too. If you can just be lucky enough to approach her the right way. You have to have the right gifts for handling her to get your work done."

It *is* true that she has spent most of her thirty years of stardom avoiding her fans, the press, the public. It is something that even people who are fond of her don't always understand or rationalize. "As for this Garbo syndrome," one of her friends says, "this whole business of 'I don't want to be approached, I don't want to be recognized, I don't want to speak to my fans'—Well, excuse me, when you go into something as public as acting, *that's* the deal. That's why they pay you all that money. The whole business of 'I want to be alone' is foolish. If you want to be left alone, what are you doing putting your image out in front of hundreds of millions of people? It's a dichotomy which doesn't play. . . . If you really want to be private, you have to be Emily Dickinson."

She continues to strike some people as being distant, very much absorbed in her own insulated, rarefied world. "Does Barbra Streisand think she's the queen of the United States right now?" Roseanne Arnold, another modern-day show business icon, asked after President Clinton's inauguration. Arnold added of Streisand, "I could only aspire to that kind of ego. We [she and her husband, Tom] went to dinner with her once. She has her own planet going on."

Maybe so. But, at least it's an environmentally-friendly planet, where women are *not* oppressed, and referendums are *not* enacted that sanction discrimination against gays, lesbians, or any particular group of people.

Moreover, she has come a long way in her personal odyssey, and the passage has not been an easy one.

"She is like a filter that filters out everything except what relates to herself," reported a friend of Barbra's in 1964, during the glory days of *Funny Girl*'s run on Broadway. "If I said, 'There's been an earthquake in Brazil, she would answer, 'Well, there aren't any Brazilians in the audience tonight, so it doesn't matter.' "

The same statement could *never* be made about Barbra Streisand today. There are buildings all over the world that bear her (and her father's) name. And there are Streisand scholarships, and Streisand endowments, and Streisand schools, and Streisand performance centers. The Streisand Foundation has, as of this writing, contributed from $4 to $7 million, depending on the source, to charitable causes around the world. Not only is this a sign of her generosity, but it is a reflection of her humanity, and her very real desire to *belong.*

It is one of the great challenges of Barbra's life to get *outside* of herself. To empower herself by integrating into the world around her, rather than retreating, as she is inclined to do, into the fantasy world which had been created in self-defense during her childhood.

It is, of course, an ongoing process, and she is nothing if not a work in progress. Today, she is more willing to extend herself, in a philanthropic, political, *and* personal sense, than at any other time in her life.

"She has always been a very defensive, isolating kind of person," says her old friend, Bob Schulenberg. *"Very* introverted. I think that's the surprise. I don't think that anybody realizes that this is one of the major introverts of our time." He adds, however, *"The Prince of Tides,* I thought, was Barbra being kind of healthy. . . . I hope so."

But, where will this evolution take her? How *far* will she extend herself?

Shortly after the 1992 presidential election, one New York newspaper ran a story, entitled "Senator Yentl," contending that Barbra had plans to run for the United States Senate in the state of New York.

She denied it, responding, "Running for the Senate is out of the question. There should be no confusion between someone with political passion and someone with political ambition."

Still, speculation suggests she is seeking some "honorary commission," or other such political assignment. Perhaps she is laying the groundwork for something to be pursued years down the line. "I can't tell you what might happen ten years from now," she answered when asked about her long-term political aspirations.

Could there be a political future for Barbra Streisand? Could the most powerful woman in Hollywood find a place on the Senate Judiciary Committee? Or in a debate with Jesse Helms on the floor of the U.S. Senate?

"Well, she *is* someone who would have instant name recognition," George McGovern says, warily. "But I'm not sure that would be wise for Barbra to move in that direction. I don't know how well informed she is on public issues."

He adds, *"But,* on the other hand, she shouldn't be excluded [from consideration] *because* she's a Hollywood celebrity. I mean, who knows, she might turn into a really effective, articulate, powerful figure. I think the best answer to that is to let her test it out."

When reminded that one Hollywood actor had crossed over into politics and made it to the White House, the former senator says, "Well, that prompts me to think it's not a very good idea."

But, Susan Estrich is probably on target when she says of Barbra, "I don't know what kind of political future she wants. I mean, I can't *imagine* she wants to run for Congress. I'd rather be Barbra Streisand than a member of Congress, you know?"

On Friday night, July 30, 1993, Barbra's friend, songwriter Carole Bayer Sager, gave a dinner party in her honor to celebrate the success of *Back to Broadway.* Attending the intimate gathering, which was held at Sager's Malibu home, were Warren Beatty, Annette Bening, Carol Burnett, Faye Dunaway, Neil Diamond, Clint Eastwood, and Bette Midler. Seated beside Barbra throughout the night was Richard Baskin.

After dinner was served, Barbra, wearing a white dress, got up in front of the room, thanked everyone for coming, and announced that she was going to sing a couple of songs.

"Well," says one of the invited guests, "Barbra left the stage because she wanted to go and change, and everyone in the room started talking, excitedly, about seeing Barbra sing. And then, like out of a Dracula movie, this fog filled the stage and the lights dimmed, and Barbra, now in a black dress, came out on the stage. She started to sing ["Somewhere"], and the movements and mannerisms started, and everyone really thought it was Barbra."

It turned out, however, that Barbra was actually playing a joke on her friends. She wasn't onstage at all, it was Streisand illusionist Jim Bailey.

After the first number, the *real* Barbra snuck into the back of the room and gleefully watched her friends watching what they thought was a performance by her.

"Slowly," the guest continues, "people turned around and saw that Barbra was *not* on stage. She was smiling and laughing, and seemed like she was having fun. It was like she was a girl pulling off the best show-and-tell for her entire class; like she had told the best joke in years."

The incident reveals not only that Barbra is capable of playing a joke on her friends but that she is able to laugh at *herself,* something she could not seem to do a few years before. The release and success of *The Prince of Tides* has been a liberating, emancipating experience for her.

She appears to be more comfortable with her fame, and more hopeful about the world around her. She also seems more committed to improving things that she *can,* and accepting things that she can not. And, finally, perhaps for the first time in her life, she has begun to accept not only the frailties of others, but also herself.

"I don't know what else there is in life," she says "to be able to be a mature adult, and with some distance and consciousness go back to your past and really grieve and rediscover that pure self that you were. And not think you're so awful because you were told you were awful. And not live out other people's opinions of you. But discover that true child, that true self. With an adult's maturity you can handle so many things. You can embrace all the parts of yourself."

She stood in front of the bathroom mirror at her home in Beverly Hills at the age of fifty-one. Hers is not a classically beautiful face, but a striking one. Bangs fall down her forehead, and into eyes, big and blue and shining with clarity. Her nose, strong and defiant, is a symbol of obstacles overcome. Her mouth is wide and generous, and one that usually has a great deal to say.

It is a face in which everything seems to fit.

Source Notes

An enormous amount of text and archival research was conducted for this book, and I acknowledge here the sources for quotations appearing in the text. In addition, over two hundred interviews were conducted for this book. Many of those interviewed requested anonymity. Those whose words *could* be attributed are listed below. For the sake of space, such an interview source is listed only once, at first appearance, though the source is usually quoted more than once in a chapter and sometimes throughout the book.

Chapter 1: Conducting Symphonies

"I couldn't understand . . .": Hilary de Vries, "Streisand the Storyteller," *Los Angeles Times Magazine,* December 8, 1991.

"You can't write . . .": Amy Rennert, "Family Secrets," *San Francisco Focus,* December 1991.

"a consummately violent . . .": Ibid.

"When I read the book . . .": Scott Siegel and Barbara Siegel, "The Prince of Tides," *Drama-Logue,* December 19, 1991.

"I know that . . .": John Voland interview.

"All my life . . .": *Halliwell's Filmgoer's Companion,* 9th ed. (New York: Harper and Row, 1990), p. 921.

"It was really odd . . .": Bonnie Lee interview.

"Remember, she was coming off . . .": Anne Thompson interview.

"Barbra, I have nothing . . .": Rennert, op. cit.

"We talked a great deal . . .": Robert Epstein, "Magnolias, Palms: 'Tides' Author Meets Hollywood," *Los Angeles Times,* December 26, 1991.

"I now know my place . . .": Ibid.

"There was a lot . . .": Nina J. Easton interview.

"Even the numbers . . .": Streisand interview, New York press junket, Columbia Pictures, November 1991.

"It was like . . .": Ibid.

Chapter 2: Tea Sets and Party Dresses

"She's mainly interested . . .": Charles Brossard, "New Singing Sensation," *Look,* November 19, 1963.

"love at first sight . . .": Georgia Holt and Phyllis Quinn, with Sue Russell, *Star Mothers* (New York: Simon & Schuster, 1988), p. 231.

"It was Manny . . .": Ibid.

"He played squash . . .": Anne Fadiman, "Barbra Puts Her Career on the Line with *Yentl,*" *Life,* December 1983.

"My father was . . .": Sheldon Spiro interview.

"I don't know . . .": Holt et al., op. cit., p. 225.

"It was a frightening situation . . .": Ibid.

"such a healthy . . .": Ibid.

"We never had . . .": Fadiman, op. cit.

"decent, hard-working people . . .": Brad Darrach, "Celebration of a Father," *People,* December 12, 1983.

"I didn't have any toys . . .": Ibid.

"He can play . . .": Ira Mothner, "Mama Barbra," *Look,* July 25, 1967.

"I was raised . . .": interview by Nancy Collins, "Entertainment Tonight."

"I remember his mother . . .": Thomas B. Morgan, "Superbarbra," *Look,* April 5, 1966.

"I remember their taking off . . .": Lawrence Grobel, "Playboy Interview: Barbra Streisand," *Playboy,* October 1977.

"I believed in God . . .": Hilary de Vries, "Streisand the Storyteller," *Los Angeles Times Magazine,* December 8, 1991.

"I remember listening . . .": Fadiman, op. cit.

"I always wanted . . .": Earl Wilson, "Barbra Starts Film Career," *Los Angeles Herald-Examiner,* June 8, 1967.

"Was I happy . . .": Holt et al., op cit., p. 227.

"I used to go . . .": Rona Jaffe, "Barbra Streisand, 'Sadie, Sadie . . . Married Lady . . .,'" *Cosmopolitan,* April 1969.

"I remember a long time ago . . .": Ray Loynd, "Barbra's Outdoor Jam-In," *Los Angeles Herald-Examiner,* July 9, 1967.

"I hadda . . .": Shana Alexander, "A Born Loser's Success and Precarious Love," *Life,* May 22, 1964.

"When I was nine . . .": Grobel, op. cit.

"We were very close . . .": Ed Frankel interview.

"I've never seen . . .": James Spada, *Streisand: The Woman and the Legend* (Garden City, N.Y.: Doubleday Dolphin, 1981), p. 21.

"He was mean . . .": interview with Mike Wallace, "60 Minutes," November 24, 1991.

"He was really mean . . .": Darrach, op. cit.

Chapter 3: Metamorphosis

"I remember singing . . .": appearance on "Larry King Live," February 6, 1992.

"I felt sure . . .": Shaun Considine, *Barbra Streisand: The Woman, the Myth, the Music* (New York: Delacorte Press, 1985), p. 11.

"when they said . . .": Georgia Holt and Phyllis Quinn, with Sue Russell, *Star Mothers* (New York: Simon & Schuster, 1988), p. 228.

"My mother hated it . . .": Edwin Miller, *"Seventeen" Interviews Film Stars and Superstars* (New York: Macmillan, 1970), p. 146.

"I used to spend . . .": "Show Business/Broadway," *Time,* April 10, 1964.

"Somehow, it made . . .": Thomas P. Morgan, "Superbarbra," *Look,* April 5, 1966.

"I was a very strange kid . . .": *People,* n.d.

"I always knew . . .": Morgan, op. cit.

"My mother never said . . .": interview with Mike Wallace, "60 Minutes," November 24, 1991.

"I was always trying . . .": Lawrence Grobel, "Playboy Interview: Barbra Streisand," *Playboy,* October 1977.

"She'd pay her . . .": Maggie Savoy, "Barbra's Top Fan Makes It on Her Own," *Los Angeles Times,* March 14, 1969.

"They couldn't fly me . . .": Ibid.

"Mother and her chicken soup . . .": Ibid.

"I met Barbara . . .": Diane Lemm interview.

"Let me just . . .": Marilyn Saposh interview.

"I never *heard* . . .": Frederic Ansis interview.

"I used to steal . . .": Peter Hamill, "Good-bye Brooklyn, Hello Fame," *Saturday Evening Post,* July 27, 1963.

"We'll just do . . .": Barbra Streisand, "Just for the Record . . ." Pamphlet. Columbia Records, 1991.

"I did a speech . . .": Hilary de Vries, "Streisand the Storyteller," *Los Angeles Times Magazine,* December 8, 1981.

"I remember thinking . . .": *People,* n.d.

"She couldn't stand . . .": Holt et al., op cit., p. 229.

"At the last minute . . .": *"Seventeen" Interviews Film Stars and Superstars* (New York: Macmillan, 1970), p. 147.

"Can't you just . . .": Ibid.

"Can you imagine . . .": Holt et al., op cit., p. 229.

"In my family . . .": Grobel, op. cit.

"She came to me . . .": Allan Miller interview.

"Once, I thought . . .": Sidney Skolsky, "Tintypes: Barbra Streisand," *Hollywood Citizen-News,* June 13, 1969.

"She was not . . .": Holt et al., op. cit., p. 228.

Chapter 4: The Fountainhead

"It was the kind . . .": Lawrence Grobel, "Playboy Interview: Barbra Streisand," *Playboy,* October 1977.

"I liked the high . . .": Joan Rivers, *Enter Talking* (New York: Delacorte Press, 1986), p. 90.

"I had four kids . . .": Kevin Sessums, "Queen of Tides," *Vanity Fair,* September 1991.

"She had blockaded . . .": Allan Miller, *A Passion for Acting* (New York: Backstage Books, 1992), pp. 34–36.

"Open a bakery . . .": Ibid.

"I hope you will . . .": Ibid.

"I wasn't the ingenue . . .": Gloria Steinem, "Barbra Streisand Talks About Her 'Million-Dollar Baby,' " *Ladies Home Journal,* August 1966.

"People looked at me . . .": David Henderson, "Barbra—Born Loser Wins Broadway," *Players Showcase,* Winter 1964.

"You'll be sorry . . .": Cecil Smith, "Barbra—A Person Who Needs People," *Los Angeles Times,* March 16, 1965.

"I *knew* I was good . . .": Steinem, op. cit.

"I can't force . . .": Smith, op. cit.

"What did surprise . . .": Eli Rill interview.
"didn't have anything . . .": Renée Taylor interview.
"I was designing . . .": Terry Leong interview.
"I bought that stuff . . .": Shana Alexander, "A Born Loser's Success and Precarious Love," *Life,* May 22, 1964.
"[In thrift shops] . . .": *New York Herald Tribune,* 1964.
"When I heard . . .": René Jordan, *The Greatest Star* (New York: G. P. Putnam's Sons, 1975), p. 65.
"I thought if they . . .": Charles Brossard, "New Singing Sensation," *Look,* November 19, 1963.

Chapter 5: Illusions

"I managed The Lion . . .": Burke McHugh interview.
"She certainly doesn't . . .": Lawrence Grobel, *Conversations With Capote* (New York: New American Library, 1985), p. 55.

Chapter 6: Crossroads

"It was the first . . .": Bob Schulenberg interview.
"She was afraid . . .": Georgia Holt and Phyllis Quinn, with Sue Russell, *Star Mothers* (New York: Simon & Schuster, 1988), p. 228.
"I hadn't really heard . . .": Gloria Steinem, "Barbra Streisand Talks About Her 'Million-Dollar Baby,' " *Ladies Home Journal,* August 1966.
"I'm an actress . . .": Charles Brossard, "New Singing Sensation," *Look,* November 19, 1963.
"I never sang . . .": Edwin Miller, *"Seventeen" Interviews Film Stars and Superstars* (New York: Macmillan, 1970), p. 148.
"The Bon Soir . . .": Robert Richards interview.

Chapter 7: Before Stonewall

"I think I'm . . .": Edwin Miller, *"Seventeen" Interviews Film Stars and Superstars* (New York: : Macmillan, 1970), p. 148.
"I sometimes feel . . .": Charles Brossard, "New Singing Sensation," *Look,* November 19, 1963.
"On my good . . .": Liz Smith, "The People-Need-People Girl," *Cosmopolitan,* May 1965.
"She's very extraordinary . . .": "Bea, Billie, and Barbra," *Newsweek,* June 3, 1963.
"Barbra forgets about . . .": Ted Rozar interview.
"What happened was . . .": Irvin Arthur interview.
"I hired my . . .": Thomas P. Morgan, "Superbarbra," *Look,* April 5, 1966.
"Let me get this . . .": Kevin Sessums, "Queen of Tides," *Vanity Fair,* September 1991.
"Barbra is the . . .": Pete Hamill, "Good-bye Brooklyn, Hello Fame," *Saturday Evening Post,* July 27, 1963.

Chapter 8: Distant Voices, Other Lives

"She had great pitch . . .": Neil Wolfe interview.
"I am a very . . .": Arthur Alpert, "Barbra Sticks by Her Name," *New York World-Telegram and Sun,* May 24, 1961.

"She looked like . . .": Joe Weiss, "Barbra Streisand and Joe Franklin," *Celebrity,* June 1978.
"As soon as I . . .": Ibid.
"I had her on the . . .": Ibid.
"When they called . . .": Martha Weinman Lear, "She Is Tough, She Is Earthy, She Is Kicky," *New York Times,* July 4, 1965.
"I think a lot . . .": John Softness interview.
"There was a little place . . .": Don Softness interview.
"At that time in . . .": Jeff Harris interview.
"The show was really . . .": Glenn Jordan interview.
"I don't think that . . .": Abba Bogin interview.

Chapter 9: New Faces of 1963

"There were a lot . . .": May Muth interview.
"Everyone turned and looked . . .": Ashley Feinstein interview.
"There were a few other people . . .": Harold Rome interview.
"In our original . . .": Jerome Weidman, "I Remember Barbra," *Holiday,* November 1963.
"When you have . . .": Pete Hamill, "Good-bye Brooklyn, Hello Fame," *Saturday Evening Post,* July 27, 1963.
"She was a skinny . . .": Ibid.
"I was dead-on . . .": David Galligan, "Elliott Gould," *Drama-Logue,* October 8, 1981.
"She was so . . .": David Colker, "In the '80s, All That Glitters Isn't Gould," *Los Angeles Herald-Examiner,* October 2, 1981.
"Like out of . . .": Shana Alexander, "A Born Loser's Success and Precarious Love," *Life,* May 22, 1964.
"She needs to be . . .": "Show Business/Broadway," *Time,* April 10, 1964.
"I first noticed . . .": Wilma Curley interview.

Chapter 10: The Revenge of Yetta Tessye Marmelstein

"Elliott put up a . . .": Mike Mansdorf interview.
"After I got good . . .": Edwin Miller, *"Seventeen" Interviews Film Stars and Superstars* (New York: Macmillan, 1970), p. 150.
"They say I'm . . .": Sidney Fields, "A Happy Confusion of Talent," *New York Daily Mirror,* April 1, 1962.
"I didn't want . . .": Miller, op. cit., p. 150.
"It was a thrilling . . .": Marilyn Cooper interview.
"When I met her . . .": Richard Falk interview.
"I must admit . . .": Richard Warren Lewis, "Playboy Interview: Elliott Gould," *Playboy,* November 1970.
"By the time . . .": Guy Flatley, "What Ever Happened to Elliott Gould? Plenty!" *New York Times,* March 4, 1973.
"She says she . . .": David Colker, "In the '80s, All That Glitters Isn't Gould," *Los Angeles Herald-Examiner,* October 2, 1981.
"I don't think . . .": "Coming Star," *New Yorker,* May 19, 1962.

Chapter 11: Getting Her Act Together (or Trying to) and Taking It Out on the Road

"There were no microphones . . .": Stanley Simmonds interview.
"She's nineteen years . . .": Joe Morgenstern, "Streisand's Rite of Passage," *Los Angeles Herald-Examiner,* November 13, 1983.
"She was easily . . .": "The 'Moron' Signed the 'Kookiest' Kid," *San Francisco Chronicle,* March 24, 1963.
"I was scared . . .": John McKinney, "The Trouble With Not Being Ingenue," *San Francisco Chronicle,* April 7, 1963.
"I am really . . .": Ibid.
"I'm sure our . . .": Mike Douglas, *Mike Douglas: My Story* (New York: G. P. Putnam's Sons, 1978), p. 226.
"They tell me . . .": Pete Hamill, "Good-bye Brooklyn, Hello Fame," *Saturday Evening Post,* July 27, 1963.
"If you maintain . . .": "Bea, Billie and Barbra," *Newsweek,* June 3, 1963.
"People always want . . .": Ibid.
"It was like . . .": Shana Alexander, "A Born Loser's Success and Precarious Love," *Life,* May 22, 1964.
"Barbra, did you *have* . . .": Merv Griffin, *Merv* (New York: Simon & Schuster, 1980), p. 70.
"He's a great-looking . . .": Judy Michaelson, "The New Stars," *New York Post,* September 13, 1963.
"All the people . . .": Said to columnist Leonard Feather.
"I'm going to take . . .": Bob Thomas, *Liberace* (New York: St. Martin's Press, 1987), p. 163.
"Here's what . . .": Ibid., p. 163.
"Maybe you should . . .": Ibid., p. 164.
"I can remember . . .": Bruce Weber, "Barbra Streisand—Talent Plus," *Beacon News,* September 5, 1963.
"Just think, one . . .": *Daily Variety,* August 21, 1963.
"I read a lot . . .": Charles Brossard, "New Singing Sensation," *Look,* November 19, 1963.

Chapter 12: Going With the Kid

"If ever they . . .": Sheila Graham, "Barbra Streisand and Elegant Tea," *Hollywood Citizen-News,* April 9, 1966.
"I know the perfect . . .": Radie Harris, *Radie's World* (New York: G. P. Putnam's Sons, 1975), p. 152.
"There is no . . .": Herbert G. Goldman, *Fanny Brice* (New York: Oxford University Press, 1992), p. 214.
"[Hire] Anne Bancroft . . .": Amy Archerd, "Just for Variety," *Variety,* June 26, 1981.

Chapter 13: Two Stars Passing in Flight

"Here was a girl . . .": Pete Hamill, "Good-bye Brooklyn, Hello Fame," *Saturday Evening Post,* July 27, 1963.
"We were in Palm Beach . . .": Dolores Hope interview.
"I'm never going . . .": Coyne Steven Sanders, *Rainbow's End* (New York: William Morrow and Co., 1990), p. 202.

"A man I hardly knew . . .": Joshua Logan, *Movie Stars, Real People, and Me* (New York: Delacorte Press, 1978), p. 263.

"Listen, kid, . . .": Martin Gottfried, *All His Jazz* (New York: Bantam Books, 1990), p. 162.

Chapter 14: Under the Hot Glare of an Awaiting Marquee

"It's a great opportunity . . .": Judy Michaelson, "The New Stars," *New York Post,* September 13, 1963.

"That was the . . .": Royce Wallace interview.

"In Boston, the word . . .": Lee Allen interview.

"We all knew that . . .": Buzz Miller interview.

"It *was* pretty bad . . .": Luther Henderson interview.

"I got up my . . .": Marvin Hamlisch and Gerald Gardner, *The Way I Was* (New York: Charles Scribner's Sons, 1992), p. 64.

"Unfortunately, we had someone . . .": Blair Hammond interview.

"Sydney had one gorgeous . . .": Marc Jordan interview.

"The show is . . .": William Glover, Associated Press, 1964.

"I'm so much . . .": Michaelson, op. cit.

"Fanny and Barbra . . .": Leonard Harris, "Funny How Streisand Plays Perfect Fanny," *New York World-Telegram and the Sun,* March 26, 1964.

"You know you've . . .": Allan Miller, *A Passion for Acting* (New York: Backstage Books, 1982), p. 51.

Chapter 15: Hello, Gorgeous

"I understand I . . .": Polly Rose Gottlieb, *The Nine Lives of Billy Rose* (New York: Crown Publishers, 1968), p. 186.

"No one in the . . .": Sheila Graham, "Barbra Streisand and Elegant Tea," *Hollywood Citizen-News,* April 9, 1966.

"Now that I'm . . .": Joanne Stang, "She Couldn't Be Medium," *New York Times,* April 5, 1964.

"The other night . . .": Liz Smith, "The People-Need-People Girl," *Cosmopolitan,* May 1965.

"Please, please . . .": Associated Press, June 6, 1965.

"What does it . . .": Shana Alexander, "A Born Loser's Success and Precarious Love," *Life,* May 22, 1964.

"You know, I hate . . .": Shaun Considine, *Barbra Streisand: The Woman, the Myth, the Music* (New York: Delacorte Press, 1985), p. 72.

"We know the talent . . .": Cecil Smith, "For People Who Need Barbra," *Los Angeles Times,* July 2, 1964.

"the most important . . .": "Money Girl," *Newsweek,* July 6, 1964.

"It's okay, I . . .": "Nielsen's Newest," *Time,* July 3, 1964.

"Guest stars? . . .": Kay Gardella, "Star Born in Brooklyn Solos 1st TV Special," *New York Daily News,* April 4, 1965.

"Noel Coward was an . . .": Richard Lewine interview.

"I've switched my . . .": "Television: Streisand at Twenty-three," *Time,* April 30, 1965.

"I used to hate . . .": "People," *Time,* April 2, 1965.

"It's the most . . .": Marylin Bender, "Streisand Dons Mink by Partos," *New York Times,* March 23, 1965.

"A cloth coat . . .": Smith, op. cit.

"a boa can . . .": *New York Times,* 1965.
"It was like . . .": Martha Weinman Lear, "She Is Tough, She Is Earthy, She Is Kicky," *New York Times,* July 4, 1965.

Chapter 16: Her Name Is Barbra

"She has cut . . .": Christina Kirk, "Will Success Unspoil Barbra?" *New York Daily News,* September 15, 1968.
"She took advantage . . .": Arnold Abrams, "Streisand: Lonely 'Funny Girl,' " *W,* March 21, 1964.
"First of all . . .": Ibid.
"She'll drive you . . .": "Show Business/Broadway," *Time,* April 10, 1964.
"She can repeat something . . .": Sid Ramin interview.
"I'm sort of . . .": *New York Post,* August 28, 1964.
"One of the big . . .": *On View,* April 1969.
"That was really . . .": Georgia Holt and Phyllis Quinn, with Sue Russell, *Star Mothers* (New York: Simon & Schuster, 1988), p. 231.
"To say I love . . .": Shana Alexander, "A Born Loser's Success and Precarious Love," *Life,* May 22, 1964.
"I have to be . . .": Ibid.
"Barbra's favorite . . .": Diana Lurie, " 'Funny Girl' and Me," *Ladies Home Journal,* August 1969.
"I used to be . . .": Ibid.
"He's a lovely . . .": Judy Michaelson, "The New Stars," *New York Post,* September 13, 1963.
"He does it so . . .": Liz Smith, "The People-Need-People Girl," *Cosmopolitan,* May 1965.
"Barbra mistrusts anyone . . .": Lurie, op. cit.
"I really fought . . .": Interview with Elliott Gould, *Los Angeles Times,* June 8, 1969.
"After *Drat! The Cat!* . . .": Ibid.
"Sitting in the . . .": Associated Press, June 6, 1965.
"I wanted to be . . .": *Newsday,* January 21, 1973.
"I'm constantly depressed . . .": "Dialogue Between Barbra Streisand and Marcello Mastroianni," *Redbook,* July 1965.
"I can't say . . .": Kay Gardella, "Star Born in Brooklyn Solos 1st TV Special," *New York Daily News,* April 4, 1965.
"I know I . . .": Diana Lurie, "They All Come Thinking I Can't Be That Great," *Life,* March 18, 1966.
"Most of them . . .": Ibid.
"When I am performing . . .": Ibid.

Chapter 17: Slowing Down for the Crossings

"Tell the audience . . .": Diana Lurie, "They All Come Thinking I Can't Be That Great," *Life,* March 18, 1966.
"She watched the playback . . .": Ray Diffen interview.
"You'll be hoarse . . .": Lurie, op. cit.
"You have to do . . .": Gerald Nachman, "Whatever Happened to Barbra Streisand?" *New York Post,* March 27, 1966.
"Get rid of . . .": Rex Reed, "Color Barbra Very Bright," *New York Times,* March 27, 1966.

"Too many people . . .": Ibid.
"Two years ago . . .": "TV-Radio: Barbra," *Newsweek,* March 28, 1966.
"The point of the trip . . .": Joan Glynn interview.
"What's this new . . .": "Spot News," *Newsweek,* February 14, 1966.
"I'm more talented . . .": Interview with Elliott Gould, *New York Post,* 1970.
"I don't think . . .": Associated Press, April 14, 1966.
"My kid's going . . .": Robert Musel, "Barbra Will Sing Tunes for Her 'Million-Dollar Baby,' " *Los Angeles Times,* April 26, 1966.
"If it's a girl . . .": Ibid.
"This pregnancy . . .": Gloria Steinem, "Barbra Streisand Talks About Her 'Million-Dollar Baby,' " *Ladies Home Journal,* August 1966.
"It's the only . . .": *New York Daily News,* April 19, 1966.
"I get so self- . . .": Steinem, op. cit.
"The woman is . . .": Interview with Michel Legrand, *Une Femme Libre,* by Guy Abitan.
"I watched her . . .": Ibid.
"I don't want . . .": Steinem, op. cit.
"My son . . .": Ira Mothner, "Mama Barbra," *Look,* July 25, 1967.

Chapter 18: Rolling Out the (Blood) Red Carpet

"He has his father's . . .": "A Star Is Borne," *Newsweek,* January 23, 1967.
"It's a whole . . .": Ira Mothner, "Mama Barbra," *Look,* July 25, 1967.
"If I were . . .": Ibid.
"The first thing . . .": Ibid.
"I'll have a problem . . .": Sheila Graham, "Barbra Streisand and Elegant Tea," *Hollywood Citizen-News,* April 9, 1966.
"I was at that . . .": David Dworski interview.
"My face?": Bob Thomas, "Barbra's Ambitious to Star in Films," Associated Press, May 16, 1966.
"We were all . . .": Interview with Herb Ross, University of Southern California Cinema-Television Library: Tape PAC 10:9.
"We had been having . . .": Bob Scheerer interview.
"I found her to be . . .": Imero Fiorentino interview.

Chapter 19: Lights, Camera, Perfectionism!

"When friends ask . . .": "Movies Are Hard Work, Says Barbra," *Los Angeles Times,* July 20, 1967.
"There are seven . . .": Charles Champlin, "Perfection Important to Barbra Streisand," *Los Angeles Times,* November 27, 1967.
"Barbra asked me if . . .": Ben Lane interview.
"Gertrude was a wonderful . . .": Vivienne Walker interview.
"I think she was very . . .": Libby Dean interview.
"I feel things . . .": Champlin, op. cit.
"She has youth . . .": Jack Hamilton, "Barbra Streisand: On a Clear Day You Can See Dolly," *Look,* December 16, 1969.
"Okay, Barbra, . . .": Ibid.
"Her relationship with Harry . . .": Marshall Schlom interview.
"I wouldn't have . . .": Vernon Scott, "Wyler and Barbra: 'Things Were Ironed Out,' " *Memphis Commercial Appeal,* February 23, 1969.
"She was a bit . . .": Ibid.
"She fusses over . . .": Axel Madsen, *William Wyler* (New York: T. Y. Crowell, 1973).

"She's so wrapped . . .": Bernard Kantor, Irwin Blacker, Anne Kramer, *Directors at Work* (New York: Funk & Wagnalls, 1970), p. 409.

"She would come . . .": Alta Maloney, " 'Funny Girl' Banned in Egypt," *Boston Herald,* September 29, 1968.

"She had to be . . .": "Symbiosis Is Continued: Director William Wyler and Actress Barbra Streisand Discuss Theirs on 'Funny Girl,' " *Action!* n.d.

"She doesn't go . . .": Kantor et al., op. cit., p. 409.

"I waited for . . .": Doris Klein, "Anne Francis Tells Her Side of Story in Five Months of 'Funny Girl' Filming," *Hollywood Reporter,* January 12, 1968.

"a view of my . . .": Ibid.

"two minutes of . . .": Ibid.

"Every day, Barbra . . .": Ibid.

Chapter 20: Middle East Accord, West Coast Wrap

"My daughter is . . .": Omar Sharif, *The Eternal Male* (Garden City, N.Y.: Doubleday & Co., 1977), p. 79.

"We're in America . . .": Ibid.

"Barbra's villa . . .": Ibid.

"We led the very . . .": Ibid.

"If all Jews . . .": Marjory Adams, "Wyler, Streisand Hit It Off," *Boston Globe,* September 29, 1968.

"I have so . . .": Joyce Haber, "Omar Sharif Loves to Live, Lives to Love," *Los Angeles Times,* October 27, 1968.

"I would love to . . .": Interview with Omar Sharif, "Donahue," 1991.

"Getting women . . .": Haber, op. cit.

"I stayed for twenty . . .": Anne Francis to columnist Sheila Graham.

Chapter 21: Clash of the Co-Starring Titans

"I love Barbra . . .": Interview with Ray Stark, *New York Post,* April 24, 1968.

"I was angling . . .": Interview with Carol Channing, *Los Angeles Herald-Examiner,* July 30, 1967.

"I am wary . . .": Ibid.

"I guess Carol . . .": Charles Champlin, "Barbra Streisand—One of Brooklyn's Sturdy Trees," *Los Angeles Times,* July 3, 1967.

"It's so ridiculous . . .": *Chicago Tribune Magazine,* August 27, 1967.

"The only thing . . .": Ira Mothner, "Barbra," *Look,* October 15, 1968.

"I'm not doing . . .": *Chicago Tribune Magazine,* August 27, 1967.

"We expected this . . .": Richard Zanuck to Ernest Lehman, Ernest Lehman Collection, USC Cinema-Television Library.

"We've created a new . . .": Kevin Thomas, "Gene Kelly Puts 'Hello, Dolly!' Together," *Los Angeles Times,* August 20, 1968.

"Irene is a wonderful . . .": Memo, Ernest Lehman Collection, USC Cinema-Television Library.

"I thought she was . . .": Interview with Ray Stark, New York Post, April 24, 1968.

"She came into the . . .": Murray Spivack interview.

"I think Howard died . . .": Marvin Laird interview.

"He was divine . . .": Mart Crowley interview.

"I think this . . .": Earl Wilson, "This 'Dolly' Smashing," *Los Angeles Herald-Examiner,* May 6, 1968.

"When I heard . . .": Earl Wilson, Ibid.

"He didn't have . . .": Joe Morgenstern, "Streisand's Rite of Passage," *Los Angeles Herald-Examiner*, November 13, 1983.

"They were just . . .": Clive Hirschhorn, *Gene Kelly* (Chicago: Henry Regnery Co., 1975), p. 293.

"You must be . . .": Morgenstern, op. cit.

"The only way to . . .": Earl Wilson, op. cit.

"Stop directing the . . .": Hirschhorn, op. cit., p. 295.

"Cool it . . .": Christina Kirk, "Will Success Unspoil Barbra?" *New York Daily News*, September 15, 1968.

"Nobody in this . . .": Peter Evans Kirk, "From Barbra Streisand—The Last Word," *Cosmopolitan*, February 1974.

"Okay, baby . . .": Michael Leahy, "Wanna Bet Walter Matthau Would Rather Play the Horses," *TV-Guide*, March 3, 1990.

"I'd love to . . .": Allan Hunter, *Walter Matthau* (New York: St. Martin's Press, 1984), p. 94.

"I'm afraid they . . .": Associated Press, July 13, 1968.

"There were things . . .": Hirschhorn, op. cit., p. 296.

Chapter 22: Shattered Hopes, Realized Dreams

"I guarantee you . . .": Earl Wilson, "Barbra's Gala Party," *Los Angeles Herald-Examiner*, September 25, 1968.

"The guys go for . . .": Joyce Haber, "Star Gazing at 'Funny Girl' Fete," *Los Angeles Times*, October 14, 1968.

"In all the years . . .": Interview with Walter Scharf, USC Cinema-Television Library.

"I see that . . .": Peter Noble, "London," *Hollywood Reporter*, January 21, 1969.

"Streisand treated me . . .": Rex Reed, *People Are Crazy Here* (New York: Delacorte Press, 1974), p. 297.

"All the others . . .": Sidney Skolsky, "Tintypes: Barbra Streisand," *Hollywood Citizen-News*, June 13, 1969.

"She'll never accept . . .": Jack Hamilton, "Barbra Streisand: On a Clear Day You Can See Dolly," *Look*, December 16, 1969.

"I know that my . . .": A. H. Weiler, "Three Stars Form Film Production Unit," *New York Times*, June 12, 1969.

"I have had to . . .": John L. Scott, "Elliott Gould—Actor, Auditor, and Husband," *Los Angeles Times*, September 22, 1967.

"Barbra lives her . . .": Diana Lurie, " 'Funny Girl' and Me," *Ladies Home Journal*, August 1969.

"My wife is . . .": Interview with Elliott Gould, *Family Weekly*, April 13, 1969.

"I'm much happier . . .": Sheila Graham, "Streisand-Sharif Date," *Hollywood Citizen-News*, December 4, 1967.

"I didn't hit . . .": Interivew with Elliott Gould, *Los Angeles Times*, June 8, 1969.

"instigated, urged, and . . .": Court documents, Superior Court of California, County of Los Angeles, no. 942542.

"Well, I was very . . .": Ibid.

"I've made up . . .": Dorothy Manners, *Los Angeles Herald-Examiner*, March 6, 1969.

Chapter 23: Private Portraits, Public Failures

"Don't forget . . .": Judy Klemesrud, "Barbra and Rozie's Mother Used to Hope for Her Own Name Up in Lights," *New York Times*, February 23, 1970.

"After all, I . . .": Phyllis Battelle, "Little Sister Syndrome," *Los Angeles Times,* May 28, 1969.

"more power, more . . .": Ibid.

"I don't have . . .": May Campbell, "Barbra Streisand's Half-Sister Starting Closer to the Top," *Los Angeles Times,* February 17, 1969.

"I'm not bold . . .": Ibid.

"Mommy, you're . . .": Dorothy Manners, *Modern Screen,* July 1969.

"It's unnatural to . . .": Richard Warren Lewis, "Playboy Interview: Elliott Gould," *Playboy,* November 1970.

"As your co-director . . .": Telegram, William Wyler to Barbra Streisand, May 16, 1969, William Wyler Collection, UCLA, Arts Special Collections.

"Absolutely not . . .": Albert Goldman, *Elvis* (New York: McGraw-Hill, 1981), pp. 436–37.

"I was aloof . . .": Charles Champlin, "Streisand: A Scintillating Show of Gifts," *Los Angeles Times,* August 5, 1969.

"She sucks! . . .": Goldman, op. cit.

"What did you . . .": Fred L. Worth and Steve D. Tamerius, *Elvis: His Life From A–Z* (Chicago: Contemporary Books, 1988), p. 190.

"Marty Erlichman invited me . . .": Artie Butler interview.

"She began to lose . . .": Clive Davis, *Clive: Inside the Record Business* (New York: Ballantine, 1976), p. 252.

"Your album sales . . .": Ibid.

"Imagine, Warren Beatty . . .": *Photoplay,* June 1970.

"It happened to be . . .": Lawrence Grobel, "Playboy Interview: Barbra Streisand," *Playboy,* October 1977.

Chapter 24: The Fall of the Skyscraper Hairdo

"She was the . . .": Interview with Herb Ross, USC Cinema Television Library.

"I was in a very . . .": John Robert Lloyd interview.

"She only calls me . . .": Wayne Warga, "It Took Lots of Persuasion to Do Barbra's Nude Scene," *Los Angeles Times,* 1970.

"She had the greatest . . .": Jack Solomon interview.

"Harry was like . . .": Don Cash, Jr., interview.

"John Wayne won . . .": Melvyn Bragg, *Richard Burton: A Life* (Boston: Little, Brown, 1988), p. 329.

"No autographs . . .": "Newsmakers," *Newsweek,* November 2, 1970.

"I'm the hottest . . .": Judy Klemesrud, "Now Who's the Greatest Star?" *New York Times,* October 5, 1969.

"She *hated* being . . .": Wayne Bernath interview.

Chapter 25: Bringing Up Barbra

"My principal function . . .": Tom Burke, "The Sheik of Malibu," *Esquire,* September 1972.

"I read the script . . .": Jacoba Atlas and Steve Jaffe, "Barbra and Ryan in Bogdanovich's Salute to the Zany Comedians of the '30s—What's Up Doc?" *Show,* April 1972.

"That's the way . . .": Ibid.

"She's not ambitious . . .": Richard Warren Lewis, "Playboy Interview: Elliott Gould," *Playboy,* November 1970.

"I am Barbra's . . .": Earl Wilson, *Show Business Laid Bare* (New York: G. P. Putnam's Sons, 1974), p. 254.

"I'd never done a . . .": Atlas and Jaffe, op. cit.

"I was lucky because . . .": Ibid.

"He asked me to do . . .": Ibid.

"She doesn't work . . .": Ibid.

"Ryan, we're in . . .": Ibid., p. 20.

"Do you think . . .": Ibid.

"She has a tendency . . .": Jerry Tallmer, "Director Peter Bogdanovich," *New York Post,* March 1972.

"We did it with . . .": Ibid.

"I knew about . . .": Rex Reed, *Valentines and Vitriol* (New York: Delacorte Press, 1977), p. 247.

"I got a glimpse . . .": Ibid., p. 247.

"She thought that . . .": Crist, op. cit., p. 20.

"I hated it . . .": Joseph Gelmis, "On Being Barbra," *Newsday,* January 21, 1973.

"In making a . . .": Ibid.

"I had ideas . . .": Said to Bob Thomas, Associated Press, 1972.

"Equal job opportunities . . .": Ibid.

"All of a sudden . . .": Elizabeth Kaye, "Barbra, The Superstar Who Wants to Be a Woman," *McCall's,* April 1975.

"It was a wonderful . . .": Ibid.

"Because I am . . .": Gelmis, op. cit.

"With me and . . .": Dorothy Manners, "Barbra Streisand: Finished With Musicals?" *Los Angeles Herald-Examiner,* May 7, 1972.

"I asked a . . .": Earl Wilson, "Barbra Likes 'Sandbox,' " *Los Angeles Herald-Examiner,* December 28, 1972.

"Spanking. It saves . . .": Judy Klemesrud, "Barbra and Rozie's Mother Used to Hope for Her Own Name Up in Lights," *New York Times,* February 23, 1970.

"And never give . . .": Ibid.

"My name is . . .": Guy Flatley, "Bewitched, Barbra'd, and Bewildered," *New York Times,* January 21, 1973.

"When a nice . . .": James Bacon, "Streisand: I Work Like a Dog," *Los Angeles Herald-Examiner,* December 19, 1972.

Chapter 26: Intersecting Icons

"She has a tendency . . .": Peer J. Oppenheimer, "Streisand, Our Poll Winner, As Seen by Three Friends," *Family Weekly,* May 5, 1974.

"Honey, when . . .": Interview with James Woods, *New York Post,* October 27, 1989.

"Barbra finds it . . .": Oppenheimer, op. cit.

"I think of . . .": Judith Crist, *Take 22* (New York: Viking, 1984), p. 222.

"She's inquisitive . . .": Oppenheimer, op. cit.

"Other people . . .": *Halliwell's Filmgoer's Companion,* 9th ed. (New York: Harper and Row, 1990), p. 921.

"You must realize . . .": Oppenheimer, op. cit.

"I went up . . .": Elizabeth Kaye, "Barbra: The Superstar Who Wants to Be a Woman," *McCall's,* April 1975.

"I was learning . . .": Ibid.

"Redford's the best . . .": Joyce Haber, "The Bergmans: The Way They Are," *Los Angeles Times,* March 10, 1974.

"I had to beg . . .": Rex Reed, *Valentines and Vitriol* (New York: Delacorte Press, 1977), p. 227.

"A week before . . .": Jack Haley, Jr., to columnist Joyce Haber.

"I felt I . . .": Lawrence Grobel, "Barbra Streisand: I'm Just Beginning to Accept Myself," *Newsday,* October 16, 1977.

"Watching it on . . .": Interview with Glenda Jackson, *New York Times.*

"Dwight, *you* . . .": *London Sunday Times,* 1973.

Chapter 27: The Normal Heart

"When I took the . . .": *Advocate,* May 19, 1976.

"Jon is a very . . .": Anne Fadiman, "Barbra Puts Her Career on the Line with *Yentl,*" *Life,* December 1983.

"people took their . . .": Jean Cox, "Barbra and Jon: The Way They Are," *Women's Wear Daily,* March 4, 1974.

"I actually enjoy . . .": Ibid.

"When Ray Stark . . .": Amy Archerd, "Barbra Farewells Ray Stark: Future as She Dictates," *Variety,* July 17, 1974.

"Barbra isn't crazy . . .": "Brice Twice," *Newsweek,* July 18, 1974.

"Have you checked . . .": Interview with Ray Stark, *Los Angeles Times,* October 27, 1989.

"Figuratively speaking . . .": Judith Crist, *Take 22* (New York: Viking, 1984), p. 286.

"Herbie had to . . .": Ibid.

"Herbie took the . . .": Ibid.

"It's hard, when . . .": Wayne Warga, "Streisand, Caan Making a Lady Out of 'Funny Girl,' " *Los Angeles Times,* June 2, 1974.

"They've recorded . . .": Joyce Haber, "Barbra's 'Butterfly' Album Untracked?" *Los Angeles Times,* June 25, 1974.

"I don't even . . .": Joyce Haber, "Streisand 'Happiest She's Ever Been,' " *Los Angeles Times,* June 27, 1974.

"Bloody awful . . .": "Playboy Interview: David Bowie," *Playboy,* September 1976.

"I'm not going . . .": Anna Quindlen, "Barbra Streisand, Superstar," *New York Post,* March 15, 1975.

"Two men in . . .": James Bacon, *Los Angeles Herald-Examiner,* March 21, 1975.

"Dear Miss . . .": Joyce Haber, "Barbra Finds Time for Fans," *Los Angeles Times,* May 9, 1974.

Chapter 28: Somewhere Over the Rainbow Road

"James Taylor and . . .": John Gregory Dunne, "Gone Hollywood," *Esquire,* September 1976.

"Barbra Streisand just . . .": Cher interview by Randall Riese and James Carreira, 1977.

"The world is waiting . . .": Marie Brenner, "Collision on *Rainbow Road,*" *New Times,* January 24, 1975.

"beautiful, sensual . . .": Jerry Parker, "Producer Peters: I'm Fighting for What I Believe In," *Los Angeles Times,* November 7, 1976.

"Jon has a way . . .": Elizabeth Kaye, "Barbra: The Superstar Who Wants to Be a Woman," *McCall's,* April 1975.

"[He's] a man . . .": Lee Grant, "Streisand in 'Star Is Born': The Way It Is," *Los Angeles Times,* May 19, 1976.

"It's very fragile . . .": Lesley Ann Warren, "Snip, Snip," *People,* July 19, 1976.

"She's worried about . . .": Joyce Haber, "And Now, Heeere's—," *Los Angeles Times,* July 14, 1975.

"How could I . . .": Frank Pierson, "My Battles With Barbra and Jon," *New York,* November 15, 1976.

"I couldn't just . . .": Ibid.

"I don't feel . . .": Ibid.

"He will be . . .": Mary Murphy, "Kris Set for 'Star Is Born' Lead," *Los Angeles Times,* September 20, 1975.

"She had recorded . . .": Paul Williams interview.

"How can I . . .": Pierson, op. cit.

Chapter 29: The Final Cut

"If this film . . .": Frank Pierson, "My Battles With Barbra and Jon," *New York,* November 15, 1976.

"Jon and I . . .": *Advocate,* May 19, 1976.

"Who knows who's . . .": " 'A Star Is Born' Films in Arizona," *Hollywood Reporter,* April 19, 1976.

"Hey, you *motherfuckers! . . .": Advocate,* May 19, 1976.

"Who's the . . .": Arthur Bell, "Barbra Streisand Doesn't Get Ulcers—She Gives 'Em," *Village Voice,* April 26, 1976.

"You owe my . . .": "Newsmakers," *Newsweek,* April 5, 1976.

"I'm scared to . . .": "People," *Time,* April 5, 1976.

"It's the hardest . . .": Lawrence B. Eisenberg, "Barbra Streisand: Tough, Temperamental, Tremendous," *Cosmopolitan,* March 1977.

"My fucking . . .": Ibid.

"I gave him . . .": Mary Blume, "Flip-flop Life of Elliott Gould," *Los Angeles Times,* December 9, 1973.

"Listen, where . . .": Pierson, op. cit.

"Frank is a very . . .": Peter Zinner interview.

"Sometimes these maids . . .": Georgia Holt and Phyllis Quinn, with Sue Russell, *Star Mothers* (New York: Simon & Schuster, 1988), p. 367.

"She's in there . . .": Jerry Parker, "Producer Peters: I'm Fighting for What I Believe In," *Los Angeles Times,* November 7, 1976.

"I heard everything . . .": Francesco Scavullo quoting Streisand during an appearance on "Geraldo," January 2, 1991.

"I did two . . .": Barbara Walters, "Barbara's Off-Camera Secrets," *Star,* April 21, 1987.

"I don't have . . .": "The Crowd Gaped On as the 'Star' Was Borne Away by Limo," *Variety,* December 21, 1976.

Chapter 30: A Star Is Bored

"Nothing like it . . .": "Peoplescape: How Plucky Can Ya Get?" *Los Angeles,* May 1976.

"had a vicious nature . . .": Court documents, Superior Court of the State of California, County of Los Angeles, no. WEC 50878.

"You just don't . . .": Kevin Kelly, *One Singular Sensation: The Michael Bennett Story* (Garden City, N.Y.: Doubleday, 1990), p. 168.

"[Barbra] knew that . . .": Andrew Yule, *Sean Connery* (New York: Donald I. Fine, 1992), p. 229.

"Good God . . .": Ibid.

"All of a sudden . . .": Michael Barackman, "Pop Duets: A Top-10 Marriage," *Los Angeles Times,* November 26, 1978.

"Should I wear it . . .": *Look,* April 2, 1979.

"I told him . . .": "Paul Jabara, "Streisand and Summer Team Up for a Duet of Disco and Egos," *Us,* November 13, 1979.

"Barbra and Donna . . .": Ibid.

"She never liked to . . .": Liz Brooks interview.

"It was the . . .": Interview with Roslyn Kind, *Los Angeles Herald-Examiner,* December 27, 1973.

"Barbra has *never* helped . . .": Richard Gordon interview.

"It's mostly my . . .": Allan Hunter, *Gene Hackman* (London: W. H. Allen, 1987), p. 162.

"the part was . . .": Interview with Jean-Claude Tramont, *Los Angeles Herald-Examiner,* March 13, 1981.

"very difficult on . . .": *Los Angeles Times,* May 14, 1980.

"You know how . . .": Roderick Mann, "Lisa Eichhorn Says Her Luck Has Turned," *Los Angeles Times,* January 15, 1981.

"She was just . . .": Ibid.

"I suppose it . . .": Ibid.

Chapter 31: "After Her Father's Death . . ."

"I want to be . . .": Edwin Miller, *"Seventeen" Interviews Film Stars and Superstars* (New York: Macmillan, 1970), p. 150.

"Barbra called me because . . .": Ted Allan interview.

"I want you to . . .": Chaim Potok, "Barbra and Chaim Potok," *Esquire,* October 1982.

"She met with me . . .": Rabbi Daniel Lapin interview.

"I think there . . .": Wayne Warga, "Barbra Streisand's Search for Her Father," *McCall's,* January 1984.

"First of all . . .": USC Cinema-Television Library.

"it just wasn't . . .": Ibid.

"I'm in love . . .": Steven Bach, *Final Cut* (New York: New American Library, Plume, 1986), p. 393.

"No buts . . .": Ibid.

"The picture nobody . . .": Ibid., p. 394.

"Like Auerbach . . .": Ibid., p. 395.

"That's why you . . .": Ibid., p. 401.

"I sold it . . .": Sally Ogle Davis, "Why Isn't This Funny Girl Laughing?" *Los Angeles,* November 1983.

"Even I can't . . .": Ibid.

"Believe me, there's . . .": Dale Pollack, "Barbra Streisand and Her 'Yentl,' " *Los Angeles Times,* October 16, 1983.

"It was time . . .": Warga, op. cit.

"Barbra was always . . .": Anne Fadiman, "Barbra Puts Her Career on the Line With *Yentl,*" *Life,* December 1983.

"It's not so . . .": Ibid.

"I found that . . .": USC Cinema-Television Library.

"Do you know . . .": Cliff Jahr, "Barbra Streisand's Biggest Gamble," *Ladies Home Journal,* December 1983.

"A man can . . .": Bob Thomas, "Barbra Did It Her Way," *Orange Coast Daily Pilot,* January 15, 1984.

"Please, we're going . . .": Pollack, op. cit.

"The leading actress . . .": Isaac Bashevis Singer, "I. B. Singer Talks to I. B. Singer About the Movie 'Yentl,' " *New York Times,* January 29, 1984.

"I did not . . .": Ibid.

Chapter 32: Homecoming

"I'm trying to . . .": Brad Darrach, "Celebration of a Father," *People,* December 12, 1983.

"to show people . . .": Nat Segaloff, *Hurricane Billy* (New York: William Morrow & Co., 1990), p. 246.

"She and I jumped . . .": Paul Grein, "Erlichman Back as Streisand's Manager," *Billboard,* February 15, 1986.

"I never have . . .": Jim Watters, "The Movies, the Magic, the Madness, the Memories," *Life,* May 1986.

"That's what I love . . .": Interview by Gene Shalit, "The Today Show," November 1987.

"I'd like to . . .": Streisand quoting Martin Ritt, ibid.

"I felt totally . . .": Ibid.

"Dear Dustin . . .": Martin Ritt to Dustin Hoffman, June 17, 1986, Martin Ritt Collection, Special Collections, Academy of Motion Picture Arts and Sciences.

"For some time . . .": "Just for the Record," pamphlet by Barbra Streisand, Columbia Records, 1991.

"I was surprised . . .": Pamela Lansden, "Take One," *People,* February 1, 1988.

"If I want . . .": *Long Beach Press-Telegram,* March 9, 1988.

"I'm putting myself . . .": David Wallace, "Sonny Side Up," *Us,* October 3, 1988.

"He has enormous . . .": Ibid.

"What lens are . . .": Nina J. Easton, "From 'Vice' to 'Sweet Hearts,' " *Los Angeles Times,* September 21, 1988.

"I decided there . . .": Wallace, op. cit.

"I remember somebody said . . .": Lance Brown interview.

"I'm happy . . .": Jenny Cullen, "Streisand in Love," *Ladies Home Journal,* June 1988.

"I had met his trainer . . .": Pam Loubman interview.

"I think he had . . .": Tony Sands interview.

"Don wanted to work . . .": Diane Albright interview.

"I always have . . .": David Wallace, op. cit.

"Barbra was more willing . . .": Judy Ellis, "Copy Again," *Life,* April 1989.

"We genuinely tried . . .": Ibid.

"We all consider . . .": Ibid.

Chapter 33: Casting Caution to the Tides

"I asked [Harris] . . .": Scott Siegel and Barbara Siegel, "The Prince of Tides," *Drama-Logue,* December 19, 1991.

"It makes the penis . . .": Stephanie Mansfield, "Nick Nolte, Up From the Gutter," *Gentleman's Quarterly,* October 1991.

"I hear you've been . . .": Ibid.

"There haven't been many women . . .": Michelle Green and David Wallace, "He's No Teacher's Pet," *People,* November 5, 1984.

"I saw a lot of pain . . .": Siegel and Siegel, op. cit.

"I decided this was . . .": Hilary de Vries, "Streisand the Storyteller," *Los Angeles Times Magazine,* December 8, 1991.

"I had a theory . . .": Interview with Nick Nolte by Steve Kmetko, KCBS News, Los Angeles, 1991.

"I looked at all . . .": Ed Blank, " 'Tides' Turning for Barbra," Scripps-Howard News Service, December 20, 1991.

"I thought *I* was . . .": New York press junket, Columbia Pictures, November 1991.

"Needless to say . . .": Columbia Pictures press release, 1991.

"There are, of course . . .": Ibid.
"She was expensively dressed . . .": Pat Conroy, *The Prince of Tides* (Boston: Houghton Mifflin, 1986), p. 47.
"By any measure . . .": Ibid., p. 123.
"Her beauty . . .": Ibid., p. 377.
"Parents can put you . . .": Blank, op. cit.
"When I first met Barbra . . .": Robert Epstein, "Magnolias, Palms: 'Tides' Author Meets Hollywood,", *Los Angeles Times,* December 26, 1991.
"It's just scary . . .": Siegel and Siegel, op. cit.
"Jason has never . . .": Joe Morgenstern, "Barbra Streisand," *Cosmopolitan,* October 1991.
"Barbra showed me . . .": Epstein, op. cit.
"Bernard should be . . .": Siegel and Siegel, op. cit.
"No, no, no . . .": Ibid.
"I always think he . . .": Ibid.
"She pulled up at . . .": Lydia Encinas interview.

Chapter 34: Southern Exposure

" 'Great God!' . . .": Jim McDill interview.
"Right now, regrettably . . .": Frank P. Jarrell, "Royal Welcome Awaits 'Prince,' " *Charleston Post-Courier,* May 13, 1990.
"Streisand was going to . . .": John Williams interview.

Chapter 35: The Undertow

"These were just regular . . .": John C. Williams, " 'Prince of Tides' Filming Gets Under Way," *Savannah Morning News,* June 19, 1990.
"She seemed delicate and . . .": Nancy Rhett interview.
"I think she flirts . . .": Paul Sylbert interview.
" 'Bridge?' . . .": Don Rhodes, "Director Streisand Has an Eye for Detail," *Augusta Chronicle,* July 15, 1990.
"They had on our . . .": Ibid.
"She is very precise . . .": Frank P. Jarrell, "Actress Absorbs Southern Style," *Charleston Post-Courier,* July 15, 1990.
"She's got eight . . .": Frank P. Jarrell, "Under Production," *Charleston Post-Courier,* August 12, 1990.
"In a film there . . .": Ibid.
"Basically, Sylbert said . . .": Frank Jarrell interview.
"She came in at . . .": Becky Kilby interview.
"*That* was one thing . . .": Norma Woods interview.

Chapter 36: Guards at the Gate

"I can understand . . .": Fred Trask interview.
"Her nails . . .": Paddy Calistro, "Barbra! Scratch the Nails," *Los Angeles Times,* January 17, 1992.
"Women who aren't . . .": Ibid.
"She wants us . . .": Ibid.
"My nightmare is . . .": Lawrence Grobel, "Playboy Interview: Barbra Streisand," *Playboy,* October 1977.

"Talk about beating . . .": John C. Williams, "T-Shirt Sales Almost Cost Beaufort Artist 'Princely' Court Fight," *Savannah Morning News,* August 3, 1990.

"I didn't expect . . .": Jane Fuhrman and Kay Graves, "Beaufort Is Going Bonkers for Barbra," *Savannah Morning News,* July 1, 1990.

"Nick Nolte was like . . .": Evelyn Grayson interview.

"What he basically wanted . . .": Charlotte Gunnells, "Nolte Wows Academy Students," *Beaufort Gazette,* May 14, 1990.

"That was the most . . .": T. C. Hunter, "TCL Instructor Helps Nick Nolte Learn Wingo's Lowcountry Lingo," *Beaufort Gazette,* June 5, 1990.

"the upper echelon . . .": Dannye Romine, "Prince and Princess of Tides," *Charlotte Observer,* July 29, 1990.

"The idea of reading . . .": Bill Thompson, "Her Name Is Barbra," *Charlotte Post-Courier,* December 22, 1981.

"[Nolte] had some . . .": John C. Williams, "Nolte's Role Gives Accent Flavor," *Savannah Morning News,* June 10, 1990.

"I went up into his . . .": Steve Dollar, "Filming of 'Prince of Tides' to Begin in Beaufort," *Savannah Morning News,* June 17, 1990.

"The helicopter swooped . . .": Fred Trask, "The Casualties of Moviemaking," *Beaufort Gazette,* July 23, 1990.

"not in a respectable . . .": Ibid.

"There were plenty of . . .": Ibid.

Chapter 37: Director at Work

"My mother had . . .": Scott Siegel and Barbara Siegel, "The Prince of Tides," *Drama-Logue,* December 19, 1991.

"Barbra Streisand is up . . .": Cindy Adams, *New York Post,* August 28, 1990.

"I always do . . .": New York press junket, Columbia Pictures, 1991.

"You don't get good . . .": Joe Morgenstern, "Barbra Streisand," *Cosmopolitan,* October 1991.

"I didn't know what . . .": Don Rhodes, " 'The Prince of Tides' Filmed in South Carolina," *Augusta Chronicle,* December 20, 1991.

"It's been pounded . . .": Siegel and Siegel, op. cit.

"Acting can either . . .": Hilary de Vries, "Prisoner of His Image," *Los Angeles Times,* November 17, 1991.

"When we were doing . . .": Siegel and Siegel, op. cit.

"He [Nick] was getting . . .": *USA Today,* December 21, 1991.

"The shy actress . . .": New York press junket, Columbia Pictures, 1991.

"I got a feeling . . .": Siegel and Siegel, op. cit.

"I like audiences . . .": *USA Today,* December 21, 1991.

"Hi, I'm Barbra . . .": Morgenstern, op. cit.

"I don't know Jason . . .": David Knight interview.

"I filmed my . . .": New York press junket, Columbia Pictures, 1991.

Chapter 38: Sudden Shock of Light

"I had spent twelve . . .": Bill Harris interview.

"The argument that . . .": Andy Marx, "Who Are These People?" *Los Angeles Times,* March 29, 1992.

"[Streisand] conjures up . . .": Andy Marx, "Director's Chair," *Los Angeles Times,* November 10, 1991.

"Women are so . . .": Paul Rosenfield, "Barbra's New Direction," *Ladies Home Journal,* February 1992.

"She would ask to . . .": Elaine Joyce interview.

Chapter 39: A Woman's Reach

"I can't say . . .": Diane Haithman, "Hollywood's Party Politics," *Los Angeles Times,* January 31, 1992.

"Our foreign policy . . .": Pete Hamill, "Barbra the Great: Talented Girl on a Triumphal March," *Cosmopolitan,* February 1968.

"I will unabashedly . . .": Judy Klemesrud, "Shirley: Let's Tax Diapers," *New York Times,* August 8, 1971.

"It was a fundraiser . . .": Sen. George McGovern interview.

"I can't understand . . .": Guy Flatley, "Bewitched, Barbra'd, Bewildered," *New York Times,* January 21, 1973.

"It was April . . .": Timothy K. Smith, "What Does Barbra Believe In, Anyway?" *Wall Street Journal,* May 14, 1993.

"Our technology . . .": Clarke Taylor, "Streisand: Women in Film Have 'Special Role,' " *Los Angeles Times,* May 3, 1986.

"She started with . . .": Ronald Brownstein, *The Power and the Glitter* (New York: Pantheon Books, 1980), p. 309.

"Why take the risk . . .": Ibid., p. 312.

"I am convinced . . .": Aleene MacMinn, "Morning Report: Largess," *Los Angeles Times,* May 31, 1989.

"Barbra Streisand has . . .": Aids Project, Geoffrey-Martin Cyr, "Streisand, Geffen Honors," *Los Angeles Optimist,* Winter 1992–93.

"Elizabeth Taylor is an . . .": David Lacaillade interview.

Chapter 40: Emancipation

"We were climbing the . . .": Terry Schleder interview.

"Has someone asked . . .": Jane Galbraith, "Telluride Cites Its Record, Calls Boycott Unfair," *Los Angeles Times,* December 17, 1992.

"Since she announced her . . .": Terry White interview.

"I don't like the way you . . .": Anecdote related by Liz Smith *New York Daily News,* 1993.

"She was also in town . . .": Eleanor Clift interview.

"I am *not* . . .": Mick Brown, "Daddy, Can You Hear Me Now?" *London Guardian,* March 31, 1984.

"In general, Washington is . . .": Mary Matalin interview.

"The inauguration was probably . . .": Susan Estrich interview.

"She's my version . . .": Maureen Dowd, "Film Star Cheers; Tennis Star Loses," *New York Times,* July 1, 1993.

"She's not knocked . . .": Clarke Taylor, "Streisand: Women in Film have 'Special Role,' " *Los Angeles Times,* May 3, 1986.

"As she's gotten . . .": Kevin Sessums, "Queen of Tides," *Vanity Fair,* September 1991.

"Does Barbra . . .": "Interview with Roseanne Arnold," *Advocate,* March 9, 1973.

"She is like . . .": "Show Business/Broadway," *Time,* April 10, 1964.

"I don't know what else . . .": New York press junket, Columbia Pictures, November 1991.

Select Bibliography

ABRAMS, ARNOLD. "Streisand: Lonely 'Funny Girl.' " *W*, March 21, 1964.

ALEXANDER, SHANA. "A Born Loser's Success and Precarious Love." *Life*, May 22, 1964.

ATLAS, JACOBA, AND STEVE JAFFE. "Barbra and Ryan in Bogdanovich's Salute to the Zany Comedies of the '30s—What's Up, Doc?" *Show*, April 1972.

BACH, STEVEN. *Final Cut: Dreams and Disaster in the Making of Heaven's Gate*. New York: William Morrow and Co., 1985.

BLANK, ED. " 'Tides' Turning for Barbra." Scripps-Howard News Service.

BRENNER, MARIE. "Collision on *Rainbow Road.*" *New Times*, January 24, 1975.

BROWNING, NORMA LEE. "Will Barbra Make It Big in Movies?" *Sunday News*, September 24, 1967.

BROWNSTEIN, RONALD. *The Power and the Glitter*. New York: Pantheon, 1990.

CONROY, PAT. *The Prince of Tides*. Boston: Houghton Mifflin Co., 1986.

CONSIDINE, SHAUN. *Barbra Streisand: The Woman, the Myth, the Music*. New York: Delacorte Press, 1985.

CRIST, JUDITH. *Take 22: Moviemakers on Moviemaking*. New York: Viking, 1984.

DE VRIES, HILARY. "Streisand the Storyteller." *Los Angeles Times Magazine*, December 8, 1991.

DUNNE, JOHN GREGORY. "Gone Hollywood." *Esquire*, September 1976.

EPSTEIN, ROBERT. "Magnolias, Palms: 'Tides' Author Meets Hollywood." *Los Angeles Times*, December 26, 1991.

FADIMAN, ANNE. "Barbra Puts Her Career on the Line With *Yentl.*" *Life*, December 1983.

GAVIN, JAMES. *Intimate Nights: The Golden Age of New York Cabaret*. New York: Grove Weidenfeld, 1991.

GRAHAM, SHEILA. *Confessions of a Hollywood Columnist*. New York: William Morrow and Co., 1969.

GROBEL, LAWRENCE. "Playboy Interview: Barbra Streisand." *Playboy*, October 1977.

HAMILL, PETE. "Good-bye Brooklyn, Hello Fame." *Saturday Evening Post*, July 27, 1963.

HARVEY, STEPHEN. *Directed by Vincente Minnelli*. New York: Harper and Row, 1989.

HOLDEN, STEPHEN. "Barbra Streisand Talks (a Lot) About Fame and 'Prince of Tides.' " *New York Times*, 1991.

HOLT, GEORGIA, AND PHYLLIS QUINN, WITH SUE RUSSELL. *Star Mothers*. New York: Simon & Schuster, 1988.

JARRELL, FRANK P. "Under Production." *Charleston Post-Courier,* August 12, 1990.

JORDAN, RENE. *The Greatest Star.* New York: G. P. Putnam's Sons, 1975.

KANTOR, BERNARD, IRWIN BLACKER, AND ANNE KRAMER. *Directors at Work.* New York: Funk & Wagnalls, 1970.

KAYE, ELIZABETH. "Barbra: The Superstar Who Wants to Be a Woman." *McCalls,* April 1975.

KLEIN, DORIS. "Anne Francis Tells Her Side of Story in Five Months of 'Funny Girl' Filming." *Hollywood Reporter,* January 12, 1968.

LURIE, DIANA. " 'Funny Girl' and Me." *Ladies Home Journal,* August 1969.

——. "They All Come Thinking I Can't Be That Great." *Life,* March 18, 1966.

McDONNELL, ANNA. "Cracking *Nuts.*" *Premiere,* December 1987.

MADSEN, AXEL. *William Wyler.* New York: T. Y. Crowell, 1973.

MICHAELSON, JUDY. "The New Stars." *New York Post,* September 13, 1963.

MILLER, ALLAN. *A Passion for Acting.* New York: Backstage Books, 1992.

MILLER, EDWIN. *"Seventeen" Interviews Film Stars and Superstars.* New York: Macmillan, 1970.

MORGAN, THOMAS B. "Superbarbra." *Look,* April 5, 1966.

MOTHNER, IRA. "Mama Barbra." *Look,* July 25, 1967.

OPPENHEIMER, PEER J. "Streisand, Our Poll Winner; As Seen by Three Friends." *Family Weekly,* May 5, 1974.

PIERSON, FRANK. "My Battles With Barbra and Jon." *New York,* November 15, 1976.

POGREBIN, LETTY COTTIN. *Deborah, Golda, and Me: Being Female and Jewish in America.* New York: Crown Publishers, 1991.

POTOK, CHAIM. "Barbra Streisand and Chaim Potok." *Esquire,* October 1982.

REED, REX. *Do You Sleep in the Nude?* New York: New American Library, 1968.

RENNERT, AMY. "Family Secrets." *San Francisco Focus,* December 1991.

RHODES, DON. "Director Streisand Has an Eye for Detail." *Augusta Chronicle,* July 15, 1990.

ROMINE, DANNYE. "Prince and Princess of Tides." *Charlotte Observer,* July 29, 1990.

ROSENFIELD, PAUL. "Barbra's New Direction." *Ladies Home Journal,* February 1992.

SANDERS, COYNE STEVEN. *Rainbow's End: The Judy Garland Show.* New York: William Morrow and Co., 1990.

SAVOY, MAGGIE. "Barbra's Top Fan Makes It on Her Own." *Los Angeles Times,* March 14, 1969.

SESSUMS, KEVIN. "Queen of Tides." *Vanity Fair,* September 1991.

SHARIF, OMAR. *The Eternal Male.* Garden City, N.Y.: Doubleday, 1976.

"Show Business/Broadway." *Time,* April 10, 1964.

SIEGEL, SCOTT, AND BARBARA SIEGEL. "The Prince of Tides." *Drama-Logue,* December 19, 1991.

SMITH, JOE. *Off the Record,* ed. by Mitchell Fink. New York: Warner Books, 1988.

SPADA, JAMES, WITH CHRISTOPHER NICKENS. *Streisand: The Woman and the Legend.* Garden City, N.Y.: Doubleday Dolphin, 1981.

STEINEM, GLORIA. "Barbra Streisand Talks About Her 'Million-Dollar Baby.' " *Ladies Home Journal,* August 1966.

WALLACE, DAVID. "Sonny Side Up." *Us,* October 3, 1988.

WARGA, WAYNE. "Barbra Streisand's Search for Her Father." *McCall's,* January 1984.

WEIDMAN, JEROME. "I Remember Barbra." *Holiday,* November 1963.

WILSON, EARL. *The Show Business Nobody Knows.* New York, 1974.

Acknowledgments

Since she burst forth on the national scene in Broadway's *Funny Girl* at the age of twenty-one, *so* much has been said, written, rumored, speculated, insinuated, and propagated about Barbra Joan Streisand that separating legend from fact was one of the great challenges of this book. It was not, suffice it to say, an easy task.

My job was exacerbated by the fact that Barbra Streisand, arguably the most powerful woman in Hollywood (and then some), is infamous within her group of friends, acquaintances, coworkers, and the industry at large, for not wanting *anything* said about her to the press—negative, positive, or otherwise. Several of the people contacted for this book, who declined to be interviewed, prefaced their apologies with, "I'd *like* to talk to you, but . . . "

People, it seems, are afraid of rousing the wrath of Streisand. It is understandable, then, that many of the more than two hundred people who *did* talk to me did so under the cloak of anonymity. Nevertheless, *they* know who they are, and I am grateful for their recollections and insights.

I am even more indebted to Barbra's friends, former friends, acquaintances, and coworkers who not only agreed to speak with me, but also allowed me to print their names herein. Among them were many who have never before spoken about Barbra, or their relationship with her, for publication. Although numerous interviews were conducted with people connected to all phases of Barbra's life, I am particularly indebted to those who helped shed light on her early days, which has heretofore been shrouded in myth and mystery. Among them: Sheldon Spiro, whose father, Nathan, was a close friend of Barbra's father, Emanuel Streisand; Ed Frankel, Barbra's childhood neighbor and playmate;

Diane Lemm, Barbra's high school girlfriend; Allan Miller, Barbra's first acting teacher, friend, and surrogate parent when she was sixteen; Burke McHugh, the man who first discovered her and hired her for his night-club when she was eighteen; Ted Rozar, her first manager; Irvin Arthur, her first agent; Donald and John Softness, her first press agents; and Glenn Jordan, the director of her first Off-Broadway musical.

Particularly rewarding to me was the work conducted regarding Barbra's political activism, and my interview with former United States Senator George McGovern. It was McGovern's 1972 campaign that marked Barbra's first real interest in presidential politics. I also enjoyed the sharp wit and astute observations of Susan Estrich, a professor of law at USC and former campaign manager for Michael Dukakis; Mary Matalin, former campaign manager for George Bush; and Eleanor Clift, political correspondent for *Newsweek*.

For their various contributions to this work, I would also like to acknowledge the following:

Paul Adamo
Rupert Adkisson
Diane Albright
Ted Allan
Lee Allen
J. B. Allin
Frederic Ansis
Ellen Aron
Buddy Barnett
Greg Harrett
Dr. Nessa Bell
Wayne Bernath
Gordon Berry
Christine Bocek
Abba Bogin
Liz Brooks
Lance Brown
Chris Bull
Artie Butler
Stephen Campbell
Bernicia and Gilbert Carreira
James Carreira
Don Cash, Jr.

Rose Clark
Liz Collumb
Ned Comstock
Marilyn Cooper
Steve Coz
Mart Crowley
Wilma Curley
Alan Davies
Francisco "Chico" Day
Libby Dean
Matt DeHaven
Dom DeLuise
Barry Dennen
Ray Diffen
Roy and Sachi Domingo
Jacqueline Duobinis
David Dworski
Nina J. Easton
Lydia Encinas
Christopher Esposito
Richard Falk
Ashley Feinstein
Vivienne Feuerstein

Imero Fiorentino
Jules Fisher
Hugh Brian Fleming
Theresa Frank
Joe Franklin
Jerry George
Tammy Gill
Joan Glynn
Michael Glynn
Sylvia Gold
Hazel Golden
Joyce Golden
Terry Golden
Richard Gordon
Evelyn Grayson
Martin Gross
Charlene M. Gunnells
Blair Hammond
Bill Harris
George Harvell
Tiger Haynes
Luther Henderson
Peter Hoffman
Dolores Hope
Don Hunstein
Angela Hynes
Frank Jarrell
Lorri L. Jean
Marc Jordan
Elaine Joyce
Joy Kashiwagi
Linda Kashiwagi
Aaron Kass
Becky Kilby
David Knight
Florence Kominsky
Nancy Koplin
David Lacaillade
Marvin Laird
Ben Lane
Rabbi Daniel Lapin

Linda Laucella
Bonni Lee
Terry Leong
Richard Lewine
Pamela Loubman
Bob Luthardt, Jr.
Mike Mansdorf
Jim McDill
Sandy Meehan
Buzz Miller
Joanne Mitchell
Martha Moffett
Joanna Molloy
Charlie Montgomery
Michael Musto
May Muth
Chris Nickens
Neal Peters
Alice Phillips
Lathornia E. Pierry
Phil Piga
Sid Ramin
Nancy Rhett
Robert Richards
Eli Rill
Howard Roessel
Harold Rome
Jonathan Rosenthal
Joel Rothschild
William Roy
George Rush
Ruth Ryon
Mariann Sabol
Coyne Steven Sanders
Tony Sands
Marilyn Saposh
Robert Scheerer
Terry Schleder
Marshall Schlom
Bob Schulenberg
Robert J. Schwartz

Stanley Simmonds
Barbra Solomon
Jack Solomon
Jim Spada
Murray Spivack
Roz Starr
Dan Striepeke
Paul Sylbert
Renee Taylor
Anne Thompson
Faye Thompson
Fred Trask
Cherry Vanilla

Jim Vidakovich
Val Virga
John Voland
Frank Volpe
Vivienne Walker
Royce Wallace
Barbara Westerland
John Williams
Paul Williams
Neil Wolfe
Norma Woods
Peter Zinner

I would also like to acknowledge the following organizations, libraries, archival institutions, and their staffs:

The Academy of Television Arts and Sciences, North Hollywood
The American Film Institute, Los Angeles
Aspen Gay and Lesbian Community Services Center, Aspen
Beaufort Chamber of Commerce, Beaufort, South Carolina
The Beverly Hills Public Library, Beverly Hills
The Billy Rose Theatre Collection, Lincoln Center Library for the Performing Arts, New York City
Boycott Colorado, Denver
Brooklyn Chamber of Commerce, Brooklyn
Brooklyn Historical Society, Brooklyn
Erasmus Hall High School, Brooklyn
Frances Howard Goldwyn Library, Hollywood
Los Angeles Gay and Lesbian Community Services Center, Los Angeles
Margaret Herrick Library, Academy of Motion Picture Arts and Sciences, Beverly Hills
Museum of Television and Radio, New York
National Academy of Recording Arts and Sciences, Burbank
National Library on Money and Politics, Washington, D.C.
New York Public Library, New York City
San Francisco Public Library, San Francisco
University of California at Los Angeles Library, Westwood
University of Southern California, Cinema-Television Library, Los Angeles

I am also appreciative for having been given access to papers and documents from the following special collections:

The Ernest Lehman Collection, USC, Cinema-Television Library
The Martin Ritt Collection, AMPAS, Special Collections
The William Wyler Collection, UCLA, Arts Special Collections

I approached working with a new publisher with some trepidation. Going into this project, it was my intention to write a fair, objective biography of Barbra Streisand. I had no way of knowing for sure whether or not my publisher would share that vision. I ended up being pleasantly surprised, and more than a little impressed. The people at Carol Publishing Group are dedicated, talented professionals, and I am extremely grateful for their contributions to this work. Hillel Black, my editor, not only was encouraging, but was as concerned about the integrity of the material as I was. I am also much appreciative of the unwavering support shown by the company's publisher and its president, Steven Schragis and Bruce Bender, respectively. I would also like to recognize the fine work and reassuring words of associate editor Denise O'Sullivan, and editorial assistant Susan Hayes.

The work of the production department at Carol was no less than exemplary. My sincere gratitude to Donald Davidson, copy chief; Al Marill, production editor (and resident movie maven); and Deborah Dwyer, copy editor. I must also acknowledge the gifted art department: Steve Brower, for his stunning cover design; Joanie Schwarz for her hand-tinting of the cover; and David Goodnough for the clean, artful lines of his text design.

I would also like to thank, for their various contributions, Meryl Earl, Gordon Allen, Ted Macri, Ben Petrone, Gary Fitzgerald, and Lisa Cushine.

Finally, I would like to thank my attorney Melvin Wulf of Beldock, Levine & Hoffman, whose steady voice and rational explanations were very much appreciated.

*   *   *

On a more personal note, I would like to acknowledge my friends for helping me get through months of arduous, twenty-hour working days. In particular, I would like to express my heartfelt appreciation to Neal Hitchens for his fine research assistance, and to Mark Goins, for his generous, selfless support. Mostly, though, I would like to thank them for their encouragement and their inspiration. Most people are lucky to find one partner in life. I have been blessed with two.

Index